MW00800505

WEST ACADEMIC PUBLISHING'S
LAW SCHOOL ADVISORY BOARD

JESSE H. CHOPER
Professor of Law and Dean Emeritus,
University of California, Berkeley

JOSHUA DRESSLER
Distinguished University Professor, Frank R. Strong Chair in Law
Michael E. Moritz College of Law, The Ohio State University

YALE KAMISAR
Professor of Law Emeritus, University of San Diego
Professor of Law Emeritus, University of Michigan

MARY KAY KANE
Professor of Law, Chancellor and Dean Emeritus,
University of California, Hastings College of the Law

LARRY D. KRAMER
President, William and Flora Hewlett Foundation

JONATHAN R. MACEY
Professor of Law, Yale Law School

ARTHUR R. MILLER
University Professor, New York University
Formerly Bruce Bromley Professor of Law, Harvard University

GRANT S. NELSON
Professor of Law, Pepperdine University
Professor of Law Emeritus, University of California, Los Angeles

A. BENJAMIN SPENCER
Earle K. Shawe Professor of Law,
University of Virginia School of Law

JAMES J. WHITE
Robert A. Sullivan Professor of Law Emeritus,
University of Michigan

TRADE SECRET LAW

CASES AND MATERIALS

Second Edition

■ ■ ■

Elizabeth A. Rowe

Professor of Law
Distinguished Teaching Scholar
Levin College of Law
University of Florida

Sharon K. Sandeen

Director of IP Institute and Professor of Law
Mitchell Hamline School of Law

AMERICAN CASEBOOK SERIES®

WEST
ACADEMIC
PUBLISHING

The publisher is not engaged in rendering legal or other professional advice, and this publication is not a substitute for the advice of an attorney. If you require legal or other expert advice, you should seek the services of a competent attorney or other professional.

American Casebook Series is a trademark registered in the U.S. Patent and Trademark Office.

© 2012 Thomson Reuters
© 2017 LEG, Inc. d/b/a West Academic
      444 Cedar Street, Suite 700
      St. Paul, MN 55101
      1-877-888-1330

West, West Academic Publishing, and West Academic are trademarks of West Publishing Corporation, used under license.

Printed in the United States of America

ISBN: 978-1-63460-592-2

To Fred, Jonathan, and Victoria

E.A.R.

In loving memory of my mother, whose initials are L.A.W.S.

S.K.S.

PREFACE TO THE SECOND EDITION

As the first casebook of its type on the market, we are very proud of the first edition of this casebook, and the extremely positive feedback we received from instructors and students about the book's innovative organization and style. We think you will find that the second edition is even better.

We describe the unique features of this casebook and how to approach teaching it in the *Preface to the First Edition*, which follows, and in the available *Teacher's Manual*. Of particular significance is our belief that a course in trade secret law provides the perfect opportunity to reinforce and re-learn many of the foundational concepts of law that law students are taught in the first year of law school, including contract law, tort law, civil procedure, property law, criminal law, and constitutional law. It also provides the vehicle to put trade secret law into various contexts, particularly the business, employment and litigation contexts. Because of the breadth of the subject matter and the approach of this casebook, Professors who teach a trade secret course, as well as their students, do not have to be experts in intellectual property law.

Based upon our experience teaching from the book over the past four years and the input of other adopters, we reorganized some of the material, deleted some cases, and added new cases. For instance, in Chapter 6 we added the important U.S. Supreme Court case, *Bonito Boats, Inc. v. Thunder Craft Boats, Inc.*, in order to provide students with more information about the policy rationales that underlie the "proper" and "improper" acquisition of information. We also added an excerpt from Pamela Samuelson's and Suzanne Scotchmer's important economic analysis of reverse engineering.

Chapter 7, the chapter that explores the breach of a duty of confidentiality prong of trade secret misappropriation, has been re-worked and streamlined to focus on relationships, including the employment relationship, which might give rise to a duty of confidentiality. It was revised to focus attention on how implied duties of confidentiality might arise, requiring students to remember what they learned in their course on Contract Law about the difference between implied-in-fact contracts and implied-at-law (or quasi) contracts.

The most significant changes to the second edition, however, are the timely additions relating to the Defend Trade Secrets Act of 2016 (DTSA) and the EU Trade Secret Directive, two laws that went into effect in mid-2016 and which are certain to change the landscape of trade secret law in the United States and Europe. Details about both laws are set forth in each chapter, particularly in Notes 1 and 2, and in the newly added Appendices. Appendix A provides the text of the DTSA overlaid over the existing Economic Espionage Act of 1996 (EEA) so that students can see how the DTSA amended the EEA. Appendix B is a verbatim copy of the EU Trade Secret Directive as it was published in the *Official Journal* of the EU. We are grateful that the EU has a policy that allows its published materials to be distributed in this manner.

Even without the recent adoptions of the DTSA and the EU Trade Secret Directive, there are many questions about the scope, requirements, and limitations of trade secret law that are unanswered or require more study. While it is too early to determine if and how the DTSA and the EU Trade Secret Directive will answer these questions, it is not too early to identify the questions, which we do throughout the book. Thus, this casebook provides numerous opportunities to discuss the legislative process and the process and rules of legislative interpretation. Teaching trade secret law from this book also provides the perfect opportunity to get students thinking about intellectual property, innovation, and information policy more broadly.

We continue to thank all those we acknowledged in the First Edition. In addition, we would like to especially acknowledge the many professors who have chosen to teach trade secrecy and the students who have embraced the course. The rising importance of this area of law, and the ongoing feedback that we receive from all of you, including our own students, has been inspiring and humbling. Special thanks to David S. Levine and Camilla Hrdy for their suggestions for revisions to the book. For excellent research assistance on the Second Edition, we thank John Schank at the University of Florida and Jacob Crawford, Derek Harvieux and Briar Schnuckel of Mitchell Hamline School of Law.

Finally, thanks to our respective families and friends for their continuing support. Sharon also thanks her dog, Abbie, for always cuddling next to her as she writes and edits.

ELIZABETH A. ROWE

SHARON K. SANDEEN

September 2016

PREFACE TO THE FIRST EDITION

We are pleased to present the first casebook in the United States devoted exclusively to trade secret law. This book fills a void among casebooks on intellectual property law by addressing an area of law that is of major import to businesses of all types and sizes. While trade secret law has received brief mention in general casebooks on intellectual property that are often used in survey courses, none of the books have been entirely focused on the law, theories, and policies underlying trade secret law in the United States. We have written this casebook to support a stand-alone 2 or 3 credit course in trade secrecy.

Why study the law of trade secrets? From a practical perspective, the study of trade secret law is important because trade secrets are among the most valuable intangible assets of a company and a company's ultimate survival may depend on its ability to protect its trade secrets. Although patent, copyright, and trademark protection tend to get most of the glory, trade secret protection is appealing to businesses because of its broad scope of protectable information and the relative ease with which a business can claim such protection. For this reason, trade secrets are important to businesses of all sizes, to industry, and to the economy. Indeed, as you will see from the cases in this book, every kind of company, from restaurants to high-technology companies, own trade secrets and trade secret disputes abound. The interesting and varied factual scenarios make the subject relatable, engaging, and relevant to students and professors alike.

From a pedagogical perspective, a course on trade secret law provides the perfect vehicle to reinforce the foundational knowledge, skills, and values that are the focus of U.S. legal education. With respect to the knowledge component, because trade secret law touches upon many other areas of law—including property law, contract law, tort law, criminal law, and employment law—a course on trade secret law enables students to review what they have learned in other courses and to make connections between various legal doctrines. Additionally, because trade secret law is based primarily upon state rather than federal law, a course on trade secret law allows principles of federalism to be reviewed and discussed and enables students to see how policy differences among states can alter the outcome of seemingly similar cases.

The skills that a trade secret course can teach are many. In addition to improving and reinforcing analytical reasoning skills, the highly fact-specific nature of trade secret analysis will help students to improve their fact-finding skills. Also, because the predominant source of trade secret law in the United States is the Uniform Trade Secrets Act, students will learn how to read, interpret, and apply statutory law and how to look for differences among states regarding the interpretation and application of a uniform law. Opportunities exist for teaching students how to conduct trade secret audits, to develop a trade secret protection program, and to craft enforceable confidentiality and non-compete agreements.

Our casebook is designed to be used by law students (and business students) with no prior background in intellectual property law. One of our main objectives was to create a casebook that would be challenging yet user-friendly to students in order to facilitate their reading of the material and their understanding and analysis of the concepts. To that end, we made conscious and thoughtful decisions about the way in which the information throughout the casebook is presented and organized. We have departed from a hide-the-ball approach and adopted a more guided approach that provides students with direction and context for each chapter. For instance, we begin each chapter with "Anticipated Learning Outcomes" that state in a few sentences the learning objectives for the chapter. The feedback from our students on the relatively innovative approach used in this Casebook has been very positive.

The general organization of the casebook follows a logical analytical approach to understanding trade secret law, with the chapters progressing from proving the essential elements of a trade secret claim to defensive tactics and remedies. These chapters are followed by a chapter on managing trade secrets and one on criminal actions. Through the use of "Special Issues" at the end of each of the twelve chapters of the Casebook, we have organized and written the casebook to provide professors with great flexibility in deciding which materials to cover based on their backgrounds and interests.

Each chapter contains explanatory text preceding the cases for each subtopic. Because trade secret cases can appear to be repetitive in their analytical approach, the cases have been edited to include only the most relevant material to the issue or issues for which they are presented. In order to guide the students' focus while reading the case, we have included a "Reading Guidance" question before each case. At the end of each case, we include questions that are directly related to the case and that can be readily answered by a careful reading of the case. These can also serve as questions for discussion in class. The notes at the end of each chapter are not focused on raising questions, but provide additional explanatory and reference material to students and professors.

We wish to acknowledge those who have contributed and supported this project, including our respective law schools and members of the small, but active group of trade secret scholars. In particular, we thank Professors Eric Johnson and Eric Claeys for agreeing to review portions of this book and for providing generous comments and insights. We received excellent research assistance from Seth Jones, Daniel Mahfood, Abood Shebib, and Adrianna Swedowski at the University of Florida Levin College of Law and Zachery Jacobson, Michael Mangold, and Mike Ryan at Hamline University School of Law. Thank you also to the students in our Trade Secret classes at Hamline and Florida who inspired this casebook, provided comments and criticisms, and served as "testers" for our manuscript. Our friends and family provided much needed support and motivation along the way. Professor Rowe is especially grateful to her husband and children for enduring this project. Professor Sandeen is thankful for the love, support, and encouragement of her family and friends. Finally, we most gratefully acknowledge West Publishing for recognizing the need for this casebook and bringing it to market.

ELIZABETH A. ROWE

SHARON K. SANDEEN

A Word About the Materials in This Casebook

All of the cases and excerpts from secondary sources that are used in this casebook have been **edited by the authors in one or more of the following ways**. Accordingly, if you want to reference or quote these materials you should obtain an unedited version.

1. Many of the internal citations have been deleted.

2. Where the internal citations have been maintained, the names of all cases and titles of the secondary sources have been italicized and the references to the applicable reporter service, law review, or publisher have been deleted.

3. In most instances, the cases and excerpts from law review articles have been edited to exclude applicable footnotes. Where footnotes were deemed important to an understanding of the material, they were included using the original footnote number.

4. Passages of cases that were deemed duplicative or unnecessary for an understanding of the case, were deleted. Such deletions are indicated by the use of ellipses (* * *). The same applies to excerpts from law review articles and other sources.

5. To improve ease of reading or to highlight different steps in the courts' analyses, paragraph breaks were added to lengthy sections of a case where appropriate. Also, in older cases, old-English terminology was replaced by its modern equivalent. Apparent typographical errors were also fixed.

6. Summaries of portions of cases or explanatory materials written by the authors of this casebook are shown in brackets ([ ]).

7. References within a case to pleadings, trial testimony, or exhibits have been deleted in most cases.

8. The formatting of the cases, including the headings used within cases, has been changed as necessary to maintain a consistent look.

ACKNOWLEDGMENTS

The excerpts of the *Restatement (First) of the Law of Torts* (© 1939 by the American Law Institute), the *Restatement (Third) of Unfair Competition* (© 1995 by the American Law Institute), and the *History of the American Law Institute and the First Restatement of Law (1932–1944)* (© 1945 by the American Law Institute), are reprinted with the permission of the American Law Institute. All rights reserved.

The sections of the Uniform Trade Secrets Act and excerpts of relevant commentary to the UTSA are reprinted with permission of the Uniform Law Commission (also known as the National Conference of Commissioners of Uniform State Laws). All rights reserved.

The excerpts from *Working Knowledge: Employee Innovation and the Rise of Corporate Intellectual Property, 1800–1930* by Catherine L. Fisk are reprinted with permission of Professor Fisk and the University of North Carolina Press. © 2009 University of North Carolina Press. Used by permission of the publisher. www.uncpress.unc.edu.

The excerpt of the article by Herbert David Klein is reprinted by special permission of Northwestern University Pritzker School of Law, *Northwestern University Law Review.*

Appendix A was prepared by Professor Sandeen based upon the early 2016 text of the Economic Espionage Act of 1996, as amended, and the text of the Defend Trade Secret Act of 2016. Appendix B is the final text of the EU Trade Secret Directive as published in the *Official Journal* of the EU, © European Union, http://eur-lex.europa.eu/, 2016. We are grateful for U.S. and EU policies that allow such materials to be copied and distributed.

The excerpts of the other law review articles and books that appear in this casebook are reprinted with the permission of the referenced authors or publishers. All rights reserved.

We are grateful to the American Law Institute, the Uniform Law Commission, and our colleagues in the legal academy and the legal profession for allowing us to utilize portions of their works.

SUMMARY OF CONTENTS

TABLE OF CONTENTS

TABLE OF CASES

The principal cases are in bold type.

TRADE SECRET LAW
CASES AND MATERIALS

Second Edition

CHAPTER 1

INTRODUCTION

■ ■ ■

Anticipated Learning Outcomes

At the conclusion of this chapter, you will have a general understanding of the factual situations that give rise to trade secret claims. You will acquire an appreciation for the historical circumstances that led to the development of trade secret law and will be able to articulate why it developed. You will also begin to make connections and distinctions between principles of trade secret law, tort law, contract law, property law, and unfair competition law.

A. TRADE SECRET LAW TODAY

With this edition of the casebook, trade secret law in the United States (and in Europe) enters a new era. On May 11, 2016, President Barack Obama signed the Defend Trade Secrets Act of 2016 (DTSA). Why is this a big deal? The DTSA is the first federal law in the United States to create a federal civil cause of action for trade secret misappropriation. For nearly one hundred and eighty years before the enactment of the DTSA, the development of civil trade secret law in the United States was the exclusive domain of state courts and legislatures (with an assist from NCCUSL, now known as the Uniform Law Commission). The DTSA amended the earlier enacted Economic Espionage Act of 1996 (EEA) which designated trade secret misappropriation as a federal crime and which is the focus of Chapter 12. (See Appendix A for the EEA as amended by the DTSA.) The enactment of the DTSA also changes the status of trade secrets as the only type of intellectual property which was not covered by a federal civil statute, and arguably puts trade secret law on par with its intellectual property siblings: patent, copyright, and trademark law.

If you saw the film *The Social Network* about the founding days of Facebook or the more recent movie, *Joy*, you got a glimpse into what trade secret law is all about. Someone has an idea, an invention, or a piece of information that he (or she) believes is of value. He could keep this information to himself and try to use it or implement it on his own, but usually ideas and inventions (particularly if they involve technology) have to be disclosed to someone in order to be implemented. If the information is not covered by a valid patent and the owner blurts out the information and thereby discloses it to others, it is free for anyone to use. Trade secret law provides a middle ground. If the requirements of trade secret law are met, the holder of an idea or other bits of information can share it with others without losing legal protection. In this way, trade secret law is believed to: (1) promote business ethics; (2) encourage innovation, invention, and creativity; and (3) facilitate the sharing of information.

Trade secrets are very important to U.S. companies and the economy. Indeed, they are arguably more important to companies now than ever before in our history. Since the revisions to our patent laws in 2011, many believe that trade secrets are even more important than patents, particularly with respect to hidden processes and computer software. For many large companies, it is estimated that trade secrets comprise over two-thirds of their intangible assets. Even for the smallest companies, there is no escaping the fact that every company probably owns trade secrets—even if they may not know it. This is because the types of information that can be protected by trade secret law is very broad. Trade secret protection is not limited like copyright protection to "original works of authorship fixed in tangible form" and the information does not have to meet the stringent requirements and strict deadlines of patent law to be protected. Theoretically, any bit of information that is "secret" and of potential "independent economic value" can be protected by trade secret law as long as it is subject to "reasonable efforts to maintain its secrecy."

Even though the DTSA is in effect, its development is just beginning and it does not preempt the long existing and rich state laws that form the current trade secret jurisprudence in this country. Indeed, the DTSA is modeled after and is likely to be heavily influenced by the interpretations of the uniform law, the Uniform Trade Secrets Act (UTSA), which has been adopted by most states. Accordingly, learning trade secret law continues to require an understanding of the UTSA and the common law of trade secrecy. As you will learn in the pages of this casebook, the highly fact-specific and policy-laden nature of trade secret analysis makes it an unpredictable (and fun) area of law. Like the Facebook example, it usually involves two sides with very different views of the identity and value of the alleged trade secret information and the circumstances of its acquisition, disclosure, or use. It is up to attorneys who handle trade secret cases to discover all of the relevant facts and apply the law and policy arguments to determine who has the better case.

The two cases that follow provide an introductory glimpse into the world of trade secret law. The remainder of the book provides detailed information about key aspects of trade secret law that will enable you to represent the next Mark Zuckerberg (or maybe the current one).

As you read all of the cases in this casebook, you should identify: (1) the information that is claimed as a trade secret; (2) the nature and scope of the relationship between the parties; (3) how the claimed trade secrets were protected by their owner; (4) how the trade secrets are alleged to have been misappropriated; (5) the remedies that are sought by the plaintiff; and (6) the arguments being asserted by the defendant.

CLOROX CO. v. S.C. JOHNSON & SON, INC.

United States District Court, E.D. Wis., 2009.
627 F.Supp.2d 954.

* * *

J.P. STADTMUELLER, DISTRICT JUDGE.

On April 21, 2009, plaintiff The Clorox Company ("Clorox") filed a complaint in this district seeking injunctive relief against defendant S.C. Johnson & Son, Inc. ("SCJ") pursuant to Rule 65 of the Federal Rules of Civil Procedure. * * * In the complaint, Clorox alleges that SCJ is threatening to misappropriate and may have already misappropriated Clorox's trade secrets by hiring away a Clorox executive, in violation of Wisconsin's Uniform Trade Secrets Act, Wis. Stat. § 134.90. * * *

Along with its complaint, Clorox filed an emergency motion for a temporary restraining order ("TRO") and preliminary injunction, as well as motions for expedited discovery and for a protective order governing disclosure of confidential information in this case. * * * Clorox further requested that a hearing be held on its motion for a TRO and a preliminary injunction. Before holding a hearing on the motion, the court provided SCJ an opportunity to file a response. In its response, SCJ asserted that the court lacks subject matter jurisdiction over this case because Clorox has not adequately pleaded the requisite amount in controversy, and because the former Clorox executive who is alleged to be the conduit of Clorox's trade secrets is an indispensable party whose joinder as a defendant would destroy complete diversity of citizenship.

* * *

BACKGROUND

The parties in this case need little introduction. Clorox is a publicly traded company incorporated in Delaware with its principal place of business located in Oakland, California. * * * Clorox bills itself as "a leading manufacturer and marketer of consumer products," with "some of consumers' most trusted and recognized brand names," including Clorox brand cleaners, Liquid-Plumr brand clog remover and Glad brand bags, wraps and containers. * * * SCJ is a private company incorporated in Wisconsin with its principal place of business located in Racine, Wisconsin. * * * SCJ also manufactures and markets consumer products with widely recognized brand names, including Scrubbing Bubbles brand cleaners, Drano brand clog remover, Ziploc brand bags and containers and Saran brand wraps. * * * Both companies have also ventured into what Clorox refers to as "natural cleaning products," with Clorox using the brand name GreenWorks and SCJ using the brand name Nature's Source. * * *

The dispute between these two consumer products giants arose from the sudden departure of Clorox's Vice President of Product Supply Timothy Bailey ("Bailey") on April 14, 2009. * * * Clorox hired Bailey in 1996, and promoted him to Vice President of Product Supply in 2005. * * * In that position, Bailey was responsible for Clorox's global supply chain. * * * In 2008, Bailey received a total compensation package from Clorox of nearly $1,000,000.00. * * * Bailey also sat on Clorox's three senior governance "teams": the corporate strategy team, the business operations leadership team, and the people and culture team. As a member of these teams, Bailey is alleged to have received detailed financial information and strategic plans, including disclosures made at meetings held on April 13, 2009. * * * Clorox alleges that Bailey had ongoing access and detailed knowledge of the cost structure for Clorox suppliers, as well as pricing strategies for Clorox's entire global products offerings. * * * As recently as March of 2009, Bailey also allegedly participated in meetings regarding a Clorox research and development project, where he was "exposed" to specific designs and attributes of "a key component used in a number of products common to Clorox and S.C. Johnson." * * * Clorox further alleges that in January of 2009, Bailey received Clorox's play book for release and launch of its GreenWorks products in specific countries around the world through 2014.

* * *

On the morning of April 14, 2009, Bailey informed Clorox management that he would be leaving Clorox to take a new position at SCJ. * * * Clorox alleges that it subsequently uncovered evidence that Bailey may have taken sensitive confidential information with him to SCJ. Clorox lists the following as examples of "suspicious acts": (1) Bailey had his assistant order a shredder to destroy papers in his office four days before resigning; (2) Bailey was recorded on surveillance video entering Clorox's offices the weekend before his resignation with a briefcase, and later leaving the offices with a large bag on rollers; (3) Bailey entered Clorox's offices in the wee hours of April 14, 2009, and may have downloaded information from his office laptop to a USB drive, including Microsoft Excel files named "Comparison Spreadsheets" as well as files named "CLX Computer" and "Contacts." * * * Clorox alleges that it protects its trade secrets through internal confidentiality and data security policies and through a confidentiality agreement, a version of which Bailey signed in 1996.

At SCJ, Bailey will take the position of Senior Vice President Product Supply. In that position, SCJ asserts that Bailey will be responsible for its plant management, supply planning and customer service, warehouse and transportation logistics, procurement, product safety and quality control, and engineering of "work systems." Bailey will also sit on SCJ's executive team. He was not a member of Clorox's executive team.[3]

* * *

III. SCJ'S MOTION TO DISMISS FOR FAILURE TO STATE A CLAIM

Having found that California law applies to Clorox's misappropriation claim, the court now turns to SCJ's final contention in its motion to dismiss: that Clorox has failed to state a claim upon which relief can be granted. * * * In considering a motion to dismiss under Rule 12(b)(6), the court accepts all factual allegations of the complaint as true and draws all reasonable inferences in favor of the plaintiff. * * * The court will grant a motion to dismiss only where it appears beyond doubt from the pleadings that the plaintiff can prove no set of facts in support of his claims which would entitle him to relief. * * *

In general, to make a prima facie claim for misappropriation of trade secrets under California's Uniform Trade Secrets Act ("CUTSA"), a plaintiff must demonstrate: "(1) the plaintiff owned a trade secret, (2) the defendant acquired, disclosed, or used the plaintiff's trade secret through improper means, and (3) the defendant's actions damaged the plaintiff." * * * CUTSA further provides that an "[a]ctual or threatened misappropriation may be enjoined." Cal. Civ. Code § 3426.2. Threatened misappropriation may be demonstrated by showing either that the defendant possesses trade secrets and has misused or disclosed those secrets in the past, that the defendant intends to misuse or disclose those secrets, or that the defendant possesses trade secrets and wrongfully refuses to return them after a demand for return is made. * * *

SCJ argues that Clorox has failed to state a claim under California law because Clorox has not alleged that SCJ has actually acquired or used any of Clorox's trade secrets, because Clorox has not alleged that SCJ is threatening to do so, and because Clorox's only theory of liability relies on the inevitable disclosure doctrine. * * *

In its complaint, Clorox makes the general allegation that SCJ has misappropriated, and/or has threatened to misappropriate Clorox's trade secrets. * * * Specifically, the complaint alleges that Bailey was given access to, and is in possession of, Clorox's trade secrets. * * * The complaint further summarizes Clorox's claim as follows:

> 55. It is inevitable that Bailey will use or rely on the information that he obtained while working for Clorox in connection with his position at S.C. Johnson and, upon information and belief, Bailey

---

[3]   In conjunction with SCJ's opposition brief, Bailey submitted an affidavit outlining his reasoning for leaving Clorox and taking a job with SCJ. In the affidavit, Bailey asserts that he decided to go to SCJ because he believed Clorox was not properly valuing his role, because SCJ offered him a competitive compensation package, and for family reasons. * * *

and S.C. Johnson have used, disclosed or threatened to use or disclose Clorox's confidential, proprietary, and trade secret information with full knowledge that this information was acquired under circumstances giving rise to a duty to maintain its secrecy or limit its use. Thus, S.C. Johnson and Bailey threaten the unlawful misappropriation of Clorox's trade secret information.

Rule 8 of the Federal Rules of Civil Procedure states that a pleading must contain "a short and plain statement of the claim showing that the pleader is entitled to relief." * * * Rule 8 establishes a notice standard of pleadings, which requires only that a plaintiff set forth "the bare minimum facts necessary to put the defendant on notice of the claim so that he can file an answer." * * * Therefore, a plaintiff "need not plead facts or legal theories; it is enough to set out a claim for relief." * * *

Here, Clorox has set out a claim for relief based almost entirely on its legal theory of inevitable disclosure. However, notwithstanding Clorox's legal theory, and making all reasonable inferences in favor of Clorox, the court finds that Clorox has set forth the bare minimum facts to state a claim of misappropriation of trade secrets. The complaint alleges that Bailey obtained trade secrets, and that "upon information and belief, Bailey and S.C. Johnson have used, disclosed or threatened to use or disclose Clorox's confidential, proprietary, and trade secret information with full knowledge that this information was acquired under circumstances giving rise to a duty to maintain its secrecy or limit its use." * * * Moreover, Clorox, through its allegations that Bailey may have taken Clorox files, could present a set of facts establishing that SCJ is actually threatening to misappropriate Clorox's trade secrets by using Bailey as a conduit of information. * * * Therefore, the court is obliged to deny SCJ's motion to dismiss for failure to state a claim.

IV. TRO AND PRELIMINARY INJUNCTION

The court now turns to Clorox's motion for a TRO and preliminary injunction. Clorox seeks an order against SCJ and anyone acting in concert with it, prohibiting them from using or disclosing Clorox's confidential proprietary and/or trade secrets and prohibiting SCJ from employing, contracting or affiliating with Bailey. * * * Before the court will issue preliminary injunctive relief, the party seeking such relief must first demonstrate the following: (1) a reasonable likelihood of success on the merits of the party's claim; (2) that the party had no adequate remedy at law; and (3) that the party will suffer irreparable harm in the absence of injunctive relief. * * * If the moving party fails to demonstrate any of these threshold elements, the court must deny preliminary injunctive relief. * * * If, however, the moving party meets the first three threshold elements, the court must then weigh the irreparable harm the moving party would suffer in the absence of an injunction against the irreparable harm the nonmoving party would suffer if the injunction were issued. * * * The court must also consider the effects of granting or denying preliminary injunctive relief on any nonparties. * * *

The court's analysis of Clorox's TRO and preliminary injunction motion begins and ends, for the most part, on Clorox's likelihood of success on the merits of its claim. This relatively low threshold is met if the moving party shows "a 'better than negligible' chance of success on the merits of at least one of its claims." * * * Clorox's complaint sets forth two counts, both of which claim misappropriation of its trade secrets. In its brief in support of its motion, Clorox hinges its success on the merits of its claim entirely on the inevitable disclosure theory of trade secret misappropriation as set forth in the *PepsiCo.* case. Specifically, Clorox alleges that Bailey is in possession of Clorox's valuable trade secrets and will inevitably disclose them, or use them on behalf of SCJ, during the course of his employment with SCJ. * * *

Even if Clorox had demonstrated a reasonable likelihood of success on the merits, the court would still be inclined to deny preliminary injunctive relief. The court recognizes that the loss of trade secrets regarding time-sensitive business strategies to an arch-competitor could rise to the level of irreparable harm that cannot be adequately addressed through later recovery of damages. Clorox's allegation that Bailey may improperly disclose or use information regarding Clorox's imminent strategic plans for its GreenWorks products, or the pending redesign of a Clorox product line, might fit the irreparable harm test. However, when balancing this potential irreparable harm Clorox may suffer if an injunction were denied, against the harms that SCJ would suffer by being deprived of a top employee for the near future, the court considers the scales to be evenly weighted. SCJ has represented to the court that it has instructed Bailey not to disclose to SCJ Clorox's confidential information. * * * Bailey also presumably remains bound by the confidentiality agreement he signed with Clorox. But the balancing does not end with the countervailing harms Clorox and SCJ may suffer. The court must also consider the effect an injunction would have on certain nonparties. The scales tip against granting a preliminary injunction on this measure. For if an injunction were granted, Bailey would suffer tangible harm by being unable to pursue his career with SCJ.

Accordingly, because Clorox has not met the threshold showing of a reasonable likelihood of success on the merits of its claim, the court is obliged to deny Clorox's motion for a TRO and a preliminary injunction.

* * *

IT IS ORDERED that plaintiff's emergency motion for temporary restraining order and preliminary injunction (Docket # 6) be and the same is hereby DENIED; * * *.

IT IS FURTHER ORDERED that defendant's motion to dismiss the complaint (Docket #44) be and same is hereby DENIED[.]

[handwritten: —affirmed trial ct.'s order for preliminary injunction — 4 factor test for preliminary injunction]

BIMBO BAKERIES USA, INC. V. BOTTICELLA

United States Court of Appeals, Third Circuit, 2010.
613 F.3d 102.

GREENBERG, CIRCUIT JUDGE.

I. INTRODUCTION

This matter comes on before this Court on an interlocutory appeal from an order of the District Court dated February 9, 2010, and entered on February 12, 2010, granting appellee's motion for a preliminary injunction. * * * The issue on appeal is whether the District Court erred in enjoining appellant Chris Botticella, formerly a senior executive at appellee Bimbo Bakeries USA, Inc. ("Bimbo"), from working for one of Bimbo's competitors until after the Court resolved the merits of Bimbo's misappropriation of trade secrets claim against Botticella. * * *

II. BACKGROUND

A. *Botticella's Employment at Bimbo*

[handwritten: —baking industry]

Bimbo, a Delaware corporation with its principal place of business in Pennsylvania, is one of the four largest companies in the United States baking industry. Bimbo and its affiliates produce and distribute baked goods throughout the country under a number of popular brand names including Thomas', Entenmann's, Arnold, Oroweat, Mrs. Baird's, Stroehmann, and Boboli. Botticella, a California resident, who already had experience in the baking industry, began working for Bimbo in 2001 and was, until January 13, 2010, its Vice President of Operations for California. In that position in which Botticella earned an annual salary of $250,000, he was directly responsible for five production facilities and oversaw a variety of areas including product quality and cost, labor issues, and new product development. In addition, Botticella worked closely with Bimbo's sales staff on sales promotion and capacity planning, and also was responsible for overseeing the operations of "co-packers" in his region, i.e., third-party manufacturers under contract with Bimbo.

[handwritten: D's knowledge of confd. info.]

As one of Bimbo's senior executives, Botticella had access to and acquired a broad range of confidential information about Bimbo, its products, and its business strategy. For example, he was one of a select group of individuals with access to the code books containing the formulas and process parameters for all of Bimbo's products. He also regularly attended high-level meetings with other top Bimbo executives to discuss the company's national business strategy. Significantly, as Bimbo repeatedly has noted throughout these proceedings, Botticella was one of only seven people who possessed all of the knowledge necessary to replicate independently Bimbo's popular line of Thomas' English Muffins, including the secret behind the muffins' unique "nooks and crannies" texture. Thomas' English Muffins is the source of approximately half a billion dollars' worth of Bimbo's annual sales income.

While employed at Bimbo, Botticella signed a "Confidentiality, Non-Solicitation and Invention Assignment Agreement" with Bimbo on March 13, 2009, in which he agreed not to compete directly with Bimbo during the term of his employment, not to use or disclose any of Bimbo's confidential or proprietary information during or after the term of his employment with Bimbo, and, upon ceasing employment by Bimbo, to return every document he received from Bimbo during the term of his employment. The agreement, however, did not include a covenant restricting where Botticella could work after the termination of his employment with Bimbo. The agreement contained a choice of law provision providing that Pennsylvania law would govern any dispute arising from the agreement.

signed non-compete

* * *

B.   *The Hostess Job Offer*

On September 28, 2009, one of Bimbo's primary competitors in the baking industry—Interstates Brand Corporation, which later changed its name to Hostess Brands, Inc. (collectively, "Hostess")—offered Botticella a position in Texas as Vice President of Bakery Operations for its eastern region. The proposed position carried a base salary of $200,000, along with various stock option and bonus opportunities. On October 15, 2009, Botticella accepted the Hostess position and agreed to begin in January 2010. Botticella did not disclose his plans to Bimbo for several months, and he therefore continued to be engaged fully in his work at Bimbo and to have full access to Bimbo's confidential and proprietary information even after he accepted the Hostess position. Botticella maintains that he continued working for Bimbo notwithstanding his acceptance of the Hostess position in order to receive his 2009 year-end bonus and to complete two Bimbo projects for which he had responsibility.

job offer at competitor

After Botticella accepted the Hostess offer and while Bimbo still employed him, Hostess directed him to execute an "Acknowledgment and Representation Form," which essentially indicated that Hostess was not interested in any confidential information, trade secrets, or other proprietary information that Botticella had acquired from Bimbo, and that Botticella would not disclose such information to Hostess. * * * Botticella signed the form on December 7, 2009.

Botticella informed his supervisor at Bimbo on January 4, 2010, that he was planning to leave Bimbo on January 15. But Botticella did not at that time indicate that he was leaving to work for a competitor. Moreover, there is no indication in the record that Bimbo asked him about his future employment plans. On January 12, Hostess announced that its Vice President of Bakery Operations for the eastern region was retiring and that Botticella would be replacing him, effective January 18. Bimbo personnel learned of the announcement and the next day, January 13, the company's Vice President for Human Relations requested that Botticella contact him. Botticella did so at approximately 10:00 a.m. PST and in the course of the ensuing telephone conversation disclosed his intention to work for Hostess. Bimbo directed Botticella to vacate its offices that day.

C.   *Botticella's Use of Confidential Information Following the Hostess Offer*

In the period between when Botticella accepted the Hostess offer on October 15, 2009, and when he ceased working for Bimbo on January 13, 2010, he continued to have all the access to Bimbo's confidential and proprietary information befitting a trusted senior executive. For instance, Botticella attended a meeting with Bimbo's president and other Bimbo officers in December 2009 at which the participants discussed confidential information regarding the company's strategic plan for California. Botticella concedes that if he had disclosed his intention to work for Hostess, Bimbo would have restricted his access to this and other types of information. Indeed, Botticella maintains that he no longer felt "comfortable" being privy to Bimbo's confidential information following his acceptance of the Hostess offer and that, accordingly, when he received emails and electronic documents containing confidential information, he deleted them, and that when he was exposed to confidential information during presentations at meetings, he "blocked it" out of his head. * * *

In one instance over the Christmas holiday, Botticella deleted a number of documents from his company-issued laptop computer. These documents included both items of a personal nature, such as his resume, and a number of work-related documents containing confidential information. Botticella claimed that he deleted these documents because he "didn't think th[ey] would [have] any value to anybody." * * * Nevertheless, when Botticella returned to his office at Bimbo on January 4, 2010, he asked a computer technician to restore the files because "he wanted to have them back just in case for the next weeks we needed to have a meeting or something." * * * Bimbo's technician then restored the files to the computer.

Following Botticella's departure, Bimbo hired E. Brian Harris, a computer forensics expert, to investigate Botticella's use of his company laptop during December 2009 and January 2010. Harris's testing revealed that a user who logged in as Botticella had accessed a number of confidential documents during the final weeks of Botticella's employment at Bimbo. In particular, the testing revealed that the person logging in as Botticella had accessed twelve files within a span of thirteen seconds on January 13, 2010, Botticella's last day at Bimbo. Significantly this access occurred minutes after the phone call in which Botticella finally disclosed to Bimbo his plans to work for Hostess and Bimbo told him to cease working for it.

There were several similar patterns of access in the weeks leading up to January 13. According to Harris, this type of activity-multiple files being accessed more or less simultaneously—was "inconsistent with an ordinary usage whereby individual files are opened and either read or edited." * * * Harris concluded that the activity was, however, consistent with copying a group of files at the same time, but he could not determine conclusively whether the files Botticella had accessed had been copied and deleted or never copied at all. * * * The testing also revealed that three external storage devices—a portable device known as a "thumb" or "flash" drive and two external hard drives—had at one time or another been connected to Botticella's computer, although it was unclear exactly when these devices had been used. Bimbo located the thumb drive and one of the hard drives but Harris could not determine conclusively whether or not any files had been copied onto the devices from Botticella's computer. Harris was not provided with the second external hard drive. According to Bimbo, that device "is unaccounted for." * * *

A number of the files accessed from Botticella's laptop during his final days at Bimbo were highly sensitive and their possession by a competitor would have been damaging to Bimbo. As described by the District Court, these documents include "Bimbo's cost-reduction strategies, product launch dates, anticipated plant and line closures, labor contract information, production strengths and weaknesses of many Bimbo bakeries, and the cost structure for individual products by brand." * * * There were, however, more mundane documents such as a presentation titled "Safety Short-Wet Floors" included in these groups of files. * * * In his video-taped deposition, portions of which were presented at the preliminary injunction hearing, Botticella admitted to copying files periodically from his laptop to external devices during his final weeks at Bimbo, but maintained that he had done so only to practice his computer skills in preparation for his new position at Hostess. Despite an earlier denial, he eventually admitted to conducting such "practice" exercises in January 2010. The District Court found that Botticella's explanation of his use of the laptop computer and the external devices was "confusing at best" and "not credible." * * *

[handwritten margin note: — sensitive files △ accessed]

D.   *Procedural History*

After Botticella left Bimbo and joined Hostess, Bimbo brought this action seeking to protect its trade secrets and then promptly moved for preliminary injunctive relief. * * * The District Court granted Bimbo's motion and preliminarily enjoined Botticella from commencing employment with Hostess and from divulging to Hostess any confidential

[handwritten margin note: trial ct.]

or proprietary information belonging to Bimbo. The Court further ordered Botticella to return to Bimbo any of the company's confidential or proprietary information in his possession. * * * Botticella appealed from the February 9, 2010 order to this Court on February 16, 2010. * * * We have expedited our consideration of this appeal.

* * *

IV. DISCUSSION

In determining whether to grant a preliminary injunction, a court must consider whether the party seeking the injunction has satisfied four factors: "(1) a likelihood of success on the merits; (2) he or she will suffer irreparable harm if the injunction is denied; (3) granting relief will not result in even greater harm to the nonmoving party; and (4) the public interest favors such relief." * * *

A. *Likelihood of Success on the Merits*

* * * Under the Pennsylvania Uniform Trade Secrets Act ("PUTSA"), which is applicable in this case, a trade secret is defined as:

> Information, including a formula, drawing, pattern, compilation including a customer list, program, device, method, technique or process that:
>
> (1) Derives independent economic value, actual or potential, from not being generally known to, and not being readily ascertainable by proper means by, other persons who can obtain economic value from its disclosure or use.
>
> (2) Is the subject of efforts that are reasonable under the circumstances to maintain its secrecy.

12 Pa. Cons. Stat. Ann. § 5302 (West 2004). * * *

Applying these standards, the District Court determined that during Botticella's employment at Bimbo, he had access to and acquired a number of Bimbo's trade secrets, including:

> a. Information in Bimbo's code books, as well as and including formulas and designs for Thomas' English Muffins, Oroweat brand products, Sandwich Thins products, and other Bimbo products.
>
> b. Bimbo's strategy for increasing profitability, embodied in a road map in January of 2009, which included line closures, plant closures, new process improvements, formula optimizations, and new product launches, and which achieved cost savings of $75 million over the course of a year.
>
> c. Knowledge of how Bimbo produces bread 'from scratch' instead of using pre-mixed ingredients.

d. Documents copied by [Botticella] from his work computer onto an external storage device with no credible explanation. . . .

e. Bimbo's promotional strategies with respect to specific customers.

f. Bimbo's cost positions.

g. Identities of Bimbo's customers targeted for upcoming bids.

The District Court then determined that Bimbo likely would be able to prove at trial that Botticella would misappropriate these trade secrets if allowed to work at Hostess.

A person has misappropriated a trade secret under Pennsylvania law when he acquires knowledge of another's trade secret in circumstances giving rise to a duty to maintain its confidentiality and then discloses or uses that trade secret without the other's consent. * * * A court may enjoin the actual or threatened misappropriation of a trade secret. * * * After determining that Bimbo was seeking an injunction on the basis of threatened misappropriation, the District Court found there was "a substantial likelihood, if not an inevitability, that [Botticella] will disclose or use Bimbo's trade secrets in the course of his employment with Hostess." * * * Accordingly, the Court concluded that Bimbo had demonstrated a likelihood of succeeding on the merits of its claim.

trade secret misappropriation

Botticella contends this conclusion was wrong as a matter of law because (a) a court only can enjoin a defendant from beginning a new job to protect a former employer's technical trade secrets, (b) such an injunction only can issue where it would be "virtually impossible" for the defendant to perform his new job without disclosing trade secrets, (c) Bimbo did not present any evidence from which the District Court could conclude that Botticella's responsibilities at Hostess would lead him to disclose Bimbo's trade secrets, and (d) the District Court drew impermissible adverse inferences against Botticella in a way that effectively shifted the burden of proof from Bimbo to Botticella.

* * *

[After rejecting each of the foregoing arguments, the court ruled that:] Accordingly, the District Court did not abuse its discretion by determining that Bimbo demonstrated a likelihood of success on its misappropriation of trade secrets claim.

B. *Irreparable Harm*

The District Court concluded that Bimbo would suffer irreparable harm absent injunctive relief because the disclosure of its trade secrets to Hostess would put Bimbo at a competitive disadvantage that a legal remedy could not redress. On appeal, Botticella does not contest this finding apart from arguing that any harm Bimbo potentially might suffer from Botticella's employment at Hostess could be prevented by a narrow injunction—to which Botticella would stipulate—prohibiting Botticella only from disclosing Bimbo's trade secrets. We recognize that the evidence at trial may show that if Bimbo is entitled to relief that relief might be narrow yet adequate, just as Botticella suggests. Nevertheless, at this preliminary stage of the proceedings, the District Court did not abuse its discretion when, faced with evidence of Botticella's suspicious conduct during his final weeks at Bimbo, it determined that a stronger remedy was needed in the interim to protect Bimbo from imminent irreparable harm. * * *

C. *Harm to Botticella Caused by Injunctive Relief*

The District Court concluded that the harm of Bimbo's trade secrets being disclosed to Hostess outweighed the harm to Botticella of not being able to commence employment at Hostess until the Court made a final determination of the merits following a trial, which it scheduled to start about two months from the date it issued the preliminary injunction. The Court noted that Botticella would continue to receive compensation for the eleven weeks of vacation time that he had accrued before leaving Bimbo. We agree with the District Court's determination. In so doing, however, we note that even a temporary injunction prohibiting someone from pursuing his livelihood in the manner he chooses operates as a severe restriction on him that a court should not impose lightly. Nevertheless, such a temporary restriction on his employment is warranted where, as here, the facts demonstrate that the restriction is necessary to prevent greater irreparable harm from befalling another party. Following a disposition on the merits which in the normal course of events will follow the disposition of this appeal and the remand of the case to the District Court, if the Court holds that Bimbo is entitled to relief, the Court should fashion a remedy appropriate to protect Bimbo's trade secrets without unduly imposing on Botticella's right to pursue his chosen occupation.

D. *The Public Interest*

We agree with the District Court's conclusion that granting the preliminary injunction was consistent with the public interest. There are several public interests at play in this case. As noted by the District Court, there is a generalized public interest in "upholding the inviolability of trade secrets and enforceability of confidentiality agreements." * * * Additionally, there is a public interest in employers being free to hire whom they please and in employees being free to work for whom they please. Of these latter two interests, Pennsylvania courts consider the right of the employee to be the more significant. * * * We are satisfied on the facts of this case that the public interest in preventing the misappropriation of

Bimbo's trade secrets outweighs the temporary restriction on Botticella's choice of employment. * * *

V. CONCLUSION

For the reasons stated above, we will affirm the order of the District Court dated February 9, 2010, and entered on February 12, 2010, granting Bimbo's motion for a preliminary injunction and will remand the case to that Court for further proceedings.

B. THE THEORIES, ORIGINS, AND EVOLUTION OF TRADE SECRET LAW

As the foregoing cases reveal, the classic (but not exclusive) factual scenario in which trade secret claims arise involve a claim by one business owner that the defendant is about to disclose or is wrongfully using "his" secret process, method, or formula. Usually, these complaints arise after a valued employee (or, in an earlier time, a valued apprentice) leaves the employ of one company and begins work at a competing company. As explained by Professor Catherine Fisk:

> In the pre-industrial economy, craft knowledge was transmitted through families or from master to apprentice. The secrecy of recipes and techniques that passed from generation to generation enabled a family or a firm to gain a reputation and to retain exclusive control of production. * * * As the concentration of production associated with industrialization eliminated the possibility of owning a workshop in most trades, the master-apprentice relationship eroded and soon was no longer the dominant form of work organization. One of the most significant consequences of the decline of the artisan relationship by which the master was obligated to train apprentices was a change in the way that knowledge was transmitted among generations and within trades. The mutual obligations to instruct and guard the secrets of the craft were eventually supplanted by a new set of rules.

Catherine L. Fisk, *Working Knowledge: Trade Secrets, Restrictive Covenants in Employment, and the Rise of Corporate Intellectual Property, 1800–1930*, 52 HASTINGS L. J. 441, 450–451 (2001).

While in recent years trade secret protection has often been labeled as a form of intellectual property, as originally conceptualized (and in most of the world outside of the United States), the protection of business secrets had more to do with the maintenance of business ethics and the prevention of unfair competition than with the protection of a property or proprietary interest. In fact, in many other countries, there is great resistance to labelling trade secrets as a form of intellectual property.

The various theories underlying the common law development of trade secret principles (which has evolved and expanded over time) are summarized in the following excerpt from a 1960 law review article.

THE TECHNICAL TRADE SECRET QUADRANGLE: A SURVEY
Herbert David Klein.
55 Northwestern Univ. L. Rev. 437 (1960).

The diverse treatment of trade secrets under the topics of torts, contracts, agency, trusts and restitution results from the multiplicity of doctrines on which their protection is based. One of these doctrines, the concept that a trade secret is a property right, was recognized early in the nation's history. . . . As property, a trade secret can be held in trust, can constitute the subject of a license agreement, is transferable *inter vivos* and by descent and distribution, is taxable, and becomes part of a bankrupt's estate.

An English judge over one-hundred years ago invoked not only the property concept, but also the concepts of contract and trust or confidence. Mr. Justice Holmes in following this reasoning doubted the usefulness of the property theory of protection and preferred to base his holding on the confidential relations of the defendant employee with the plaintiff employer. This violation-of-trust doctrine was quoted with approval in a recent decision which in disposing of the contract theory of protection, emphasized instead the concept of breach of duty from which the courts protect the owner of [a] trade secret.

Intimately connected with the breach of confidence is the act of impropriety thereby committed which leads to the third doctrine, that of unfair competition resulting in unjust enrichment. A "fundamental Doctrine of Equity . . . requires that a person shall not use a position of advantage naturally arising from the relationship of the parties to profit at the expense of the other," and the courts will not permit one to profit from acts of unfair competition or violation of business ethics.

––––––

Given the common law origins of trade secret law and the flexibility of the common law process, it is understandable that the theories upon which early trade secret cases were brought differed depending upon the facts of each case, the courts in which the cases were brought (whether law or equity), and the remedies that were sought.

1. THE EMERGENCE OF THE COMMON LAW OF TRADE SECRECY (1800 TO 1939)

From the early 1800s through 1988, trade secret law in the United States was primarily governed by common law rather than statute. Like other unfair competition and business torts of the time, including trademark infringement and interference with contract, trade secret law developed in a series of cases that were brought to resolve disputes between businesses. This meant that lawyers handling such cases had two basic choices. They could identify an existing common law cause of action or equitable claim that fit their client's situation and provided the relief they sought or they could try to make new law.

At common law a lawyer's toolbox is limited to two basic civil wrongs: one based on contract law and the other based on tort law. Although there are different theories, philosophies, and explanations for contract and tort law, it is generally recognized that contract law is used to order the interactions of individuals and companies *ex ante* (before they occur) by specifying the obligations of the contracting parties. Assuming there is a valid and enforceable contract, a cognizable wrong is committed when there is a material breach of contract. In contrast, it is generally recognized that tort law is designed to remedy perceived wrongdoing *ex post* (after a wrong has occurred) and in so doing to deter behavior that society deems wrongful. Usually (although there are exceptions), the civil justice system will not provide a remedy in either situation unless the plaintiff can establish that he has actually been harmed in some way.

While the existence of an agreement of confidentiality—particularly an express agreement—provided a ready basis upon which to impose liability against one who wrongfully used or disclosed secrets in contravention of the agreement, common law claims for relief based upon contract law were not always ideal for several reasons. First, contract claims depend upon the existence of a binding and enforceable contract. In the absence of an express (written or oral) agreement of confidentiality, plaintiffs in trade secret cases are forced to argue that the circumstances give rise to an implied-in-fact agreement of confidentiality; an argument that could not always be proven in early cases. Not only was it likely that a given set of facts did not give rise to either an express of an implied contract, as noted by Professor Fisk, it was not until the late 1800s that courts became more comfortable imposing implied contractual obligations on employees. Catherine L. Fisk, WORKING KNOWLEDGE AND THE RISE OF CORPORATE INTELLECTUAL PROPERTY, 1800–1930, (University of North Carolina Press, 2009).

Second, even if an express or implied contract can be proven, the remedies for breach of contract do not typically include injunctive relief (what is known under contract law as "specific performance"). Thus, early trade secret plaintiffs who desired injunctive relief to prevent the use or disclosure of their secrets were required to: (1) establish the basis for specific performance under contract law (typically based either upon the assertion of property rights or the alleged breach of an obligation of confidentiality); (2) plead and prove the commission of a tort for which injunctive relief was available; or (3) seek relief in a court of equity which generally had greater powers than a court of law to "do justice" and issue equitable relief, including injunctive relief and restitution.

(3) Third, contract-based claims for relief are not useful in situations where the plaintiff's trade secrets fall into the hands of a third-party, meaning someone who was not directly involved in the initial misappropriation of the trade secrets. *See* Sharon K. Sandeen, *The Third Party Problem: Assessing the Protection of Information Through Tort Law,* *in* INTELLECTUAL PROPERTY PROTECTION OF FACT-BASED WORKS (Robert Brauneis, ed. 2009). Because only parties who are in privity of contract are bound by the terms of the contract, trade secret cases that were based upon breach of contract claims could only reach the contracting parties and not others. In order to reach third-parties, it was necessary for tort and equitable principles to emerge that provided a way to impose a duty on third-parties to maintain the confidentiality of trade secrets in certain circumstances.

The limited scope and remedies of contract law also forced early attorneys and judges to consider alternative theories of relief for alleged trade secret misappropriation. The principal approaches that emerged from the common law are the property and unfair competition approaches as represented by the following two cases which, despite other labels, focus on duties of confidentiality.

As you will learn, a broader conception of trade secret misappropriation to include the improper acquisition of trade secrets, in addition to the original claim of breach of a duty of confidentiality, emerged later and must be understood as a different type of "wrong" than a breach of a duty of confidentiality. *See* Note, *Nature of Trade Secrets and Their Protection,* 42 HARV. L. REV. 254 (1928) (discussing the early development of this type of trade secret misappropriation). How different and how such differences affect trade secret remedies are questions that are explored in subsequent chapters of this casebook.

> ### Reading Guidance
>
> *On what basis does the court find that the defendant owed a duty to the plaintiff?*

CINCINNATI BELL FOUNDRY CO. V. DODDS

Ohio Superior Court, 1887.
10 Ohio Dec. Reprint 154, 1887 WL 469.

TAFT, J.

Plaintiff alleges that it is the owner by purchase of a secret process for the manufacture of bells, and that it has been selling bells of this manufacture for two years last past; that the business is a valuable one, having been made so by the excellence of the bell and the extensive advertising done, by plaintiff and its predecessors in ownership for twenty years; that defendant John B. Dodds was the foreman of the Blymyer Manufacturing Company, from whom the bell business was purchased by plaintiff, and which continued to manufacture bells for plaintiff after the sale; that Dodds as foreman acquired a knowledge of this secret process under an injunction of secrecy and now proposes to use this process in the manufacture and sale of bells for the firm of John B. Dodds & Son, consisting of himself and his co-defendant Robert H. Dodds, and to communicate the secret to the Eureka Foundry Company, to enable the latter company to manufacture the bells for this firm. * * * The prayer is for an injunction to prevent the manufacture, or sale of the bells, the communication of the secret process to any one * * *.

When the petition was filed, a preliminary injunction was granted. A motion to dissolve has been made, which is now to be considered.

It is clearly established in the case of *Peabody v. Norfolk*, that he who discovers and keeps secret a process of manufacture, whether a proper subject for a patent or not, has a property in it which a court of equity will protect against one who in violation of contract and breach of confidence undertakes to apply it to his own use, or to disclose it to third persons. He has not an exclusive right to it as against the public or against those who, in good faith, acquire knowledge of it. * * *

The property in a secret process is the power to make use of it to the exclusion of the world. If the world knows the process, then the property disappears. There can be no property in a process, and no right of protection if knowledge of it is common to the world. It would be a violation of every right of the employee of a manufacturer to prevent the former from using, in a business of his own, knowledge which he acquired in the employ of the latter, when he might have acquired such knowledge in the employ of other manufacturers. Indeed, a contract not to do so would probably fail of enforcement because in restraint of trade.

The principles of law governing in the consideration of this case therefore are:

1st. That the inventor of a secret process has a property right in it which he may call upon a court of equity to protect him in against the use or disclosure of the secret by any person acquiring knowledge of it in confidence.

2d. That the inventor may sell the secret and all his property in it and thereby vest in the purchaser as full rights as he himself has to protection against its use or disclosure by any who have acquired knowledge of it in confidence from the inventor or himself.

3d. That the process must be a secret process, not common to the trade, to entitle the plaintiff to protection.

Coming now to apply these principles at bar, there seems to be no doubt that John B. Dodds proposes to make exactly the same bell that was made by the Blymyer Manufacturing Company, and that he has made a contract with the Eureka Foundry Company to make this bell for him, necessitating the disclosure of the process of manufacture to third persons. * * * It further appears that the Blymyer Manufacturing Co. sold this process, together with the good-will of the bell business, to the plaintiff's assignor in Nov. 1884. From what has been said it follows that plaintiff has the same remedy against defendants that the Blymyer Manufacturing Co. would have had against them, had no assignment taken place. The questions of fact are simplified to two.

1st. Was the process a secret one?

2d. Did John B. Dodds acquire knowledge of it in confidence, and under an implied obligation not to use or disclose it?

The manufacture of bells has been extensive for many centuries. The metal of which they were made was copper and tin. This is known as bell-metal, and is still the metal generally used, while iron in recent years has been used for small bells. The particular mixture of metals used by plaintiff for bell material is of very recent date, and was for years of doubtful success. Mr. W. H. Clark seems to have experimented for several years in making bells of this mixture. His experiments included not only the mixture of certain metals, but the proper form and size and weight of the bells adapted to produce the best result. It seems that the size, weight and form of a bell have as much to do with the tone as the metals used.

* * * There is no evidence tending to show that at the present time, there is any other manufacturer engaged in making bells of the same proportions of form, size, weight and mixture of metals. * * * It is important at this point, to say that because bells of plaintiff have been sold everywhere, and it would be easy therefore to make patterns from the bells, it does not follow that the use of those forms with a certain mixture of metals may not constitute a secret. The result from those forms and sizes with any other mixture of metal than the one used, as copper and tin for instance, or white iron, would be entirely different from the result obtained from these forms and sizes with the metal mixture which is used. Knowledge of the fact that these forms, sizes and weights made a good bell, and that these metals made a good bell-metal mixed in a certain proportion, would not be knowledge of plaintiff's process, unless it was accompanied by knowledge of the fact that a good bell was made by a combination of this bell-metal with these forms, sizes and weights. The success of the plaintiff's bells for so many years, and its continued manufacture, without competition, except by bells of other metals, is itself evidence that the process which was used was one either not known at all, or at best so imperfectly understood, as to make it impossible for anybody else to succeed in making merchantable

bells of this variety. That is a trade secret, which is not well enough or exactly enough known by any person but the inventor or owner as to enable other persons to make use of it in trade.

* * *

Many affidavits have been filed of persons formerly in the employ of the Blymyer Manufacturing Co. as to the publicity with which this process of bell-making was carried on. The knowledge thus acquired by the affiants seems to have been largely confined to the fact that certain metals were used in the mixture. It is very doubtful whether the knowledge which these subordinate employees had, was knowledge which could be used to reproduce the bell made by the Blymyer Company. They were fellow-employees of Mr. Dodds. As was said in the case of *Peabody v. Norfolk*, cited above, "Although the process is carried on in a large factory, the workmen may not understand or be entrusted with the secret, or may have acquired a knowledge of it upon like confidence. A secret of trade or manufacture does not lose its character by being confidentially disclosed to agents or servants, without whose assistance it could not be made of any value, even if, as argued in support of the demurrer, the process is liable to be inspected by the assessor of internal revenue or other public officer. The owner is not the less entitled to protection against those who in, or with knowledge of, violation of contract and breach of confidence, undertake to disclose it or reap the benefit of it."

[handwritten margin note: even if others heard it, may not necessarily understand, know how to use it to make bells]

At bar it does not appear that the Blymyer Manufacturing Co. attempted to enjoin secrecy upon their many subordinate employees, but preferred rather to rely upon the difficulty there would be in acquiring such a complete knowledge of the bell-making as to enable them to communicate it or use it if they wanted to. The fact that in twenty years, the process does not seem to have been successfully reproduced, indicates that such a course has sufficiently protected the secret. The bill of sale of the process as a secret by the Blymyer Manufacturing Co. to David W. Blymyer, in November, 1884, before there was any fear of disclosure or use by other persons, is evidence that the process was so considered by its owners.

On this question of whether the process is a secret, there has been introduced a great deal of testimony, oral, by deposition and by affidavit. In some respects it is quite conflicting, and raises doubts whether the process is a real secret. Cross examination of witnesses and the sifting process of a trial are necessary to a complete determination of the question. I have considered it rather with a view to determining what probability there is of the plaintiffs maintaining the existence of a secret at the trial, and it seems to me that there is such a probability. I may add that the claim made by John B. Dodds & Son, in their letter of April 25, 1887, to Farrington & Taylor, in which they claim that the process to be used by them in making bells is only known to J. B. Dodds, is an admission which tends to strengthen me in this conclusion.

I come now to the last question; is John B. Dodds under an obligation not to use or disclose the secret? Mr. Dodds says that he knew that the combination of these metals would make a bell-metal, from working at another foundry, in 1862 and 1863, where bells were so made. That, as I have said, was probably rather an experiment than a business, and one which was abandoned. The testimony of D. W. Blymyer, W. H. Blymyer, and the witness Alford shows that Dodds knew and understood and was told that the process was a secret which it was his duty to use every effort to preserve. He denies that he had any such understanding, or instruction. The weight of the evidence is against him. Moreover, if there was a secret, as I have found probable, and he came to know it because he was foreman and had to know it that it might be used, and knew that it was a secret, then I am inclined to think that his obligation to preserve such secret as the property of his employer must be implied, even though nothing was said to him on the subject.

implied duty to Maintain Confd.

* * *

From what has been said it will be seen that I deem it my duty to continue this injunction. I reach this conclusion the more readily, because this is only a preliminary hearing, and not final. To decide against the plaintiff on this hearing on the question of the secret, would be equivalent to a final decree in advance. The mischief, if any there is, would be done, no matter what the final decree. It is, therefore, plainly the duty of the court in such a case to continue the injunction if there is a possibility of plaintiff's sustaining its case on final hearing.

Motion overruled, and injunction continued in a modified form.

DID YOU GET IT?

1. What are the claimed trade secrets and who owns them?

2. What is the relationship between the plaintiff and the defendant(s)?
   D is fmr. employee of D's fmr Parent. Co.

3. The court found that Dodds was, at a minimum, under an implied duty to maintain the confidentiality of the trade secrets. Does this mean there was a contract between the parties?

4. Why didn't the court accept the defendant's argument that the alleged trade secrets had already been disclosed to others?
   —they didn't know how to use it.

The *Cincinnati Bell* case is an example of an early trade secret case that emphasized the property nature of a claim for trade secret misappropriation. The next case is an example of an early trade secret case that emphasized the unfair competition aspects of a trade secret claim.

┌───┐
│ *Reading Guidance* │
│ *What "wrong" was committed by each of the defendants?* │
└───┘

ALLEN-QUALLEY CO. V. SHELLMAR PRODUCTS CO.

United States District Court, N.D. Illinois, 1929.
31 F.2d 293.

WALTER C. LINDLEY, DISTRICT JUDGE.

Plaintiff's bill seeks an injunction to bar defendant from making, using, or selling combination confection wraps of the kind made and sold by the plaintiff, and from using, revealing, or making known the processes and machinery likewise used by plaintiff in said manufacture, and a decree that the defendant be compelled to assign to plaintiff United States patent No. 1,640,052, covering candy packages or wrappers consisting of a combination of transparent and opaque materials, issued August 23, 1927, and purchased by the defendant from the patentee, Olsen, on December 14, 1927.

Plaintiff is in the candy manufacturing business in St. Paul. In the early part of 1927 two of its employees perfected a new wrapper for candy packages, which contains a ribbon of transparent material called cellophane, and when wrapped about the candy affords a clear view of the contents of the package without unwrapping the same. So far as the defendant and plaintiff are concerned, at least, this was a new device. * * *

Defendant had been and was then manufacturing other wraps for plaintiff, but the latter designed a machine for the manufacture of this one in its own plant. The perfecting of the wrap, the process for making it, and the machine by which it was manufactured [took] from 12 to 15 months. Thereafter on November 25, 1927, Mair, the then general manager of plaintiff, met Martin, a representative of defendant, in Chicago and said to him that a new wrap had been designed; that the plaintiff's officers desired to make it themselves; but that he personally felt that it would be better to allow defendant to make it. This witness testifies that he told Martin that what he said to the former about the wrap was in confidence; that application for patent would be made, but had not yet been filed; that Martin agreed that the confidence would be respected, was most enthusiastic and said that the principle used in making the wrap was just what the trade was looking for.

A few days later Martin and Miller, another representative of defendant, went to St. Paul and there interviewed the general manager, president, and secretary of plaintiff. They said they had come to see and confer with plaintiff concerning the new wrapper, and that they did not want to "let the grass grow under their feet." They stayed two days. The testimony of three witnesses for the plaintiff is to the effect that Martin and Miller were eager to secure the right to manufacture the wrap and use the process previously designed; that upon an agreement that the information should be confidential, the details of the machine and process were fully disclosed; that after a full conference an oral agreement was entered into, by virtue of which defendant was to be allowed to manufacture the wrap upon a specified royalty; that it was further agreed that a written contract should be prepared embodying this oral agreement.

Martin and Miller returned to Chicago, and a few days later, in pursuance of an engagement, plaintiff's officers met defendant's patent counsel and defendant's representatives in separate conferences in Chicago. Counsel for defendant advised plaintiff he would not permit his clients to pay the royalty previously tentatively agreed upon by the parties. Defendant's patent counsel advised plaintiff that they were making a search of the patent records in Washington. After considerable negotiation, defendant refused to sign a written contract, and on December 14th, 1927, purchased the [Olsen] patent above mentioned by long distance telephone communications to San Francisco for the sum of $1,000. Thereafter, claiming it had a right so to do, defendant manufactured and sold wraps of the character mentioned, made by machines, which according to the testimony of one Angle, then employed by defendant, were based upon plaintiff's machine.

This witness testified that directly after Miller returned from St. Paul he exhibited the wrap to Angle, and asked the latter if he could make the same and devise a machine for the making of the same; that at that time Miller described plaintiff's machine seen in St. Paul; that he (Angle) could not at first understand the directions; but that as he proceeded he began to understand them. This machine was started directly after the return of the defendant's representatives from St. Paul, before the Olsen patent was purchased. Later defendant secured a standard machine from another source, but with the knowledge that it had of plaintiff's machine, made very material and substantial modifications in the machine it had purchased so as to adapt it to the making of this specific wrap.

It is evident that the parties entered into a tentative oral agreement in St. Paul, whereby defendant was to manufacture plaintiff's wrap; that the plaintiff in Chicago and St. Paul disclosed to the defendant, in confidence, all of the details concerning the wrap, the process of making the same and the machine for its manufacture; and that the defendant refused to execute a written contract in accordance with its tentative agreement because it believed the royalty demanded was too great and the arrangement inequitable.

* * *

In this situation the question at issue is whether or not the plaintiff is entitled to an injunction against the defendant's manufacture of the wrap and the use of its process in such manufacture and to the assignment of the patent purchased upon the payment of the purchase price thereof. The basic question involved is: Were plaintiff and defendant dealing at arms' length, or were their negotiations of such character as to put defendant in such position that in equity and good faith it was bound to respect the information given it by plaintiff and not to use the same for its own benefit and against plaintiff's interest?

Plaintiff's witnesses swear they told defendant's representatives that the disclosure of the wrapper, the manufacturing process, and the machine was strictly confidential. One of defendant's witnesses says that he asked plaintiff to keep all of said facts secret and that plaintiff replied there was no necessity for maintaining secrecy, because plaintiff was fully protected by patent. One of them says, not that plaintiff did not ask that the disclosure be treated as confidential, but that he remembers no such request.

— π says Convo was confidential

Defendant learned in confidence that plaintiff had what it called an invention for a wrapper; that plaintiff had designed a machine for producing the wrapper. It had seen the wrapper and the machine and knew that plaintiff considered both of great value and anticipated substantial profits from the same. Defendant was enthusiastic about the merits of the wrapper and was negotiating for a license to manufacture it. Could it, with knowledge of these facts, buy a so-called prior patent to which its attention had been called by reason of the disclosure made, cut off negotiations with plaintiff, and assert that it has the right to use plaintiff's process, to use plaintiff's machine or an adaptation thereof, or to make plaintiff's wrapper without accounting to plaintiff in any manner? Was it not under the duty to say to plaintiff, "We are not further interested," and cease its search and desist from making that which plaintiff had disclosed? If it discovered a so-called prior patent, was it not bound to disclose the same to plaintiff, and if it purchased same, to offer it to plaintiff? Are the demands of commercial integrity satisfied by the actions of defendant? If men in the business world are to respect the rights of others, if we are to insist upon morality in contractual dealings, if honesty is to prevail in commercial intercourse between citizens, a court of equity must put the stamp of disapproval upon what defendant has done here.

* * *

The question is not one of contracts, of patents, or of professional conduct of counsel. It is a question of the validity in equity of the acts of defendant in receiving in confidence, pending making contractual relationship, under an agreement to treat the same as confidential, a disclosure of the plaintiff's secrets, using such disclosure to locate a patent, directing its machinist to make a machine like plaintiff's machine, procuring an assignment of patent it claimed covered the alleged invention, and refusing to account to plaintiff. * * *

It is well established that equity will enjoin the use and disclosure of trade secrets, such as processes, formulae, and inventions learned in confidence. The difference between secret processes and patents is that the owner of a patent has a monopoly against all the world, while the owner of a secret process has no right "except against those who have contracted, expressly or by implication, not to disclose the secret, or who have obtained it by unfair means." * * * The jurisdiction of equity to protect such trade secrets is founded upon trust or confidence. The court "fastens the obligation upon the conscience of the party, and enforces it against him in the same manner as it enforces against a party to whom a benefit is given, the obligations of performing a promise on the faith of which the benefit has been conferred." * * * Whether the subject-matter is patentable or not, if the designer discovers and keeps secret a process of manufacture, though he will not have an exclusive right to it as against the public, after he shall have published it, or against those who in good faith acquire knowledge of it, yet he has a property right, which a court of chancery will protect against one who in bad faith and breach of confidence undertakes to apply it to his own use. * * *

The plaintiff at the time it divulged the information to defendant was not yet exhibiting the product to the world. It was giving information to nobody except to the defendant, as a proposed licensee, and under an agreement that the information should be treated as confidential. The relationship between them was one of trust and confidence. The language of Mr. Justice Holmes in *E. I. DuPont de Nemours Powder Co. v. Masland* is peculiarly pertinent, when he says: "Whether the plaintiffs have any valuable secret or not the defendant knows the facts, whatever they are, through a special confidence that he accepted. The property may be denied but the confidence cannot be." The same justice, in discussing the rights of the Chicago Board of Trade in quotations on prices of grain collected by itself, in *Board of Trade of Chicago v. Christie G. & S. Co.*, says: 'It stands like a trade secret. The plaintiff has the right to keep the work which it has done, or paid for doing, to itself. The fact that others might do similar work, if they might, does not authorize them to steal the plaintiff's.

It is apparent that it is immaterial in exercising this particular jurisdiction of equity, so far as the immediate parties are concerned, whether there is a valid patent owned by plaintiff or not. The basis for the jurisdiction is that the inventor is not required to apply for a patent, but is entitled to a protection of his process and device against a publication thereof and the misuse thereof by one who is guilty of a violation of trust and confidence. * * * It should be observed, moreover, that by revealing the wrap to the world, after the defendant had begun to violate the confidence reposed in it, and after applying for a patent therefore, plaintiff did not lose its rights as against defendant, and that it has never revealed to the world the particular process for making the wrap. * * *

Patent counsel, at the request of defendant, secured the Olsen patent. The circumstances were such that the purchase of this patent was, so far as defendant is concerned, a violation of trust, and the patent itself is therefore imbued with a trust relationship. * * *

It may well be that if defendant had never been in a confidential relationship with the plaintiff, upon the plaintiff's publication to the world of its wrap, the defendant might rightfully have purchased the same. Not by any action of plaintiff, but by its own violation of confidence, it has deprived itself of that opportunity, which is open to the rest of the world. It cannot obtain in confidence the details of an alleged invention, of the process for making the same, and of the machine by which it is made, and proceed to make the product by that or similar process, or by equivalent or similar machine or methods before the plaintiff makes its publication to the world, and then assert that it is a member of the public to whom the publication has been made. A court of equity cannot approve such breach of confidence.

There will be a decree for the relief prayed.

DID YOU GET IT?

1. What are the claimed trade secrets and who owns them?
    — process for making candy wrappers
2. What is the relationship between the plaintiff and the defendant?
    D— manu co. working for π candy business
3. What "wrong" did the defendant commit?
    — disclosing + using the process
4. Were plaintiff's alleged trade secrets disclosed to the public?
    No.

2. THE RESTATEMENT (FIRST) OF TORTS

Based upon cases from the nineteenth century and early twentieth century, a body of common law related to the protection of business secrets emerged. As Professor Fisk notes in the following excerpts from her book, the period also marked a shift from employee ownership of intellectual property rights to corporate ownership.

WORKING KNOWLEDGE AND THE RISE OF CORPORATE INTELLECTUAL PROPERTY, 1800–1930

Catherine L. Fisk.
University of North Carolina Press, 2009.

In the years bracketing the Civil War, much changed in American law and society. The agrarian republic imagined by Jefferson disappeared with early industrialization and the rise of commerce in the North. The "market revolution" that began in the Jacksonian era—the growth of commerce within the settled East and the expansion of commerce into the fast-growing West—opened up new opportunities for entrepreneurship through inventing, manufacturing, and selling. Factory production developed, first in textiles and armaments in New England, and then in clocks and other goods. The construction of roads, canals, and railroads opened up new possibilities for commerce and the extraction and processing of raw materials, including iron, lumber, and all sorts of minerals. In 1860, the United States trailed Great Britain, France, and Germany in industrial output, but by 1900 American industrial production exceeded that of these three countries combined. In those four decades, freedom in the economic sense shifted from the freedom of the yeoman farmers to work their lands to the freedom of white men to use their energy, ingenuity, and knowledge to make their way, and maybe their fortune, in the expanding markets.

* * *

Contract emerged in the 1870s as a unified body of law with the particular purpose of facilitating the formation of productive exchanges that would enrich the parties to the contract and, therefore, society as a whole. The development of laissez-faire contract, and its particularly enthusiastic embrace by judges confronting employment cases, was the dominant feature of the intellectual landscape of the late nineteenth-century law of the workplace. The rise of the scientific view of law and highly formalist approach to contracts, especially in the areas of master-servant, intellectual property, and equity, changed the perspective of judges and legal treatises on the employment relationship. Employment was a contract whose terms were determined by the employer and freely accepted by the employee.

* * *

In sum, during the latter half of the nineteenth century, a muscular new law of contract redefined the obligations of the employment relation for skilled craft workers. As the growing manufacturing firms sought ways to wrest control of the production process from their skilled workers and to expand their market power through control of patents, their lawyers found a sympathetic ear in judges who considered employee control of workplace knowledge "a reprehensible practice," as one put it, or not a "good custom," as said by another.

* * *

The transformation of craft knowledge into trade secrets occurred relatively quickly in a series of cases in the late 1880s and early 1890s. Using implied contract, courts revised traditional workplace norms while insisting that they were simply enforcing a bargain. Trade secret law grew from a relatively limited obligation to guard a particular and highly confidential piece of information or to convey a secret recipe along with the sale of a business, into a general prohibition on using a wide range of firm-specific information in subsequent employment. As courts expanded trade secrets and non-compete agreements to protect employer control over workplace knowledge, they transformed the nature of ownership of what had been regarded as artisanal knowledge. It ceased being an attribute of skilled craft workers and became an asset of corporate employers.

———

Beginning in 1938, the American Law Institute (the ALI) set about to "restate" the body of trade secret law that had developed to that point in a volume of the *Restatement (First) of Torts* (volume IV) dealing with "Interference with Business Relations" (hereinafter "the *Restatement of Torts*"). When Volume IV of the *Restatement of Torts* was published in 1939, it contained three sections dealing with confidential business information (set forth below with permission of the ALI) Section 757 sets forth the general principle of liability for the disclosure or use of another's trade secret. Section 758 concerns liability in the event of the "innocent discovery" of another's trade secret, essentially attempting to deal with the problem of trade secrets falling into the hands of third-parties who are not under a duty of confidentiality. Section 759 addresses the improper acquisition of "business information" (not otherwise meeting the definition of a trade secret) when such information is used "for the purpose of advancing a rival business interest."

While the trade secret principles that are set forth in the *Restatement of Torts* have since been modified by the Uniform Trade Secrets Act (the UTSA), the *Restatement (Third) of Unfair Competition*, and the Defend Trade Secrets Act of 2016 (the DTSA), it is important to understand how trade secret law was envisioned in the early part of the twentieth century and how it has evolved since.

RESTATEMENT (FIRST) OF TORTS
Section 757

One who discloses or uses another's trade secret, without privilege to do so, is liable to the other if:

(a) he discovered the secret by improper means, or

(b) his disclosure or use constitutes a breach of confidence reposed in him by the other in disclosing the secret to him, or

(c) he learned the secret from a third person with notice of the facts that it was secret and that the third person discovered it by improper means or that the third person's disclosure of it was otherwise a breach of duty to the other, or

(d) he learned the secret with notice of the facts that it was secret and that its disclosure was made by mistake.

Section 758

One who learns another's trade secret from a third person without notice that it is secret and that the third person's disclosure is a breach of his duty to the other, or who learns the secret through a mistake without notice of the secrecy and the mistake,

(a) is not liable to the other for a disclosure or use of the secret prior to receipt of such notice, and

(b) is liable to the other for a disclosure or use of the secret after the receipt of such notice, unless prior thereto has in good faith paid value for the secret or has so changed his position that to subject him to liability would be inequitable.

Section 759

[handwritten margin note: — for business info that does not meet definition of trade secret]

One who, for the purpose of advancing a rival business interest, procures by improper means information about another's business is liable to the other for the harm caused by his possession, disclosure or use of the information.

———

As a concise and accessible statement of an emerging body of law, the *Restatement of Torts* provisions on trade secrecy, together with the accompanying commentary and a growing body of case law, proved to be very influential and served as the primary source for an understanding of trade secret law in the United States for at least 50 years (from 1939 to 1989). However, beginning in the 1960s, concern was expressed by legal commentators and the practicing bar that trade secret law was not developing in a consistent fashion and that it was too amorphous and unpredictable. *See* Sharon K. Sandeen, *The Evolution of Trade Secret Law and Why Courts Commit Error When They Do Not Follow the Uniform Trade Secrets Act*, 33 HAMLINE L. REV. 493 (2010). For instance, a commentator of the time wrote:

> At the threshold of any discussion of the protection of trade secrets it seems most appropriate to define what the term "trade secrets" actually means. The term seems to imply the existence of some sort of property and suggests that a trade secret ought to be definable as such. . . . In fact, this is rarely the case.

Mathias Correa, *Protection of Trade Secrets*, 18 BUS. LAW. 531 (1963).

According to one commentator, the slow, unclear and inconsistent development of trade secret law was due, at least in part, to the inherent features of the *Restatement* series.

> Jurisdictions considering [the *Restatement's*] pronouncements are free to adopt or reject them in whole or in part . . . [and] they have

interpreted the *Restatement* differently.... The second factor limiting the overall effectiveness of the *Restatement* is that it treated some areas of trade secrets law inadequately, and others not at all.

Ramon Klitzke, *The Uniform Trade Secrets Act*, 64 MARQ. L. REV. 277, 282–83 (1980); *see also*, note 3 of Chapter 2 for a discussion of the differences between a *Restatement* and a uniform law. The differences also reflect the nature of the common law process, including the fact that the common law cannot develop until a case is brought. — *Know what fits into the definition*

Food for Thought

Consider why members of the practicing bar (and their clients) wanted uniformity in trade secret law. What are the pros and cons of uniform versus non-uniform laws? Is perfect uniformity ever possible? Why or why not?

---

3. THE UNIFORM TRADE SECRETS ACT

Under the auspices of the American Bar Association (the ABA), an effort was launched in the mid-1960s to draft a uniform law to govern trade secrets, ultimately leading to the adoption of the Uniform Trade Secrets Act (UTSA) by the National Conference of Commissioners of Uniform State Laws (NCCUSL, but now known as the Uniform Law Commission) in August of 1979. Based upon a review of the various drafts of the UTSA, the principal issues of concern to the drafters of the UTSA were:

1. The definition of a trade secret;
2. The meaning of misappropriation; *(umbrella term)*
3. The availability and scope of injunctive relief;
4. The nature and extent of monetary relief, including punitive damages and attorney's fees;
5. The treatment of trade secrets during litigation; and
6. The effect of the UTSA on other causes of action. *— less emphasis on these*

The UTSA was later amended in 1985 and since 1989, after the State of Alaska became the twenty-sixth state to enact its version of the UTSA, it has been the primary source of trade secret law in the United States. As of the publication of this book, the UTSA has been enacted (in substantial form) by forty-seven states, the District of Columbia, Puerto Rico, and the U.S. Virgin Islands. The three states that have not yet adopted the UTSA are: Massachusetts, New York, and North Carolina. Instead, Massachusetts and New York follow common law principles as expressed in the *Restatement of Torts,* the *Restatement (Third) of Unfair Competition,* or applicable case precedents. North Carolina has adopted a statute which is very similar, though not identical, to the UTSA but is not recognized as an "official" version of the UTSA by the Uniform Law Commission.

Although the *Restatement of Torts* provisions on trade secrecy were replaced by similar provisions in the *Restatement (Third) of Unfair Competition* in 1995, a declining number of courts still cite the *Restatement of Torts*. The *Restatement (Third) of Unfair Competition* is not cited as much as the applicable statutory version of the UTSA because it was published in 1995 after the UTSA was adopted and because most of its provisions mirror the UTSA. However, because the *Restatement (Third) of Unfair Competition* addresses some issues that are not directly addressed by the UTSA (such as ownership and implied duties of confidentiality) and contains extensive comments and illustrations, it is a helpful resource for general information concerning the meaning and application of trade secret law. Another helpful resource for understanding trade secret law is *Milgrim on Trade Secrets*, a treatise first published in 1967. *See* Roger M. Milgrim and Eric E. Bensen, MILGRIM ON TRADE SECRETS (2016), hereinafter referred to as *"Milgrim on Trade Secrets."* For a shorter summary of U.S. trade secret law, see Sharon K. Sandeen and Elizabeth A. Rowe, TRADE SECRET LAW IN A NUTSHELL (2013), with a second edition expected in late 2017.

In the remainder of this casebook, the wording, meaning, and application of the UTSA is carefully examined, particularly with respect to its definition of a trade secret and the act of misappropriation. However, because several states have yet to adopt the UTSA, and the *Restatement* provisions on trade secret law continue to be relied upon by courts in both UTSA and non-UTSA jurisdictions, the *Restatement of Torts* and the *Restatement (Third) of Unfair Competition* are also discussed where appropriate.

With respect to state trade secret law, the law and case decisions of each applicable state must be consulted to determine the details and nuances of trade secret law that apply in each state. *See* Brian M. Malsberger, et al., TRADE SECRETS: A STATE-BY-STATE SURVEY (5th ed. 2015). While state trade secret law is primarily uniform, there are some differences in both the wording and application of the law that may make a big difference in the outcome of particular cases.

4. THE DEFEND TRADE SECRET ACT OF 2016 AND THE EU TRADE SECRET DIRECTIVE

This casebook also discusses relevant provisions of the Defend Trade Secrets Act of 2016 (DTSA) that was signed by President Obama and went into effect on May 11, 2016 and the *Directive (EU) 2016/943 of the European Union and European Council of 8 June 2016 on the protection of undisclosed know-how and business information (trade secrets) against their unlawful acquisition, use and disclosure* (EU Trade Secret Directive) that entered into force on July 5, 2016. The codified version of the DTSA, as it amended the previously existing Economic Espionage Act of 1996, is set forth in the Appendix A to this casebook. The EU Trade Secret Directive is reprinted in Appendix B.

With respect to both the DTSA and the EU Trade Secret Directive, because they were only recently enacted at the time this casebook was published, there is little jurisprudence concerning their interpretation and application. However, because the DTSA was modeled after the UTSA, with the DTSA adopting much of the language of the UTSA verbatim, it is likely that the language that the DTSA "borrowed" from the UTSA will be interpreted consistently with the UTSA. How the "new" language will be interpreted remains to be seen. *See* Sharon K. Sandeen and Christopher B. Seaman, *Toward a Federal Jurisprudence of Trade Secret Law* (expected publication in late 2017).

C. SPECIAL ISSUE: ARE TRADE SECRETS PROPERTY AND WHY DOES IT MATTER?

Since the emergence of trade secret law in the United States in the 1800s there has been an enduring debate among lawyers, judges, and legal scholars about whether and when trade secrets should be considered a form of property. Comment a. to the *Restatement of Torts*, section 757, reads:

> The suggestion that one has a right to exclude others from the use of his trade secret because he has a right of property in the idea has been frequently advanced and rejected. The theory that has prevailed is that the protection is afforded only by a general duty of good faith and that the liability rests upon breach of this duty; that is, breach of contract, abuse of confidence or impropriety in the method of ascertaining the secret. Apart from breach of contract, abuse of confidence or impropriety in the means of procurement, trade secrets may be copied as freely as devices or processes which are not secret.

1. DU PONT V. MASLAND

Fueling the debate about whether trade secret principles are based upon property theory or principles of unfair competition is an oft-cited passage from *E.I. Du Pont de Nemours Powder Co. v. Masland*, 244 U.S. 100 (1917), in which Justice Holmes wrote:

> The case has been considered as presenting a conflict between a right of property and a right to make a full defense; and it is said that if the disclosure is forbidden to one who denies that there is a trade secret, the merits of his defense are adjudged against him before he has a chance to be heard or to prove his case. We

approach the question somewhat differently. The word "property" as applied to trademarks and trade secrets is an unanalyzed expression of certain secondary consequences of the primary fact that the law makes some rudimentary requirements of good faith. Whether the plaintiffs have any valuable secret or not the defendant knows the facts, whatever they are, through a special confidence that he accepted. The property may be denied, but the confidence cannot be. Therefore, the starting point for the present matter is not property or due process of law, but that the defendant stood in confidential relations with the plaintiffs, or one of them. These have given place to hostility, and the first thing to be made sure of is that the defendant shall not fraudulently abuse the trust reposed in him. It is the usual incident of confidential relations. If there is any disadvantage in the fact that he knew the plaintiffs' secrets, he must take the burden with the good.

As with all legal characterizations, one must consider the context in which they are made. Although *Masland* involved a claim of trade secret misappropriation, the specific issue before the Supreme Court was whether the lower court erred in denying an injunction that "forbade only the disclosure of processes claimed by [plaintiffs], including the disclosure to experts or witnesses produced during the taking of proofs, but excepting the defendant's counsel." The defendant, Masland, wanted to disclose the alleged secrets to his expert witnesses and argued that his right to due process should trump plaintiff's alleged property right. Justice Holmes disagreed, choosing instead to focus on the unfair competition aspects of the underlying claim.

Justice Holmes' reluctance in 1917 to categorize trade secrets as a form of property may have reflected his personal views concerning the scope and nature of property rights, but it was also consistent with the prevalent view of the time. As Professor Fisk explained:

> Today, a sophisticated lawyer asked to name the first thing that popped into her head at the mention of the word "property" might say copyrights or trademarks, in addition to real estate, personal property, or financial assets. But in the early nineteenth century, ideas were not easily assimilated to the concept of property. Rather, the focus was on physical things. Not until the late nineteenth century were trade secrets characterized as property in either legal or popular parlance. Until the twentieth century, thing-ness was necessary for knowledge to be conceived in legal terms as property. . . . Courts ordered the return of trade secrets if they were things but did not enjoin the use of the knowledge expressed in those things. Judges emphasized the presence of physical things in part because they did not understand inchoate

knowledge to be a firm's asset. Antebellum courts focused on protecting the physical property rather than the idea. * * *

Catherine L. Fisk, WORKING KNOWLEDGE AND THE RISE OF CORPORATE INTELLECTUAL PROPERTY, 1800–1930, (University of North Carolina Press, 2009).

2. RUCKELSHAUS V. MONSANTO CO.

The case that is frequently cited for the proposition that trade secrets are a form of private, albeit intangible, property is *Ruckelshaus v. Monsanto Co.*, 467 U.S. 986 (1984) (reprinted in part in Chapter 11). In that case the Supreme Court considered whether certain provisions of the Federal Insecticide, Fungicide, and Rodenticide Act were unconstitutional. Monsanto argued that the provisions of the law that required it to disclose certain information and data were unconstitutional because they amounted to a taking of property without just compensation in violation of the Fifth Amendment to the U.S. Constitution. For such a claim to be successful, Monsanto had to first establish it had a property interest in the information. In finding a property interest in Monsanto's data, the Court in *Ruckelshaus* explained:

> Because of the intangible nature of a trade secret, the extent of the property right therein is defined by the extent to which the owner of the secret protects his interest from disclosure to others. * * * Information that is public knowledge or that is generally known in an industry cannot be a trade secret. * * * If an individual discloses his trade secret to others who are under no obligation to protect the confidentiality of the information or otherwise publicly discloses the secret, his property right is extinguished.
>
> * * *
>
> Although this Court never has squarely addressed the question whether a person can have a property interest in a trade secret, which is admittedly intangible, the Court has found other kinds of intangible interests to be property for purposes of the Fifth Amendment's Takings Clause. * * *
>
> We therefore hold that to the extent that Monsanto has an interest in its health, safety, and environmental data cognizable as a trade-secret property right under Missouri law, that property right is protected by the Takings Clause of the Fifth Amendment.

The court went on to note, however, that Monsanto's takings claim was based upon the wording of the applicable statute which created an "investment-backed expectation" that the information that Monsanto submitted to the government would be protected from disclosure for a period of fifteen years. There is no requirement imposed upon governments to write laws which promise confidentiality of submitted information, except for limited data exclusivity requirements set-forth in various international agreements (discussed in Chapter 11).

Professor Pamela Samuelson critiqued the Supreme Court's decision in *Ruckelshaus* by noting:

> [T]o the extent that information is coming to be regarded as property, there is a clear need for some serious thought about how to draw lines between information that can be protected as property and information that cannot. One possible line of demarcation which would be consistent with [*Ruckelshaus*] is that secret information is protectable as property until no longer secret. Another possible line might distinguish between complex patterns of information that have been fixed in some medium, * * * and individual or unfixed isolated bits of data. * * * We must approach the process of drawing such distinctions carefully and deliberately, with full appreciation of the consequences of their inherent characterizations. A world in which all information is property under all circumstances is, at present, unthinkable. But arriving at a coherent theory concerning when information is property, and when it is not, is a task to which little thought has been given, and much must be.

See Pamela Samuelson, *Information as Property: Do Ruckelshaus and Carpenter Signal a Changing Direction in Intellectual Property Law?*, 38 CATH. U. L. REV. 365 (1989).

Food for Thought

Why, as Professor Samuelson argues, is it important to determine when and under what circumstances information (including trade secrets) will be treated as property? What might happen if all information is treated as private property? How does intangible property differ from tangible property?

---

3. ALDERSON V. U.S.

Although it is clear from the language of *Ruckelshaus* that the U.S. Supreme Court limited its holding to information that qualifies for trade secret protection, Professor Samuelson's concern that the holding of *Ruckelshaus* might be used to claim property rights in lesser forms of information was prescient. In *Alderson v. United States*, 718 F.Supp.2d 1186 (2010), an individual who successfully brought a False Claims Act *qui tam* action argued that the information concerning Medicare fraud that he provided to the government was his property. He did so because he wanted the money he was awarded for such information to be taxed at the lower capital gains rate instead of the ordinary income rate.

In denying the plaintiff a property interest in the information he provided to the government, the court explained:

> The Ninth Circuit has distilled a three-part test for determining whether a property right exists: "First, there must be an interest capable of precise definition; second, it must be capable of exclusive control; and third, the putative owner must have established a legitimate claim to exclusivity." * * *

> Here, it is clear that Alderson did not have the right to exclude others from obtaining his "secret information" and "know-how." The "secret information" and "know-how" was nothing more than the knowledge that Alderson's employer was engaged in wrongdoing. Alderson's "information" and "know-how" was also known by Alderson's employer.

Applying the foregoing definition of property rights, some bodies of information may qualify, but not others. It also suggests that knowledge that another has engaged in wrongdoing cannot be a property interest.

4. WHY DOES A PROPERTY CHARACTERIZATION MATTER?

The foregoing illustrates that whether information is characterized as property can have real world consequences and that when deciding whether information will be treated as property, context matters. Combining the Supreme Court's definition of property from *Ruckelshaus* and the Ninth Circuit's definition from *Alderson*, information that meets the definition of a trade secret is property to the extent it can be precisely defined and is maintained within the exclusive control of the putative trade secret owner. But under well-established trade secret doctrine, proving the existence of a property right (a trade secret), alone, is not enough to state a trade secret claim.

In the commentary to section 39 (Definition of Trade Secret) of the *Restatement (Third) of Unfair Competition*, it is explained:

> The dispute over the nature of trade secret rights has had little practical effect on the rules governing civil liability for the appropriation of a trade secret. The cases generally require that the plaintiff establish both the existence of a trade secret under the principles described in this Section and the fact of misconduct by the defendant under the rules stated in § 40. Many cases acknowledge that the primary issue is the propriety of the defendant's conduct as a means of competition. The substantive scope of the rights recognized under the law of trade secrets thus

reflects the accommodation of numerous interests, including the trade secret owner's claim to protection against the defendant's bad faith or improper conduct, the right of competitors and others to exploit information and skills in the public domain, and the interest of the public in encouraging innovation and in securing the benefits of vigorous competition.

The foregoing quote brings us back to the question: Why does a property characterization even matter? Whether you label a trade secret as property or not, you still have to prove all of the elements of a trade secret misappropriation claim in order to prevail.

As explained in *Milgrim on Trade Secrets,* "the primary answer to the question is that different legal consequences might flow from the characterization, including potentially different statute of limitations, admissibility of evidence principles and remedies." *See* MILGRIM ON TRADE SECRETS, § 3.01 (2016). But there are other potential consequences of a property characterization. As noted by Professor Robert Bone, commenting on the early trade secret case of *Peabody v. Norfolk*, ". . . classifying secret information as 'property' meant that a contract to convey that information could not be an unlawful restraint on trade. Moreover, classifying the information as property meant that the court could restrain Cook even though he was not in privity with Peabody." Robert G. Bone, *A New Look at Trade Secret Law: Doctrine in Search of Justification*, 85 CAL. L. REV. 241, 253–54 (1998). Professor Eric Claeys observes that if trade secrets are property, then everyone (other than the trade secret owner) owes a duty in tort not to take the trade secrets. Eric R. Claeys, *Intellectual Usufructs: Trade Secrets, Hot News, and the Property Paradigm at Common Law*, in INTELLECTUAL PROPERTY AND THE COMMON LAW, (Shyamkrishna Balganesh, ed., 2013).

Professor Samuelson notes that the characterization of trade secrets as property may impact the applicability of a First Amendment defense (discussed in Chapter 9) to trade secret misappropriation. Pamela Samuelson, *Principles for Resolving Conflicts Between Trade Secrets and the First Amendment*, 58 HASTINGS L. J. 777, 808–11 (2007). Charles Tait Graves argues that "a property conception best serves the interests of promoting employee mobility and the freedom to use information in the public domain." Charles Tait Graves, *Trade Secrets as Property: Theory and Consequences*, 15 J. INTELL. PROP. L. 39 (2001). In his article, *The Surprising Virtues of Treating Trade Secrets as Intellectual Property,* Professor Mark Lemley argues:

If we give protection to things that are public, we defeat the [disclosure] purpose [of trade secret law] and give windfalls to people who may not be inventors (what we might call "trade secret trolls"). Courts that think of trade secret law as a common law tort rather than an IP right are apt to overlook the secrecy requirement in their zeal to reach "bad actors." But it is the courts that emphasize secrecy, not appropriation, as the key element of the cause of action that have it right.

61 STAN. L. REV. 311, 313 (2008).

In summary, whether (and when) trade secrets are characterized as property can result in a number of ancillary effects. It is also important to understand that the debate whether trade secret law is grounded in property rights is part of a broader and ongoing philosophical debate about the proper grounding of a variety of legal doctrines. Grounding an area of law in a particular theory or philosophy can serve a number of important functions, including defining (and thereby limiting) the scope of the law, explaining the law, and making it easier to apply. More importantly, the underlying justifications for a particular body of law can help to make the law more understandable by the public at large and, hopefully, more respected. As expressed by Professor Eric Claeys in an article that explores the justifications for trade secret law:

> Socially, people are inclined not to obey or submit to government coercion without some persuasive explanation why the law claims legitimate authority over them. Ordinarily, people expect that such a claim appeals at some level to their interests. Copycat competitors will have the same expectation as other competitors. It will not do to assert, without serious qualification to copycats: "You must suffer so that your up-market competitors as a whole or society as a whole may be better off." Copycatting is perfectly legitimate in many situations—as trade secrecy itself confirms, by making it legitimate to copy and use business information that falls within common industry knowledge, is readily ascertainable by skilled competitors, or has not been marked off by reasonable precautions. Without any explanation why it is wrong to copy and use valid trade secrets, a judgment of misappropriation seems to a down-market competitor a raw assertion of government power favoring up-market elites.

See Eric Claeys, *Private Law Theory and Corrective Justice in Trade Secrecy*, 4 J. TORT L. 1, 19 (2011).

Food for Thought

With the foregoing quote in mind, what do you think makes the protection of trade secrets legitimate? Would you be more inclined to respect a property based regime or an unfair competition based regime? Which justification do you think has the most rhetorical power?

The contract, unfair competition, and property justifications of trade secret law all have appeal from the standpoint of the down-market competitor who wants to understand why it is "wrong" to use someone else's information. Under contract law, the wrong is the breach of contract. Under unfair competition principles, the wrong is engaging in some act or acts deemed contrary to business ethics. Under property law, the wrong is interfering with or destroying someone else's property. But all three justifications also have problems. As noted above, the breach of contract justification does not always work for the simple reason that there may be no binding contractual obligation. An emphasis on unfair competition principles may result in too much information being protected as courts focus more on the bad acts of the defendant than on the secrecy of the information sought to be protected. Conversely, an undue emphasis on trade secrets as property rights may cause courts to deemphasize the importance of free competition and employee mobility that individuals and businesses should enjoy.

As a practical matter, concluding that a particular set of information is property is only the beginning of the analysis. Although the rhetoric of property rights may suggest that all forms of property are the same, this is not the case. Some forms of property, such as real property, may be stronger than others. Thus, even if trade secrets are categorized as a form of property, we still need to consider the proper metes and bounds of such a property right. *See* Michael A. Carrier, *Cabining Intellectual Property through a Property Regime*, 54 DUKE L.J. 1 (2004).

This is a debate that is ongoing in trade secret circles, details of which you will learn throughout this casebook. Generally, to understand the scope of any legal right (including property rights), you need to know: (1) the theoretical scope of protection; (2) the requirements for protection; (3) applicable limitations on the scope of protection; (4) the essential elements of a claim to enforce such rights; (5) applicable defenses; and (6) available remedies. You also need to understand the public policy that underlies such matters. These issues are the focus of the remainder of this casebook.

Food for Thought

As you proceed through the remainder of this casebook, consider which justification of trade secret law (property, contract, or unfair competition) seems most appropriate to you and how the varying justifications might help either the plaintiff or defendant to prevail.

NOTES

1. **The DTSA and the Commerce Clause.** Unlike similar federal laws governing patents and copyrights, but like the EEA and the federal law which governs trademarks (known as the Lanham Act), the DTSA was not adopted pursuant to Congress' powers under the intellectual property clause of the U.S. Constitution (Article 1, Section 8, Clause 8). Rather, it was adopted pursuant

to its Commerce Clause powers. The Commerce Clause (Article 1, Section 8, Clause 3) reads: "The Congress shall have power . . . [t]o regulate commerce with foreign nations, and among the several states, and with the Indian tribes; . . ."

Recall from your knowledge of Constitutional law that the power of Congress is limited but that the Commerce Clause is often used to justify the adoption of federal laws. When adopting a federal law under the Commerce Clause, Congress usually includes a provision in the law that is designed to provide the necessary Commerce Clause (or Constitutional) hook. The DTSA provision reads as follows:

> An owner of a trade secret that is misappropriated may bring a civil action under this subsection if the trade secret is related to a product or service used in, or intended for use in, interstate or foreign commerce.

Food for Thought

How far do you think this provision extends? Will it cover all trade secret cases or just some? If you were the plaintiff's attorney in a trade secret case and you wanted to bring the case in federal court based upon federal subject matter jurisdiction, what would you need to plead and prove to meet the factual predicates of the foregoing provision? How difficult do you think it would be to prove those factual predicates and what might your client have to reveal in the process?

---

2. **Introduction to the EU Trade Secret Directive.** Principles of trade secret law, particularly of the breach of confidentiality variety, have existed in many countries for many years. *See* Elizabeth A. Rowe and Sharon K. Sandeen, TRADE SECRECY AND INTERNATIONAL TRANSACTIONS (2015). However, it was not until the adoption of the World Trade Organization Agreement on Trade-related Aspects of Intellectual Property (the TRIPS Agreement) that a major international agreement specifically required countries to provide legal protection for trade secrets. Since 1995 when the TRIPS Agreement went into effect for most countries of the European Union (EU), the trade secret laws of the EU have been a hodge-podge of laws and legal principles. Some common law countries (like England) relied upon principles developed through case law while other countries (particularly civil law countries) relied upon written code, but most often not stand-alone statutes that focus on trade secrets. *See* European Commission, *Study on Trade Secrets and Confidential Business Information in the Internal Market*, Final Study, April 2013.

The EU Trade Secret Directive (reprinted in Appendix B) is significant in that it requires all EU-member countries to conform their laws to more detailed requirements concerning the scope and limits of trade secret rights and remedies. While largely modeled after the UTSA, the EU Trade Secret Directive includes a number of explicit exceptions that serve to limit the scope of trade secret rights.

3. **The stated purposes of trade secret law.** As with the evolution of trade secret law generally, the stated purposes of trade secret law have also evolved through the years. In the early years, the primary purpose of trade secret law was the preservation of commercial ethics. *Kewanee Oil Company v. Bicron Corporation*, 416 U.S. 470, 481–482 (1974) ("The maintenance of standards of commercial ethics and the encouragement of invention are the broadly stated policies behind trade secret law.") Later, as corporate and business interest in intellectual property increased and trade secrets began to be seen as a form of property, another purpose of trade secret law was identified, namely, to encourage invention and innovation. *Id.* at p. 482–484 ("Certainly the patent policy of encouraging invention is not disturbed by the existence of another form of incentive to invention.") A third, but seemingly illogical, purpose emerged out of *Kewanee* when the Supreme Court had to explain how state trade secret law did not interfere with the disclosure purpose of patent law. The court concluded that trade secret law did not conflict with the disclosure goals of U.S. patent law because it facilitates the sharing of information, albeit on a smaller scale than U.S. patent law. *Id.* at p. 484–489; *see also* Sharon K. Sandeen, *Kewanee Revisited: Returning to First Principles of Intellectual Property Law to Determine the Issue of Federal Preemption*, 12 MARQ. L. REV. 299 (2008).

4. **The economics of trade secrecy.** Historically, there has not been much study or analysis of the economics of trade secret law including, for instance, whether trade secret protection is actually needed to encourage invention and innovation. This changed markedly in the past two decades with the publication of a number of articles and essays that address the economics of trade secrecy, including: Michael Risch, *Trade Secret Law and Information Development Incentives*, *in* THE LAW AND THEORY OF TRADE SECRECY: A HANDBOOK OF CONTEMPORARY RESEARCH (Rochelle C. Dreyfuss and Katherine J. Strandburg eds., 2011); Michael Risch, *Why Do We Have Trade Secrets?*, 11 MARQ. INTELL. PROP. L. REV. 1 (2007); Pamela Samuelson and Suzanne Scotchmer, *The Law and Economics of Reverse Engineering*, 111 YALE L.J. 1577, 1650 (2002); William A. Landes and Richard A. Posner, *The Economics of Trade Secrecy Law*, *in* THE ECONOMIC STRUCTURE OF INTELLECTUAL PROPERTY LAW (2003); Peter S. Menell, *Intellectual Property: General Theories*, *in* ENCYCLOPEDIA OF LAW & ECONOMICS (Boudewijn Bouckaert and Gerrit De Geest eds., 2000); David D. Friedman, William M. Landes, and Richard A. Posner, *Some Economics of Trade Secret Law*, 5 JOURNAL OF ECONOMIC PERSPECTIVES 61–72 (1991); Steven N. S. Cheung, *Property Rights in Trade Secrets*, 20 ECON. INQUIRY 40 (1982); Edmund W. Kitch, *The Law and Economics in Rights in Valuable Information*, 9 J. OF LEGAL STUDIES 683 (1980).

5. **The use of contracts to protect trade secrets.** As we will learn in Chapter 9, the adoption of the Uniform Trade Secrets Act did not displace or preclude breach of contract claims. Thus, while the UTSA was specifically designed to preclude competing tort theories of recovery, claims based upon breach of an express or implied-in-fact agreement of confidentiality can still be

brought. Indeed, one scholar argues that in light of the uncertain foundations of trade secret law and other considerations, "trade secret liability should be governed mainly by contract principles." *See* Robert G. Bone, *A New Look at Trade Secret Law: A Doctrine in Search of Justification*, 86 CAL. L. REV. 241 (1998).

Of course, when contract claims are brought to protect trade secrets, the plaintiff has the burden of proving all of the elements of a breach of contract claim and is limited to remedies for breach of contract. *See* Sharon K. Sandeen, *A Contract by Any Other Name is Still a Contract: Examining the Effectiveness of Trade Secret Clauses to Protect Databases*, 45 IDEA 119 (2005). Also, it is well-established that contracts cannot be used to create trade secret rights; they must exist independent of the contract. MILGRIM ON TRADE SECRETS, vol. 1, § 1.03 n. 8 (2016). What is an unsettled aspect of trade secret law (or more broadly "information law") is the extent to which contracts or other tort theories can be used to protect information that does not qualify for trade secret protection. *See* Raymond T. Nimmer, NIMMER ON INFORMATION LAW, vol. 1, § 5:4 (2015); Robert Unikel, *Bridging the Trade Secret Gap: Protecting Confidential Information Not Rising to the Level of Trade Secrets*, 29 LOY. U. CHI. L.J. 841 (1998). Those who own vast amounts of information and data often argue for broad protection, while those who value a rich public domain argue for limits on the type and scope of information that can be protected by contract. As the Supreme Court has repeatedly noted: "[F]ederal laws require that all ideas in general circulation be dedicated to the common good unless they are protected by a valid patent." *Lear, Inc. v. Adkins*, 395 U.S. 653, 668 (1969). The drafters of the UTSA adopted the narrower approach when they decided not to include *Restatement of Torts,* Section 759 (reprinted above) in the UTSA.

Theoretically, an express or implied contract could be used to protect a broader set of information than would qualify for protection under trade secret law. However, not all information would provide the necessary consideration for a binding contract. Arguably, in order to serve as consideration for an agreement of confidentiality, the subject information should have some degree of novelty, although not the level of novelty needed for patent protection. *See* discussion of idea submission claims in the Special Issue section of Chapter 4. Also, for public policy reasons, some argue that there are bodies of information that we should preclude from being the subject of a contract. *See, e.g.*, J. H. Reichman & Jonathan A. Franklin, *Privately Legislated Intellectual Property Rights: Reconciling Freedom of Contract with Public Good Uses of Information*, 147 U. PA. L. REV. 875 (1999). The general skill and knowledge that we all possess, some of which we acquired through our work experiences, is an example of information that, arguably, should not be the subject of contractual restrictions on use. *See* discussion of the difference between trade secret information and general skill and knowledge in the Special Issue section of Chapter 3.

Food for Thought

As you study the materials in this book, consider the consequences of using contracts to protect trade secrets and other business information. Is it possible for a trade secret owner to enter into contracts with all who may be exposed to the trade secrets? What type of defendants would be able to avoid liability under a pure contract-based theory of trade secret liability?

---

6. **Bibliographic note:** In addition to the references above, for more information on the topics discussed in this chapter, see MILGRIM ON TRADE SECRETS §§ 1.01, 2.01 (2016); Robert G. Bone, *Steps Toward Evidence-Based IP: the (Still) Shaky Foundations of Trade Secret Law*, 92 TEX. L. REV. 1803 (2014); Jasmine McNealy, *Who Owns Your Friends?: Phonedog v. Kravitz and Business Claims of Trade Secret in Social Media Information*, 39 RUTGERS COMPUTER & TECH. L.J. 30 (2013); David S. Almeling, *Seven Reasons Why Trade Secrets Are Increasingly Important*, 27 BERKELEY TECH. L.J. 1091 (2012); Richard A. Epstein, *Trade Secrets as Private Property: Their Constitutional Protection* (Univ. Chi. John M. Olin Law & Econ. Working Paper No. 190, 2d Series (2003)); Jacqueline Lipton, *Balancing Private Rights and Public Policies: Reconceptualizing Property in Databases*, 18 BERKELEY TECH. L.J. 773 (2003); James W. Hill, *Trade Secrets, Unjust Enrichment and the Classification of Obligation*, 4 VA. J.L. & TECH. 2 (1999); Vincent Chiapetta, *Myth, Chameleon or Intellectual Property Olympian? A Normative Framework Supporting Trade Secret Law*, 8 GEORGE MASON L. REV. 69 (1999); Michael Deutch, *The Property Concept of Trade Secrets in Anglo-American Law: An Ongoing Debate*, 31 U. RICH. L. REV. 313 (1997); Robert P. Merges, *The End of Friction? Property Rights and Contract in the "Newtonian" World of On-Line Commerce*, 12 BERKELEY TECH. L.J. 115 (1997); Niva Elkin-Koren, *Copyright Policy and the Limits of Freedom of Contract*, 12 BERKELEY TECH L. J. 93 (1997); Raymond T. Nimmer & Patricia A. Krauthaus, *Information as Property Databases and Commercial Property,* 1 INT'L J.L. & INFO. TECH. 3 (1993); Wendy J. Gordon, *Intellectual Property and Corrective Justice*, 78 VA. L. REV. 283 (1992).

CHAPTER 2

WHAT CAN BE A "TRADE SECRET"?

■ ■ ■

> ### Anticipated Learning Outcomes
>
> At the conclusion of this chapter you will have an understanding of the kinds of information that are eligible for trade secret protection and the elements required to create a trade secret. To satisfy this objective, the chapter introduces the definitions of a trade secret as presented in the *Restatement (First) of Torts*, the Uniform Trade Secrets Act (UTSA), the *Restatement (Third) of Unfair Competition*, and the Defend Trade Secrets Act of 2016 (DTSA) (which amended the definition of a trade secret that was originally enacted as part of the Economic Espionage Act of 1996).

A. INTRODUCTION

In this chapter we explore the various sources of law that help define the term "trade secret." You will see that the term has special significance. It covers a small subset of information, not just any information that a company considers confidential. Accordingly, understanding the elements of a trade secret is critical to determining whether information that a putative trade secret owner alleges is a trade secret actually meets the legal criteria to be a trade secret.

While almost any kind of business information can qualify for trade secret protection, proper application of the definition of a trade secret serves to filter out true trade secrets from: (1) other confidential and proprietary information; (2) trivial information; and (3) information that is free for everyone to use. As you read the cases in this and the subsequent three chapters, note that the best analyses spend a fair amount of time examining whether the plaintiff (and putative trade secret owner) has presented sufficient evidence to meet each of the elements of the definition of a trade secret.

As discussed in Chapter 1, until 2016, trade secret law in the United States came from three main sources: common law as expressed in the *Restatement of Torts* and *the Restatement (Third) of Unfair Competition*, and statutory law as expressed in the UTSA. With the adoption of the Defend Trade Secret Act of 2016 (DTSA), a fourth source of law now exists, but one that remains to be interpreted by the federal judiciary. (See

Appendix A.) The *Restatement of Torts* represents the oldest of the four sources, with the UTSA, the *Restatement (Third) of Unfair Competition*, and the DTSA being the modern versions. *not necessarily settled*

Under all sources of trade secret law, certain categories of information are not protectable as trade secrets. For important public policy reasons, unprotectable information includes: (1) information that is generally known or readily ascertainable; (2) abstract ideas; and (3) an individual's personal or professional skills (we focus more specifically on these categories in Chapter 3). Often in trade secret cases, particularly those that involve so-called "combination trade secrets" or compilations of data, the central issue in the case relates to the ability of the parties to articulate which part of the combination or compilation is protectable and which part is not.

Assuming information does not fall into a category of unprotectable information, it must also meet additional requirements to be deemed a trade secret. According to both the UTSA and the DTSA, it must be secret, the owner must have made reasonable efforts to preserve its secrecy, and it must have sufficient value. One of the problems with the cases interpreting the UTSA is that these concepts are often merged, such that, for example, the analysis of "generally known" or "readily ascertainable" becomes intertwined with the analysis of value and reasonable efforts.

The convergence of concepts will become apparent to you as each of the requirements for trade secrecy is addressed more fully in subsequent chapters. In this chapter, you will see why the term "trade secret" has special legal significance. To do so, we turn to the definitions.

B. DEFINITIONS OF A TRADE SECRET

Since the UTSA has been widely adopted in the United States and was the model for both the DTSA and the EU Trade Secret Directive, this casebook focuses on the UTSA definition of a trade secret. However, it is important to understand the key similarities and differences between and among the UTSA, the DTSA, and the *Restatements,* particularly in cases that are brought in non-UTSA jurisdictions. Indeed, in analyzing any trade secret case, one must first understand the source of law applicable to that case since it could be outcome determinative.

The *Restatement of Torts* was the first major effort at synthesizing the law of trade secrecy. Although the text of the *Restatement of Torts* (reprinted in Chapter 1) does not include a definition of a trade secret, comment b to section 757 provides that:

A trade secret may consist of any formula, pattern, device or compilation of information which is used in one's business, and which gives him an opportunity to obtain an advantage over competitors who do not know or use it.

* * *

It differs from other secret information in a business (*see* § 759) in that it is not simply information as to a single or ephemeral events in the conduct of the business, as for example, the amount or other terms of a secret bid for a contract * * *. A trade secret is a process or device for continuous use in the operation of a business.

As noted in Chapter 1, a principal motivating factor behind the adoption of the UTSA was the perceived need to more precisely define the parameters of a trade secret. Section 1(4) of the UTSA defines a trade secret as:

> [I]nformation, including a formula, pattern, compilation, program, device, method, technique, or process, that: (i) derives independent economic value, actual or potential, from not being generally known to, and not being readily ascertainable by proper means by, other persons who can obtain economic value from its disclosure or use, and (ii) is the subject of efforts that are reasonable under the circumstances to maintain its secrecy.

In substantial part, the foregoing is also the definition of a trade secret under federal law as expressed in the Economic Espionage Act of 1996 and the DTSA. Two differences are: (1) the definition of a trade secret applicable to both EEA and DTSA claims includes a list of types of protected "information;" and (2) a more comprehensive list of examples. *See* 18 U.S.C. § 1839(3), reprinted in Appendix A. Whether these differences will make a difference in the application of the DTSA remains to be seen.

When the *Restatement (Third) of Unfair Competition* was adopted by the American Law Institute in 1995, it largely replicated the language of the UTSA. However, there are some differences in terminology and coverage. With respect to the definition of a trade secret, section 39 of the *Restatement (Third) of Unfair Competition* provides that:

> A trade secret is any information that can be used in the operation of a business or other enterprise and that is sufficiently valuable and secret to afford an actual or potential economic advantage over others.

Note that the foregoing definition is different from the UTSA and DTSA definitions in that it does not mention reasonable efforts to maintain secrecy. This difference is explored in greater detail in Chapter 5.

Among the main differences between the earlier *Restatement of Torts* definition of a trade secret and the more modern UTSA and *Restatement (Third) of Unfair Competition* definitions are that the latter do not require that the secret be "in use" by the owner to qualify for protection. The fact that the information has potential use or value is sufficient. Moreover, the UTSA places greater emphasis on the trade secret owner's efforts to keep the information secret due in large part to the notice function of such efforts.

While the EEA and DTSA do not include a use requirement in the definition of a trade secret, because both the EEA and DTSA were enacted pursuant to Congress' powers under the Commerce Clause of the United States Constitution, the subject trade secrets must be "related to a product or service used in, or intended for use in, interstate or foreign commerce." *See* Appendix A, 18 U.S.C. §§ 1832(a) and 1836(b)(1). Also, like the UTSA, the definition of a trade secret under the EEA and DTSA requires that the trade secret owner engage in reasonable efforts to maintain the secrecy of the information.

Food for Thought

Can you identify the types of information that a business may own that is of value to it even though it is not used? Do you think secret information that is not put to use should be protected by trade secret law? If so, should there be a limit on the length of protection for unused information?

Reading Guidance

Did the price book in this case meet the definition of a trade secret under the Missouri UTSA?

LYN-FLEX WEST, INC. V. DIECKHAUS

Missouri Court of Appeals, Eastern District, 1999.
24 S.W.3d 693.

PAUL J. SIMON, JUDGE.

Lyn-Flex West, Inc., plaintiff, appeals the judgment entered following the grant of a directed verdict in favor of defendants, Wayne Dieckhaus (Wayne), Dick Dieckhaus (Dick), George Convy, and Walk Easy Manufacturing Co., Inc., (collectively defendants), in an action for misappropriation of trade secrets, tortious interference with a business expectancy, and conspiracy. * * *

The record, in the light most favorable to the plaintiff, reveals that plaintiff is a national corporation engaged in the business of shoe insole manufacturing. Walk Easy is also engaged in the same business and is currently one of plaintiff's two competitors, manufacturing the same products and servicing many of plaintiff's former customers at prices pennies lower than plaintiff's. In many instances, plaintiff's product codes are used by Walk Easy. Defendants Wayne, Dick and Convy, formerly officers of plaintiff, currently are officers of Walk Easy.

For years, plaintiff has compiled the identity of its customers, the technical and detailed information concerning products manufactured for each of those customers, the materials used in the production and manufacturing of each product, and the precise dimensions of each part comprising the insole, including notes and codes unique to each customer in a Detailed Price and Specifications Book (price book).

Plaintiff's current and former employees testified that the book was kept in an office with limited access and locked at night. Although it was not kept in a lock box or stamped confidential, office employees understood it to be such and that it would not be shown to competitors or those who had no need to see its contents. Dick acknowledged that the possession of the book in the hands of a competitor would give an advantage, at least in the area of pricing. Only Gary Hahn, plaintiff's computer technician, had the ability to print out a price book and it was distributed only to those who had a need to use it.

Peter Leher was the sole stockholder of plaintiff until his death. Wayne served as plaintiff's president, with Dick as general manager, and Convy as head of sales. Following Leher's death, plaintiff was operated by United Missouri Bank (UMB) as trustee of his estate. UMB contacted Wallace McNeill, an investor, to inquire whether he was interested in purchasing plaintiff. * * *

On November 7, 1997, McNeill purchased all of the company's stock and the purchase was announced to plaintiff's employees. The next day, Wayne, Dick and Convy announced to McNeill that they were leaving. The three officers left on November 12, 1997 and established Walk Easy, using a corporate name registered to Convy and his son. The lease for the manufacturing facility of Walk Easy had been negotiated one day earlier by Wayne. Dick had been shopping for equipment the week before he left plaintiff. Shortly before he left, Dick asked Jane Folker, who shortly thereafter went to work for Walk Easy, to ask Gary Hahn to print out a new price book for him. That price book has not been found on plaintiff's premises.

In a deposition, Jane Folker admitted to seeing one of plaintiff's price books in Dick's office at Walk Easy, and stated that she had observed Dick use the book on occasion. After these statements were made, the police searched the premises of Walk Easy and recovered a price book of plaintiff. At trial, Dick maintained that the book was given to him by Leher to be kept at his home. He admitted at trial that he did occasionally use the price book for reference in pricing to see how Walk Easy prices compared to plaintiff's. While he maintained at trial that he developed Walk Easy's specifications from memory, reflecting his many years at plaintiff, when asked at trial, he could not recall those specifications. Some of Walk Easy's customers also stated that they did not provide Dick with specifications for their products. As a result of the competition, plaintiff lost several customers to Walk Easy, including Justin Boot and its subsidiaries, costing plaintiff hundreds of thousands of dollars in lost sales.

Plaintiff brought suit in the circuit court in Franklin County, alleging misappropriation of trade secrets, tortious interference with a business expectancy and conspiracy. At the close of plaintiff's evidence, the defendants made an oral motion for a directed verdict on the basis that plaintiff had failed to produce evidence to support a finding that the price book was a trade secret and thus had failed to show that any trade secrets had been misappropriated * * *.

The trial judge sustained the oral motion, indicating that he did not believe that the price book was a trade secret, by stating "I don't think they made sufficient effort to protect the books before plaintiff bought the company. And all the evidence is that they used those old books." The trial court found that the book was not a trade secret and ruled that plaintiff had not established evidence sufficient to show misappropriation, absence of a justification for tortious interference and an unlawful act for conspiracy. The trial court made no written findings of fact and conclusions of law.

In its first point on appeal, plaintiff contends that the trial court erred in directing a verdict against plaintiff on its claims for damages for misappropriation of trade secrets under the Uniform Trade Secrets Act. Plaintiff argues that it presented evidence sufficient to allow a reasonable jury to conclude that defendants had misappropriated trade secrets of plaintiff by removing a confidential price book belonging to plaintiff, using the information in such book to compete against plaintiff and that as a result plaintiff was thereby harmed. Defendants contend that the price book does not constitute a trade secret because the information contained in the book is generally known and no efforts were made to maintain its secrecy.

The Uniform Trade Secrets Act, sections 417.450 to 417.467, has been adopted in Missouri. * * * The definition section 417.453 provides, in pertinent part: * * *

    (4) "Trade secret", information, including but not limited to, technical or nontechnical data, a formula, pattern, compilation, program, device, method, technique, or process, that:

        (a) Derives independent economic value, actual or potential, from not being generally known to, and not being readily ascertainable by proper means by other persons who can obtain economic value from its disclosure or use; and

        (b) Is the subject of efforts that are reasonable under the circumstances to maintain its secrecy.

Prior to the act's adoption in 1995, we applied the definition of a trade secret found in the first Restatement.

The Restatement defined a trade secret as: any formula, pattern, device or compilation of information which is used in one's business, and which gives him an opportunity to obtain an advantage over competitors who do not know or use it. (Citing Rest. (First) of Torts Section 757 comment b.)

Further, the Restatement set forth six factors to be considered in the determination of whether given information constitutes a trade secret:

(1) the extent to which the information is known outside of his business;

(2) the extent to which it is known by employees and others involved in his business;

(3) the extent of measures taken by him to guard the secrecy of the information;

(4) the value of the information to him and to his competitors;

(5) the amount of effort or money expended by him in developing the information;

(6) the ease or difficulty with which the information could be properly acquired or duplicated by others.

Although the Restatement's factors are not part of the Uniform Trade Secrets Act, the act essentially incorporates these factors in its definition of trade secrets. Further, courts in states that have adopted the Act, have found that those factors provide guidance in determining whether the information in a given case constitutes trade secrets within the definition of the Act.

The threshold issue which permeates all of plaintiff's points on appeal is whether the price book constitutes a trade secret. The existence of a trade secret is a conclusion of law based on the applicable facts.

Although the price book is not part of the record on appeal, the evidence indicates that it is a detailed compilation of technical and non-technical data including customer contacts, specifications for each listed product, product numbers, material requirements and price information.

In addition to showing that the price book is a compilation of data, plaintiff produced evidence to show that the information in the book was subject to reasonable efforts to maintain its secrecy. Further, plaintiff established evidence to support that the price book derived independent economic value from not being generally known to or readily ascertainable by proper means by others who can obtain economic value from its disclosure or use. We examine the restatement factors, as they are helpful in our inquiry. First, there is evidence that the information is not known outside of the business. Hans Hansen, who formerly worked for a competitor, and is currently an officer of plaintiff, testified that he did not know the details contained in the book until he began to work for plaintiff. Second, there is evidence to support that all of the information in the book was not independently known by employees, in that employees, even Dick who had worked for the company for many years, referred to the book for reference when giving pricing and specification information. * * *

Plaintiff presented witnesses who testified as to the measures taken to ensure confidentiality. There was testimony that employees knew the price book was confidential, that access was limited, it was locked in an office at night and old copies were shredded. There was evidence that the price book was not taken from the office except during sales calls. Gary Hahn, the technical support engineer, was the only person with the capability to print it.

Defendants point to the fact that the price book was not stamped as confidential as evidence that the price books were not confidential and thus not trade secrets. The lack of a confidential stamp is not dispositive here, as there are other indications, previously indicated, that the book was treated confidentially. Further, defendants argue that the price book was not intended by plaintiff to be confidential, nor treated as such as no confidentiality agreements were signed by plaintiff's employees having access to the price book. While the existence of a confidentiality or noncompete agreement may be further evidence of the book's confidentiality, the lack of such agreements is not conclusive, as officers of a corporation owe independent fiduciary duties to the corporation to protect trade secrets from disclosure. * * *

The information in the book would be valuable to competitors, as is established by the testimony of Hans Hansen and by the statement of defendant Dick, who admitted that it would be advantageous to a competitor at least in terms of pricing. Fifth, the book represented a compilation of many years of experience in the business of manufacturing insoles and thus a great deal of time and effort was obviously expended in its preparation. Finally, the specifications and price information could not be easily duplicated or properly acquired by others. Hans Hansen testified that he did not know of the information in the price book before he began to work for plaintiff. Even Dick, who had worked in pricing and specifications for many years using plaintiff's price book could not correctly state the specifications of the insoles made for one of Walk Easy's major customers. Additionally, the evidence showed that it would take a year or more to recreate the information contained in the price book. These factors, taken together are sufficient to show that the price book is a trade secret. * * *

Since plaintiff has established facts sufficient to support a finding that the book was a compilation of data, deriving independent economic value and the subject of reasonable efforts to maintain secrecy, and that the individual defendants, who were officers of plaintiff misappropriated plaintiff's trade secrets by taking the price book and using it for the benefit of defendant Walk Easy, the trial court erroneously applied the law and erred in directing a verdict against plaintiff on the misappropriation count.

* * *

Judgment reversed and remanded.

DID YOU GET IT?

1. How does the Missouri Uniform Trade Secrets Act define a trade secret?

2. How does the court apply that definition to the facts of the case?

3. How does the court use the six factors from the *Restatement of Torts*?

C. WHAT IS PROTECTABLE?

The modern view of trade secret law under the UTSA and the DTSA defines the 'information" that might be a trade secret very broadly. Virtually any information of competitive value to a company can be a trade secret as long as it meets the three requirements of trade secret protection: secrecy, independent economic value, and reasonable efforts. Although many trade secrets are comprised of scientific and technical information that may be patentable (often referred to as "technical trade secrets"), a wide range of confidential business information that would not otherwise qualify for patent protection can be protected under trade secret law. Thus, similar to the price book in *Lyn-Flex,* marketing information, customer information, and sales information are all within the realm of trade secret subject matter.

While the universe of protectable information appears quite large, several requirements serve to limit its breadth. One practical limitation is the requirement that the putative trade secret owner be able to articulate in a very concrete way exactly what it is claiming to be a trade secret. Thus, the claimed information cannot be a vague or abstract concept. Trade-secret owners often have difficulty identifying with specificity the exact nature of the information that they claim as a trade secret. The tendency is to try to claim as much as possible, but ultimately that can be a mistake. *See, e.g., Imax Corp. v. Cinema Technologies, Inc.,* 152 F.3d 1161 (9th Cir. 1998) (finding that plaintiff's discovery responses failed to specifically identify which dimensions and tolerances of its projectors were trade secrets).

The defense strategy of forcing a plaintiff in a trade secret case to divulge the details of its trade secrets is discussed in Chapter 9. In Chapter 10 (the chapter dealing with remedies), the potential consequences of over-asserting trade secret rights are discussed. For now, the cases that follow explore the general question of what limits (if any) should be placed on the types of information that can be protected by trade secret law. The three requirements for trade secret protection are examined in greater depth in Chapters 3, 4, and 5.

Reading Guidance
Can a pineapple be protected as a trade secret? Is a plant information?

[handwritten margin notes: TT made MD-2 pineapple variety / Δ bought MD 2 / plant from patent third party Co.]

DEL MONTE FRESH PRODUCE COMPANY
v. DOLE FOOD COMPANY, INC.
United States District Court, S.D. of Florida, 2001.
136 F.Supp.2d 1271.

GOLD, DISTRICT JUDGE.

[handwritten margin notes: denies Motion to dismiss on Count I / grants on Count II (specify what TT is protecting)]

The plaintiffs in this case are Del Monte Fresh Produce Company, a Delaware corporation, and Del Monte Fresh Produce, N.A., Inc., a Florida corporation (collectively referred to as "Del Monte"); each has its principal place of business in Florida. The defendants are Dole Food Company, Inc., a Hawaii corporation, and Dole Fresh Fruit Company, a Nevada corporation (collectively referred to as "Dole"); each has its principal place of business in California. The parties in this case are engaged in the development, growth, processing, and distribution of fruits and vegetables. This litigation concerns a dispute over the growth, marketing, and distribution of a certain variety of pineapple.

Del Monte's complaint alleges that, over the course of many years, it and its predecessors developed a new variety of pineapple, which is known as MD-2. The testing and development of the MD-2 variety occurred in Hawaii. Sometime after, Del Monte sent MD-2 plant materials to Costa Rica for further study in the nurseries of that country. These pineapples had the advantage of a higher vitamin C content, a sweeter taste, more fiber, brighter color, a more pleasant smell, and a milder texture. In time, Del Monte ascertained that the MD-2 variety flourished in the soil and climate of Costa Rica, so it began to propagate the pineapples in its plantations located in that country. In 1996, Del Monte began to sell the MD-2 variety in the United States under the name of "Del Monte Gold Extra Sweet." At present, this brand of pineapple accounts for approximately forty-five percent of the pineapple market in the United States.

In 1991, a Costa Rican farm known as Cabo Marzo, which was a seller of pineapple to Dole, allegedly obtained Del Monte's MD-2 variety plant material. Del Monte claims that Cabo Marzo obtained the MD–2 variety unlawfully from Del Monte's Costa Rican plantations. In 1995, Dole purchased the MD–2 plant material from Cabo Marzo and began to propagate it to compete with Del Monte. In 1999, Dole began to sell the pineapples that it allegedly had developed from the MD–2 variety throughout the United States under the brand name of "Dole Premium Select." According to Del Monte, both Cabo Marzo and Dole knew that the MD–2 variety belonged exclusively to Del Monte. Del Monte further claims that when Dole represented to the pineapple trade that it had developed the "Dole Premium Select" brand of pineapple as a "new, super sweet" variety to compete with the "Del Monte Gold Extra Sweet," Dole knew or should have known its representations were false.

* * *

Misappropriation of Trade Secrets

FL's law – UTSA

Del Monte has brought a claim against Dole under sections 688.001 et seq. of the Florida Statutes for misappropriation of trade secrets. Florida's Uniform Trade Secret Act displaces tort law regarding trade secret misappropriation. In order to plead such a claim successfully, a plaintiff must aver that: (1) the plaintiff possessed secret information and took reasonable steps to protect its secrecy and (2) the secret it possessed was misappropriated, either by one who knew or had reason to know that the secret was improperly obtained or by one who used improper means to obtain it. *See* Fla. Stat. § 688.002. To qualify as a trade secret, the information that the plaintiff seeks to protect must derive economic value from not being readily ascertainable by others and must be the subject of reasonable efforts to protect its secrecy. Additionally, if the information in question is generally known or readily accessible to third parties, it cannot qualify for trade secret protection.

Whether the MD–2 Variety Is a Trade Secret

Count II of Del Monte's complaint is for misappropriation of trade secrets under the Florida Trade Secrets Act. Dole claims that Del Monte cannot state a claim for misappropriation of trade secrets under Florida law because a pineapple cannot be protected as a trade secret. * * *

Dole further states that a pineapple is not information, so as to qualify under the definition of trade secret contained in Florida statutes, section 688.002(4), which defines a trade secret as "information, including a formula, pattern, compilation, program, device, method, technique, or process. . . ." Dole's argument is flawed in several respects. First, Del Monte does not seek to protect any pineapple as a trade secret. Rather, it seeks to protect its proprietary interest in the MD–2 variety of pineapple.

Δ's argument – ct. rejects

* * *

– Del Monte develops MD-2
– farmer Cabo Marzo gets MD-2 somehow (illegally)

The court's research has revealed only one case that directly addresses the issue of whether a plant's genetic material constitutes a trade secret. In *Pioneer Hi-Bred International v. Holden Foundation Seeds, Inc.,* the court held that certain corn seeds developed by the plaintiff and sold by the defendant as its own were trade secrets. The Eighth Circuit arrived at this conclusion even though the seeds were readily available to any purchaser on the market and the defendant had obtained the plaintiff's seeds by taking them from a local farmer's corn field. *Pioneer Hi-Bred International* establishes that at least one Federal Circuit has squarely recognized that plant material can constitute a trade secret, even if it is readily available to the public. The Eighth Circuit's rationale is particularly applicable to this case because, in *Pioneer Hi-Bred International,* the court was interpreting Iowa's Uniform Trade Secrets Act, which is identical to Florida's Uniform Trade Secrets Act.

Dole asks that the court distinguish *Pioneer Hi-Bred International* from this case on the grounds that the plants appropriated by the defendants in that case reproduced sexually while the plants in this case reproduce asexually. Dole argues that because pineapples can be reproduced simply by planting them in the ground and watering them, they cannot be a trade secret. There simply is no legal or logical basis for such a distinction. Dole has failed to establish a connection between sexual or asexual plant reproduction and the question of whether the MD–2 variety is protected information. Moreover, Dole has failed to show that a pineapple is significantly different from a corn seed, which will eventually develop into an edible plant when planted and watered.

Absent clear authority that such information is not protected under Florida's Uniform Trade Secrets Act, Del Monte's complaint will not be dismissed on the basis that the MD–2 variety is not a trade secret. This is because whether a particular type of information constitutes a trade secret is a question of fact. The law is clear that questions of fact cannot be resolved on motions to dismiss because the court must accept the plaintiff's allegations of the plaintiff's complaint as true. In this case, Del Monte has alleged that the MD–2 variety is a trade secret, and the court must take that and the supporting statements as true. Once the parties have completed discovery, Dole may raise this issue again in a motion for summary judgment, at which time the court will apply the appropriate standard to the evidence submitted by Del Monte in support of its allegations.

While it is clear that Del Monte seeks to protect MD–2, Dole correctly states that "it is unclear exactly what aspect of MD–2 Del Monte claims is entitled to trade secret protection." Does Del Monte seek to protect MD–2's genetic code, growth technique, or some other quality? Because this case involves complex factual matters, Dole's motion to dismiss count II is granted without prejudice so that Del Monte can plead more specifically what aspect of MD–2 it seeks to protect as a trade secret.

* * *

DID YOU GET IT?

1. What source of law provides the definition of a trade secret in this case? *FL trade secrets act (based on UTSA)*

2. What does Del Monte seek to protect as a trade secret? *MD-2 variety of pineapple*

3. In light of the court's ruling, if you represent Del Monte, how might *Process/* you articulate what you are seeking to protect as a trade secret? — *form ~ to create/ growth this pineapple*

> ### Reading Guidance
> *Can a religious or other non-profit organization own trade secrets?*

—Ct held *—Church of Scientology*
TT failed to **RELIGIOUS TECHNOLOGY CENTER V. NETCOM**
show/define its trade secrets **ON-LINE COMMUNICATION SERVICES, INC.**

United States District Court, N.D. California, 1995.
923 F.Supp. 1231.

—whether writings written by a Church qualify as trade secrets

WHYTE, DISTRICT JUDGE.

This case involves the scope of intellectual property rights on the Internet. Plaintiffs, two Scientology-affiliated organizations claiming copyright and trade secret protection for the writings of the Church's founder, L. Ron Hubbard, brought this suit against defendant Dennis Erlich ("Erlich"), a former Scientology minister turned vocal critic of the Church, who allegedly put plaintiffs' protected works onto the Internet.

* * *

BACKGROUND

— A fmr. member of the Church

Defendant Dennis Erlich was a member of the Church of Scientology ("the Church") from approximately 1968 until 1982. During his years with the Church, Erlich received training to enable him to provide ministerial counseling services, known as "auditing." While with the Church, Erlich had access to various Scientology writings, including those of the Church's founder, L. Ron Hubbard ("Hubbard"), which the Church alleges include published literary works as well as unpublished confidential materials (the "Advanced Technology works"). According to plaintiffs, Erlich had agreed to maintain the confidentiality of the Advanced Technology works.

Since leaving the Church, Erlich has been a vocal critic of Scientology and he now considers it part of his calling to foster critical debate about Scientology through humorous and critical writings. Erlich has expressed his views about the Church by contributing to the Internet "Usenet newsgroup" called "alt.religion.scientology" ("the newsgroup"), which is an on-line forum for the discussion of issues related to Scientology. * * *

Plaintiff Religious Technology Center ("RTC"), a nonprofit religious corporation, "was formed by Scientologists, with the approval of [Hubbard], to act as the protector of the religion of Scientology and to own, protect, and control the utilization of the Advanced Technology[7] in the United States."

RTC allege[s] that Erlich infringed the copyrights in the Exhibit A and B works. RTC also alleges that Erlich misappropriated its trade secrets in the Exhibit B works, the confidentiality of which it alleges has been the subject of elaborate security measures. RTC further claims that those works are extremely valuable to the Church. Erlich admits to having posted excerpts from some of the works, but argues that the quotations were used to provide context for debate and as a basis for his criticism. Erlich further argues that he has neither claimed authorship of any of the works nor personally profited from his critique, satire, and commentary. Erlich contends that all of the Exhibit B documents he posted had been previously posted anonymously over the Internet, except for item 1, which he claims he received anonymously through the mail.

From August to December 1994, plaintiffs exchanged a series of letters with Erlich, warning him to stop posting their protected writings onto the newsgroup. Plaintiffs also demanded that defendants Netcom and Klemesrud take actions to prevent Erlich's continued postings of protected materials. Erlich indicated that he would not stop, claiming he had a right to continue with his criticism and satire. On February 8, 1995, plaintiffs filed this action against Erlich, Klemesrud, and Netcom for copyright infringement and, against Erlich alone, for misappropriation of trade secrets, seeking actual, statutory, and punitive damages, injunctive relief, impoundment of the infringing materials and equipment, and attorneys' fees and costs.

On February 10, 1995, the court granted plaintiffs' ex parte application for a temporary restraining order ("TRO") prohibiting Erlich from making unauthorized use of works identified in the exhibits to the complaint and an order directing the clerk to issue a writ of seizure under 17 U.S.C. § 503(a). On February 13, 1995, in execution of the writ of seizure, local police officers entered Erlich's home to conduct the seizure. The officers were accompanied by several RTC representatives, who aided in the search and seizure of documents related to Erlich's alleged copyright infringement and misappropriation of trade secrets. Erlich alleges that RTC officials in fact directed the seizure, which took approximately seven hours. Erlich alleges that plaintiffs seized books, working papers, and personal papers.

---

[7]   These works are part of the "course" materials used in the upper-levels of Scientology training, and are only available to those Scientologists who have successfully completed all of the lower courses.

After locating Erlich's computers, plaintiffs allegedly seized computer disks and copied portions of Erlich's hard disk drive onto floppy disks and then erased the originals from the hard drive. Although plaintiffs returned to Erlich's counsel some of the articles seized, Erlich contends that plaintiffs have not returned all of the seized articles, including ones that are unrelated to the litigation.

* * *

In the third cause of action, plaintiff RTC alleges that Erlich misappropriated its trade secrets. California has adopted a version of the Uniform Trade Secret Act ("UTSA"), Cal.Civ.Code § 3426.1 et seq. The UTSA defines a trade secret as

CA TSA

> information, including a formula, pattern, compilation, program, device, method, technique, or process, that:
>
> (1) Derives independent economic value, actual or potential, from not being generally known to the public or to other persons who can obtain economic value from its disclosure or use; and
>
> (2) Is the subject of efforts that are reasonable under the circumstances to maintain its secrecy.
>
> * * *

To establish its trade secret claim, RTC must show, *inter alia,* that the Advanced Technology works (1) have independent economic value to competitors and (2) have been kept confidential.

1. Nature of Works

Δ's argument

As a preliminary matter, Erlich argues that the Advanced Technology works cannot be trade secrets because of their nature as religious scriptures. In *Wollersheim,* the Ninth Circuit rejected the Church's application for a preliminary injunction on the basis of a trade secret claim against a splinter Scientology group that had acquired stolen copies of the Advanced Technology. The Church argued not that the works gave them a competitive market advantage but that disclosure of the works would cause its adherents "religious harm . . . from premature unsupervised exposure to the materials." Although the Ninth Circuit rejected plaintiffs' trade secret argument based on the *spiritual* value of the harm, it later noted that it had left open the question of whether the Advanced Technology works could qualify as trade secrets, assuming plaintiffs could prove that the secrets confer on them an actual *economic* advantage over competitors. Nonetheless, the court noted that such an allegation would "raise grave doubts about [the Church's] claim as a religion and a not-for-profit corporation."

The Church contends that the Advanced Technology works consist of "*processes* and the theory behind those processes . . . that are to be used precisely as set forth by L. Ron Hubbard to assist the parishioner in achieving a greater spiritual awareness and freedom." Erlich responds that the works are essentially religious texts. Erlich argues that the Church cannot have trade secrets because trade secret law is necessarily related to commerce. The Church contends that, like other organizations, it must pay bills, and that licensing fees from these documents allow it to continue operating.

D's argument

The Church's status as a religion does not itself preclude it from holding a trade secret. Restatement § 39 cmt. d, at 429 ("[N]onprofit entities such as . . . religious organizations can also claim trade secret protection for economically valuable information such as lists of prospective members or donors."); UTSA § 3426.1(c) (defining "person" to include a "corporation . . . or any other legal or commercial entity"); With the exception of the *Vien* case, there is little authority to support a finding that religious materials can constitute trade secrets. However, there is "no category of information [that] is excluded from protection as a trade secret because of its inherent qualities."

Nor is there any authority to support Erlich's argument that the Church's religious texts cannot be trade secrets because, unlike most trade secrets, these secrets are not *used* in the production or sales of a commodity but *are the commodities themselves*. The Church's Advanced Technology "course" materials, which are an integral part of the Church's spiritual counseling techniques, do not appear fundamentally different from the course manuals upheld as trade secrets in *SmokEnders, Inc. v. Smoke No More, Inc.*

The [SmokEnders ("SE")] program requires attendees to follow a rigid structured regimen comprised of specific assignments and detail[ed] concepts as recited in [the manual]. . . .

The SE program is a step-by-step regimented program which requires that each person attending a SE program perform each act of the program at a particular time. Each act required by a SE seminar attendee must be performed by attendees at the same time in the program, with each a minimum departure from the program.

The SE trade secret resides in the composite program as it is arranged for step-by-step delivery to the attendees.

SmokEnders is arguably distinguishable because only the "moderators" and not the attendees were given access to the course materials in that case. However, the adherents of the Church, unlike the attendees and like the moderators in *SmokEnders,* are under a duty of confidentiality as to the materials. This case is analogous to *SmokEnders* because in both cases the "commodity" that is produced from the trade secrets is the result achieved by the person using the course materials and their techniques (whether it be stopping smoking or reaching a "higher spiritual existence").

Thus, there is at least some precedent for granting trade secret status to works that are techniques for improving oneself (though not specifically spiritually). Conversely, there is no authority for excluding religious materials from trade secret protection because of their nature. Indeed, there is no authority for excluding any type of information because of its nature. While the trade secret laws did not necessarily develop to allow a religion to protect a monopoly in its religious practices, the laws have nonetheless expanded such that the Church's techniques, which clearly are "used in the operation of the enterprise," Restatement § 39, at 425, are deserving of protection if secret and valuable.

Although trade secret status may apply to works that are techniques for spiritually improving oneself, the secret aspect of those techniques must be defined with particularity. It appears that plaintiffs are claiming that the entire works themselves, which they describe as "processes and the theory behind those processes," constitute the trade secrets. This definition is problematic because it is impossible to determine when the "secret" has been lost after portions of the works have been disclosed. Although plaintiffs' definition has at least some support in *SmokEnders,* where the court upheld as a trade secret a "composite [stop-smoking] program" found in an instructional manual, 184 U.S.P.Q. at 312, this court is not satisfied that plaintiffs have identified their trade secrets with sufficient definiteness to support injunctive relief.

* * *

Because RTC is the plaintiff, and because it is moving for injunctive relief, it bears the burden of proving its trade secrets. The court finds that RTC has failed to adequately define its trade secrets and, at least as to those works that have been made available to the public through previous Internet postings not by Erlich, RTC has failed to meet its burden on the issue of secrecy. Therefore, RTC has failed to show a likelihood of success on its trade secret misappropriation claim.

* * *

DID YOU GET IT?

1. What is Erlich's argument challenging the plaintiff's trade secret claim? *—religion cannot have TS b/c is not commerce— works are relig. texts here*

2. What does the California UTSA require to establish trade secrecy? *—secrecy   —indep. econ. value*

3. Why did the court find that "RTC has failed to adequately define its trade secrets"? *—too broad —hard to know what exact part/portion of the work contains the secret*

[handwritten margin notes: —affirms trial ct.'s decision —printer technology]

[handwritten note above title: TS owner]

ALTAVION, INC. v. KONICA MINOLTA SYSTEMS LABORATORY INC.

California Court of Appeals, First District, 2014.
226 Cal.App.4th 26.

SIMONS, J.

* * *

Appellant and defendant Konica Minolta Systems Laboratory, Inc. (KMSL), is a research and development subsidiary of a multinational corporation that, among other things, manufactures multifunction printers (also known as multifunction peripherals) (MFP's) and other devices with printing, scanning, and copying functionalities. Respondent and plaintiff Altavion, Inc. (Altavion), is a small company that invented a process for creating self-authenticating documents through the use of barcodes that contain encrypted data about the contents of the original documents. The trial court concluded that KMSL misappropriated trade secrets disclosed by Altavion during negotiations aimed at exploiting Altavion's technology. The negotiations were subject to a nondisclosure agreement and centered around the possibility of embedding Altavion's invention in one of KMSL's MFP's. During the negotiations, the invention was described as Altavion's "digital stamping technology" (DST). After the negotiations failed, Altavion discovered KMSL had filed for patents encompassing Altavion's DST. Altavion brought suit and, following a bench trial, the trial court found KMSL misappropriated Altavion's trade secrets—both Altavion's DST concept as a whole and specific DST design concepts. The court awarded Altavion damages, prejudgment interest, and attorney fees.

[handwritten margin note: trial ct. held Δ liable for TS misapp]

On appeal, KMSL contends it was improper for the trial court to base its ruling on misappropriation of Altavion's DST concept as a whole, and any other trade secrets the court found misappropriated were not adequately identified in the court's decision. KMSL further contends Altavion's DST was not protectable as a trade secret, either as a combination secret or as particular design concepts, because ideas and design concepts are not protectable trade secrets. * * *

Altavion's DST

Dr. Ali Moussa is the president and founder of Altavion. He founded Altavion in 2000 with the goal of developing DST to enable the self-authentication of digital and paper documents.

Altavion's DST was designed to encode the content of an original document into a small (maximum one inch by one inch) barcode (also called a "stamp") printed on the document. In order to create the barcode, a scanned version of the original document would be divided into cells and the pixel-level data about each cell would be represented in the barcode in a highly compressed form. By comparing the data encrypted in the barcode with a subsequent version of the document, Altavion's DST would show whether and where the document had been altered by searching for alterations at the pixel-level. Because the barcode would permit the document to be authenticated without involvement of a third party, Altavion claimed its DST would create "self-authenticating" documents. Altavion's DST was implemented by software programmed to execute the algorithms necessary to perform the various barcode creation and authentication functions.

Altavion's barcode, and especially its color barcode, could contain far more data in a small space than existing barcodes. Grayscale or color barcodes, as compared to black and white barcodes, represent data with higher density, enabling more data to be represented in a given area. However, the development of a color barcode presented a distinct technical challenge because over time the colors on a printed barcode are subject to degradation, which can inhibit read back of the data contained in the barcode. Altavion resolved this problem by using "color reference cells" to aid in reconstruction of the encoded data. The company's implementation of the approach was unique, in that Altavion's barcode employed multiple reference cells for each color, and by an averaging process a range of values could be determined to represent each color.

Altavion's Relationship with KMSL

* * *

Altavion was introduced to KMSL through William Zivic, a salesman employed at the time by Minolta Business Solutions. Although the terms of the agreement are unclear, in July 2003 Altavion and KMSL entered into a nondisclosure agreement (NDA), in which the companies agreed that any confidential information disclosed during their subsequent negotiations would be kept confidential. Prior to discussions with Altavion, KMSL had no digital stamping projects in progress or products in development. Indeed, Tomita admitted "the first consideration [he] had ever given to [DST] was brought about by [his] discussions with Altavion."

KMSL's interest in Altavion's DST was in developing technology for authenticating printed documents, rather than for documents that remain only in a digital environment. For a variety of reasons, it is more difficult to authenticate printed documents than electronic documents (an issue known as the "closed loop problem"). For example, an expert for KMSL at trial explained that problems can arise in the printing, storage, and scanning processes that make it more difficult to authenticate a paper document with a stamp.

In a December 15, 2003 letter to Moussa, Tomita wrote, "At [KMSL] we are studying using your unique technology for digital stamping for possible use in multiple applications in current and future products and for jointly developing it further for even better utilization." The parties sought to negotiate terms by which Altavion's DST could be embedded in a KMSL MFP. Altavion and KMSL discussed the possibility of a pay-per-stamp revenue model.

* * *

On August 31, 2004, KMSL and Altavion executed a memorandum of understanding (MOU), which stated that KMSL "will continue to recognize that Altavion's unique implementation of [DST] is Altavion's own intellectual property and will continue to protect [it]." Unbeknownst to Altavion, even before execution of the MOU, KMSL had already begun filing a series of patent applications encompassing Altavion's DST. Specifically, on June 28 and August 9, 2004, KMSL filed patent applications for color barcode producing methods, with KMSL's Ming listed as the inventor on the June application and Ming and Tomita listed as inventors on the August application. Both applications described a method "to keep the integrity or authenticity of the color barcode" through the use of color reference cells in the barcode. KMSL ultimately filed 24 United States DST patent applications, and eight United States patents were issued. The patents and applications identified varying combinations of Tomita, Ming, Cattrone, and Pathak as inventors.

* * *

In September 2004, shortly after execution of the MOU, KMSL hired software engineer Pathak to work on the digital stamping project and, specifically, to develop "closed loop technologies." Pathak had access to the evaluation software provided by Altavion. In a September 17 e-mail to Tomita, Cattrone said he had "asked [Pathak] to analyze the Altavion software and think about ways in which we can achieve similar results with the focus on a closed loop digital stamp." He also wrote, "[Pathak] understands and knows well that there are many ways to achieve similar Altavion'esque results within the digital domain." The e-mail also asserted there were problems in the relationship with Altavion. For example, Cattrone opined, "It is unlikely that we will get a digital stamping SDK from Altavion in the near future—our signing of the MOU meant nothing to [Moussa]."

KMSL and Altavion reached an impasse in their negotiations in the fall of 2004. The parties were unable to agree on the terms for KMSL's payment of a development fee to Altavion, or the scope of an SDK to be provided to KMSL.

The Present Lawsuit

In October 2006, Moussa learned about KMSL's patent filings. In November 2007, Altavion filed the present lawsuit. In the second amended and operative complaint (Complaint), Altavion sued KMSL, Cattrone, and four other Konica Minolta entities. Altavion alleged causes of action for trade secret misappropriation, breach of the NDA, and a variety of other torts. KMSL filed a cross-complaint alleging (among other things) fraud based on Moussa's false statements that he had applied for patents.

* * *

The court found in favor of Altavion and against KMSL (but not against the other Konica Minolta defendants) on Altavion's misappropriation claim. The trial court awarded damages of $1 million and prejudgment interest of $513,400, for a total of $1,513,400. After further proceedings, the trial court awarded attorney fees to Altavion in the amount of $3,297,102.50, as well as amounts for expert fees and costs. The court also awarded costs to three of the Konica Minolta companies that had not been found liable for misappropriation.

DISCUSSION

* * *

Did Altavion's DST Design Concepts Constitute Protectable Trade Secrets?

As noted previously, the UTSA defines a "[t]rade secret" as "information, including a formula, pattern, compilation, program, device, method, technique, or process, that: [¶] (1) Derives independent economic value, actual or potential, from not being generally known to the public or to other persons who can obtain economic value from its disclosure or use; and [¶] (2) Is the subject of efforts that are reasonable under the circumstances to maintain its secrecy." (§ 3426.1, subd. (d).)

" 'Information' has a broad meaning under the [UTSA]." "The definition of trade secret is . . . unlimited as to any particular class or kind of matter and may be contrasted with matter eligible for patent or copyright protection, which must fall into statutorily defined categories."

A. *Ideas Are Protectable as Trade Secrets.*

As explained below, the trade secret information at issue in the present case is principally comprised of the design concepts underlying Altavion's DST. In the words of the trial court, "the issue is whether [KMSL's] ideas set forth in the patents and patent applications are founded upon and disclose any trade secret 'ideas' [it] learned from [Altavion]." Because the trade secret information at issue in this case is a set of ideas rather than a set of products or specific formulae, it is important to address KMSL's assertion in its brief on appeal that "[g]eneralized ideas and inventions are protectable by patents and thus cannot be trade secrets."

Although KMSL fails to provide a citation for that assertion, KMSL proceeds to quote language in *Silvaco* drawing a distinction between patent law and trade secret law. *Silvaco* explained, "The sine qua non of a trade secret . . . is the plaintiff's possession of information of a type that can, at the possessor's option, be made known to others, or withheld from them, i.e., kept secret. This is the fundamental difference between a trade secret and a patent. A patent protects an *idea,* i.e., an invention, against appropriation by others. Trade secret law does not protect ideas as such. Indeed, a trade secret may consist of something we would not ordinarily consider an *idea* (a conceptual datum) at all, but more a *fact* (an empirical datum), such as a customer's preferences, or the location of a mineral deposit. In either case, the trade secret is not the idea or fact itself, but *information* tending to communicate (disclose) the idea or fact to another. Trade secret law, in short, protects only *the right to control the dissemination of information.*" (*Silvaco,* 184 Cal.App.4th 210, 220–221 (2010).)

In isolation, the statement "[t]rade secret law does not protect ideas as such" is easily misunderstood. In fact, *Silvaco* plainly does *not* hold that secret ideas are not protectable under trade secret law, and KMSL cites no authority for its apparent claim that the definition of "information" in section 3426.1, subdivision (d), excludes patentable ideas. "[A]lthough a trade secret may be a device or process which is patentable, patentability is not a condition precedent to the classification of a trade secret. Thus, it has been said that a trade secret may be a device or process which is clearly anticipated in the prior art or one which is merely a mechanical improvement on a machine or device. Novelty and invention are not requisite for a trade secret as they are for patentability. In harmony with these precepts, it has been held that *a trade secret in the broad sense consists of any unpatented idea which may be used for industrial and commercial purposes.*" * * *

An inventor who fails to obtain a patent for a patentable idea incurs significant risks. The secret may leak, or other circumstances may arise that frustrate the inventor's right to obtain a patent. (*Kewanee Oil Co. v. Bicron Corp., supra,* 416 U.S. at p. 490.) Nevertheless, the "long-standing principle" is "that an inventor who chooses to exploit his invention by private arrangements is entirely free to do so, though in so doing he may thereby forfeit his right to a patent." * * *

In conclusion, it is clear that if a patentable idea is kept secret, the idea itself can constitute information protectable by trade secret law. In that situation, trade secret law protects the inventor's *"right to control the dissemination of information"*)—the information being the idea itself— rather than the subsequent use of the novel technology, which is protected by patent law. In other words, trade secret law may be used to sanction the misappropriation of an idea the plaintiff kept secret. This is consistent with the proposition that "The sine qua non of a trade secret . . . is the plaintiff's possession of information of a type that can, at the possessor's option, be made known to others, or withheld from them, i.e., kept secret."

B.	*Design Concepts Underlying Altavion's DST Constitute Protectable "Information."*

* * * The information at issue in the present case can readily be divided into three tiers of specificity and secrecy. The least specific and least secret level of information is Altavion's general idea for a barcode allowing for self-authentication of documents with identification of alterations. This level of information is not a protectable trade secret because the general idea was disclosed to other companies without the benefit of an NDA. At the other extreme, the most specific and secret level of information includes Altavion's algorithms and source code that execute Altavion's DST. Such information is unquestionably protectable by trade secret law, but it could not form the basis for Altavion's misappropriation claim because Altavion did not share its algorithms and source codes with KMSL.

The middle tier of information is comprised of the design concepts that underlie Altavion's DST, many of which might be evident to a software end user. There is no evidence such information was disclosed to anyone other than KMSL, pursuant to an NDA, and, thus, misappropriation of these secret design concepts (separately and in combination) provides a basis for Altavion's claim.

* * *

The two other levels of information arguably at issue in the present case are the most secret level—Altavion's algorithms and source code—and the middle tier of information, comprised of the design concepts underlying Altavion's DST. The record shows Altavion did not disclose those levels of information to other companies. The record also shows that, although it is well-established that source code can constitute a protectable trade secret, Altavion did *not* disclose its source code and algorithms to KMSL. Accordingly, the information at issue in the present case is the *design concepts underlying* Altavion's DST, which Altavion kept secret from other companies but indisputably disclosed to KMSL subject to an NDA.

KMSL argues Altavion's DST design concepts are not protectable trade secrets, characterizing *Silvaco* as standing for the proposition that "although a finished product might have distinctive characteristics resulting from a specific design, those characteristics cannot constitute trade secrets." KMSL is mistaken. *Silvaco* merely held that the design of a software program is not a trade secret *to the extent the design elements are disclosed and evident to the end user*. The plaintiff in that case, Silvaco, was the developer of software used to design electronic circuits and systems. Silvaco filed suit against the defendant Intel, alleging Intel had misappropriated certain trade secrets used by Silvaco in its software. "The primary gist of the claims was that Intel had used software acquired from another software concern with knowledge that Silvaco had accused that concern of incorporating source code, stolen from Silvaco, in its products." The main issue in the case was whether Intel could be liable for misappropriation of Silvaco's source code where it never had access to the actual source code.

As relevant to the present case, *Silvaco* also held that one category of purported trade secrets—described as "various features, functions, and characteristics of the design and operation of Silvaco's software products"—did not include trade secrets at all. That was because those software design concepts ceased to be protectable trade secrets to the extent the finished program disclosed the underlying design. As *Silvaco* explained, "The design may constitute the *basis* for a trade secret, such that *information concerning it* could be actionably misappropriated; but it is the information—not the design itself—that must form the basis for the cause of action. And while the finished (compiled) product might have distinctive characteristics resulting from that design—such as improved performance—they cannot constitute trade secrets because they are not secret, but are evident to anyone running the finished program." Thus, *Silvaco* makes a distinction between source code and software design concepts, concluding design concepts are not protected by trade secret law where they can be ascertained by the end software user. * * *

Although *Silvaco* supports the proposition that *disclosed* software design concepts are not trade secrets, "A potent distinction exists between a trade secret which *will* be disclosed if and when the product in which it is embodied is placed on sale, and a 'trade secret' embodied in a product which has been placed on sale, which product admits of discovery of the 'secret' upon inspection, analysis, or reverse engineering." Consistent with that proposition, cases have extended trade secret protection to computer programs and aspects of computer programs that the plaintiffs kept confidential. For example, in *Integrated Cash Mgmt. Serv. v. Digital Transactions,* the plaintiff alleged that former employees misappropriated the design and "architecture" of the plaintiff's computer programs in creating a program for another company. The appellate court extended trade secret protection to "the manner in which several non-secret utility programs are arranged to create" the plaintiff's "computer software product." The court noted that the manner in which the plaintiff's programs interacted was not generally known or readily ascertainable, and that the combination of programs "was not disclosed in [the plaintiff's] promotional literature, which contains merely a user-oriented description of the advantages of [the plaintiff's] product."

* * *

In the present case, although the trial court extended trade secret protection to design concepts analogous to those at issue in *Silvaco,* we conclude *Silvaco* does not preclude Altavion's misappropriation claim because the evidence shows that Altavion did not disclose its DST design concepts to anyone other than KMSL, and the disclosure to KMSL was subject to an NDA.

* * *

The trial court's judgment is affirmed. Costs on appeal are awarded to Altavion.

DID YOU GET IT?

1. Can you articulate the difference between a mere idea or concept and a protectable trade secret?

2. Can ideas that are not patentable be trade secrets? Why or why not?

3. What aspects of a computer program could be protected using trade secrecy?

D. SPECIAL ISSUE: HOW DOES TRADE SECRET LAW INTERACT WITH FEDERAL PATENT AND COPYRIGHT LAWS?

There is a substantial body of federal law which generally provides that state law cannot be applied or enforced if it unduly conflicts with federal law. Known as the federal preemption doctrine, the issue of federal preemption may arise as a defense anytime a plaintiff asserts a cause of action based upon state law if there is a similar federal law or when federal law specifies, either explicitly or impliedly, that state law is preempted. *See, e.g.,* John E. Nowak & Ronald D. Rotunda, CONSTITUTIONAL LAW § 9.1, at 393–94 (8th ed. 2010).

The doctrine of federal preemption was applied by the U.S. Supreme Court to limit the application of state unfair competition law in the famous companion cases of *Sears, Roebuck & Co. v. Stiffel Co.,* 376 U.S. 225 and *Compco Corp. v. Day-Brite Lighting, Inc.,* 376 U.S. 234, decided on the same date in March 1964. Noting a conflict between the unfair competition laws of Illinois that prohibited product simulation and federal patent law, the court ruled that the Illinois statute was preempted and could not be enforced.

Although the *Sears/Compco* cases involved a conflict between the unfair competition laws of Illinois and federal patent law, it immediately raised concerns about the continued viability of state trade secret law. *See* Sharon K. Sandeen, *The Evolution of Trade Secret Law and Why Courts Commit Error When They Do Not Follow the UTSA,* 33 HAMLINE L. REV. (2010). It was not until 1974 when the U.S. Supreme Court issued its decision in *Kewanee Oil Co. v. Bicron* that it became clear that state trade secret law, or at least the U.S. Supreme Court's understanding of Ohio's trade secret law, was not preempted by federal patent law and could be enforced. *See* Sharon K. Sandeen, *Kewanee Revisited: Returning to First Principles of Intellectual Property Law to Determine the Issue of Federal Preemption*, 12 MARQ. INTELLECTUAL PROP. L. REV. 299 (2008).

While the general view from *Kewanee* is that trade secret law and patent law can and do co-exist, practical questions often arise involving the interaction between trade secret law and patent law or trade secret law and copyright law. The two cases below touch on these questions. Specifically, how does the presence of a patent or copyright affect the trade secret status of the information? If, for instance, an inventor files a patent application that is rejected by the USPTO, can the inventor keep the information contained in the application as a trade secret? As you will see in *Bondpro v. Siemens* which follows, patent applications are usually published eighteen months after they are filed. This means that even if the patent application is ultimately rejected, its contents still becomes public. But is it possible (and should it be possible) for patent applicants to patent their inventions but keep some information as trade secrets?

While patent and trade secret law protect inventions and information, copyright law covers original expression fixed in tangible form. However, the existence of a copyright can affect a trade secret claim depending on whether the copyrighted material was published or otherwise made publicly available. Also, as you will see in *Computer Associates v. Altai*, below, a state trade secret claim may be preempted by federal copyright law where the rights as granted or enforced under the state law are equivalent to those granted under the federal copyright law. *See also, Spear Marketing, Inc. v. Bancorpsouth Bank*, 791 F.3d 586 (2015) (holding that state law claims based upon ideas fixed in tangible form are preempted by section 301(a) of the Copyright Act where the alleged wrongdoing falls within the exclusive rights of a copyright owner.)

Yet to be determined is how the adoption of the DTSA might affect the preemption analysis. It is clear that Congress did not intend for the DTSA to preempt state trade secret law (*see* 18 U.S.C. § 1838, reprinted in Appendix A), but it is less clear how conflicts between federal patent, copyright, and trade secret laws will be resolved in the future.

Food for Thought

What legal and policy arguments do you think underlie the federal preemption doctrine? Why does federal law preempt state law sometimes and not others? What are some of the reasons why Congress might want to enact a federal law that explicitly preempts state law?

> ### Reading Guidance
> *How did the Supreme Court address the concern that state trade secret law was preempted by the federal patent law?*

[handwritten: focused on objectives of patent law vs. TS law]

KEWANEE OIL CO. V. BICRON CORP.

United States Supreme Court, 1974.

416 U.S. 470.

[handwritten: — fed. patent law did not preempt State trade secret law.]

Mr. CHIEF JUSTICE BURGER delivered the opinion of the Court.

* * *

Ohio has adopted the widely relied-upon definition of a trade secret found at *Restatement of Torts* s 757, comment b (1939). According to the Restatement,

> "(a) trade secret may consist of any formula, pattern, device or compilation of information which is used in one's business, and which gives him an opportunity to obtain an advantage over competitors who do not know or use it. It may be a formula for a chemical compound, a process of manufacturing, treating or preserving materials, a pattern for a machine or other device, or a list of customers."

The subject of a trade secret must be secret, and must not be of public knowledge or of a general knowledge in the trade or business. This necessary element of secrecy is not lost, however, if the holder of the trade secret reveals the trade secret to another "in confidence, and under an implied obligation not to use or disclose it." These others may include those of the holder's "employees to whom it is necessary to confide it, in order to apply it to the uses for which it is intended." Often the recipient of confidential knowledge of the subject of a trade secret is a licensee of its holder.

The protection accorded the trade secret holder is against the disclosure or unauthorized use of the trade secret by those to whom the secret has been confided under the express or implied restriction of nondisclosure or nonuse. The law also protects the holder of a trade secret against disclosure or use when the knowledge is gained, not by the owner's volition, but by some "improper means," which may include theft, wiretapping, or even aerial reconnaissance. A trade secret law, however, does not offer protection against discovery by fair and honest means, such as by independent invention, accidental disclosure, or by so-called reverse engineering, that is by starting with the known product and working backward to divine the process which aided in its development or manufacture.

Novelty, in the patent law sense, is not required for a trade secret "Quite clearly discovery is something less than invention" modified to increase scope of injunction. However, some novelty will be required if merely because that which does not possess novelty is usually known; secrecy, in the context of trade secrets, thus implies at least minimal novelty.

The subject matter of a patent is limited to a "process, machine, manufacture, or composition of matter, or . . . improvement thereof," which fulfills the three conditions of novelty and utility as articulated and defined in 35 U.S.C. ss 101 and 102, and nonobviousness, as set out in 35 U.S.C. s 103.8 If an invention meets the rigorous statutory tests for the issuance of a patent, the patent is granted, for a period of 17 years [now 20 from date of filing], giving what has been described as the "right of exclusion." This protection goes not only to copying the subject matter, which is forbidden under the Copyright Act, 17 U.S.C. s 1 et seq., but also to independent creation.

The first issue we deal with is whether the States are forbidden to act at all in the area of protection of the kinds of intellectual property which may make up the subject matter of trade secrets.

Article I, s 8, cl. 8, of the Constitution grants to the Congress the power

> "(t)o promote the Progress of Science and useful Arts, by securing for limited Times to Authors and Inventors the exclusive Right to their respective Writings and Discoveries . . . "

In the 1972 Term, in *Goldstein v. California,* we held that the cl. 8 grant of power to Congress was not exclusive and that, at least in the case of writings, the States were not prohibited from encouraging and protecting the efforts of those within their borders by appropriate legislation. The States could, therefore, protect against the unauthorized rerecording for sale of performances fixed on records or tapes, even though those performances qualified as "writings" in the constitutional sense and Congress was empowered to legislate regarding such performances and could pre-empt the area if it chose to do so. This determination was premised on the great diversity of interests in our Nation—the essentially non-uniform character of the appreciation of intellectual achievements in the various States. Evidence for this came from patents granted by the States in the 18th century.

Just as the States may exercise regulatory power over writings so may the States regulate with respect to discoveries. States may hold diverse viewpoints in protecting intellectual property to invention as they do in protecting the intellectual property relating to the subject matter of copyright. The only limitation on the States is that in regulating the area of patents and copyrights they do not conflict with the operation of the laws in this area passed by Congress, and it is to that more difficult question we now turn.

The question of whether the trade secret law of Ohio is void under the Supremacy Clause involves a consideration of whether that law "stands as an obstacle to the accomplishment and execution of the full purposes and objectives of Congress." We stated in *Sears, Roebuck & Co. v. Stiffel Co.*, that when state law touches upon the area of federal statutes enacted pursuant to constitutional authority, "it is 'familiar doctrine' that the federal policy 'may not be set at naught, or its benefits denied' by the state law. This is true, of course, even if the state law is enacted in the exercise of otherwise undoubted state power."

The laws which the Court of Appeals in this case held to be in conflict with the Ohio law of trade secrets were the patent laws passed by the Congress in the unchallenged exercise of its clear power under Art. I, s 8, cl. 8, of the Constitution. The patent law does not explicitly endorse or forbid the operation of trade secret law. However, as we have noted, if the scheme of protection developed by Ohio respecting trade secrets "clashes with the objectives of the federal patent laws," then the state law must fall. To determine whether the Ohio law "clashes" with the federal law it is helpful to examine the objectives of both the patent and trade secret laws.

analysis = objectives

The stated objective of the Constitution in granting the power to Congress to legislate in the area of intellectual property is to "promote the Progress of Science and useful Arts." The patent laws promote this progress by offering a right of exclusion for a limited period as an incentive to inventors to risk the often enormous costs in terms of time, research, and development. The productive effort thereby fostered will have a positive effect on society through the introduction of new products and processes of manufacture into the economy, and the emanations by way of increased employment and better lives for our citizens. In return for the right of exclusion—this "reward for inventions,"—the patent laws impose upon the inventor a requirement of disclosure. To insure adequate and full disclosure so that upon the expiration of the 17-year period 'the knowledge of the invention enures to the people, who are thus enabled without restriction to practice it and profit by its use,' the patent laws require that the patent application shall include a full and clear description of the invention and "of the manner and process of making and using it" so that any person skilled in the art may make and use the invention. When a patent is granted and the information contained in it is circulated to the general public and those especially skilled in the trade, such additions to the general store of knowledge are of such importance to the public weal that the Federal Government is willing to pay the high price of 17 years of exclusive use for its disclosure, which disclosure, it is assumed, will stimulate ideas and the eventual development of further significant advances in the art. The Court has also articulated another policy of the patent law: that which is in the public domain cannot be removed therefrom by action of the States.

- objectives of fed. patent law

- promote progress of sci...

> "(F)ederal laws requires that all ideas in general circulation be dedicated to the common good unless they are protected by a valid patent."

The maintenance of standards of commercial ethics and the encouragement of invention are the broadly stated policies behind trade secret law. "The necessity of good faith and honest, fair dealing, is the very life and spirit of the commercial world." *National Tube Co. v. Eastern Tube Co.*, 3 Ohio Cir.Cr.R., N.S. at 462. In *A. O. Smith Corp. v. Petroleum Iron Works Co.*, the Court emphasized that even though a discovery may not be patentable, that does not "destroy the value of the discovery to one who makes it, or advantage the competitor who by unfair means, or as the beneficiary of a broken faith, obtains the desired knowledge without himself paying the price in labor, money, or machines expended by the discover."

In *Wexler v. Greenberg*, the Pennsylvania Supreme Court noted the importance of trade secret protection to the subsidization of research and development and to increased economic efficiency within large companies through the dispersion of responsibilities for creative developments.

Having now in mind the objectives of both the patent and trade secret law, we turn to an examination of the interaction of these systems of protection of intellectual property—one established by the Congress and the other by a State—to determine whether and under what circumstances the latter might constitute "too great an encroachment on the federal patent system to be tolerated."

As we noted earlier, trade secret law protects items which would not be proper subjects for consideration for patent protection under 35 U.S.C. s 101. As in the case of the recordings in *Goldstein v. California*, Congress, with respect to nonpatentable subject matter, "has drawn no balance; rather, it has left the area unattended, and no reason exists why the State should not be free to act."

Since no patent is available for a discovery, however useful, novel, and nonobvious, unless it falls within one of the express categories of patentable subject matter of 35 U.S.C. s 101, the holder of such a discovery would have no reason to apply for a patent whether trade secret protection existed or not. Abolition of trade secret protection would, therefore, not result in increased disclosure to the public of discoveries in the area of nonpatentable subject matter. Also, it is hard to see how the public would be benefited by disclosure of customer lists or advertising campaigns; in fact, keeping such items secret encourages businesses to initiate new and individualized plans of operation, and constructive competition results. This, in turn, leads to a greater variety of business methods than would otherwise be the case if privately developed marketing and other data were passed illicitly among firms involved in the same enterprise.

Congress has spoken in the area of those discoveries which fall within one of the categories of patentable subject matter of 35 U.S.C. s 101 and which are, therefore, of a nature that would be subject to consideration for a patent. Processes, machines, manufactures, compositions of matter and improvements thereof, which meet the tests of utility, novelty, and nonobviousness are entitled to be patented, but those which do not, are not. The question remains whether those items which are proper subjects for consideration for a patent may also have available the alternative protection accorded by trade secret law.

Certainly the patent policy of encouraging invention is not disturbed by the existence of another form of incentive to invention. In this respect the two systems are not and never would be in conflict. Similarly, the policy that matter once in the public domain must remain in the public domain is not incompatible with the existence of trade secret protection. By definition a trade secret has not been placed in the public domain.

— the two IP are not in conflict.

The more difficult objective of the patent law to reconcile with trade secret law is that of disclosure, the quid pro quo of the right to exclude. We are helped in this stage of the analysis by Judge Henry Friendly's opinion in *Painton & Co. v. Bourns, Inc.* There the Court of Appeals thought it useful, in determining whether inventors will refrain because of the existence of trade secret law from applying for patents, thereby depriving the public from learning of the invention, to distinguish between three categories of trade secrets:

"(1) the trade secret believed by its owner to constitute a validly patentable invention; (2) the trade secret known to its owner not to be so patentable; and (3) the trade secret whose valid patentability is considered dubious."

Trade secret protection in each of these categories would run against breaches of confidence—the employee and licensee situations—and theft and other forms of industrial espionage.

Cat 1

As to the trade secret known not to meet the standards of patentability, very little in the way of disclosure would be accomplished by abolishing trade secret protection. With trade secrets of nonpatentable subject matter, the patent alternative would not reasonably be available to the inventor. "There can be no public interest in stimulating developers of such (unpatentable) knowhow to flood an overburdened Patent Office with applications (for) what they do not consider patentable." *Ibid.* The mere filing of applications doomed to be turned down by the Patent Office will bring forth no new public knowledge or enlightenment, since under federal statute and regulation patent applications and abandoned patent applications are held by the Patent Office in confidence and are not open to public inspection.

Cat 2

Even as the extension of trade secret protection to patentable subject matter that the owner knows will not meet the standards of patentability will not conflict with the patent policy of disclosure, it will have a decidedly beneficial effect on society. Trade secret law will encourage invention in areas where patent law does not reach, and will prompt the independent innovator to proceed with the discovery and exploitation of his invention. Competition is fostered and the public is not deprived of the use of valuable, if not quite patentable, invention.

Even if trade secret protection against the faithless employee were abolished, inventive and exploitive effort in the area of patentable subject matter that did not meet the standards of patentability would continue, although at a reduced level. Alternatively with the effort that remained, however, would come an increase in the amount of self-help that innovative companies would employ. Knowledge would be widely dispersed among the employees of those still active in research. Security precautions necessarily would be increased, and salaries and fringe benefits of those few officers or employees who had to know the whole of the secret invention would be fixed in an amount thought sufficient to assure their loyalty. Smaller companies would be placed at a distinct economic disadvantage, since the costs of this kind of self-help could be great, and the cost to the public of the use of this invention would be increased. The innovative entrepreneur with limited resources would tend to confine his research efforts to himself and those few he felt he could trust without the ultimate assurance of legal protection against breaches of confidence. As a result, organized scientific and technological research could become fragmented, and society, as a whole, would suffer.

Another problem that would arise if state trade secret protection were precluded is in the area of licensing others to exploit secret processes. The holder of a trade secret would not likely share his secret with a manufacturer who cannot be placed under binding legal obligation to pay a license fee or to protect the secret. The result would be to hoard rather than disseminate knowledge. Instead, then, of licensing others to use his invention and making the most efficient use of existing manufacturing and marketing structures within the industry, the trade secret holder would tend either to limit his utilization of the invention, thereby depriving the public of the maximum benefit of its use, or engage in the time-consuming and economically wasteful enterprise of constructing duplicative manufacturing and marketing mechanisms for the exploitation of the invention. The detrimental misallocation of resources and economic waste that would thus take place if trade secret protection were abolished with respect to employees or licensees cannot be justified by reference to any policy that the federal patent law seeks to advance.

Nothing in the patent law requires that States refrain from action to prevent industrial espionage. In addition to the increased costs for protection from burglary, wire-tapping, bribery, and the other means used to misappropriate trade secrets, there is the inevitable cost to the basic decency of society when one firm steals from another. A most fundamental human right, that of privacy, is threatened when industrial espionage is condoned or is made profitable; the state interest in denying profit to such illegal ventures is unchallengeable.

The next category of patentable subject matter to deal with is the invention *Cat. 3* whose holder has a legitimate doubt as to its patentability. The risk of eventual patent invalidity by the courts and the costs associated with that risk may well impel some with a good-faith doubt as to patentability not to take the trouble to seek to obtain and defend patent protection for their discoveries, regardless of the existence of trade secret protection. Trade secret protection would assist those inventors in the more efficient exploitation of their discoveries and not conflict with the patent law. In most cases of genuine doubt as to patent validity the potential rewards of patent protection are so far superior to those accruing to holders of trade secrets, that the holders of such inventions will seek patent protection, ignoring the trade secret route. For those inventors "on the line" as to whether to seek patent protection, the abolition of trade secret protection might encourage some to apply for a patent who otherwise would not have done so. For some of those so encouraged, no patent will be granted and the result "will have been an unnecessary postponement in the divulging of the trade secret to persons willing to pay for it. If (the patent does issue), it may well be invalid, yet many will prefer to pay a modest royalty than to contest it, even though Lear allows them to accept a license and pursue the contest without paying royalties while the fight goes on. The result in such a case would be unjustified royalty payments from many who would prefer not to pay them rather than agreed fees from one or a few who are entirely willing to do so."

The point is that those who might be encouraged to file for patents by the absence of trade secret law will include inventors possessing the chaff as well as the wheat. Some of the chaff—the nonpatentable discoveries—will be thrown out by the Patent Office, but in the meantime society will have been deprived of use of those discoveries through trade secret-protected licensing. Some of the chaff may not be thrown out. This Court has noted the difference between the standards used by the Patent Office and the courts to determine patentability. In *Lear, Inc. v. Adkins*, the Court thought that an invalid patent was so serious a threat to the free use of ideas already in the public domain that the Court permitted licensees of the patent holder to challenge the validity of the patent. Better had the invalid patent never issued. More of those patents would likely issue if trade secret law were abolished. Eliminating trade secret law for the doubtfully patentable invention is thus likely to have deleterious effects on society and patent policy which we cannot say are balanced out by the speculative gain which might result from the encouragement of some inventors with doubtfully patentable inventions which deserve patent protection to come forward and apply for patents. There is no conflict, then, between trade secret law and the patent law policy of disclosure, at least insofar as the first two categories of patentable subject matter are concerned.

(at. 1)

The final category of patentable subject matter to deal with is the clearly patentable invention, i.e., that invention which the owner believes to meet the standards of patentability. It is here that the federal interest in disclosure is at its peak; these inventions, novel, useful and nonobvious, are "the things which are worth to the public the embarrassment of an exclusive patent." *Graham v. John Deere Co.* (quoting Thomas Jefferson). The interest of the public is that the bargain of 17 years of exclusive use in return for disclosure be accepted. If a State, through a system of protection, were to cause a substantial risk that holders of patentable inventions would not seek patents, but rather would rely on the state protection, we would be compelled to hold that such a system could not constitutionally continue to exist. In the case of trade secret law no reasonable risk of deterrence from patent application by those who can reasonably expect to be granted patents exists.

Trade secret law provides far weaker protection in many respects than the patent law. While trade secret law does not forbid the discovery of the trade secret by fair and honest means, e.g., independent creation or reverse engineering, patent law operates "against the world," forbidding any use of the invention for whatever purpose for a significant length of time. The holder of a trade secret also takes a substantial risk that the secret will be passed on to his competitors, by theft or by breach of a confidential relationship, in a manner not easily susceptible of discovery or proof. Where patent law acts as a barrier, trade secret law functions relatively as a sieve. The possibility that an inventor who believes his invention meets the standards of patentability will sit back, rely on trade secret law, and after one year of use forfeit any right to patent protection, 35 U.S.C. s 102(b), is remote indeed.

Nor does society face much risk that scientific or technological progress will be impeded by the rare inventor with a patentable invention who chooses trade secret protection over patent protection. The ripeness-of-time concept of invention, developed from the study of the many independent multiple discoveries in history, predicts that if a particular individual had not made a particular discovery others would have, and in probably a relatively short period of time. If something is to be discovered at all very likely it will be discovered by more than one person. Singletons and Multiples in Science (1961), in R. Merton, The Sociology of Science 343 (1973); J. Cole & S. Cole, Social Stratification in Science 12–13, 229–230 (1973); Ogburn & Thomas, Are Inventions Inevitable?, 37 Pol.Sci.Q. 83 (1922). Even were an inventor to keep his discovery completely to himself, something that neither the patent nor trade secret laws forbid, there is a high probability that it will

— unlikely that an inventor will rely on State law over fed. law if their invention is eligible for protection for both

be soon independently developed. If the invention, though still a trade secret, is put into public use, the competition is alerted to the existence of the inventor's solution to the problem and may be encouraged to make an extra effort to independently find the solution thus known to be possible. The inventor faces pressures not only from private industry, but from the skilled scientists who work in our universities and our other great publicly supported centers of learning and research.

We conclude that the extension of trade secret protection to clearly patentable inventions does not conflict with the patent policy of disclosure. Perhaps because trade secret law does not produce any positive effects in the area of clearly patentable inventions, as opposed to the beneficial effects resulting from trade secret protection in the areas of the doubtfully patentable and the clearly unpatentable inventions, it has been suggested that partial pre-emption may be appropriate, and that courts should refuse to apply trade secret protection to inventions which the holder should have patented, and which would have been, thereby, disclosed. However, since there is no real possibility that trade secret law will conflict with the federal policy favoring disclosure of clearly patentable inventions partial pre-emption is inappropriate. Partial pre-emption, furthermore, could well create serious problems for state courts in the administration of trade secret law. As a preliminary matter in trade secret actions, state courts would be obliged to distinguish between what a reasonable inventor would and would not correctly consider to be clearly patentable, with the holder of the trade secret arguing that the invention was not patentable and the misappropriator of the trade secret arguing its undoubted novelty, utility, and nonobviousness. Federal courts have a difficult enough time trying to determine whether an invention, narrowed by the patent application procedure and fixed in the specifications which describe the invention for which the patent has been granted, is patentable. Although state courts in some circumstances must join federal courts in judging whether an issued patent is valid, *Lear, Inc. v. Adkins, supra*, it would be undesirable to impose the almost impossible burden on state courts to determine the patentability—in fact and in the mind of a reasonable inventor—of a discovery which has not been patented and remains entirely uncircumscribed by expert analysis in the administrative process. Neither complete nor partial pre-emption of state trade secret law is justified.

Our conclusion that patent law does not pre-empt trade secret law is in accord with prior cases of this Court. Trade secret law and patent law have co-existed in this country for over one hundred years. Each has its particular role to play, and the operation of one does not take away from the need for the other. Trade secret law encourages the development and exploitation of those items of lesser or different invention than might be accorded protection under the patent laws, but which items still have an important part to play in the technological and scientific advancement of the Nation. Trade secret law promotes the sharing of knowledge, and the efficient operation of industry; it permits the individual inventor to reap the rewards of his labor by contracting with a company large enough to develop and exploit it. Congress, by its silence over these many years, has seen the wisdom of allowing the States to enforce trade secret protection. Until Congress takes affirmative action to the contrary, States should be free to grant protection to trade secrets.

Since we hold that Ohio trade secret law is not preempted by the federal patent law, the judgment of the Court of Appeals for the Sixth Circuit is reversed, and the case is remanded to the Court of Appeals with directions to reinstate the judgment of the District Court.

It is so ordered.

Reversed and remanded for reinstatement of District Court judgment.

Mr. JUSTICE POWELL took no part in the decision of this case.

Mr. JUSTICE MARSHALL, concurring in the result.

Unlike the Court, I do not believe that the possibility that an inventor with a patentable invention will rely on state trade secret law rather than apply for a patent is "remote indeed." State trade secret law provides substantial protection to the inventor who intends to use or sell the invention himself rather than license it to others, protection which in its unlimited duration is clearly superior to the 17-year monopoly afforded by the patent laws. I have no doubt that the existence of trade secret protection provides in some instances a substantial disincentive to entrance into the patent system, and thus deprives society of the benefits of public disclosure of the invention which it is the policy of the patent laws to encourage. This case may well be such an instance.

But my view of sound policy in this area does not dispose of this case. Rather, the question presented in this case is whether Congress, in enacting the patent laws, intended merely to offer inventors a limited monopoly in exchange for disclosure of their invention, or instead to exert pressure on inventors to enter into this exchange by withdrawing any alternative possibility of legal protection for their inventions. I am persuaded that the former is the case. State trade secret laws and the federal patent laws have co-existed for many, many years. During this time, Congress has repeatedly demonstrated its full awareness of the existence of the trade secret system, without any indication of disapproval. Indeed, Congress has in a number of instances given explicit federal protection to trade secret information provided to federal agencies. Because of this, I conclude that there is "neither such actual conflict between the two schemes of regulation that both cannot stand in the same area, nor evidence of a congressional design to pre-empt the field." I therefore concur in the result reached by the majority of the Court.

DID YOU GET IT?

1. How did the majority perceive the hierarchy between patent law and *— patent*
    trade secret law and the resulting effect on inventors? *— inventors → select patent* *— trade secret.*

2. What conflict is presented between trade secret law and patent law as
    to inventions that are not patentable?

3. What is the crux of Justice Marshall's position in his concurring
    opinion? *interpreted Congress only gave 17 yr limited protection, not TS, which could be forever*

> ### *Reading Guidance*
> *What is the effect of disclosing a trade secret in a patent application?*

BONDPRO CORPORATION V. SIEMENS POWER GENERATION, INC.

United States Court of Appeals, Seventh Circuit, 2006.
463 F.3d 702.

POSNER, CIRCUIT JUDGE.

* * *

BondPro is a small company that manufactures products * * * that require
the bonding of dissimilar materials. Siemens (a subsidiary of the German
conglomerate), the defendant, makes electrical generators. The generators
produce electrical power by spinning rotors over magnets. The rotors have
slots into which copper coils are wedged. The outer layer of each coil
consists of insulation material in the form of a U-shaped "slot cell." Siemens
manufactures slot cells by first placing the insulation material in a U-
shaped ("female") container and then pressing a "male" mold on top and
applying heat. This process compresses the insulation into a rigid U-
shaped material that can slide into the slots. The process resembles putting
material into a bowl and pressing another, slightly smaller bowl into the
first bowl to compress and harden the material inside that bowl.

The disadvantage of the process is that the slot cell may emerge with
wrinkles in the insulation material that are difficult to smooth out.
BondPro developed (though it has never marketed) a process that
dispenses with the female mold. Instead the insulating material is placed
on the outside of the male mold and pressed against it by placing the mold
and the insulation material in a vacuum bag so that air pressure
compresses the material against the mold. Any remaining wrinkles are
smoothed by hand. The ensemble consisting of the mold and the insulation
material pressed against it is then placed in an autoclave, a container in
which high levels of heat and air pressure are applied to the contents. The
heat and pressure compress the insulation coating the mold into the
desired rigid shape and it is then removed from the male mold and slid into
a rotor's slot.

In 2001, Scott Wang, BondPro's principal, explained and later demonstrated the process to Mark Miller, a materials engineer employed by Siemens. Though there were some negotiations, they resulted only in agreement (as we shall see) on confidentiality; Siemens didn't seek a license from BondPro to use the process, even though BondPro had made clear in the course of the negotiations that it believed it had proprietary rights to it. Instead Miller filed a patent application on behalf of Siemens for a process similar to BondPro's (more precisely, similar to the description of BondPro's process in its appeal briefs) although among other differences it does not specify the use of an autoclave for the final step of hardening the insulation materials coating the male mold. There are other ways of applying heat and pressure; no particular way is specified in the patent application.

The Patent Office rejected Siemens' application and Siemens has never used the process. Nor for that matter has BondPro, except to make some prototypes to show Siemens. There may have been some use of BondPro's process by other companies, but if so there is no evidence of the value of such use.

Anybody other than Siemens can use the BondPro process without liability because, as BondPro acknowledges and indeed asserts, the process was disclosed to the world in Siemens's patent application. A trade secret that becomes public knowledge is no longer a trade secret. The mere fact of mention in a public document is not controlling; no one may have noticed the document. Publication in a patent destroys the trade secret, because patents are intended to be widely disclosed—that is the quid for the quo of the patentee's exclusive right to make and sell the patented device. But patent applications are not patents, and they used to be secret. However, now they have to be published after 18 months, the aim of this rule being to disseminate the knowledge revealed in the application to the inventor community so that other inventors can build upon it. Published patent applications are in fact studied by inventors in the relevant field, and so a secret disclosed in them will ordinarily (we need not decide whether invariably) lose its status as a trade secret. Of course a patent application that is rejected, as Siemens' was, is less likely to contain information that other inventors would want to use, but it might, since patent examiners are not infallible and a patent application might disclose some novel features or bring to light some forgotten prior art.

But had it not been for the alleged theft of BondPro's secret by Siemens, there would have been no patent application. So while someone who learned about BondPro's process from the application or some other source traceable to Siemens would have no liability for using the process without BondPro's consent, Siemens would be liable to BondPro for the consequences of enabling the innocent copying by revealing BondPro's trade secret to the world.

* * *

The answers to the questions posed in the preceding paragraph depend on just what BondPro's claimed trade secret is. Is it merely the manufacture of rotor-coil insulation by applying heat and air pressure to insulation materials draped as it were around the fittingly named "male mold," as BondPro sometimes suggests? This was something Miller and others in the trade knew already because a company named Torr Technologies had described this method in advertising materials that Miller, doubtless along with others, had been given at a trade convention that he had attended in 2000. * * *

So if BondPro really had an invention that was concealed from Siemens, there would have to be more detail to it than we have thus far indicated; but we cannot find the detail. In places BondPro hints that the trade secret includes not just the heat and the air pressure but that these forces are exerted in an autoclave. Yet in its brief, in listing nine components that constitute the trade secret (some of them almost risible, such as "Stacking of Materials on Mold"), there is no mention of an autoclave, just of "Application of Simultaneous Heat and Pressure," which could be done by other means, as by combining a convection oven to provide heat with a shrink-tape process ("shrink tape," as the term implies, is a wrapping that squeezes by shrinking) to provide pressure.

One expects a trade secret to be rich in detail, because a process described in general terms (squeeze insulation materials draped on the male mold with heat and air pressure rather than pressing the male mold into a female mold containing the materials) will usually be widely known and thus not worth incurring costs to try to conceal and so not a trade secret. In its reply brief BondPro acknowledges that "many of the elements of the BondPro slot cell manufacturing process were in the public domain" but states that "the precise execution of each element, in conjunction with the precise execution of each additional element, renders BondPro's process a secret." But BondPro has not told us what those details of execution or implementation are. For example, in the list of nine components the temperature and the duration of the application of heat are stated as a broad range rather than as specific numbers—and anyway Wang obtained the range from Siemens! And a broad range was all that Siemens's patent application disclosed—so if BondPro's trade secret resides in specifics that have not been disclosed to us, Siemens is not responsible for their disclosure.

AFFIRMED.

DID YOU GET IT?

1. Did the patent office's rejection of Siemens' patent application affect the trade secret status of BondPro's process?

2.   Does the disclosure of the trade secret in the patent application affect Siemens' liability to BondPro for trade secret misappropriation?

3.   Could Siemens have patented a trade secret that it stole from Bondpro?

Reading Guidance

Can a plaintiff maintain claims for both copyright infringement and trade secret misappropriation of the same information?

COMPUTER ASSOCIATES INTERNATIONAL, INC. v. ALTAI, INC.

United States Court of Appeals, Second Circuit, 1992.
982 F.2d 693.

WALKER, CIRCUIT JUDGE.

* * *

In its complaint, [Computer Associates] CA alleged that Altai misappropriated the trade secrets contained in the ADAPTER program. Prior to trial, while the proceedings were still before Judge Mishler, Altai moved to dismiss and for summary judgment on CA's trade secret misappropriation claim. Altai argued that section 301 of the Copyright Act preempted CA's state law cause of action. Judge Mishler denied Altai's motion, reasoning that " [t]he elements of the tort of appropriation of trade secrets through the breach of contract or confidence by an employee are not the same as the elements of a claim of copyright infringement.' "

The parties addressed the preemption issue again, both in pre- and post-trial briefs. Judge Pratt then reconsidered and reversed Judge Mishler's earlier ruling. The district court concluded that CA's trade secret claims were preempted because "CA—which is the master of its own case—has pleaded and proven facts which establish that one act constituted both copyright infringement *and* misappropriation of trade secrets [namely, the] copying of ADAPTER into OSCAR 3.4. . . ."

* * *

General Law of Copyright Preemption Regarding Trade Secrets and Computer Programs

Congress carefully designed the statutory framework of federal copyright preemption. In order to insure that the enforcement of these rights remains solely within the federal domain, section 301(a) of the Copyright Act expressly preempts

> all legal or equitable rights that are equivalent to any of the exclusive rights within the general scope of copyright as specified by section 106 in works of authorship that are fixed in a tangible

medium of expression and come within the subject matter of copyright as specified by sections 102 and 103. . . .

This sweeping displacement of state law is, however, limited by section 301(b), which provides, in relevant part, that

> [n]othing in this title annuls or limits any rights or remedies under the common law or statutes of any State with respect to . . . activities violating legal or equitable rights that are not equivalent to any of the exclusive rights within the general scope of copyright as specified by section 106. . . .

17 U.S.C. § 301(b)(3). Section 106, in turn, affords a copyright owner the exclusive right to: (1) reproduce the copyrighted work; (2) prepare derivative works; (3) distribute copies of the work by sale or otherwise; and, with respect to certain artistic works, (4) perform the work publicly; and (5) display the work publicly. *See* 17 U.S.C. § 106(1)–(5).

Section 301 thus preempts only those state law rights that "may be abridged by an act which, in and of itself, would infringe one of the exclusive rights" provided by federal copyright law. But if an "extra element" is "required instead of or in addition to the acts of reproduction, performance, distribution or display, in order to constitute a state-created cause of action, then the right does not lie 'within the general scope of copyright,' and there is no preemption." 1 Nimmer § 1.01[B], at 1–14–15.

A state law claim is not preempted if the "extra element" changes the "nature of the action so that it is *qualitatively* different from a copyright infringement claim." To determine whether a claim meets this standard, we must determine "what plaintiff seeks to protect, the theories in which the matter is thought to be protected and the rights sought to be enforced." An action will not be saved from preemption by elements such as awareness or intent, which alter "the action's scope but not its nature. . . ."

Following this "extra element" test, we have held that unfair competition and misappropriation claims grounded solely in the copying of a plaintiff's protected expression are preempted by section 301. We also have held to be preempted a tortious interference with contract claim grounded in the impairment of a plaintiff's right under the Copyright Act to publish derivative works.

However, many state law rights that can arise in connection with instances of copyright infringement satisfy the extra element test, and thus are not preempted by section 301. These include unfair competition claims based upon breaches of confidential relationships, breaches of fiduciary duties and trade secrets.

Trade secret protection, the branch of unfair competition law at issue in this case, remains a "uniquely valuable" weapon in the defensive arsenal of computer programmers. Precisely because trade secret doctrine protects the discovery of ideas, processes, and systems which are explicitly precluded from coverage under copyright law, courts and commentators alike consider it a necessary and integral part of the intellectual property protection extended to computer programs.

The legislative history of section 301 states that "[t]he evolving common law rights of . . . trade secrets . . . would remain unaffected as long as the causes of action contain elements, such as . . . a breach of trust or confidentiality, that are different in kind from copyright infringement." *House Report,* at 5748. Congress did not consider the term "misappropriation" to be "necessarily synonymous with copyright infringement," or to serve as the talisman of preemption. *Id.*

Trade secret claims often are grounded upon a defendant's breach of a duty of trust or confidence to the plaintiff through improper disclosure of confidential material. The defendant's breach of duty is the gravamen of such trade secret claims, and supplies the "extra element" that qualitatively distinguishes such trade secret causes of action from claims for copyright infringement that are based solely upon copying.

The district court stated that:

> Were CA's [trade secret] allegations premised on a theory of illegal *acquisition* of a trade secret, a charge that might have been alleged against Arney, who is not a defendant in this case, the preemption analysis might be different, for there seems to be no corresponding right guaranteed to copyright owners by § 106 of the copyright act.

However, the court concluded that CA's trade secret claims were not grounded in a theory that Altai violated a duty of confidentiality to CA. Rather, Judge Pratt stated that CA proceeded against Altai solely "on a theory that the misappropriation took place by Altai's *use* of ADAPTER—the same theory as the copyright infringement count." The district court reasoned that "the right to be free from trade secret misappropriation through 'use', and the right to exclusive reproduction and distribution of a copyrighted work are not distinguishable." Because he concluded that there was no qualitative difference between the elements of CA's state law trade secret claims and a claim for federal copyright infringement, Judge Pratt ruled that CA's trade secret claims were preempted by section 301.

We agree with CA that the district court failed to address fully the factual and theoretical bases of CA's trade secret claims. The district court relied upon the fact that Arney—not Altai—allegedly breached a duty to CA of confidentiality by stealing secrets from CA and incorporating those secrets into OSCAR 3.4. However, under a wrongful acquisition theory based on *Restatement (First) of Torts* § 757 (1939), Williams and Altai may be liable for violating CA's right of confidentiality. Section 757 states in relevant part:

> One who discloses or uses another's trade secret, without a privilege to do so, is liable to another if. . . . (c) he learned the secret from a third person with notice of the fact that it was a secret and that the third person discovered it by improper means or that the third person's disclosure of it was otherwise a breach of his duty to the other. . . .

* * * In response to CA's complaint, Altai rewrote OSCAR 3.4, creating OSCAR 3.5. While we agree with the district court that OSCAR 3.5 did not contain any expression protected by copyright, it may nevertheless still have embodied many of CA's trade secrets that Arney brought with him to Altai. Since Altai's rewrite was conducted with full knowledge of Arney's prior misappropriation, in breach of his duty of confidentiality, it follows that OSCAR 3.5 was created with actual knowledge of trade secret violations. Thus, with regard to OSCAR 3.5, CA has a viable trade secret claim against Altai that must be considered by the district court on remand. This claim is grounded in Altai's alleged use of CA's trade secrets in the creation of OSCAR 3.5, while on actual notice of Arney's theft of trade secrets and incorporation of those secrets into OSCAR 3.4. The district court correctly stated that a state law claim based *solely* upon Altai's "use", by copying, of ADAPTER's non-literal elements could not satisfy the governing extra element test, and would be preempted by section 301. However, where the use of copyrighted expression is simultaneously the violation of a duty of confidentiality established by state law, that extra element renders the state right qualitatively distinct from the federal right, thereby foreclosing preemption under section 301.

* * *

DID YOU GET IT?

1. What was the district court's reasoning on the preemption issue?

2. What test does the appellate court apply in analyzing the preemption issue?

3. Under what circumstances will a trade secret claim be preempted by copyright law?

4. Is the placement of a copyright notice on a document inconsistent with trade secret protection? How about registering one's copyrights?

Food for Thought

Now that you have been introduced to the doctrine of preemption, how is the issue likely to be raised in a trade secret case and by whom? Does the fact that the foregoing cases each found that the subject trade secret claims were not preempted resolve the issue of preemption for all trade secret cases?

NOTES

1.   **The definition of a trade secret in the EEA and DTSA.** As noted previously, the definition of a trade secret that is contained in the Economic Espionage Act of 1996 (EEA), was amended by the DTSA. The amendment is noted in the following stricken and underlined text of 18 U.S.C. § 1839(3):

> [T]he term "trade secret" means all forms and types of financial, business, scientific, technical, economic, or engineering information, including patterns, plans, compilations, program devices, formulas, designs, prototypes, methods, techniques, processes, procedures, programs, or codes, whether tangible or intangible, and whether or how stored, compiled, or memorialized physically, electronically, graphically, photographically, or in writing if—

> **(A)**   the owner thereof has taken reasonable measures to keep such information secret; and

> **(B)**   the information derives independent economic value, actual or potential, from not being generally known to, and not being readily ascertainable through proper means by, ~~the public~~ another person who can obtain economic value from the disclosure or use of the information.

This definition is now more consistent with the UTSA definition, but is not identical, thereby raising the question whether the definition of a trade secret under the EEA/DTSA will cover the same information as is covered under the UTSA. Can you see the differences? There are three: (1) a specific list of protectable information; (2) a longer list of illustrative examples; and (3) the memorialization clause.

2.   **Del Monte's Plant Patents.** Apparently not content with potential trade secret protection, Del Monte applied for and received U.S. Plant Patent protection for two varieties of pineapple that were developed after the variety that is the subject of the foregoing case. (*See* Plant Patent numbers: USPP16,328 P3 and USPP25,763 P3.)

Food for Thought

Assuming that there are elements of a plant that need not be disclosed in a Plant Patent, should companies be able to also assert trade secret rights for elements of the same plant? Or, should companies be required to choose between different means of protection?

---

3.   **The difference between a *Restatement* and a uniform law.** There are important differences between the *Restatement of the Law* and a uniform law that should be understood as you think about how to apply the law that is applicable in a given case. As explained by Professor Sharon Sandeen:

> The Restatement series was and is an explication of applicable law as divined by members of the American Law Institute (ALI),

consisting of a collection of judges, academics and practitioners. The purpose of the Restatement was not to codify the law, but rather to clarify and simplify the law by providing an easily accessible and clear statement of what the members of the ALI thought was the majority view of the states on various points of law. * * *

* * *

In contrast to the Restatement series, the purpose of the uniform law process is not merely to restate existing law, but to make and codify the law. * * * Thus, as a body of law, the UTSA—particularly as codified in each of the * * * jurisdictions that have adopted it—has a different status than the Restatement series. Whereas the Restatement series is secondary authority of what the law is, the UTSA is primary authority. As a matter of statutory interpretation, therefore, the first place that courts in UTSA jurisdictions should look to understand trade secret law is the language of the UTSA itself.

Sharon K. Sandeen, *The Evolution of Trade Secret Law and Why Courts Commit Error When They Do Not Follow the Uniform Trade Secrets Act*, 33 HAMLINE L. REV. 493, 539–540 (2010).

As explained in a history of the *Restatement* series, the *Restatements* were not intended to fix the law for all time, but were designed to be an easy reference for attorneys and judges who, in 1939, did not have access to the internet and may not have had easy access to judicial opinions:

> The first Restatement of the Law is done. We started with the belief that out of the mass of case authority and legal literature could be made clear statements of the rules of the common law today operative in the great majority of our States, expressed as simply as the character of our complex civilization admits. The result shows that this belief was justified. The Restatement of each subject expresses as nearly as may be the rules which our courts will today apply. These rules cover not merely situations which have already arisen in our courts but by analogy rules applicable to situations likely to arise. The Restatement of a subject is thus more than a picture of what has been decided; it is a picture of present law expressed by the foremost members of the profession. * * * Though the rules are expressed in the form of a code, except in sporadic instances, there never has been any desire to give them statutory authority. The Restatement is an agency tending to promote the clarification and unification of the law in a form similar to a Code. But it is not a Code or statute. It is designed to help preserve not to change the common system of expressing law and adapting it to changing conditions in a changing world.

William Draper Lewis, *How We Did It* in HISTORY OF THE AMERICAN LAW INSTITUTE AND THE FIRST RESTATEMENT OF THE LAW, RESTATEMENT IN THE COURTS PERMANENT EDITION 1932–1944.

4.   **Establishing rights for the first time in litigation.** Trade secret law permits a putative trade secret holder to establish its trade secret rights for the first time in litigation. The trade secret owner bears the burden of establishing that the information in question was entitled to trade secret protection before it was allegedly misappropriated. One of the biggest challenges for most plaintiffs lies in identifying the trade secret(s) with specificity. This is an especially important requirement in trade secret law because there is no government registration or certification of a trade secret prior to litigation, nor is there a presumption of validity. Elizabeth A. Rowe, *Trade Secret Litigation and Free Speech: Is it Time to Restrain the Plaintiffs?*, 50 BOSTON COLLEGE L. REV. 1425, 1447 (2009).

5.   **Bibliographic note:** In addition to the references above, for more information on the topics discussed in this chapter, *see* MILGRIM ON TRADE SECRETS §§ 1.06, 1.09, 9.03 (2016); Edward D. Manzo, *The Impact of the America Invents Act on Trade Secrets*, 13 J. MARSHALL REV. INTELL. PROP. L. 497 (2014); Charles Tait Graves and Elizabeth Tippett, *UTSA Preemption and the Public Domain; How Courts Have Overlooked Patent Preemption of State Law Claims Alleging Employee Wrongdoing*, 65 RUTGERS L. REV. 59 (2012); J. Jonas Anderson, *Secret Inventions*, 26 BERKELEY TECH. L. J. 917 (2011); Eric R. Claeys, *The Use Requirement at Common Law and Under the Uniform Trade Secrets Act*, 33 HAMLINE L. R. 583 (2010); Charles Tait Graves & Brian D. Range, *Identification of Trade Secret Claims in Litigation: Solutions for a Ubiquitous Dispute*, 5 NW. J. TECH. & INTELL. PROP. 68, 70–71 (2006); Howard B. Abrams, *Copyright, Misappropriation, and Preemption: Constitutional and Statutory Limits of State Law Protection*, 1983 SUP. CT. REV. 509 (1983).

CHAPTER 3

PUBLIC AVAILABILITY AND SECRECY

• • •

— generally known
— readily ascertainable

Anticipated Learning Outcomes

At the conclusion of this chapter, you will have a better understanding of the fundamental requirement that only secret information can be a trade secret. This will be accomplished through discussion of the UTSA's and DTSA's exclusion from trade secret protection of information that is "generally known" or "readily ascertainable." You will also learn to differentiate between potential trade secrets and general skill and knowledge.

A. INTRODUCTION

It is a fundamental and long-standing principle of intellectual property law that publicly available information cannot qualify for legal protection under patent, copyright, or trade secret law or under general principles of unfair competition. As the Supreme Court explained in *Bonito Boats, Inc. v. Thunder Craft Boats, Inc.*, 489 U.S. 141, 156 (1989), ". . . concepts within the public grasp, or those so obvious that they readily could be, are the tools of creation available to all. They provide the baseline of free competition. . . ." With respect to trade secrets, the Supreme Court noted in *Kewanee* that "[t]he subject of a trade secret must be secret, and must not be of public knowledge or of a general knowledge in the trade or business." (416 U.S. 470, 475 (1974)). This fundamental and consistent axiom of trade secret law is expressly incorporated into the modern definition of a trade secret under the UTSA and the DTSA.

Recall from Chapter 2 that the UTSA defines a trade secret as:

Information . . . that (i) derives independent economic value . . . *from not being generally known to, and not being readily ascertainable by proper means* by, other persons who can obtain economic value from its disclosure or use, and (ii) is the subject of efforts that are reasonable under the circumstances to maintain its secrecy. (Emphasis added.)

In this chapter we explore the "not generally known" and "not readily ascertainable" requirements of the UTSA and DTSA which, in effect, define the meaning of secrecy. In a sense, these requirements reflect the principle that in order to be protectable as a trade secret, information must not be easily available or publicly known. However, as you will see in the cases that follow, whether information is known or available is not as easy to determine as one may think. One reason for this difficulty is that the requirements place the burden on the plaintiff (the putative trade secret owner) to prove the non-existence of generally known or readily ascertainable information. In practice, however, it is often the defendant who presents evidence about known and available information. Another reason is due to the tendency of courts to merge the two requirements into one. Ultimately, the question should focus on ensuring that only information that is truly secret is protected.

Food for Thought

What does it mean for information to be "in the public grasp"? Must the information be published in a book, magazine, or newspaper of general circulation? Is it enough for the information to be available somewhere? What if you cannot find it using a Google® search?

One place where the generally known and readily ascertainable inquiries often arise is in cases involving "combination trade secrets" or "compilations of data" where part of the information composing the alleged trade secret may be publicly available, but not all of it. In *Penalty Kick Management Ltd. v. Coca-Cola Co.*, 164 F.Supp.2d 1376, 1379 (N.D. Ga. 2001), the court explained the commonly-held view in the U.S. that:

> The fact that some or all of the components of the trade secret are well-known does not preclude protection for a secret combination, compilation, or integration of the individual elements. [A] trade secret can exist in a combination of characteristics and components, each of which, by itself, is in the public domain, but the unified process, design and operation of which in unique combination, affords a competitive advantage and is a protectible secret.

> [A] trade secret can include a system where the elements are in the public domain, but there has been accomplished an effective, successful and valuable integration of the public domain elements and the trade secret gave the [trade secret owner] a competitive advantage which is protected from misappropriation. (internal citations omitted)

The challenge in combination trade secret cases is for the plaintiff to articulate how the combination of known information produces something different, identifiable, and valuable. *See* Charles Tait Graves, Alexander D. MacGillivray, *Combination Trade Secrets and The Logic Of Intellectual Property*, 20 SANTA CLARA COMPUTER & HIGH TECH. L.J. 261 (2004). Courts also must be careful not to confuse the public portions of combined information with the totality of the combined information and to differentiate between trade secrets that are created by combining known elements ("combination trade secrets") and trade secrets that may be distinct and identifiable parts of compilations of data.

The first case in this chapter, _Rohm and Haas Co._, represents a dispute over a combination trade secret and the question whether trade secrets can exist in information when part, but not all, of the information is publicly available. A separate question, addressed as part of the determination of remedies (see Chapter 10), is how to value trade secrets when they are only a part of a good or service.

Another type of case where the issue of the public availability of information arises, is with respect to mass distributed products. The central question in those cases is whether the trade secrets that are embodied in the goods have been disclosed to the public by virtue of the sale of the goods themselves. The _Peggy Lawtons, Louis Hutchison_, and _Editions Play Bac_ cases (involving recipes, processes for preparing food, and software products) are examples of these types of cases.

Because technology has become part of the fabric of our daily lives, the internet can affect the generally known and readily ascertainable analyses. Two Church of Scientology cases later in the chapter, _Netcom_ and _Lerma_, highlight the internet problem. The Special Issue in this chapter looks at another category of information that falls outside the ambit of trade secret protection: a person's general skill and knowledge. This information is not necessarily known to the public, but is learned by people in the field through education, work, and life experiences.

B. EXPLORING THE MEANING OF "GENERALLY KNOWN" AND "READILY ASCERTAINABLE"

The comments to the UTSA state that "generally known" does not necessarily mean known by the general public. Specifically, the official comments to section 1 of the UTSA read:

> The language "not generally known to and not being readily ascertainable by proper means by other persons" does not require that information be generally known to the public for trade secret rights to be lost. If the principal persons who can obtain benefit from the information are aware of it, there is no trade secret. A method of casting metal, for example, may be unknown to the general public but readily known within the foundry industry.

Thus, in order to apply the generally known limitation it is necessary to know (or learn) both the general state of knowledge in the field of the alleged trade secrets and the knowledge within the applicable industry. The process is similar to a "prior art" search under patent law. Only by comparing what is already known widely or within a specific industry can one determine whether the plaintiff's information is not generally known.

[handwritten marginalia: does not req. full knowledge of public for TS to be broken]

To apply the "readily ascertainable" requirement requires a similar but somewhat different fact-finding mission. Instead of looking for what is generally known among the public or within an industry, the inquiry focuses on what is knowable. As one court noted, the readily ascertainable inquiry "is heavily fact dependent and simply boils down to assessing the ease with which a trade secret could have been independently discovered." *MicroStrategy, Inc. v. Business Objects*, 331 F.Supp. 2d 396, 417 (E.D. Va. 2004). As explained in the comments to the UTSA, "[i]nformation is readily ascertainable if it is available in trade journals, reference books, or published materials. Often the nature of the product lends itself to being readily copied as soon as it is available on the market." In other words, the information is available to the members of the public but may not have been seen by them so it is not yet part of their "knowledge."

It is interesting that the drafters of the UTSA chose a conjunctive between "generally known" and "readily ascertainable." This implies that each term has a separate meaning and purpose. However, as the foregoing suggests, many of the facts that are examined to determine whether information is generally known are also examined to determine if information is readily ascertainable. Thus, it is not surprising that in practice, courts seem to struggle with determining the meaning of the labels. Often they do not consider the readily ascertainable prong as a separate factor, but instead appear to collapse it into the generally known prong. Those courts that separate the two concepts often look for evidence of the time, trouble, and effort that it took the plaintiff to develop the alleged trade secrets as an indication of whether the information is readily ascertainable. *See, e.g., Editions PlayBac, supra*, and *AvidAir Helicopter Supply, Inc. v. Rolls Royce Corp.*, 663 F.3d 966, 973 (2011).

Some states that have adopted the UTSA, like California and Illinois, have removed the readily ascertainable language from their definition of a trade secret due, in part, to concerns about the ability of putative trade secret owners to prove a negative. *See* CAL. CIV. CODE § 3426.1(d) (2016); 765 Ill. Comp. Stat. 1065/2(d) (2016). However, the issue can still be raised as a defense rather than as part of plaintiff's prima facie case. In California it goes to the issue of misappropriation. *Abba Rubber Co. v. Seaquist*, 286 Cal.Rptr. 518, 529, n. 9 (C.A.1991). In Illinois it relates to the issue of whether there is a trade secret in the first instance. *Delta Med. Sys. v. Mid-Am. Med. Sys., Inc.*, 331 Ill.App. 3d 777, 791 (2002).

Food for Thought

Looking at the UTSA's and DTSA's definition of a trade secret, what do you think "generally known" and "readily ascertainable" means? Who has to know the information for it to be generally known? Do you think information can be readily ascertainable and not generally known? How easy must it be to find information for it to be readily ascertainable?

> ### Reading Guidance
>
> *What evidence and arguments did the plaintiff present on the issue of whether its formula for paint was generally known?*

[handwritten: Combination-trade secret]

ROHM AND HAAS CO. V. ADCO CHEMICAL CO.

[handwritten: process]
United States Court of Appeals, Third Circuit, 1982.
[handwritten: for creating paint vehicle] 689 F.2d 424.

JAMES HUNTER, III, CIRCUIT JUDGE.

[handwritten margin notes: Ct. reversed trial ct.'s holding — the process is a TS = combination of elements despite some knowledge of indiv. elements]

* * *

Prior to the development of the process claimed to be a trade secret, plaintiff had sold latex paint vehicles[1] made using a process disclosed in Patent No. 2,795,564. In 1955 plaintiff embarked on a research campaign to develop a "second generation" latex paint vehicle "with improved qualities." As the result of a seven year effort, plaintiff developed the process involved here (the "Process"), which plaintiff used in producing a paint vehicle with the desired qualities. Plaintiff used this vehicle in the manufacture of four highly successful products. Other manufacturers have tried to offer vehicles competitive with plaintiff's second generation vehicle, but failed. The defendants alone have been able to market vehicles with the same desirable qualities. Plaintiff contends that only revelations by one of plaintiff's former employees, Joseph Harvey, enabled defendants to produce these vehicles.

[handwritten margin note: fmr. employee]

Joseph Harvey joined plaintiff in 1959 as a laboratory technician. From the outset of his employment, Harvey worked under plaintiff's scientists in the development of latex paints, including those incorporating the Process involved here. Plaintiff's laboratory notebooks in Harvey's handwriting contain repeated descriptions of the Process which Harvey carried out pursuant to plaintiff's instructions. Harvey's duties also gave him access to plaintiff's commercial process descriptions which detailed the Process.

In March 1967 Harvey signed an employment agreement in which he acknowledged that "any business or trade secrets, including secret processes of manufacture of Rohm and Haas Company, are the property of Rohm and Haas Company" and agreed "not to divulge such information to outsiders or other unauthorized persons either while employed by Rohm and Haas Company or afterwards." During Harvey's tenure at Rohm and Haas, extensive security measures were in effect which Harvey

---

[1] Appellant's Brief explains:

A paint vehicle is the liquid portion of the paint and it is usually colorless. Pigment is added to the vehicle for coloration. The vehicle is a two component substance, i.e., thinner and binder. The thinner is the volatile component of the paint-water in the case of latex paints-which evaporates when the paint dries, leaving behind the solid paint film. The binder is the non-volatile component of the vehicle which functions to bind the pigment particles into a uniform paint film and to adhere the film to the surface being painted.

acknowledged were intended to "keep the secrets in." App. Harvey was reminded at his exit interview in June 1967 that he possessed confidential information and that he should contact plaintiff if he had any question concerning the extent of his obligation to preserve confidentiality. Harvey never contacted plaintiff.

Defendants, Adco and Thibaut & Walker, are related corporations engaged in the manufacture and sale respectively of various chemicals. In 1968 defendants initiated a program to copy two of plaintiff's products which were made using the Process. To accomplish this task, defendants hired a Ph.D. chemist, Victor Meyer, whom defendants had retained as an independent consultant since 1963.

After nearly two years of work, Dr. Meyer advised defendants that he had successfully developed a match for plaintiff's products. Defendants, based on this report, prepared an advertising and promotional campaign for their matching products. In September 1970 Dr. Meyer attempted to implement the process he had developed on a commercial scale. This attempt failed. Nevertheless, defendants promoted their matching products at an October 1970 paint show. At this show and during this period, defendants represented to the trade that their matching products were available. In order to fill orders from customers based on these representations, defendants purchased plaintiff's products, repackaged them as their own, and sold them without informing customers of the substitution. Defendants made the acquisition of a "match" for plaintiff's products their highest priority.

During the October 1970 paint show, defendants' president was referred by a former employee of the plaintiff to Joseph Harvey, who was seeking employment at the time. Defendants' president immediately contacted Harvey, and, after one interview, Harvey was hired by defendants to develop latex paint compounds including acrylics.[3]

Harvey began work on November 17, 1970. His first assignment was to duplicate one of plaintiff's products made using the Process which had been the object of Dr. Meyer's research efforts. During his first week at work and without assistance, Harvey prepared a laboratory replication of the product; the first entry in the laboratory notebook which Harvey maintained for the defendants was the complete Process which Harvey had learned for making plaintiff's products. Harvey stated in his deposition:

---

[3] Defendants knew at the time of the hiring that Harvey was not a college graduate, that he had been fired from one of the two jobs he had held since leaving plaintiff, and that he had been unemployed for long periods. Defendants also knew that Harvey had been employed by plaintiff in its research laboratories working on acrylic latex technology. Defendants were also aware that plaintiff was the only company for which Harvey had performed work relating to acrylic latexes. Defendants offered Harvey a job at a salary nearly twenty-five percent higher than he had previously earned.

Q: This process that is referred to at pages 4 through 6 of your (Adco) notebooks, that process did not come from Dr. Meyer at all, did it?

Harvey: No.

Q: This was a Rohm and Haas process, Mr. Harvey?

Harvey: Yes.

Later in his deposition Harvey made clear that the "Harvey process" was one he had learned at and brought from Rohm and Haas.

Harvey soon revealed his process to defendants. Defendants never asked Harvey about the origin of the "Harvey process." Within a few weeks defendants sent samples to prospective customers and ordered Harvey to duplicate the "Harvey process" on a commercial scale. Harvey's attempt to do so proved unsuccessful due to his own mathematical errors. Because Harvey had no idea what was wrong, defendants called in Dr. Meyer and others to make the "Harvey process" work. One of those called in testified:

Q: In those discussions that you had with Mr. Harvey, was it apparent to you that Mr. Harvey knew a formula but knew nothing with respect to what made it work, or why it worked, or what its variances would be?

A: I'd agree with that.

Defendants subsequently were successful in duplicating the "Harvey process" on a commercial scale, and the Meyer process was set aside. By mid-1971 defendants were selling duplicates of plaintiff's products using the "Harvey process." Plaintiff filed suit in October, 1971.

After a nine-day trial, * * * [t]he court rejected the trade secret claim, stating that plaintiff had failed to show that the Process was a trade secret. Plaintiff appeals.

trial ct. rejected TS claim - Said it was not a TS.

* * *

The Existence of a Trade Secret

New Jersey and Pennsylvania have adopted the definition of a trade secret provided in the Restatement of Torts:

A trade secret may consist of any formula, pattern, device or compilation of information which is used in one's business and which gives him an opportunity to obtain an advantage over competitors who do not know or use it.

law

As we have stated above, plaintiff proved that it used the Process in its business to obtain a distinct advantage over its competitors, including defendants. The district court acknowledged the competitive value of the Process in its finding that "some kind of useful information was inevitably obtained (by the defendants) out of the hiring of Joseph Harvey." Nonetheless, the district court held that the plaintiff had failed in its attempt to show that the Process was not a matter of general knowledge within the industry.

Plaintiff's proof that the Process was its secret consisted of demonstrating by the realities of the marketplace that this valuable method of producing latex paint vehicles was unknown to its competitors. Apart from defendants, plaintiff was the only manufacturer to use the Process and as a result it could offer four superior products. Other competitors had tried and failed to put competing products on the market. Defendants' Dr. Meyer, a Ph.D. chemist, had been unable over the course of two years to develop competing products without plaintiff's Process. Defendants' expert admitted that the publications claimed to reveal the elements of the Process were unknown both to defendants and to him prior to this lawsuit, leaving no reason to suspect that defendants could have duplicated the Process through skill and effort using the available literature.[5] Only after defendants acquired the "Harvey process" could they field a match for the plaintiff's products. None of these facts were seriously contested by the defendants below, and none turned on a question of the credibility of witnesses.

Under both New Jersey and Pennsylvania law, these facts were sufficient to establish that the alleged secret is in fact the secret of a particular employer, and not a matter of general knowledge within the industry. Plaintiff, having thus proven the existence of a trade secret as well as every other element of his trade secret claim, was entitled to relief.

What the trial ct. held

The district court nonetheless concluded that the Process was a matter of general knowledge in the industry. It gave two grounds for its conclusion. First, it held that the plaintiff had not defined its alleged trade secret sufficiently to remove it from "the kind of information that goes with knowledge, skill and experience in the field (that) is more likely to accompany the employee without protection." Second, the district court held that most if not all of the elements of plaintiff's Process were "long and widely known in the trade."

We conclude that the district court erred in rejecting plaintiff's proof that the Process is a trade secret. Both of the grounds set forth are legally inadequate to defeat plaintiff's claim for relief.

* * *

The legal inference made by the district court is at odds with the facts. Harvey himself admitted that his swift "discovery" of the "Harvey process" was the result not of any heightened chemical prowess, but of his

---

[5]   Harvey, too, admitted that he had not consulted the publication which he believed revealed the Process before he divulged the Harvey process to the defendants.

recollection of plaintiff's Process. Harvey's background and the testimony of defendants' agent as to Harvey's grasp of the "Harvey process," supra, leave little doubt that memory, not ability, was the source of Harvey's revelation. On this record, regardless of the specificity of plaintiff's definition of its trade secret, the legal conclusion drawn by the district court is without basis, and is thus an error of law.

The district court * * * held that because defendants had shown that some or all of the individual elements of plaintiff's Process were widely known in the trade, the Process itself as a matter of law must be considered to be general knowledge.

The trade secret law of Pennsylvania and New Jersey is directly contrary to the legal conclusion drawn by the district court. The law of these states provides that even though each and every element of plaintiff's Process is known to the industry, the combination of those elements may be a trade secret if it "produces a product superior to that of competitors." Plaintiff proved that the Process produced a superior product. The district court's * * * ground for concluding that plaintiff's Process was widely known in the industry, based on a misreading of the applicable law, thus is erroneous.

[handwritten margin note: — knowledge of combo of elements may be a TS even if some ppl know certain indiv. elements]

The district court denied plaintiff's claim only by imposing these additional and incorrect legal standards of secrecy on the plaintiff's trade secret. Reversal of the district court and remand for the entry of judgment for the plaintiff is therefore appropriate. * * *

The judgment of the district court will be reversed. The case will be remanded for entry of judgment for plaintiff and for proceedings consistent with this opinion to grant the plaintiff all relief to which it is entitled.

DID YOU GET IT?

1. Did the process in this case qualify as a trade secret in light of its alleged public availability? *[handwritten: Yes b/c combination of elements met the req. (secrecy, value)]*

2. What facts supported the court's holding in this case? *[handwritten: value of info, gaining advantage]*

3. Do you think the process was readily ascertainable? If so, what facts lead you to that conclusion?

4. What part of a combination trade secret is protected?

[handwritten: The combination has value in not being known.
Fact that the
Not just the individual elements.]

[handwritten margin notes: "- recipe for baking chocolate chip cookies - this was a TS."]

> ### Reading Guidance
> *Can one have a trade secret in a chocolate chip cookie recipe?*

PEGGY LAWTON KITCHENS, INC. V. HOGAN
Appeals Court of Massachusetts, 1984.
18 Mass. App. Ct. 937.

Before ARMSTRONG, CUTTER and KASS, JJ.

Nothing is sacred. We have before us a case of theft of a recipe for baking chocolate chip cookies. The issue is whether the plaintiff, Peggy Lawton Kitchens, Inc. (Kitchens), possessed a protected trade secret.

A Superior Court judge found that Kitchens first added chocolate chip cookies to its line of prepackaged bakery products in 1960. They were an indifferent success. In 1963, Lawton Wolf, a principal officer of Kitchens, mixed the chaff from walnuts ("nut dust" he called it) in his chocolate chip cookie batter. This, as the judge found, "produced a distinctive flavor. It was an immediate commercial success." Lawton Wolf, in his testimony, described what nut dust did for his cookies in rhapsodic terms: "Miraculous." Sales, he said, "took off immediately. It did to the cookies what butter does to popcorn or salt to a pretzel. It really made the flavor sing."

[handwritten margin note: "nut dust"]

The judge found that, from the beginning of its use, Kitchens carefully guarded the cookie recipe. One copy of the recipe was locked in an office safe. A duplicate was secured in the desk of William Wolf, Lawton's son. To satisfied customers who asked for the recipe, Kitchens wrote that the formula was a trade secret. For work day use, Kitchens broke down the formula into baking ingredients, small ingredients (e.g., the nut dust), and bulk ingredients. The three components were kept on separate cards which contained gross weights. Even though those cards concealed the true proportions of the ingredients, access to the cards was limited to long-time trusted employees. The defendant Terence Hogan, whose responsibilities at Kitchens were plant and equipment maintenance and safety, was not among those entrusted with the ingredients cards. Hogan, the judge found, had gained access to the cards through a pretext, and after Hogan left Kitchens' employ, a master key, which could open the vault and the office in which William Wolf's desk was located, was found in Hogan's desk.

[handwritten margin note: "- Δ = fmr employee"]

Hogan and his wife organized a bakery business to sell prepackaged bakery products under the trade name Hogie Bear. Among the first products Hogie Bear made was a chocolate chip cookie. It had the same recipe, including the miraculous nut dust. The judge found that about forty brands of chocolate chip cookies were sold in New England. Except for those made by Kitchens and Hogie Bear, no two are alike. The judge found Hogie Bear's cookie "similar in appearance, color, cell construction, texture, flavor and taste. They are 'formulated' in a similar fashion. They are the same."

* * *

1. *Was there a trade secret?* No doubt, the basic ingredients, flour, sugar, shortening, chocolate chips, eggs, and salt, would be common to any chocolate chip cookie. The combination in which those ingredients are used, the diameter and thickness of the cookie, and the degree to which it is baked would, however, constitute a formula which its proprietor could protect from infringement by an employee who either gains access to the formula in confidence or by improper means. In any event, the insertion of the nut dust into the mix served to add that modicum of originality which separates a process from the every day and so characterizes a trade secret. Lawton Wolf's testimony that "sales took off immediately" supports a determination that the improved recipe had competitive value so far as Kitchens was concerned.

* * *

Judgments affirmed.

— nut dust added
modicum of originality

DID YOU GET IT?

1. Was the plaintiff's recipe a trade secret? *Yes. Combo of ingredients (formula)*

2. What effect does the list of ingredients on the product's label have on the finding of trade secrecy in this case?

3. To what extent did the defendant's conduct affect the finding of a protectable trade secret? *Used same exact formula, texture, flavor.*

Reading Guidance
When is a process generally known or readily ascertainable?

— was not a TS
all elements were
readily ascertainable

HUTCHISON V. KFC CORPORATION

United States Court of Appeals, Ninth Circuit, 1995.
51 F.3d 280.
[Unpublished opinion, case No. 93-16847.]

— skinless fried chicken recipe — not "secret"
— trial ct. granted S.J. in favor of △
— the method was readily ascertainable

NORRIS, WIGGINS, and FERNANDEZ, CIRCUIT JUDGES.

Plaintiffs-appellants Louis Hutchison, Gayle Reese, and RHR, Inc. (collectively, "Hutchison") appeal the district court's grant of summary judgment in favor of defendant-appellee Kentucky Fried Chicken Corp. ("KFC"). Hutchison brought the action under Nevada's version of the Uniform Trade Secrets Act, in the District Court for the District of Nevada pursuant to that court's diversity jurisdiction. We affirm the order of summary judgment for KFC because the material that Hutchison disclosed to KFC in confidence did not constitute a protectible trade secret.

facts

Hutchison developed an allegedly proprietary process for making skinless fried chicken. When KFC was considering purchasing the process from Hutchison, Hutchison disclosed information about the process to KFC's agents, subject to written confidentiality agreements. KFC declined to purchase the process. KFC later began to market a skinless fried chicken product. Hutchison sued for misappropriation of his trade secret.

trial ct. held it wasn't a TS

The district court granted KFC's motion for summary judgment, ruling that Hutchison's process was generally known or readily ascertainable and therefore could not constitute a trade secret. The court held that Hutchison's allegedly secret process consisted of nothing more than "the general process of cutting, skinning, marinating, dipping and breading, and frying the chicken." The court pointed out that certain aspects of the process could have constituted trade secrets (*e.g.*, the recipes for the batter, flour mixtures, and marinade; the cooking temperatures; and the contents of the cooking oils), but Hutchison had not alleged that KFC had misappropriated those aspects.

* * *

To be a trade secret, the subject matter must in fact be secret: it must "[d]erive independent economic value, present or potential, from not being generally known to, and not being readily ascertainable by proper means by, other persons who can obtain economic value from its disclosure or use." The threshold for "ready ascertainability" is not a high one: the process need not satisfy the "non-obviousness" standard necessary for patent protection. Nevertheless, if a process is generally known in the industry, or readily ascertainable from public sources, section 600A.030 does not protect it even if it was previously unknown to the recipient.

secrecy

For Hutchison's process, the element of secrecy potentially could exist either in the combination of steps for the process as a whole or in the individual steps. We conclude that the element of secrecy was present in neither.

Combination of Steps:

Hutchison's combination of steps was not a trade secret. Skinless fried chicken had been on public sale by Pudgie's Famous Chicken, a chain of quick service restaurants, since 1981. From the idea of serving skinless chicken, the basic sequence of steps (skinning, marinating, dipping, breading, freezing if necessary, and frying) is readily ascertainable.

Hutchison has failed to produce evidence distinguishing its general process either from that generally in use, or from the process KFC has been using for years. He has also been unable to show that his exact combination of steps would not suggest itself to anyone seeking to achieve the same end product.[2] The overall sequence, therefore, was not a trade secret.

Individual Steps:

Having determined that the sequence of steps was readily ascertainable, we turn to the two individual steps, deskinning and tumble marination, that Hutchison claims were proprietary to him.[3] We conclude that, at the level of generality in which the individual steps were disclosed to KFC, they were generally known or readily ascertainable and therefore not trade secrets.

Deskinning:

The allegedly proprietary component of Hutchison's deskinning process is "the technique for doing it manually, so that you didn't need to use any machinery, which could still be done at a rate of at least two chickens per minute." The technique consists of slipping a hand under the skin of the chicken and pulling the skin off, allegedly in a manner that achieves superior speed.[4]

We find that the deskinning technique is readily ascertainable. Other than the claim of speed, Hutchison's description of the process contains no details that differentiate his technique from what anyone else might do when faced with a chicken in need of flaying. Hutchison asserts that speed made his process "economical," but he has presented no evidence that the speed he achieved was anything unusual in the industry.

Furthermore, there is no evidence that KFC actually used Hutchison's method to deskin its chickens. According to KFC's unrebutted affidavits, when KFC introduced its skinless product in 1991, it deskinned chickens by fitting them with a teflon cone, using an air hose to blow the skin away from the chicken, and pulling the skin off by hand.[5] Therefore, even if the deskinning process were proprietary to Hutchison, summary judgment would be warranted because there is no evidence that KFC misappropriated it.

Tumble Marination:

Hutchison's process calls for tumble marinating the chicken in a commercially available tumble marinator, which brings out a natural

---

[2]   Reverse engineering of an unpatented product to discover the process by which it was made is legal and does not constitute misappropriation under Nev.Rev.Stat. § 600A.030, assuming a sample of the product was obtained legitimately.

[3]   Hutchinson has conceded that none of the following steps were individually proprietary to him: cutting the chicken into nine pieces; dipping the chicken in batter; running the dipped chicken through a flour mix to bread it; or preparing chicken in a pressure cooker. KFC does not even use a pressure cooker to cook its skinless crispy chicken.

[4]   KFC had the opportunity to learn the technique when a representative from KFC witnessed Hutchinson's son deskinning a chicken.

[5]   In mid-1992, KFC switched to an entirely mechanical deskinning process.

protein gel in the chicken, which in turn coats the chicken with a tacky substance that acts as a substitute skin and helps the breading to adhere to the meat. Hutchison disclosed to KFC that the chicken was tumble marinated with commercially available equipment to create a substitute skin, but Hutchison did not reveal the contents of the marinade.

Hutchison has not rebutted KFC's claim that it has been tumble marinating certain product lines (*e.g.*, "Extra Crispy Chicken") since the mid-1970s. For its skinfree chicken product, KFC initially used a tumble marination procedure, but at the end of 1991, KFC switched to an injection marination system.

Because tumble marination was already known to and used by KFC and others in the industry, and because tumble marinators were commercially available, the concept cannot be proprietary to Hutchison. Hutchison's specific marinade was not disclosed and therefore could not be misappropriated.

Hutchison's process, insofar as it was disclosed to KFC, is not a trade secret entitled to protection under Nevada's law of trade secrets. It contained no element, singly or in combination, that was not generally known or readily ascertainable. The order of summary judgment is AFFIRMED.

DID YOU GET IT?

1. What facts support the court's finding on whether Hutchinson's process was generally known or readily ascertainable?

2. How does this case compare to *Peggy Lawton Kitchens v. Hogan*? What facts may explain the difference in outcomes of the two cases?

3. How does the extent of disclosure to KFC play into the court's analysis?

Reading Guidance

Was the game concept in this case readily ascertainable or generally known?

EDITIONS PLAY BAC, S.A. V. WESTERN PUB. CO., INC.

United States District Court, S.D. New York, 1993.
1993 WL 541219.
[Not Reported in F.Supp.]

MARTIN, DISTRICT JUDGE:

Plaintiffs Editions Play Bac ("Play Bac") and Editions Hatier ("Hatier") are French corporations engaged in the joint production of an educational question-and-answer card game called "Les Incollables." Plaintiff Workman Publishing Co. ("Workman") currently holds the U.S. license to market an English-language version of "Les Incollables," which it markets under the name "Brain Quest." On May 18, 1992, plaintiffs commenced this

[handwritten: — π sought injunction]

action seeking to enjoin the defendant, Western Publishing Co.
("Western"), from selling, marketing or advertising a game called "Ask
Me!", which plaintiffs allege is based on the misappropriation of the trade
secret used in its own game, "Les Incollables." * * *

FACTUAL BACKGROUND

An early version of "Les Incollables" was first marketed in France
beginning in June 1989. The current version of the game has been on sale
in France since May 1990, and in all relevant respects is the same as the
earlier version. The game was very successful in France, and was widely
advertised and written up in the French press. Its American "debut"
occurred in June 1990, when the Executive Director of Play Bac, Gaetan
Burrus ("Burrus"), attended the American Book Publishers Association
Conference for the purpose of finding American companies interested in
licensing an American version of "Les Incollables". Burrus met George Oess
("Oess"), a representative of Western, who expressed a serious interest in
the product. While Burrus had merely shown other publishing company
representatives the game, he gave Oess a sample of "Les Incollables" to
take back to the company's Wisconsin headquarters with him.

[handwritten: — π looked for co.'s that wanted to license]

On July 12, 1990, at Oess's invitation, Burrus met with Barrie Simpson
("Simpson"), another Western representative, in New York. Simpson and
Burrus held further discussions about a potential relationship between the
two companies. Subsequently, Burrus and Francois Dufour ("Dufour"), a
principal and co-founder of Play Bac, met with seven Western employees
at Western's Racine headquarters on August 23, 1990. The Western
contingent consisted of four creative staff members, two marketing staff
members and James Pisors, who was in charge of license arrangements for
ideas and inventions at Western. At this meeting, Burrus and Dufour gave
a detailed presentation on the concepts behind "Les Incollables" as well as
a booklet containing reproductions of French advertisements, press
releases and press clippings about the French game. In addition, proposed
licensing terms and royalties were discussed. There is no evidence of any
express confidentiality agreement or waiver made before, during or after
the meeting.

[handwritten: — π disclosed info re game at mtg w/ Δ]

The information disclosed by Play Bac at the August 23rd meeting is the
subject of this dispute. Plaintiffs characterize that information as their
"Game Concept," which consists of the following elements: a) the
packaging, physical design, construction and appearance of the product; b)
the arrangement, number, placement and sequence of questions and
answers; c) the subject matter of the questions; d) the know-how, principles
and techniques for formulating and selecting the questions and answers;
and e) the pricing and merchandising techniques Play Bac used to market
the product.

[handwritten: Game concept info]

In their complaint, plaintiffs allege that the defendant misappropriated the "Game Concept" and used it to create its own competing product. In addition, plaintiffs contend that Western breached the confidentiality under which the "Game Concept" for "Les Incollables" was presented to Western. Plaintiffs also argue that Western breached an agreement—which plaintiffs assert was both explicit and implied in fact as well as in law—not to use Play Bac's concept without Play Bac's permission.

Western has moved for summary judgment on the grounds that the information disclosed by Play Bac was not a trade secret, and that even if such information did have trade secret status, Western did not misappropriate any information in designing its competing product, "Ask Me!". Western also asserts there was no confidential relationship formed by the negotiations and that there is no evidence of any agreement to limit the use of Play Bac's concept.

[handwritten margin note: Δ's arguments]

For the reasons stated below, defendant's motion for summary judgment is denied.

DISCUSSION

* * *

The Applicable Substantive Law on Trade Secrets

The parties have agreed that Wisconsin law applies. In 1986, Wisconsin adopted the Uniform Trade Secret Act ("UTSA"), Wis.Stat. § 134.90. * * * While the essence of plaintiffs' claim is an alleged misappropriation of the "Game Concept," the critical issue for purposes of this motion is whether or not the "Game Concept" is a trade secret. The Wisconsin statute defines "trade secret" as:

> information, including a formula, pattern, compilation, program, device, method, technique or process to which *all of the following* apply:
>
> 1. The information derives independent economic value, actual or potential, from not being generally known to, and not being readily ascertainable by proper means by, other persons who can obtain economic value from its disclosure or use.
>
> 2. The information is the subject of efforts to maintain its secrecy that are reasonable under the circumstances.

Wis.Stat. § 134.90(1)(c) (emphasis added).

The threshold analysis under the Wisconsin UTSA is whether the "Game Concept" is a trade secret within the meaning of § 134.90(1)(c). Under Wisconsin law, a trade secrets claim presents issues of both law and fact. While the ultimate question of whether certain information constitutes a trade secret is one of law for the court, there may be issues of fact to be resolved before such a determination can be made.

① not generally know
② indep. econ. value
③ reas. measures to maintain secrecy

With the UTSA definition in mind, the Court turns to the question of whether plaintiffs have introduced evidence sufficient to create a factual issue regarding the trade secret status of the information disclosed on August 23rd. The Court concludes that plaintiffs have produced evidence raising genuine issues of material fact regarding each piece of the trade secret analysis delineated in § 130.90(1)(c) of the UTSA. Specifically, there are factual issues presented regarding a) whether the information is not readily ascertainable or generally known; b) whether the information derives independent economic value from not being generally known; and c) whether plaintiffs took reasonable measures to maintain secrecy. Until a fact finder resolves these factual disputes, the Court cannot make a determination on the legal question of whether the "Game Concept" qualifies as a trade secret.

"Generally Known" or "Readily Ascertainable"

Defendant asserts that much of the "Game Concept" is either readily ascertainable by proper means from the commercially available product or is information which is generally known in the educational publishing industry. *See* Wis.Stat. § 134.90(1)(c)(1).

The "Game Concept," as described by plaintiffs, is a combination of ideas and the reasons behind them. It is clear that certain elements of the "Game Concept" are readily ascertainable from a physical inspection of the product, and therefore cannot be trade secrets. "That which is placed in the public domain cannot remain secret." 1 Roger M. Milgrim, *Milgrim on Trade Secrets* § 2.03 (1993). Even a relatively cursory examination of "Les Incollables" reveals the packaging, physical design, construction, number, placement and sequence of questions and answers, the subject matter and topical categories of the questions, and the relative proportion of topical categories.

In addition, defendant has produced Play Bac's own promotional materials, which list the subjects covered and point out that the questions cover a "full year's curriculum for grades 1–7." The French press coverage also highlights the fact that "there are ten questions per card, nine of which are taken from school curriculum. The last is an entertainment question to relax the atmosphere." Even the creator of "Les Incollables," Gaetan Burrus, admitted in deposition testimony that the subject matter, arrangement and number of questions and answers, and the physical design of the game were readily apparent from a physical inspection.

Moreover, plaintiffs have presented insufficient evidence to create a triable question of fact on this issue. For example, in support of their contention that the screw-shaped clip which holds the cards together is not readily ascertainable, plaintiffs point to Burrus's testimony that the clip was not easy to take apart and appeared to be a screw, but in fact was not one. Plaintiffs also point to Burrus's testimony to the effect that the fact that the two decks of cards contained different sets of questions was not immediately apparent from a visual inspection.

These evidentiary offerings evince a misunderstanding of the meaning of "readily ascertainable". Rather than the overly narrow and restrictive meaning plaintiffs ascribe to the term, "readily ascertainable" must be given its common usage meaning, namely, discoverable "with a fair degree of ease, without much difficulty." *See Webster's Third New International Dictionary* (1986). There is no evidence showing that the clip construction and other design features are not discoverable with a fair degree of ease, although perhaps not at first glance. No reasonable jury could conclude that the above elements of the "Game Concept" in themselves were not readily ascertainable from the product being sold on the French market. Accordingly, the Court finds that these elements of the "Game Concept" cannot satisfy the first requirement of the UTSA definition, and are therefore not trade secrets.

However, plaintiff's "Game Concept" also contains information which is not necessarily readily apparent, namely, the "how and why", or "know-how", behind the game. Defendant asserts that the principles and techniques for developing the questions and answers for "Les Incollables" are methods which are generally known in the industry, and therefore cannot be trade secrets. *See* Wis.Stat. § 134.90(1)(c)(1). In addition, defendant asserts that the marketing strategies disclosed by Play Bac are also generally known or readily ascertainable and therefore not worthy of trade secret protection. The Court finds that plaintiffs have produced evidence sufficient to raise a triable issue of fact on the question of whether this information meets the criteria set forth in § 134.90(1)(c)(1).

"Know-how", in the context of trade secret law, is the informational and experiential expertise which can be applied to a product. Where the secret use of such know-how creates a competitive advantage, the know-how may be considered a trade secret. Such information may often include marketing methods and pricing strategy.

Moreover, while individual elements of an idea might be well-known in the industry or generally known, the combination of otherwise well-known principles may be a trade secret. In the case of plaintiffs' "Game Concept," the principles and techniques for formulating and selecting the questions and answers and the reasons behind the specific marketing strategies chosen may all be considered "know-how" and may merit protection.

Defendant points to deposition testimony by Sally Kovalchick, an educational projects editor at Workman Publishing, and an affidavit by Eugene M. Malecki, an official at PSI, the company Western hired to develop questions for "Ask Me!," as proof that the principles and techniques Play Bac used to formulate its questions and answers are generally known and used by others in the educational publishing industry. Ms. Kovalchick testified that she always instructed her authors that the questions they wrote should be "fun", "interesting", "easily understood", and "precise". These instructions are, defendant argues, identical to those contained in the question-writing recipe plaintiffs assert is a trade secret.

Mr. Malecki, who was the Director of Operations at PSI and the person most closely involved in the preparation of questions for Western, testified that it was common industry practice in writing questions for curriculum-based games to consult textbooks for the appropriate grade levels and to consult curriculum developers and teachers.

In response, plaintiffs have produced affidavit testimony stating that they had developed their particular technique for formulating the content and form of the questions and answers over the course of two years of experimentation and that these techniques were not commonly known in the industry. According to Burrus's testimony, Play Bac's "recipe" required questions to be "clear and immediately understandable", the entertainment questions could not be too "trendy", the answers had to be "short, definite and unique, . . . indisputably right or wrong." Burrus also testified that Play Bac's requirement of a single answer to every question was not common to question-and-answer games.

The amount of effort or money expended by Play Bac developing its information is relevant in determining whether or not information is a trade secret under the UTSA. Burrus testified that Play Bac's method of choosing only those particular parts of the curriculum which were actually taught for inclusion in the game was developed through experimentation and was not readily ascertainable or generally known. Francois Dufour's testimony further asserts that Play Bac developed this particular method of writing their own questions after consulting textbooks and curricula, testing them on children, and then having teachers review them.

The Court is not permitted on a motion for summary judgment to assess the weight or credibility of the evidence presented. Plaintiffs have submitted more than enough evidence, which when construed in the light most favorable to plaintiffs, establishes a genuine material issue of fact on the question of whether Play Bac's question-writing techniques were generally known in the industry.

* * *

Accordingly, summary judgment is denied as to these claims.

SO ORDERED.

DID YOU GET IT?

1. What does the plaintiff claim as its trade secrets?
2. What is the defendant's argument as to why the information is not a trade secret?

3. What is the court's reasoning on whether the game concept is generally known or readily ascertainable? *It may be considered "know how"*

4. Should the fact that the game was published in France and in the French language change the analysis? *Formulation was kept secret.*
Not if the reasoning behind q-n Formulation was kept secret.

C. PROTECTION OF TECHNICAL VERSUS BUSINESS INFORMATION

The universe of information that can qualify for trade secret protection generally falls into two broad categories: technical information and business information. Technical information is the kind of information that we traditionally consider deserving of patent protection and is often referred to as "technical trade secrets." It includes information about how things are manufactured, designed, or operated. Formulas, devices, and processes are examples of technical information that are protectable under trade secret law.

The rubric "business information" is generally used to refer to non-technical information that is commercially useful in a business, including financial information, pricing information, marketing information, and strategic plans. One type of business information that is often the subject of trade secret litigation is customer information. Whether or not customer lists are trade secrets is a point of controversy in many cases. In recent years, the asserted value of customer information has given rise to claims that social media sites, including the LinkedIn pages of individual employees, are employer-owned trade secrets. *See Cellular Accessories for Less, Inc. v. Trinitas, LLC*, below.

While both categories of information are equally protectable under the UTSA and the DTSA, assuming the particular information at issue meets the other requirements to qualify as a trade secret, courts in trade secret cases sometimes appear to be more impressed by technical information. Thus, putative trade secret owners seeking to protect technical information can have an easier time convincing a court that the information is "worthy" of trade secret protection.

Interestingly, to the extent the hierarchy between technical and business information was originally borrowed from patent law, times have changed. The scope of patentable subject matter has expanded over time to now include business methods. *See Bilski v. Kappos,* 361 U.S. 593, 594 (2010) ("Section 101 similarly precludes a reading of the term 'process' that would categorically exclude business methods."). Prior to the late 1990s, business information was not considered patentable. Indeed, recall that the Supreme Court in *Kewanee* noted that the kind of business information that may be protected under trade secret law would not be considered patentable. Professor Sharon Sandeen explained that:

In *Kewanee*, the Supreme Court relied heavily upon its understanding that patent protection was not available for advertising schemes and business methods. This is no longer the case. Although the wording of Section 101 of the Patent Act has not changed since 1974, the interpretation and application of that provision has changed dramatically. At the time of *Kewanee*, a number of judicially created doctrines existed to preclude the patentability of life forms, business methods, and computer software. Due to post-1974 developments, including the Supreme Court's decision in *Diamond v. Chakrabarty*, these doctrines no longer apply. Instead, as artfully stated in *Chakrabarty*, an inventor can seek a patent for "anything under the sun that is made by man."

Sharon K. Sandeen, *Kewanee Revisited: Returning to First Principles of Intellectual Property Law to Determine the Issue of Federal Preemption*, 12 MARQ. INTELL. PROP. L. REV. 299, 328 (2008).

While the 2014 case of *Alice Corp. v. CLS Bank*, 134 S.Ct. 2347, 2357 (2014) has once again limited the scope of patentable subject matter, particularly with respect to computer software, it did not explicitly overrule the *Bilski* court's assertion that business methods are patentable.

The following case is a classic example of a case involving a customer list. Pay attention to some of the rules presented in the next case that help provide guidelines as to when customer information is likely to be protected and when it is not. The *Cellular Accessories* case involving LinkedIn information follows.

Reading Guidance
Under what circumstances can customer lists receive trade secret protection?

[handwritten: firework company]

PYRO SPECTACULARS NORTH, INC. V. SOUZA

United States District Court, E.D. of California, 2012.
861 F.Supp.2d 1079.

[handwritten: —this was a TS —customer list w/ specified info for each customer. —not just a list of phone #'s]

GREGORY G. HOLLOWS, UNITED STATES MAGISTRATE JUDGE.

Presently pending before the court is plaintiffs' Pyro Spectaculars, Inc.; Pyro Spectaculars North, Inc.; and Pyro Events, Inc.'s ("PSI") motion for a preliminary injunction, which came on for hearing before the undersigned on March 15, 2012. * * *

BACKGROUND FACTS

PSI is a business originally started by the Souza family in the early 1900s and is currently one of the largest fireworks production companies in the United States. Notwithstanding its size, PSI remains a tight-knit, family-

[handwritten: —It was ascertainable, but not readily ascertainable]

operated and managed business. PSI states that its success in the commercial market is highly dependent on its established relationships with customers, vendors, and pyrotechnic operators. PSI employs commissioned sales executives to market and sell pyrotechnic displays and services to its customers, which are often ongoing customers that purchase fireworks displays regularly from PSI.

According to Ian Gilfillan, PSI's Executive Vice President and husband of Nancy Souza, PSI has compiled its list of customers over the decades of its business from advertising, website contacts, publicity, customer referrals, and other sources of leads that have been gathered and forwarded to its account executives to make a sale for PSI. Customer lists include "the name, address, and phone number of the customer; the 'contact person'; the amount of money previously spent; line item budgets and breakdown of costs of the displays the client purchased; and a breakdown of the specific products used in the individual displays, and a listing of every pyrotechnic operator PSI used for different accounts." It also includes "customer feedback, complaints and customer preferences, site surveys concerning the size of the fireworks that can be shot in the customer's area, notes about how to improve the customer's shows in the future, as well as special requirements, preferences and procedures of the authorities that have jurisdiction over the displays." Furthermore, "PSI has compiled lists of pyrotechnic operators, their experience, training, qualifications and requirements, as well as a list of Hazardous Materials Drivers and their experience, training, qualifications and requirements, among other lists that it keeps confidential." These lists and information were stored in a program on PSI's company database known as the "Booking Form" program.

On or about November 1, 1995, PSI hired defendant Steven Souza as an account executive. Defendant was hired both to serve PSI's existing customers and accounts as well as to seek additional accounts. His responsibilities included the marketing and sales of pyrotechnic displays and show production for Northern California and Hawaii. Mr. Gilfillan passed this territory on to defendant when he moved up in position with PSI. PSI expended resources for defendant to visit and develop new and existing PSI clients, and throughout his career at PSI, defendant enjoyed access to PSI's business information, data, and documents. Indeed, defendant admitted that he learned all of his pyrotechnics customer contact information through his employment at PSI. Defendant's access to the company database was limited to the "Booking Form" program.

Shortly after being hired, on November 8, 1995, defendant signed a document titled "Pyro Spectaculars, Inc. Account Executives Duties and Responsibilities–1994" which provided in part:

Account executives agree that all account or customer lists, trade secrets, unique display designs or knowledge gained are the exclusive property of Pyro Spectaculars, Inc. and the Account Executive hereby waives any rights therein. Account Executives further agree that they will not divulge any knowledge, trade secrets, formulas, patents or unique display designs to anyone outside Pyro Spectaculars, Inc.

During his employment, defendant also signed and acknowledged multiple versions of PSI's employee handbook, including the PSI Employee Handbook issued November 2008, which plaintiff received on November 30, 2008 and signed on December 5, 2008. Section One of the PSI Employee Handbook issued November 2008 provides, in part:

The protection of confidential business information and trade secrets is vital to the interests and the success of Company. Such confidential information includes, but is not limited to, the following examples:

- Computer processes

- Computer programs and codes

- Customer lists

- Customer preferences

- Financial information

- Marketing strategies

- New materials research

- Pending projects and proposals

- Proprietary production processes

- Scientific data

- Scientific formulae

- Technological data

All employees may be required to sign a non-disclosure agreement as a condition of employment. Employees who improperly use or disclose Company trade secrets or confidential operational business information will be subject to disciplinary action, up to and including termination of employment and legal action, even if they do not actually benefit from the disclosed information.

Section 7 of that handbook also states, in pertinent part, that:

Employees are responsible for all Company property, materials, or written information issued to them or in their possession or control. Employees must return all Company property immediately upon request or upon termination of employment. Company may take all action deemed appropriate under the law to recover or protect its property issued to employees.

By signing the acknowledgment of receipt of handbook form, defendant acknowledged that he read and understood all of its provisions.

Around the first week of December 2011, defendant decided in his own mind to resign from PSI. However, he must have been seriously considering such a move as somewhat before that, in November 2011, defendant downloaded and printed 52 individual customer Booking Forms from the Booking Form program. In discussions with his then-prospective new employer and PSI competitor, J & M Displays/Hi-Tech FX, LLC, defendant projected that he could bring approximately $500,000–$600,000 in client revenue to the table, 70–80% of which would be attributable to existing PSI customers. Defendant later acknowledged that J & M Displays/Hi-Tech FX, LLC had only a few customers in Northern California prior to his resignation from PSI. He also stated that he had not heard of J & M Displays prior to J & M Displays recruiting him, was not aware of any advertising by J & M Displays in California, and that J & M Displays were not hiring any other sales people in California apart from defendant.

Defendant actually tendered his resignation on January 14, 2012, to be effective on January 16, 2012. On January 16, 2012, he allegedly informed PSI Assistant Office Manager, Cindy Allie, that he had no other employment lined up. However, by that time defendant had already signed an employment contract with J & M Displays/Hi-Tech FX, LLC on January 14, 2012, which actually overlapped his employment with PSI by two days. Defendant purportedly told Ms. Allie that she may not want to keep in touch with him after he takes business away from PSI. Defendant's wife, Sherry Souza, also informed a PSI employee that she hated defendant's family and that defendant and her would "take as many shows as we can."

Furthermore, shortly after defendant's resignation, PSI started receiving reports from some of its customers that defendant had been contacting them and soliciting their business on behalf of his new employers. Mark Silveira, PSI's Madeira Facilities Manager, also reported that, around mid-December 2011, defendant had asked him who built PSI's fireworks racks, adding that he was starting his own company and looking for a supplier.

In light of this information, PSI retained a computer forensics expert to analyze defendant's former PSI-assigned laptop. The forensics report indicated that, on January 14, 2012 (the date of his resignation), defendant transferred over 60 PSI files from his PSI-assigned laptop to a Western Digital external hard drive and to additional USB drives. Thereafter, a wiping software called "Disk Redactor" was used to delete and write over several computer files on the PSI-assigned laptop. It was later established that defendant retained the services of a computer expert to help him delete various files and folders from his PSI-assigned laptop. Despite the deletion, the computer forensics expert was able to recover the names of some of the files transferred, which were mostly concerning specific PSI clients and projects.

Additionally, it is undisputed that defendant retained an older version of PSI's Booking Form program and accessed it after his resignation. (He kept a separate Excel database of PSI customer and show information that was derived from PSI documents and databases. Defendant also admitted that he accessed and funneled information from PSI Booking Forms to Mark Johnson at J & M Displays to prepare proposals to customers on behalf of J & M Displays, even though defendant was no longer a PSI employee and knew that it was something he was not permitted to do. Defendant further testified as follows:

> Q. And how many proposals did you make in January after you left?
>
> A. Probably 20.
>
> Q. And how were you able to make so many proposals so quickly?
>
> A. Get my information and—I didn't make the proposal. J & M— Mark at J & M made the proposal. I fed him the information. He could probably put out four or five, six a day out of their system.

This deposition testimony was further corroborated by PSI's computer forensics expert, whose analysis of one of defendant's personal computers revealed multiple contracts and proposals from J & M Displays to PSI customers within 2 weeks of defendant's resignation from PSI. Some of these proposals from J & M Displays had a similar format to PSI's previous proposals and offered slightly more product for the same budget.

Defendant also testified that he called, e-mailed, and visited several PSI customers in person since he resigned from PSI, using the above-mentioned Excel database of PSI customer information. Defendant's wife, Sherry Souza, who is herself a pyrotechnics operator and has shot shows for PSI in the past, assisted defendant with addressing and mailing cards to customers. She also indicated that she had discussions with individuals at J & M, including Brian Panther and Mark Johnson, regarding expenses for a pyrotechnics show for a former PSI customer.

PSI claims that, in the weeks since defendant's resignation, at least 6 of its customers have or may have signed contracts with J & M Displays. Moreover, J & M Displays is apparently offering a 5% increase in product for the same price if a customer is willing to sign a multi-year agreement. PSI contends that unless defendant is enjoined, his conduct will continue to damage PSI's business, goodwill, and reputation.

* * *

DISCUSSION

* * *

Defendant's briefing confirms there is no dispute that defendant downloaded and retained PSI documents and information after his resignation. Nor is there any dispute that he funneled PSI documents and information, including PSI Booking Forms, to his new employer to formulate proposals to PSI customers. Thus, assuming for the moment that the information constituted a trade secret, the element of misappropriation is satisfied, because defendant disclosed and used PSI documents and information without its consent, knowing that his acquisition of such information gave rise to a duty not to unduly disclose it, or was acquired by virtue of his former status as a PSI employee. Indeed, defendant's counsel conceded at oral argument that the only issue is whether the information constitutes a trade secret.

For purposes of CUTSA, a trade secret is defined as follows:

> [I]nformation, including a formula, pattern, *compilation,* program, device, method, technique, or process that:
>
> (1) Derives independent economic value, actual or potential, from not being generally known to the public or to other persons who can obtain economic value from its disclosure or use; and
>
> (2) Is the subject of efforts that are reasonable under the circumstances to maintain its secrecy.

Cal. Civ.Code § 3426.1(d) (emphasis added).

Defendant argues that PSI's Booking Forms and Booking Form program contain information that is generally known to the public and not secret, and that PSI does not protect the information on its Booking Form program. Both contentions will be addressed separately below.

Secrecy of Information

Although PSI's Booking Form program also contains pyrotechnics operator and vendor information, the parties address most of their briefing to the secrecy of the specific customer information contained on individual Booking Forms and the program as a whole.

In *Morlife, Inc. v. Perry,* 56 Cal.App.4th 1514 (1997), the California Court of Appeal for the First District extensively summarized California law with respect to when a customer list can be protected as a trade secret:

> With respect to the general availability of customer information, courts are reluctant to protect customer lists to the extent they embody information which is readily ascertainable through public sources, such as business directories . . . On the other hand, where

identifies /locations
of customers

PROTECTION OF TECHNICAL VERSUS

SEC. C   BUSINESS INFORMATION   117

Customers' particular
needs / characteristics

the employer has expended time and effort identifying customers with particular needs or characteristics, courts will prohibit former employees from using this information to capture a share of the market. Such lists are to be distinguished from mere identities and locations of customers where anyone could easily identify the entities as potential customers . . . As a general principle, the more difficult information is to obtain, and the more time and resources expended by an employer in gathering it, the more likely a court will find such information constitutes a trade secret . . . The requirement that a customer list must have economic value to qualify as a trade secret has been interpreted to mean that the secrecy of this information provides a business with a substantial business advantage . . . In this respect, a customer list can be found to have economic value because its disclosure would allow a competitor to direct its sales efforts to those customers who have already shown a willingness to use a unique type of service or product as opposed to a list of people who only might be interested . . . Its use enables the former employee to solicit both more selectively and more effectively.

Id. at 1521–22.

Δ's argument

Defendant asserts that PSI's customer identities are widely known throughout the industry and easily ascertainable. "A competitor can easily find very long lists of customers of PSI through a very simple and swift search on Google. A competitor certainly could contact the Fire Marshall's office, call customers and operators, contact local fire jurisdictions or agencies, but this is not necessary, as the Internet offers such a speedy method of learning the identities of such a large number of entities that have purchased shows from PSI." In support of these assertions, defendant's and his wife's declarations attach numerous permit applications and related documentation for PSI pyrotechnics shows done for private and public entities in various counties obtained through public records requests. The permit applications show relatively detailed information regarding individual shows, including plot plans, customer names and contacts, as well as shell counts and descriptions. Sherry Souza's declaration also attaches PSI proposals, contracts, and city council meeting minutes regarding shows put on for public entities found on the Internet, and these documents often include the prices PSI charged for these shows. Furthermore, defendant points out that PSI itself provides information about its shows and customers on its website.

To be sure, if the identities and contact information of PSI's customers, operators, and vendors were the only information at issue, the court would be inclined to agree with defendant. It is not very hard to determine which entities regularly have fireworks shows, and these shows are often widely publicized. It is also probably true that one can ascertain the names of all licensed pyrotechnics operators in California, and that the names and contact information for pyrotechnics vendors are available in public directories. However, the true value of PSI's Booking Form program lies in its comprehensive, if not encyclopedic, compilation of customer, operator, and vendor information, both with respect to each individual customer Booking Form and in the aggregate.

As outlined above, it includes contact information for the "contact person" at each customer; detailed financial, costs, and budgeting information for shows; a breakdown of the specific products used in individual shows; customer special preferences and requirements; notes of customer complaints and how a customer's shows can be improved; as well as information regarding operators and Hazardous Materials Drivers, including their experience, training, qualifications, and requirements. PSI compiled this information "over the decades of its business from advertising, website contacts, publicity, customer referrals, and other sources of leads that have been gathered and forwarded to its account executives, including Defendant, to make a sale for PSI." It has been "developed at great expense and labor" and "gives PSI a competitive advantage in the industry."

While defendant persuasively argues that many of the individual pieces of information in the Booking Forms program can be ultimately ascertained by requesting and scouring public records, calling customers and operators, and reverse engineering videos and CDs, that misses the point. The Booking Forms program provides a virtual encyclopedia of specific PSI customer, operator, and vendor information at a competitor's fingertips, allowing the competitor to solicit both more selectively and more effectively without having to expend the effort to compile the data. It is this type of compilation that may be entitled to trade secret protection. Another federal district court reached the same conclusion in a case involving remarkably similar facts and allegations:

> "Customer lists containing merely public information that can easily be compiled by third parties will not be protected as trade secrets; however, where the party compiling the customer lists, while using public information as a source, . . . expends a great deal of time, effort and expense in developing the lists and treats the lists as confidential in its business, the lists may be entitled to trade secret protection . . . While the information contained on the lists and the notes is ultimately ascertainable from public sources, it is not readily ascertainable from public sources: A third party wishing to duplicate the information could not do so without investing a significant amount of time, effort, and expense. . . ."

Fireworks Spectacular, Inc. v. Premier Pyrotechnics, Inc., 147 F.Supp.2d 1057, 1062–63, 1066 (D.Kansas 2001) (involving former employee of a pyrotechnics company who started his own competing business).

Finally, defendant's argument that all of the information ~~Forms~~ is readily available to the public is undercut by h this case. If the information is truly that readily availabl raises the question of why it was necessary for defendant download, retain, and funnel the Booking Forms and othe to his new employer in the first place.

* * *

DID YOU GET IT?

1. What is the defendant's argument as to why the customer information is not a trade secret? *It is available + discoverable to public by google, etc.*

2. What is the plaintiff's argument as to why this customer information is more than just a list of names and is thus entitled to trade secret protection? *It is not readily ascertainable — Sweat of the brow.*

3. What facts support the court's finding that the customer list was not readily ascertainable? *Specific info particularized to each customer.*

Food for Thought

Do you think all customer lists should be protected as trade secrets? What facts would you want to know to determine if a customer list is a protectable trade secret? Should Facebook be able to protect the information that is posted by Facebook users as its own trade secrets?

Reading Guidance

What was the nature of the customer information at issue in this case?

CELLULAR ACCESSORIES FOR LESS, INC. v. TRINITAS LLC

United States District Court, C. D. of California, 2014.
2014 WL 4627090, at *2.

PREGERSON, DISTRICT JUDGE.

* * *

I.   BACKGROUND

Cellular and Trinitas are both sellers of mobile phone accessories to businesses. David Oakes worked for Cellular as a "Sales Account Manager" from June 2, 2004 to December 27, 2010, when he was terminated. Oakes signed an "Employment Agreement" at the start of his employment in 2004. The Employment Agreement contained a clause reading: "CAFL [i.e., Cellular] requests that proprietary information remains the property of this organization and may not leave, either physically or electronically unless approved in writing by [Mitchell Langstein]." That clause also included Cellular's "customer base" within the sweep of "proprietary information."

Oakes also signed a "Statement of Confidentiality" on January 7, 2008, which stated that he would not "knowingly disclose, use, or induce or assist in the use or disclosure of any Proprietary Information . . . or anything related to Proprietary Information . . . without the Company's prior express written consent." "Proprietary Information" was defined in the Statement as:

> information (a) that is not known by actual or potential competitors of the company or is generally unavailable to the public, (b) that has been created, discovered, developed, or which has otherwise become known to the Company . . . and (c) that has material economic value or potential material economic value to the Company's present or future business.

The parties agree that Oakes signed the Statement; however, they disagree as to whether a valid contract was formed thereby.

In late 2010, shortly before being terminated, Oakes emailed himself a digital file created with the ACT computer program ("ACT file") containing the contact information for some 900+ business and personal contacts. He also maintained his LinkedIn contact information after his termination. Finally, Plaintiff alleges that he also emailed himself the direct contact information for the purchasing agents of certain clients, information on clients' billing preferences and procedures, clients' past pricing requests, and at least one internal strategy document regarding a client, Honeywell.

Plaintiff also alleges that Oakes emailed or otherwise contacted clients after his termination and accused Cellular of "major unethical and deceitful acts done deliberately by management towards its clients."

After leaving Cellular, Oakes started his own company in Texas which eventually became the company known as Trinitas. Trinitas directly competes with Cellular for business in the corporate mobile phone accessory market. * * *

III. DISCUSSION

* * *

Three different types of information might be subject to trade secret law in this case. First, the parties do not dispute that Oakes emailed himself the ACT file, as well as numerous additional items described above. Second, the parties also do not dispute that Oakes retained contacts in his LinkedIn social networking account that he created while employed at Cellular. Third, Cellular alleges, and provides exhibits to show, that Oakes emailed himself a number of other files and documents relating to customers, including the direct contact information for those with the power to do business, information about purchasing and billing preferences or requirements, and specific strategy information relating to one client, Honeywell. Defendants do not directly deny that Oakes took all the documents alleged in this third category of information, but neither do they precisely admit it. Defendants' Reply does admit that Oakes took certain documents relating to Honeywell and its "purchasing requirements."

The removal of the ACT file, containing customer information, is the primary point of contention. "It is well-established that a customer list may constitute a protectable trade secret." *Gable Leigh, Inc. v. North Am. Miss.* However, such lists are not automatically trade secrets, because many customer lists contain no information which is not "easily discoverable through public sources." *Scott v. Snelling & Snelling, Inc.* But where "the employer has expended time and effort identifying customers with particular needs or characteristics," the list can be a protectable trade secret. *Mor-Life, Inc. v. Perry.* Thus, the chief factual issue in determining whether a customer list is a trade secret is the amount of effort involved in compiling it. If the methods used to compile the information are "sophisticated," "difficult," or "particularly time consuming," that tends to show that it is a trade secret. *Am. Paper & Packaging Products, Inc. v. Kirgan.* The underlying rationale for requiring that customer lists be the product of some significant effort is that information which is easily and publicly available does not convey enough "independent economic value" to its holder to satisfy the first prong of the § 3426.1 definition. *Scott,* at 1044.

Defendants argue that Plaintiff has failed to carry its burden of showing that the ACT file is the product of significant effort. Defendant contends that all the information in the ACT file is easily obtained through public sources. "Anyone can easily get extensive information about Fortune 1000 companies, through a standard internet search."

However, whether the information in Oakes' ACT file could be so easily obtained is in dispute. Cellular CEO Mitchell Langstein declares that "[t]o build a list of cellular accessories procurement officers requires the expenditure of a significant amount of time and money," that "Cellular hires and pays employees who are tasked with cold-calling companies and working their way past the 'gatekeepers' to reach the right procurement officer," that David Oakes was similarly required, during his employment with Cellular, to make such calls, that Oakes and other employees were encouraged to "network" with employees at prospect companies, that Oakes made such networking contacts in the course of his employment, and that, in short, "information found in [the] customer list is not available in public directories."

Indeed, Oakes' own declaration supports this narrative: "I was directed to generate business. . . . I was given no leads or customer lists, but was told to begin making cold calls to generate new business for the company. . . . Getting business usually depended on a number of factors, including the relationships I was able to form with the individuals. . . . As I began to make calls, I would put their information into my ACT file."

On the other hand, Oakes also says that "All individuals I talked to-at any company-had already been contacted by other competitors," and that LinkedIn suggested contacts to him automatically-facts which, if true, tend to show that his information-gathering techniques were not especially "sophisticated" or "difficult." *Kirgan*.

In short, there is a genuine issue of fact as to how difficult the information in the ACT file was to obtain.

Defendants also argue that David Oakes' LinkedIn contacts were not a trade secret, because Cellular encouraged its employees to create and use LinkedIn accounts and Oakes' LinkedIn contacts would have been "viewable to any other contact he has on LinkedIn." Plaintiff argues, on the other hand, that LinkedIn information is only available to the degree that the user chooses to share it. Therefore, according to Plaintiff's declarant, it is not automatically the case that contact information is "viewable to any other contact." Oakes' declaration does not say whether this characterization of the functionality of LinkedIn is accurate, or if it is, whether he had set his contacts to be viewable. Because the Court declines to take judicial notice of the functions of LinkedIn, and because the parties' declarants do not make sufficiently clear whether and to what degree Oakes' LinkedIn contacts were indeed made public (and whether this was done with Cellular's explicit or implicit permission), there remain issues of material fact as to the LinkedIn information.

As to the third type of information-the emails containing contact information, emails indicating customer preferences, and internal memo-Defendant does not address the matter separately, but asserts that Oakes retained the Honeywell documents "for posterity," and that information about clients' purchasing requirements or preferences cannot be a trade secret because the cellular accessories business is a "commodity business that shifts and changes all the time." But it seems clear that if a customer list (gathered with a sufficient amount of effort) can provide independent economic value to a business, documentation of the past behavior and preferences of those customers can be, too-even if market conditions change. As to the Honeywell memo, it appears to describe a successful method for meeting a customer's needs, which could likewise provide independent economic value. "Cellular uses its customer information, in conjunction with additional trade secret information, such as customer product, pricing and payment preferences, to win business from [and] maintain relationships with clients." Thus, there is a genuine issue of material fact with regard to the economic value of this information, too.

* * *

Defendant's motion for summary judgment as to trade secret misappropriation is denied.

DID YOU GET IT?

1. What types of information was allegedly taken by the defendants?

2. What is the defendants' argument as to why the ACT file is not a trade secret?

3. How do you think the protectability of LinkedIn contacts differ, if at all, from the other types of customer information in the case?

4. What is the procedural posture of this case?

D. INTERNET DISCLOSURES AND PUBLIC AVAILABILITY

As the previous case reveals with respect to LinkedIn information, the power of the internet has added complexity and challenges to the framework upon which trade secrecy is built. The clash between the need to maintain secrecy while living and doing business surrounded by a medium that so easily makes information publicly available is readily apparent. Professor Elizabeth Rowe has written about the challenges that the internet presents to trade secrets.

CONTRIBUTORY NEGLIGENCE, TECHNOLOGY, AND TRADE SECRETS
Elizabeth A. Rowe.
17 George Mason L. Rev. 1, 21–22 (2009).

[T]he Internet is a dangerous place for trade secrets. Many courts assume that a trade secret posted on the Internet is generally known and consequently has lost its trade secret status. Even when a party posting trade secret information may not have intended to cause harm to the trade secret owner, the nature of the Internet is such that the secret could nonetheless be destroyed.

Unlike other mass media, the Internet has no editors who scrutinize submissions and decide what materials will be published. Any person sitting at a computer can post proprietary information onto the Internet, resulting in immediate and irreparable harm. * * *

The nature of the Internet is such that the trade secret owner may never know the identity of the person making the disclosure. Furthermore, the person posting the information may very well be far removed from the person who originally misappropriated the secret, making it difficult to even identify potential defendants in misappropriation actions involving disclosures on the Internet.

Because the value of a trade secret lies in its secrecy, most misappropriators who acquire another's trade secrets and plan to use them for their own competitive advantage have no incentive to publicize the secret. The culture of the Internet, however, has led to a higher likelihood that those in possession of another's trade secrets will make them public, rather than continuing to keep them secret for personal gain. The great ease with which virtually anyone can post information on the Internet, coupled with its "disinhibiting effect," and a general decline in employee loyalty in the workplace, have allowed disgruntled employees to achieve the ultimate revenge against their former employers by destroying trade secrets.

———

The earliest analyses of the effect of trade secrets appearing on the internet come from a series of cases involving the Church of Scientology pursuing actions against former church members who allegedly misappropriated the Church's trade secrets. Recall the *RTC v. Netcom* case that you read in Chapter 2 on the issue of whether religious texts can qualify for trade secret protection. In this chapter, that case and another help to illustrate the analysis that a court may follow in deciding how to treat alleged trade secret information that is posted on the internet.

Reading Guidance

How does the internet play into the defendant's argument as to why the Church's information was not a trade secret?

RELIGIOUS TECHNOLOGY CENTER V. NETCOM ON-LINE COMMUNICATION SERVICES, INC.

United States District Court, N.D. California, 1995.
923 F.Supp. 1231.

WHYTE, DISTRICT JUDGE.

[For the background facts and other information about this case, see Chapter 2. Also, note that this case was based upon the internet as it existed before the widespread use of the world-wide web (which was introduced in 1991) and the advent of Facebook and Google.]

* * *

Erlich argues that the Church's trade secrets have been made available to the public through various means. The unprotected disclosure of a trade secret will cause the information to forfeit its trade secret status, since "[i]nformation that is generally known or readily ascertainable through proper means by others . . . is not protectable as a trade secret." Once trade secrets have been exposed to the public, they cannot later be recalled.

Erlich argues that many of the Advanced Technology documents have been available in open court records in another case, *Church of Scientology Int'l v. Fishman,* destroying the necessary element of secrecy. However, the *Fishman* court recently issued an order sealing the file pending a decision on whether the documents are trade secrets. Even if those records were temporarily open to the public, the court will not assume that their contents have been generally disclosed, especially when this question is still pending before the district court in *Fishman.* Such a disclosure, without evidence that the secrets have become generally known, does not necessarily cause RTC to forfeit its trade secrets. The contrary result would mean that if documents were ever filed without a sealing order, even for a short time, the court would not be able to decide that they should be sealed because the documents would have lost their potential trade secret status by virtue of the temporary unsealing. The only fair result would be to allow trade secret status for works that are otherwise protectable as trade secrets unless they were somehow made generally available to the public during the period they were unsealed, such as by publication.

* * *

Finally, Erlich newly emphasizes in his Reply that the works he posted were not secrets because he received them through proper means: eight of the documents were allegedly previously posted anonymously to a public portion of the Internet and one of the documents (item 1 of Exhibit B) allegedly came to Erlich anonymously through the U.S. mail. Erlich claims that because the alleged trade secrets were received from "public sources," they should lose their trade secret protection. Although the Internet is a new technology, it requires no great leap to conclude that because more than 25 million people could have accessed the newsgroup postings from which Erlich alleges he received the Exhibit B works, these works would lose their status as secrets. While the Internet has not reached the status where a temporary posting on a newsgroup is akin to publication in a major newspaper or on a television network, those with an interest in using the Church's trade secrets to compete with the Church are likely to look to the newsgroup. Thus, posting works to the Internet makes them "generally known" to the relevant people-the potential "competitors" of the Church.

The court is troubled by the notion that any Internet user, including those using "anonymous remailers" to protect their identity, can destroy valuable intellectual property rights by posting them over the Internet, especially given the fact that there is little opportunity to screen postings before they are made. Nonetheless, one of the Internet's virtues, that it gives even the poorest individuals the power to publish to millions of readers, can also be a detriment to the value of intellectual property rights. The anonymous (or judgment proof) defendant can permanently destroy valuable trade secrets, leaving no one to hold liable for the misappropriation. Although a work posted to an Internet newsgroup remains accessible to the public for only a limited amount of time, once that trade secret has been released into the public domain there is no retrieving it.

While the court is persuaded by the Church's evidence that those who made the original postings likely gained the information through improper means, as no one outside the Church or without a duty of confidence would have had access to those works, this does not negate the finding that, once posted, the works lost their secrecy. Although Erlich cannot rely on his own improper postings to support the argument that the Church's documents are no longer secrets, evidence that another individual has put the alleged trade secrets into the public domain prevents RTC from further enforcing its trade secret rights in those materials. Because there is no evidence that Erlich is a privy of any of the alleged original misappropriators, he is not equitably estopped from raising their previous public disclosures as a defense to his disclosure. The court is thus convinced that those postings made by Erlich were of materials that were possibly already generally available to the public. Therefore, RTC has not shown a likelihood of success on an essential element of its trade secret claim.

* * *

DID YOU GET IT?

1. Why does it matter whether the Church's information was available on the internet?

2. What if Erlich did not receive the information that he disclosed directly from the internet? Does it alter the trade secret analysis?

3. Would the court's analysis be different given the current state of the internet?

4. Is all information that is posted on the internet "readily ascertainable"? What about all information that is available in a library?

> ### Reading Guidance
> *In this related case, decided a few months after Netcom, what was the continuing effect of the Church's materials having appeared on the internet?*

RELIGIOUS TECHNOLOGY CENTER V. LERMA
United States District Court, E.D. Virginia, 1995.
908 F.Supp. 1362.

* * *

BRINKEMA, DISTRICT JUDGE.

* * *

The essential facts are not in dispute. In 1991, the Church of Scientology sued Steven Fishman, a disgruntled former member of the Church of Scientology, in the United States District Court for the Central District of

California. On April 14, 1993, Fishman filed in the open court file what has come to be known as the Fishman affidavit, to which were attached 69 pages of what the Religious Technology Center ("RTC") describes as various Advanced Technology works, specifically levels OT–I through OT–VII documents. Plaintiff claims that these documents are protected from both unauthorized use and unauthorized disclosure under the copyright laws of the United States and under trade secret laws, respectively.

In California, the RTC moved to seal the Fishman affidavit, arguing that the attached AT documents were trade secrets. That motion was denied and the Ninth Circuit upheld the district court's decision not to seal the file. The case was remanded for further proceedings and the district court again declined to seal the file, which remained unsealed until August 15, 1995.

Defendant Arnaldo Lerma, another former Scientologist, obtained a copy of the Fishman affidavit and the attached AT documents. Lerma admits that on July 31 and August 1, 1995, he published the AT documents on the Internet through defendant Digital Gateway Systems ("DGS"), an Internet access provider. RTC, which regularly scans the Internet, discovered the publication of documents and on August 11, 1995, warned Lerma to return the AT documents and not publish them any further. After Lerma refused to cooperate, RTC obtained a Temporary Restraining Order prohibiting Lerma from any further publication of the documents and a seizure warrant which authorized the United States Marshal to seize Lerma's personal computer, floppy disks and any copies of the copyrighted works of L. Ron Hubbard, the author of the AT documents.

During the same time period, on or about August 5 or 6, 1995, Lerma sent a hard copy of the Fishman affidavit and AT attachments to Richard Leiby, an investigative reporter for The Washington Post. On August 12, 1995, counsel for RTC discovered this disclosure and approached The Post, which was told that the Fishman affidavit might be stolen. In response to the RTC's representations, The Post returned the actual copy which Lerma had given it. However, The Post had by then learned that a copy of the same Fishman affidavit was available in the open court file in the United States District Court for the Central District of California. On August 14, 1995, The Post sent Kathryn Wexler, a news aide stationed in California, to that court to obtain a copy of the Fishman affidavit. The Clerk's office made a copy for Wexler, who then mailed it to Washington. Although it is undisputed that RTC staff members had been checking that file out and holding it all day to prevent anyone from seeing it, the file was not sealed and obviously was available, upon request, to any member of the public who wished to see it.

The day after The Post obtained its copy of the Fishman affidavit, the RTC applied for a sealing order and the trial judge ordered the file sealed.

However, there is no evidence in the record that the judge ordered The Post to return the copy made by the Clerk's office or that any kind of a restraining order was issued by that court against The Post.

Five days later, on August 19, 1995, The Post published a news article, entitled "Church in Cyberspace: Its Sacred Writ is on the Net. Its Lawyers are on the Case," written by defendant Marc Fisher. In that article, RTC's lawsuit against Lerma and the seizure of his computer equipment were discussed, as was the history of Scientology litigation against its critics and the growing use of the Internet by Scientology dissidents. The article included three brief quotes (totaling 46 words) from three of the AT documents. On August 22, 1995, the RTC filed its First Amended Verified Complaint for Injunctive Relief and Damages in which it added The Washington Post and its two reporters, Fisher and Leiby, as additional defendants. A Second Amended Verified was later filed and is now the subject of this summary judgment motion.

* * *

The Post argues persuasively that the AT documents were no longer trade secrets by the time The Post acquired them. They point to the following undisputed facts. First, the Fishman affidavit had been in a public court file from April 14, 1993 until August 15, 1995, for a total of 28 months. Although RTC has shown that it went to extraordinary efforts to control access to that file by having church members sign out the file and keep it in their custody at the courthouse, the file nevertheless was an open file, available to the public. The Post was able to obtain a copy of the Fishman affidavit without any difficulty, by merely asking the Clerk of the court to copy it. Thus, having been in the public domain for an extensive period of time, these AT documents cannot be deemed "trade secrets."

Of even more significance is the undisputed fact that these documents were posted on the Internet on July 31 and August 1, 1995. On August 11, 1995, this Court entered a Temporary Restraining Order among other orders which directed Lerma to stop disseminating the AT documents. However, that was more than ten days after the documents were posted on the Internet, where they remained potentially available to the millions of Internet users around the world.

As other courts who have dealt with similar issues have observed, "posting works to the Internet makes them 'generally known'" at least to the relevant people interested in the news group. Once a trade secret is posted on the Internet, it is effectively part of the public domain, impossible to retrieve. Although the person who originally posted a trade secret on the Internet may be liable for trade secret misappropriation, the party who merely downloads Internet information cannot be liable for misappropriation because there is no misconduct involved in interacting with the Internet.

Even if one were to assume that the AT documents are still trade secrets, under Virginia law, the tort of misappropriation of trade secrets is not committed by a person who uses or publishes a trade secret unless that person has used unlawful means, or breached some duty created by contract or implied by law resulting from some employment or similar relationship.

It is the *employment of improper means to procure the trade secret, rather than the mere copying or use,* which is the basis of [liability] . . . Apart from breach of contract, abuse of confidence or impropriety in the means of procurement, trade secrets may be copied freely as devices or processes which are not secret.

The RTC claims that because The Post was on notice of the RTC's allegations that the AT documents were stolen and were both trade secrets and unpublished copyrighted works, The Post was under a legal obligation not to copy or use the documents. This Court knows of no law which required The Post to sit on its hands and do no further investigation into what was obviously becoming a newsworthy event and newsworthy documents. The RTC's allegations are still just allegations. The very court from which the Fishman affidavit was obtained still has under advisement the issue of whether the AT documents are trade secrets. Although The Post was on notice that the RTC made certain proprietary claims about these documents, there was nothing illegal or unethical about The Post going to the Clerk's office for a copy of the documents or downloading them from the Internet.

Because there is no evidence that The Post abused any confidence, committed an impropriety, violated any court order or committed any other improper act in gathering information from the court file or downloading information from the Internet, there is no possible liability for The Post in its acquisition of the information. This is true regardless of the documents status as trade secrets. As for the disclosure of the information, The Post did nothing more than briefly quote from publicly available materials. These acts simply do not approach a trade secret misappropriation, and, therefore, summary judgment must be entered for the defendants.

* * *

DID YOU GET IT?

1. What was the Washington Post's argument as to why it did not misappropriate a "trade secret"?

2. Was it enough that the information was available on the internet or did it need to actually be accessed by members of the public for it to be "generally known"?

3. What could the Church have done in both this case and *RTC v. Netcom* to make a stronger showing of its efforts to keep its sacred script secret?

E. SPECIAL ISSUE: WHERE IS THE DIVIDING LINE BETWEEN A TRADE SECRET AND ONE'S GENERAL SKILL & KNOWLEDGE?

As the *Rohm and Haas* case reveals, a tension often presented in trade secret cases is the right of an employee to use the information that is in his or her head versus an employer's right to stake a claim to that information. The general rule is that a former employee may use the general knowledge, skills, and experience acquired during his or her employment, even in competition with his or her former employer. "This principle effectuates the public interest in labor mobility, promotes the employee's freedom to practice a profession, and freedom of competition." *CVD, Inc. v. Raytheon Co.*, 769 F.2d 842, 852 (1st Cir. 1985). However, the former employee may not use the confidential or trade secret information of the former employer. The following concurring opinion explains the policy considerations related to the general rule. The case that follows the concurrence is an example of how the general rule is applied in practice.

> ### Reading Guidance
> *Why is it important to distinguish between general skill and knowledge and trade secrets?*

SI HANDLING SYSTEMS, INC. v. HEISLEY
United States Court of Appeals, Third Circuit, 1985.
753 F.2d 1244.

* * *

ADAMS, CIRCUIT JUDGE concurring.

Although I concur with the result reached by the majority, I believe that a number of the contentions raised in this appeal are sufficiently important to warrant additional comment. When deciding the equitable issues surrounding the request for a trade secret injunction, it would seem that a court cannot act as a pure engineer or scientist, assessing the technical import of the information in question. Rather, the court must also consider economic factors, since the very definition of "trade secret" requires an assessment of the competitive advantage a particular item of information affords to a business. Similarly, among the elements to be weighed in determining trade secret status are the value of the information to its owner and to competitors, and the ease or difficulty with which the information may be properly acquired or duplicated. *International Election Systems Corp. v. Shoup* (applying Pennsylvania law of trade secrets).

While the majority may be correct in suggesting that the trial court need not always "engage in extended analysis of the public interest," the court on occasion must apply the elements of sociology. This is so since trade secret cases frequently implicate the important countervailing policies served on one hand by protecting a business person from unfair competition stemming from the usurpation of trade secrets, and on the other by permitting an individual to pursue unhampered the occupation for which he or she is best suited. *See Wexler v. Greenberg.* "Trade secrets are not . . . so important to society that the interests of employees, competitors and competition should automatically be relegated to a lower position whenever trade secrets are proved to exist." Robison, *The Confidence Game: An Approach to the Law About Trade Secrets.*

These observations take on more force, I believe, when a case such as the present one involves the concept of "know-how." Under Pennsylvania law an employee's general knowledge, skill, and experience are not trade secrets. *E.g., Van Products Co. v. General Welding & Fabricating Co.* Thus in theory an employer generally may not inhibit the manner in which an employee uses his or her knowledge, skill, and experience-even if these were acquired during employment. * * * When these attributes of the employee are inextricably related to the information or process that constitutes an employer's competitive advantage—as increasingly seems to be the case in newer, high-technology industries, *see generally* Note, *Trade Secrets and the Skilled Employee in the Computer Industry*—the legal questions confronting the court necessarily become bound up with competing public policies.

It is noteworthy that in such cases the balance struck by the Pennsylvania courts apparently has favored greater freedom for employees to pursue a chosen profession. *See Comment, The Trade Secret Quagmire in Pennsylvania: A Mandate for Statutory Clarification.* The courts have recognized that someone who has worked in a particular field cannot be expected to forego the accumulated skills, knowledge, and experience gained before the employee changes jobs. Such qualifications are obviously very valuable to an employee seeking to sell his services in the marketplace. A person leaving one employer and going into the marketplace will seek to compete in the area of his or her greatest aptitude. In light of the highly mobile nature of our society, and as the economy becomes increasingly comprised of highly skilled or high-tech jobs, the individual's economic interests will more and more be buffeted by employers' perceived needs to maintain their competitive advantage. Courts must be cautious not to strike a balance that unduly disadvantages the individual worker.

In achieving a proper balance, courts should be guarded in their use of older precedents. Perhaps the most "influential Pennsylvania holdings in the field of trade secrets" were decided in the early 1960's. *See* Comment, *supra.* Yet, quite significantly, those cases pre-date the rapid growth of several high-tech industries and the innovations which those industries have spawned.

Furthermore, society has a fundamental interest in allowing an individual reasonable freedom to change his or her job and to make full use of acquired skills and experience for new employment. Reasonable movement promotes competition and the dissemination of ideas, which in turn benefit the consumer. *Accord ILG Industries, Inc. v. Scott.* Important values are served when the resources of skill and information are allocated in such a manner that they are utilized most efficiently to produce goods and services. * * *

DID YOU GET IT?

1. Why does Judge Adams think that courts should sometimes apply "elements of sociology" when ruling on trade secret cases?

2. According to this concurrence, in which direction has Pennsylvania courts typically struck the balance between protecting employees versus protecting employers' trade secrets?

3. How do consumers benefit when employees are allowed to change jobs freely?

Reading Guidance

Was the former employee in this case using his general knowledge and skill, or the plaintiff's trade secret?

TEMPO INSTRUMENT, INC. V. LOGITEK, INC.
United States District Court, E.D. New York, 1964.
229 F.Supp. 1.

* * *

ZAVATT, CHIEF JUDGE.

* * *

Plaintiff is a domestic corporation engaged primarily in the manufacture of an electronic timing device known as a Time Delay Relay. It claims to be the assignee of a patent issued on March 19, 1963 (United States Letters Patent No. 3,082,329) directed to an electronic circuit referred to as the Gate circuit. The individual defendant, Herbert L. Fischer, was employed by the plaintiff as an engineer from April 1959 until May 1960. In September 1961 Fischer organized the corporate defendant, Logitek, Inc., which also engaged in the manufacture of time delay relays. In sum, the plaintiff alleges that the defendants are making, using and selling articles which infringe upon its patent and that the defendants are availing themselves of trade secrets disclosed to the defendant, Fischer, during his employment with the plaintiff.

* * *

With regard to the question of unfair competition, the plaintiff's allegations may be separated into two basic claims. To begin with, the plaintiff alleges that its Gate circuit has always been maintained as a trade secret; that it notified all key personnel, including the defendant Fischer, of this fact; that Fischer, in breach of his confidential relationship with the plaintiff, and the defendant Logitek are currently utilizing Fischer's knowledge of the Gate circuit in the manufacture of time delay relays which are being sold in competition with the plaintiff's products. For present purposes only, the court will assume arguendo that this Gate circuit is of such substantial value as to qualify as a trade secret; that the plaintiff maintained a sufficient degree of secrecy as to the nature of this circuit; and that the defendants are actually utilizing information gained by Fischer in a confidential relationship with the plaintiff. Naturally, the actual truth or falsity of these allegations will have to be established at a full trial. * * *

It would appear that the main thrust of the plaintiff's unfair competition allegation is that the defendants have utilized aspects of manufacture and production which were not disclosed by the issuance of the patent. Thus it is alleged that the defendants have violated a confidential relationship by making use of information such as plaintiff's costs and prices, its techniques for purchasing and using components necessary to manufacture and the testing techniques used by the plaintiff. As a result of such activities it is alleged that Logitek, Inc. has successfully underbid the plaintiff on numerous occasions and has thereby competed unfairly.

At the outset it must be noted that there has been little showing that such purchasing, manufacturing and testing techniques would qualify as trade secrets, i.e., that they are of such value as to be afforded judicial protection. * * *

Moreover, while the plaintiff has made some showing that the actual Gate circuit was maintained as a trade secret by Tempo, the papers now before this court give little evidence of such secrecy surrounding the plaintiff's purchasing, manufacturing and testing techniques.

The court is of the opinion that this know-how, alleged to have been disclosed to the defendant Fischer in a confidential relationship and then wrongly utilized by him, constitutes nothing more than the general knowledge and experience gained by an employee in any business and is, therefore, not actionable. The defendant Fischer, like many engineers, has been employed by numerous electronic firms. It appears that several of these positions involved work upon transistor circuits and that his duties at each of these companies provided him with knowledge which made his services desirable to the plaintiff.

The plaintiff, having drawn upon Fischer's prior experiences, can hardly now complain that he has added his Tempo experiences to the sum total of his knowledge and is utilizing this knowledge at Logitek. Fischer's "experience, his skill, his unmatured thoughts and designs were his own. That they had been gained at the expense of the plaintiff certainly gave the latter no legal right to them." *New York Automobile Co. v. Franklin.* "An employee, upon the termination of his employment, is free to draw upon his general knowledge, experience, memory and skill, howsoever gained, provided he does not use, disclose or impinge upon any of the secret processes or business secrets of his former employer." 2 Callmann, Unfair Competition and Trade-Marks, § 55.2(a) at 824 (2d ed. 1950). This court is convinced upon the papers before it that the defendant Fischer did not draw upon any such secret processes or business secrets of Tempo, since it does not appear that this know-how was in fact a trade secret. The findings of the New York Supreme Court in *Richard M. Krause, Inc. v. Gardner* are apposite: * * *

"The plaintiff claims that one of the trade secrets wrongfully used by the defendants was the plaintiff's method of estimating costs. The defendants readily admitted that they knew the plaintiff's method, and that the defendant corporation used it. (There has been no such admission in the instant case.) But this is no trade secret, the use of which this court will enjoin. It is a matter of experience, knowledge of the business, and judgment. The factors to be considered in making estimates are fundamental—inside costs, outside costs, overhead, and profit. The amount of money making up each factor necessarily fluctuates with the market. There is nothing secret in the decision of how much of a mark-up percentage is necessary for a good profit. Good estimating in this industry has the same common denominators as in others—experience and intelligence. The defendants are accused of having learned the plaintiff's sources of supply and the prices that the plaintiff charged to various customers. This information constitutes part of the general knowledge and experience that a person acquires in any business. The use of that knowledge and experience will not be enjoined."

This court noted with approval the finding in *S. W. Scott & Co., Inc. v. Scott,* that an "employee may make use in his new employment of the knowledge he had acquired in the old. If it involves no breach of confidence, it is not unlawful, 'for equity has no power to compel a man who changes employers to wipe clean the slate of his memory." *Peerless Pattern Co. v. Pictorial Review Co.*

For the foregoing reasons the plaintiff's motion for a preliminary injunction is denied.

DID YOU GET IT?

1. What did the plaintiff claim as its trade secret?

2. Why was the court persuaded that the information used by the defendant was part of his general knowledge and experience?

3. What was the court's logic? Did the court reason that: (a) the plaintiff's information was not a trade secret and was therefore general knowledge of the defendant; or (b) that the information was part of defendant's general knowledge and skill and therefore not a trade secret?

Food for Thought

We would not allow landlords to "contract around" the laws that prohibit discrimination; should we allow businesses to contract around legal principles that were specifically designed to limit the scope and anti-competitive effects of trade secret law? Should employers be allowed to contractually restrict an employee's ability to use his general skill and knowledge when working for a future employer?

The issues posed in the last *Food for Thought* are examined in Chapter 8 when the enforceability of Non-compete, Non-disclosure, Non-solicitation, and Invention Assignment Agreements is discussed.

NOTES

1. **The DTSA and general skill and knowledge.** As noted previously, the definition of a trade secret that is contained in the EEA, as amended by the DTSA (see Appendix A), is nearly identical to the UTSA except for a list of types of information, a longer list of illustrative examples, and a memorialization clause. Another difference is that neither the EEA nor the DTSA is accompanied by interpretative commentary, including the commentary in the UTSA stating that trade secrets do not include "general skill and knowledge." Thus, it remains to be seen whether federal courts will interpret the DTSA to include this important limitation, which arose out of common law.

Arguably, the limitation on the protection of general skill and knowledge is consistent with the broad principles expressed in *Kewanee* (see Chapter 2) and *Bonito Boats* (see Chapter 6), but those (and other cases) focus on the public policies of information diffusion and free competition, while the general skill and knowledge limitation focuses on the public policy of employee mobility, an issue that federal courts have not addressed as much.

Faced with criticism related to issues of employee mobility, the DTSA includes the following "new" language in 18 U.S.C. § 1836 (emphasis added):

(3) REMEDIES.—In a civil action brought under this subsection with respect to the misappropriation of a trade secret, a court may—

(A) grant an injunction—

(i) to prevent any actual or threatened misappropriation described in paragraph (1) on such terms as the court deems reasonable, *provided the order does not—*

(I) *prevent a person from entering into an employment relationship, and that conditions placed on such employment shall be based on evidence of threatened misappropriation and not merely on the information the person knows; or*

(II) *otherwise conflict with an applicable State law prohibiting restraints on the practice of a lawful profession, trade, or business;*

(ii) if determined appropriate by the court, requiring affirmative actions to be taken to protect the trade secret; and

(iii) in exceptional circumstances that render an injunction inequitable, that conditions future use of the trade secret upon payment of a reasonable royalty for no longer than the period of time for which such use could have been prohibited;

2. **The express limitation of the EU Trade Secret Directive.** In contrast to the DTSA, the EU Trade Secret Directive has several express provisions that recognize the importance of labor mobility, including a provision that states that the general skill and knowledge of an employee cannot be protected as a trade secret. *Directive (EU) 2016/943 of the European Parliament and of the Council of 8 June 2016 for the protection of undisclosed know-how and business information (trade secrets) against their unlawful acquisition, use and disclosure*, Article 1.3(b), reprinted in Appendix B.

3. **A note on the use of contracts to protect trade secrets.** In Note 5 of Chapter 1, the issue was raised concerning the possible use of contracts to protect business information and, specifically, whether a contract could be used to protect information not meeting the substantive requirements for trade secret protection (for instance because the information does not have the required "independent economic value"). A separate but related question is whether contracts can be used to protect information that trade secret doctrine says can never be protected as a trade secret (namely, publicly available and readily ascertainable information and one's general skill and knowledge) or to prevent the otherwise allowed acts of reverse engineering and independent development. The question is similar to the debates under copyright law whether contracts can be used to force a waiver of fair use rights. *See, e.g.,* Niva

Elkin-Koren, *Copyright Policy and the Limit of Freedom of Contract,* 12
BERKELEY TECH. L. J. 93 (1997).

While freedom of contract suggests that contracts can be used to modify
existing law, where the law reflects important issues of public policy, a counter-
argument is that such a contract is unenforceable as against public policy.
Neither the UTSA nor the DTSA addresses this issue directly, leaving the issue
to be resolved by the courts. Moreover, it is clear that contracts cannot be used
to create trade secrets, leaving only a potential breach of contract action for
information that does not qualify for trade secret protection.

4.   **A benefit of trade secret licenses.** Although a trade secret may
not be created by agreement if it never existed in fact, information that was a
secret at the time of the agreement but has since become public may continue
to generate royalties under certain circumstances. Thus, for instance, parties
may agree to continue the payment of royalties for secrets after they have been
generally disclosed. *See, e.g., Warner-Lambert Pharmaceutical Company v.
John J. Reynolds, Inc.,* 178 F.Supp. 655 (S.D.N.Y. 1959) (The licensee of the
formula for Listerine mouthwash sued to terminate royalty payments after the
formula entered the public domain. The court denied the request, holding that
the plaintiff had received an enormous benefit from the head start it received).
See also Aronson v. Quick Point Pencil, 440 U.S. 257 (1979), and *Nova
Chemicals, Inc. v. Sekisui Plastics Co.,* 579 F.3d. 319 329 (3d Cir. 2009).

5.   **The types of trade secrets most often litigated.** As you learned
in this chapter, most trade secrets fall into two main categories: business
information and technical information. A 2011 survey of reported cases shed
light on the difference in litigation rates between these categories in state and
federal courts.

> Of the varied subject matter that can qualify as a trade secret, two
> categories comprise the vast majority (94%) of trade secrets litigated
> in state courts: internal business trade secrets (i.e., customer lists
> and internal business information) and technical trade secrets (i.e.,
> formulas, technical information, and software or computer
> programs). Internal business trade secrets were litigated in 70% of
> state cases, and technical trade secrets were litigated in 36%. Those
> figures compare to 48% and 56%, respectively, in federal cases.

David S. Almeling et al., *A Statistical Analysis of Trade Secret Litigation in
State Courts,* 46 GONZ. L. REV. 57, 60 (2011).

6.   **Bibliographic note:** In addition to the references noted above, for
more information on the topics discussed in this chapter, *see* MILGRIM ON
TRADE SECRETS §§ 1.03, 17.03 (2016); Zoe Argento, *Killing the Golden Goose,
The Dangers of Strengthening Domestic Trade Secret Rights in Response to
Cyber-Misappropriation,* 16 YALE J. L. & TECH., 172, 177 (2014); Eric E.
Johnson, *Trade Secret Subject Matter,* 33 HAMLINE L. REV. 545 (2010); Victoria
A. Cundiff, *Reasonable Measures to Protect Trade Secrets in a Digital
Environment,* 49 IDEA 359 (2009); Elizabeth A. Rowe, *Saving Trade Secret*

Disclosures on the Internet Through Sequential Preservation, 42 WAKE FOREST LAW REVIEW 1 (2007); Sharon K. Sandeen, *A Contract By Any Other Name Is Still A Contract: Examining The Effectiveness Of Trade Secret Clauses To Protect Databases*, 45 IDEA 119 (2005).

CHAPTER 4

THE ECONOMIC VALUE REQUIREMENT OF TRADE SECRECY

■ ■ ■

Anticipated Learning Outcomes

By the conclusion of this chapter, you will acquire a further understanding of the definition of a trade secret, particularly with respect to the UTSA's and DTSA's "independent economic value" requirement, and learn how to read, interpret, and apply a statute. You will also be able to articulate differences between trade secret misappropriation claims and idea submission claims.

A. INTRODUCTION

As detailed in Chapter 2, although the definition of a trade secret under the UTSA is not numbered as such, it is generally understood that it has three components. In short-hand, information will be protected as a trade secret if it: (1) is secret; (2) has independent economic value to others because of its secrecy; and (3) is the subject of reasonable efforts to maintain its secrecy. In Chapter 3, the meaning of secrecy was examined. This Chapter examines the independent economic value requirement. The pertinent language (emphasized below) is contained in Section 1(4)(i) of the UTSA.

UNIFORM TRADE SECRETS ACT

Section 1(4)

"Trade Secret" means information, including a formula, pattern, compilation, program, device, method, technique, or process, that:

(i) *derives independent economic value, actual or potential*, from not being generally known to, and not being readily ascertainable by proper means by, *other persons who can obtain economic value from its disclosure or use*, and

(ii) is the subject of efforts that are reasonable under the circumstances to maintain its secrecy. (Emphasis added.)

————

This language from the UTSA (and also included in the DTSA, see Appendix A) suggests two important, yet often overlooked, aspects of the independent economic value requirement. First, the information must "derive independent economic value" because of its secrecy, rather than from the inherent value of the information. In other words, it must have demonstrable commercial value *because* it is secret. Second, the UTSA's language suggests that the information must have value to "other persons," not just to the owner of the information. Thus, if the information is only of value to the owner's internal operations, and not to others, it may not meet the economic value requirement.

After initially quoting from the UTSA, however, many courts give the economic value requirement little or no additional attention. In some cases, it is simply assumed that the asserted trade secrets must have value because otherwise the plaintiff would not have brought a suit for misappropriation. In other cases, (perhaps due to the structure of section 1(4)(i) which places the secrecy and economic value requirements in the same subsection) the requirement is often subsumed in an exploration of the meaning of secrecy and is not examined as a separate requirement. In still other cases, evidence of economic value is required and evaluated, but is often misapplied.

In the following excerpt from a law review article, Professor Eric Johnson summarizes how courts have applied (or misapplied) the economic value requirement, and how they often read the word "independent" out of the definition.

TRADE SECRET SUBJECT MATTER

Eric E. Johnson.
33 Hamline L. Rev. 545, 557–58 (2010).

An initial reading of the UTSA should reveal that "independent economic value" is intended to be key limiting language. Yet some treatise authors have declared the issue to be more or less moot. Roger E. Schechter and John R. Thomas have written, "Value is seldom a practical issue in trade secret cases. The high cost of enforcing intellectual property rights suggests that plaintiffs will only commence litigation concerning information of considerable value." But, for a couple of reasons, this declaration appears to be in error. To the extent value is not an issue in very many cases, that would seem largely to be because courts have no clear guidance on how to construe the issue. That being the case, courts often choose to ignore it, finding other reasons to rule as they do. But more importantly, Schechter and Thomas's observation reads words out of the statutory language. Trade secrets must not merely have "value," they must have *independent economic value.* That is, postponing for the moment the discussion of whatever it is that "independent economic" means, just because litigation concerns something of value, it does not follow that the value is of the *independent economic type.*

As it turns out, the meaning of the phrase "independent economic value" has been contested in many reported cases. But a review of them is not terrifically illuminating. Summing them up, treatise-writer Melvin F. Jager has concluded that the meaning of independent economic value is "unclear." His somewhat grim assessment is that "[i]maginative lawyers and courts will continue to have a field day in defining . . . 'independent economic value.' "

Courts confront the chaos in numerous ways. One beginning question is: For whom must the information have value? The courts are not all in agreement on an answer. Some courts have held that the core inquiry in determining whether information has independent economic value relates to the value placed by the plaintiff, the putative trade secret owner, on keeping the information secret from persons who could exploit it to the owner's relative disadvantage. Other courts have held that information has economic value if the defendant, the putative trade secret thief, derives value from using it. Still other courts have understood "economic value" as potentially going both ways, meaning that the information has value to either the owner or a competitor.

The question of to whom the value must accrue is uninteresting to some courts, which have used a sweat-of-the brow theory to explain value. These courts hold that the key factor in determining whether information has independent economic value is the amount of effort and expense that goes into developing it.

Other courts mix and match. In Maine, courts use a five-factor test to determine whether an alleged trade secret has the requisite independent economic value. The factors are: (1) the value of the information to the plaintiff, (2) the amount of effort or money spent developing the information, (3) the measures utilized to protect the information from discovery, (4) the relative ease or difficulty faced by one trying to develop the information for themselves, and (5) the degree to which third parties have placed the information in the public domain or rendered it easily accessible, for instance, through patent applications or in the course of marketing products. This list combines value-to-the-plaintiff and sweat-of-the-brow, then adds three factors that are redundant in various ways of the requirement that the information actually be successfully held as secret.

> ### Food for Thought
>
> *What do you think the economic value language of the UTSA means? Using Professor Johnson's summary of applicable case law, which approach do you think is most beneficial for the plaintiff? For the defendant? Which approach is likely to lead to less information being protected?*

B. APPLYING THE ECONOMIC VALUE REQUIREMENT

The confused and unsettled state of the economic value requirement, coupled with the large number of reported trade secret cases, means that it is likely that either side in a trade secret misappropriation case can find precedent to support their interpretation of the requirement. Since the plaintiff in a civil case has the burden to prove each and every element of its claim, it will be inclined to downplay the economic value requirement either by suggesting that it is not a separate and distinct requirement, or by arguing that it is easy to prove. The defendant will argue exactly the opposite in an effort to make it more difficult for the plaintiff to prove its case.

Whenever lawyers (and law students) are confronted with an unclear and confusing area of law, the best approach is to consider the issue from multiple angles, including matters of policy and fairness. Where a statute is involved, as is the case with the economic value requirement of both the UTSA and the DTSA, a critical question is: What is the proper interpretation of the statute? This usually requires an understanding of the background and purpose of the statute.

Because Minnesota was one of the first two states to adopt the UTSA (the other being Louisiana), an early case that considered the economic value requirement, particularly as a separate and distinct requirement of the UTSA, is *Electro-Craft Corporation v. Controlled Motion, Inc.* As you consider *Electro-Craft* and the cases that follow it, pay close attention to the types of evidence and arguments that are made on the issue of independent value and whether the evidence presented is direct or circumstantial.

> ### *Reading Guidance*
> *What must the plaintiff prove to satisfy the economic value requirement?*

ELECTRO-CRAFT CORP. V. CONTROLLED MOTION, INC.

Minnesota Supreme Court, 1983.
332 N.W.2d 890.

— fmr. employee case

COYNE, JUSTICE.

Respondent Electro-Craft Corporation ("ECC") sued appellants Controlled Motion, Inc. ("CMI") and CMI's president, John Mahoney, (a former employee of ECC) for misappropriation of trade secrets. ECC claimed that CMI and Mahoney improperly copied the designs of ECC's electric motors. The district court found that misappropriation had occurred and also found appellants in contempt for violating a temporary restraining order. We reverse the order for judgment based on misappropriation and affirm the order finding appellants in contempt.

— three initial Motors

THE PRODUCTS

ECC, a Minnesota corporation, manufactures D.C. iron core motors, moving coil motors, brushless motors, and other products. ECC has four plants, three of which manufacture motors and motor parts. The total employment of those three plants is around 500.

CMI is a Minnesota corporation which manufactures moving coil motors. John Mahoney is the president and founder of CMI. Mahoney was formerly national sales manager for ECC. While at ECC, Mahoney established ECC's customer relationships with Storage Technology Company and IBM, customers for the motors involved in this lawsuit.

ECC and CMI manufacture high performance D.C. motors, called "servo" motors, which are able to start and stop at least 30 times per second. These motors are useful for such high technology applications as computer disc drives and printers and industrial robots. In this action ECC claims misappropriation of trade secrets with respect to one moving coil motor and one brushless motor.

* * *

According to Mr. Edward Kelen, president of ECC, ECC was one of only three significant producers of small moving coil motors in 1980. Also, although seven companies produced brushless servo motors, ECC had more than half of the private sector domestic market. Motors made for the producer's own use and motors produced for military or foreign markets were not included in Kelen's evaluations, but it seems clear that ECC's share of the overall servo motor market is substantial. Moreover, Kelen testified that the total brushless motor market is growing rapidly; in five

— it has "value" if it gives the newcomer/competitor a "headstart"/competitive advantage

years (from 1980) it was projected to grow from two million dollars to fifty or sixty million dollars per year. * * *

ECC began work on moving coil motors in 1966. At this time Honeywell had already applied for a patent on a moving coil motor. ECC began making primitive moving coil motors in 1967; ECC developed its 1030/1040 motor to meet the needs of users of a comparable Honeywell motor, the 33 V.M. The two motors are nearly identical, and Designer Erland Persson had a 33 Honeywell V.M. in his possession when he designed ECC's 1030/1040. Persson testified that he had problems with the adhesives and supporting materials for the 1030/1040 and that it took ECC from six to eight months to develop the armature for the motor.

About 1974, Robert Schept, Engineering Manager at ECC, designed the successful ECC 1600 moving coil motor. Schept studied various other motors on the market to try to determine the best combination of dimensions for the motor. Subsequently, Schept designed the 1125 moving coil motor for ECC. He did this by scaling down the ECC 1600 while keeping its performance basically the same. Schept testified that it took four to five months to design prototypes for the 1125 and around a year to start actual production. The 1125 is now used for a variety of applications; for each application ECC produces a different model 1125 with different dimensions. The model involved in this case is the 1125–03–003, designed for a specific computer system built by Storage Technology Co.

ECC's brushless motors are of more recent origin than that of ECC's moving coil motors. Nonetheless, a long process of trial and error, using new developments in technology and costing approximately two million dollars, has been involved in the development of workable models. ECC initially sent prototypes to several customers. Finally, ECC worked with IBM to develop a prototype motor for an IBM printer. This model was a very successful enterprise for ECC, since ECC became the only known source of motors for the IBM project. For around five years, ECC has also been working with Ford Motor Company on a new application for ECC brushless motors. This application involves using larger ECC motors in automated assembly lines. ECC has produced several prototypes for Ford and hopes to begin production in 1983.

THE EVENTS

In May of 1980, John Mahoney, while employed by ECC, began to explore the possibility of starting his own business. Mahoney already had many contacts in the business, including people at Storage Technology and at IBM—ECC customers for the ECC 1125–03–003 and brushless motors. Mahoney had also guided development of the IBM project and the Ford project. On June 12, 1980, Mahoney hired an attorney as counsel for the proposed new business, and counsel helped Mahoney prepare a prospectus which was circulated to prospective investors. Mahoney met with several prospective investors during June and July but apparently received no investments before August 1980.

The prospectus indicates that Mahoney proposed to compete with ECC in its IBM and Ford applications. Mahoney planned to complete prototypes for IBM in twelve weeks and obtain IBM approval in another week. Mahoney planned to try eventually to enter the market for the Ford systems. The prospectus projected revenues in the third month from sales of the prototype brushless motors but projected no research and development expenses for the first few months.

In June of 1980 Mahoney met with several of his fellow ECC employees about their joining the new business. On August 6, 1980, Mahoney resigned from ECC. Mahoney and ECC's president, Kelen, met briefly regarding trade secrets and Mahoney told Kelen not to worry. On September 16, 1980, four other ECC employees resigned in order to work for Mahoney's company, now called CMI. * * *

All of these employees, as well as Mahoney, had signed confidentiality agreements when hired by ECC. None of these agreements, however, included a non-competition clause. When these four employees left ECC, ECC's management conducted exit interviews. The employees were asked to sign acknowledgment forms which outlined the areas that ECC considered confidential; only Anderson signed the acknowledgment.

* * *

On September 18, Mahoney traveled to Colorado to meet representatives of Storage Technology Co. Mahoney received the specifications for a moving coil motor to meet Storage Technology's application, at that time supplied by the ECC 1125–03–003 and a Honeywell motor. Mahoney delivered prototypes of a CMI motor, the CMI 440, to Storage Technology on December 15, 1980; the motor was finally approved on March 1, 1981.

The evidence is conflicting as to how CMI produced the 440. The CMI 440 is almost identical in dimensions and tolerances to the ECC 1125–03–003. William Craighill, the former ECC employee who developed the CMI 440, testified that he did not copy, nor even possess, an ECC 1125 motor when he designed the CMI 440. Craighill claimed that he used only a similar Honeywell motor, the Storage Technology specifications, and his own calculations to develop the CMI 440. On the other hand, circumstantial evidence pointed to the conclusion that CMI employees copied the ECC 1125. The similarity of the motors suggests copying, although the motors are not absolutely identical. Furthermore, the manufacturing processes, adhesives, and other materials are nearly identical. * * *

THE ACTION

On September 26, 1980, about six weeks after Mahoney's resignation, ECC sued CMI and Mahoney (hereinafter referred to together as "CMI") claiming that CMI misappropriated ECC's trade secrets. On October 1, 1980, Judge William Posten issued an order which enjoined CMI from accepting orders from ECC's principal "Customer" (not named in the complaint but later shown to be IBM) with respect to "brushless" motors. After a preliminary hearing Judge Lindsay Arthur of the Hennepin County District Court granted a temporary injunction in favor of ECC on April 16, 1981. * * *

A trial was held before Judge Arthur, without a jury, from June 15, 1981 to July 7, 1981. By order of October 19, 1981, Judge Arthur found that CMI had misappropriated ECC's trade secrets and enjoined CMI from producing or selling any "brushless or low inertia electric motor or tachometer" with dimensions within 10% of the dimensions of ECC's 1125 motor or ECC's brushless motor produced for IBM. * * * The court also awarded ECC $50.00 in exemplary damages (but no compensatory damages) for each offending motor sold.

CMI appealed * * * [and] ECC filed a notice of review of the district court's final order, seeking compensatory damages, attorney fees, and further injunctive relief, and seeking recovery against John Mahoney individually. The appeals have been consolidated for consideration.

* * *

A.   *Trade Secret Status.*

The Uniform Trade Secrets Act, * * * allows the protection of certain types of information through an action for misappropriation. Misappropriation is defined as improper acquisition, disclosure, or use of a "trade secret." Minn. Stat. § 325C.01, subd. 3. Without a proven trade secret there can be no action for misappropriation, even if defendants' actions were wrongful.

1.   In defining the existence of a trade secret as the threshold issue, we first focus upon the "property rights" in the trade secret rather than on the existence of a confidential relationship. . . . We recognize that the confidential relationship is also a prerequisite to an action for misappropriation, *Jostens, Inc. v. National Computer Systems, Inc.,* and that the elements of trade secret status and the confidentiality of the relationship "should not be artificially separated for purposes of analysis since, in a significant sense, they are interdependent." * * * However, without the finding of a trade secret, we cannot grant relief to ECC. Otherwise this court would come dangerously close to expanding the trade secrets act into a catchall for industrial torts.

2.   In order to determine the existence of trade secrets, we must first determine what trade secrets are claimed by ECC and what trade secrets were found by the district court. * * *

* * * On the record before us, ECC did not meet its burden of showing that certain features of the brushless motor were protectable trade secrets

which might be misappropriated in the future. Furthermore, given ECC's lack of specificity, it was impossible for the district court to fashion a meaningful injunction which would not overly restrict legitimate competition for the IBM project.

With respect to the moving coil motors, however, ECC claims that the dimensions, tolerances, adhesives, and manufacturing processes of the ECC 1125–03–003 motor are trade secrets. The thrust of ECC's claim is that the specific combination of details and processes for the 1125 motor is a trade secret, and the evidence of the specific features of the 1125 motor sold to Storage Technology adequately identifies the information which ECC claims constitutes a trade secret. We believe that ECC's claim was specific enough in identifying its trade secrets to support a misappropriation action with respect to the 1125.

what the TS actually is.

3.   In determining whether ECC has proven the existence of a trade secret in the 1125 motor, we look to the common law and the Uniform Trade Secrets Act, * * *. The Act, which became effective on August 1, 1980, carries forward, explains, and clarifies many of the rules of the common law of trade secrets. To the extent, however, that the Act modifies the common law, we are constrained to give effect to the statutory language.

* * *

Applying the statutory test, we hold that, like the plaintiff in *Jostens* [*v. National Computer Systems*], ECC has not met its burden of proving the existence of any trade secrets. Therefore, we must reverse the district court's order even though the district court in this case found trade secrets to exist and made specific findings leading up to that ultimate conclusion. Because we do not lightly reverse the district court, we feel compelled to discuss all three elements of trade secret status under the Act as they relate to the evidence and the findings of the district court.

(a)   *Not generally known, readily ascertainable.* The trial court found the information regarding the ECC 1125–03–003 to be secret. This finding was not clearly erroneous. First, the trial court found on conflicting evidence that CMI could not *readily* (i.e. quickly) reverse engineer a motor with exactly the same dimensions, tolerances, and materials as the ECC 1125–03–003. This finding was not clearly erroneous. Reverse engineering time is certainly a factor in determining whether information is readily ascertainable. *ILG Industries, Inc. v. Scott.* The complexity and detail of dimensional data also bears on its ascertainability. * * *

Second, the district court found that the exact combination of features of the 1125–03–003 is unique, even though none of the processes or features are unique in the industry and the 1125–03–003 is not the only way to achieve the required performance. Novelty is not a requirement for trade secrets to the same extent as for patentability. *E.g., Clark v. Bunker.* On the other hand, some novelty is required; mere variations on widely used processes cannot be trade secrets. Thus, in *Jostens,* a type of computer system was held not to be secret where it merely combined known subsystems (and where defendant had produced a different system). In the present case the exact combination of features of the 1125–03–003 could be characterized as a unique solution to the needs of one customer in the industry.

* * *

This is not to suggest that ECC could make out a claim for trade secret status for the entire class of ECC moving coil motors, or even for the ECC 1125 in general. If a new customer devised an application for the ECC 1125 and CMI modified its 440 motor to meet those new specifications, ECC could not object. In that case ECC would be trying to protect, not a specific combination of features, but the design process of trial and error, (including the talent of ECC's employees), by which those features are adapted to a given use. The law of trade secrets will not protect talent or expertise, only secret information. *See, Dynamics Research Corp. v. Analytic Sciences Corp.* (engineering management system really involved talent of consultants, not information, so not a trade secret), and cases cited therein.

(b) *Independent economic value from secrecy.* This statutory element carries forward the common law requirement of **competitive advantage.** The trial court found ECC to have a competitive advantage in the ECC 1125–03–003, not over all competitors, but over "any company which has not, through its own efforts or through license, obtained similar information." CMI claims that ECC was required to show a competitive advantage over all competitors, including those competitors already successfully producing motors.

The statute requires that a trade secret "[derive] independent economic value ... from not being generally known ... and not being readily ascertainable. . . ." This does not mean, as CMI contends, that the owner of the trade secret must be the only one in the market. Several developers of the same information, for example, may have trade secret rights in that information. *Uniform Trade Secrets Act § 1, Commissioner's Comment (1979).* If an outsider would obtain a valuable share of the market by gaining certain information, then that information may be a trade secret if it is not known or readily ascertainable.

It is true that, as CMI contends, the trial court's stated reasons for its finding of a competitive advantage are not valid as to the 1125–03–003. First, the court cited a "dearth of effective competitors for its principal customer" as evidence of advantage. The trial court could only have meant *brushless* motors customer IBM, since Honeywell is an approved source for the 1125 motor sold to Storage Technology. Second, the court cited the time and money ECC reasonably expended in developing its motors. That ECC expended time and money between 1966 and 1975 in the development of the 1125 motor and its predecessors does not support a finding of competitive advantage unless, under the present state of the art, a prospective competitor could not produce a comparable motor without a similar expenditure of time and money.[12] The trial court found, however, that such time and money *would* be required of a prospective competitor today, and that finding was supported by some evidence. The ECC 1125, therefore, did provide ECC with economic value from its secrecy, as the statute requires—value that ECC would lose if any prospective competitor could enter the market (cutting into ECC's market share) without a substantial development expense.

[The *Electro-Craft* court's examination of the reasonable efforts requirement was deleted. It was on the basis of a finding that such efforts were inadequate that the court found that there were no trade secrets and decided to reverse the trial court's ruling.]

* * *

We reverse the district court's final order of October 19, 1981. * * *

DID YOU GET IT?

1. What are the claimed trade secrets and who owns them?

2. What evidence of value did the court rely upon in finding that ECC established that the identified trade secrets had independent economic value?

3. Is the amount of money ECC spent to develop its secrets relevant to the question of economic value?

Reading Guidance
What evidence of independent economic value did RTC present?

RELIGIOUS TECHNOLOGY CENTER V. NETCOM ON-LINE COMMUNICATION SERVICES, INC.
United States District Court, N.D. California, 1995.
923 F.Supp. 1231.

[The facts of this case and the discussion of the nature of the protectable trade secrets were covered in Chapter 2. The following is the court's discussion of the economic value of the alleged trade secrets.]

* * *

---

[12]   Therefore, the third common law element of trade secret status, that the information must have been developed at plaintiff's expense, is not completely eliminated by the Act, as we suggested in *Jostens.* Under the Act it becomes a possible element of proof that the information provides a competitive advantage.

2.   Independent Economic Value

A trade secret requires proof of "independent economic value, actual or potential, from not being generally known to the public or to other persons who can obtain economic value from its disclosure or use." A trade secret must have sufficient value in the owner's operation of its enterprise such that it provides an actual or potential advantage over others who do not possess the information.

RTC's president, Warren McShane, attests that:

> [t]he Advanced Technology is a source of substantial revenue for RTC in the form of licensing fees paid by Churches that are licensed to use the Advanced Technology. These Churches themselves receive a significant amount of their income from donations by parishioners for services based upon the Advanced Technology. These Churches pay RTC a percentage of the donations paid by parishioners for the services based upon the Advanced Technology. These donations and fees provide the majority of operating expenses of these various Church organizations.

The Church's need for revenues to support its services is no less because of its status as a religion. RTC points out that it receives six percent of what the individual churches receive in licensing fees. This evidence is sufficient to establish the value of the Advanced Technology works to the Church.

Erlich also argues that, to constitute a trade secret, information must give its owner a *competitive* advantage, which implies that the Church must have competitors, as it did in *Vien*. Although Erlich is clearly not a "competitor" of the Church, there is no requirement that a trade secret have any value to the *defendant;* the value can be to *others* who do not possess it. The Church has admitted, however, that it currently has no "competitors." However, the definition of trade secret does not require that there *currently* be competitors, only that there be actual or *potential* value from the information being secret. Thus, potential competition is sufficient. This evidence can be shown by direct evidence of the impact of the information on the business or by circumstantial evidence of the resources invested in producing the information, the precautions taken to protect its secrecy, and the willingness of others to pay for its access.

The several past instances of breakaway Scientology-like groups exploiting RTC's Advanced Technology works for their profit constitute reasonable circumstantial evidence that these works give the Church a competitive advantage. In fact, McShane's declaration constitutes direct evidence that the works have a significant impact on the donations received by the Church, providing a majority of its operating expenses. The status of the Advanced Technology works as trade secrets should not depend on Erlich's use of them. Accordingly, this court finds support for the court's conclusion in *Vien* that the Church has shown independent economic value.

DID YOU GET IT?

1. What are the claimed trade secrets and who owns them?

2. Is it possible to articulate an economic value for trade secrets that are not clearly defined?

3. How does RTC attempt to establish value?

4. Can non-profit corporations derive economic value from trade secrets?

> ### Reading Guidance
> *How does the court define "independent economic value"?*

LEATT CORP. V. INNOVATIVE SAFETY TECHNOLOGY, LLC

U.S. District Court, S.D. California, 2010.
2010 WL 1526382.
[Not reported in F.Supp.2d]

IRMA E. GONZALEZ, CHIEF JUDGE.

This is a case about alleged trade secret misappropriation. Currently before the Court is Plaintiffs' motion for a preliminary injunction, which seeks to enjoin Defendants (1) from using or disclosing Plaintiffs' trade secrets, (2) from manufacturing or selling the DefNder product in the United States, (3) requiring Defendants to return all of Plaintiffs' trade secrets in Defendants' possession or control, and (4) from competing unfairly with Plaintiffs in any manner. * * *

BACKGROUND

I.   Factual background

Plaintiffs Leatt Corporation ("Leatt") and Exceed Holdings (Pty) Ltd. ("Xceed") allege to have spent many years of independent research and development to create neck safety braces for use in motorsports. The effort was spearheaded by the founder of both corporations, Dr. Christopher Leatt, whose personal acquaintance was fatally injured in a motorcycle event in 2000–2001 when he fell and broke his neck. * * *

At the same time as Dr. Leatt was working on developing a neck brace for motorcycles, he was also working on a neck brace for cars. This brace, subsequently known as Moto-R, was first sold in or around July/August 2004. At that time, one of the major devices available for neck protection in motorsports and the only device that was approved by the world's top motorsport authority, the Federation Internationale de l'Automobile ("FIA"), was the "HANS" device. According to Plaintiffs, the Moto-R was superior to the HANS device, which apparently made insufficient provision for side impact and did not optimally apply its restraining force in a horizontal direction.

Xceed, formerly known as Leatt Brace Holdings (Pty) Limited ("Leatt Brace"), was established in 2005 and was responsible for the development of safety devices for motorsports, including neck braces or restraint devices. * * * Leatt was established in or around May 2005 and was responsible for the commercialization of the safety devices developed by Xceed. Leatt now also assists in the development and manufacture of new safety devices.

During the latter half of 2005 and 2006, after the Moto-R was launched, most of Plaintiffs' efforts were diverted to finalizing the development, manufacturing, and launch of the Moto-GPX, a brace for use with motorcycles. The Moto-GPX brace was launched at the end of 2006, and was enormously successful, largely due to the need for such a product and the absence of any competing protective equipment for the protection of motorcyclists' necks.

At about the same time in 2006, Leatt began commercializing the original Moto-R. However, while the U.S. safety body approved the Moto-R, it had not yet been approved by the European safety body, the FIA. Accordingly, Leatt focused on improving the Moto-R to a level where it would be approved by the FIA. To that end, a new version of Moto-R was allegedly prototyped in or around the late summer and/or early fall of 2006 ("Prototype 1"). According to Plaintiffs, substantial sums were expended on research and development during 2007 and up to the beginning of 2008. Leatt designed and built a second prototype around the summer of 2007 ("Prototype 2").

Two employees of Leatt, Grant Nelson and Karl Ebel, tested Prototype 2 around August and November 2007 at the Delphi test center in Ohio, after which they traveled to the Dakar Rally in Spain. Both employees worked for Xceed and then Leatt from at least 2005, and both had entered into employment and confidentiality agreements with Leatt on or around May 7, 2007, providing that they would maintain strictly confidential any and all information acquired during their employment by Leatt, including the "know-how as well as any and all result which has been or will be achieved or used with the Project," "the description of the Project," and "any other information which is not publicly available." * * *

Shortly after their return from the Dakar Rally, both Nelson and Ebel resigned from Leatt. Nelson resigned on January 11, 2008, effective January 25, 2008, and Ebel resigned in early February 2008. Plaintiffs allege that in less than a month after leaving Leatt, Nelson had already designed a prototype of a neck brace with a raised stabilizer bar similar to Prototype 2 ("the DefNder") and had drafted a document for his patent attorney describing his "invention." In March 2008, either Nelson or Ebel reserved a spot at the PRI tradeshow in Florida to launch the DefNder product. Nelson began testing the DefNder by May 2008, branding was complete by June 2008, and pre-orders were being taken by August 2008. In or around June 2008, Nelson, Ebel, and an investor (Doug Williams) formed Defendant Innovative Safety Technology, LLC ("IST"), which listed all three as managers or members. IST is presently in the business of selling safety braces, namely the DefNder. Williams is now the majority shareholder of the IST.

In summer or fall of 2008, IST entered into a distribution agreement with Defendant Kevin Heath, who arranged for the DefNder to be manufactured in China and to be imported and sold in the United States. Heath accomplished this through two of his companies: E.V. Technology ("EVT"), a Chinese business entity, and Kevin Heath Enterprises, Inc. ("KHE"), a California corporation. Defendant EVT was to manufacture the DefNder product, while Defendant KHE was to manufacture, import, market, and sell the product. By November 2008, when KHE began to manufacture the DefNder, Heath alleges he had already expended approximately $105,950 on testing, marketing, and obtaining tooling, labor, and other services.

Defendant KHE currently has a contract to sell the DefNder, and is the owner of the <defNderneckbrace.com> domain name. The [DefNder] website * * * <defNderneckbraces.com> provides information and advertising for the DefNder product, and also allows online purchases of the DefNder. * * *

* * *

III. Current proceedings

Plaintiffs commenced the present action in this Court on June 16, 2009. * * * The FAC asserts three causes of action against corporate Defendants IST, KHE, and EV, and the individual Defendant Heath: (1) trade secret misappropriation, (2) unfair competition, and (3) tortious interference.

* * *

LEGAL STANDARD

A party seeking a preliminary injunction must demonstrate "that he is likely to succeed on the merits, that he is likely to suffer irreparable harm in the absence of preliminary relief, that the balance of equities tips in his favor, and that an injunction is in the public interest." *Winter v. Nat. Res. Def. Council, Inc.* * * * "In each case, courts must balance the competing claims of injury and must consider the effect on each party of the granting or withholding of the requested relief." *Indep. Liv. Cntr. of Southern Cal., Inc. v. Maxwell-Jolly* * * *.

DISCUSSION

I.   Likelihood of success on the merits

A.   *Misappropriation of trade secrets*

To state a cause of action for misappropriation of trade secrets under the California's Uniform Trade Secrets Act ("UTSA"), a plaintiff must establish two elements: (1) the existence of a trade secret, and (2) misappropriation of the trade secret. * * *

i.   *Trade secrets*

The Heath Defendants first argue there are no "trade secrets" involved in this case. The UTSA defines a trade secret as "information, including a formula, pattern, compilation, program, device, method, technique, or process, that: (1) [d]erives independent economic value, actual or potential, from not being generally known to the public or to other persons who can obtain economic value from its disclosure or use; and (2) [i]s the subject of efforts that are reasonable under the circumstances to maintain its secrecy." CAL. CIV.CODE § 3426.1(d).

At the outset, the Court rejects the Heath Defendants' arguments that there is no independent economic value to the information Plaintiffs are trying to safeguard, or that Plaintiffs have failed to use reasonable efforts to maintain its secrecy. To have independent economic value, the information must be " 'sufficiently valuable and secret to afford an actual or potential economic advantage over others.' " *Yield Dynamics, Inc. v. TEA Systems Corp.* (quoting RESTATEMENT (THIRD) OF UNFAIR COMPETITION § 39). "The advantage 'need not be great,' but must be 'more than trivial.' " *Id.* In the present case, Plaintiffs are attempting to protect disclosure of certain features of Prototype 2, such as the harness channels and their strategic placement, the stabilizer bars, and the overall shape of the brace. * * * According to Plaintiffs, they spent a significant amount of time and resources in developing and testing these features. * * *

Information that is kept confidential and that was obtained as a result of a significant expenditure of time and resources undoubtedly has "independent economic value" to its owner. *See, e.g., Religious Tech. Ctr. v. Netcom On-Line Commc'n Servs., Inc.,* (noting that independent economic value can be shown by "circumstantial evidence of the resources invested in producing the information, the precautions taken to protect its secrecy, and the willingness of others to pay for its access") * * *. Likewise, information can have independent economic value even if there is no actual product on the market utilizing the information or it relates solely to test failures. *See, e.g., Camacho* (noting that the definition of a trade secret " 'includes information that has commercial value from a negative viewpoint,' " such as " 'the results of lengthy and expensive research which proves that a certain process will not work'" (citation omitted)). Accordingly, the design features Plaintiffs are trying to protect in the present case have the requisite "independent economic value."

* * *

iii. Conclusion

For the foregoing reasons, Plaintiffs have sufficiently shown that they are likely to succeed on the merits of their misappropriation claim.

* * *

DID YOU GET IT?

1. How did the court define economic value? Does such definition differ from that which was applied in the previous case?

2. What evidence did the court rely upon to establish the existence of economic value?

3. Looking at the economic value language of the UTSA, do you agree with the court's definition of economic value? Why or why not?

Reading Guidance
Is it possible for information to be valuable to a business, but not have the required "independent economic value"?

BUFFETS, INC. V. KLINKE
United States Court of Appeals, Ninth Circuit, 1996.
73 F.3d 965.

D.W. NELSON, CIRCUIT JUDGE.

Appellant Buffets Inc., doing business as Old Country Buffets ("OCB"), brought this action against Appellee Paul Klinke, et al., ("The Klinkes"), for misappropriation of trade secrets and violation of Washington's Consumer Protection Act [which includes Washington's version of the UTSA]. OCB alleges that the Klinkes misappropriated its recipes and its job training manuals, both of which it claims are trade secrets, in order to open a buffet restaurant. The district court granted summary judgment for the Klinkes on the Consumer Protection Act claim and following a bench trial, entered judgment in favor of the Klinkes on the remaining claims. We affirm.

FACTUAL AND PROCEDURAL BACKGROUND

Buffets Inc., a Minnesota corporation, operates a nationwide chain of budget buffet restaurants under the name Old Country Buffet. * * * Dennis Scott, one of the principal founders of OCB, developed the first OCB menus and instituted the OCB practice of "small batch cooking": rather than preparing and storing large quantities of food at a time, which is standard practice in many buffet restaurants, Scott instead prepared small batches of food to insure freshness. Scott had a significant amount of experience in the restaurant business and adapted many of the recipes he acquired previously to this type of "small-batch" cooking. In 1989, Scott formed a new company, Evergreen Buffets, which opened its first OCB restaurant in Vancouver, Washington. Scott's partner, Joel Brown, hired Appellee Mark Miller to work at one of the Evergreen restaurants. Miller was fired in 1991, however, for alleged "financial improprieties."

In 1990, Scott met the Appellees Klinkes and gave them a tour of one of the OCB restaurants. The Klinkes were themselves successful restaurateurs, having operated a number of franchise restaurants for over 40 years. The Klinkes asked if they could buy an OCB franchise, but were told that OCB was not franchising. Paul Klinke, who was acquainted with Miller, later arranged for one of his former employees, Jack Bickle, to begin working at one of the OCB restaurants.

In March 1991, Scott, who had by now left OCB, again met with the Klinkes and told them that Miller might assist them in opening a buffet restaurant. Paul Klinke contacted Miller and Miller began working with him in April of 1991. Moreover, on March 19, 1991, Paul Klinke had dinner with Bickle and asked Bickle to provide him with OCB recipes and to get his son, Greg, a job as a cook at one of the OCB stores. Paul offered Bickle $60.00, but Bickle refused both the money and the opportunity to perform those services.

Between March 19, 1991 and April 2, 1991, Greg Klinke and Miller discussed the possibility of Greg's obtaining work at one of the OCB restaurants. On April 2, Greg applied for a job as a cook. On his application, however, he did not disclose either his true residence or his experience as a cook working for his parents. Nor did he reveal the fact that he was still on his parents' payroll.

That summer, Miller asked one of Scott's former administrative assistants to help him compile an employee's manual. Miller provided the bulk of the material for the manuals; the district court found that the new manuals were "almost exact copies of OCB position manuals." In August, Miller gave a licensed transcriber a box of recipes to retype and subsequently delivered to the Klinkes what the district court described as the "OCB recipes." The district court found that when the Klinkes first opened their buffet restaurant, Granny's, they used the copied position manuals to train their employees and the OCB recipes to prepare their dishes. The court granted the Klinkes' motion for summary judgment on the Washington Consumer Protection Act claim, maintaining that the Klinkes' alleged wrongful conduct did not impact the public interest. After a bench trial, it held that neither the recipes nor the job manuals were trade secrets.

* * *

I.   *Trade Secret Status of the Recipes*

RCW § 19.108.010(4) defines a trade secret as "information, including a formula, pattern, compilation, program, device, method, technique or process that:

> (a) Derives independent economic value, actual or potential, from not being generally known to, and not being readily ascertainable by proper means by, other persons who can obtain economic value from its disclosure or use; and

> (b) Is the subject of efforts that are reasonable under the circumstances to maintain its secrecy."

In *Boeing Co. v. Sierracin Corp.*, the Washington Supreme Court makes the important distinction between copyright law and trade secrets law, noting that "[c]opyright does not protect an idea itself, only its particular expression. . . . By contrast, trade secrets law protects the author's very ideas if they possess *some novelty* and are undisclosed or disclosed only on the basis of confidentiality." OCB argues that novelty is not a requirement for trade secret protection; this contention, however, clearly contradicts Washington law. Moreover, contrary to OCB's assertions, the district court's finding that the recipes were more detailed than those of its competitors does not mandate a finding of novelty, for as is discussed below, the court held that even these detailed procedures were readily ascertainable.

Many of OCB's remaining arguments on appeal appear to misunderstand the logic of the district court's holding. The district court did *not* hold, as OCB contends, that the recipes were not trade secrets merely because they had their origins in the public domain, but also because many of them were "basic American dishes that are served in buffets across the United States." This finding was certainly not erroneous. The recipes were for such American staples as BBQ chicken and macaroni and cheese and the procedures, while detailed, are undeniably obvious. Thus, this is not a case where material from the public domain has been refashioned or recreated in such a way so as to be an original product, but is rather an instance where the end-product is itself unoriginal.

* * *

The district court further held that the recipes had no independent economic value, a finding OCB fails to address adequately on appeal. OCB's argument focuses only on that portion of the district court's opinion that held that the recipes had no independent value because OCB had not proven that its food offerings were "superior in quality to that of its rivals." This, however, was not the sole basis for the court's holding. The court held that even though OCB food tasted better than that of its rivals and few of its rivals were succeeding, "OCB [had] failed to establish by a preponderance of the evidence that its rivals [were] not succeeding because of inferior food quality." The court thus notes that there was no demonstrated relationship between the lack of success of OCB's competitors and the unavailability of the recipes, i.e., OCB failed to provide that it necessarily derived any benefit from the recipes being kept secret. The court also noted that "limiting food costs is crucial to the profitability of a buffet" and explained that OCB failed to demonstrate that its recipes play a role in limiting costs.

Further weighing against any finding of economic value was the court's finding that OCB's recipes had to be simplified because of the limited reading skills of its cooks. Given this fact, it appears unlikely that the recipes themselves conferred any economic benefit upon OCB because it was from "translated" versions of these recipes, rather than the highly detailed versions now at issue, that OCB cooks prepared its well-celebrated food.

* * *

The judgment of the district court is AFFIRMED.

DID YOU GET IT?

1. What are the claimed trade secrets and who owns them?

2. Why did the court affirm the lower court's finding of no economic value? What evidence was missing?

3. If the recipes are of value, but not because they are secret, why are they valuable?

Food for Thought

In the last case, the court found that the plaintiff had presented insufficient evidence to establish the existence of independent economic value. If you were the plaintiff's attorney in a trade secret misappropriation case and had to prove independent economic value, what types of evidence would you present on the issue? Must you be able to prove a specific monetary value?

For reasons that are explained in greater detail in Chapter 11, a significant number of trade secret issues arise in the context of requests for information from the government under the U.S. Freedom of Information Act (FOIA) and similar state laws. Indeed, trade secret issues can arise in a variety of cases that do not directly involve claims of misappropriation, such as breach of contract, product liability, and environmental pollution cases.

In FOIA cases, the public's interest in information about the activities of government often must be balanced against trade secret rights that are claimed in such information. Thus, courts in FOIA cases tend to more carefully apply the three requirements of trade secrecy, including the independent economic value requirement. The next case is an example.

Reading Guidance

How is value determined in this case?

TAYLOR V. BABBITT

United States District Court, District of Columbia, 2011.
760 F.Supp.2d 80.

RICARDO M. URBINA, DISTRICT JUDGE.

I.   INTRODUCTION

This matter is before the court on the Federal Aviation Administration's ("FAA") motion for summary judgment and the plaintiff's cross-motion for summary judgment or, in the alternative, for discovery. The plaintiff, an aircraft enthusiast, submitted a request to the FAA under the Freedom of Information Act ("FOIA"), 5 U.S.C. § 552, seeking design specifications for a 1930s-era antique aircraft, the Fairchild F–45. The FAA denied the request on the grounds that the requested materials constituted trade secrets and were thus exempt from disclosure under 5 U.S.C. § 552(b)(4) ("Exemption 4").

The plaintiff has moved for summary judgment, asserting that the requested materials are not trade secrets for Exemption 4 purposes because they are neither secret nor commercially valuable. * * * The FAA has also moved for summary judgment, arguing that the materials are both secret and commercially valuable, and as such are exempted from FOIA disclosure under Exemption 4. * * *

II.   FACTUAL & PROCEDURAL BACKGROUND

A.   The F–45 Type Certificate Application

In 1935, the Fairchild Aircraft Corporation ("FAC") submitted an application to the Civil Aeronautics Authority ("CAA"), the predecessor to the FAA, for a type certificate for a new aircraft model, the F–45 airplane. Pursuant to CAA regulations, FAC submitted numerous materials along with its type certification application, including "technical blueprints depicting the design, materials, components, dimensions and geometry of the aircraft, engineering analyses and engineering test reports."

* * *

In 1955, FEAC sent a letter ("the 1955 Letter") to the CAA authorizing the agency to "loan" the F–45 type certification materials to members of the public who wished to make repairs to their aircraft. Although the 1955 Letter specified that FEAC was not authorizing individuals to manufacture or sell parts built in accordance with the materials, it did not impose any confidentiality requirements on individuals requesting the materials. Despite this authorization, neither the CAA nor the FAA ever disclosed the F–45 type certification materials to members of the public.

* * *

C. The *Herrick* Litigation

In 1997, Greg Herrick, the owner of one of the few remaining F–45 airplanes, submitted a FOIA request to the FAA for the F–45 type certification materials for the purpose of restoring his airplane. *Herrick v. Garvey.* The FAA informed Herrick that it had contacted Fairchild, which objected to the release of the type certification materials. As a result, the FAA denied Herrick's request, asserting that the materials were exempt from disclosure as trade secrets under FOIA Exemption 4.

Herrick filed suit in the United States District Court for the District of Wyoming, asserting that the FAA had improperly applied the trade secrets exemption. The district court granted summary judgment to the FAA, and the Tenth Circuit affirmed. * * *

D. Procedural History of This Case

In August 2002, the plaintiff submitted his own FOIA request to the FAA, seeking copies of the "plans, blueprints, specifications, engineering drawings and data submitted in support of the Type Certificate for the Fairchild F 45." The materials requested were identical to those sought by Herrick. *See Herrick v. Garvey* (stating that the plaintiff sought "certain technical drawings and other data provided . . . by the Fairchild Aircraft Corporation in 1935 in connection with its 'Application for Approved Type Certificate' for an aircraft known as the Fairchild F–45"). Indeed, the plaintiff brought his FOIA request after Herrick requested his assistance with repairs to Herrick's F–45.

In February 2003, after receiving no response from the FAA, the plaintiff filed a complaint in this court. The court stayed the action in April 2003 because of a disagreement as to whether the FAA had actually received the plaintiff's FOIA request. Thereafter, the FAA denied the plaintiff's request and his subsequent appeal.

* * *

III. ANALYSIS

* * *

FOIA affords the public access to virtually any federal government record that FOIA itself does not specifically exempt from disclosure. 5 U.S.C. § 552. FOIA confers jurisdiction on the federal district courts to order the release of improperly withheld or redacted information. 5 U.S.C. § 552(a)(4)(B). In a judicial review of an agency's response to a FOIA request, the defendant agency has the burden of justifying nondisclosure, and the court must ascertain whether the agency has sustained its burden of demonstrating that the documents requested are exempt from disclosure under FOIA and that the agency has adequately segregated exempt from non-exempt materials. * * * An agency may meet its burden by providing the requester with a *Vaughn* index, adequately describing each withheld document and explaining the reason for the withholding.

B.   The Court Grants the Plaintiff's Motion for Summary Judgment and Denies the FAA's Motion for Summary Judgment

The FAA contends that the materials requested by the plaintiff constitute trade secrets and are therefore not subject to disclosure pursuant to FOIA Exemption 4. The plaintiff counters that the materials are not trade secrets for purposes of FOIA Exemption 4 because they are neither secret nor commercially valuable.

Exemption 4 of FOIA authorizes the government to withhold "trade secrets and commercial or financial information obtained from a person and privileged or confidential." 5 U.S.C. § 552(b)(4). A trade secret, for purposes of Exemption 4, is "a secret, commercially valuable plan, formula, process, or device that is used for the making, preparing, compounding, or processing of trade commodities and that can be said to be the end product of either innovation or substantial effort." * * * Furthermore, there must exist "a direct relationship between the information at issue and the productive process." *Id.* If information qualifies as a trade secret, it is protected from disclosure under Exemption 4 and the inquiry ends. *Id.*

In this case, the parties do not dispute that the F–45 type certification materials were directly related to the productive process of the F–45 aircraft. Rather, the parties' dispute centers on two issues: (1) whether the F–45 type certification materials are, in fact, "secret," and (2) whether these materials are "commercially valuable," as required for trade secret protection under Exemption 4. The court considers these matters in turn.

1.   The Requested Materials Are Not Secret

The plaintiff contends that the F–45 type certification materials do not fall under Exemption 4 because they are not "secret." Specifically, the plaintiff asserts that the 1955 Letter from FEAC granting the CAA permission to "loan" the F–45 materials effectively eliminated their secret status. The FAA responds that the 1955 Letter did not remove the trade secret status of the materials, as it only authorized the CAA and the FAA to release the materials for certain specified purposes, and in any case, the materials were never actually disclosed to the public. Furthermore, the FAA contends that even if the 1955 Letter removed the materials' secret status, Fairchild effectively restored the secrecy of the materials by revoking its grant of permission in response to Herrick's FOIA request in 1997.

It is well established that the actual public disclosure of trade secrets eliminates the trade secret status of such information. *See, e.g., Ruckelshaus v. Monsanto Co.* (noting that public disclosure of trade secrets "extinguishe[s]" the owner's property right in the information) * * *.

In *Herrick,* the Tenth Circuit considered whether the 1955 Letter authorizing the disclosure of the F–45 type certificate materials meant that those materials could not be considered secret for Exemption 4 purposes. Noting that the letter placed no restrictions on the further dissemination of the type certificate materials, the court stated that

> [w]hen a submitter grants the government permission to loan or release specific information to the public, the submitter clearly indicates that he has no further intention to keep the information secret. It is therefore a reasonable inference that the submitter himself would be willing to release the information to the public if requested to do so. Thus, once a submitter grants the government permission to loan or release the information to the public, there is no reason for Exemption 4 to apply because the submitter no longer intends the information to be "secret." An examination of the plain meaning of the word "secret" leads to a similar conclusion. Most people would agree that if a person was given a piece of information and was told that the information could be revealed to anyone who asked about it, the information would not constitute a "secret."

> *Id.* (footnote omitted).

Thus, the court concluded, "where the submitter or owner of documents held by the government grants the government permission to loan or release those documents to the public, those documents are no longer 'secret' for purposes of Exemption 4. In such a situation, FOIA creates an obligation for the government to release the documents."

Like the Tenth Circuit, this court concludes that once FEAC authorized the CAA to disclose the F–45 type certificate materials to outside parties without any obligation to maintain the confidentiality of the information, the materials were no longer secret for purposes of Exemption 4. *Id.; see also Ruckelshaus* (observing that "[o]nce the data that constitute a trade secret are disclosed to others, *or others are allowed to use those data,* the holder of the trade secret has lost his property interest in the data") (emphasis added); *Nova Chems., Inc. v. Sekisui Plastics Co.* (holding that information disclosed pursuant to a licensing agreement that did not require the licensee to maintain its secrecy could not be considered a trade secret).

* * * The court cannot conclude that Fairchild's denial of Herrick's FOIA request, following a forty-year period in which it authorized the disclosure

of the materials and took no steps to maintain the secrecy of the information, restores the secret status of the materials at issue.

Accordingly, the court concludes that the F–45 type certificate materials are not secret and therefore do not constitute trade secrets for purposes of Exemption 4. Although this conclusion is sufficient to resolve the parties' cross-motions for summary judgment, the court nonetheless proceeds to consider the second disputed issue—whether the requested materials are commercially valuable—as the resolution of this issue also supports the court's conclusion.

2. The F–45 Type Certification Materials Are Not Commercially Valuable

Although it is undisputed that the F–45 type certification materials were commercially valuable when originally submitted in 1935, the parties dispute whether the materials remain commercially valuable today. The plaintiff contends that for purposes of Exemption 4, information protected as trade secrets must be commercially valuable because of its use in making a trade commodity. Thus, the plaintiff asserts that the F–45 materials, which consist of outdated, seventy-year-old technology, are not commercially valuable because they are not "valuable in manufacturing planes." The FAA does not contend that the materials are valuable based on their current usefulness in manufacturing aircraft. Rather, the FAA asserts that the materials are commercially valuable in the antique aircraft market as a result of their "obvious utility in repairing any of the few remaining F–45s."

"Very little case law exists which interprets and applies the D.C. Circuit's definition of 'trade secret.' " * * * Indeed, this Circuit has not had occasion to consider whether trade secret protection may be afforded to information whose value is unrelated to the present-day production of a commodity, nor has it offered a precise definition of the term "commercially valuable."

The Supreme Court has, however, observed that "the value of a trade secret lies in the competitive advantage it gives its owner over competitors." *Ruckelshaus.* Accordingly, courts have routinely found that information that provides its owner an advantage over its competitors is commercially valuable. *See, e.g., Pac. Sky Supply v. Dep't of Air Force* (concluding that design drawings of airplane parts were commercially valuable because the manufacturer enjoyed substantial commercial success in sales of the airplane parts covered by the drawings during the previous five years and had orders pending for over $150,000 in the parts). On the other hand, obsolete information that provides no competitive advantage is not commercially valuable and cannot constitute a trade secret. *See, e.g., Fox Sports Net North, LLC v. Minn. Twins P'ship.* (stating that "obsolete information cannot form the basis for a trade secret claim because the information has no economic value"); *MicroStrategy, Inc. v. Business*

Objects, S.A., (finding that a document was not worthy of trade secret protection because "the products it references have not been on the market for over half a decade, and the market for these products is constantly changing"); *Applied Indus. Materials Corp. v. Brantjes,* (refusing to extend trade secret protection to information that was "so outdated that it lack[ed] current economic value").

The FAA concedes that the F–45 type certification materials are not commercially valuable based on their usefulness in manufacturing aircraft. After all, the technical information in the F–45 type certificate is surely obsolete. Moreover, although Fairchild presently engages in the distribution of aircraft and aircraft components, Fairchild no longer manufactures aircraft. Accordingly, the F–45 materials are not commercially valuable vis-à-vis the aircraft manufacturing industry.

Instead, the FAA contends that the commercial value of the F–45 type certification materials arises from their value in the antique aircraft market. The FAA has produced evidence showing that the design drawings and specifications included in the F–45 type certification materials are valuable in restoring and repairing F–45s and other aircraft of 1930s vintage, as well as in producing replicas.

But even if the F–45 type certification materials may be valuable within the antique aircraft market, there is no evidence that these materials are commercially valuable to Fairchild with respect to any business interest it has in the antique airplane market. Nowhere does the FAA assert that Fairchild currently competes in the antique aircraft market or that it has any intention to do so in the future. Indeed, the FAA cannot even assert that there exists an identifiable market for F–45 plans.

While the FAA need not provide detailed information regarding Fairchild's business endeavors within the antique aircraft market, the FAA may not rely merely on broad conclusions that the disclosure of the F–45 plans would negatively impact Fairchild's competitive position in that market. *See Pac. Architects & Eng'rs, Inc. v. Renegotiation Bd.* (stating that agencies may not "thwart[ ] the intent of the [FOIA] by making 'conclusory and generalized allegations of exemptions'") (quoting *Vaughn v. Rosen*); *see also Nat'l Parks & Conservation Ass'n v. Kleppe* (providing that under the second prong of Exemption 4, a court "need only exercise its judgment in view of the nature of the material sought and *the competitive circumstances in which the [submitters] do business,* relying at least in part on relevant and credible opinion testimony" (emphasis added)).

Because trade secret protection is ultimately grounded in the "economic value . . . [from] the competitive advantage over others that [the owner] enjoys by virtue of its exclusive access to the data," *Ruckelshaus,* the F–45 type certification materials are not commercially valuable because their economic value does not derive from the competitive advantage they confer upon Fairchild within the antique aircraft market. Thus, although the FAA asserts that the F–45 type certification materials are valuable in the antique aircraft market, the FAA has not shown that the F–45 materials confer a competitive advantage upon Fairchild in the antique aircraft market. Consequently, the court concludes that the F–45 type certification materials are not commercially valuable, and thus do not constitute trade secrets under Exemption 4.

In sum, the FAA has not demonstrated that the materials sought by the plaintiff are secret and commercially valuable, as necessary to demonstrate that they are trade secrets protected from disclosure by Exemption 4. The court therefore grants the plaintiff's motion for summary for summary judgment and denies the FAA's motion for summary judgment.

IV. CONCLUSION

For the foregoing reasons, the court grants the plaintiff's motion for summary judgment, denies the FAA's motion for summary judgment and denies the plaintiff's motion for discovery as moot. * * *

DID YOU GET IT?

1. What are the claimed trade secrets and who owns them?

2. What does the defendant argue to prove the non-existence of value?

3. Is the standard for commercial value discussed in *Babbitt* the same as the independent economic value required under the UTSA and DTSA?

4. Do you think the public interest in access to information held by the government played a role in the court's decision?

C. THE DRAFTING HISTORY OF THE ECONOMIC VALUE REQUIREMENT OF THE UTSA

Because of the case method of instruction used in most law school courses, law students are understandably prone to think that the meaning of the law can be derived from reported case decisions. This approach works well when a principle of law is well developed and clear, but it can be misleading when, as with the economic value requirement of trade secret law, a particular point of law has been under-examined or misapplied. In the absence of a clear and settled statement of the law or, at the very least, a well-reasoned judicial opinion, lawyers have to resort to resources and arguments that are not case-based. These resources include common sense, theory, and policy arguments. In the case of statutes, it may also include information concerning the context and intent of the statute.

Various rules of statutory interpretation and canons of construction have been developed to assist attorneys and judges to interpret and apply statutes. *See, e.g.,* Linda D. Jellum, MASTERING STATUTORY INTERPRETATION (2nd ed. 2013); Einer Elhauge, STATUTORY DEFAULT

RULES: HOW TO INTERPRET UNCLEAR LEGISLATION (2008); and Frank B. Cross, THE THEORY AND PRACTICE OF STATUTORY INTERPRETATION (2009). Usually, the process of statutory interpretation begins with a careful reading of the statute itself. The general rule is that statutes and regulations will be interpreted in accordance with the common meaning of the words used, unless applicable law provides a different meaning. Thus, a starting point for understanding the meaning of a statute is often a dictionary. Where applicable, the definitions section of the applicable statute or related or similar statutes should be consulted.

When a reading of a statute does not result in clarity of meaning or courts want to understand the purpose of the statute, other materials are consulted as an aid to understanding the meaning of the statute. This may include information concerning the background and context of the subject legislation and its legislative history. In the case of uniform laws such as the UTSA, the drafting history of the uniform laws can help to provide meaning. This includes the official comments to uniform laws which many courts use as persuasive authority.

The following excerpt from an article by Professor Sharon Sandeen explains the drafting history of the UTSA's economic value requirement. As you read the excerpt, consider the purpose and function of the economic value requirement.

THE EVOLUTION OF TRADE SECRET LAW AND WHY COURTS COMMIT ERROR WHEN THEY DO NOT FOLLOW THE UNIFORM TRADE SECRETS ACT

Sharon K. Sandeen.
33 Hamline L. Rev. 493, 525–26 (2010).

The economic value requirement of the UTSA was not simply a definitional flourish but was specifically designed to increase the plaintiff's burden of proof in order to ensure that a claim for relief was not provided for illusory information or information of little import. The first draft of the UTSA prepared by the PTC [the ABA Committee that started the project] contained a tangibility requirement that would have required trade secret plaintiffs to prove that their trade secrets had been fixed in some tangible form. The purpose of the tangibility requirement was explained as follows:

> You get into these cases, and the plaintiff tries to get strong relief and disclose as little of what his real secret is as he can; and the idea is that trade secret protection should not be available unless, prior to misappropriation, the plaintiff has provided an evidentiary embodiment of that which he seeks protection for.

After it was pointed out that sometimes the worst way to protect a secret is to write it down (as was the case with the Pentagon Papers that were then in the news), the decision was made to delete the tangibility requirement. Later, when concern was raised that the absence of a tangibility requirement might create rights in inchoate ideas, Professor Dole [the Reporter for the UTSA drafting project] explained: "We did not mean to grant protection to abstract ideas—period. An abstract idea wouldn't have commercial value." In lieu of a tangibility requirement, the UTSA requires proof of commercial value and reasonable efforts to maintain secrecy.

As originally drafted, the economic value requirement used the term "commercial value." Section 1(4) of the version of the UTSA that was adopted by NCCUSL in 1979 reads:

> (i) derives independent actual or potential *commercial value* from not being generally known to, and not being readily ascertainable by proper means by, other persons who can obtain *economic value* from its *commercial use.* . . .

The Review Committee had earlier agreed that "commercial value" was a better concept than "economic value," but both terms were still used. Following the formal adoption of the UTSA in August 1979, NCCUSL's Committee on Style (as is its purpose and practice) reviewed the language of the UTSA for grammatical and style problems. Apparently noting confusion or inartfulness in the use of both the terms "commercial" and "economic," the Style Committee changed the foregoing language to read as follows:

> (i) derives independent economic value, actual or potential, from not being generally known to, and not being readily ascertainable by proper means by, other persons who can obtain *economic value* from its disclosure or use. . . .

Apparently, the Committee on Style viewed the terms "commercial" and "economic" as being synonymous. In light of this drafting history, the economic value requirement can be read to include a requirement that the alleged trade secret information be of value to others due to its actual or potential commercial use.

———

The transcripts of the proceedings at which various drafts of the UTSA were discussed contain very little about the meaning and purpose of the economic value requirement. However, the fact that some form of "value" or "advantage" language was in most of the drafts of the UTSA suggests that it was considered to be an important criterion. In one piece of drafting history from 1972 it was explained: "The competitive advantage factor means that a trade secret must have actual or potential commercial utility." This is consistent with common law and comment b to Section 757 of the *Restatement First of Torts* which lists "the value of the information [to the trade secret owner] and to his competitors" as one of six factors that courts should consider in determining the existence of a trade secret. It is also consistent with the language of the *Restatement (Third) of Unfair Competition*, Section 39, which requires that the information be "sufficiently valuable and secret to afford an actual or potential economic advantage over others."

Food for Thought

With the foregoing drafting history in mind, what do you think the economic value requirement means? What would you argue if you were representing the plaintiff in a trade secret misappropriation case? What would you argue if you were representing the defendant?

D. SPECIAL ISSUE: WHAT ARE IDEA SUBMISSION CASES AND DO THEY DIFFER FROM TRADE SECRET CASES?

While trade secret law was developing through a series of cases brought between competing businesses, another body of cases was developing as a result of claims made by so-called "idea men." *See, e.g., Desny v. Wilder*, 46 Cal.2d 715, 299 P.2d 257 (1956) and *Johnson v. Benjamin Moore & Co.*, 788 A.2d. 906 (N.J. Super. Ct. App. Div. 2002); *see also* Mary LaFrance, *Something Borrowed, Something New: The Changing Role of Novelty in Idea Protection Law*, 34 SETON HALL L. REV. 485 (2009). Often referred to as "idea submission" cases, these cases typically involve an individual who develops an idea that he thinks would be of value to a business, the submission of that idea to a business (usually unsolicited), and the alleged use of the idea by the business without compensation. Often they involve ideas of potential interest to the entertainment industry, such as a concept for a new television show, but they can include any idea that may be of interest to a business, such as ideas for new products like a new mop, ways to improve business processes, or the idea for Facebook.

To the extent an idea was secret before it was disclosed to a prospective user or purchaser, there is a possible overlap between idea submission claims and trade secret claims. If the idea qualifies for trade secret protection, then the idea man is likely to assert a trade secret misappropriation claim if his idea is disclosed or used by another without his consent. If the idea is not a trade secret, then the idea man needs to resort to other legal doctrines, principally contract law, to support any claim against one who is accused of wrongly using or disclosing the idea. This is because, as is discussed in Chapter 10, in many states that have adopted Section 7 of the UTSA, common law tort claims for the wrongful use or disclosure of business information (including ideas) are precluded, leaving only potential claims for breach of an express or implied contract.

The first case that follows is an example of an idea submission case that is brought as a trade secret claim. The *Reeves* case is an idea submission case based upon contract principles.

Reading Guidance
What is the idea that plaintiff disclosed to defendant?

DAKTRONICS, INC. V. MCAFEE
Supreme Court of South Dakota, 1999.
1999 S.D. 113.

* * *

AMUNDSON, JUSTICE.

Miles McAfee and David Baker appeal the trial court's grant of summary judgment in favor of Daktronics for claims relating to development of a baseball pitch speed indicator. We affirm.

FACTS

In March 1988 Baker, a baseball coach at Bacone College in Oklahoma, contacted Daktronics by letter expressing he had an idea which Daktronics would be interested in, but was unable to provide further information without disclosing the idea in its entirety. In April 1988 Baker initiated a meeting with Daktronics, where Baker disclosed an idea of a pitch speed indicator that would display the type and speed of a pitched baseball to spectators at a baseball game. Baker requested Daktronics develop a prototype of such a pitch speed indicator.

Daktronics built a prototype for Baker by interfacing a radar gun with a console and digital display board. All of the materials necessary for the prototype were readily available on the market. The radar gun was purchased by Baker from MPH Industries and the console and display boards were manufactured by Daktronics.

After manufacture of the prototype, Miles McAfee became Baker's partner. Baker and McAfee contacted various major league ballparks for the sale of their product. They advertised the product, in conjunction with Daktronics, at the Major League Baseball Annual Conference in Atlanta, Georgia, and the NCAA Conference in Nashville, Tennessee. Between 1988 and 1992, McAfee and Baker ordered four pitch speed indicators from Daktronics.

In the fall of 1996 Daktronics began manufacturing pitch speed indicators for use in major league ballparks.

Baker and McAfee claim the speed pitch indicators Daktronics sold to major league baseball teams are essentially the same as the idea first discussed with Daktronics in early 1988. Daktronics sued McAfee seeking a declaratory judgment. McAfee counterclaimed, bringing four causes of action: misappropriation of trade secret, unjust enrichment, conversion, and breach of fiduciary duty. The trial court granted summary judgment in favor of Daktronics.

* * *

DECISION

1.   Trade secrets claim.

McAfee and Baker contend the trial court erred in granting summary judgment because genuine issues of material fact exist as to their claim for misappropriation of a trade secret.

* * *

McAfee and Baker bear the burden of establishing the existence of a trade secret. *Weins v. Sporleder.* "Without a proven trade secret, there can be no action for misappropriation, even if defendants' actions were wrongful." * * * McAfee claims that the "trade secret" in this case is displaying for public viewing the speed and type of pitch thrown within a ballpark.

SDCL 37–29–1(4) defines "trade secret" as:

> [I]nformation, including a formula, pattern, compilation, program, device, method, technique or process that:
>
> (i)   Derives independent economic value, actual or potential, from not being generally known to, and not being readily ascertainable by proper means by, other persons who can obtain economic value from its disclosure or use; and
>
> (ii) Is the subject of efforts that are reasonable under the circumstances to maintain its secrecy.

In *Weins,* this Court concluded the existence of a trade secret is a mixed question of law and fact. The legal question is, " 'whether the information in question could constitute a trade secret under the first part of the definition of trade secret' " under SDCL 37–29–1(4). * * *

McAfee and Baker claim a trade secret in the concept of displaying speed and type of pitch thrown for the public to view at a ballpark. However, " 'the commonly accepted definition of a trade secret does not include a marketing concept or new product idea submitted by one party to another.' " * * * Therefore, simply possessing a non-novel idea or concept without more is generally, as a matter of law, insufficient to establish a trade secret. * * *.

Even if McAfee's product passed the legal inquiry of SDCL 37–39–1(4), it fails under the remaining subsections. The first subsection requires there to be economic value that is not readily ascertainable by other means. * * * In *Weins,* we adopted the Seventh Circuit Court of Appeals definition that, " 'this requirement precludes trade secret protection for information

SEC. D

WHAT ARE IDEA SUBMISSION CASES AND DO
THEY DIFFER FROM TRADE SECRET CASES?

171

generally known within an industry even if not to the public at large.'"
* * *

Baker and McAfee argue that the issue of whether information is generally known or readily ascertainable is a question of fact. * * * Ordinarily, this is true. * * * However, a court may determine a question of fact by summary judgment if it appears to involve no genuine issues of material fact and the claim fails as a matter of law. * * *

Baker and McAfee's concept involved combining the use of a radar gun, a console, and a display. It is undisputed that all of these items were readily available on the market. "Combining these materials cannot be considered a trade secret if the formula was 'within the realm of general skills and knowledge' in the relevant industry." *Weins.* "Thus, the focus turns to the 'ease with which information can be developed through other proper means: if the information can be readily duplicated without involving considerable time, effort or expense, then it is not secret.'" *Weins.*

There is nothing novel about combining these materials to display speeds and types of pitches thrown for the public's view. It is undisputed Daktronics had itself utilized a speed indicator with a display in sporting events such as ski jumping prior to 1988. Further, prior to 1988, the Jugs corporation had developed and been using such a speed pitch indicator to display the speed of a pitched baseball in amusement arcades. The product in which McAfee and Baker claim a trade secret was within the general knowledge of the relevant industry, and, in fact, already existed, albeit for different use.

In addition, this Court notes that Daktronics is not alone in designing speed pitch displays for major league baseball stadiums. As of the time of the motion for summary judgment, the speed of pitches were displayed at Houston's Astrodome, the Veterans Stadium in Philadelphia, Pittsburgh's Three River Stadium, San Francisco's Candlestick Park and the Skydome in Toronto. Competitors of Daktronics had designed the display systems for each of these ballparks.

Considering the above, clearly the concept in which McAfee and Baker claim to possess a trade secret contains ingredients that were all in the public realm, could be easily duplicated and, in fact, were already in existence. * * *

The trial court found, based on the submissions in resistance to the motion for summary judgment, that Baker and McAfee failed to carry their burden to establish a trade secret.

* * *

3.   Conversion.

Baker and McAfee also allege that the information imparted by them to Daktronics was proprietary in nature and was converted by Daktronics. "Conversion is the act of exercising control or dominion over personal property in a manner that repudiates the owner's right in the property or in a manner that is inconsistent with such right." * * * Baker and McAfee appear to argue that Daktronics converted their idea or concept of displaying the speed and type of pitch thrown to the public view.

The trial court concluded the claim of conversion failed because it depends on a wrongful interference with a property interest. We agree. McAfee and Baker have failed to show a property interest. Ideas which are not novel and "are in the public domain may freely be used by anyone with impunity." *Murray v. National Broad. Co., Inc.* Since there was no property interest, there could be no conversion.

We have considered the other issue raised by appellants, and conclude that it is without merit.

Affirmed.

DID YOU GET IT?

1.   What is the relationship between the plaintiff and the defendant?

2.   Why did plaintiff's trade secret claim fail?

3.   Can you articulate a difference between a trade secret and an idea?

4.   Why didn't plaintiff bring a breach of contract claim?

Food for Thought

Should an idea be protectable if it does not meet the requirements for trade secret protection? If so, under what circumstances? Should any limits be placed on the protection of mere ideas?

SEC. D

WHAT ARE IDEA SUBMISSION CASES AND DO
THEY DIFFER FROM TRADE SECRET CASES?

173

Reading Guidance

What does a plaintiff in a non-trade-secret idea submission case have to prove that is different from what it would have to prove in a trade secret case?

REEVES V. ALYESKA PIPELINE SERVICE CO.

Supreme Court of Alaska, 1996.
926 P.2d 1130.

* * *

PER CURIAM.

I. INTRODUCTION

This case raises issues concerning the protection of ideas. * * *

II. FACTS AND PROCEEDINGS

In 1985 Alyeska created a visitor turnout at Mile 9 of the Steese Highway between Fox and Fairbanks. The turnout had informational signs and provided visitors a view of the Trans-Alaska Pipeline. Before Alyeska constructed the turnout, visitors gained access to the pipeline by a nearby road and trespassed on the Trans-Alaska Pipeline right-of-way.

John Reeves, owner of Gold Dredge No. 8, a tourist attraction outside Fairbanks and near the turnout, contacted Alyeska in January 1991 to discuss a tourism idea he had. He spoke with Keith Burke, Alyeska's Fairbanks Manager. After receiving Burke's assurance that the tourism idea was "between us," Reeves orally disclosed his idea to build a visitor center at the turnout. He proposed that Alyeska lease him the land and he build the center, sell Alyeska merchandise, and display a "pig"[2] and a cross-section of pipe.

Burke told him the idea "look[ed] good" and asked Reeves to submit a written proposal, which Reeves did two days later. The proposal explained Reeves' idea of operating a visitor center on land leased to him by Alyeska. The proposal included plans to provide small tours, display a "pig," pipe valve, and section of pipe, sell refreshments and pipeline memorabilia, and plant corn and cabbage.

After submitting the proposal, Reeves met with Burke once again. At this meeting Burke told Reeves the proposal looked good and was exactly what he wanted. In Reeves' words, Burke told him, "We're going to do this deal, and I'm going to have my Anchorage lawyers draw it." Reeves claimed he and Burke envisioned that the visitor center would be operating by the 1991 summer tourist season.

---

[2] A "pig" is a device which passes through the pipeline to clean interior pipe walls, survey interior pipe shape and detect corrosion.

Reeves alleges that Alyeska agreed during this meeting (1) to grant access to the turnout for twenty years; (2) to allow Reeves to construct and operate an information center; and (3) to allow Reeves to sell merchandise and charge a $2.00 admission fee. Reeves stated that, in exchange, he agreed to pay Alyeska ten percent of gross receipts.

Over the next several months, Burke allegedly told Reeves that the deal was "looking good" and not to worry because it takes time for a large corporation to move. However, in spring 1991, Burke told Reeves that the visitor center was such a good idea that Alyeska was going to implement it without Reeves. By August 1991 Alyeska had installed a portable building at the turnout to serve as a visitor center; it built a permanent log cabin structure in 1992.

The members of the Alyeska Pipeline Club North (APCN) operated the visitor center and sold T-shirts, hats, and other items. APCN does not charge admission. A section of pipeline and a "pig" are on display. APCN employees provide information and answer visitors' questions. Members of APCN had suggested in 1987 that Alyeska create a visitor center at the turnout. However, Alyeska had rejected the idea at that time. Before meeting with Reeves, Burke did not know that APCN's visitor center idea had been raised and rejected by Alyeska in 1987.

Approximately 100,000 people visited the visitor center each summer in 1992 and 1993. It grossed over $50,000 in sales each year. The net profit for 1993 was calculated to be $5,000–$15,000. APCN received all the profit.

* * *

III. DISCUSSION

* * *

Reeves sued Alyeska on claims of breach of oral contract, promissory estoppel, breach of implied contract, quasi-contract (unjust enrichment and quantum meruit), breach of the covenant of good faith and fair dealing, breach of license and/or lease agreement, and various torts related to the contractual relationships alleged.

This case presents several questions of first impression concerning the protection of business ideas. * * *

A.   *Protection of Ideas*

The law pertaining to the protection of ideas must reconcile the public's interest in access to new ideas with the perceived injustice of permitting some to exploit commercially the ideas of others. Federal law addresses the protection of new inventions and the expression of ideas. Federal patent law protects inventors of novel, nonobvious, and useful inventions by excluding others from "making, using, or selling the invention" for a period of seventeen years. Federal copyright law protects an individual's tangible *expression* of an idea, but not the intangible idea itself. Copyright law creates a monopoly for the author that allows him or her to benefit economically from the author's creative efforts. It does not create a monopoly on the idea from which the expression originates; the idea remains available for all to use. Reeves' claims do not fall under these federal protections because his idea is not a new invention, nor is it expressed in a copyrighted work. Nevertheless, federal law is not the only protection available to individuals and their ideas.

Creating a middle ground between no protection and the legal monopolies created by patent and copyright law, courts have protected ideas under a variety of contract and contract-like theories. These theories protect individuals who spend their time and energy developing ideas that may benefit others. It would be inequitable to prevent these individuals from obtaining legally enforceable compensation from those who voluntarily choose to benefit from the services of the "idea-person." * * *

We have not had occasion to address these theories in the context of the protection of ideas. In addressing each of Reeves' claims we must determine whether the special nature of ideas affects the application of traditional contract and contract-like claims. In making these determinations we are mindful of the competing policies of retaining the free exchange of ideas and compensating those who develop and market their ideas. On the one hand, protecting ideas by providing compensation to the author for their use or appropriation rewards the idea person and encourages the development of creative and intellectual ideas which will benefit humankind. On the other hand, protecting ideas also inevitably restricts their free use, potentially delaying or restricting the benefit any given idea might confer on society. * * *

Reeves argues that requiring novelty and originality, as did the trial court, erroneously imports property theories into contract-based claims. He contends that so long as the parties bargained for the disclosure of the idea, the disclosure serves as consideration and the idea itself need not have the qualities of property. Alyeska argues that novelty and originality should be employed as limiting factors in idea cases because these cases are based on a theory of idea as intellectual property. Alyeska contends that in order to be protected, an idea must have "not been suggested to or known by the public at any prior time."

We find that the manner in which requirements such as novelty or originality are applied depends largely on which theory of recovery is pursued. Thus, we will address the parties' arguments concerning novelty as they apply to each of Reeves' theories of recovery.

B. *Express Contract Claims*

Reeves argues that he and Alyeska entered into three different oral contracts: (1) a confidentiality or disclosure agreement by which Alyeska promised not to use Reeves' idea without his participation, if Reeves disclosed the idea; (2) a lease agreement by which Alyeska promised to lease the turnout to Reeves in exchange for a percentage of the center's profits; and (3) a memorialization agreement by which Alyeska promised to commit the agreement to writing.

* * *

1.   *The Disclosure Agreement*

Reeves alleges that in exchange for the disclosure of his idea, Alyeska promised to keep the idea confidential and not to use the idea without entering into a contract with Reeves to implement the idea. Reeves' deposition testimony, when all inferences are taken in his favor, supports the existence of a disclosure agreement. Reeves testified that in his early conversations with Burke, he told Burke that he was in the tourism industry and had an idea that would help Alyeska. Reeves stated that Burke told him the idea "was between us." Reeves testified that he "didn't offer anything to Keith Burke until [Reeves] was told by [Burke] that we had a deal. This was between me and him, and this was going no place else." Reeves also testified that Burke had promised confidentiality and that Reeves believed that he and Burke had a "done deal."

Alyeska does not respond separately to Reeves' disclosure agreement claim. It instead argues that, notwithstanding Reeves' assertion there were three agreements, Reeves actually alleged only one contract, which included a purported twenty-year lease agreement. It argues that the statute of frauds applies because the alleged agreement concerns a lease for a period longer than one year and because performance would not be completed within one year.

We conclude that the statute of frauds does not apply to the alleged disclosure agreement. That alleged agreement was to be completed within one year. If Alyeska chose to implement the idea, it was to enter into a lease agreement with Reeves by the summer tourist season. * * *

[The court's discussion of the alleged Lease Agreement and the Memorialization Agreement is deleted. The court held that there was no Lease Agreement because, pursuant to Alaska's Statute of Frauds, agreements involving real estate had to be in writing. With respect to the alleged Memorialization Agreement, the court held that "an oral promise to execute a written contract, where a written contract is necessary to satisfy the statute of frauds, must itself satisfy the statute of frauds."]

C.   *Implied-in-Fact Contract*

The trial court's opinion did not address whether Reeves established a contract implied-in-fact. Reeves argues that he "submitted uncontroverted evidence sufficient to find as a matter of law that Alyeska's actions established a contract implied in fact." We conclude that Alyeska failed to carry its burden of showing that it is entitled to judgment as a matter of law on this claim.

Reeves has made out a prima facie case for an implied contract. We have held that an implied-in-fact contract, like an express contract, is based on the intentions of the parties. "It arises where the court finds from the surrounding facts and circumstances that the parties intended to make a contract but failed to articulate their promises and the court merely implies what it feels the parties really intended." * * *

There are three primary factual scenarios under which ideas may be submitted to another. The first involves an unsolicited submission that is involuntarily received. The idea is submitted without warning; it is transmitted before the recipient has taken any action which would indicate a promise to pay for the submission. Under this scenario, a contract will not be implied.

The second involves an unsolicited submission that is voluntarily received. In this situation, the idea person typically gives the recipient advance warning that an idea is to be disclosed; the recipient has an opportunity to stop the disclosure, but through inaction allows the idea to be disclosed. * * * Under California law, if the recipient at the time of disclosure understands that the idea person expects to be paid for the disclosure of the idea, and does not attempt to stop the disclosure, inaction may be seen as consent to a contract.

This view has been criticized as unfairly placing a duty on the recipient to take active measures to stop the submission. The critics argue that inaction generally should not be considered an expression of consent to a contract.

We believe that a contract should not be implied under this scenario. An implied-in-fact contract is based on circumstances that demonstrate that the parties intended to form a contract but failed to articulate their promises. Only under exceptional circumstances would inaction demonstrate an intent to enter a contract.

The third scenario involves a solicited submission. Here, a request by the recipient for disclosure of the idea usually implies a promise to pay for the idea if the recipient uses it. * * *

Reeves argues that Alyeska solicited his idea. He alleges that Burke asked him what the idea was, and later requested a written proposal. He contends that the request and Alyeska's later use of the idea created an implied contract for payment. These allegations are sufficient to survive summary judgment. A reasonable fact-finder could determine that Burke's actions implied a promise to pay for the disclosure of Reeves' idea. A fact-finder could also determine that Reeves volunteered the idea before Burke took any affirmative action that would indicate an agreement to pay for the disclosure. These possible conclusions present genuine issues of material fact.

Relying largely on cases from New York, Alyeska argues that novelty and originality should be required in an implied-in-fact claim. Reeves responds that we should follow California's example and not require novelty as an essential element of this sort of claim.

Idea-based claims arise most frequently in the entertainment centers of New York and California, but New York requires novelty, whereas California does not. *Compare Murray v. National Broadcasting Co.*, with *Donahue.*

We prefer the California approach. An idea may be valuable to the recipient merely because of its timing or the manner in which it is presented. In *Chandler v. Roach*, the court stated that "the fact that the [recipient of the idea] may later determine, with a little thinking, that he could have had the same ideas and could thereby have saved considerable money for himself, is no defense against the claim of the [idea person]. This is so even though the material to be purchased is abstract and unprotected material." *Id.*

Implied-in-fact contracts are closely related to express contracts. Each requires the parties to form an intent to enter into a contract. It is ordinarily not the court's role to evaluate the adequacy of the consideration agreed upon by the parties. The bargain should be left in the hands of the parties. If parties voluntarily choose to bargain for an individual's services in disclosing or developing a non-novel or unoriginal idea, they have the power to do so. The *Desny* court analogized the services of a writer to the services of a doctor or lawyer and determined there was little difference; each may provide a product that is not novel or original. It held that it would not impose an additional requirement of novelty on the work. Although Reeves is not a writer, his ideas are entitled to no less protection than those of writers, doctors, or lawyers. Therefore, Reeves should be given the opportunity to prove the existence of an implied-in-fact contract for disclosure of his idea.

* * *

E.   *Quasi-Contract Claim*

Reeves argues that Alyeska was unjustly enriched because it solicited and received Reeves' services, ideas, and opinions without compensating Reeves. He argues that the trial court erred in granting summary judgment to Alyeska on his quasi-contract cause of action.

We have required the following three elements for a quasi-contract claim:

  1)   a benefit conferred upon the defendant by the plaintiff;

  2)   appreciation by the defendant of such benefit; and

3)   acceptance and retention by the defendant of such benefit under such circumstances that it would be inequitable for him to retain it without paying the value thereof.

Quasi-contracts are "judicially-created obligations to do justice." "Consequently, the obligation to make restitution that arises in quasi-contract is not based upon any agreement between the parties, objective or subjective." * * *

The trial court understood Reeves to be arguing that his idea was a property right that was stolen by Alyeska. Reeves, however, argues that "Alyeska took Reeves' concept, proposal *and services* without any payment to Reeves." (Emphasis added.) Reeves' quasi-contract claims must be divided into two categories. His claim that Alyeska appropriated his idea for a visitor center is necessarily a property-based claim that seeks recovery for the value of the idea itself; Reeves seeks a recovery based on "his" idea. His claims that Alyeska benefitted from his proposal and services, however, do not necessarily rely on the visitor center idea being property; these claims are based on his services of disclosing and drafting the proposal. The property and non-property claims are treated differently.

An idea is usually not regarded as property because our concept of property implies something that can be owned and possessed to the exclusion of others. To protect an idea under a property theory requires that the idea possess property-like traits. Courts consider the elements of novelty or originality necessary for a claim of "ownership" in an idea or concept. These elements distinguish protectable ideas from ordinary ideas that are freely available for others to use. It is the element of originality or novelty that lends value to the idea itself.

If the idea is not distinguished in this manner, its use cannot satisfy the requirements of a quasi-contract claim. The idea, even if beneficial to the defendant, cannot be conferred if the plaintiff has no right of possession. With no right of possession, the idea cannot be said to have been conferred by the plaintiff. Despite Reeves' protestations, the idea of establishing a visitor center near the pipeline is neither original nor novel.

Nevertheless, not all of Reeves' quasi-contract claims require that his idea be considered property and consequently novel or original. Reeves argues that Alyeska was unjustly enriched "by Reeves' efforts on its behalf, not merely on the 'concept that [Reeves'] idea was intellectual property.'" Therefore, we must analyze whether the parties' transactions give rise to a quasi-contract.

The facts alleged by Reeves demonstrate that Burke specifically asked Reeves to draw up a proposal and that Alyeska was going to "do this deal." There is also evidence Reeves was familiar with the Fairbanks summer tourist industry and had special expertise in that area. These facts present a genuine issue of fact as to whether Alyeska benefited from Reeves' experience or his written plan. Thus, there is a question of fact whether Reeves' idea had value to Alyeska in its timing or in how it was presented, rather than in its novelty or originality. Reeves' endorsement of the idea, in combination with his experience in the Fairbanks tourism industry, may have also been valuable to Alyeska. The fact that Alyeska rejected a similar idea in 1987 may indicate that some feature of Reeves' plan or presentation caused Alyeska to go forward with a visitor center. If Reeves' services unjustly enriched Alyeska, he should be compensated for the value of those services.

* * *

IV. *CONCLUSION*

For the reasons stated above, we REVERSE that part of the summary judgment entered for Alyeska on Reeves' express contract, implied contract, promissory estoppel, quasi-contract, breach of implied covenant of good faith and fair dealing, and related tort claims based on the alleged disclosure agreement, and REMAND to the trial court for further proceedings consistent with this opinion. We AFFIRM the summary judgment entered for Alyeska on the remainder of Reeves' claims, including those based on the alleged lease and memorialization agreements. * * *

DID YOU GET IT?

1. What are the claimed ideas and who owns them?

2. What is the relationship between the plaintiff and the defendants?

3. What are the nature and required elements of plaintiff's claims?

4. Does the court recognize any limits on the types of information that can be protected by an express contract, an implied-in-fact contract, or an implied-at law (quasi)-contract?

———

As the *Daktronics* case suggests, given the right set of facts, it is possible that the plaintiff in an idea submission case will have a trade secret misappropriation claim. Roger Milgrim and Eric Bensen argue in their treatise that the likelihood of such overlap was increased in UTSA jurisdictions when the use requirement of the *Restatement of Torts,* Section 757, was eliminated. MILGRIM ON TRADE SECRETS, § 9.05[4] (2016). Comment h to Section 39 of the *Restatement (Third) of Unfair Competition* explains:

> With the rejection under the Uniform Trade Secrets Act and under this section of any requirement of use by the owner of a trade secret, * * * there is no longer a formal distinction between trade secrets and the ideas that form the subject matter of the submission cases. The developing rules governing the rights of

submitters and recipients of ideas in the absence of an express or implied-in-fact contract can thus be understood as specific applications of the general rules stated here. The rules in this Restatement relating to the protection of trade secrets are therefore applicable, either directly or by analogy, to claims in tort alleging the appropriation of ideas.

But consider how the requirements of the UTSA and DTSA, particularly the independent economic value requirement, might operate to limit the types of ideas that could serve as the basis for a trade secret claim.

As the *Reeves* case demonstrates, idea submission cases are not necessarily dependent on the existence of a trade secret or even a novel idea. If the plaintiff in an idea submission case can prove the existence of an express, implied-in-fact, or quasi-contract, some courts are willing to provide recovery for ideas that would not qualify for trade secret protection. Contractual claims based upon an express or implied-in-fact contract are not precluded by the enactment of the UTSA (*see* Chapter 9). However, there is ongoing debate about the types of information that can be protected by contract.

In many idea submission cases, the courts resort to language of concreteness or novelty in an attempt to distinguish between information that can be the subject of a successful idea submission claim and that which cannot. In so doing, they recognize that even outside the context of trade secret litigation there should be limits on the type of information that can be protected under the law. What those limits are and how to articulate and apply them is an unsettled aspect of what has fairly recently been labeled "information law." As Raymond Nimmer explains in his book, *Information Law:*

> [A]n inevitable effect of the digital transformation of society consists of increasingly sharp conflicts between competing perspectives on information and its exchange. One perspective emphasizes proprietary control and commercial potential, whereas the other emphasizes free use and equal access as a fundamental social value.

See Raymond Nimmer, INFORMATION LAW, § 1.4 (2016).

Idea submission claims that are based upon the existence of an "implied-at-law" or "quasi-contract" are another story. Arguably, claims based upon ideas that are disclosed under a quasi-contract are precluded by section 7 of the UTSA unless they can be brought as trade secret claims. (*See* discussion of Section 7 of the UTSA in Chapter 9.) Additionally, when idea submission claims are brought as trade secret misappropriation claims they are usually of the breach of confidentiality variety. (*See* Chapter 7.) In such cases, it is not enough for the plaintiff to prove the existence of a duty of confidentiality. As *Daktronics* demonstrates, the plaintiff must also prove that the subject information was a trade secret at the time of disclosure.

> ### *Food for Thought*
> *On what side of the information protection debate do you fall? Do you think there should be limits on the type of information that can be protected by contract? If so, how would you draw the line between protectable ideas and information and non-protectable ideas and information? Should the rules you suggest be waivable or non-waivable?*

NOTES

1. **The value requirement of the Defend Trade Secrets Act.** The DTSA includes a value requirement in its definition of a trade secret. Consistent with the UTSA, the DTSA language reads: "independent economic value, actual or potential, from not being generally known to, and not being readily ascertainable through proper means by, another person who can obtain economic value from the disclosure or use of the information." 18 U.S.C. § 1839(3)(B), reprinted in Appendix A. How this provision will be interpreted by the federal courts remains to be seen.

2. **The value requirement of the EU Trade Secret Directive.** The EU Trade Secret Directive also includes a value requirement in its definition of a trade secret, but it is worded differently from the DTSA. The EU Directive requires "commercial value because it is secret," which is consistent with the language or Article 39 of the TRIPS Agreement. *See Directive (EU) 2016/943 of the European Parliament and of the Council of 8 June 2016 for the protection of undisclosed know-how and business information (trade secrets) against their unlawful acquisition, use and disclosure*, Article 2(1)(b). *See* Appendix B.

3. **The novelty requirement in idea submission cases.** As noted above, some courts resort to the concept of novelty to differentiate between protectable and unprotectable ideas, particularly when they are uncomfortable about the plaintiff's claims. *See Murray v. National Broad. Co., Inc.*, 844 F.2d 988 (2d Cir. 1988). However, the novelty that they refer to is not the stringent type of novelty that is required for patent protection. Professor Lionel S. Sobel explained:

> The role that novelty plays in determining whether the defendant actually used the plaintiff's idea—rather than another idea—was explained by the New York Court of Appeals in *Apfel v. Prudential-Bache Securities*. . . . The court explained that in each case where novelty is required, the contract was made before the idea was disclosed and "no separate post-disclosure contract for use of the idea [was] made." Thus, those cases "present[ed] the issue of whether the idea the buyer was using was, in fact, the seller's." The court observed that "there is no equity in enforcing a seemingly valid contract when, in fact, it turns out upon disclosure that the buyer already possessed

> the idea. In such instances, the disclosure, though freely bargained
> for, is manifestly without value." Where a post-disclosure agreement
> is entered into, there is no question that the idea had value to the
> recipient, and thus novelty is not required."

Lionel S. Sobel, *The Law of Ideas, Revisited*, 1 UCLA ENT. L. REV. 9, 62–63
(1994). Thus, the novelty requirement of idea submission law (where it is
applied) is conceptually similar to the generally known and economic value
provisions of the UTSA. Ideas that are generally known cannot serve as the
basis of a pre-disclosure contract claim because the public availability of the
ideas means they are of no actual value to the buyer. In other words, the
alleged contract fails for want of adequate consideration. As the court in *Reeves*
notes, however, there can be value in knowing information sooner rather than
later.

    4.   **Staleness.** As suggested in *Taylor v. Babbitt*, the concept of staleness
has also been used by some courts to limit the protection that is afforded to
information. The basic idea is that although information may have had
economic value at one time, the value of the information was subsequently lost.
Taylor v. Babbitt, 760 F.Supp.2d 80, 88 (D.D.C. 2011) ("[I]nformation that
provides its owner an advantage over its competitors is commercially valuable.
On the other hand, obsolete information that provides no competitive
advantage is not commercially valuable and cannot constitute a trade secret.")
See also Fox Sports Net N., L.L.C. v. Minnesota Twins P'ship, 319 F.3d 329 (8th
Cir. 2003) ("[O]bsolete information cannot form the basis for a trade secret
claim because the information has no economic value.")

    5.   **More on the use of legislative history to interpret statutes.** The
use of legislative history to interpret a statute is not without its critics. A major
critique of the process is that the record of correspondence and debates
concerning a statute can, at best, only reveal what the individuals who were
engaged in the correspondence and debates actually believed or understood; it
cannot explain what every legislator who voted for the legislation intended.
The range of views on the relevance of legislative history is best exemplified by
the writings of Judge Guido Calabresi and Justice Antonin Scalia.

    Judge Calabresi has expressed the view that without looking to the
legislative history of a law, its meaning is often difficult if not impossible to
discern: "[T]here are often differing interpretations that can be given a law,
since vagueness in certain crucial statutory terms will frequently be a
prerequisite for gaining approval from all the groups that could block
enactment." Guido Calabresi, A COMMON LAW FOR THE AGE OF STATUTES, 31–
43 (1982). Justice Scalia, on the other hand, objected to the use of legislative
history, asserting that the intent of the legislature is not "the proper criterion
of the law." He further argued:

> [The use of legislative history] does not even make sense for those
> who *accept* legislative intent as the criterion. It is much more likely
> to produce a false or contrived legislative intent than a genuine one.
> The first and most obvious reason for this is that, with respect to

99.99 percent of the issues of construction reaching the courts, there *is* no legislative intent, so that any clues provided by the legislative history are bound to be false.

Antonin Scalia, A MATTER OF INTERPRETATION: FEDERAL COURTS AND THE LAW, 31–31 (1997).

One need not take sides in the foregoing debate to observe that legislative history is often used by attorneys and judges to explain or understand the meaning and purpose of statutes. Indeed, reported case decisions frequently provide detailed explanations of the history, context, meaning, and intended purpose of statutes. However, it is also true that there are different types of materials that comprise the legislative history of a statute, with some being more helpful for an understanding of a statute than others.

Sometimes legislatures will debate and enact intent language or, as in the case of the UTSA, interpretative commentaries, for example, the "Sense of Congress" provisions of the DTSA. Although not codified law, these materials are likely to reflect the views of most (if not all) of the individuals who supported the legislation because they are typically reviewed or debated at the same time as the subject legislation. Similarly, materials that document a give-and-take between numerous legislators on an issue that resulted in amendments to draft legislation are more valuable for an understanding of the meaning of a statute than one legislator's statement of what he intended.

In the final analysis, it is up to each judge who handles a case involving a statute or regulation to interpret its meaning and intent. The information the judge relies upon will depend on the rules of statutory and regulatory interpretation that apply in the subject jurisdiction and what information the judge believes is relevant. As a practical matter, it also depends upon what arguments and research are provided by counsel. If legislative history might help your client to win its case, you should present it.

6. **The desire for predictability.** Information concerning the historical context in which legislation was enacted, including an understanding of the problem that was sought to be solved, can be extremely valuable for an understanding of a statute. At the time the UTSA was adopted in 1979, trade secret law had developed sufficiently that it could be "restated" by the American Law Institute in the *Restatement (First) of Torts*. It is important, therefore, to consider the factors that motivated the adoption of the UTSA. Why, if trade secret law had been included in the *Restatement (First) of Torts* for more than forty years, did the drafters of the UTSA feel compelled to draft a new "uniform" law?

One answer lies in the practical differences between standards and rules, and the value that the business community perceives in the predictability of law. Although it is common to think of the adoption of statutes as creating new rights and responsibilities, it is often the case that statutes (including uniform laws) are enacted to "fix" or alter laws that already exist. The Uniform Commercial Code is an obvious example of this approach. Well-developed principles of contract and commercial law existed before the adoption of the Uniform Commercial Code, but in order to streamline commercial practice and reduce transactions costs, it was felt that various default rules should be adopted.

Sometimes the common law development of legal principles is too slow or inconsistent to serve as a suitable basis for predicting the outcome of a case. When businesses know what their rights and obligations are, they can plan accordingly. It is the unexpected obligation that is likely to cut into their bottom-line. Thus, if given a choice between a clear but demanding legal obligation and an uncertain but less demanding legal obligation, businesses often prefer the former. This is one of the stories behind the UTSA. The business community was not happy with the slow and inconsistent development of trade secret law and decided that a uniform law was needed to replace the common law of trade secrecy.

7.   **Bibliographic note:** In addition to the references noted above, for more information on the topics discussed in this chapter, *see* MILGRIM ON TRADE SECRETS §§ 1.02, 9.05 (2016); Robert C. Denicola, *The New Law of Ideas*, 28 HARV. J. LAW & TECH. 195 (2014); Eric R. Claeys, *The Use Requirement at Common Law and Under the Uniform Trade Secrets Act*, 33 HAMLINE L. REV. 583 (2010); Shyamkrishna Balganesh, *The Pragmatic Incrementalism of Common Law Intellectual Property*, 63 VAND. L. REV. 1543 (2010); Arthur R. Miller, *Common Law Protection for Products of the Mind: An "Idea" Whose Time Has Come*, 119 HARV. L. REV. 703 (2006); Adrian Vermeule, *The Cycles of Statutory Interpretation*, 68 U. CHI. L. REV. 149 (2001); William N. Eskeridge, Jr., Philip P. Frickey & Elizabeth Garrett, LEGISLATION AND STATUTORY INTERPRETATION (2d ed. Foundation Press 2006); Robert Unikel, *Bridging the Trade Secret Gap: Protecting Confidential Information Not Rising to the Level of Trade Secrets*, 29 LOY. U. CHI. L. J. 841 (1998); and Ronald Caswell, *A Comparison and Critique of Idea Protection in California, New York, and Great Britain*, 14 LOY. L.A. INT'L & COMP. L.J. 717 (1992).

CHAPTER 5

REASONABLE EFFORTS TO MAINTAIN SECRECY

■ ■ ■

Anticipated Learning Outcomes

At the conclusion of this chapter, you will have a deeper understanding of the reasonable efforts requirement that is at the heart of trade secret protection. You will be introduced to the concept of relative secrecy and the factors that courts consider in assessing the reasonableness of a putative trade secret owner's security measures.

A. INTRODUCTION

The reasonable efforts requirement is probably the most important factor in determining whether an information holder owns a protectable trade secret. Whether a state follows the *Restatement of Torts*, the *Restatement (Third) of Unfair Competition*,[1] or the UTSA, the reasonable efforts requirement is a critical part of the analysis in every trade secret case. As discussed in greater detail in Chapter 11, in order to satisfy the requirement, trade secret owners must carefully assess risks, both internal and external. Although the requirement is stated a bit differently in the UTSA (and DTSA) versus the *Restatements,* generally the putative trade secret owner must establish that it undertook affirmative steps to protect its trade secret information, and not just express an intent to protect such information. The number and nature of the steps taken is the key.

Both the UTSA and DTSA include reasonable efforts as part of the definition of a trade secret. They require that in order to qualify for trade secret protection the information must be "the subject of efforts that are reasonable under the circumstances to maintain its secrecy." The comments to the *Restatement of Torts* include consideration of the measures taken to guard the secrecy of information as one of six factors to be considered in determining whether information qualifies as a trade secret. In determining whether a defendant's acquisition of a trade secret was improper, the commentary to the *Restatement (Third) of Unfair*

---

[1] The *Restatement (Third) of Unfair Competition* does not include a reasonable efforts requirement in its definition of a trade secret, but the commentary to the definition section (section 39) states that: "Precautions taken to maintain the secrecy of information are relevant in determining whether the information qualifies for protection as a trade secret."

Competition calls for an evaluation of whether sufficient precautions were taken, and if the trade secret owner's failure to take reasonable precautions facilitated the misappropriation of the trade secret.

Reasonableness is a relative term that depends on the particular circumstances. As stated in *Kewanee* and other cases, trade secrets are lost if they are shared with others outside of a confidential relationship. (This has been referred to by Professor Sandeen as the third-party doctrine of trade secrecy, which is conceptually similar to the similar doctrine under Fourth Amendment jurisprudence.) However, because trade secret owners often need to share their trade secrets with others (such as employees and vendors) to derive any benefit therefrom, the standard of secrecy under trade secret law is one of relative secrecy not absolute secrecy. Thus, what may be reasonable to protect a secret in one business environment or relationship may not be reasonable in another. Accordingly, whether the measures taken by a trade secret owner are sufficient to satisfy the reasonableness standard is usually a question of fact for the jury.

Efforts to protect the secrecy of information are also related to the economic value requirement of trade secret law, which you learned about in Chapter 4. Indeed, whether or not a company took adequate steps to protect a secret is often used as evidence of the information holder's subjective belief that the information was a trade secret and thus worthy of legal protection. Furthermore, as a policy matter, we expect trade secret owners will make sufficient efforts to protect that which is valuable to their businesses. When a business fails to take the initiative and expend the resources required for the protection of its information, the civil justice system should not use its power to bar others from using the information. As one court noted:

> [I]f the person entitled to a trade secret wishes to have its exclusive use in his own business, he must not fail to take all proper and reasonable steps to keep it secret. He cannot lie back and do nothing to preserve its essential secret quality, particularly when the subject matter of the process becomes known to a number of individuals involved in its use or is observed in the course of manufacture within plain view of others. "(O)ne may not venture on liberties with his own secret, may not lightly or voluntarily hazard its leakage or escape, and at the same time hold others to be completely obligated to observe it."

J. T. Healy & Son, Inc. v. James A. Murphy & Son, Inc., 260 N.E.2d 723, 731 (Mass. 1970).

The foregoing principle, among others, is expressed by Judge Posner in the case that follows, *Rockwell Graphic Systems v. Dev Industries, Inc.*, and in a host of other state cases, as represented by *Dicks v. Jensen*. This chapter also presents cases involving considerations of reasonableness within various confidential relationships (both between employers and employees, and business-to-business). The chapter concludes with an examination of reasonableness in a digital world and in "the Cloud."

> ### Food for Thought
> *If you owned a business that possessed valuable trade secrets, what efforts would you engage in to maintain the secrecy of your valuable information? How would you decide if the security measures you undertake are enough?*

B. APPLYING THE REASONABLE EFFORTS REQUIREMENT

> ### Reading Guidance
> *What is Judge Posner's view of reasonableness in this case?*

[handwritten: — need more evidence, cannot decide an S.J. here]

ROCKWELL GRAPHIC SYSTEMS v. DEV INDUSTRIES, INC.

[handwritten: — π]

United States Court of Appeals, Seventh Circuit, 1991.
925 F.2d 174.

[handwritten: — reverses S.J. grant — genuine issue of material fact re whether efforts were reasonable "reasonable"]

POSNER, CIRCUIT JUDGE.

This is a suit for misappropriation of trade secrets. Rockwell Graphic Systems, a manufacturer of printing presses used by newspapers, and of parts for those presses, brought the suit against DEV Industries, a competing manufacturer, and against the president of DEV, who used to be employed by Rockwell. * * *

When we said that Rockwell manufactures both printing presses and replacement parts for its presses—"wear parts" or "piece parts," they are called—we were speaking approximately. Rockwell does not always manufacture the parts itself. Sometimes when an owner of one of Rockwell's presses needs a particular part, or when Rockwell anticipates demand for the part, it will subcontract the manufacture of it to an independent machine shop, called a "vendor" by the parties. When it does this it must give the vendor a "piece part drawing" indicating materials, dimensions, tolerances, and methods of manufacture. Without that information the vendor could not manufacture the part. Rockwell has not tried to patent the piece parts. It believes that the purchaser cannot, either by inspection or by "reverse engineering" (taking something apart in an effort to figure out how it was made), discover how to manufacture the part; to do that you need the piece part drawing, which contains much information concerning methods of manufacture, alloys, tolerances, etc. that cannot be gleaned from the part itself. So Rockwell tries—whether hard enough is the central issue in the case—to keep the piece part drawings secret, though not of course from the vendors; they could not

[handwritten right margin: gave to vendor?]

[handwritten bottom: — physical security — contractual security]

[handwritten bottom: issue — could've done a little more, but debatable]

manufacture the parts for Rockwell without the drawings. DEV points out that some of the parts are for presses that Rockwell no longer manufactures. But as long as the presses are in service—which can be a very long time—there is a demand for replacement parts.

Rockwell employed Fleck and Peloso in responsible positions that gave them access to piece part drawings. Fleck left Rockwell in 1975 and three years later joined DEV as its president. Peloso joined DEV the following year after being fired by Rockwell when a security guard caught him removing piece part drawings from Rockwell's plant. This suit was brought in 1984, and pretrial discovery by Rockwell turned up 600 piece part drawings in DEV's possession, of which 100 were Rockwell's. DEV claimed to have obtained them lawfully, either from customers of Rockwell or from Rockwell vendors, contrary to Rockwell's claim that either Fleck and Peloso stole them when they were employed by it or DEV obtained them in some other unlawful manner, perhaps from a vendor who violated his confidentiality agreement with Rockwell. Thus far in the litigation DEV has not been able to show which customers or vendors lawfully supplied it with Rockwell's piece part drawings.

The defendants persuaded the magistrate and the district judge that the piece part drawings weren't really trade secrets at all, because Rockwell made only perfunctory efforts to keep them secret. Not only were there thousands of drawings in the hands of the vendors; there were thousands more in the hands of owners of Rockwell presses, the customers for piece parts. The drawings held by customers, however, are not relevant. They are not piece part drawings, but assembly drawings. (One piece part drawing in the record is labeled "assembly," but as it contains dimensions, tolerances, and other specifications it is really a piece part drawing, despite the label.) An assembly drawing shows how the parts of a printing press fit together for installation and also how to integrate the press with the printer's other equipment. Whenever Rockwell sells a printing press it gives the buyer assembly drawings as well. These are the equivalent of instructions for assembling a piece of furniture. Rockwell does not claim that they contain trade secrets. It admits having supplied a few piece part drawings to customers, but they were piece part drawings of obsolete parts that Rockwell has no interest in manufacturing and of a safety device that was not part of the press as originally delivered but that its customers were clamoring for; more to the point, none of these drawings is among those that Rockwell claims DEV misappropriated.

The distinction between assembly and piece part drawings is not esoteric. *A.H. Emery Co. v. Marcan Products Corp.*, marks it, and along with other cases declares—what is anyway obvious—that a firm's act in making public some of its documents (or part of a document) does not destroy the status as trade secrets of information contained in other documents (or another part of the same document). It is immaterial that Rockwell affixed the same legend enjoining the user to confidentiality to its assembly drawings as it did to its piece part drawings. Perhaps thinking of the doctrine of patent misuse DEV suggests that if a firm claims trade secret protection for information that is not really secret, the firm forfeits trade secret protection of information that is secret. There is no such doctrine—even the patent misuse doctrine does not decree forfeiture of the patent as the sanction for misuse—and it would make no sense. This is not only because there are any number of innocent explanations for Rockwell's action in "overclaiming" trade secret protection (if that is what it was doing)—such as an excess of caution, uncertainty as to the scope of trade secret protection, concern that clerical personnel will not always be able to distinguish between assembly and piece part drawings at a glance, and the sheer economy of a uniform policy—but also because it would place the owner of trade secrets on the razor's edge. If he stamped "confidential" on every document in sight, he would run afoul of what we are calling (without endorsing) the misuse doctrine. But if he did not stamp confidential on every document he would lay himself open to an accusation that he was sloppy about maintaining secrecy—and in fact DEV's main argument is that Rockwell *was* impermissibly sloppy in its efforts to keep the piece part drawings secret.

On this, the critical, issue, the record shows the following. (Because summary judgment was granted to DEV, we must construe the facts as favorably to Rockwell as is reasonable to do.) Rockwell keeps all its engineering drawings, including both piece part and assembly drawings, in a vault. Access not only to the vault, but also to the building in which it is located, is limited to authorized employees who display identification. These are mainly engineers, of whom Rockwell employs 200. They are required to sign agreements not to disseminate the drawings, or disclose their contents, other than as authorized by the company. An authorized employee who needs a drawing must sign it out from the vault and return it when he has finished with it. But he is permitted to make copies, which he is to destroy when he no longer needs them in his work. The only outsiders allowed to see piece part drawings are the vendors (who are given copies, not originals). They too are required to sign confidentiality agreements, and in addition each drawing is stamped with a legend stating that it contains proprietary material. Vendors, like Rockwell's own engineers, are allowed to make copies for internal working purposes, and although the confidentiality agreement that they sign requires the vendor to return the drawing when the order has been filled, Rockwell does not enforce this requirement. The rationale for not enforcing it is that the vendor will need the drawing if Rockwell reorders the part. Rockwell even permits unsuccessful bidders for a piece part contract to keep the drawings, on the theory that the high bidder this round may be the low bidder the next. But it does consider the ethical standards of a machine shop before

[margin note: π's methods for secrecy]

[handwritten note at bottom: — employee engineers sign confid. agmt — vendors sign confid. agmt.]

making it a vendor, and so far as appears no shop has ever abused the confidence reposed in it.

The mere fact that Rockwell gave piece part drawings to vendors—that is, disclosed its trade secrets to "a limited number of outsiders for a particular purpose"—did not forfeit trade secret protection. On the contrary, such disclosure, which is often necessary to the efficient exploitation of a trade secret, imposes a duty of confidentiality on the part of the person to whom the disclosure is made. But with 200 engineers checking out piece part drawings and making copies of them to work from, and numerous vendors receiving copies of piece part drawings and copying them, tens of thousands of copies of these drawings are floating around outside Rockwell's vault, and many of these outside the company altogether. Although the magistrate and the district judge based their conclusion that Rockwell had not made adequate efforts to maintain secrecy in part at least on the irrelevant fact that it took no measures at all to keep its assembly drawings secret, DEV in defending the judgment that it obtained in the district court argues that Rockwell failed to take adequate measures to keep even the piece part drawings secret. Not only did Rockwell not limit copying of those drawings or insist that copies be returned; it did not segregate the piece part drawings from the assembly drawings and institute more secure procedures for the former. So Rockwell could have done more to maintain the confidentiality of its piece part drawings than it did, and we must decide whether its failure to do more was so plain a breach of the obligation of a trade secret owner to make reasonable efforts to maintain secrecy as to justify the entry of summary judgment for the defendants. * * *

The greater the precautions that Rockwell took to maintain the secrecy of the piece part drawings, the lower the probability that DEV obtained them properly and the higher the probability that it obtained them through a wrongful act; the owner had taken pains to prevent them from being obtained otherwise. * * *

If Rockwell expended only paltry resources on preventing its piece part drawings from falling into the hands of competitors such as DEV, why should the law, whose machinery is far from costless, bother to provide Rockwell with a remedy? The information contained in the drawings cannot have been worth much if Rockwell did not think it worthwhile to make serious efforts to keep the information secret.

The remedial significance of such efforts lies in the fact that if the plaintiff has allowed his trade secret to fall into the public domain, he would enjoy a windfall if permitted to recover damages merely because the defendant took the secret from him, rather than from the public domain as it could have done with impunity. It would be like punishing a person for stealing property that he believes is owned by another but that actually is abandoned property. If it were true, as apparently it is not, that Rockwell had given the piece part drawings at issue to customers, and it had done so without requiring the customers to hold them in confidence, DEV could have obtained the drawings from the customers without committing any wrong. The harm to Rockwell would have been the same as if DEV had stolen the drawings from it, but it would have had no remedy, having parted with its rights to the trade secret. This is true whether the trade secret is regarded as property protected only against wrongdoers or * * * as property protected against the world. In the first case, a defendant is perfectly entitled to obtain the property by lawful conduct if he can, and he can if the property is in the hands of persons who themselves committed no wrong to get it. In the second case the defendant is perfectly entitled to obtain the property if the plaintiff has abandoned it by giving it away without restrictions.

It is easy to understand therefore why the law of trade secrets requires a plaintiff to show that he took reasonable precautions to keep the secret a secret. If analogies are needed, one that springs to mind is the duty of the holder of a trademark to take reasonable efforts to police infringements of his mark, failing which the mark is likely to be deemed abandoned, or to become generic or descriptive (and in either event be unprotectable). The trademark owner who fails to police his mark both shows that he doesn't really value it very much and creates a situation in which an infringer may have been unaware that he was using a proprietary mark because the mark had drifted into the public domain, much as DEV contends Rockwell's piece part drawings have done.

But only in an extreme case can what is a "reasonable" precaution be determined on a motion for summary judgment, because the answer depends on a balancing of costs and benefits that will vary from case to case and so require estimation and measurement by persons knowledgeable in the particular field of endeavor involved. On the one hand, the more the owner of the trade secret spends on preventing the secret from leaking out, the more he demonstrates that the secret has real value deserving of legal protection, that he really was hurt as a result of the misappropriation of it, and that there really *was* misappropriation. On the other hand, the more he spends, the higher his costs. The costs can be indirect as well as direct. The more Rockwell restricts access to its drawings, either by its engineers or by the vendors, the harder it will be for either group to do the work expected of it. Suppose Rockwell forbids *any* copying of its drawings. Then a team of engineers would have to share a single drawing, perhaps by passing it around or by working in the same room, huddled over the drawing. And how would a vendor be able to make a piece part—would Rockwell have to bring all that work in house? Such reconfigurations of patterns of work and production are far from costless; and therefore perfect security is not optimum security.

Policy

There are contested factual issues here, bearing in mind that what is reasonable is itself a fact for purposes of Rule 56 of the civil rules. Obviously Rockwell took some precautions, both physical (the vault security, the security guards—one of whom apprehended Peloso *in flagrante delicto*) and contractual, to maintain the confidentiality of its piece part drawings. Obviously it could have taken more precautions. But at a cost, and the question is whether the additional benefit in security would have exceeded that cost. We do not suggest that the question can be answered with the same precision with which it can be posed, but neither can we say that no reasonable jury could find that Rockwell had done enough and could then go on to infer misappropriation from a combination of the precautions Rockwell took and DEV's inability to establish the existence of a lawful source of the Rockwell piece part drawings in its possession.

This is an important case because trade secret protection is an important part of intellectual property, a form of property that is of growing importance to the competitiveness of American industry. Patent protection is at once costly and temporary, and therefore cannot be regarded as a perfect substitute. If trade secrets are protected only if their owners take extravagant, productivity-impairing measures to maintain their secrecy, the incentive to invest resources in discovering more efficient methods of production will be reduced, and with it the amount of invention. And given the importance of the case we must record our concern at the brevity of the district court's opinion granting summary judgment (one and a half printed pages). Brevity is the soul of wit, and all that, and the district judge did have the benefit of a magistrate's opinion; but it is vital that commercial litigation not appear to be treated as a stepchild in the federal courts. The future of the nation depends in no small part on the efficiency of industry, and the efficiency of industry depends in no small part on the protection of intellectual property.

The judgment is reversed and the case remanded to the district court for further proceedings consistent with this opinion * * *

REVERSED AND REMANDED.

DID YOU GET IT?

1. Based on Judge Posner's analysis in this case, how do we evaluate the fact that a trade secret owner could have done more to protect its trade secret? *— concerns about doing the work efficiently balanced w/ secrecy effects*

2. How should a plaintiff trade secret owner balance secrecy protections and costs? *— whether additional protections exceed the cost or burden business as a whole*

3. Why does Judge Posner reason that reasonableness often cannot be determined on summary judgment?

B/c it's industry-specific. Can't say a jury wouldn't find certain efforts reasonable just b/c could've done a little more or less.

case-by-case
fact + industry specific

> **Reading Guidance**
>
> *Did this court have enough evidence to decide the issue of reasonableness on summary judgment?*

— affirms S.J.
in favor of D

π

DICKS V. JENSEN

Supreme Court of Vermont, 2001.
172 Vt. 43.

— Customer list for
lodge resort / senior
citizens

JOHNSON, J. *— no evidence π took measures*
to keep list secret

Plaintiff James Dicks appeals from an order of the Windham Superior Court granting summary judgment to defendants Cary and Brenda Jensen. Plaintiff claims that defendants violated the Vermont Trade Secrets Act, 9 V.S.A. §§ 4601–4609, when they left plaintiff's employ at the Lodge at Mount Snow and solicited the Lodge's bus tour customers to start their own lodge in Bennington, Vermont. Plaintiff also alleges that defendants breached a fiduciary duty, the covenant of good faith and fair dealing, and intentionally interfered with business relations. We affirm.

Plaintiff has owned the Lodge at Mount Snow (Lodge) in Dover, Vermont since 1971. During the nonwinter months, the Lodge relies heavily on business from bus tours of senior citizen groups. These tours are run by organizers who return to the Lodge year after year. The bus tour industry is highly competitive with various hotel owners in the region aggressively soliciting business from the tour groups. In 1991, plaintiff hired defendants to manage the Lodge and market and run a bus tour business at the Lodge. The defendants worked without an employment agreement and ran most aspects of the Lodge's business. They were responsible for advertising, soliciting, and organizing the Lodge's bus tours. Securing tour groups to visit the Lodge involved mass mailings to lists of senior citizen tour groups collected through chambers of commerce, agencies on aging, and mail order catalogs throughout the Eastern United States. Because these mass mailings typically have a very low response rate, defendants had to send additional promotional material, followed by direct telephone solicitation. The telephone solicitations resulted in twenty to sixty actual bookings from an initial mailing of ten to fifteen thousand. Booking a tour required about six months of lead time.

In 1997, defendants left the Lodge to open their own competing lodge, the Autumn Inn, in Bennington. Defendants contacted Lodge customers to inform them of the move. They also solicited business from the Lodge's regular bus tour customers. Nine of eleven tours booked by defendants their first season were with customers who had reservations booked at the Lodge who canceled their reservations and rebooked with defendants.

Plaintiff filed suit alleging, inter alia, that defendants had misappropriated the Lodge's customer list, violating the Vermont Trade Secrets Act; that, in soliciting the Lodge's customers, defendants had breached their fiduciary duty and the covenant of good faith and fair dealing to plaintiff; and that defendants had tortiously interfered with the Lodge's business relations. The trial court, on a motion for summary judgment by defendants, ruled that defendants did not violate the Trade Secrets Act. The court noted that a customer list could not be a trade secret if the content was readily ascertainable from publically available sources. Because the court found that the Lodge's customer list was not developed by "extraordinary effort," it was, therefore, readily ascertainable and not protected. * * *

On appeal, plaintiff alleges that summary judgment on the trade secrets claim was inappropriate because there were genuine issues of material fact as to whether the list is a trade secret. * * *

Vermont Trade Secrets Act

The Vermont Trade Secrets Act, was enacted in 1996 to prevent the misuse of business information. The statute allows injunctive relief and damages for misappropriation of trade secrets. The Act was explicitly designed to displace other common law remedies for misappropriation of trade secrets. A "trade secret" is defined as:

> [I]nformation, including a formula, pattern, compilation, program, device, method, technique, or process, that: (A) derives independent economic value, actual or potential, from not being generally known to, and not being readily ascertainable by proper means by, other persons who can obtain economic value from its disclosure or use; and (B) is the subject of efforts that are reasonable under the circumstances to maintain its secrecy.

* * *

As indicated by the statutory definition of trade secret, there are two components to the test for whether some information deserves trade secret protection. The first is whether the information has independent economic value that is not readily ascertainable to others; the second is whether reasonable efforts were made to maintain the information's secrecy. Although the trial court based its decision primarily on the first element, plaintiff must satisfy both elements for his list to be protected under the statute. * * *

A customer list can be a protected trade secret. As the Ninth Circuit recognized, a list of people who have already purchased a product is substantially more valuable than a list of people who might only be interested in purchasing. The process of parsing a customer list from a directory of potentially profitable customers from entries not worth pursuing injects that list with value. But, the threshold amount of time and money that must be invested before a customer list is accorded statutory protection varies considerably. * * *

The second part of the definition of trade secret requires the party seeking protection to make reasonable efforts to ensure the information's secrecy. It would be anomalous for the courts to prohibit the use of information that the rightful owner did not undertake to protect. Other jurisdictions have used several factors to determine the reasonableness of efforts to maintain the information's secrecy, including whether parties had a written agreement not to compete, whether knowledge was confined to any restricted group of employees, and the extent of measures to guard access to the information. Thus the burden is on the plaintiff to demonstrate that he "pursued an active course of conduct designed to inform his employees that such secrets and information were to remain confidential." If the owner of the information has attempted to protect information, however, others who have access to it are under an obligation to respect those measures.

[handwritten margin note: Secrecy factors]

In this case, there is no evidence in the record that plaintiff took any measures to indicate that the customer list was confidential. Plaintiff does not identify any agreement between the parties, written or oral, that encompasses an understanding that the customer list was confidential. Nor does plaintiff identify any procedures or measures taken to ensure that the customer list was secure and access to it restricted. In fact, defendants provided statements that the names of tour groups were posted on a large reservation board in an office where all employees and any office visitor could see. The customer names were not locked and were available to all employees. Plaintiff's response was only that at some point the Lodge stopped putting the full names of tours on the reservation board, and that the full names of the customers were kept in defendants' office. Absent any attempt by plaintiff to maintain the customer list's secrecy, enforcing just the first part of the statute would protect all business information that had independent economic value, without regard to the parties' own actions to protect it. This interpretation would render the second part of the statutory test superfluous. * * *

[handwritten margin notes: — no confid. agmt — no phys. security]

On the record before us, therefore, there is no dispute of material fact, and summary judgment is appropriate for this statutory element. Because plaintiff has adduced no evidence that he took reasonable efforts to maintain the secrecy of the customer information, we hold, as a matter of law, that this customer list is not a trade secret. * * *

DID YOU GET IT?

1. How did the evidence of reasonableness in this case compare to that in *Rockwell?* *[handwritten: — here, no evidence of any secrecy efforts]*

2. What evidence did the plaintiff put forth to meet his burden of demonstrating that he "pursued an active course of conduct designed

to inform his employees that [his] secrets and information were to remain confidential"? — Moved list from reservation board to A's office

3.   Do you think Judge Posner would have agreed with this decision? — probably b/c it's so drastic.

C. REASONABLENESS AND CONFIDENTIAL RELATIONSHIPS

but maybe not under industry specific analysis

The foregoing cases both involved the employment relationship. As you may have noticed so far (and as is discussed in greater detail in Chapter 7), relationships are very important in trade secret misappropriation cases. Relationships can be particularly relevant for the reasonable efforts analysis because courts often need to decide what efforts the plaintiff took with respect to notifying the defendant about the importance of keeping the disputed information secret.

As is discussed in Chapters 7 and 8, courts often hold that employees owe an implied duty of confidentiality to their employers, but there is also a practical need to identify the alleged trade secrets. Thus, the question of reasonable efforts usually centers on whether the employer adequately informed its employees of the identity of its claimed trade secrets. The analysis changes in circumstances where the putative trade secret owner discloses its secrets to non-employees where the creation of a duty of confidentiality is often the focus.

The presence of a written confidentiality agreement with those who will be exposed to a trade secret has become a basic expectation in showing steps to protect a secret. A study of trade secret cases confirmed that "confidentiality agreements with employees and business partners are the most important factors in the courts' analysis of reasonable measures." *See* David Almeling, Darin Synder et al., *A Statistical Analysis of Trade Secret Litigation in State Courts*, 46 GONZAGA L. REV. 57, 82–83 (2010). In the absence of such express agreements, courts are left to interpret the facts surrounding the relationship to determine whether an implied agreement can be inferred. Often, the nature of the relationship between the parties affects whether courts are willing to imply confidentiality in the absence of an express agreement and, consequently, whether a putative trade secret owner's security efforts were reasonable.

Although it is possible that security efforts that are engaged in without a duty of confidentiality will be deemed sufficient (for instance when dealing with a case of the improper acquisition of trade secrets where the defendant had no relationship with the plaintiff), in cases where a putative trade secret owner voluntarily discloses its information to another, the non-existence of a duty of confidentiality may trump all other considerations. This is due to what Professor Sharon Sandeen has labeled "the third-party doctrine of trade secrecy," which is similar to the third-party doctrine of Fourth Amendment jurisprudence. *See* Sharon K. Sandeen, *Lost in the*

Cloud? Information Flows and the Implications of Cloud Computing for Trade Secret Protection, 19 VIRG. JOUR. OF LAW & TECH. (JOLT) 1 (2014) (discussing the possible loss of trade secrets stored in the Cloud).

For instance, as you learned in the Special Issue section of Chapter 4, many trade secret cases arise in situations where a person submits an idea to a company and then alleges that the idea was misappropriated or otherwise used without permission. Under current law, the key to prevailing in an idea submission case is to prove either the elements of a trade secret misappropriation claim or a breach of contract claim. One issue that arises in idea submission cases based upon trade secret principles is whether the "idea man" was reasonable in the way he handled his idea. Unlike the employment relationship or an ongoing business relationship, proving reasonableness in idea submission cases can be particularly challenging due to the short-term nature of the relationship between the parties. Generally, if one hands over an idea without an understanding or agreement, it is considered a gift. Thus, without a pre-disclosure agreement, the plaintiff in an idea submission case will have difficulty proving that the "idea" which it communicated to the defendant qualifies as a trade secret and that it took the requisite steps to protect the idea.

In cases where a pre-disclosure agreement can be proven, the principal question under the reasonable efforts analysis is whether such an agreement, alone, is enough. Usually more efforts are required, and the best practice is for information owners to engage in efforts that are designed to prevent the misappropriation of their trade secrets in the first instance.

The cases that follow explore the meaning of reasonable efforts in two factual situations not involving the employment relationship. The first two cases are classic idea submission cases, pursued as trade secret claims, where there was no prior relationship between the parties. The third case involves a vendor/vendee relationship.

Food for Thought

Should the nature of the relationship between the trade secret owner and the person or company to whom it discloses its trade secrets be a factor in determining the reasonableness of protection efforts? Is it enough for a trade secret owner to focus on efforts that are undertaken to protect information that it shares with others or must it also be concerned with risks posed by strangers?

Reading Guidance

What was the nature of the relationship between the parties in this case?

INCASE INC. v. TIMEX CORP.

United States Court of Appeals, First Circuit, 2007.
488 F.3d 46.

STAHL, SENIOR CIRCUIT JUDGE.

* * *

Incase is a designer and manufacturer of injection-molded plastic packaging products, located in Hopedale, Massachusetts. In late 1997 and early 1998, Incase had discussions with Timex, a manufacturer of watches and other electronics based in Middlebury, Connecticut, about providing packaging for some of Timex's watches. Following these meetings, Incase began working on several packaging products for Timex, including the watch holders at issue here.

Incase's usual procedure is to provide design services in conjunction with its manufacturing. Incase does not charge directly for the design services, but their expectation is that, if the design is satisfactory to the client, then Incase would receive a contract to manufacture the product.

The products at issue in this case are two watch packages, known as the "S–4" and "S–5." Each is comprised of a series of integrated plastic components, including a ring or collar (which functions like a wrist) on a fixed base. The whole package allows for secure retail display of the watch without having to remove it from its packaging. The S–4 and S–5 differed in the way the "price flag" was incorporated into the package. The price flag is a small plastic component attached to the base that can display the price, SKU, or other information. In the S–4, the price flag is fixed, while in the S–5, the price flag is moveable and removable. The removable price flag was important to Timex, since it allowed for better use of its automated manufacturing and distribution system, and because it allowed retailers to use the same watch holder for both promotional and everyday display. Timex had used moveable and removable price flags before, but prior designs had only two positions, while the S–5's price flag had three, and later four. The removable price flag is the focus of Incase's misappropriation of trade secrets claim. * * *

Incase and Timex had begun working on the S–5 design, with the removable price flag. Over the course of 1998, the parties went back and forth with specifications, design ideas, and at least twenty prototypes. The design was largely complete by May 1999, but Timex never placed any orders or entered into a contract for the manufacturing of the units.

By August 1999, Timex, unbeknownst to Incase, was in discussions with Yuhing, a Philippines manufacturing concern, with a view toward their producing the S–5. In its dealings with Yuhing, Timex relied on Incase's drawings and prototypes of the S–5. The S–5 that Yuhing ultimately produced differed in some minor respects from the S–5 that Incase had developed, though each incorporated the removable price flag. By May 2000, Yuhing was manufacturing S–5 units for Timex. Ultimately, Timex purchased 3,569,000 S–5 units from Yuhing.

Timex never notified Incase that it had given the manufacturing work for the S–5 to a different company. In March 2001, Frank Zanghi, vice president of Incase, was in a Target store when he noticed Timex products displayed in Yuhing's S–5 package, with the price flag derived from Incase's price flag design. Incase subsequently brought suit in Massachusetts state court against Timex, alleging breach of contract to purchase six million S–4 holders, misappropriation of trade secrets for the S–5 price flag, unjust enrichment/implied contract for use of Incase's S–5 design, and unfair and deceptive trade practices in violation of Mass. Gen. Laws ch. 93A, § 11 ("Chapter 93A"). Timex removed the case to United States District Court based on diversity of citizenship.

Following trial on the contract, implied contract, and trade secret claims, a jury returned a verdict for Incase on all claims. Timex moved for a judgment as a matter of law, and the district court granted the motion with respect to the trade secret [claim]. * * * Incase appeals from the court's judgment as a matter of law on the trade secret claim. * * *

To prevail on a claim of misappropriation of trade secrets, a plaintiff must show: 1) the information is a trade secret; 2) the plaintiff took reasonable steps to preserve the secrecy of the information; and 3) the defendant used improper means, in breach of a confidential relationship, to acquire and use the trade secret. In issuing its judgment as a matter of law, the court held that Incase had not presented any evidence that the information was secret or that it had taken reasonable steps to preserve the secrecy of the information. Timex also argues here that there was no confidential relationship formed between the parties, and that the trade secret was not even the property of Incase in the first place.

The appeal on this claim turns on the second element of the misappropriation cause of action: whether Incase took reasonable steps to preserve the secrecy of the price flag design. The district court noted that no documents were marked "confidential" or "secret"; there were no security precautions or confidentiality agreements; Incase had not told Timex the design was a secret; and Incase's principal designer on the project, Bob Shelton, did not think the design was a secret. Timex adds that Frank Zanghi, Incase's vice president, did not tell anyone at Timex that the design was confidential.

Incase argues that the jury could have found evidence of steps to preserve secrecy in the fact that Incase showed the designs only to Timex; the trade practices of the watch packaging industry; and the fact that Timex treated the designs as confidential in its dealings with Yuhing. It also argues that Shelton's testimony should not have been given the weight it was by the court, since he was speaking for himself, not the company, when he said that he did not believe the design was secret. Incase also points to other testimony by Shelton where he said that he did not show the work to anyone other than Timex.

After a careful review of the record, we have not found any evidence to support Incase's argument that it took reasonable steps to preserve the secrecy of the price flag design. Although Frank Zanghi testified, for example, that when Incase works on a project, it is treated as "confidential between Incase and the company," that the design is "proprietary" and "our property," and that he believed that the price flag designs were secret. He admitted under cross-examination that this policy was never articulated to Timex. The fact that Incase kept its work for Timex private from the world is not sufficient; discretion is a normal feature of a business relationship. Instead, there must be affirmative steps to preserve the secrecy of the information as against the party against whom the misappropriation claim is made. Here, there is no evidence that any such steps were taken. Therefore, we affirm the district court's judgment as a matter of law on the misappropriation of trade secrets claim. * * *

For the forgoing reasons, we *affirm*.

DID YOU GET IT?

1. What was the nature of the relationship between Timex and Incase?

2. What facts support a finding of no reasonable efforts in this case?

3. The court notes that "discretion is a normal feature of a business relationship." What more is required (beyond discretion) to be considered a reasonable measure to protect confidentiality in a business relationship?

4. What does this case suggest about the type of evidence a defendant in a trade secret case should try to discover in an effort to show the non-existence of trade secrets?

Food for Thought

Is there any advantage to defending against an idea submission claim by arguing (as the defendant in the Daktronics case in Chapter 4 did) that the information was generally known and readily ascertainable, versus arguing that the information was not subject to reasonable efforts to maintain secrecy? How would you decide which argument is better?

LEARNING CURVE TOYS, INC. V. PLAYWOOD TOYS, INC.

United States Court of Appeals, Seventh Circuit, 2003.
342 F.3d 714.

RIPPLE, CIRCUIT JUDGE.

* * *

In 1992, Robert Clausi and his brother-in-law, Scott Moore, began creating prototypes of wooden toys under the name PlayWood Toys, Inc., a Canadian corporation. Clausi was the sole toy designer and Moore was the sole officer and director of PlayWood. Neither Clausi nor Moore had prior experience in the toy industry, but Clausi had "always been a bit of a doodler and designer," and the two men desired to "create high-quality hard-wood maple toys for the independent toy market." As a newly formed corporation, PlayWood did not own a facility in which it could produce toys. Instead, it worked in conjunction with Mario Borsato, who owned a wood-working facility. Subject to a written confidentiality agreement with PlayWood, Borsato manufactured prototypes for PlayWood based on Clausi's design specifications.

PlayWood's first attempt to market publicly its toys was at the Toronto Toy Fair on January 31, 1992. PlayWood received favorable reviews from many of the toy retailers in attendance; PlayWood also learned that the best way to get recognition for its toys was to attend the New York Toy Fair ("Toy Fair") the following month. Based on this information, Clausi and Moore secured a position at the Toy Fair in order to display PlayWood's prototypes. It was during this Toy Fair that Clausi and Moore first encountered Learning Curve representatives Roy Wilson, Harry Abraham and John Lee.

On the morning of February 12, 1993, the first day of the Toy Fair, Roy Wilson stopped at PlayWood's booth and engaged Clausi and Moore in conversation. Wilson identified himself as Learning Curve's toy designer and explained that his company had a license from the Britt Allcroft Company to develop Thomas the Tank Engine & Friends™ (hereinafter "Thomas") trains and accessories. Wilson commented that he was impressed with the look and quality of PlayWood's prototypes and raised the possibility of working together under a custom manufacturing contract to produce Learning Curve's line of Thomas products. Clausi and Moore responded that such an arrangement would be of great interest to PlayWood. Later that same day, Harry Abraham, Learning Curve's vice president, and John Lee, Learning Curve's president, also stopped by PlayWood's booth. They too commented on the quality of PlayWood's prototypes and indicated that PlayWood might be a good candidate for a manufacturing contract with Learning Curve.

Clausi and Moore continued to have discussions with Learning Curve's representatives over the remaining days of the Toy Fair, which ended on February 14. During these discussions, Lee indicated that he would like two of his people, Abraham and Wilson, to visit PlayWood in Toronto the day after the Toy Fair ended in order to determine whether the two parties could work out a manufacturing arrangement for some or all of Learning Curve's wooden toys. Clausi, feeling a little overwhelmed by the suggestion, requested that their visit be postponed a few days so that he could better acquaint himself with Learning Curve's products. The parties ultimately agreed that Abraham and Wilson would visit PlayWood at Borsato's facility on February 18, 1993, four days after the conclusion of the Toy Fair. Clausi spent the next several days after the Toy Fair researching Learning Curve's products and considering how PlayWood could produce Learning Curve's trains and track.

On February 18, 1993, Abraham and Wilson visited PlayWood in Toronto as planned. The meeting began with a tour of Borsato's woodworking facility, where the prototypes on display at the Toy Fair had been made. After the tour, the parties went to the conference room at Borsato's facility. At this point, according to Clausi and Moore, the parties agreed to make their ensuing discussion confidential. Clausi testified:

> After we sat down in the board room, Harry [Abraham of Learning Curve] immediately said: "Look, we're going to disclose confidential information to you guys, and we're going to disclose some designs that Roy [Wilson of Learning Curve] has that are pretty confidential. If Brio were to get their hands on them, then we wouldn't like that. And we're going to do it under the basis of a confidential understanding."
>
> And I said: "I also have some things, some ideas on how to produce the track and produce the trains now that I've had a chance to look at them for the last couple of days, and I think they're confidential as well. So if we're both okay with that, we should continue." So we did.

Moore testified to the existence of a similar conversation:

> It was at this point that Harry Abraham told us that they were going to disclose some confidential documents, drawings, pricing, margins, and asked us if we would keep that information confidential.
>
> I believe it was Robert [Clausi] who said that, you know, absolutely, we would keep it confidential. In fact, we had some ideas that we felt would be confidential we would be disclosing to

them, and would they keep it, you know, confidential? Would they
reciprocate? And Harry [Abraham] said: "Absolutely." And then
we proceeded to go along with the meeting.

Immediately after the parties agreed to keep their discussion confidential,
Wilson, at Abraham's direction, showed Clausi and Moore drawings of
various Thomas characters and provided information on the projected
volume of each of the products. Clausi testified that he considered the
documents disclosed by Learning Curve during the meeting confidential
because they included information on products not yet released to the
public, as well as Learning Curve's projected volumes, costs and profit
margins for various products. After viewing Wilson's various drawings, the
parties discussed PlayWood's ideas on how to manufacture Learning
Curve's trains. Clausi suggested that they might use a CNC machine,
which he defined as a computer numerically controlled drill that carves in
three dimensions, to create Learning Curve's trains out of a single piece of
wood (as opposed to piecing together separate pieces of wood).

The parties' discussion eventually moved away from train production and
focused on track design. Wilson showed Clausi and Moore drawings of
Learning Curve's track and provided samples of their current product. At
this point, Abraham confided to Clausi and Moore that track had posed "a
bit of a problem for Learning Curve." Abraham explained that sales were
terrific for Learning Curve's Thomas trains, but that sales were abysmal
for its track. Abraham attributed the lack of sales to the fact that Learning
Curve's track was virtually identical to that of its competitor, Brio, which
had the lion's share of the track market. Because there was "no
differentiation" between the two brands of track, Learning Curve's track
was not even displayed in many of the toy stores that carried Learning
Curve's products. Learning Curve had worked unsuccessfully for several
months attempting to differentiate its track from that of Brio.

After detailing the problems with Learning Curve's existing track,
Abraham inquired of Clausi whether "there was a way to differentiate" its
track from Brio's track. Clausi immediately responded that he "had had a
chance to look at the track and get a feel for it [over] the last few days" and
that his "thoughts were that if the track were more realistic and more
functional, that kids would enjoy playing with it more and it would give the
retailer a reason to carry the product, especially if it looked different than
the Brio track." Clausi further explained that, if the track "made noise and
[ ] looked like real train tracks, that the stores wouldn't have any problem,
and the Thomas the Tank line, product line would have [ ] its own different
track" and could "effectively compete with Brio." Abraham and Wilson
indicated that they were "intrigued" by Clausi's idea and asked him what
he meant by "making noise."

Clausi decided to show Abraham and Wilson exactly what he meant. Clausi took a piece of Learning Curve's existing track from the table, drew some lines across the track (about every three-quarters of an inch), and stated: "We can go ahead and machine grooves right across the upper section . . . , which would look like railway tracks, and down below machine little indentations as well so that it would look more like or sound more like real track. You would roll along and bumpity-bumpity as you go along." Clausi then called Borsato into the conference room and asked him to cut grooves into the wood "about a quarter of an inch deep from the top surface." Borsato left the room, complied with Clausi's request, and returned with the cut track three or four minutes later. Clausi ran a train back and forth over the cut piece of track. The track looked more realistic than before, but it did not make noise because the grooves were not deep enough. Accordingly, Clausi instructed Borsato to cut the grooves "just a little bit deeper so that they go through the rails." Borsato complied with Clausi's request once again and returned a few minutes later with the cut piece of track. Clausi proceeded to run a train back and forth over the track. This time the track made a "clickety-clack" sound, but the train did not run smoothly over the track because the grooves were cut "a little bit too deep." Based on the sound produced by the track, Clausi told Abraham and Moore that if PlayWood procured a contract with Learning Curve to produce the track, they could call it "Clickety-Clack Track."

Both Abraham and Wilson indicated that Clausi's concept of cutting grooves into the track to produce a clacking sound was a novel concept. Thereafter, Wilson and Clausi began to discuss how they could improve the idea to make the train run more smoothly on the track, but Abraham interrupted them and stated: "No, focus. You guys have to get the contract for the basic product first, and then we can talk about new products, because . . . it takes [our licensor] a long time to approve new products and new designs." The meeting ended shortly thereafter without further discussion about Clausi's concept for the noise-producing track. Before he left, Wilson asked Clausi if he could take the piece of track that Borsato had cut with him while the parties continued their discussions. Clausi gave Wilson the piece of track without hesitation. The piece of track was the only item that Abraham and Wilson took from the meeting. Clausi and Moore did not ask Wilson for a receipt for the cut track, nor did they seek a written confidentiality agreement to protect PlayWood's alleged trade secret. After the meeting, Clausi amended PlayWood's confidentiality agreement with Borsato to ensure that materials discussed during the meeting would remain confidential. Clausi also stamped many of the documents that he received from Learning Curve during the meeting as confidential because they included information on products not yet released to the public. PlayWood never disclosed the contents of Learning Curve's documents to anyone.

During March of 1993, PlayWood and Learning Curve met on three separate occasions to discuss further the possibility of PlayWood manufacturing Learning Curve's Thomas products. At one of the meetings, and at Learning Curve's request, PlayWood submitted a manufacturing proposal for the Thomas products. Learning Curve rejected PlayWood's proposal. Learning Curve told Clausi that its licensor wanted the Thomas products to be made in the United States.

Thereafter, PlayWood had no contact with Learning Curve until late October of 1993, when Abraham contacted Clausi to discuss another possible manufacturing contract because Learning Curve's secondary supplier was not providing enough product. Again, PlayWood submitted a manufacturing proposal at Learning Curve's request, but it too was rejected. Learning Curve later stated that its new business partner had decided to manufacture the product in China.

Clausi and Moore continued to work on PlayWood's toy concepts. After the 1994 New York Toy Fair, which was not particularly successful for PlayWood, Clausi and Moore began to focus their efforts on refining PlayWood's concept for the noise-producing track. During this time, Clausi and Moore made no attempt to license or sell the concept to other toy companies because they believed that PlayWood still had "an opportunity to get in the door" with Learning Curve if they could perfect the concept and also because they believed that they were bound by a confidentiality agreement.

In December of 1994, while shopping for additional track with which to experiment, Moore discovered that Learning Curve was selling noise-producing track under the name "Clickety-Clack Track." Like the piece of track that Clausi had Borsato cut during PlayWood's February 18, 1993, meeting with Learning Curve, Clickety-Clack Track™ has parallel grooves cut into the wood, which cause a "clacking" sound as train wheels roll over the grooves. Learning Curve was promoting the new track as

> the first significant innovation in track design since the inception of wooden train systems. . . . It is quite simply the newest and most exciting development to come along recently in the wooden train industry, and it's sure to cause a sensation in the marketplace. . . . [I]t brings that sound and feel of the real thing to a child's world of make-believe without bells, whistles, electronic sound chips or moving parts.

Moore was "stunned" when he saw the track because he believed that Learning Curve had stolen PlayWood's concept. He testified: "This was our idea. This is what we've been working on even up to that day to go back to [Learning Curve] as an opportunity to get in the door, and there it is on the shelf." Moore purchased a package of Clickety-Clack Track™ and showed it to Clausi. Clausi testified that he was disappointed when he saw the track because he believed that Learning Curve had taken PlayWood's name and design concept "almost exactly as per [their] conversation" on February 18, 1993.

PlayWood promptly wrote a cease and desist letter to Learning Curve. The letter accused Learning Curve of stealing PlayWood's concept for the noise-producing track that it disclosed to Learning Curve "in confidence in the context of a manufacturing proposal." Learning Curve responded by seeking a declaratory judgment that it owned the concept.

Previously, on March 16, 1994, Learning Curve had applied for a patent on the noise-producing track. The patent, which was obtained on October 3, 1995, claims the addition of parallel impressions or grooves in the rails, which cause a "clacking" sound to be emitted as train wheels roll over them. The patent identifies Roy Wilson of Learning Curve as the inventor.

Clickety-Clack Track™ provided an enormous boost to Learning Curve's sales. Learning Curve had $20 million in track sales by the first quarter of 2000, and $40 million for combined track and accessory sales.

District Court Proceedings

Learning Curve responded to PlayWood's cease and desist letter by seeking a declaratory judgment that it owned the concept for noise-producing toy railroad track, as embodied in Clickety-Clack Track.™ PlayWood counterclaimed against Learning Curve, as well as its representatives, Roy Wilson, Harry Abraham and John Lee. PlayWood asserted that it owned the concept and that Learning Curve had misappropriated its trade secret Learning Curve voluntarily dismissed its complaint for declaratory relief, and PlayWood's claim for trade secret misappropriation proceeded to trial. The jury returned a verdict in favor of PlayWood. The trial court declined to enter judgment on the verdict and instead asked the parties to brief Learning Curve's Rule 50 motion on the issue of whether PlayWood had a protectable trade secret under the Illinois Trade Secrets Act, 765 ILCS 1065/1 *et seq.* The district court granted Learning Curve's motion and entered judgment in its favor on the ground that PlayWood presented insufficient evidence of a trade secret. Specifically, the court determined that PlayWood did not have a trade secret in its concept for noise-producing toy railroad track under Illinois law because: (1) PlayWood did not demonstrate that its concept was unknown in the industry; (2) PlayWood's concept could have been easily acquired or duplicated through proper means; (3) PlayWood failed to guard the secrecy of its concept; (4) PlayWood's concept had no economic value; and (5) PlayWood expended no time, effort or money to develop the concept.

*Trade Secret Status * * **

The parties agree that their dispute is governed by the Illinois Trade Secrets Act ("Act"). To prevail on a claim for misappropriation of a trade secret under the Act, the plaintiff must demonstrate that the information at issue was a trade secret, that it was misappropriated and that it was used in the defendant's business. The issue currently before us is whether there was legally sufficient evidence for the jury to find that PlayWood had a trade secret in its concept for the noise-producing toy railroad track that it revealed to Learning Curve on February 18, 1993.

The Act defines a trade secret as:

> [I]nformation, including but not limited to, technical or non-technical data, a formula, pattern, compilation, program, device, method, technique, drawing, process, financial data, or list of actual or potential customers or suppliers, that:
>
> (1) is sufficiently secret to derive economic value, actual or potential, from not being generally known to other persons who can obtain economic value from its disclosure or use; and
>
> (2) is the subject of efforts that are reasonable under the circumstances to maintain its secrecy or confidentiality.

Both of the Act's statutory requirements focus fundamentally on the secrecy of the information sought to be protected. However, the requirements emphasize different aspects of secrecy. The first requirement, that the information be sufficiently secret to impart economic value because of its relative secrecy, "precludes trade secret protection for information generally known or understood within an industry even if not to the public at large." The second requirement, that the plaintiff take reasonable efforts to maintain the secrecy of the information, prevents a plaintiff who takes no affirmative measures to prevent others from using its proprietary information from obtaining trade secret protection.

Although the Act explicitly defines a trade secret in terms of these two requirements, Illinois courts frequently refer to six common law factors (which are derived from § 757 of the Restatement (First) of Torts) in determining whether a trade secret exists: (1) the extent to which the information is known outside of the plaintiff's business; (2) the extent to which the information is known by employees and others involved in the plaintiff's business; (3) the extent of measures taken by the plaintiff to guard the secrecy of the information; (4) the value of the information to the plaintiff's business and to its competitors; (5) the amount of time, effort and money expended by the plaintiff in developing the information; and (6) the ease or difficulty with which the information could be properly acquired or duplicated by others.

* * *

The existence of a trade secret ordinarily is a question of fact. As aptly observed by our colleagues on the Fifth Circuit, a trade secret "is one of the most elusive and difficult concepts in the law to define." In many cases, the existence of a trade secret is not obvious; it requires an ad hoc evaluation of all the surrounding circumstances. For this reason, the question of whether certain information constitutes a trade secret ordinarily is best "resolved by a fact finder after full presentation of evidence from each side." We do not believe that the district court was sufficiently mindful of these principles. The district court, in effect, treated the Restatement factors as requisite elements and substituted its judgment for that of the jury. PlayWood presented sufficient evidence for the jury reasonably to conclude that the Restatement factors weighed in PlayWood's favor.

1. Extent to which PlayWood's concept for noise-producing toy railroad track was known outside of PlayWood's business

PlayWood presented substantial evidence from which the jury could have determined that PlayWood's concept for noise-producing toy railroad track was not generally known outside of PlayWood's business. It was undisputed at trial that no similar track was on the market until Learning Curve launched Clickety-Clack Track™ in late 1994, more than a year after PlayWood first conceived of the concept. * * * [I]n this case, there was additional evidence from which the jury could have determined that PlayWood's concept was not generally known within the industry.

First, there was substantial testimony that Learning Curve had attempted to differentiate its track from that of its competitors for several months, but that it had been unable to do so successfully.

Furthermore, PlayWood's expert witness, Michael Kennedy, testified that PlayWood's concept, as embodied in Clickety-Clack Track,™ was unique and permitted "its seller to differentiate itself from a host of competitors who [were] making a generic product." Kennedy explained that the look, sound and feel of the track made it distinct from other toy railroad track: "[W]hen a child runs a train across this track, he can feel it hitting those little impressions. And when you're talking about young children [,] having the idea that they can see something that they couldn't see before, feel something that they couldn't feel before, hear something that they couldn't hear before, that is what differentiates this toy from its other competitors."

Finally, PlayWood presented evidence that Learning Curve sought and obtained a patent on the noise-producing track. It goes without saying that the requirements for patent and trade secret protection are not synonymous. Unlike "a patentable invention, a trade secret need not be novel or unobvious." "The idea need not be complicated; it may be intrinsically simple and nevertheless qualify as a secret, unless it is common knowledge and, therefore, within the public domain." However, it is commonly understood that "[i]f an invention has sufficient novelty to be entitled to patent protection, it may be said a *fortiori* to be entitled to protection as a trade secret." In light of this evidence, we cannot accept

Learning Curve's argument that no rational jury could have found that PlayWood's concept was unknown outside of its business.

2. Extent to which PlayWood's concept was known to employees and others involved in PlayWood's business

The district court did not address the extent to which PlayWood's concept was known to employees and others involved in PlayWood's business. However, we agree with PlayWood that the evidence was sufficient to establish that its concept for noise-producing track was known only by key individuals in its business.

At the outset, we note briefly that PlayWood was a small business, consisting only of Clausi and Moore. Illinois courts have recognized on several occasions that the expectations for ensuring secrecy are different for small companies than for large companies. Apart from Clausi (PlayWood's sole toy designer and the person who conceived of the concept for noise-producing track) and Moore (PlayWood's sole officer and director), the only person who knew about the concept was Borsato, the person who physically produced PlayWood's prototype at Clausi's direction. The concept was disclosed to Borsato in order for PlayWood to develop fully its trade secret. Moreover, Borsato's actions were governed by a written confidentiality agreement with PlayWood. Indeed, as an extra precaution, Clausi even amended PlayWood's confidentiality agreement with Borsato immediately after the February 18, 1993, meeting to ensure that materials discussed during the meeting would remain confidential. From this evidence, the jury reasonably could have determined that this factor also weighed in favor of PlayWood.

3. Measures taken by PlayWood to guard the secrecy of its concept

There also was sufficient evidence for the jury to determine that PlayWood took reasonable precautions to guard the secrecy of its concept. The Act requires the trade secret owner to take actions that are "reasonable under the circumstances to maintain [the] secrecy or confidentiality" of its trade secret; it does not require perfection. Whether the measures taken by a trade secret owner are sufficient to satisfy the Act's reasonableness standard ordinarily is a question of fact for the jury. Indeed, we previously have recognized that "only in an extreme case can what is a 'reasonable' precaution be determined [as a matter of law], because the answer depends on a balancing of costs and benefits that will vary from case to case."

Here, the jury was instructed that it must find "by a preponderance of the evidence that PlayWood's trade secrets were given to Learning Curve as a result of a confidential relationship between the parties." By returning a verdict in favor of PlayWood, the jury necessarily found that Learning Curve was bound to PlayWood by a pledge of confidentiality. The jury's determination is amply supported by the evidence. Both Clausi and Moore testified that they entered into an oral confidentiality agreement with

Abraham and Wilson before beginning their discussion on February 18, 1993. In particular, Clausi testified that he told Abraham and Wilson: "I also have some things, some ideas on how to produce the track and produce the trains now that I've had a chance to look at them for the last couple of days, and I think they're confidential as well. So if we're both okay with that, we should continue." In addition to this testimony, the jury heard that Learning Curve had disclosed substantial information to PlayWood during the February 18th meeting, including projected volumes, costs and profit margins for various products, as well as drawings for toys not yet released to the public. The jury could have inferred that Learning Curve would not have disclosed such information in the absence of a confidentiality agreement. Finally, the jury also heard (from several of Learning Curve's former business associates) that Learning Curve routinely entered into oral confidentiality agreements like the one with PlayWood.

PlayWood might have done more to protect its secret. As Learning Curve points out, PlayWood gave its only prototype of the noise-producing track to Wilson without first obtaining a receipt or written confidentiality agreement from Learning Curve-a decision that proved unwise in hindsight. Nevertheless, we believe that the jury was entitled to conclude that PlayWood's reliance on the oral confidentiality agreement was reasonable under the circumstances of this case. First, it is well established that "[t]he formation of a confidential relationship imposes upon the disclosee the duty to maintain the information received in the utmost secrecy" and that "the unprivileged use or disclosure of another's trade secret becomes the basis for an action in tort." Second, both Clausi and Moore testified that they believed PlayWood had a realistic chance to "get in the door" with Learning Curve and to produce the concept as part of Learning Curve's line of Thomas products. Clausi and Moore did not anticipate that Learning Curve would violate the oral confidentiality agreement and utilize PlayWood's concept without permission; rather, they believed in good faith that they "were going to do business one day again with Learning Curve with respect to the design concept." Finally, we believe that, as part of the reasonableness inquiry, the jury could have considered the size and sophistication of the parties, as well as the relevant industry. Both PlayWood and Learning Curve were small toy companies, and PlayWood was the smaller and less experienced of the two. Viewing the evidence in the light most favorable to PlayWood, as we must, we conclude that there was sufficient evidence for the jury to determine that PlayWood took reasonable measures to protect the secrecy of its concept.

4.   Value of the concept to PlayWood and to its competitors

There was substantial evidence from which the jury could have determined that PlayWood's concept had value both to PlayWood and to its competitors. It was undisputed at trial that Learning Curve's sales skyrocketed after it began to sell Clickety-Clack Track™. In addition,

PlayWood's expert witness, Michael Kennedy, testified that PlayWood's concept for noise-producing track had tremendous value. Kennedy testified that the "cross-cuts and changes in the [track's] surface" imparted value to its seller by causing the track to "look different, feel different and sound different than generic track." Kennedy further testified that, in his opinion, the track would have commanded a premium royalty under a negotiated license agreement because the "invention allows its seller to differentiate itself from a host of competitors who are making a generic product with whom it is competing in a way that is proprietary and exclusive, and it gives [the seller] a significant edge over [its] competition."

* * *

It is irrelevant under Illinois law that PlayWood did not actually use the concept in its business. "[T]he proper criterion is not 'actual use' but whether the trade secret is 'of value' to the company." Kennedy's testimony was more than sufficient to permit the jury to conclude that the concept was "of value" to PlayWood. It is equally irrelevant that PlayWood did not seek to patent its concept. So long as the concept remains a secret, *i.e.,* outside of the public domain, there is no need for patent protection. Professor Milgrim makes this point well: "Since every inventor has the right to keep his invention secret, one who has made a patentable invention has the option to maintain it in secrecy, relying upon protection accorded to a trade secret rather than upon the rights which accrue by a patent grant." It was up to PlayWood, not the district court, to determine when and how the concept should have been disclosed to the public.

5. Amount of time, effort and money expended by PlayWood in developing its concept

PlayWood expended very little time and money developing its concept; by Clausi's own account, the cost to PlayWood was less than one dollar and the time spent was less than one-half hour. The district court determined that "[s]uch an insignificant investment is . . . insufficient as a matter of Illinois law to establish the status of a 'trade secret'." We believe that the district court gave too much weight to the time, effort and expense of developing the track.

Although Illinois courts commonly look to the Restatement factors for guidance in determining whether a trade secret exists, as we have noted earlier, the requisite statutory inquiries under Illinois law are (1) whether the information "is sufficiently secret to derive economic value, actual or potential, from not being generally known to other persons who can obtain economic value from its disclosure or use;" and (2) whether the information "is the subject of efforts that are reasonable under the circumstances to maintain its secrecy or confidentiality." A significant expenditure of time and/or money in the production of information may provide evidence of value, which is relevant to the first inquiry above. However, we do not understand Illinois law to require such an expenditure in all cases.

* * *

6.   Ease or difficulty with which PlayWood's concept could have been properly acquired or duplicated by others

Finally, we also believe that there was sufficient evidence for the jury to determine that PlayWood's concept could not have been easily acquired or duplicated through proper means. PlayWood's expert witness, Michael Kennedy, testified: "This is a fairly simple product if you look at it. But the truth is that because it delivers feeling and sound as well as appearance, it isn't so simple as it first appears. It's a little more elegant, actually, than you might think." In addition to Kennedy's testimony, the jury heard that Learning Curve had spent months attempting to differentiate its track from Brio's before Clausi disclosed PlayWood's concept of noise-producing track. From this evidence, the jury could have inferred that, if PlayWood's concept really was obvious, Learning Curve would have thought of it earlier.

Despite this evidence, the district court concluded that PlayWood's concept was not a trade secret because it could have been easily duplicated, stating that "[h]ad PlayWood succeeded in producing and marketing [the] notched track, the appearance of the track product itself would have fully revealed the concept PlayWood now claims as a secret." Of course, the district court was correct in one sense; PlayWood's own expert recognized that, in the absence of patent or copyright protection, the track could have been reverse engineered just by looking at it. However, the district court failed to appreciate the fact that PlayWood's concept was not publicly available. As Professor Milgrim states: "A potent distinction exists between a trade secret which *will be* disclosed if and when the product in which it is embodied is placed on sale, and a 'trade secret' embodied in a product which has been placed on sale, which product admits of discovery of the 'secret' upon inspection, analysis, or reverse engineering." "Until disclosed by sale the trade secret should be entitled to protection." Reverse engineering can defeat a trade secret claim, but only if the product could have been properly acquired by others, as is the case when the product is publicly sold. Here, PlayWood disclosed its concept to Learning Curve (and Learning Curve alone) in the context of a confidential relationship; Learning Curve had no legal authority to reverse engineer the prototype that it received in confidence. Accordingly, we must conclude that the jury was entitled to determine that PlayWood's concept could not easily have been acquired or duplicated through proper means. * * *

Conclusion

For the foregoing reasons, the judgment of the district court is reversed, and the jury's verdict is reinstated. The case is remanded to the district court for a jury trial on exemplary damages and for consideration of attorneys' fees by the court. PlayWood may recover its costs in this court.

REVERSED AND REMANDED.

DID YOU GET IT?

1. What standard of reasonableness does this court apply in its analysis?

2. What facts were relevant to determining whether PlayWood's actions were reasonable to protect its alleged trade secret?

3. What framework or test did this court use to guide its analysis of whether PlayWood's concept was a protectable trade secret?

> ### Reading Guidance
> *How does this case contrast with PlayWood?*

NIEMI V. AMERICAN AXLE MFG. & HOLDING, INC.
Court of Appeals of Michigan, 2007.
2007 WL 29383.
[Not Reported in N.W. 2d]

OWENS, WHITE, HOEKSTRA, J.J.

PER CURIAM.

* * *

AAM, a manufacturer of automotive stabilizer bars, contracted with defendant Springfield to build stabilizer bar benders that combined the functions of forming, flattening, and piercing (referred to as "FFP") the bars. Springfield contracted with plaintiffs for the design of the benders. Plaintiffs prepared the designs and drawings for the machines in accordance with AAM's specifications, on AAM title block paper, and submitted them to Springfield pursuant to Springfield's purchase orders. Plaintiffs did not mark the documents as "confidential," or otherwise agree in writing that defendants were to keep the designs confidential. Springfield paid plaintiffs' invoices in full for the design work. It is undisputed that Springfield built the benders according to plaintiffs' designs, and AAM used the benders to manufacture stabilizer bars for General Motors Corporation GMT 800 and GMT 360 truck platforms. * * *

Plaintiffs brought this action against AAM and Springfield asserting claims for misappropriation of trade secrets in violation of the Michigan Uniform Trade Secrets Act (MUTSA), MCL 445.1901 *et seq.,* and breach of contract. Plaintiffs do not allege that defendants disclosed the design to any other parties. Rather, their misappropriation claim is based on an allegation that defendants continued to use plaintiffs' designs in the manufacture of stabilizer bars without additional compensation. The trial court granted AAM's motion for summary disposition with respect to both claims, and granted Springfield's motion for summary disposition with respect to the misappropriation claim. * * *

Plaintiffs argue that the trial court erred in dismissing their claim for misappropriation of a trade secret because there was a genuine issue of material fact whether they exercised reasonable efforts to maintain the confidentiality of their designs. We disagree.

The MUTSA, which provides a statutory basis for relief from the misappropriation of a trade secret, defines the term "trade secret" as follows:

> (d) "Trade secret" means information, including a formula, pattern, compilation, program, device, method, technique, or process, that is both of the following:
>
>> (i) Derives independent economic value, actual or potential, from not being generally known to, and not being readily ascertainable by proper means by, other persons who can obtain economic value from its disclosure or use.
>>
>> (ii) Is the subject of efforts that are reasonable under the circumstances to maintain its secrecy. [MCL 445.1902.]

Plaintiffs argue that the trial court erred in determining that they failed to demonstrate reasonable efforts to maintain the secrecy of their technological information. Plaintiffs maintain that the parties implicitly understood, based on a 30-year relationship, that the technological information was meant to remain confidential, and that confidentiality was in the interests of all of the parties. Plaintiffs aver that both Springfield and AAM required their employees to keep the information confidential, and that AAM emphasized the need for confidentiality in its internal memoranda. Plaintiffs contend that these efforts were reasonable under the circumstances, pursuant to MCL 445.1902(d)(ii).

Viewing the evidence in a light most favorable to plaintiffs, the only "effort" plaintiffs made to maintain confidentiality was their reliance on an implied agreement that Springfield and AAM would not release the information because they understood the proprietary value of it. Plaintiffs acknowledge that they did not enter into written confidentiality agreements, or label the documents confidential. They do not identify any express oral agreement regarding confidentiality. Plaintiffs emphasize that there were internal confidentiality agreements within defendants' companies, but these do not reflect any effort by plaintiffs to impose confidentiality. Under these circumstances, there is no genuine issue of material fact that plaintiffs failed to make reasonable efforts to safeguard the confidentiality of their designs.

Furthermore, the nature of plaintiffs' complaint is not that defendants disclosed the designs to outsiders, but that they failed to restrict their own use of the designs in accordance with plaintiffs' expectations. Assuming, arguendo, that the parties had an implied agreement to keep plaintiffs' designs concealed from outside parties, this is not sufficient to establish that the parties had an implied agreement to limit defendants' use of plaintiffs' designs. Under these circumstances, the trial court correctly granted summary disposition of plaintiffs' misappropriation of trade secrets claim in favor of defendants.

In reaching this conclusion, we reject plaintiffs' reliance on *Learning Curve Toys, Inc. v. PlayWood Toys, Inc.,* and *Rockwell Graphic Systems, Inc. v. DEV Industries, Inc.,* as support for their contention that their efforts to maintain secrecy were reasonable. In both of these cases, the party asserting the trade secret made efforts to preserve confidentiality that were reasonable for the surrounding circumstances. In *Learning Curve Toys, Inc.,* representatives from the defendant toy manufacturer met with representatives from the plaintiff to discuss combining efforts to produce wooden train sets. The parties orally agreed that their discussion would be kept confidential, and each revealed potentially valuable information. The court determined that the defendant's efforts to preserve confidentiality by an express oral agreement were reasonable under the circumstances. These circumstances included the fact that the defendant was a small, inexperienced firm hoping to take advantage of a potential opportunity.

Here, plaintiffs did not produce evidence of an express oral confidentiality agreement. Rather, they suggest that there was an implied understanding of confidentiality. Plaintiffs contend that they are a small firm, like the defendant in *Learning Curve Toys, Inc.,* but plaintiffs were neither inexperienced, nor were they a fledgling company hoping to take advantage of a new opportunity.

Similarly, *Rockwell, supra,* does not support plaintiffs' position. Although the court in *Rockwell* held that summary judgment is rarely appropriate with respect to the question of reasonable efforts to maintain confidentiality, that holding is not applicable here. The plaintiff in *Rockwell* tried to preserve the confidentiality of its "piece part drawings" by making them confidential, storing them in a locked vault, and monitoring who had access to them. Although the plaintiff did not always strictly enforce these measures, the court recognized that these lapses must be balanced against the plaintiff's interest in efficiency and cost-effectiveness. * * * The court remarked that "only in an extreme case can what is a 'reasonable' precaution be determined on a motion for summary judgment, because the answer depends on a balancing of costs and benefits that will vary from case to case" depending on the particular circumstances.

Although the court in *Rockwell* considered it the exception rather than the rule to decide the question of "reasonable efforts" at the summary disposition stage, summary disposition was proper in this case. Plaintiffs did not make any concrete efforts to preserve the confidentiality of the designs provided to defendants. They did not mark the documents as confidential, or require an express agreement of confidentiality from Springfield. Nor did they control what Springfield or AAM did with the documents while they had them in their possession. Even if plaintiffs made reasonable efforts to guard against disclosure to their competitors, their efforts were not reasonable to restrict defendants' use of the alleged trade secret. Accordingly, the trial court properly granted summary disposition with respect to plaintiffs' misappropriation of trade secrets claim. * * *

Affirmed.

DID YOU GET IT?

1. What was the nature of the relationship between these parties?

2. Why did the court find that the efforts to preserve confidentiality in this case were different from those in *PlayWood*?

3. What is the distinction that the court makes here between the plaintiff's efforts to protect against disclosure of the secret versus use of the secret?

D. SPECIAL ISSUE: WHAT ARE REASONABLE EFFORTS IN A DIGITAL AND CYBER WORLD?

Technology presents an interesting dilemma for the modern law of trade secrecy and the way in which courts evaluate reasonable efforts. How do we keep information secret in a world where technology makes it so easily accessible and where it can be stored in computer servers located anywhere in the world? There is no question that trade secrets have become more vulnerable because of the technological tools now available in the workplace. The facts of one case highlight, in a rather dramatic way, how such misappropriation can occur.

The story in *Four Seasons Hotels & Resorts B.V. v. Consorcio Barr, S.A*, 267 F.Supp.2d 1268 (S.D. Fla. 2003), occurs mostly in Caracas, Venezuela, where the corporate defendant, Consorcio, was the owner of the building which housed the Four Seasons Hotel Caracas. Consorcio entered into various agreements with Four Seasons Hotels whereby Four Seasons would manage the operations of the hotel and license its brand name and trademarks to Consorcio in connection with the operation of the hotel. Pursuant to these agreements, Consorcio could request hard copy print-outs of guest histories from Four Seasons. However, it was not entitled to any of the proprietary electronic data that Four Seasons considered trade secret information, such as detailed guest information in databases and financial management information.

When Four Seasons refused to grant Consorcio access to the electronic data, Consorcio took drastic measures to obtain the information. As explained by the court:

> [A] group of Consorcio's personnel, including armed security guards, forcibly entered the Four Seasons' computer systems room [and u]nder the pretext of self-executing a Venezuelan court order downloaded onto back-up tapes all of the guest information and data stored electronically on [one of Four Seasons' servers] in Caracas, as well as all of the financial information and data stored electronically on [another Four Seasons] server.

Consorcio personnel (specifically, the former assistant to the Four Seasons' Manager of Information Technology) then transferred the downloaded information to a laptop, and using the Four Seasons' IT Director's password gained full access to the databases. Prior to that time, Consorcio also took other steps to acquire Four Seasons' proprietary data by, for instance, intercepting the hotel's e-mail communications and using a program to attempt to crack Four Seasons' passwords.

Consorcio also hired Bencomo, the former Assistant Systems Administrator at the Four Seasons, who came equipped with inside knowledge of the Four Seasons computer networks, as well as the administrative and user passwords. A forensic examination of Bencomo's laptop revealed thirty-eight e-mails sent to Consorcio that contained Four Seasons' data in encrypted spreadsheets. Bencomo was also believed to have engaged in "spoofing" to access the Four Seasons network. As described in the case, spoofing occurs when a person, in attempting to gain access to a network, sets up a fake internet protocol ("IP") address which is not traceable back to their own IP address.

———

Because cases like *Four Seasons* and many other smaller-scale acts of digital misappropriation can occur daily in the course of conducting business, it is imperative that trade secret owners be proactive in trying to protect their trade secrets. *See* Victoria A. Cundiff, *Reasonable Measures to Protect Trade Secrets in a Digital Environment*, 49 IDEA 359 (2009). Professor Elizabeth Rowe argues, in the first excerpt that follows, that in conducting a reasonable efforts analysis, courts should pay attention to the choices made by a trade secret owner to protect digital information. In the second excerpt, she proposes a further refinement of the reasonable efforts requirement in the context of cybersecurity. The case that follows these excerpts provides a glimpse into the security measures that may be needed when dealing with digital information. Finally, the excerpt from Professor Sandeen's article raises concerns about the storage of trade secrets in "the Cloud."

Contributory Negligence, Technology and Trade Secrets

Elizabeth A. Rowe.
17 George Mason L. Rev. 1, 12–13, 27–29 (2009).

When alleged misappropriation occurs by electronic means, many cases analyzing reasonable precautions nonetheless continue to focus on traditional facilities-based security measures. Thus, for instance, courts generally examine the use of non-disclosure agreements, steps to secure the facility, notice to employees about protecting trade secrets, and the use of passwords. In more recent cases, however, courts are beginning to pay more attention to technical protection measures, going beyond the use of traditional measures. * * *

Unfortunately, the only thing consistent about the way in which the courts analyze reasonable efforts in these digital misappropriation cases is the inconsistency in both the approach and outcomes. In one case, the court found that the plaintiff had taken reasonable measures to protect a trade secret that was kept on a computer and protected by a password because the plaintiff used licensing agreements, a password protected Web site, and generally kept the secrets out of the public display at conventions. In another case, a court found that the use of encrypted e-mail to transmit the alleged trade secret and password protection were insufficient to meet the requirement given the lack of other security measures. Still, other courts do not address the issue directly, disposing of the cases on other grounds. * * *

[B]ecause the [reasonable efforts] requirement mandates consideration of what is reasonable under the circumstances, * * * the changing circumstances that have come about as a result of new technology require a reexamination of what security measures are reasonable. Reasonableness requires not necessarily a checklist of specific items, but a conscious, risk assessment approach that better anticipates and ultimately stems the inappropriate dissemination or disclosure of the secrets. This reflects both a normative and prescriptive observation about the appropriate direction for digital misappropriation cases. * * *

To that end, * * * Courts should pay greater attention to the technical measures and processes that companies use to protect their trade secrets, rather than merely focusing on the traditional facilities-based measures. In light of the foreseeability of the greater dangers posed by technology, reasonableness requires evidence of a risk analysis and steps to address those risks. Trade secret owners must avoid ex post facto justifications and explanations for trade secret protection and instead show affirmative measures generated from conscious recognition and assessment of the need to protect putative trade secrets. * * *

Thus, in determining reasonableness, the court ought to not only review evidence of the cost-benefit analysis that the plaintiff trade secret owner might have considered, but also the nature of the risks involved, with special consideration to the known technological risks that may or may not have been considered by the trade secret owner. Factors that could aid in that determination include: (1) the nature of the industry, (2) the nature of the trade secrets and how they were stored, (3) the nature of the measures taken to protect the secrets, and (4) the known risks from storage and protection choices. While some of these are interrelated, the benefit of having each considered separately is that it allows a more comprehensive, methodical, and consistent analysis of the reasonable efforts requirement in each case, something that is currently lacking in the case law.

RATS, TRAPS, AND TRADE SECRETS
Elizabeth A. Rowe.
57 Boston College L. Rev. 381, 412–15 (2016).

In order to effectively combat the kinds of remote access tools, or RATs, that can remotely control a victim's computer and access their files, it is necessary that companies take a more active stance to protect their trade secrets. Accessing remotely without needing to be on the same premises has opened up the world of potential perpetrators, setting up an unwieldy cat and mouse game. Accordingly, [I propose] the acronym TRAP for "technologically responsive active protection" to serve as a guiding principle that further refines the reasonable efforts requirement for the protection of trade secrets. Consistent with every putative trade secret owner's duty to protect its trade secrets, rather than being passive in its efforts, TRAP reinforces the need to take initiative and be self-reliant in preparing and implementing security plans to protect against trade secret misappropriation through electronic means.

The enormous challenges that technology presents through the interconnected framework of the Internet raises the stakes in protecting proprietary information. The larger problem of cybersecurity and espionage is clearly a matter of national concern, and a cooperative stance between the public and private sectors will always be essential. Nevertheless, each company must build its own fortress in this "war," rather than rely on external sources for protection. Active protection certainly requires consideration of technological tools. The use of such tools to protect, hide, or fight back must be considered. For example, some companies build fake networks, create fake documents, or build beacons into their documents that provide more information about who has taken property, not just that it was compromised. Although many of these tools are considered passive, other more aggressive techniques are beginning to emerge as options. Hacking back is an example of an active defense mechanism, but one that is controversial. * * *

Many companies do not invest sufficiently in cybersecurity and protecting their trade secret information. Moreover, to the extent that a company's network may be interconnected with others, vulnerability can be shared on a larger scale as companies increasingly connect over the Internet. Thus, guarding and protecting one's own secrets and assets has benefits beyond each individual company. The private sector can therefore, as a practical matter, play an important role in increasing security.

Companies may choose not to invest, or to invest minimally, in security for a host of reasons. The financial costs associated with shoring up networks and computers can be a deterrent, especially when for many companies the return on investment is uncertain. This problem can be particularly acute with small businesses. Not only are the financial costs more likely to be burdensome, but these businesses might be more likely to underestimate or downplay their risks. Small businesses are also less likely to have the kinds of internal policies in place to secure their information.

Technologically responsive active protection encompasses the view that as a result of technology, trade secret protection has become far more difficult. As such, effective approaches must account for these technological advances, including the interconnectedness of all systems and the intangibility of the kinds of information that companies seek to protect. Accordingly, reasonable efforts to protect trade secrets in this context must be active and ongoing, and must integrate people and processes for optimal protection. Indeed, because the existence of technological controls might in itself create a false sense of security, it is imperative that the role of the people in implementing technological processes effectively be underscored. * * *

A well-considered security plan will include analysis of both internal and external risks, consider the nature of the trade secret information to be protected, appropriately tailor reasonable security measures to protect the sensitive information, and ensure ongoing assessment and review of the security plan in order to update what weaknesses appear. Experts believe that even the most basic steps to protect against cyber intrusions could prevent about eighty percent of such attacks. How money is spent is also of significance. For instance, it is best that companies do more than just protect against perimeter attacks generally designed to detect breaches, and become more aware of developing intelligence about threats. It is also highly recommended that companies encrypt information so that even if it is stolen, it will have no value to the thief.

Reading Guidance

*Did the plaintiff use reasonable measures to protect its software in this
case?*

QSRSOFT, INC. V. RESTAURANT TECHNOLOGY, INC.

United States District Court, N.D. of Illinois, 2006.
84 U.S.P.Q. 2d 1297.

DER-YEGHIAYAN, J.

This matter is before the court on Plaintiff QSRSoft, Inc.'s ("QSRSoft")
motion for entry of a preliminary injunction against Defendant Restaurant
Technology, Inc. ("RTI"). For the reasons stated below, we grant QSRSoft's
motion for a preliminary injunction.

BACKGROUND

QSRSoft contends that every McDonald's Restaurant has a McDonald's
Corporation computer system, an in store processor ("ISP"), that stores
data about the restaurant's sales performance and status. McDonald's
Corporation allegedly provides restaurant operators with limited reports,
called R2D2, but in no relation to Star Wars, generated from the ISP data.
Additionally, QSRSoft alleges that McDonald's Corporation has approved
QSRSoft and RTI as back-office vendors, meaning that each has access to
the data stored in the ISP. Both QSRSoft and RTI provide software tools to
McDonald's Restaurant franchise owners and operators ("franchisees").
QSRSoft contends that both companies' software tools use data extracted
from the ISP.

QSRSoft alleges that it developed the DotComm System, an internet-based
computer system that assists franchisees in analyzing information
collected from the restaurants. QSRSoft contends that the DotComm
System differs from other competitors' systems in that it more quickly
collects and processes information from restaurants, provides automatic
information transfer backup, and provides underlying detail or reports.
QSRSoft alleges that if a franchise wants to use the DotComm System, the
franchisee must first obtain a licensing agreement, which includes a
provision that only key management personnel are permitted to access the
DotComm System due to its proprietary nature. According to QSRSoft, a
franchisee is provided with the opportunity to evaluate the DotComm
System for thirty days under the terms of a software evaluation licensing
agreement. QSRSoft contends that once the franchisee agrees to the
licensing agreement and identifies a list of the key personnel that will have
access to the DotComm System, QSRSoft sends the franchisee an access
code and unique password. QSRSoft alleges that the DotComm System
automatically instructs the user to change the password during the first

time the franchisee accesses the system. According to QSRSoft, the franchisee informs QSRSoft of the updated password.

QSRSoft claims that in January 2006, RTI, who provides predominantly accounting software to fast food restaurants, contacted F.A.F., Inc. d/b/a McDonald's Restaurant ("FAF"), which operates nine McDonald's restaurants in Fargo, North Dakota, to obtain information from QSRSoft about the DotComm System. QSRSoft contends that in February 2006, Gregg Matejka ("Matejka"), FAF's director of operations, contacted QSRSoft about evaluating the DotComm System in one of FAF's McDonald's restaurants. QSRSoft claims that it subsequently sent a licensing agreement ("Agreement") to FAF and requested that the Agreement be executed and returned to QSRSoft. QSRSoft further alleges that on February 8, 2006, QSRSoft sent an access code and password to FAF in anticipation of receiving the executed Agreement from FAF. Although FAF did not return the Agreement, QSRSoft contends that FAF understood that FAF was accepting the terms of the Agreement and would use the DotComm System subject to such terms. QSRSoft claims that on February 8, 2006, FAF accessed the DotComm System using the newly provided access code and password, a process that required FAF to change the initial password. According to QSRSoft, on or about February 9, 2006, FAF provided RTI with the access code and the recently changed password ("FAF password").

QSRSoft alleges that RTI used the FAF password from February 2006 until April 30, 2006 in order to gain access to the DotComm System, view, download, save, print, and copy each web page on the DotComm System, as well as to download the QSRSoft Data Engine, the backbone of the DotComm System's ability to extract restaurant information. QSRSoft claims that RTI was able to use the information it received from accessing the DotComm System to develop Reports, a similar RTI product for McDonald's franchises. * * *

DISCUSSION

* * *

Trade Secret Misappropriation

Under the ITSA, the court may issue an injunction if there is "actual or threatened misappropriation of a trade secret." 765 ILCS 1065/3(a). QSRSoft claims that RTI misappropriated "at least two of" its trade secrets: the Specific ISP Data and the 100 web-page displays ("Screen Shots"). For QSRSoft to show a "better than negligible chance on succeeding on its ITSA trade secret misappropriation claim, QSRSoft must show that (1) there is a trade secret; (2) the trade secret was misappropriated by RTI; and (3) RTI used the trade secret for business purposes.

Existence of Trade Secrets

The ITSA defines a trade secret as:

> [I]nformation, including but not limited to, technical or non-technical data, a formula, pattern, compilation, program, device, method, technique, drawing, process, financial data, or list of actual or potential customers or suppliers, that:
>
> (1) is sufficiently secret to derive economic value, actual or potential, from not being generally known to other persons who can obtain economic value from its disclosure or use; and
>
> (2) is the subject of efforts that are reasonable under the circumstances to maintain its secrecy or confidentiality.

765 ILCS 1065/2(d).

The ITSA therefore "precludes trade secret protection for information generally known or understood within an industry even if not to the public at large," *Pope v. Alberto-Culver Co.*, and "requires a plaintiff to take 'affirmative measures' to prevent others from using [the] information." *Jackson v. Hammer*; *see Learning Curve Toys, Inc. v. PlayWood Toys, Inc.* (noting that the ITSA "prevents a plaintiff who takes no affirmative measures to prevent others from using its proprietary information from obtaining trade secret protection"). * * *

The evidence shows that QSRSoft is likely to succeed in establishing the existence of valid trade secrets. First, although the ISP data is not stored on QSRSoft computers and the ISP data is owned by McDonald's franchisees, how QSRSoft compiles and manipulates the Specific ISP Data for use in the DotComm System is not known to competitors in the industry. Second, QSRSoft has taken reasonable measures to protect its trade secrets from the general public and competitors through the use of licensing agreements, a password protected website, and generally keeping its trade secrets out of the public display at conventions. Third, QSRSoft has presented evidence that show it invested "over two and a half years, more than $2,000,000, and employed three full-time software developers and system architects" to develop the DotComm System. Finally, due to the amount of data contained in the ISP, approximately 315 tables consisting of approximately one million pieces of information, and the fact that the Specific ISP Data represents approximately one percent of the data in the ISP, competitors would have to spend a large amount of time and effort, just as QSRSoft has done, in order to ascertain the precise data needed to determine the Specific ISP Data.

RTI contends that QSRSoft does not have valid trade secrets in the ISP Data or Screen Shots, noting that QSRSoft "spends only two of fifteen pages in its Motion discussing its alleged trade secret claim. . . ." RTI argues that QSRSoft cannot show the validity of the QSRSoft trade secrets because

QSRSoft never introduced either the Specific ISP Data or Screen Shots into evidence. RTI further states that QSRSoft "failed to put into evidence exactly what information [QSRSoft] is referring to when it refers to its Specific ISP Data and DotComm Screen Shots as trade secrets." * * *

RTI alternatively argues that QSRSoft did not reasonably maintain the secrecy of QSRSoft's trade secrets and QSRSoft thereby waived the trade secrets. RTI contends that in *Ruckelshaus v. Monsanto Co.*, "the United States Supreme Court has stated expressly that trade secrets are "*extinguished*" when provided to a third-party that is not obligated to protect the confidentiality of the trade secrets." RTI contends that the Supreme Court has stated:

> Because of the intangible nature of a trade secret, the extent of the property right therein is defined by the extent to which the owner of the secret protects his interest from disclosure to others. Information that is public knowledge or that is generally known in an industry cannot be a trade secret. *If an individual discloses his trade secret to others who are under no obligation to protect the confidentiality of the information, or otherwise publicly discloses the secret, his property right is extinguished.*

(citing *Ruckelshaus*) (emphasis in brief).

However, in *Ruckelshaus*, the Supreme Court was faced with the question of whether the Takings Clause of the Fifth Amendment applied to the Environmental Protection Agency's ("EPA") public disclosure of a trade secret, an intangible property, in the same way it would to tangible property. The particular phrase cited by RTI was used by the Supreme Court to compare trade secrets to tangible property in finding that the plaintiff, Monsanto, had a property right that is protected by the Takings Clause since trade secrets have many of the characteristics of tangible property. Thus, the statement referred to by RTI is not a "clear" statement that any disclosure to a third-party waives a trade secret, but rather is a general statement of the law.

* * *

In the instant action, the evidence establishes that QSRSoft's trade secrets were sufficiently guarded from the public. The efforts taken by QSRSoft to hide its trade secret from competitors such as RTI include: guarding the DotComm System with licensing agreements and a password protected website; not showing the Specific ISP Data or Data Engine to potential customers and competitors at conventions; typically only showing prospective customers and competitors less than five percent of the DotComm System at conventions; typically only showing prospective customers and competitors less than five percent of the Screen Shots at conventions; not showing the DotComm web interface during demonstrations; and not allowing customers and competitors to view the

DotComm source code. These efforts are more than reasonable to establish a better than negligible chance that QSRSoft will be able to show that it did not waive its trade secrets. *See, e.g., Web Communications Group, Inc. v. Gateway 2000, Inc.* (holding that the plaintiff's trade secret misappropriation claim failed "because [plaintiff] took virtually no steps to protect the confidentiality" of the trade secret) (noting that none of the documents relating to the trade secret were marked as confidential (as was the plaintiff's policy with trade secrets), there was not a confidentiality agreement with the defendant, the plaintiff disclosed "either dummies or specifications" for the trade secret at issue to suppliers and competitors, and the plaintiff's president acknowledged that the competitor would be able to use the disclosed information for its own benefit); *Stampede Tool Warehouse* (finding that trade secret had not been waived when reasonable efforts were taken to protect secrecy of trade secrets from competitors).

RTI also argues that because an authorized user accessed the DotComm System and since QSRSoft did not immediately discontinue access to the DotComm System for that user, that QSRSoft has placed its trade secrets into the public domain. However, the evidence supports the finding that the only reported breach of QSRSoft's efforts to keep its trade secrets hidden was performed and traced back to RTI employees, Clutter and Starkey, who viewed, downloaded, and printed information while on the password protected website. Additionally, the fact that RTI understood that the DotComm System could only be accessed with the correct login information supports the claim that RTI was aware that QSRSoft had taken measures to protect its trade secrets. RTI's surreptitious access to the password protected website does not negate the fact that QSRSoft took reasonable efforts to protect its trade secrets. Therefore, based on the evidence, we find that there is a strong likelihood that QSRSoft's claimed trade secrets are protected by the ITSA.

The evidence also shows that QSRSoft has a strong likelihood of showing that RTI misappropriated QSRSoft's trade secrets. [The remainder of the court's misappropriation analysis has been deleted]. * * *

CONCLUSION

Based on the foregoing analysis, we grant QSRSoft's motion for a preliminary injunction.

DID YOU GET IT?

1. What was the nature of the plaintiff's trade secrets and how were they stored?

2. What specific measures did the plaintiff take to preserve the secrecy of the information?

3. How did the defendants allegedly gain access to the trade secrets?

———

The *QSRSoft* case provides a glimpse of the efforts that a business must engage in to protect information that it stores in digital form. If a business maintains its own network of computers and servers, it can retain IT experts that will help it to implement the necessary passwords, firewalls, and encryption protocols that will protect its information. It can also instruct its employees to limit the information that is communicated over the internet and require in-person, intranet, or hard-copy communications of important trade secrets. As Professor Sandeen explains in the following excerpt, however, once a business chooses to store its information with a third-party service (for instance through the use of cloud storage providers), the analysis of reasonable efforts changes because the company must also worry about the security measures that are employed by the third-party. Businesses that choose to utilize third-party services to store their information must also be concerned about the nature of the relationship between the business and the third-party.

LOST IN THE CLOUD: INFORMATION FLOWS AND THE IMPLICATIONS OF CLOUD COMPUTING FOR TRADE SECRET PROTECTION

Sharon K. Sandeen.
19 Va. J.L. & Tech. (JoLT) 1, 48 (2014).

While there is some debate among courts whether a putative trade secret owner can do little or nothing intra-enterprise and still establish the existence of trade secrets for purposes of a misappropriation claim, there is no debate that the decision of a putative trade secret owner to share information outside the confines of its own business requires it to tread carefully. Generally, when a trade secret owner voluntarily decides to share information with another, it risks waiving whatever trade secrecy may exist in such information even in situations where the information does not become generally known of readily ascertainable. * * *

* * *

While some cloud storage services may be willing to provide an express promise of confidentiality, they often disclaim any responsibility or liability for the security of stored information. This not only undermines the creation of an express promise of security, but hampers the ability of the trade secret owner to prove an implied-in-fact promise since a well-established rule of contract law provides that implied obligations cannot be inferred where express obligations of the same nature are disclaimed. Further, unlike other relationships where an implied-at-law duty of confidentiality has been found, the disclosure or use of trade secrets is not necessary to further a business relationship between a cloud storage service and its customers. Thus, although it is conceivable that a cloud storage service might be held to an implied-at-law duty of confidentiality under a special set of facts (even when it has expressly disclaimed liability for stored data), the chances are high that no such duty will be found. This is particularly so since the information that is being stored in the cloud is not likely to be stored in a manner that gives the cloud storage service notice of the existence of trade secrets.

Without the existence of either an express or implied confidential relationship with its cloud storage service, a company that pursues trade secret misappropriation claims for information that is (or has been) stored in the cloud is likely to confront defense arguments that such information is no longer (or never has been) entitled to trade secret protection due to the fact that it was stored in the cloud. In this regard, the defendant will argue that it was not reasonable to store information in the cloud without first securing an express promise of confidentiality. In response, the trade secret owner may produce evidence of the efforts it engaged in to protect its trade secrets intra-enterprise, but such efforts are likely to be insufficient if the same information was shared with one or more third-parties who were not under a duty of confidentiality. This is because, no amount of intra-enterprise reasonable efforts is sufficient to prevent the loss of trade secrecy that results from a voluntary, non-confidential disclosure of trade secrets to third-parties and it will be difficult to establish that extra-contractual duties of confidentiality exists.

Some courts may be troubled by the foregoing analysis and may seek to liberalize traditional notions of confidential relationships in order to avoid the forfeiture of trade secret rights for information stored in the cloud. Or, they may interpret the Stored Communications Act or similar laws to impose a legal duty of confidentiality despite disclaimers to the contrary. While these approaches might solve the problem of trade secrets stored in the cloud, an expansion of the definition of confidential relationships to cover relationships in the cloud could have deleterious effects with respect to other information flows, such as the law governing the unsolicited submission of ideas by so-called "idea-men." Rather than making it easier for duties of confidentiality to be formed in the cloud, I believe that more attention should be paid to the proper definition of "disclosure" under trade secret law and that a better taxonomy is needed to differentiate between trade secret destroying "disclosures" and non-trade secret destroying "mere transfers."

NOTES

1.   **The reasonable efforts requirement of the DTSA and the EU Trade Secret Directive.** Consistent with the language of the UTSA and Article 39 of the TRIPS Agreement, both the DTSA and the EU Trade Secret Directive include reasonable efforts requirements, although in the EU it is

labeled "reasonable steps". What "reasonable efforts" means under each regime remains to be seen.

2. **Reasonable efforts in academic research.** As you have seen, trade secrets exist in virtually every business environment. Research labs and academic environments are no exception. As with every other setting, the extent of efforts to protect such secrets are critical and it is important that professors and researchers (who may not be used to thinking about trade secrets) have policies and measures in place, just like companies, to ensure secrecy. As an example of a dispute involving professors, graduate students, and research assistants, see *Seng-Tiong Ho v. Taflove*, 648 F.3d 489 (7th Cir. 2011).

3. **Bibliographic note:** In addition to the references noted above, for more information on the topics discussed in this chapter, see MILGRIM ON TRADE SECRETS §§ 1.04, 17.03 (2016); Andrea M. Matwyshyn, *Imagining The Intangible*, 34 DEL. J. CORP. L. 965 (2009); Michael Risch, *Why Do We Have Trade Secrets?*, 11 MARQ. INTELL. PROP. L. REV. 1 (2007); Elizabeth A. Rowe, *Introducing a Take-Down for Trade Secrets on the Internet*, 2007 WISCONSIN L. REV. 1041 (2007); Elizabeth A. Rowe, *Saving Trade Secret Disclosures on the Internet Through Sequential Preservation*, 42 WAKE FOREST L. REV. 1 (2007); Andrew-Beckerman-Rodau, *Trade Secrets—The New Risks to Trade Secrets Posed by Computerization*, 28 RUTGERS COMPUTER & TECH. L. J. 227 (2002).

CHAPTER 6

THE MEANING OF MISAPPROPRIATION: IMPROPER MEANS

■ ■ ■

Anticipated Learning Outcomes

At the conclusion of this chapter, you will know the definition of "misappropriation" under the UTSA and DTSA and understand the "improper means" pathway for proving misappropriation. You will also learn the types of wrongful acts (principally, wrongful acquisition) that may be considered improper and those (like independent discovery and reverse engineering) that are proper.

A. INTRODUCTION

Merely proving the existence of a trade secret and defendant's acquisition, disclosure, or use of that secret is not enough to establish a successful claim for trade secret misappropriation. Consistent with general principles of tort law and the concept of "fault," there must also be both some form of wrongdoing and proof of the requisite mindset. As explained in comment g to the *Restatement of Torts*, Section 757:

> Liability under the rule stated in this Section is based not on the actor's purpose to discover another's trade secret but on the nature of the conduct by which the discovery is made. The actor is free to engage in any proper conduct for the very purpose of discovering the secret. So long as his conduct is proper, his purpose does not subject him to liability.

Although the definition of misappropriation set forth in both the UTSA and DTSA is lengthy and is divided into eight subparts, when you read it carefully, four pathways for proving misappropriation (or "wrongdoing") emerge: (1) the improper means pathway; (2) the breach of confidentiality pathway; (3) the accident or mistake pathway and (4) the third-party liability pathway. Additionally, there are three specified wrongful actions: acquisition, disclosure, or use.

UNIFORM TRADE SECRETS ACT
Section 1(2)

As used in this [Act], unless the context requires otherwise:

(2) "Misappropriation" means:

   (i) acquisition of a trade secret of another by a person who knows or has reason to know that the trade secret was acquired by improper means; or — *can be industry/context specific*

   (ii) disclosure or use of a trade secret of another without express or implied consent by a person who

   direct acquirer

   (A) used improper means to acquire knowledge of the trade secret; or

   (B) at the time of disclosure or use, knew or had reason to know that his knowledge of the trade secret was

   (I) derived from or through a person who had *downstream acquirer* utilized improper means to acquire it;

   (II) acquired under circumstances giving rise to a duty to maintain its secrecy or limit its use; or

   (III) derived from or through a person who owed a duty to the person seeking relief to maintain its secrecy or limit its use; or

   not frequently litigated

   (C) before a material change of his [or her] position, knew or had reason to know that it was a trade secret and that knowledge of it had been acquired by accident or mistake.

———

This chapter explores the types of wrongdoing that can constitute acquisition by "improper means," that is, activities that may constitute actual or threatened wrongful acquisition of trade secrets. It also presents cases that illustrate permissible ways to discover a trade secret, like independent discovery and reverse engineering. The Special Issue section explores the difference between competitive intelligence and corporate espionage.

B. THE MEANING AND LIMITS OF "IMPROPER MEANS"

Many of the cases that have been examined in the preceding chapters involve the alleged breach of a duty of confidentiality that arose either in the employment context or in a business-to-business relationship. These sorts of cases make up the bulk of trade secret litigation in the U.S. and are explored more fully in Chapter 7 when misappropriation by "wrongful" disclosure or use is explored. As noted in Chapter 1, it was from such relationships that the law of trade secrets developed, with the concept of a claim for wrongful acquisition of trade secrets emerging much later. *See* Note, *Nature of Trade Secrets and Their Protection*, 42 HARV. L. REV. 254 (1928).

Although not as numerous, lawsuits involving the alleged acquisition of trade secrets by improper means tend to have greater rhetorical power because they often include allegations of criminal behavior, such as theft, bribery, and cyber-espionage. Because they are not dependent on the existence of a confidential relationship, however, they also present important questions concerning the requisite knowledge of the accused defendant, proof of harm, and the available remedies. A very practical problem is that the desire to punish the defendant for bad behavior often causes courts and juries to overlook the need to prove the other elements of a trade secret claim.

According to Section 1(1) of the UTSA, "improper means" includes "theft, bribery, misrepresentation, breach or inducement of a breach of a duty to maintain secrecy, or espionage through electronic means." However, the comments to Section 1 go on to quote comment f to the *Restatement of Torts* which explains: "a complete catalogue listing of improper means is not possible." Thus, while the list that is contained in Section 1(1) of the UTSA suggests the kinds of actions that are deemed contrary to standards of business ethics, it is not an exclusive list. Plaintiffs in trade secret cases who are unable to prove theft, bribery, misrepresentation, inducement, breach of confidentiality, or espionage are allowed to argue that defendant's actions were nonetheless improper. The critical question for purposes of trade secret analysis is determining what these actions might be.

The DTSA includes language that is identical to the UTSA language, but with an explicit, statutory exception. Title 18, section 1839(6) states:

[T]he term 'improper means'—

(A) includes theft, bribery, misrepresentation, breach or inducement of a breach of a duty to maintain secrecy, or espionage through electronic or other means; and

(B) does not include reverse engineering, independent derivation, or any other lawful means of acquisition.

The UTSA does not use the term "lawful means." Instead, it uses and defines the terms "improper means" in the text of the UTSA and "proper means" in the commentary. The meaning of "lawful means" under the DTSA will have to be interpreted by the federal courts.

> ### *Food for Thought*
> *Must the actions of the defendant constitute a crime or a tort, or can otherwise legal activities be deemed "improper" because the defendant's purpose is to acquire trade secrets? What types of "lawful means of acquisition" would not be misappropriation under the DTSA?*

Although the foregoing questions are still open to debate, there are some activities that trade secret law recognizes as proper. This includes the activities of reverse engineering and independent development which, as noted above, were made an explicit part of the DTSA.

The comments to Section 1 of the UTSA provide the following non-exclusive list of 5 activities that are deemed "proper means" to acquire a trade secret:

1. Discovery by independent invention;

2. Discovery by "reverse engineering," that is, by starting with the known product and working backward to find the method by which it was developed. The acquisition of the known product must, of course, also be by fair and honest means, such as purchase of the item on the open market for reverse engineering to be lawful;

3. Discovery under a license from the owner of the trade secret;

4. Observation of the item in public use or on public display; [and]

5. Obtaining the trade secret from published literature.

In the cases that follow you will see how the focus on the defendant's conduct is critical to the improper means analysis.

> ### *Food for Thought*
> *Can you identify actions, not listed in Section 1(1) of the UTSA, that you believe constitute "improper means" of acquiring trade secrets? Conversely, can you identify additional "proper means" for acquiring trade secret information other than those listed above?*

Reading Guidance

What was improper about the defendant's conduct in this case?

PIONEER HI-BRED INT'L V. HOLDEN FOUNDATION SEEDS, INC.

United States Court of Appeals, Eighth Circuit, 1994.
35 F.3d 1226.

JOHN R. GIBSON, SENIOR CIRCUIT JUDGE.

This case involves a dispute between competing breeders of corn seed. The district court awarded $46,703,230.00 to Pioneer Hi-Bred International based on Holden Foundation Seeds, Inc.'s misappropriation of the genetic make-up of certain seed corn. Holden contests the district court's liability determination and damage award on numerous grounds. * * * We affirm.

trial ct. - P won.

* * *

The sale of hybrid seed corn is a multi-billion dollar industry. Pioneer is a vertically integrated seed corn company. It conducts a breeding program, develops parent seed, and produces hybrid seed corn for the retail market. The superior performance of its products, obtained in part through millions of dollars spent annually on corn research and development, has enabled it to gain a sizeable portion of the retail seed corn market. Its marketed seed corns include Pioneer hybrids 3780 (Pioneer's leader in sales for several years) and 3541—which share a common parent, designated H3H.

P

Holden indirectly competes with Pioneer. Holden is a foundation seed company that develops inbred parent seed lines and sells these lines to its customers, also seed corn companies, which use them to produce hybrid seed in competition with Pioneer. During the 1980s, Holden's LH38, LH39, and LH40 ("LH38–39–40") were among its most popular parent lines.

D

Pioneer sued Holden on a number of legal theories, claiming that Holden developed LH38–39–40 from misappropriated Pioneer H3H or H43SZ7—protected trade secrets of Pioneer ("H3H/H43SZ7"). During discovery, the district court decided, at Pioneer's request that the nature of this dispute required that Holden "freeze in" a particular story regarding the development of LH38–39–40. The court did so to prevent Holden from altering its story to conform to the scientific evidence eventually introduced. Holden claimed that although LH38–39–40 demonstrated some similarity to Pioneer's seed lines, Holden developed LH38–39–40 from an internal line, designated L120. The district court held that the genetic make-up of H3H/H43SZ7 is a protected trade secret of Pioneer. The court determined that although LH38–39–40 differed in some respects from Pioneer's seed, the lines had nonetheless been derived from misappropriated Pioneer material. The district court based its decision on expert testimony that LH38–39–40 derived from H3H/H43SZ7 and

Holden's inability to offer adequate evidence of its "L120 story." * * * The district court awarded over 46 million dollars in damages to Pioneer. Holden appeals. * * *

Much of Holden's argument before this court focused on the district court's ruling that Holden misappropriated Pioneer's protected trade secret. According to Iowa law, a plaintiff must generally show three elements to prevail in a trade secret action: "(1) existence of a trade secret, (2) acquisition of the secret as a result of a confidential relationship, and (3) unauthorized use of a secret." We review determinations of state law de novo, giving the district court no deference.

Iowa Law

Holden does not argue on appeal that genetic messages cannot qualify as trade secrets. Ronald Holden, Holden's chief operating officer, testified that he does not "have any problem" with the idea that there is a claimed proprietary interest in inbreds and parent lines. Thus, we assume without deciding that genetic messages can qualify for trade secret status. Holden instead argues that it should not be liable for misappropriating H3H/H43SZ7 because Pioneer failed: (1) to keep the genetic messages secret; (2) to prove that Holden actually possessed the protected genetic messages; and (3) to prove that Holden obtained the material by improper means. The district court rejected each of Holden's arguments. * * *

Holden argues that H3H/H43SZ7 are not trade secrets because Pioneer failed to maintain their secrecy. * * * The district court found that the genetic messages of H3H and H43SZ7 were trade secrets. The district court found that the "formula" did not exist outside Pioneer's and its contractors' fields, and that Pioneer took reasonable precautions to protect the secrecy of the genetic message. Pioneer takes several measures to preserve the secrecy of its inbreds. Growers operate under contracts which prohibit disclosure of the seed. Fields have no labels indicating what seed is being grown, and all seed bags are coded to avoid identification. Pioneer removes male inbred lines and commingles them with other corn, thereby frustrating those seeking to obtain the inbred seed. * * *

Although there is conflicting evidence on whether Pioneer had maintained the secrecy of the genetic messages, there is sufficient evidence to support the district court's finding that Pioneer took reasonable precautions to protect the secrecy of the genetic message of H3H/H43SZ7. * * * Holden's claim that the message was "widely disseminated" because it could be obtained from seed elevators and farmers' seed bags is overstated. Although a Pioneer employee, Thomas Urban, acknowledged that the male corn could get into a seed bag as a contaminant, he also stated "it's almost impossible." Urban explained that Pioneer had "many, many employees who stood looking at corn ears . . . [and] [t]he chances of that happening are not very great." Urban knew of no instances of the male corn being found in bags of hybrid seed. Moreover, the seed in the bags and elevators is mixed, and a grower would have no way of easily identifying the desired male seed from the many other seeds in the overall mix. "The more difficult, time consuming and costly it would be to develop the information, the less likely it is 'readily' ascertainable." It is also relevant that the possible means identified by Holden of obtaining H3H/H43SZ7 were not the means by which Holden claimed it developed LH38–39–40. Many courts have held that the fact that one "could" have obtained a trade secret lawfully is not a defense if one does not actually use proper means to acquire the information. This evidence does not lead us to conclude that the district court clearly erred in finding that Pioneer maintained the requisite secrecy for trade secret protection of H3H/H43SZ7. * * *

Holden also argues that Pioneer's trade secret claim is invalid because insufficient evidence supports the district court's finding that Holden possessed H3H or H43SZ7. Holden contends that since none of the tests can conclusively prove parentage, the district court clearly erred in finding possession. * * * We believe that there is sufficient evidence to warrant a finding that Holden derived LH38–39–40 from H3H/H43SZ7. Holden does not attack the qualifications of the various experts, and our review of their testimony convinces us that the experts established by a preponderance of the evidence that Holden derived LH38–39–40 from H3H/H43SZ7. * * * The various tests, according to Pioneer's witnesses, indicated that Holden more likely than not used Pioneer's trade secrets to develop LH38–39–40. One Pioneer expert, Dr. Donald Duvick, estimated the likelihood of Holden's independent development of L120 to be approximately one in a trillion. Sprague stated that he found it "extremely difficult" to buy Holden's L120 story. Although reasonable minds could differ as to the merits of the experts' various conclusions, the testimony certainly permitted the court to do far more than "speculate or guess" about possession. The combined results of all the tests, when viewed together, provide sufficient evidence of possession.

* * *

We next consider Holden's argument that Pioneer failed to prove the second requisite element of a trade secret action. Although frequently listed as such, a "confidential relationship" is not in fact a prerequisite to a trade secret action. Holden admits that a contractual or confidential relationship is not required to maintain a trade secret action. The district court held, and the parties agree, that a plaintiff may prevail in the absence of such a relationship by showing that the secret was obtained by improper means. *See Restatement of Torts* § 757(a) (1939) (the critical inquiry is whether the defendant obtained the secret by "improper means").

Conduct which is not otherwise unlawful may nonetheless be improper. *Dupont v. Christopher* (use of aircraft to view partially-completed, guarded building of competitor held to be "improper means"). Holden contends, however, that Pioneer failed to prove improper means. In support of its position, Holden suggests there is absolutely no evidence of misappropriation or improper means. Thus, Holden argues we must reverse because mere possession of a trade secret cannot support a trade secret award. *See Restatement of Torts* § 757, cmt. a (1939) ("[i]t is the employment of improper means to procure the trade secret, rather than the mere copying or use, which is the basis of the liability"); *cf. Kewanee Oil* ("trade secret [law] . . . does not offer protection against discovery by fair and honest means, such as by independent invention, accidental disclosure, or by so-called reverse engineering, that is by starting with the known product and working backward to divine the process which aided in its development or manufacture").

After considering Holden's arguments, the district court found "that Pioneer has met its burden regarding misappropriation." Although the court failed to elaborate upon the precise facts which supported its finding of improper means, such elaboration is not required.

Certainly, the issue is close. Pioneer presented no direct evidence regarding how Holden obtained H3H/H43SZ7. However, "direct evidence of industrial espionage is rarely available" and not required. "Wrongful taking of a trade secret can be found based on circumstantial evidence." Roger M. Milgrim, *Trade Secrets* § 15.01[1]. Moreover, the fact that Holden may have altered Pioneer's secret does not insulate it from liability. Slight alteration of a competitor's protected secret implicates the same concerns as cases of outright misappropriation.

The record displays a long history of Holden attempts to obtain Pioneer's genetic material. Roland Holden, the now-retired founder of Holden's Foundation Seeds, Inc., testified about his repeated searches for Pioneer's seed. As the court stated, "it is very clear that for a number of years, Roland Holden was doing anything he could to try to find out more about and grow Pioneer lines." These efforts included searching "friendly farms" for stray inbred plants (e.g., H3H)—a process by which he admitted obtaining possession of several Pioneer lines. Although the court concluded that "Pioneer has not specifically shown" that these efforts were the "exact source" of L120, the testimony supports such an inference. Holden's inadequate explanation of its faulty record-keeping and the untimely disposal of all L120 seed also give rise to an inference of misappropriation. An inference of misappropriation from limited facts is especially warranted in situations such as this where the secret itself is so unique that any form of duplication would probably be improper. *Rockwell Graphic v. DEV Indus.* (stating that if a plaintiff can show that the probability of the defendant obtaining the trade secret by proper means is slight, then "it will have taken a giant step toward proving what it must prove" to recover in a trade secret action). Unlike the situation where a competitor is found to have possession of a process, product or fact which is similar to plaintiff's "secret," this case involves possession of a product *derived from* the protected secret. Proof of derivation removes the possibility of independent development, further supporting the court's finding that Holden misappropriated genetic material from Pioneer.

The court did not end its analysis after determining that Pioneer met its burden as to misappropriation or improper means. Rather, the court concluded that since Pioneer "met this burden, Holden has the burden of showing that H3H and/or H43SZ7 were lawfully acquired"—a burden which the court concluded Holden did not meet. Holden construes this language as expressing the court's decision to place upon it, and not Pioneer, the burden of proof on the issue of improper means.

There is authority supporting a shift in the burden of proof once a plaintiff proves that the defendant obtained and used the trade secret. However, the cases employing a burden-shifting analysis typically involve breaches of confidential relationships. Nonetheless, a burden-shifting analysis may be appropriate in those instances, such as this case, where the defendant actively pursued plaintiff's secrets, discarded highly relevant information, consistently denied obtaining the protected material through any means, and possessed secrets shown to have probably been derived from (not merely exhibiting similarities to) plaintiff's secret.

* * * In light of the evidence discussed above, and after reviewing the entire record, we cannot say the district court's finding of misappropriation was clearly erroneous.

DID YOU GET IT?

1. The defendant argued that there was no evidence of improper means. Why did the court find otherwise?

2. Is it a crime or a tort to take seeds from a "friendly field"?

3. What is the significance of the fact that the defendant's product was derived from the plaintiff's product?

4. Is the fact that a plaintiff's trade secret is in a defendant's possession sufficient to find improper means?

5. How did the reasonable efforts requirement intersect with the improper means analysis in this case?

Food for Thought

Look again at the definition of misappropriation under the UTSA, set forth above. What must the defendant Holden have known about the alleged trade secrets? Was that proven? If so, how?

---

held aerial photos of plant was improper means of obtaining TS
construction

> ### Reading Guidance
>
> What laws did the defendants violate in the process of taking photographs in this case? *Texas Restatement Torts §757*

E.I. DUPONT DENEMOURS & CO. V. CHRISTOPHER

United States Court of Appeals, Fifth Circuit, 1970.
431 F.2d 1012.

GOLDBERG, CIRCUIT JUDGE.

- D photogs took photos via plane directly on top of construction site.
- to determine process for making methanol

This is a case of industrial espionage in which an airplane is the cloak and a camera the dagger. The defendants-appellants, Rolfe and Gary Christopher, are photographers in Beaumont, Texas. The Christophers were hired by an unknown third party to take aerial photographs of new construction at the Beaumont plant of E. I. duPont deNemours & Company, Inc. Sixteen photographs of the DuPont facility were taken from the air on March 19, 1969, and these photographs were later developed and delivered to the third party.

DuPont employees apparently noticed the airplane on March 19 and immediately began an investigation to determine why the craft was circling over the plant. By that afternoon the investigation had disclosed that the craft was involved in a photographic expedition and that the Christophers were the photographers. DuPont contacted the Christophers that same afternoon and asked them to reveal the name of the person or corporation requesting the photographs. The Christophers refused to disclose this information, giving as their reason the client's desire to remain anonymous. Having reached a dead end in the investigation, DuPont subsequently filed suit against the Christophers, alleging that the Christophers had wrongfully obtained photographs revealing DuPont's trade secrets which they then sold to the undisclosed third party. DuPont contended that it had developed a highly secret but unpatented process for producing methanol, a process which gave DuPont a competitive advantage over other producers. This process, DuPont alleged, was a trade secret developed after much expensive and time-consuming research, and a secret which the company had taken special precautions to safeguard. The area photographed by the Christophers was the plant designed to produce methanol by this secret process, and because the plant was still under construction parts of the process were exposed to view from directly above the construction area. Photographs of that area, DuPont alleged, would enable a skilled person to deduce the secret process for making methanol. DuPont thus contended that the Christophers had wrongfully appropriated DuPont trade secrets by taking the photographs and delivering them to the undisclosed third party. In its suit DuPont asked for damages to cover the loss it had already sustained as a result of the wrongful disclosure of the trade secret and sought temporary and permanent injunctions prohibiting

relief sought

any further circulation of the photographs already taken and prohibiting any additional photographing of the methanol plant.

The Christophers answered with motions to dismiss for lack of jurisdiction and failure to state a claim upon which relief could be granted. Depositions were taken during which the Christophers again refused to disclose the name of the person to whom they had delivered the photographs. DuPont then filed a motion to compel an answer to this question and all related questions.

On June 5, 1969, the trial court held a hearing on all pending motions and an additional motion by the Christophers for summary judgment. The court denied the Christophers' motions to dismiss for want of jurisdiction and failure to state a claim and also denied their motion for summary judgment. The court granted DuPont's motion to compel the Christophers to divulge the name of their client. Having made these rulings, the court then granted the Christophers' motion for an interlocutory appeal under 28 U.S.C.A. § 1292(b) to allow the Christophers to obtain immediate appellate review of the court's finding that DuPont had stated a claim upon which relief could be granted. Agreeing with the trial court's determination that DuPont had stated a valid claim, we affirm the decision of that court.

This is a case of first impression, for the Texas courts have not faced this precise factual issue, and sitting as a diversity court we must sensitize our Erie antennae to divine what the Texas courts would do if such a situation were presented to them. The only question involved in this interlocutory appeal is whether DuPont has asserted a claim upon which relief can be granted. The Christophers argued both at trial and before this court that they committed no "actionable wrong" in photographing the DuPont facility and passing these photographs on to their client because they conducted all of their activities in public airspace, violated no government aviation standard, did not breach any confidential relation, and did not engage in any fraudulent or illegal conduct. In short, the Christophers argue that for an appropriation of trade secrets to be wrongful there must be a trespass, other illegal conduct, or breach of a confidential relationship. We disagree.

[margin note: D's argument]

It is true, as the Christophers assert, that the previous trade secret cases have contained one or more of these elements. However, we do not think that the Texas courts would limit the trade secret protection exclusively to these elements. On the contrary, in *Hyde Corporation v. Huffines*, the Texas Supreme Court specifically adopted the rule found in the Restatement of Torts which provides:

> 'One who discloses or uses another's trade secret, without a privilege to do so, is liable to the other if (a) he discovered the secret by improper means, or (b) his disclosure or use constitutes a breach of confidence reposed in him by the other in disclosing the secret to him * * *.' Restatement of Torts § 757 (1939).

Thus, although the previous cases have dealt with a breach of a confidential relationship, a trespass, or other illegal conduct, the rule is much broader than the cases heretofore encountered. Not limiting itself to specific wrongs, Texas adopted subsection (a) of the Restatement which recognizes a cause of action for the discovery of a trade secret by any 'improper' means.

The defendants, however, read *Furr's Inc. v. United Specialty Advertising Co.*, as limiting the Texas rule to breach of a confidential relationship. The court in Furr's did make the statement that "The use of someone else's idea is not automatically a violation of the law. It must be something that meets the requirements of a 'trade secret' and has been obtained through a breach of confidence in order to entitle the injured party to damages and/or injunction."

We think, however, that the exclusive rule which defendants have extracted from this statement is unwarranted. In the first place, in Furr's the court specifically found that there was no trade secret involved because the entire advertising scheme claimed to be the trade secret had been completely divulged to the public. Secondly, the court found that the plaintiff in the course of selling the scheme to the defendant had voluntarily divulged the entire scheme. Thus the court was dealing only with a possible breach of confidence concerning a properly discovered secret; there was never a question of any impropriety in the discovery or any other improper conduct on the part of the defendant. The court merely held that under those circumstances the defendant had not acted improperly if no breach of confidence occurred. We do not read Furr's as limiting the trade secret protection to a breach of confidential relationship when the facts of the case do raise the issue of some other wrongful conduct on the part of one discovering the trade secrets of another. If breach of confidence were meant to encompass the entire panoply of commercial improprieties, subsection (a) of the Restatement would be either surplusage or persiflage, an interpretation abhorrent to the traditional precision of the Restatement. We therefore find meaning in subsection (a) and think that the Texas Supreme Court clearly indicated by its adoption that there is a cause of action for the discovery of a trade secret by any "improper means."

The question remaining, therefore, is whether aerial photography of plant construction is an improper means of obtaining another's trade secret. We conclude that it is and that the Texas courts would so hold. The Supreme Court of that state has declared that "the undoubted tendency of the law has been to recognize and enforce higher standards of commercial morality in the business world." That court has quoted with approval articles indicating that the proper means of gaining possession of a competitor's secret process is "through inspection and analysis" of the product in order to create a duplicate. Later another Texas court explained:

> 'The means by which the discovery is made may be obvious, and the experimentation leading from known factors to presently unknown results may be simple and lying in the public domain. But these facts do not destroy the value of the discovery and will not advantage a competitor who by unfair means obtains the knowledge without paying the price expended by the discoverer.'

We think, therefore, that the Texas rule is clear. One may use his competitor's secret process if he discovers the process by reverse engineering applied to the finished product; one may use a competitor's process if he discovers it by his own independent research; but one may not avoid these labors by taking the process from the discoverer without his permission at a time when he is taking reasonable precautions to maintain its secrecy. To obtain knowledge of a process without spending the time and money to discover it independently is improper unless the holder voluntarily discloses it or fails to take reasonable precautions to ensure its secrecy.

In the instant case the Christophers deliberately flew over the DuPont plant to get pictures of a process which DuPont had attempted to keep secret. The Christophers delivered their pictures to a third party who was certainly aware of the means by which they had been acquired and who may be planning to use the information contained therein to manufacture methanol by the DuPont process. The third party has a right to use this process only if he obtains this knowledge through his own research efforts, but thus far all information indicates that the third party has gained this knowledge solely by taking it from DuPont at a time when DuPont was making reasonable efforts to preserve its secrecy. In such a situation DuPont has a valid cause of action to prohibit the Christophers from improperly discovering its trade secret and to prohibit the undisclosed third party from using the improperly obtained information.

We note that this view is in perfect accord with the position taken by the authors of the Restatement. In commenting on improper means of discovery the savants of the Restatement said:

> 'f.   Improper means of discovery. The discovery of another's trade secret by improper means subjects the actor to liability independently of the harm to the interest in the secret. Thus, if one uses physical force to take a secret formula from another's pocket, or breaks into another's office to steal the formula, his conduct is wrongful and subjects him to liability apart from the rule stated in this Section. Such conduct is also an improper means of procuring the secret under this rule. But means may be improper under this rule even though they do not cause any other harm than that to the interest in the trade secret. Examples of such means are fraudulent misrepresentations to induce

disclosure, tapping of telephone wires, eavesdropping or other espionage. A complete catalogue of improper means is not possible. In general, they are means which fall below the generally accepted standards of commercial morality and reasonable conduct.'

In taking this position we realize that industrial espionage of the sort here perpetrated has become a popular sport in some segments of our industrial community. However, our devotion to free wheeling industrial competition must not force us into accepting the law of the jungle as the standard of morality expected in our commercial relations. Our tolerance of the espionage game must cease when the protections required to prevent another's spying cost so much that the spirit of inventiveness is dampened. Commercial privacy must be protected from espionage which could not have been reasonably anticipated or prevented. We do not mean to imply, however, that everything not in plain view is within the protected vale, nor that all information obtained through every extra optical extension is forbidden. Indeed, for our industrial competition to remain healthy there must be breathing room for observing a competing industrialist. A competitor can and must shop his competition for pricing and examine his products for quality, components, and methods of manufacture. Perhaps ordinary fences and roofs must be built to shut out incursive eyes, but we need not require the discoverer of a trade secret to guard against the unanticipated, the undetectable, or the unpreventable methods of espionage now available.

In the instant case DuPont was in the midst of constructing a plant. Although after construction the finished plant would have protected much of the process from view, during the period of construction the trade secret was exposed to view from the air. To require DuPont to put a roof over the unfinished plant to guard its secret would impose an enormous expense to prevent nothing more than a school boy's trick. We introduce here no new or radical ethic since our ethos has never given moral sanction to piracy. The market place must not deviate far from our mores. We should not require a person or corporation to take unreasonable precautions to prevent another from doing that which he ought not do in the first place. Reasonable precautions against predatory eyes we may require, but an impenetrable fortress is an unreasonable requirement, and we are not disposed to burden industrial inventors with such a duty in order to protect the fruits of their efforts. "Improper" will always be a word of many nuances, determined by time, place, and circumstances. We therefore need not proclaim a catalogue of commercial improprieties. Clearly, however, one of its commandments does say "thou shall not appropriate a trade secret through deviousness under circumstances in which countervailing defenses are not reasonably available."

Having concluded that aerial photography, from whatever altitude, is an improper method of discovering the trade secrets exposed during construction of the DuPont plant, we need not worry about whether the flight pattern chosen by the Christophers violated any federal aviation regulations. Regardless of whether the flight was legal or illegal in that sense, the espionage was an improper means of discovering DuPont's trade secret.

The decision of the trial court is affirmed and the case remanded to that court for proceedings on the merits.

DID YOU GET IT?

1. Which state's law was applicable in this case? *Texas Restatement of Torts § 757*

2. What was the defendants' argument as to why they were not liable for misappropriation via improper means? *Didn't break the law, violate confid., etc.*

3. According to the court, why shouldn't DuPont have been expected to take additional precautions to guard against the defendants' conduct? *B/c it would be unreasonable to impose huge expense*

4. *Christopher* was decided long before Texas adopted the UTSA. Would the result be the same under the UTSA? What about Texas' version of the UTSA?

Reading Guidance

How might the public policy expressed in this case help define "improper" and "proper" means of acquiring trade secrets?

BONITO BOATS, INC. V. THUNDER CRAFT BOATS, INC.

Unites States Supreme Court, 1989.
489 U.S. 141.

JUSTICE O'CONNOR delivered the opinion of the Court.

We must decide today what limits the operation of the federal patent system places on the States' ability to offer substantial protection to utilitarian and design ideas which the patent laws leave otherwise unprotected. In *Interpart Corp. v. Italia,* the Court of Appeals for the Federal Circuit concluded that a California law prohibiting the use of the "direct molding process" to duplicate unpatented articles posed no threat to the policies behind the federal patent laws. In this case, the Florida Supreme Court came to a contrary conclusion. It struck down a Florida statute which prohibits the use of the direct molding process to duplicate unpatented boat hulls, finding that the protection offered by the Florida law conflicted with the balance struck by Congress in the federal patent statute between the encouragement of invention and free competition in unpatented ideas. We granted certiorari to resolve the conflict and we now affirm the judgment of the Florida Supreme Court.

I

In September 1976, petitioner Bonito Boats, Inc. (Bonito), a Florida corporation, developed a hull design for a fiberglass recreational boat which it marketed under the trade name Bonito Boat Model 5VBR. Designing the boat hull required substantial effort on the part of Bonito. A set of engineering drawings was prepared, from which a hardwood model was created. The hardwood model was then sprayed with fiberglass to create a mold, which then served to produce the finished fiberglass boats for sale. The 5VBR was placed on the market sometime in September 1976. * * *

In May 1983, after the Bonito 5VBR had been available to the public for over six years, the Florida Legislature enacted Fla.Stat. § 559.94 (1987). The statute makes "[i]t ... unlawful for any person to use the direct molding process to duplicate for the purpose of sale any manufactured vessel hull or component part of a vessel made by another without the written permission of that other person." The statute also makes it unlawful for a person to "knowingly sell a vessel hull or component part of a vessel duplicated in violation of subsection (2)." * * *

On December 21, 1984, Bonito filed this action in the Circuit Court of Orange County, Florida. The complaint alleged that respondent here, Thunder Craft Boats, Inc. (Thunder Craft), a Tennessee corporation, had violated the Florida statute by using the direct molding process to duplicate the Bonito 5VBR fiberglass hull, and had knowingly sold such duplicates in violation of the Florida statute. Bonito sought "a temporary and permanent injunction prohibiting [Thunder Craft] from continuing to unlawfully duplicate and sell Bonito Boat hulls or components," as well as an accounting of profits, treble damages, punitive damages, and attorney's fees. * * *

II

Article I, § 8, cl. 8, of the Constitution gives Congress the power "[t]o promote the Progress of Science and useful Arts, by securing for limited Times to Authors and Inventors the exclusive Right to their respective Writings and Discoveries." The Patent Clause itself reflects a balance between the need to encourage innovation and the avoidance of monopolies which stifle competition without any concomitant advance in the "Progress of Science and useful Arts." As we have noted in the past, the Clause contains both a grant of power and certain limitations upon the exercise of that power. Congress may not create patent monopolies of unlimited duration, nor may it "authorize the issuance of patents whose effects are to remove existent knowledge from the public domain, or to restrict free access to materials already available."

From their inception, the federal patent laws have embodied a careful balance between the need to promote innovation and the recognition that imitation and refinement through imitation are both necessary to invention itself and the very lifeblood of a competitive economy. * * *

Sections 102(a) and (b) [of the Patent Act] operate in tandem to exclude from consideration for patent protection knowledge that is already available to the public. They express a congressional determination that the creation of a monopoly in such information would not only serve no socially useful purpose, but would in fact injure the public by removing existing knowledge from public use. From the Patent Act of 1790 to the present day, the public sale of an unpatented article has acted as a complete bar to federal protection of the idea embodied in the article thus placed in public commerce. * * *

* * *

Thus our past decisions have made clear that state regulation of intellectual property must yield to the extent that it clashes with the balance struck by Congress in our patent laws. The tension between the desire to freely exploit the full potential of our inventive resources and the need to create an incentive to deploy those resources is constant. * * *

What was implicit in our decision in *Sears*, we have made explicit in our subsequent decisions concerning the scope of federal pre-emption of state regulation of the subject matter of patent. Thus, in *Kewanee Oil Co. v. Bicron Corp.,* we held that state protection of trade secrets did not operate to frustrate the achievement of the congressional objectives served by the patent laws. Despite the fact that state law protection was available for ideas which clearly fell within the subject matter of patent, the Court concluded that the nature and degree of state protection did not conflict with the federal policies of encouragement of patentable invention and the prompt disclosure of such innovations.

* * *

We have since reaffirmed the pragmatic approach which *Kewanee* takes to the pre-emption of state laws dealing with the protection of intellectual property. At the same time, we have consistently reiterated the teaching of *Sears* and *Compco* that ideas once placed before the public without the protection of a valid patent are subject to appropriation without significant restraint. * * *

III

We believe that the Florida statute at issue in this case so substantially impedes the public use of the otherwise unprotected design and utilitarian ideas embodied in unpatented boat hulls as to run afoul of the teaching of our decisions in *Sears* and *Compco*. It is readily apparent that the Florida statute does not operate to prohibit "unfair competition" in the usual sense that the term is understood. The law of unfair competition has its roots in the common-law tort of deceit: its general concern is with protecting consumers from confusion as to source. While that concern may result in the creation of "quasi-property rights" in communicative symbols, the focus is on the protection of consumers, not the protection of producers as an incentive to product innovation. * * *

In contrast to the operation of unfair competition law, the Florida statute is aimed directly at preventing the exploitation of the design and utilitarian conceptions embodied in the product itself. The sparse legislative history surrounding its enactment indicates that it was intended to create an inducement for the improvement of boat hull designs. To accomplish this goal, the Florida statute endows the original boat hull manufacturer with rights against the world, similar in scope and operation to the rights accorded a federal patentee. Like the patentee, the beneficiary of the Florida statute may prevent a competitor from "making" the product in what is evidently the most efficient manner available and from "selling" the product when it is produced in that fashion. The Florida scheme offers this protection for an unlimited number of years to all boat hulls and their component parts, without regard to their ornamental or technological merit. Protection is available for subject matter for which patent protection has been denied or has expired, as well as for designs which have been freely revealed to the consuming public by their creators.

In this case, the Bonito 5VBR fiberglass hull has been freely exposed to the public for a period in excess of six years. For purposes of federal law, it stands in the same stead as an item for which a patent has expired or been denied: it is unpatented and unpatentable. Whether because of a determination of unpatentability or other commercial concerns, petitioner chose to expose its hull design to the public in the marketplace, eschewing the bargain held out by the federal patent system of disclosure in exchange for exclusive use. Yet, the Florida statute allows petitioner to reassert a substantial property right in the idea, thereby constricting the spectrum of useful public knowledge. Moreover, it does so without the careful protections of high standards of innovation and limited monopoly contained in the federal scheme. We think it clear that such protection conflicts with the federal policy "that all ideas in general circulation be dedicated to the common good unless they are protected by a valid patent." * * *

Moreover, as we noted in Kewanee, the competitive reality of reverse engineering may act as a spur to the inventor, creating an incentive to develop inventions that meet the rigorous requirements of patentability. The Florida statute substantially reduces this competitive incentive, thus eroding the general rule of free competition upon which the attractiveness of the federal patent bargain depends. The protections of state trade secret law are most effective at the developmental stage, before a product has been marketed and the threat of reverse engineering becomes real. During this period, patentability will often be an uncertain prospect, and to a certain extent, the protection offered by trade secret law may "dovetail" with the incentives created by the federal patent monopoly. In contrast, under the Florida scheme, the would-be inventor is aware from the outset of his efforts that rights against the public are available regardless of his ability to satisfy the rigorous standards of patentability. * * * Given the substantial protection offered by the Florida scheme, we cannot dismiss as hypothetical the possibility that it will become a significant competitor to the federal patent laws, offering investors similar protection without the quid pro quo of substantial creative effort required by the federal statute. * * *

It is for Congress to determine if the present system of design and utility patents is ineffectual in promoting the useful arts in the context of industrial design. By offering patent-like protection for ideas deemed unprotected under the present federal scheme, the Florida statute conflicts with the "strong federal policy favoring free competition in ideas which do not merit patent protection." We therefore agree with the majority of the Florida Supreme Court that the Florida statute is preempted by the Supremacy Clause, and the judgment of that court is hereby affirmed.

It is so ordered.

DID YOU GET IT?

1. Why is it important that not all information be protected by federal or state law?

2. Is there a Constitutional basis for the court's arguments?

3. What does the court say about reverse engineering?

> ### *Reading Guidance*
> *Can it be improper means to obtain and publish information obtained through reverse engineering?*

CHICAGO LOCK CO. v. FANBERG

United States Court of Appeals, Ninth Circuit, 1982.
676 F.2d 400.

[handwritten: reverse engineering here was proper]

ELY, CIRCUIT JUDGE:

The Chicago Lock Company ("the Company"), a manufacturer of "tubular" locks, brought suit against Morris and Victor Fanberg, locksmiths and publishers of specialized trade books, to enjoin the unauthorized dissemination of key codes for the Company's "Ace" line of tubular locks. The District Court * * * concluded that the key codes for the Company's tubular locks were improperly acquired trade secrets and enjoined distribution of the Fanbergs' compilation of those codes. For the reasons set forth in this opinion, we reverse the District Court and order that judgment be entered in favor of the Fanbergs.

THE FACTS

Since 1933 the Chicago Lock Company, a manufacturer of various types of locks, has sold a tubular lock, marketed under the registered trademark "Ace," which provides greater security than other lock designs. Tubular Ace locks, millions of which have been sold, are frequently used on vending and bill changing machines and in other maximum security uses, such as burglar alarms. The distinctive feature of Ace locks (and the feature that apparently makes the locks attractive to institutional and large-scale commercial purchasers) is the secrecy and difficulty of reproduction associated with their keys.

The District Court found that the Company "has a fixed policy that it will only sell a duplicate key for the registered series 'Ace' lock to the owner of record of the lock and on request of a bona fide purchase order, letterhead or some other identifying means of the actual recorded lock owner." In addition, the serial number-key code correlations are maintained by the Company indefinitely and in secrecy, the Company does not sell tubular key "blanks" to locksmiths or others, and keys to Ace locks are stamped "Do Not Duplicate."

If the owner of an Ace lock loses his key, he may obtain a duplicate from the Company. Alternatively, he may have a proficient locksmith "pick" the lock, decipher the tumbler configuration, and grind a duplicate tubular key. The latter procedure is quicker than the former, though more costly. The locksmith will, to avoid the need to "pick" the lock each time a key is lost, record the key code (i.e., the tumbler configuration) along with the serial number of the customer's lock. Enough duplicate keys have been made by locksmiths that substantial key code data have been compiled, albeit noncommercially and on an ad hoc basis.

Appellant Victor Fanberg, the son of locksmith Morris Fanberg and a locksmith in his own right, has published a number of locksmith manuals for conventional locks. Realizing that no compilation had been made of tubular lock key codes, in 1975 Fanberg advertised in a locksmith journal, Locksmith Ledger, requesting that individual locksmiths transmit to him serial number-key code correlations in their possession in exchange for a copy of a complete compilation when finished. A number of locksmiths complied, and in late 1976 Fanberg and his father began to sell a two-volume publication of tubular lock codes, including those of Ace locks, entitled "A-Advanced Locksmith's Tubular Lock Codes." In 1976 and 1977 Fanberg advertised the manuals in the Locksmith Ledger for $49.95 and indicated that it would be supplemented as new correlations became known. About 350 manuals had been sold at the time of trial. The District Court found that Fanberg "had lost or surrendered control over persons who could purchase the books," meaning that nonlocksmiths could acquire the code manuals.

The books contain correlations which would allow a person equipped with a tubular key grinding machine to make duplicate keys for any listed Ace lock if the serial number of the lock was known. On some models, the serial numbers appear on the exterior of the lock face. Thus, Fanberg's manuals would make it considerably easier (and less expensive) for a person to obtain (legitimately or illegitimately) duplicate keys to Ace locks without going through the Company's screening process. This is what caused consternation to the Company and some of its customers. At no time did Fanberg seek, or the Company grant, permission to compile and sell the key codes. Nor did the individual locksmiths seek authorization from the Company or their customers before transmitting their key code data to Fanberg. * * *

The [district] court found that the Company's high security policy for its Ace tubular locks, of which the confidential key code data were a part, was a "valuable business or trade secret-type asset" of the Company, and that the Fanbergs' publication of their compilation of these codes so undermined the Company's policy as to constitute "common law unfair competition in the form of an unfair business practice within the meaning of Section 3369 of the Civil Code of the State of California," as broadly interpreted in *Barquis v. Merchants Collection Association.* The court enjoined the Fanbergs from publishing or distributing any lists of key code correlations for the Company's registered series Ace tubular locks. * * *

THE TRADE SECRETS CLAIM

Appellants argue that the District Court erroneously concluded that they are liable under Section 3369 for acquiring appellee's trade secret through improper means. We agree, and on this basis we reverse the District Court.

Although the District Court's Findings of Fact and Conclusions of Law are lengthy, the thrust of its holding may be fairly summarized as follows: appellants' acquisition of appellee's serial number-key code correlations through improper means, and the subsequent publication thereof, constituted an "unfair business practice" within the meaning of Section 3369. Even though the court did not make an explicit finding that appellee's serial number-key code correlations were protectable trade secrets, both appellants and appellee premise their appeal on such an "implicit" finding. We think it clear that the District Court based its decision on a theory of improper acquisition of trade secrets, and in the following discussion we assume arguendo that appellee's listing of serial number-key code correlations constituted a trade secret.

* * *

Trade secrets are protected * * * in a manner akin to private property, but only when they are disclosed or used through improper means. Trade secrets do not enjoy the absolute monopoly protection afforded patented processes, for example, and trade secrets will lose their character as private property when the owner divulges them or when they are discovered through proper means. "It is well recognized that a trade secret does not offer protection against discovery by fair and honest means such as by independent invention, accidental disclosure or by so-called reverse engineering, that is, starting with the known product and working backward to divine the process."

Thus, it is the employment of improper means to procure the trade secret, rather than mere copying or use, which is the basis of liability. The Company concedes, as it must, that had the Fanbergs bought and examined a number of locks on their own, their reverse engineering (or deciphering) of the key codes and publication thereof would not have been use of "improper means." Similarly, the Fanbergs' claimed use of computer programs in generating a portion of the key code-serial number correlations here at issue must also be characterized as proper reverse engineering. The trial court found that appellants obtained the serial number-key code correlations from a "comparatively small" number of locksmiths, who themselves had reverse-engineered the locks of their customers. The narrow legal issue presented here, therefore, is whether the Fanbergs' procurement of these individual locksmiths' reverse engineering data is an "improper means" with respect to appellee Chicago Lock Company.

The concept of "improper means," as embodied in the Restatement, and as expressed by the Supreme Court, connotes the existence of a duty to the trade secret owner not to disclose the secret to others. "The protection accorded the trade secret holder (i.e., in this case the Company) is against the disclosure or unauthorized use of the trade secret by those to whom the secret has been confided under the express or implied restriction of disclosure or nonuse."

* * *

We find untenable the basis upon which the District Court concluded that the individual locksmiths owe a duty of nondisclosure to the Company. The court predicated this implied duty upon a "chain" of duties: first, that the locksmiths are in such a fiduciary relationship with their customers as to give rise to a duty not to disclose their customers' key codes without permission; and second, that the lock owners are in turn under an "implied obligation (to the Company) to maintain inviolate" the serial number-key code correlations for their own locks.

The court's former conclusion is sound enough: in their fiduciary relationship with lock owners, individual locksmiths are reposed with a confidence and trust by their customers, of which disclosure of the customers' key codes would certainly be a breach. This duty, however, could give rise only to an action by "injured" lock owners against the individual locksmiths, not by the Company against the locksmiths or against the Fanbergs.

The court's latter conclusion, that lock owners owe a duty to the Company, is contrary to law and to the Company's own admissions. A lock purchaser's own reverse-engineering of his own lock, and subsequent publication of the serial number-key code correlation, is an example of the independent invention and reverse engineering expressly allowed by trade secret doctrine. Imposing an obligation of nondisclosure on lock owners here would frustrate the intent of California courts to disallow protection to trade secrets discovered through "fair and honest means." Further, such an implied obligation upon the lock owners in this case would, in effect, convert the Company's trade secret into a state-conferred monopoly akin to the absolute protection that a federal patent affords. Such an extension of California trade secrets law would certainly be preempted by the federal scheme of patent regulation.

* * *

The District Court's conclusion that the Fanbergs committed an "unfair business practice" under Section 3369, therefore, must be reversed, and judgment should be entered in favor of appellants. In view of the foregoing we find it unnecessary to reach appellants' First Amendment and vagueness claims.

REVERSED AND REMANDED with instructions that judgment be entered in favor of defendants-appellants.

DID YOU GET IT?

1. How did the Fanbergs obtain the data about the locks that they published in the manual? *— asked indiv. locksmiths serial serial number-key code correlations*
2. According to the plaintiff, *Chicago Lock*, what conduct of the defendants constituted "improper means"? *— common law unfair competition*
3. The appellate court here suggests that improper means requires a duty of non-disclosure to the trade secret owner. Do you agree? Is this reasoning consistent with *DuPont v. Christopher*? *No, it just req. non-reverse engineering.*

> ### Reading Guidance
> Did the defendant in this case independently discover its information through reverse engineering?

FAIVELEY TRANSPORT MALMO AB v. WABTEC CORP.

United States Court of Appeals, Second Circuit, 2009.
559 F.3d 110.

CABRANES, CIRCUIT JUDGE

* * *

[handwritten margin note: there was no actual "reverse engineering" here b/c D already had the info.]

BACKGROUND

During the 1970s, SAB Wabco—a corporate descendant of the Westinghouse Air Brake Company and the predecessor-in-interest to plaintiff-appellee Faiveley Transport Malmo AB ("Faiveley")—developed BFC TBU, a unique air brake system designed to stop trains quickly and smoothly, if not always quietly. The original patents for the BFC TBU have since expired.

In 1993, SAB Wabco entered into a license agreement ("the 1993 Agreement") with Wabco, then a sister company. Pursuant to the 1993 Agreement, Wabco was authorized to use SAB Wabco "know-how"— including "manufacturing data, specifications, designs, plans, trade secrets" and other information, as well as "Patents, Patent Applications, and New Technology," to produce and market BFC TBU. The 1993 Agreement was originally scheduled to expire on December 31, 2003, but could be renewed annually for one-year terms after that time by agreement of the parties. Upon the expiration of the 1993 Agreement, Wabco was to "cease manufacture" of licensed products, except insofar as required to meet contracts entered into prior to the expiration of the agreement.

In 2004, Faiveley acquired SAB Wabco. As part of the acquisition, Faiveley assumed ownership of SAB Wabco's intellectual property, including that related to BFC TBU, as well as SAB Wabco's rights and obligations under the 1993 Agreement. At that time, Wabtec Corporation ("Wabtec"), the successor-in-interest to Wabco, was still producing BFC TBU parts and components pursuant to the 1993 Agreement. In December 2004, Faiveley notified Wabtec that the 1993 Agreement would not be renewed, as a result of which the 1993 Agreement terminated on December 31, 2005.

Beginning in 2005, Wabtec began to develop its own line of BFC TBU through "reverse engineering." In 2007, the New York City Transit Authority (the "Transit Authority") awarded a "sole source" contract to Wabtec whereby Wabtec was to provide BFC TBU for the City's overhaul of a certain class of subway cars. According to Faiveley, following the termination of the 1993 Agreement, Wabtec continued to use Faiveley's proprietary information to produce BFC TBU for its contract with the Transit Authority. In May 2007, Faiveley submitted a letter to the Transit Authority protesting the Wabtec-Transit Authority contract but did not succeed in having itself substituted for Wabtec. * * *

DISCUSSION

* * *

Faiveley is not entitled to preliminary relief unless it has demonstrated that Wabtec likely misappropriated a trade secret. Both parties agree that New York law governs that issue in this case. "To succeed on a claim for the misappropriation of trade secrets under New York law, a party must demonstrate: (1) that it possessed a trade secret, and (2) that the defendants used that trade secret in breach of an agreement, confidential relationship or duty, or as a result of discovery by improper means."

"A trade secret is any formula, pattern, device or compilation of information which is used in one's business, and which gives the owner an opportunity to obtain an advantage over competitors who do not know or use it." In determining whether information constitutes a trade secret, New York courts have considered:

> (1) the extent to which the information is known outside of the business; (2) the extent to which it is known by employees and others involved in the business; (3) the extent of measures taken by the business to guard the secrecy of the information; (4) the value of the information to the business and its competitors; (5) the amount of effort or money expended by the business in developing the information; (6) the ease or difficulty with which the information could be properly acquired or duplicated by others.

We detect no error in the District Court's conclusion that the BFC TBU manufacturing drawings pertaining to "dimensions and tolerances, surface finishes, material selection and treatments, lubrication specifications, and special instructions for manufacture, testing, and assembly," contain trade secrets under New York law. That this information is not widely known is evinced by the fact that no company other than Faiveley—and Wabtec pursuant to the 1993 Agreement-has produced a complete BFC TBU. Faiveley has strictly limited the access of its own employees to the information and does not permit customers to view it. It is undisputed that SAB Wabco, Faiveley's predecessor-in-interest, devoted substantial resources to the development of the BFC TBU. As demonstrated in the testimony of those who took part in Wabtec's engineering process, BFC TBU and BFC TBU components are extremely difficult to duplicate. The information contained in the manufacturing drawings provided Faiveley, as the District Court found, with "far more tha[n] [a] 'slight competitive edge.'"

Having established that Faiveley "possessed a trade secret," we now consider whether Wabtec likely used Faiveley's trade secrets "in breach of an agreement, confidential relationship or duty, or as a result of discovery by improper means." Wabtec argues that it did not misappropriate Faiveley's trade secrets because it independently discovered the same information through a "reverse engineering" process. As the Supreme Court has noted, "trade secret law . . . does not offer protection against discovery by fair and honest means, such as by independent invention, accidental disclosure, or by so-called reverse engineering, that is by starting with the known product and working backward to divine the process which aided its development or manufacture."

In this case, the record provides ample support for the District Court's conclusion that Wabtec's reverse engineering process made "important use of Faiveley's trade secrets," and was "[a]t a minimum . . . fatally tainted," by the involvement of Roland Moore, a Wabtec employee who had "frequent contact with Faiveley drawings during the course of the [1993] Agreement." Wabtec's first effort to reverse engineer BFC TBU, which did not involve Moore, produced no usable drawings. However, when Wabtec attempted for a second time to reverse engineer BFC TBU, Moore was selected to play a key role because "he [was] knowledgeable about the product." Notwithstanding Moore's "self-serving testimony that his role in the reverse engineering process was minimal," the record indicates that Moore made several specific recommendations to draftsmen. Wabtec has not presented us with any compelling reason—nor are we aware of any—to question the District Court's assessment that Moore's testimony was "self-serving."

Accordingly, we hold that the District Court did not err in finding that Faiveley is likely to succeed on the merits of its claim that Wabtec misappropriated Faiveley's trade secrets. * * *

DID YOU GET IT?

1. Why was the court not persuaded by the defendant's reverse engineering argument? *B/c D had access to P's TS info.*

2. What role does taint play in a misappropriation analysis? *Can push against a finding of reverse engineering.*

3. How might a company avoid taint in its research and development process? *Not allow person that worked w/ the info, plans, drawings of TS to work R+D to reverse engineer.*

> ### *Food for Thought*
>
> *Should parties to a contract be able to define "acquisition by improper means" or preclude acquisition by reverse engineering or independent development? What if the contractual clauses are contained in mass-distributed Terms of Use Agreements and browse-wrap agreements that no one reads? Should you be subjected to potential criminal responsibility for trade secret misappropriation because you contractually agreed not to acquire certain information, even if your acquisition of that information was otherwise lawful?*

The foregoing questions remain to be fully explored and resolved under trade secret law. On one hand, principles of freedom of contract suggest that the parties to a contract should be free to define what are "improper" and "proper" means of acquiring information, and non-disclosure agreements often contain provisions which limit access to information. On the other hand, there is a big difference between imposing liability for breach of contract and imposing tort liability and criminal penalties. Ordinarily, what constitutes a tort or a crime is defined by social norms and not by the contractual agreement of two or more parties. Additionally, there is the question whether parties should be allowed to contract-around the limitations that are built into trade secret law, in particular, the recognition that reverse engineering and independent development are proper means of acquiring information, including trade secrets.

The following excerpt from an article by Professors Samuelson and Scotchmer highlights the potential economic consequences of contractual restrictions on reverse engineering.

THE LAW AND ECONOMICS OF REVERSE ENGINEERING

Pamela Samuelson & Suzanne Scotchmer.
111 Yale L.J. 1575, 1586 (2002).

The economic effects of reverse engineering depend on a number of factors, including the purpose for which it is undertaken, the industrial context within which it occurs, how much it costs, how long it takes, whether licensing is a viable alternative, and how the reverse engineer uses information learned in the reverse engineering process. * * *

We argue that a legal right to reverse-engineer does not typically threaten an innovative manufacturer because the manufacturer generally has two forms of protection against competitors who reverse-engineer: lead time before reverse engineers can enter and costliness of reverse engineering. Lead time serves the same function as a short-lived intellectual property right. Costliness may prevent reverse engineering entirely, especially if the innovator licenses others as a strategy for preventing unlicensed entry.

Provided that the cost of reverse engineering is high enough, such licensing will be on terms that permit the innovator to recoup its R&D expenses, while at the same time constraining the exercise of market power in order to dissuade other potential entrants.

Our economic assessment of reverse engineering recognizes that this activity is only one step in what is typically a four-stage development process. The first stage of a second comer's development process is an awareness stage. This involves a firm's recognition that another firm has introduced a product into the market that is potentially worth the time, expense, and effort of reverse engineering. In some markets, recognition happens very rapidly; in others, it may take some time, during which the innovator can begin to recoup its R&D costs by selling its product and establishing goodwill with its customer base.

Second is the reverse engineering stage. This begins when a second comer obtains the innovator's product and starts to disassemble and analyze it to discern of what and how it was made. The reverse engineering stage may be costly, time-consuming, and difficult, although this varies considerably, depending mainly on how readily the innovator's product will yield the know-how required to make it when confronted by a determined and skilled reverse engineer. However, a reverse engineer will generally spend less time and money to discern this know-how than the initial innovator spent in developing it, in part because the reverse engineer is able to avoid wasteful expenditures investigating approaches that do not work, and in part because advances in technology typically reduce the costs of rediscovery over time.

Third is the implementation stage. After reverse-engineering the innovator's product, a second comer must take the know-how obtained during the reverse engineering process and put it to work in designing and developing a product to compete in the same market. This may involve making prototypes, experimenting with them, retooling manufacturing facilities, and reiterating the design and development process until it yields a satisfactory product. It may be necessary to return to the reverse engineering stage again if it becomes apparent in the implementation phase that some necessary know-how eluded the reverse engineer the first time. Information obtained during reverse engineering may, moreover, suggest possibilities for additional product innovation that will be investigated in the implementation stage. For these reasons, the second comer's implementation stage may take considerable time and require significant expense.

The fourth stage in the second comer's development process is the introduction of its product to the market. How quickly the new product will erode the innovator's market share and force the innovator to reduce prices to be competitive with the new entrant will depend on various market factors.

* * *

On balance, we conclude that a legal rule favoring reverse engineering of traditional manufactured products is economically sound. A prohibition on reverse engineering would, in effect, give firms perpetual exclusive rights in unpatented innovations. Given that the costs and time required for reverse engineering already protect most innovators, a ban on reverse engineering is unnecessary. On the positive side, a right to reverse-engineer has a salutary effect on price competition and on the dissemination of know-how that can lead to new and improved products.

C. SPECIAL ISSUE: WHAT IS THE DIFFERENCE BETWEEN COMPETITIVE INTELLIGENCE AND CORPORATE ESPIONAGE?

As you saw in *DuPont v. Christopher*, companies often engage in information gathering about their competitors. This process, when done properly, is known as competitive intelligence and it is commonplace in many industries as companies strive to remain competitive. Competitive intelligence allows companies to maintain an advantage by learning about, anticipating, and planning for competitors' business strategies in many areas, including research and development. Many companies have in-house departments or outside consultants who assist with their intelligence gathering. Competitive information can be acquired through a host of legitimate avenues such as SEC filings, industry or company websites and blogs, networking events, Freedom of Information Act (FOIA) requests, and patent filings. *See* Craig S. Fleisher and Babette E. Bensoussan, STRATEGIC AND COMPETITIVE ANALYSIS: METHODS AND TECHNIQUES FOR ANALYZING BUSINESS COMPETITION (2002).

While competitive intelligence by itself is legal and ethical, it can sometimes cross the line into trade secret misappropriation or corporate espionage. Corporate espionage is the illegal and unethical pursuit of competitive business information and those caught engaging in espionage face possible civil and criminal penalties. Virtually all kinds of competitive business information can be the target of corporate espionage including "customer lists, design manuals and drawings, financial data, food and dessert recipes, product development data, strategic planning information, manufacturing cost data, formulas, testing data, marketing strategies, installation techniques, product composition, and clustering technology." *See* Carl Pacini and Raymond Placid, *The Importance of State Trade Secret Laws in Deterring Trade Secret Espionage*, 7 BUFF. INTELL. PROP. L. J. 101, 103 (2009). In Chapter 12, we discuss the criminal penalties for espionage as provided under the Economic Espionage Act of 1996, as amended. For the purposes of this chapter, note that corporate espionage can expose a company to civil liability for trade secret misappropriation.

Companies who engage in corporate espionage use a wide range of techniques to obtain competitor's trade secrets, including deception, bribing employees, electronic eavesdropping, computer hacking, and computer theft. This behavior can be actionable under both the UTSA and the DTSA. You will see an example in the case that follows, *MicroStrategy, Inc. v. Business Objects*, where the court analyzes whether one company's efforts to obtain competitive intelligence from a competitor constitutes "improper means" under the Virginia UTSA.

Recall that in addition to prohibiting the improper acquisition of trade secrets, the UTSA and DTSA also prohibit using trade secret information that an individual or corporation acquires wrongfully or knows or should have known was wrongfully acquired by someone else. Accordingly, when corporations hire individuals or firms to conduct competitive intelligence gathering activities, they could be liable under trade secret law if those individuals or firms go beyond the ethical and legal means of intelligence gathering and engage in espionage.

Reading Guidance

Did the defendant cross the line from lawful intelligence gathering to misappropriation by improper means in this case?

MICROSTRATEGY INC. V. BUSINESS OBJECTS, S.A.

United States District Court, E.D. of Virginia, 2004.
331 F.Supp.2d 396.

FRIEDMAN, DISTRICT JUDGE.

* * *

FINDINGS OF FACT

Company Information

The plaintiff, MicroStrategy, Incorporated, founded in 1989, develops and sells business intelligence software and related maintenance, technical support, consulting, and training services to various organizations. The company competes primarily in the "high-end" segment of the business intelligence market. In 2002, MicroStrategy's revenue was $144 million. MicroStrategy's principle place of business is McLean, Virginia. During all times relevant to this case, Michael Saylor was the Chief Executive Officer of MicroStrategy; Sanju Bansal was the Chief Operating Officer of MicroStrategy; and Jeffrey Bedell was the Chief Technology Officer of MicroStrategy. The defendants, Business Objects, S.A., a French corporation, and its wholly owned subsidiary, Business Objects Americas,

Inc., compete with MicroStrategy in the business intelligence software and services industry.

Business intelligence software allows companies to access and analyze the massive quantities of data that they accumulate in their daily operations, thereby increasing corporate efficiency and productivity. At the time of the events in question, MicroStrategy's perceived number one competitor in the high-end segment of the market was Business Objects.

In 2002, Business Objects' total revenues exceeded $450 million. Business Objects' principle place of business in the United States is San Jose, California. During all times relevant to this case, Bernard Liautaud was the Chief Executive Officer of Business Objects and Clifton Thomas Weatherford, Jr. was the Chief Financial Officer. Prior to 1999, Business Objects targeted a different, lower-end customer base than MicroStrategy. Subsequently, Business Objects began targeting the same high-end customer base that MicroStrategy historically had serviced.

MicroStrategy's trade secrets are its most valuable assets. MicroStrategy goes to great lengths to protect these valuable assets from unauthorized disclosure. MicroStrategy requires all of its employees to sign the MicroStrategy Agreement as a condition of their employment. * * *

MicroStrategy utilizes a number of methods to maintain the secrecy of its proprietary information. It employs physical security, such as locked doors, limited access to its buildings through the use of badges, and the use of security cameras, to protect its corporate information and intellectual property. MicroStrategy utilizes network-type security features, including firewalls and a virtual private network that can be accessed only by MicroStrategy employees to protect its electronic information. MicroStrategy enters into non-disclosure agreements (NDA) to protect trade secrets and other proprietary and confidential information that is disclosed outside the company, such as to a beta tester, customer, or prospect. MicroStrategy protects against unauthorized use of its software products through the use of CD keys, which are only disclosed to authorized users. * * *

Business Objects' Acquisition of Information

* * * Business Objects acquired constructive or actual access to a significant amount of MicroStrategy's proprietary and confidential information, including internal email, descriptions of software architecture, sales documents, competitive intelligence, and PowerPoint presentations. This information came through a variety of means. MicroStrategy employees would send information to their friends at Business Objects. The most important method was simply soliciting information about MicroStrategy and its products from new hires formerly employed at MicroStrategy. In at least one instance, a former MicroStrategy employee, John Ennis, took a large amount of proprietary

information with him to Business Objects. Some of the information in Business Objects' possession may also have come through third parties— such as prospective or current MicroStrategy customers or industry analysts. However, no evidence of any concrete examples was introduced at trial to indicate when, if ever, this actually occurred.

The origin of much of the information is unknown. Business Objects employees had a habit of concealing their sources when forwarding such information within the company, often stating only that "a little bird" provided the information, or that they just happened upon the information. For example, in an email to the distribution list "Competitive Info" dated August 8, 2001, Business Objects employee Steve Moller attached a zip file named "Competitive presentations." Mr. Moller stated in his email: "A little bird delivered these presentations to me. . . . They were created by MicroStrategy . . . themselves. It could be valuable information when you're in competitive situations with them."

The "little bird" appears to have also provided Business Objects information to MicroStrategy. In fact, the leaking of proprietary information amongst competitors in this industry appears to be quite common. Collecting intelligence on any competitor is an accepted practice in any industry when done properly—based on the aggregation of publicly available information.

Although MicroStrategy contends Business Objects had a "spy" inside MicroStrategy, this allegation rests on a use of that term in an email that was clearly intended to be playful. The spy reference was followed by a "smiley face" emoticon. The spy in question was simply a friend of a Business Objects employee. Such an exchange of information, while improper in many, if not most, instances, seems common in any industry and does not necessarily constitute the misappropriation of a trade secret. As noted, during the relevant time frame, MicroStrategy also was in possession of Business Objects information.

The Internal MicroStrategy Email

On April 3, 2001, MicroStrategy's CEO Michael Saylor authored an internal email sent to all MicroStrategy employees that was eventually circulated within Business Objects. The contents of the email, which included details related to MicroStrategy's restructuring plans, were considered "extraordinarily sensitive" to the company. Due to press reports about MicroStrategy's restructuring, Mr. Saylor felt it was his responsibility to share the inner thinking and plans of MicroStrategy's senior management team with the company's employees. Mr. Saylor did not intend for this email to be distributed outside of MicroStrategy. Mr. Saylor testified that Business Objects' acquisition of this internal MicroStrategy email was "devastating."

The email was received by Francis Jayakumar from his friend at MicroStrategy, the alleged "spy." Jayakumar forwarded it to Jerome Tocanne and Business Objects' Vice President of Marketing, Dave Kellogg. Jerome Tocanne then circulated the internal MicroStrategy email to all Business Objects staff in the western region, as well as to the Vice President of Competitive Intelligence at Business Objects, Matthew Sell. * * *

Corey Sommers

Sommers was a former MicroStrategy employee hired by Business Objects in March 2001. While at MicroStrategy, Sommers served as a sales consultant and also worked on competitive intelligence. Sommers was placed in charge of competitive intelligence on MicroStrategy for Business Objects. As part of that job, Sommers solicited internal MicroStrategy documents. He also requested information from new hires who had worked for MicroStrategy and compiled reports based on his own experiences working for the plaintiff.

Two months after starting at Business Objects, Corey Sommers drafted the "MicroStrategy Recommended Sales Strategy." This document contained a section listing MicroStrategy's selling points. Sommers learned these key selling points as a MicroStrategy employee. On June 11, 2001, Corey Sommers circulated a draft of this document widely throughout Business Objects.

On August 29, 2001, Corey Sommers obtained MicroStrategy's volume discount schedule from a source he described as "a little bird" and forwarded this information to other Business Objects employees. MicroStrategy's volume discount schedule was also included in course materials for Business Objects University, an internal organization responsible for training all Business Objects employees.

Sommers believes he obtained this document from a customer. Other testimony indicates MicroStrategy's volume discount schedule is proprietary and confidential information that is not disclosed outside the company. Sommers testified that he believed this type of information was regularly available in the OLAP Report, an industry publication. However, he later stated that the information was "maybe more current" than that which might be found in the OLAP report, indicating this was not a document that was publicly available at the time it was disclosed.

As Sommers testified, MicroStrategy's volume discount schedule was a "valuable piece of competitive intelligence," which assisted Business Objects' sales staff in understanding MicroStrategy's pricing. A competitor in possession of such pricing information would be able to undercut MicroStrategy.

As instructed by Matthew Sell, Business Objects' Vice President of Competitive Intelligence, Corey Sommers drafted the "MicroStrategy TCO [Total Cost of Ownership] White Paper." On September 26, 2001, Corey Sommers circulated a draft of this white paper to former MicroStrategy employees Leena Shah, Tom Papp, David Fussichen, and Jeff Scudder to obtain their "feedback." Corey Sommers stated: "I believe this may be a good 4th-quarter response to the low level, technical attack document that MicroStrategy has circulated to all potential customers looking also at Business Objects. The white paper focuses on business and TCO issues rather than getting mirred [sic] in feature/function." He further stated that the draft "contains competitive items that are not disputed by MicroStrategy, several of which are even admitted to in their own attack document. These items happen to be resonating quite well with customers and have helped swing some deals over to us."

Corey Sommers obtained a proprietary and confidential MicroStrategy document, which he described as a "MicroStrategy anti-BO FUD" document. Every page of this document was marked "MicroStrategy Incorporated Confidential and Proprietary—Unauthorized use, disclosure, or duplication is strictly prohibited." It was, however, a "simplified version" of a document that had been "going around." Leena Shah included information from this document, verbatim, in her Business Objects University course materials.

Most importantly, Sommers also acquired a 44-page MicroStrategy document entitled "Business Objects Competitive Recipe." The header of each and every page stated, "Comprehensive Competitive Analysis—Business Objects" and every page of the document was marked "MicroStrategy, Inc. Confidential." The document described the means by which MicroStrategy could compete with and beat Business Objects.

MicroStrategy's CEO Michael Saylor described the contents of the "Competitive Recipe" as "everything that we as a company learned over the course of competing with Business Objects for about seven or eight years, plus everything we learned about what was critical to our customers." As Saylor testified, hundreds of people had input into this "very critical" document. MicroStrategy's competitive intelligence team prepared the "Competitive Recipe" with input from MicroStrategy's CEO Michael Saylor, COO Sanju Bansal, account executives, sales consultants, technical engineers, and customers.

The "Competitive Recipe" outlines, among other things:

(a) key themes to portray to customers, which were derived from interviews with people in the field and customers;

(b) traps MicroStrategy account executives should set for Business Objects—in other words, which weaknesses of

Business Objects the account executive should draw the customers' attention to; and

(c) MicroStrategy's weaknesses so that the field staff can anticipate traps that Business Objects may set.

MicroStrategy's COO Sanju Bansal testified that the "Competitive Recipe" is "amongst the most sensitive of all MicroStrategy information, and probably would rank right up there . . . with the source code of product [sic] itself." Mr. Bansal explained the harm to MicroStrategy resulting from Business Objects' acquisition of the "Competitive Recipe" document: "[I]f you had the document and you were competing with somebody you could anticipate their every play, their every move, and therefore, you could, before they even made the move, sort of negate the effect of that move or negate the effect of that play." Saylor testified that the document had three primary values to Business Objects: (1) It would let them know what flaws their product had; (2) Business Objects could change its marketing message to downplay such flaws; or (3) the company could alter its sales cycle to counteract these weaknesses.

To protect the "Competitive Recipe" against unauthorized disclosure, MicroStrategy limited the distribution of the document within the company to employees on a need to know basis. MicroStrategy did not authorize disclosure of the "Competitive Recipe" to Business Objects. Nor did MicroStrategy give the "Competitive Recipe" to any of its customers, not even to those with an NDA. MicroStrategy did provide a copy of the "Competitive Recipe" to the Gartner Group, an industry analyst with whom MicroStrategy has a consulting arrangement and an NDA. The document was provided to the Gartner Group in confidence as a resource for understanding how MicroStrategy compares with Business Objects and to obtain feedback on its contents. There is no evidence that the Gartner Group distributed this document outside of the company. While Business Objects implied that its receipt of the Competitive Recipe came via the Gartner Group, it offered no evidence to support this inference. Furthermore, the defendant concedes that the version of the Competitive Recipe given to the Gartner Group was different from the version in its possession. There is nothing to suggest that the Competitive Recipe was ever made publicly available and Bansal testified that he had never seen anything from the "Competitive Recipe" appear in a Gartner publication.

On October 29, 2001, Corey Sommers emailed MicroStrategy's "Competitive Recipe" to several dozen Business Objects employees, including Vice President of Marketing Dave Kellogg and Director of Consulting Brian Baillod. In his email, Mr. Sommers described the "Competitive Recipe" as "an internal sales doc, not something a customer would get" that was "overwhelming in its thoroughness." Mr. Sommers suggested that Business Objects could use this document to "make MicroStrategy look like fools with the technical decisionmakers."

There is no record that any of the recipients of this document, which included members of upper management such as Dave Kellogg, Vice-President of Marketing, expressed any concern that Sommers had obtained and circulated this document. Business Objects CEO Bernard Liautaud admitted that he would not want MicroStrategy to have a copy of a Business Objects document that explained how to beat MicroStrategy in the marketplace.

Leena Shah

In April 2001, Business Objects also hired former MicroStrategy employee Leena Shah to work in the Atlanta office as a Technical Instructor in Business Objects University. As a Business Objects employee, Leena Shah was given responsibility for developing and delivering competitive workshops on MicroStrategy to Business Objects sales and presales employees throughout North America and Europe. In order to create these workshops, Ms. Shah actively solicited and obtained information from a variety of sources concerning Business Objects competitors, which she then incorporated into her presentations. That information often came from anonymous sources as well as former and current MicroStrategy employees. She even continued to solicit ex-MicroStrategy employees for information after the instant litigation had been filed and the Chicago office of Business Objects had been made "off limits" to such queries as a result of this litigation. Finally, as noted above, other Business Objects employees, like Corey Sommers, would forward information they had obtained to her and she would incorporate that information into her training material.

Often, her solicitation of information was at the behest of Business Objects executives. For instance, on September 21, 2001, Richard Nicol, Vice President of Business Objects University, directed Leena Shah to solicit information concerning MicroStrategy from former MicroStrategy employees Alex Brown, James Watson, and John Ennis: "[P]lease find a suitable way for discussing in detail the contents [of the MicroStrategy competitive workshop] with these three people and let me know what the reactions are." Leena Shah did contact these individuals and asked for an outline of MicroStrategy's sales demonstrations and questioned them regarding the technical capabilities of MicroStrategy products.

On September 25, 2001, Alex Brown responded to Leena Shah's questions. Mr. Brown provided information related to the then-unreleased MicroStrategy 7.2 software, including functionality, the original code name, and the release date: "A little birdie told me that 7.2 got pushed to Q1." Mr. Brown provided very general comments on the overall MicroStrategy web architecture and browser functionality. Mr. Brown answered Ms. Shah's questions on technical capabilities of MicroStrategy products and product features: MicroStrategy now has a "complete UNIX web SDK that it is architecturally identical to the Windows Web SDK," and "[t]here is supposed to be a full UNIX Web front-end soon."

Shah also sought and obtained encryption keys to a variety of MicroStrategy software products. She most vigorously pursued a beta copy of MicroStrategy latest product, version 7.2, but the record offers no evidence that she ever succeeded.

On September 24, 2001, Ms. Shah asked Katarzyna Peplinska, a former MicroStrategy employee who worked in Business Objects' Chicago office, to send her a MicroStrategy CD key. On that same day, Ms. Peplinska sent Ms. Shah the CD key for MicroStrategy 7GA, MicroStrategy 7 SP1, MicroStrategy7 SP2, MicroStrategy 7.1 RC, MicroStrategy 7.1 GA (includes Administrator), Narrowcast Server, MicroStrategy 7.1.1 with OLAP Provider, and MicroStrategy 7.1 Beta 3 with OLAP Provider. MicroStrategy Chief Technology Officer Jeff Bedell confirmed that these were in fact MicroStrategy's CD keys for the listed products. MicroStrategy COO Sanju Bansal testified that MicroStrategy would never license its software products to Business Objects.

On September 25, 2001, Ms. Shah asked former MicroStrategy employees Alex Brown, James Watson, and John Ennis for a CD key to MicroStrategy 7.1.1. Alex Brown responded: "[Y]ou never know and I never told you—the enterprise key is 527528737–MST5L."

Leena Shah met with former MicroStrategy employee Suzanne Muccino on January 8, 2002, so that Shah could obtain information on new MicroStrategy product offerings: "[I] need to pick your brain about some MicroStrategy stuff . . . especially the likelihood or ability to get a hold of a copy of version 7.2." Leena Shah needed this information to update Business Objects University course materials. Muccino began working at Business Objects' Atlanta office as an account manager on December 10, 2001. Ms. Shah obtained information concerning MicroStrategy at this meeting and then scheduled a "longer meeting to get more of an insight on the Sales Strategy side of things at mstr."

On January 8, 2002 at 9:13 AM, Shah advised Ozlem Atmaca of Business Objects that she had obtained information on new MicroStrategy product offerings from Ms. Muccino and that she would continue her efforts to obtain information from former MicroStrategy employees: "[I] have got some information from Suzanne Muccino—but will meet with her for a longer meeting to get more of an insight on the Sales Strategy side of things at MicroStrategy. [S]he also gave me something that will help with v7.2 stuff."

At 10:34 AM, Shah wrote to Business Objects employee Thomas Burnes: "I have got my hands on the new product improvements for v7.2." Ms. Shah then quoted verbatim from a document entitled "What's New in MicroStrategy 7.2." Ms. Shah later covered these new MicroStrategy product improvements in courses she taught to Business Objects employees on how to compete against MicroStrategy.

At 10:48 AM, Leena Shah sent a second email to Thomas Burnes of "high importance." Ms. Shah stated: "something more comprehensive which I am sure will be of use, and also suggests that they did not have in v7.1 as this is coming from the new features of v7.2 document." *Id.* Ms. Shah then quoted two paragraphs verbatim from the "What's New in MicroStrategy 7.2" document. Ms. Shah closed her email by stating: "Tom, please keep this purely internal and confidential. It is a document that just happened to fall into my hands. Please keep for your own information until it has been decided exactly how we are going to use this info in our course and through the company in general."

Later that same day at 4:59 PM, Shah wrote to John Hawkins, District Technical Manager for the West Central Region: "I have managed to get my hands on a copy of a document that lists the new features of v7.2—[I] have only just got it so [I] need to get it in a non-MicroStrategy form before circulating." Ms. Shah admitted that there would be no need to convert publicly available information into a non-MicroStrategy form before circulating it. As this chain of emails make clear, at their meeting on the morning of January 8, 2002, Muccino provided proprietary information concerning the new features for MicroStrategy 7.2 prior to its release.

Also on January 8, 2002, Leena Shah indicated that she was going to meet with Business Objects market analyst Kate McNeel the following week. On February 8, 2002, Kate McNeel circulated the "What's New in MicroStrategy v.7.2" document throughout Business Objects: "Attached is a doc which lists new features in MicroStrategy version 7i, which is currently in Beta, and due for GA release in the next 2 months." Shah had provided to McNeel the document she had received from Muccino the day before. MicroStrategy 7.2, also known as MicroStrategy 7i, was not released until April 2002.

Jeffrey Bedell testified that MicroStrategy treats the new features of unreleased software as confidential information. However, it was clear that in a press release announcing the launch of beta testing of an earlier version of the software, MicroStrategy 7.1, some of the product's features were made public.

CONCLUSIONS OF LAW

In deciding whether any of the information disclosed in this case constituted trade secrets and whether Business Objects' receipt of such information constituted misappropriation of trade secrets, the court must be careful not to constrain legitimate competitive practices. It is apparent that in this industry, as perhaps in all others, a large amount of confidential information makes its way into the public domain eventually. It is also clear that because the software industry moves quite rapidly, what might have been a confidential trade secret yesterday is merely public competitive intelligence tomorrow. In the instant case, the important actors obviously considered much of this information to be fair game. As one Business Objects employee put it, "this happens in the industry. . . . You constantly get the other side's competitive intelligence. It's part of the game." At some point, however, a line can be crossed, and it is clear to the court that the present case evinces some instances where that occurred.

Requirements of the Virginia Uniform Trade Secrets Act

The tort of misappropriation of trade secrets is codified in the Virginia Uniform Trade Secrets Act (VUTSA), Va. Code Ann. §§ 59.1–336 to 59.1–343. * * *

Misappropriation

Once a plaintiff has demonstrated that the information in question was a trade secret, he must then prove that it was misappropriated. The VUTSA details three acts that, under the right circumstances, can constitute misappropriation: the acquisition, disclosure, or use of a trade secret. * * * Where a trade secret was acquired or learned through "improper means," any of the three acts will constitute misappropriation. There are a wide variety of methods used to acquire information that will be considered "improper" under the VUTSA. A non-exhaustive list provided by statute includes misrepresentation, breach of a duty or inducement of a breach of a duty to maintain secrecy, and espionage. Espionage is adequately defined as the use of spies to obtain information about the plans or activities of a competing company. The term spy need not carry any cloak and dagger connotations. Simply put, a spy is someone who is employed to convey the confidential information of one company to another.

Where the defendant did not utilize "improper means" to acquire a trade secret, the fact that it possessed a trade secret will not alone constitute misappropriation. Something more is required: disclosure or use. For example, if the trade secret is revealed accidentally or is thrust upon the defendant, unsolicited, the defendant will not be liable for its mere possession of the trade secret. However, should it act on that trade secret, liability will result. The distinction between improper and "innocent" acquisition is important for the present case because there are instances where Business Objects came into possession of a trade secret without having sought it out and apparently did nothing with the information once possessed. Perhaps more importantly, there are also instances where the defendant's employees claimed to have just "bumped into" confidential information or that it just fell into their laps, where it is evident that this information was actively solicited. In such cases, mere acquisition, even without disclosure or use, would be misappropriation.

In order to prevail on a claim of trade secret misappropriation, a plaintiff must produce some evidence that the information in question constitutes a trade secret. Moreover, the alleged trade secret must be described "in sufficient detail to establish each element of a trade secret." * * * It is not enough to claim generally that trade secrets were stolen. A plaintiff must identify, with particularity, each trade secret it claims was misappropriated. * * * This must be done to allow the finder of fact to distinguish that which is legitimately a trade secret from other information that is simply confidential but not a trade secret, or is publicly available information.

* * *

The Alleged Trade Secrets

In general, MicroStrategy has demonstrated that it took reasonable steps to preserve the secrecy of its information. As noted, the company had in place physical security preventing access to confidential information as well as software-related security measures. The company also ensured that its employees were contractually bound to keep such information confidential. Such contract terms were made known to employees in a number of ways, including emphasizing the need to maintain secrecy in the employee handbook in addition to the contract terms themselves.

* * *

While the elements of a misappropriation of trade secrets claim are present with regard to a number of pieces of information, the court must assess each alleged trade secret according to the requisite elements. In other words, it is not enough to say the defendant used the information in exhibit X, that the information in exhibit Y was secret, and that the information in exhibit Z had economic value. Each item must be assessed to determine if it is a trade secret and if it was misappropriated. * * *

Business Objects Competitive Recipe

As noted, Corey Sommers obtained this document, plaintiff's exhibit 5, from an unknown source. It described the means by which the MicroStrategy sales force could compete with Business Objects in obtaining business. Based on its findings of fact detailed above, the court concludes that reasonable efforts were made to maintain the secrecy of this document. It was not circulated outside of MicroStrategy with one exception and within MicroStrategy was only provided to the field sales staff. The one exception was in providing the document to the Gartner Group. The court finds the testimony of Sanju Bansall credible that this disclosure was made in confidence. It is not necessary that there have been a written agreement memorializing the confidentiality of the disclosure. Nor did this single disclosure, in confidence, render the document public.

It is also clear that this document had enormous economic value, both to MicroStrategy and to Business Objects, as demonstrated by the testimony of Michael Saylor, discussed above. The court does not accept the defendant's contention that because the document concerned Business Objects it was of no economic value to Business Objects. The document's value was, in part, premised on the fact that it detailed how MicroStrategy would counter the various aspects of Business Objects' product or exploit various weaknesses or deal with "traps" regarding its own product. The analogy to a playbook is quite apt in this instance, and Business Objects came into possession of that playbook. From the nature of the document and from Sommers' comments in circulating the document, Business Objects was well aware of the importance of this document. Even though it was ten months old at the time, there is no evidence that the information had become valueless when it was disclosed.

Finally, this document was not obtained from a public source or from a MicroStrategy customer, given the testimony from Bansal regarding the limited distribution of this document. Nor did Business Objects receive the document from the Gartner Group as it admits that the version it possessed was different than the version supplied to the Gartner Group. This document could only have been obtained from an employee of MicroStrategy, in breach of his employment agreement. Given the overwhelming evidence that this type of information was actively solicited from MicroStrategy employees by ex-employees of the company who moved on to Business Objects, like Sommers, it is clear that the document was obtained improperly. In light of these conclusions and the court's findings of fact on this particular document, the court concludes that the Competitive Recipe was a trade secret and that Business Objects misappropriated this trade secret. * * *

Features of MicroStrategy 7i

As the court has noted in its findings of fact, a document titled "What's New in MicroStrategy 7.2" was disclosed widely throughout Business Objects. This document was in Business Objects' hands two months before the general release of the software.

The defendant makes a number of arguments regarding this document: that it was not labeled confidential, that it appears to be a marketing document for customers, and that there is no evidence it was not generally known or readily ascertainable through proper means. The version produced to the court is not labeled confidential; however, it is appropriate to infer that it was stripped of any MicroStrategy-related markings. Leena Shah mentioned in one email that she had to get the document in "non-MicroStrategy" form before circulating. Furthermore, it does not appear to be intended for public consumption. Several of the comments regarding features of the product indicate as much. While the defendant cites press releases detailing features of MicroStrategy products that predate this document, it appears that these press releases concerned MicroStrategy 7.1, an earlier version of the software.

The court can easily conclude this document was misappropriated. It was solicited by Leena Shah from another ex-MicroStrategy employee in violation of that employee's agreement with MicroStrategy. The court cannot, however, conclude this document contained trade secrets. No testimony was elicited regarding the inherent economic value of this particular document, what this document actually was, or any efforts to maintain the secrecy of this document. There is no reason for the court to believe that this document was kept confidential simply on the basis of general testimony regarding MicroStrategy's attitude towards the new features of its products. This is particularly true when those statements are contradicted by exhibits wherein MicroStrategy did publicize the new features of earlier versions of the software. Additionally, Shah testified that the information was already public, and the court finds it easy to believe that high-level details of upcoming software would become generally known despite any company's efforts to maintain their secrecy. Furthermore, while more technical information regarding these features might be of economic value to a competitor, the mere knowledge that software already being beta tested and two months from release (and already long overdue for release) possesses a particular feature does not seem to provide an economic advantage to a competitor. * * *

CONCLUSION

With regard to the plaintiff's misappropriation of trade secrets claim, for the reasons discussed in this Opinion and Order, the court FINDS for the plaintiff, and will enter an appropriate injunction. * * *

It is so ORDERED.

DID YOU GET IT?

1. What was the relationship between the parties?

2. What evidence persuaded the court that the defendant used improper means to acquire MicroStrategy's trade secrets?

3. Under what theory could an employer be liable for the conduct of its employees who conduct espionage against a competitor?

NOTES

1. **The definition of "improper means" in the DTSA and the EU Trade Secret Directive.** The definition of improper means under the DTSA is identical to the definition that is set forth in the UTSA. *See* Appendix A, 18 U.S.C. § 1839(5). The comparable language in the EU Trade Secret Directive, Article 4.2 provides that:

The acquisition of a trade secret without consent of the trade secret holder shall be considered unlawful, whenever carried out by:

(a) unauthorized access to, appropriation of, or copying of any documents, objects, materials, substances or electronic files, lawfully under the control of the trade secret holder, containing the trade secret or from which the trade secret can be deduced;

(b) any other conduct which, under the circumstances, is considered contrary to honest commercial practices.

Subdivision (a) of the Directive is similar to U.S. law because the "unauthorized appropriation" language is similar to the "wrongful acquisition" language of the UTSA and the DTSA. It is different from the UTSA and the DTSA in that it also defines "unauthorized access to" and "unauthorized copying" as acts of unlawful acquisition. While both types of acts have been found to constitute "wrongful acquisition" in the U.S., those acts are not listed as examples in the UTSA's and DTSA's definitions of improper means. Additionally, in the U.S., the act of unauthorized copying may be preempted by section 301 of the Copyright Act. *See* discussion of copyright preemption in Chapters 2 and 9.

2. **A note on "commercial privacy."** As part of its holding that the defendants' aerial photography constituted an improper means of obtaining another's trade secrets, the court in *Christopher* noted that "[c]ommercial privacy must be protected from espionage which could not have been reasonably anticipated or prevented." Four years later, the Supreme Court in *Kewanee Oil Co. v. Bicron Corp.* reasoned that "[a] most fundamental human right, that of privacy, is threatened when industrial espionage is condoned or is made profitable; the state interest in denying profit to such illegal ventures is unchallengeable." According to the Court, "the basic decency of society" is threatened when companies steal from one another.

Although these two early cases appear to have laid the foundation for commercial privacy in trade secret jurisprudence, the concept has remained largely undefined. The contextual application in the *Christopher* case suggests that commercial privacy may be something more than its individual privacy counterpart. In general, trade secret laws appear to provide greater protection to corporations against surveillance by competitors than individuals receive under privacy torts for incursions by other individuals. *See* Sharon K. Sandeen, *Relative Privacy: What Privacy Advocates Can Learn from Trade Secret Law*, 2006 MICH. ST. L. REV. 667 (2006). In addition, a corporations' privacy interests under trade secret law are often interpreted more broadly than privacy interests under the Fourth Amendment. For instance, the United States Supreme Court, in a case remarkably similar to *Christopher*, found that the Environmental Protection Agency's aerial photographs of a Dow Chemical plant did not violate Dow's Fourth Amendment rights. *See Dow Chemical Co. v. United States,* 476 U.S. 227 (1986). In addition, *compare California v. Greenwood,* 486 U.S. 35 (1988) (finding the Fourth Amendment did not protect an individual's garbage which was placed in garbage bags on a curb for collection) *with Tennant Co. v. Advance Mach. Co.*, 355 N.W.2d 720 (Minn. Ct. App. 1984) (finding that company retained a property interest in trash placed in a dumpster for purposes of a trade secret claim).

3. **Does the *DuPont v. Christopher* case go too far?** If you were in a commercial airplane flying over Texas and took a picture of the landscape, the fact that your photograph captured a building under construction would not be deemed improper. If such were the case, then internet mapping and satellite services such as "Google Earth" would be in a lot of trouble for taking satellite photographs of private property that allows one to discern close-up details about the property. Thus, a number of courts and commentators believe that *DuPont v. Christopher* is on the outer edge of the line between proper and improper means. *See, e.g.*, Geraldine Szott Moohr, *The Problematic Role of Criminal Law in Regulating Use of Information: The Case of the Economic Espionage Act*, 80 N.C. L. Rev. 853, 888, 921 (2002). Of course, the actions of the Christophers were fairly obvious given the fact that they had to fly a small plane over DuPont's plant.

Food for Thought

With modern technology, such as sensitive listening devices, drones, satellites, and infrared imaging, a lot of information concerning activities occurring on private property can be obtained without anyone needing to fly-over or step-upon the property. Do you think such activities should be considered improper for trade secret purposes? Yes

---

4. **Memorization and misappropriation.** While some older cases drew a distinction between written and memorized information, the modern view disregards that difference. *See, e.g., Ed Nowogroski Ins. v. Rucker*, 971 P. 2d 936 (Wash. 1999). The modern view is reflected in the UTSA which does not make a distinction between memorized information and information that exists in tangible form. Thus, even if a defendant memorized the plaintiff's trade secret and did not take any physical or tangible embodiment of the trade secret with him, that conduct could constitute misappropriation depending upon whether the defendant wrongfully acquired or threatens to disclose or use the memorized information. Georgia is one state that will only protect customer information that is in tangible form. This is despite language in the UTSA-inspired state statute that defines information as a trade secret "without regard to form." *See* C. Geoffrey Weirich & Daniel P. Hart, *Protecting Trade Secrets and Confidential Information in Georgia*, 60 MERCER L. REV. 533, 538–40 (2009).

5. **Bibliographic note:** In addition to the references noted above, for more information on the topics discussed in this chapter, *see* MILGRIM ON TRADE SECRETS §§ 1.01, 1.05, 7.02, 7.03 (2016); Elizabeth A. Rowe, *RATs, TRAPs and Trade Secrets*, 57 B.C. L. REV. 381 (2016); Elizabeth A. Rowe, *A Sociological Approach to Misappropriation*, 58 KANSAS L. REV. 1 (2009); Samuel J. Horovitz, *If You Ain't Cheating You Ain't Trying: "Spygate" and the Legal Implications of Trying Too Hard*, 17 TEX. INTELL. PROP. L.J. 305 (2009);

Michael L. Rustad, *The Negligent Enablement of Trade Secret Misappropriation*, 22 SANTA CLARA COMPUTER & HIGH TECH. L.J. 455 (2006).

CHAPTER 7

MISAPPROPRIATION: DISCLOSURE OR USE IN BREACH OF A DUTY OF CONFIDENTIALITY
■ ■ ■

Anticipated Learning Outcomes

At the conclusion of this chapter, you will have a greater understanding of the breach of confidentiality pathway for proving misappropriation, including the wrongful behaviors of disclosure or use. You will also learn more about how duties of confidentiality are formed, the types of relationships that can give rise to an implied duty of confidentiality, and how to determine the scope of a duty of confidentiality. You will also understand the circumstances under which a third-party may be held liable for trade secret misappropriation.

A. INTRODUCTION

As noted in Chapter 6, there are four ways to establish the misappropriation element of a trade secret claim. The two primary ways are: (1) by proving that the defendant *acquired* the trade secrets by improper means; or (2) by proving that the defendant *disclosed or used* the trade secrets in breach of a duty of confidentiality. A particular defendant may also engage in both types of activities by first wrongfully acquiring trade secrets and then disclosing or using them.

In situations that involve a third-party to the original misappropriation, the third-party may be liable for trade secret misappropriation if he disclosed or used information when he "knew or should have known" that the information was: (1) acquired by another by improper means; (2) acquired from another who had a duty of confidentiality; or (3) acquired by accident or mistake, by himself or another. Technically, this is a form of direct liability, but it is one or more steps removed from the original misappropriation.

In light of the foregoing, this chapter is presented in three parts. First in Part B, it explores how duties of confidentiality may arise between trade secret owners and others, including employees. This topic was already examined in many of the previous cases, including the *Reeves* case in Chapter 4 (which should be reviewed), but it is further considered in this chapter in order to explore the parameters of an implied duty of confidentiality. A critical issue with respect to implied-in-law duties is whether trade secret owners should be required to prove the traditional elements of a quasi-contract or whether something less is required in the trade secret context.

In Part C, the meanings of "disclosure" and "use" and how to prove disclosure or use is explored. The Special Issue and Notes section of this chapter discusses third-party and secondary liability.

B. RELATIONSHIPS GIVING RISE TO A DUTY OF CONFIDENTIALITY

Although cases involving the misappropriation of trade secrets by improper means often present intriguing facts of corporate espionage by electronic or other technological methods, the majority of trade secret cases involve alleged breaches of a duty of confidentiality. This is because most trade secret cases involve disputes between a trade secret owner and a former employee—over 90% according to one empirical study. *See* David Ameling, et al, *A Statistical Analysis of Trade Secret Litigation in State Courts*, 46 GONZ. L. REV. 57, 69 (2011).

As you learned in Chapter 6, the improper means type of trade secret misappropriation focuses on the method that the defendant used to acquire the alleged trade secrets and whether it is "improper" under applicable law, social norms, or business practices. Under the duty of confidentiality type of misappropriation, the focus is on: (1) the nature of the relationship between the plaintiff and defendant; (2) whether such relationship gave rise to a duty of confidentiality; and (3) whether there is an actual or threatened disclosure or use of trade secrets in violation of the applicable duty of confidentiality.

Neither the UTSA nor the DTSA uses the phrase "duty of confidentiality" and, accordingly, do not define the scope and meaning of a duty of confidentiality in either their text or, in the case of the UTSA, in its commentary. However, they do define "improper" to include breach or inducement to breach a "duty to maintain secrecy" and "misappropriation" to include disclosing or using a trade secret of another with knowledge or reason to know that it was acquired "under circumstances giving rise to a duty to maintain its secrecy." *See* UTSA, section 1(1) and 1(2)(ii)(B)(II) and 18 U.S.C. § 1839(5) and (6).

Typically, to understand what is meant by "a duty to maintain secrecy," one must look to the common law, including applicable case law and relevant secondary sources concerning duties of confidentiality. The *Restatement (Third) of Unfair Competition* contains two provisions related to duties of confidentiality, as follows:

RESTATEMENT (THIRD) OF UNFAIR COMPETITION

Section 42

A person to whom a trade secret has been disclosed owes a duty of confidence to the owner of the trade secret for purposes of the rule stated in § 40, if:

(a) the person made an express promise of confidentiality prior to the disclosure of the trade secret; or

(b) the trade secret was disclosed to the person under circumstances in which the relationship between the parties to the disclosure or the other facts surrounding the disclosure justify the conclusions that, at the time of the disclosure,

    (1) the person knew or had reason to know that the disclosure was intended to be in confidence, and

    (2) the other party to the disclosure was reasonable in inferring that the person consented to an obligation of confidentiality.

Section 43

An employee or former employee who uses or discloses a trade secret owned by the employer or former employer in breach of a duty of confidence is liable for the appropriation of trade secrets under the rules stated in § 40.

————

Based upon the foregoing, there are two ways that a duty of confidentiality may arise. It may be based upon an actual agreement between the parties (either written, oral, or implied) or it may arise as a matter of law, either a statute or common law. The most obvious example of an express duty of confidentiality is a binding written contract. *See, e.g.,* *B.F. Goodrich v. Wohlgemuth*, 192 N.E.2d 99, 105 (1963) ("The written contract expressly binds the employee [or other] . . . not to misuse special confidential knowledge of trade secrets secured by him while the contractual relationship of employment existed.") Thus, if a trade secret owner wants to create a duty in another to maintain the confidentiality of his information, the best way to do so is to get the promise in writing before any disclosure occurs. This can take the form of a confidentiality clause in an agreement that deals primarily with other matters (for instance a clause in an employment agreement or a license agreement) or a separate "Confidentiality Agreement" or "Non-Disclosure Agreement." (*See* Chapters 8 and 11 for a fuller discussion of express agreements that impose confidentiality obligations.)

The *Reeves* case in Chapter 4 details the various ways that contractual duties of confidentiality may arise, and was covered earlier to introduce you to idea submission cases and to make the point that contractual duties of confidentiality may protect some information that would not otherwise qualify for trade secret protection. As noted in that case, contractual duties of confidentiality may be created expressly or be implied-in-fact. There are also certain types of relationships where a duty of confidentiality might exist by rule or statute, or by operation of law.

In Chapter 9, you will learn that Section 7 of the UTSA was intended to preclude common law tort claims that were previously used to protect information not meeting the requirements of trade secrecy. This means that (except in States that do not understand the purpose of Section 7 and misapply it), the only conceivable way to protect information that does not meet the definition of trade secret is through contract law. It also means that it is important to understand the difference between an implied-in-fact contract (which is based upon contract law) and an implied-at-law obligation (which is a matter of equity).

An implied-in-fact contract (like an express written or oral agreement) is based on the intentions of the parties. "It arises where the court finds from the surrounding facts and circumstances that the parties intended to make a contract but failed to articulate their promises and the court merely implies what it feels the parties really intended." *Reeves v. Aleyska Pipeline Service Company*, quoting *Martens v. Metzgar*. *See also, Restatement (Second) of Contracts* § 4 cmt. a (1981).

Implied-at-law (or quasi) contracts (or duties) are different from implied-in-fact contracts because there is no finding of intent to enter into a contract. *See Restatement (Second) of Contracts* § 4 cmt. b (1981) ("As opposed to the inferred from fact ("implied in fact") contract, the "implied in law" quasi-contract is no contract at all, but a form of the remedy of restitution") and *Restatement of Restitution*, Part I (1937). Instead, a duty is implied from the circumstances due to equitable considerations. In the trade secret context, trade secret owners often argue that the nature of the relationship between the parties coupled with the sharing of trade secret information should create either an implied-in-fact contract or an implied-at-law duty of confidentiality.

Previous cases in this book provide examples of express written and oral confidentiality agreements and implied agreements of confidentiality. The cases that follow focus more attention on the types of relationships and circumstances that might give rise to either an implied-in-fact or implied-at-law duty of confidentiality. In practice, however, no trade secret owner should put itself in the position of having to argue that an implied duty of confidentiality exists. The better practice is to obtain an express promise of confidentiality before sharing any trade secrets with another.

When reading the following cases, consider both the language from the *Restatement (Third) of Unfair Competition* that is set forth above and the following language from the *Reeves* case:

We have required the following three elements for a quasi-contract claim:

1) a benefit conferred upon the defendant by the plaintiff;

2) appreciation by the defendant of such benefit; and

3) acceptance and retention by the defendant of such benefit under such circumstances that it would be inequitable for him to retain it without paying the value thereof.

Quasi-contracts are "judicially-created obligations to do justice." "Consequently, the obligation to make restitution that arises in quasi-contract is not based upon any agreement between the parties, objective or subjective."

Food for Thought

Is there a difference between a duty to maintain secrecy and a duty of confidentiality? Could it be that the language of the UTSA was not intended to be synonymous with a duty of confidentiality?

---

1. FIDUCIARY AND TRUST RELATIONSHIPS

The most obvious example of a relationship that can give rise to a statutory or implied-at-law duty of confidentiality is a trust or fiduciary relationship. For instance, if you hire an attorney to file a patent application for you, and in the process you disclose important trade secrets, a duty of confidentiality has been created due to the mere nature of the relationship. This is because it is well-established that attorneys have a professional and ethical obligation to protect information provided to them by their clients. MODEL RULES OF PROFESSIONAL CONDUCT R. 1.6 (2013). Sometimes, like the attorney-client relationship, the relationship that is alleged in a trade secret case will involve trust or fiduciary duties that make it easy for a court to find a duty of confidentiality. A key question in such cases, however, is the scope of the duty of confidentiality and the identity of the information to be protected.

2. THE EMPLOYMENT RELATIONSHIP

Based upon principles of agency and employment law (and the statutes of some states) it is generally recognized that the employment relationship imposes a duty of confidentiality on employees, but that duty is not absolute. *See Restatement (Third) of Agency* § 8.05 cmt. c (2006). The precise scope and nature of the duty will differ depending upon the particular facts of a case and the law of a given jurisdiction, but it usually includes a duty to maintain the confidentiality of known trade secrets. In some jurisdictions, it may also require employees to maintain the confidentiality of proprietary business information that does not meet the definition of a trade secret, even in the absence of an express agreement.

The first step in determining whether an employment relationship gives rise to a duty of confidentiality is to determine if the relationship is, in fact, an employment relationship. Merely because a company "hires" or pays an individual to work for it does not mean that the individual is an employee. As the U.S. Supreme Court recognized in the famous copyright case, *Community for Creative Non-Violence v. Reid,* 490 U.S. 730 (1989), there is a substantial body of common law that defines the features and parameters of the employment relationship. "[W]hen we have concluded that Congress intended terms such as 'employee,' 'employer,' and 'scope of employment' to be understood in light of agency law, we have relied on the general common law of agency, rather than on the law of any particular State, to give meaning to these terms." *Id.* at 740. Generally, to determine whether an employment relationship exists, one must look beyond the labels that are used. *See Restatement (Third) of Agency* § 1.02 cmt. a (2006).

Under trade secret law, whether an individual is an employee or an independent contractor can affect the trade secret misappropriation analysis in at least three ways. First, as is discussed in the Special Issue section of Chapter 8, an individual's status as an employee may determine ownership and use rights in trade secrets that are created by the employee during his employment. Second, the employment relationship often gives an individual greater access to the trade secrets of a company than would be enjoyed by an outsider or independent contractor. Usually in such cases, there can be no claim that the employee wrongfully "acquired" the trade secrets but only a claim that the trade secrets were (or may be) improperly "disclosed" or "used." Third, the employment relationship gives rise to a number of implied duties which can serve as the basis for a trade secret misappropriation claim. However, in certain circumstances a court may also determine that an independent contractor owed a duty of confidentiality to the owner of a trade secret.

The two cases that follow provide examples, with divergent results, of how courts determine if an implied duty of confidentiality exists in an employment setting.

> ### Reading Guidance
> What facts are critical to the court's finding on the duty of confidentiality in this case?

TOWN & COUNTRY HOUSE & HOMES SERVICE, INC. V. EVANS

Supreme Court of Errors of Connecticut, 1963.

150 Conn. 314.

* * *

SHEA, ASSOCIATE JUSTICE.

[handwritten: -employer-employee relationship; agency law; implied duty of court'd; -non-compete; -bribery non-solicitation claim here is not preempted by UTSA87]

The plaintiff conducts a housecleaning business and provides men and machinery for that purpose. The defendant was employed by the plaintiff from May, 1957 to March, 1960. It was the plaintiff's custom to require its employees to sign covenants binding them, under certain circumstances, not to engage in the housecleaning business after the termination of their employment with the plaintiff. The defendant was requested to sign such a covenant but refused to do so. He worked for the plaintiff at the homes of various customers in Fairfield County in this state and in Westchester County in New York. During the latter part of his employment, he told a number of the plaintiff's customers that he was planning to enter the housecleaning business for himself, and he solicited business from them. Thereafter, the defendant terminated his employment and started his own housecleaning business. At the time of the trial he had fifteen regular customers, some of whom were former customers of the plaintiff.

On these facts, the trial court concluded that the relationship between the parties was the ordinary one of employer and employee; that the defendant was not entrusted with any of the plaintiff's confidential communications and did not learn any peculiar secrets or gain any private information while he was in the plaintiff's employ; that there was nothing secret about the plaintiff's list of customers; that, in the absence of fraud or express contract, the defendant had a right to start his own business and could legally solicit business from his former employer's customers; and that judgment should be rendered for the defendant.

* * *

The plaintiff has * * * assigned error in the court's conclusions, on the ground that the facts set forth in the finding do not support them. He claims that the defendant was not entitled to solicit its customers for his rival business before the termination of his employment. The defendant, as an agent of the plaintiff, was a fiduciary with respect to matters within the scope of his agency. * * * The very relationship implies that the principal has reposed some trust or confidence in the agent and that the agent or employee is obligated to exercise the utmost good faith, loyalty and honesty toward his principal or employer. * * * In the absence of clear consent or waiver by the principal, an agent, during the term of the agency, is subject to a duty not to compete with the principal concerning the subject matter of the agency. *Restatement (Second)*, 2 Agency § 393. Upon termination of the agency, however, and in the absence of a restrictive agreement, the agent can properly compete with his principal in matters for which he had been employed. "Thus, before the end of his employment, he can properly purchase a rival business and upon termination of employment immediately compete. He is not, however, entitled to solicit customers for such rival business before the end of his employment * * * in direct competition with the employer's business." *Restatement (Second)*, 2 Agency § 393, comment e. Knowledge acquired by an employee during his employment cannot be used for his own advantage to the injury of the employer during employment. * * *

The court found that the defendant solicited customers for his own business before his employment with the plaintiff was terminated. Such action was in direct competition with his employer and was contrary to the employer's interest. It was a betrayal of the employer's trust and confidence in the defendant. He is not entitled to the benefits resulting from this unlawful conduct, and he should account to the plaintiff for the profits received from any business done with former customers of the plaintiff who were solicited by him while he was in its employ. Moreover, the plaintiff is entitled to injunctive relief restraining the defendant from performing, either directly or indirectly, any service, in competition with the plaintiff, for any former customers of the plaintiff who were solicited by him prior to the termination of his employment.

The plaintiff also claims that the names of its customers constituted a trade secret and that the court erred in reaching a contrary conclusion. "A trade secret may consist of any formula, pattern, device or compilation of information which is used in one's business, and which gives him an opportunity to obtain an advantage over competitors who do not know or use it. It may be a formula for a chemical compound * * * or a list of customers." *Restatement*, 4 Torts § 757, comment b. Matters of public knowledge or of general knowledge in an industry cannot be appropriated by one as his secret. A trade secret is known only in the particular business in which it is used. It is not essential that knowledge of it be restricted solely to the proprietor of the business. He may, without losing his protection, communicate the secret to employees or to others who are pledged to secrecy. Nevertheless, a substantial element of secrecy must exist, to the extent that there would be difficulty in acquiring the information except by the use of improper means. * * *

Trade secrets are the property of the employer and cannot be used by the employee for his own benefit. The lack of any express agreement on the part of the employee not to disclose a trade secret is not significant. The law will import into every contract of employment a prohibition against the use of a trade secret by the employee for his own benefit, to the detriment of his employer, if the secret was acquired by the employee in the course of his employment. * * * A list of customers, if their trade and patronage have been secured by years of business effort and advertising and the expenditure of time and money, constitutes an important part of a business and is in the nature of a trade secret. It is the property of the employer and may not be used by the employee as his own property or to his employer's prejudice. * * * If in any particular business the list of customers is, because of some peculiarity of the business, in reality a trade secret and an employee has gained knowledge thereof as a matter of confidence, he will be restrained from using that knowledge against his employer. * * * On the other hand, where the identity of the customers is readily ascertainable through ordinary business channels or through classified business or trade directories, the courts refuse to accord to the list the protection of a trade secret. * * *

The plaintiff brought this action in equity requesting, in its prayer for relief, an accounting of profits, an injunction and damages. If the list of customers was a trade secret, the plaintiff would be entitled, in addition to any other proper relief, to an injunction restraining the defendant from performing services for customers on the list. * * * On the other hand, if the list of customers was not a trade secret, the right to injunctive relief and damages would apply only to business done with customers solicited before the end of the employment. Thus, the measure and extent of the relief to which the plaintiff may be entitled depends on a proper determination of whether the plaintiff's list of customers was a trade secret. The court's conclusion that there was nothing secret about the plaintiff's list of customers is not supported by any subordinate facts in the finding. We are unable to determine what factors were considered by the court in reaching this conclusion. Without the necessary facts to support it, it cannot stand.

There is error, the judgment is set aside and a new trial is ordered.

* * *

DID YOU GET IT?

1. What are the claimed trade secrets and who owns them?

2. Why does the employment relationship include an implied duty of confidentiality?

3. Can you articulate the scope of an employee's duty of confidentiality?

4. What must an employee do to avoid breaching the duty of confidentiality?

> ### Reading Guidance
> *What set of circumstances are necessary to create an implied duty of confidentiality between an employer and employee?*

[handwritten: —ct. held no contractual relationship here between employees + employer]

SHATTERPROOF GLASS CORP. V. GUARDIAN GLASS CO.

United States District Court, E.D. Michigan, S.Div., 1970.
322 F.Supp. 854.

* * *

TALBOT SMITH, DISTRICT JUDGE.

[handwritten: —windshield glass duplication companies]

This case concerns the bending of glass for, principally, automobile windshields. The litigants are suppliers of replacement windshields, not original equipment suppliers. For a while, years ago, all that was needed for a windshield was a pair of flat pieces of glass. One piece comprised the left side of the windshield, the other the right. In the middle was a divider strip of some kind. Then in the early 1950's all of this changed. We began to get "panoramic" windshields, "wrap-around" windshields, which were bent pieces of glass, now common on cars. They are laminated, there being a sheet of plastic sandwiched between two pieces of glass.

The bending is simplicity itself in theory, though in practice difficulties arising from the process operations are experienced. The general idea is that the two pieces of flat glass, one slightly larger than the other, are put on a frame, or mold. * * * [T]his frame is made up of three sections, * * * a center section, and two symmetrical end sections, one left, the other right. These sections are hinged so they can bend, either upwards to support the flat pieces of glass (their position at the outset) or downwards, to support the bent pieces of glass at the finish of the operation. At the start of the operation these sections are so disposed that six pars thereof support the flat glass. The frame, with its glass load is started through a furnace. As the glass heats up and softens it sags and sinks into the mold which, by means of its hinges, bends and receives it. We thus end up with bent pieces of glass. * * * Our problems in this action relate to the molds on which the bending takes place, and more particularly to such things as hinges, pivots, and points of support. In addition, the plaintiff claims that the defendant misappropriated 43 of its trade secrets. * * *

We will now consider the alleged theft of trade secrets. Basic, of course, to the whole concept of trade secrets is secrecy itself. At the very outset of our consideration of this problem, it is stressed to us, and properly so, that the plaintiff's business, concerning which it makes broad claims of secrecy, was not an original-equipment business but a replacement business. What it did was merely to duplicate (for, say, a motorist whose windshield had been broken) windshields for the replacement market. The windshields themselves (the broken ones, that is, that are to be replaced by replacement companies, such as Guardian and Shatterproof) had already been produced by the original equipment manufacturers, and had been supplied to the replacement companies with molds and specifications. In addition, it is clear that those skilled in the art are able to tell from an examination of a windshield a great deal about it, such as the hinge points, whether a hold-down was used, or whether it was "bent to size or whether it was bent block size and cut after." * * *

Equally inimical to plaintiff's trade secrets theory, moreover, is the situation with respect to the two alleged thieves, Little and Kapron. It is plaintiff's theory that it was through these men that the defendant "misappropriated" the trade secrets of Shatterproof. These men, we note at the outset, were not supervisors or even foremen. They were hourly rated employees; Little's pay being $2.75 per hour. Both were mold makers. (There were about a dozen men at Shatterproof whose trade was mold making.) Neither man was told or warned that his work involved proprietary or confidential matter, nor did they so understand, save with respect to nonproduction, experimental items. The Jendrisak testimony is revealing on this point. He knew when both Little and Kapron left that they were going to Guardian, to practice their trade in Guardian's bending operation, just as, Mr. Jendrisak admitted, he had some time back left Libbey-Owens Ford to go to Shatterproof to practice his profession or trade. At no time did he warn them that so-and-so were trade secrets, or ask them not to use them. "Did you feel," he was asked, "that either one of them were betraying you in some way?" The answer was, "Well, I don't know how I felt at the time; I felt we were losing good men, particularly Harvey Little. I certainly felt that." (Mr. Jendrisak later re-hired Mr. Kapron.) At no time had he ever accused either man of stealing trade secrets from him, nor did he ever contact and warn Guardian of a trade secret situation. The plaintiff has failed to establish the existence of any confidential relationship between it and Little and Kapron.

Plaintiff urges to us that the law, in this situation, as to these hourly rated workers "infers a confidential relationship in the same way that a client coming to a lawyer infers that the lawyer will not abuse the confidence reposed with him." The analogy is not apt. Its application to this situation would seriously impinge upon the doctrine of freedom of choice as to work and trade, and its inevitable result would be deleterious in the extreme to industrial labor, a binding workman to the particular employer for whom he originally worked in a modest, hourly-rated capacity. We are constrained to reject the argument made.

Nor do the circumstances of their hiring suggest that the defendant knew of any such relationship or participated in the breach thereof. Defendant's Vice-President Hertzberg testified that Little called him on the telephone and asked for employment, bringing Kapron with him. They were hired as fixture makers, mold makers, which Guardian required, as do all companies similarly situated. "Ford had fixture makers and mold makers. Libby-Owens had them, Pittsburgh had them. And it was a trade, as far as I was concerned. I would have advertised under ordinary circumstances had they not approached me."

From all of the testimony on this matter, pro and con, we find nothing sinister, nothing of misappropriation. This is merely life in today's industrial world, employees coming and going, bettering themselves where they can. Shatterproof itself had hired both engineering and management personnel from Libby-Owens-Ford and Pittsburgh, when it went into the glass bending business in 1952. We are not, of course, hinting at any impropriety, but speaking rather, of trade practices. It is our conclusion and our finding that there was no confidential relationship with Little and Kapron, no breach thereof, and neither irregularity nor impropriety in their hiring by Guardian.

* * *

DID YOU GET IT?

1. What are the claimed trade secrets and who owns them?
    Process to duplicate windshields
2. Why wasn't a confidential relationship recognized between the plaintiff and its employees Little and Kapron?
    They were never even told they knew TS.
3. What did the employer need to do to create a confidential relationship; in other words, what facts relate to the issue of whether a confidential relationship was established? *Warning them of TS, hesitance when they leave*
4. Is the mere sharing of trade secret information enough to create a duty of confidentiality? If not, what else is needed? *No,*

3.   INDEPENDENT CONTRACTORS

Although the employment relationship is, by far, the most common relationship that exists between plaintiffs and defendants in trade secret misappropriation cases, it is not the only relationship that may give rise to an implied duty of confidentiality. A variety of relationships have been found to provide the basis for a duty of confidentiality "under the circumstances." This includes vendor and vendee relationships, manufacturer and supplier relationships, and contractor and sub-contractor relationships.

The following case involves a relationship between a company and an independent contractor. As with the previous two cases, consider the facts that must be present to create an implied duty of confidentiality under such circumstances.

> **Reading Guidance**
>
> What is the significance for trade secret purposes of a finding that an
> individual is an independent contractor?

HICKLIN ENGINEERING, L.C. V. BARTELL

United States Court of Appeals, Seventh Circuit, 2006.
439 F.3d 346.

—Independent contractor

* * *

EASTERBROOK, CIRCUIT JUDGE.

Axi-Line Precision Products designs and makes testing equipment for auto
and truck transmissions. Since 1998 Axi-Line has been a division of Hicklin
Engineering. Between 1993 and 2000 R.J. Bartell, an engineer, worked
part-time for Axi-Line. He did not sign a restrictive covenant or
confidentiality agreement. After Bartell began a competing business (R.J.
Bartell & Associates) that sells transmission testing equipment, Hicklin
filed this suit under Wisconsin's version of the Uniform Trade Secrets Act.
* * * The parties agreed to final decision by a magistrate judge, * * * and
Bartell prevailed on summary judgment * * *. Hicklin appeals from these
decisions. * * *

* * * Magistrate Judge Gorence ordered the district clerk to keep both of
her substantive opinions under seal—not just portions that revealed trade
secrets, but the whole opinions. The resolution of this litigation thus has
been concealed from the public. The judge did not explain what authority
permits a federal court to issue entire opinions in secret. Redacting
portions of opinions is one thing, secret disposition quite another. We have
insisted that litigation be conducted in public to the maximum extent
consistent with respecting trade secrets, the identities of undercover
agents, and other facts that should be held in confidence. * * * This means
that both judicial opinions and litigants' briefs must be in the public record,
if necessary in parallel versions—one full version containing all details,
and another redacted version with confidential information omitted.
Hicklin has filed multiple briefs using this procedure; the sealed brief
contains a trade secret diagram omitted from the public brief but otherwise
is identical.

What happens in the federal courts is presumptively open to public
scrutiny. Judges deliberate in private but issue public decisions after public
arguments based on public records. The political branches of government
claim legitimacy by election, judges by reason. Any step that withdraws an
element of the judicial process from public view makes the ensuing decision
look more like fiat and requires rigorous justification. The Supreme Court
issues public opinions in all cases, even those said to involve state secrets.
* * * It is impossible to see any justification for issuing off-the-record

opinions in a dispute about drawings of transmission testing equipment. We inquired at oral argument whether the district court's opinions contain any information that Hicklin claims as a trade secret; we were told that they do not. Accordingly, there is no reason even for redaction. The Clerk of this court will place the district court's opinions in the public record. We hope never to encounter another sealed opinion.

Bartell did not promise to avoid future competition with Axi-Line. Nor did he promise in writing not to use his drawings and ideas for any other entity. The district court concluded that this means that Bartell may do as he pleases with any information that Axi-Line furnished him, plus whatever he developed on his own. The second half of this proposition is unimpeachable. As an independent contractor, Bartell presumptively owned his work product. He was free to sell engineering solutions to Axi-Line on either an exclusive or a non-exclusive basis, just as lawyers may sell their legal solutions to clients on an exclusive or non-exclusive basis. In the absence of an agreement, non-exclusivity is the norm.

Thus a lawyer who develops a new form contract, securities indenture, or tax shelter when working for Client X may reuse the language when dealing with Client Y, or may publish the language in a treatise for all to see and emulate, unless he has promised X to keep silent. A software programmer, working as an independent contractor for Client Z, who develops a novel way to organize a database may re-use the source code for another client's project, unless he promises otherwise. Norms of the trade might reverse this presumption, but Hicklin has not proffered any evidence that a mechanical engineer's human capital or knowledge, built up when working for a client, belong to that client rather than the engineer.

Things are otherwise when the client rather than the independent contractor develops the information. Then the client presumptively owns the data, and the contractor may use it only with the client's consent. Again the legal profession supplies an example. Bidder decides to make a tender offer for Target and supplies that information to Lawyer so that the necessary forms and contracts may be prepared. Lawyer is free to use (or re-use) form templates developed when working for other clients but is not free to disclose (or trade on) the impending offer, for that information is Bidder's property. By working on the deal, Lawyer did not acquire any property rights in the information Bidder supplied.

The law of trade secrets follows the same approach to ownership, both in general, see *Restatement (Third) of Unfair Competition* § 43 comment c (1995), and in Wisconsin. * * * *See* Wis. Stat. § 134.90(2)(a) plus the definition of "improper means" in § 134.90(1); *RTE Corp. v. Coatings, Inc.* ("Where what is thought to be a trade secret is disclosed [to an independent contractor], the question posed is whether, under the circumstances, the recipient of the information knew or should have known that the information is a trade secret and that the disclosure was made in confidence. . . . A confidential relationship does not arise when the parties are dealing at arm's length and the recipient has not been put on notice of the confidential nature of the disclosure."). *See also* 2–7 *Milgrim on Trade Secrets* § 7.01[9][e] (discussing the situation of consulting engineers). So Bartell did not acquire any rights in Axi-Line's trade-secret data just because he used those data in the performance of his duties.

Would the record permit a reasonable jury to find that Bartell knew that Axi-Line treated at least some of the data it provided as trade secrets? It would. The information's nature-dimensions, materials, and tolerances on the parts used to make dynamometers and other equipment-is one reason. Many of these details (especially materials and tolerances) would be hard to obtain by reverse engineering. *See United States v. Lange* (criminal conviction for disclosing information of this kind). Axi-Line's safeguards, of which Bartell knew, are another reason. The firm took standard precautions, such as perimeter fences, excluding unescorted visitors, and keeping data under lock and key. Bartell himself suggested to Axi-Line that certain plans (which Bartell had converted from hand-drawn blueprints to computer-assisted-design models) bear confidentiality legends, and Axi-Line told Bartell to include appropriate legends in his CAD models. Even bearing the legend, these detailed models (and printouts made from them) were not shown to customers or competitors.

From Bartell's knowledge, and the norm that a client's information remains its property after an independent contractor has worked with the data, a reasonable jury could infer that Bartell implicitly agreed to use the data for Axi-Line's benefit rather than his own. Wisconsin does not require an express, written contract of confidentiality. *RTE* says as much, and although that decision predates the state's adoption of the Uniform Trade Secrets Act, every decision we could find applying that statute holds that an implied undertaking to abide by the trade's norms of confidentiality suffices. * * * And breach of an implicit promise to hold information for the client's sole benefit in turn violates the Trade Secrets Act, Wis. Stat. § 134.90(2)(a).

* * * There remains the question whether Bartell did disclose or use Axi-Line's confidential information improperly. Bartell contends that he did not reveal to anyone else the CAD models that he built using Axi-Line's data but just looked at them to ensure that the new plans he was creating for his own business did not contain any obvious blunders. Whether that is permissible under Wisconsin law is an interesting question, but not one we need resolve, given Hicklin's contention that Bartell copied and used the trade secrets wholesale rather than capitalizing on more general knowledge that he had gained while working on testing gear. There will be time enough to address the legal issue if the trier of fact should conclude that Bartell's "just checking" version is the right one.

On remand the parties and trier of fact will need to separate Axi-Line's contributions (which Hicklin owns) from Bartell's (which he owns), determine which of Axi-Line's data are trade secrets, ascertain whether Bartell recognized that these data are confidential, pin down the use that Bartell made of those trade secrets, and if necessary decide whether Wisconsin law permits such a use. If Hicklin prevails on these issues, the district court will have to select an appropriate remedy.

Hicklin has presented additional legal theories, but the district court need not consider them. These common-law approaches have been superseded by the Trade Secrets Act. *See* § 7(a) of the Uniform Trade Secrets Act, enacted as Wis. Stat. § 134.90(6) * * *. They would in any event add little or nothing to the statutory remedy, so they should be put to one side if only to streamline the litigation.

* * *

The judgment is vacated (except with respect to the award under Rule 37) and the case is remanded for proceedings consistent with this opinion.

DID YOU GET IT?

1. What is the presumptive rule regarding the ownership of independent contractor information?

2. Can there be a confidential relationship between a company and an independent contractor? If so, under what circumstances?

3. Are the norms of an industry enough to create a duty of confidentiality? Should they be?

4.   OTHER BUSINESS RELATIONSHIPS

As previously noted, there are a variety of business relationships that may give rise to a duty of confidentiality "under the circumstances." As emphasized in *Hicklin*, two critical facts often determine whether an implied duty of confidentiality will be found: (1) the existence of a trade secret; and (2) the trade secret owner's act of sharing its trade secret with another. Another key fact is the knowledge that the recipient of the trade secret has (or does not have) regarding both the existence of a trade secret and the expectation of confidentiality. The following case provides an example of how courts determine whether an implied duty of confidentiality exists, but case law is replete with other examples.

> ### *Reading Guidance*
> *When does a subcontractor owe a duty of confidentiality?*

KAMIN V. KUHNAU

Supreme Court of Oregon, 1962.
232 Or. 139.

* * *

O'CONNELL, JUSTICE.

This is a suit in equity to enjoin defendants from unfairly competing with plaintiff and to recover damages resulting from such competition. Defendants appeal from a decree permanently enjoining them from engaging in unfair competition with plaintiff and from an award of damages in the amount of $19,272.48.

Plaintiff alleges that he employed defendant, Richard Kuhnau, as an independent contractor to furnish labor and materials required in the construction of garbage truck bodies embodying improvements invented by plaintiff. It is alleged that plaintiff perfected a so-called "packer" garbage truck body involving the use of a "plow" which is a power-operated device for compressing materials placed in the truck body and thereby increasing its capacity. It is asserted that these improvements were trade secrets communicated to defendant Kuhnau in the course of a confidential relationship, giving rise to a duty not to disclose or appropriate such secrets for defendant's own benefit. Plaintiff charges that defendant, in violation of this duty, manufactured packer truck bodies for his own account, sold them, and offered them for sale in competition with plaintiff. * * *

The facts are as follows. For approximately 25 years plaintiff had been employed by a knitting mill as a mechanic. In 1953 he entered into the garbage collection business. From the time plaintiff entered into the garbage collection business he began thinking of methods of facilitating the loading of garbage trucks and of compressing or packing the materials after they were loaded. By 1955 he had done some experimental work on his own truck, devising a hoist mechanism operated by hydraulic cylinders to lift a bucket from the ground to the top of the truck box. By this time he had also arrived at the conclusion that the packing of the loaded materials could best be effected through the use of a hydraulically operated plow which would move against the loaded materials and compress them against the interior of the truck. At the time plaintiff conceived this solution there were on the market garbage truck bodies containing various "packer" mechanisms, including hydraulically operated plows. However, plaintiff and defendant apparently were not aware of the use of hydraulic cylinders for this purpose and thought that plaintiff's idea was novel in this respect.

In January, 1955, plaintiff made arrangements with defendant Kuhnau, president and manager of Oregon Rental Equipment Company, to use the company's machine shop and one or more of its employees to assist plaintiff in carrying on further experimental work in developing plaintiff's ideas. This experimental work was carried on for approximately one year. According to plaintiff's evidence, all of the experimental work was done under his supervision and Kuhnau had no voice or control as to the manner in which the developmental work was to be carried on. It is Kuhnau's contention that he and the employees of Oregon Rental Equipment Company contributed suggestions and ideas which were used in the development and improvement of the truck body and compressor mechanism. * * *

When plaintiff had completed his experimental work he began to receive orders for truck bodies embodying his improvements. The first two units sold were manufactured by Oregon Rental Equipment Company.

After the sale of these two units (in the spring of 1956) Kuhnau terminated his connections with Oregon Rental Equipment Company. He rented a machine shop at another location and began business under the name of R. K. Truck Sales. Between May and October, 1956, he manufactured ten units for plaintiff. For each unit Kuhnau received an amount agreed upon by the parties. Plaintiff fixed the selling price of the unit and his profit consisted of the difference between the selling price and the amount he paid Kuhnau.

On or about October, 1, 1956, Kuhnau informed plaintiff that he was going to manufacture truck bodies in competition with plaintiff. Kuhnau testified that the relationship was terminated as a result of a disagreement over the amount he was to receive for manufacturing the unit for plaintiff. Plaintiff contends that Kuhnau terminated the relationship for the purpose of entering into competition with plaintiff. The units manufactured by Kuhnau were similar to those which he had previously manufactured for plaintiff. However, there were some differences in the design of the two units. The principal difference was that Kuhnau mounted the hydraulic cylinder operating the plow or blade under the truck bed whereas the cylinder in plaintiff's truck was above the bed. There was testimony supporting plaintiff's assertion that it was his idea to place the cylinder under the bed of the truck but that suggestion was not adopted because Kuhnau did not think it was feasible. * * *

The initial question is whether the disclosure to defendant Kuhnau of plaintiff's design for a garbage packer unit was made under such circumstances as to raise an implication of a promise by Kuhnau not to appropriate the design to his own use.

Obviously, no such implication could be made if Kuhnau had been employed simply to recreate a packer unit already on the market in the locality and commonly known to the trade. But this was not the case. It was established that garbage truck bodies of the type made by plaintiff had not been on the local market. * * *

Whether the information disclosed was intended to be appropriable by the disclosee will depend upon the relationship of the parties and the circumstances under which the disclosure was made. It is not necessary to show that the defendant expressly agreed not to use the plaintiff's information; the agreement may be implied. And the implication may be made not simply as a product of the quest for the intention of the parties but as a legal conclusion recognizing the need for ethical practices in the commercial world.

In the case at bar the relationship between plaintiff and Kuhnau was such that an obligation not to appropriate the plaintiff's improvements could be implied. Kuhnau was paid to assist plaintiff in the development of the latter's idea. It must have been apparent to Kuhnau that plaintiff was attempting to produce a unit which could be marketed. Certainly it would not have been contemplated that as soon as the packer unit was perfected Kuhnau would have the benefit of plaintiff's ideas and the perfection of the unit through painstaking and expensive experimentation. It is to be remembered that the plaintiff's experimentation was being carried on, not on the assumption that he was duplicating an existing machine, but upon the assumption that he was creating a new product. It has been recognized in the cases that a manufacturer who has been employed to develop an inventor's ideas is not entitled to appropriate those ideas to his own use. * * *

* * * In *McKinzie v. Cline*, the plaintiffs employed the defendants to manufacture a gun swivel which one of the plaintiffs had invented. The defendants discontinued manufacturing the swivel for the plaintiffs and proceeded to manufacture and sell it for their own account. It was held that defendants violated a confidential relationship which existed between the parties and that therefore plaintiffs were entitled to an injunction and damages. * * * The *McKinzie* case followed the line of authority previously discussed which de-emphasizes the elements of secrecy and novelty and stresses the breach of the confidential relation between the parties. The court adopted the higher standard of commercial ethics to which we have already alluded:

> 'If our system of private enterprise on which our nation has thrived, prospered and grown great is to survive, fair dealing, honesty and good faith between contracting parties must be zealously maintained; therefore, if one who has learned of another's invention through contractual relationship, such as exists in the present case, takes unconscionable and inequitable advantage of the other to his own enrichment and at the expense

of the latter, a court of equity will extend its broad equitable powers to protect the party injured.'

We reaffirm this declaration of business ethics and hold that defendant Kuhnau violated his duty to plaintiff by appropriating the information derived through their business relationship.

* * *

The decree [for plaintiff] is affirmed.

DID YOU GET IT?

1. What is the relationship between the plaintiff and the defendant?

2. What facts supported the court's finding that there was an implied obligation of confidentiality between Kuhnau and the plaintiff? Was it an implied-in-fact obligation or an implied-at-law obligation?

3. Was the court more concerned with the existence of a duty of confidentiality or the existence of a trade secret? Does it matter?

5.   ARM'S-LENGTH TRANSACTIONS

The term "arm's-length transaction" is a term of art that is frequently used in business-related transactions. It generally refers to the fact that the parties to a contract or other business relationship do not have an ongoing relationship. The term is defined in Black's Law Dictionary (West 2009) as follows: "Of or relating to dealings between two parties who are not related or not on close terms and who are presumed to have roughly equal bargaining power; not involving a confidential relationship."

Transactions that can truly be described as arm's-length transactions do not usually create an implied confidential relationship between the parties. However, as the foregoing cases reveal, what may appear to be an arm's-length transaction on the surface can result in duties of confidentiality in particular circumstances. Inversely, parties to an arm's-length transaction who wish to avoid the imposition of implied duties of confidentiality may specifically disclaim them. In practice, whether an arm's-length transaction creates an implied duty of confidentiality may turn on the perceived wrongfulness of the defendant's actions.

— P here did not waive
TS claim

— no explicit language in disclosure
agmt that P waived
TS claims/confid.

> ### Reading Guidance
> Can a party disclaim a confidential relationship by contract and, if so, how?

indep.
toy
inventor

BURTEN v. MILTON BRADLEY CO.
United States Court of Appeals, First Circuit, 1985.
763 F.2d 461.

toy manufactur

COFFIN, CIRCUIT JUDGE.

This case concerns the clarity of a disclosure agreement between appellants, independent toy inventors, and the Milton Bradley Co., a toy manufacturer, and whether the parties intended by their disclosure agreement to preclude the formation of a confidential relationship. * * *

Facts

"Triumph" is the name of an electronic board game invented by Coleman and Burten which they had hoped to sell to Milton Bradley. Milton Bradley has a policy to consider game ideas only from inventors known to it, and only after inventors agree to sign its "Disclosure Record" form. Appellants willingly signed Milton Bradley's standard disclosure agreement which ostensibly delineates the parties' rights pending evaluation of the product, and Triumph was accepted for review. The disclosure agreement contained language to the effect that the submission was undertaken voluntarily, that no relationship to Milton Bradley was to be implied from the company's willingness to review the idea, that Milton Bradley assumed no obligation to accept the product, and that the disclosing party was to retain all rights under United States patent laws. The disclosure agreement also authorized Milton Bradley to reproduce for its records all material submitted.

— disclosure
agmt

Appellants failed to secure a contract on the first review of Triumph, so they modified the game and resubmitted it to Milton Bradley after signing new disclosure agreements. Triumph again was rejected by Milton Bradley. This should have been the end of the story, but approximately one year later, appellants discovered that Milton Bradley was marketing a new electronic board game under the name of "Dark Tower." Because appellants believed that Dark Tower contained significant structural and design similarities to Triumph, they brought this action for trade secret misappropriation. * * *

— P signed

After the lengthy trial was concluded, the jury returned a general verdict for Coleman and Burten in the amount of $737,058.10 for royalties based on the Dark Tower profits. Milton Bradley moved for judgment notwithstanding the verdict, and the district court, after a meticulous survey of the cases, which it recognized posed a "surprisingly close

— P won at trial ct.

question," set aside the verdict. We share the court's view of the closeness of the question, but feel constrained to allow the verdict to stand.

Analysis

In Massachusetts the law of torts affords limited protection to the owner of a trade secret for the misappropriation of his ideas. * * * The essence of the wrong is generally "the breach of the duty not to disclose or to use without permission confidential information acquired from another." * * * In order to successfully establish a cause of action for misappropriation, therefore, a plaintiff must show that he or she shared a confidential relationship with the defendant, possessed a trade secret, disclosed it to the defendant, and that the defendant made use of the disclosure in breach of the confidence reposed in him. *See generally Restatement of Torts* § 757.

A confidential relationship generally arises by operation of law from the affiliations of the parties and the context in which the disclosures are offered. * * * Where the facts demonstrate that a disclosure was made in order to promote a specific relationship, e.g., disclosure to a prospective purchaser to enable him to appraise the value of the secret, the parties will be bound to receive the information in confidence. * * * As the district court indicated, a confidential relationship typically will be implied where disclosures have been made in business relationships between employers and employees, *e.g., Jet Spray Cooler, Inc. v. Crampton*, purchasers and suppliers, *e.g., Curtiss-Wright Corp. v. Edel Brown Tool & Die Co.*, or prospective licensees and licensors * * *.

The formation of a confidential relationship imposes upon the disclosee the duty to maintain the information received in the utmost secrecy; the unprivileged use or disclosure of another's trade secret becomes the basis for an action in tort. * * *

An implied confidential relationship can be defeated, however, if the disclosing party voluntarily conveys a trade secret to another without limitation upon its use * * *. Apparently the latter is what Milton Bradley intended to accomplish when it asked appellants to sign its Disclosure Record forms.[3]

---

[3]   The disclosure agreement, which is reproduced in full in the district court's opinion, *Burten v. Milton Bradley Co.*, states in relevant part:

"I submit my idea or item voluntarily and I understand that this submission by me and its acceptance by Company does not, in whole or in part, establish or create by implication or otherwise any relationship between Company and me not expressed herein. I further understand and agree that Company, in its own judgment, may accept or reject the idea or item submitted and shall not be obligated to me in any way with respect to my idea or item until Company shall at its own election enter into a properly executed written agreement with me and then only, according to all of the terms of said agreement. If no agreement is concluded, I shall rely solely upon such rights as I may have under U.S. Patent laws. . . .

Milton Bradley argues that its disclosure form waives, as a matter of law, any duties or obligations it might owe to appellants other than those under the patent laws. The language of the form, it asserts, clearly disclaims "any relationship" between it and appellants which includes a fortiori Milton Bradley's refusal to establish a confidential relationship. Milton Bradley reasons, therefore, that appellants' claim of misappropriation must fail. Finding this argument persuasive, the district court concluded that there was no issue of fact to submit to the jury regarding the parties' understanding of the disclosure agreement.

What makes the issue so close a question in this case is the use of undifferentiated or general terminology. We begin our analysis, therefore, recognizing that the disclosure agreement in the case at bar cannot stake a claim to a clearly "express disclaimer". A widely quoted statement of the law in such a case is the following:

> "[A] disclosure expressly received in confidence may create a confidential relationship. Conversely, express disclaimer by the disclosee of a confidential relationship from the outset will dispel the existence of such a relationship." *Milgrim, Trade Secrets* § 4.03 at 4–18, citing *Crown Industries, Inc. v. Kawneer Co.*

In *Crown Industries v. Kawneer*, the plaintiff's agreement to the conditions of submission for review of his idea precluded the formation of a confidential relationship. The Kawneer Company policy booklet explicitly stated:

> "1. No confidential relationship is to be established by such submission or implied from consideration of the submitted material, and the material is not to be considered to be submitted 'in confidence.' (Confidential relationships have been held to create obligations which are beyond those that the Company is willing to assume.)"

Similarly, in *Kearns v. Ford Motor Co.*, the plaintiff signed an equally unambiguous form entitled "CONFIDENTIAL DISCLOSURE WAIVER" which contained language to the effect that "Ford Motor Company cannot receive suggestions in confidence." The court in *Kearns* concluded that plaintiff's right to rely on an implied confidential relationship, to the extent it was shown to exist under the circumstances, was effectively terminated upon signing the waiver form. In both cases, therefore, the explicit waivers barred plaintiff's recovery for misappropriation of trade secrets. * * *

In contrast to the language of the above agreements, the Milton Bradley disclosure agreement contains no explicit language regarding waiver of a confidential relationship. Nor is it, as appellee contends, "almost identical"

"I further agree that Company may photograph, xerograph or otherwise reproduce for its records only any material submitted by me herewith or subsequently with respect to said idea or item whether accepted or rejected."

to the disclaimers appellants signed with Parker Brothers Games ("this suggestion is not submitted in confidence") and the Western Publishing Company ("disclosures . . . are not received or held on a confidential basis") in which the signing party's waiver of a confidential relationship is clearly addressed. By the same token, we cannot accept the district court's equating the instant agreement with those of Parker and Western as "a like disclaimer." Indeed, as we show below, the absence of an express disclaimer at best conveys an ambiguous message as to whether the agreement covers confidential relationships.

We do not dispute Milton Bradley's assertion that its form may credibly be read to waive all relationships and obligations between the parties, including a confidential relationship. So, however, can it equally be understood to address only the relationship between the parties during Milton Bradley's review procedure. The agreement clearly puts appellants on notice that they are not entitled to remuneration from Milton Bradley merely upon submission of Triumph, but it does not adequately apprise them of the rights and obligations of the parties upon Milton Bradley's affirmative use or appropriation of the ideas submitted.

In its decision denying appellee's motion for a directed verdict, the district court found the disclosure agreement to be an explicit waiver of all contract rights between the parties. The court was concerned, however, that the disclosure did not carry equal force with respect to a confidential relationship because such relationship provides the basis for an action in tort. The court suggested that the language necessary to waive contractual obligations may not be sufficient to disclaim tort liability for the misappropriation of trade secrets. Although the district court, after trial, reached a different conclusion, we find merit in this analysis.

Under Massachusetts law, parties cannot easily contract out of liability for tortious behavior. It is, for example, clearly against public policy for one party to attempt to exempt itself from liability for its own gross negligence or its own misrepresentations. *Restatement (Second) of Contracts* §§ 195, 196 (1981). Significantly, even where Massachusetts has permitted individuals to contractually disclaim liability for mere negligence, the language of the disclaimer has been clear and unambiguous to that effect.

* * * The Milton Bradley disclosure form, in contrast to those in the above cases, conspicuously lacks language which explicitly disclaims tort liability. Absent such clear language, we think that a jury could reasonably read "relationship" as it is used in the Milton Bradley form to embrace only those ties and obligations established by consensual understanding or course of dealing (under contract principles) and not those legal constructs which may be triggered by unanticipated, covert, and devious misuse.

* * *

On its face, then, we find that the disclosure agreement falls short of an unambiguous waiver of all rights in Triumph and does not, as a matter of law, bar appellants' action for misappropriation. The jury, therefore, was correctly allowed to consider evidence outside of the form to fairly assess the meaning of the agreement and the intent of the parties in signing it. A. Corbin, *3 Corbin on Contracts* § 579 (1960) (parol evidence admissible to clarify ambiguous contract).[5]

* * *

We fully recognize that a manufacturer may wish to insulate itself from claims of misuse of materials submitted in confidence, whether founded on fact, fantasy or coincidence. This objective may be clearly realized by the kinds of explicit waivers we have noted in the same industry. We see no ponderable burden attached to requiring such explicitness.

The effect of the disclosure form on the relationship between the parties was therefore a factual question appropriately submitted to the jury at the conclusion of the trial. Finally, we believe that there was sufficient evidence before the jury for it to find for the appellants. * * *

Finding all remaining arguments unpersuasive, the judgment of the district court is reversed.

DID YOU GET IT?

1. What is the relationship between the plaintiff and the defendant?

2. Was the duty of confidentiality implied-in-fact or implied-at-law?

3. What was wrong with the disclosure agreement? Why did it fail to disclaim the creation of a confidential relationship?

4. What public policies are supported by a default expectation that parties who exchange ideas do so in trust and confidence?

Food for Thought

The next time you "click to agree" to a Terms of Use Agreement for an interactive website you visit, take time to actually read the Agreement and see what it says about ideas that are submitted through the website. Sometimes, Terms of Use Agreements will not only disclaim the creation of any confidential relationship, they will include a royalty-free license to use the idea or an outright transfer of ownership of the idea.

---

[5] Of particular relevance was evidence introduced at trial which established that Milton Bradley fostered the expectation of confidentiality in a number of ways. In the words of the district court, there was:

> "an industry-wide custom among reputable game and toy companies to maintain the secrecy of ideas submitted by outside inventors and to use innovations only if royalties were paid to the inventor. The evidence further showed that not only did [Milton Bradley] adhere to this custom, but it fostered such an understanding with outside inventors. High-level [Milton Bradley] executives testified that the industry, as well as virtually all the independent professionals, shared this expectation."

C. EVIDENCE OF ACTUAL OR THREATENED MISAPPROPRIATION: DISCLOSURE OR USE

Proving the existence of a confidential relationship that includes a duty to maintain the secrecy of trade secrets is only one step in the trade secret misappropriation analysis. Before even considering the existence of a confidential relationship, the existence of a trade secret should first be established. As emphasized in *Milgrim on Trade Secrets*: "Reliance upon a confidential relationship claim cannot obscure the core principle that, absent a trade secret, no protection can be had." *See* MILGRIM ON TRADE SECRETS, § 3.03 (2016). But the existence of a trade secret and a confidential relationship, alone, is not enough to establish a trade secret misappropriation claim. The scope of the duty of confidentiality must be determined and it must be shown that the person who is under the duty of confidentiality either actually disclosed or used the plaintiff's trade secrets or threatens to disclose or use those trade secrets.

Food for Thought

Look again at the definition of misappropriation contained in the UTSA and DTSA. What act (or "wrong") must a defendant engage in to commit misappropriation of a trade secret? If you were the plaintiff's attorney in a trade secret misappropriation case, how would you attempt to prove wrongdoing by the defendant?

As a practical matter, it is easiest to prove actual disclosure of trade secrets because there is likely to be direct evidence of the defendant's disclosure of plaintiff's trade secrets, for instance, in the form of the intentional posting of the information on the internet. (*See, e.g., DVD v. Bunner,* below, and *Ford v. Lane* in Chapter 9.) The more difficult task is to prove the "threatened disclosure" of trade secrets, as the discussion of the inevitable disclosure doctrine in Chapter 8 reveals.

Proving actual or threatened "use" of plaintiff's trade secrets tends to be most difficult to prove for a variety of reasons, not the least of which is the fact that trade secret misappropriators often keep their use of plaintiff's trade secrets hidden from public view. As the court in *Veteran Medical Products, Inc. v. Bionix Development Corp.* explained:

> The plaintiff in a trade secret misappropriation action faces a difficult challenge in ferreting out evidence of misappropriation. The holder of a trade secret "takes a substantial risk that the secret will be passed on to his competitors, by theft or by breach of a confidential relationship, in a manner not easily susceptible of discovery or proof."

2008 WL 696546 (W.D. Mich. 2008) (quoting *Kewanee Oil Co. v. Bicron Corp.*).

The cases that follow provide a glimpse into difficulties that can arise in trying to establish the actual or threatened use of trade secrets.

> ### Reading Guidance
> *How much of a trade secret must be used to constitute misappropriation?*

MANGREN RESEARCH AND DEVELOPMENT CORP. V. NATIONAL CHEMICAL CO., INC.

United States Court of Appeals, Seventh Circuit, 1996.
87 F.3d 937.

ILANA DIAMOND ROVNER, CIRCUIT JUDGE.

* * *

Mangren's story is one of a grass-roots operation that made good. The company was founded in 1974 by Ted Blackman and Peter Lagergren while they were chemistry students at the University of Texas. Mangren initially manufactured dog shampoo and industrial cleaners and solvents in a garage that belonged to Blackman's father-in-law. Eventually, however, the company began to produce mold release agents. Rubber and plastics manufacturers apply such agents to the molds and presses they use in the manufacturing process. Typically, the end-product is formed by filling a mold or press with a liquified rubber or plastic and then heating, which causes the liquid to solidify and to take the shape of the vessel containing it. The mold release agent is designed to prevent the solidifying substance from sticking to the mold during this process.

In the mid-1970s, Masonite was a major user of mold release agents. At the time, Masonite was using a DuPont product called Vydax that was primarily composed of a flurotelemer (a type of fluorocarbon). Vydax was quite expensive, however, and Masonite asked Mangren to attempt to develop a cheaper mold release agent that would be even more effective. Blackman and Lagergren then began to study and to experiment with different component chemicals. They decided that the key ingredient in their mold release agent would be a fluorocarbon resin that would impart a low surface energy to the molding surface. After eighteen months of study and testing, Mangren found that a particular type of polytetrafluoroethylene ("PTFE") performed this function. This type of PTFE had three essential characteristics: (1) it was highly degraded; (2) it had a low molecular weight; and (3) it had low tensile strength. At the time, PTFEs having these characteristics were used only as additives in manufacturing processes; they had never before been used as the primary component of a mold release agent. Indeed, the available literature indicated that this type of PTFE was unsuited for such an application.

* * *

P's
Secrecy
methods

Even as its sales grew, Mangren remained a small company, never having more than six employees at any one time. Because its success depended on the uniqueness of its mold release agent, Mangren took a number of steps to ensure that its formula remained secret. First, all employees were required to sign a confidentiality agreement, and non-employees were not permitted in the company's laboratory. Once chemical ingredients were delivered to the company's premises, moreover, the labels identifying those ingredients were removed and replaced with coded labels understood only by Mangren employees. The company's financial and other records also referred to ingredients only by their code names.

The seeds of the present lawsuit were planted when Mangren made two ill-fated hiring decisions in the 1980s. First, it hired Rhonda Allen in 1986 to be its office manager. Eventually, however, Allen became Mangren's sales manager, a position that provided her access to Mangren's customers and its pricing policies. In 1988, Mangren hired Larry Venable, an organic chemist, to help Blackman develop a chromium-free mold release agent. Although Venable did not have prior experience with PTFE-based mold release agents, he and Blackman succeeded in developing a chromium-free product that also used a highly degraded PTFE with low molecular weight and low tensile strength.

For reasons not relevant here, Mangren terminated the employment of Allen and Venable in 1989. After holding two intervening jobs, Venable met William Lerch early in 1990. Lerch had recently incorporated defendant National Chemical Company, Inc. ("National Chemical"), which was but one of a number of companies he then owned. Venable told Lerch about his Mangren experience and about an idea he had for developing a mold release agent to be used in the rubber industry. Lerch was excited about the prospect and inquired about the market for such a product. Venable responded that Masonite was a large user and therefore a potential customer.

The two discussed the possibility that they might be sued by Mangren if they developed a competing mold release agent. Venable was especially concerned because he realized that any product he could develop would be similar to Mangren's mold release agent. He knew, for example, that a mold release agent using TL–102—the PTFE that Mangren used—would be "potentially troublesome" and probably would prompt a lawsuit. Lerch told Venable not to worry about a misappropriation suit and explained that he had once been accused of trade secret infringement but had won the case by changing one ingredient or proportion of ingredients in creating his product. Lerch laughed and said the same thing would happen here. Shortly thereafter, Lerch and Venable incorporated defendant National Mold Release Company to manufacture the mold release agent that National Chemical would sell.

Venable then set about developing a mold release agent that would be more effective than Mangren's product. The agent he produced, like Mangren's, used a highly degraded PTFE that had a low molecular weight and low tensile strength. For the most part, Venable used a PTFE designated as TL–10, although he at times also used TL–102, the very same PTFE used by Mangren.

Venable then recommended that Lerch hire Allen to market defendants' product. Lerch knew that Allen, too, was a former Mangren employee. Defendants hired Allen as a vice president and assigned her the responsibility of developing a customer base for their mold release agent. From their days at Mangren, Venable and Allen knew that company's customers and pricing policies. Allen therefore approached Mangren customers with the news of defendants' new mold release agent and quoted a slightly lower price for defendants' product than that charged by Mangren. Allen contacted Masonite, for example, a company with whom she had dealt on behalf of Mangren, and informed them about National Chemical and the mold release agent it had developed. Masonite expressed interest, and after at least one preliminary test and one control test, defendants were able to qualify their mold release agent for use at Masonite. Masonite then began purchasing defendants' product.

Venable and Allen left defendants in April 1991. Venable began to work as a consultant for Bash Corporation ("Bash"), a Chicago-based construction supply company. Venable provided Bash with a mold release agent formula that was substantially derived from defendants' formula. Allen, whom Bash had hired on Venable's recommendation, then presented Bash's product to Masonite as the same high quality product she had sold on behalf of National Chemical. Indeed, in a letter notifying Masonite of her association with Bash, Allen represented that:

> This change will not affect Masonite in any way, except for the better. You can still expect the same quality coatings and service I have provided you with in the past. . . . The only change will be in my company name and address. Even the names of the coatings will not change.

Because of its similarity to defendants' mold release agent, Bash was quickly able to qualify its product for use at Masonite and to begin selling to that company. Early in 1992, however, Bash went out of business, prompting Allen to incorporate Bash Chemical Corporation ("Bash Chemical") in Texas. That company then continued to manufacture and market the same mold release agent previously sold by the Illinois-based Bash.

Mangren filed this suit in May 1993, after sales of its mold release agent markedly declined in the three previous years. Mangren alleged that defendants had misappropriated its mold release agent formula, and specifically its use of a highly degraded PTFE that had a low molecular weight and low tensile strength. Mangren also alleged the misappropriation of its customer list and pricing information. Mangren sought to recover the profits it lost due to defendants' misappropriation, including profits lost through sales of PTFE-based mold release agents by defendants and Bash, and profits lost when Mangren lowered its prices to meet defendants' competition. * * *

Having determined that Mangren established a protectable trade secret in its mold release agent formula, we turn to the question of misappropriation. The ITSA defines a "misappropriation" in pertinent part as follows:

> [D]isclosure or use of a trade secret of a person without express or implied consent by another person who:
>
> * * *
>
> (B) at the time of disclosure or use, knew or had reason to know that knowledge of the trade secret was:
>
>> (I) derived from or through a person who utilized improper means to acquire it:
>>
>> (II) acquired under circumstances giving rise to a duty to maintain its secrecy or limit its use; or
>>
>> (III) derived from or through a person who owed a duty to the person seeking relief to maintain its secrecy or limit its use. . . .

Defendants argue that they did not "use" Mangren's trade secret under this definition because their mold release agent formula is not the same as Mangren's. Although they concede that the primary ingredient of their formula is also a highly degraded PTFE with a low molecular weight and low tensile strength, defendants emphasize that many of the other ingredients are different. Furthermore, the specific PTFE used in defendants' product is typically not the same as the one used by Mangren, although its essential characteristics are identical. Finally, defendants use a slightly smaller volume of PTFE in their mold release agent-twenty as opposed to twenty-three percent in Mangren's product. * * *

Defendants' argument, however, is inconsistent even with the jury instruction to which they agreed below. The jury was instructed that:

> In order for you to find that defendants misappropriated one of Mangren's trade secrets, you do not have to find that defendants copied or used each and every element of the trade secret. You may find that defendants misappropriated Mangren's trade secrets even if defendants created a new product if defendants could not have done so without use of Mangren's trade secret.

That instruction, as defendants apparently conceded below, is consistent with traditional trade secret law. We observed in *In re Innovative Constr. Sys., Inc.* for example, that "the user of another's trade secret is liable even if he uses it with modifications or improvements upon it effected by his own efforts, so long as the substance of the process used by the actor is derived from the other's secret." Although that decision involved Wisconsin law, the law of Illinois is in accord. We have observed before, in fact, that if trade secret law were not flexible enough to encompass modified or even new products that are substantially derived from the trade secret of another, the protections that law provides would be hollow indeed.

Mangren emphasizes, moreover, that the trade secret misappropriated here was not necessarily its overall formula, but the essential secret ingredient—a highly degraded PTFE having a low molecular weight and low tensile strength, which had previously been considered unsuitable for such an application. Defendants do not contest that they use a similar PTFE in their mold release agent and that it was Venable, the former Mangren employee, who revealed to them that such a PTFE could be used effectively. Once Venable let defendants in on the secret and defendants then used that secret to develop their own product, there plainly was a misappropriation even if defendants' product was not identical to Mangren's. In other words, reasonable jurors could conclude from the evidence in this case that defendants' mold release agent was substantially derived from Mangren's trade secret, for defendants could not have produced their product without using that secret. Defendants were not therefore entitled to judgment as a matter of law or to a new trial on the trade secret and misappropriation issues.

* * *

DID YOU GET IT?

1. What was defendant's argument as to why it was not liable for misappropriation?

2. What facts might support plaintiff's argument that defendant's product was substantially derived from its trade secret?

3. If another company had reverse engineered Mangren's trade secret and used it to create a competing mold release agent, would it be liable for misappropriation?

———

When there is no direct evidence that the defendant has (or will) disclose or use plaintiff's trade secrets, the plaintiff must resort to circumstantial evidence in an attempt to prove actual or threatened misappropriation. The following case discusses the use of circumstantial evidence to establish the actual use or disclosure of trade secrets. In

Chapter 8, the inevitable disclosure doctrine is examined as a form of circumstantial evidence that, in some states, can be used to prove the "threatened" use or disclosure of trade secrets.

Reading Guidance

What circumstantial evidence did the plaintiff use in an effort to prove the actual or threatened use or disclosure of his trade secrets?

STRATIENKO, M.D. V. CORDIS CORP.

United States Court of Appeals, Sixth Circuit, 2005.
429 F.3d 592.

ROGERS, CIRCUIT JUDGE.

Plaintiff Dr. Alexander Stratienko, who created a catheter device and shared his design for that device with Defendant Cordis Corporation, brought this federal diversity suit against Cordis for misappropriation of a trade secret, wrongful benefit, and breach of contract. The district court granted summary judgment to Cordis, and Dr. Stratienko appeals. * * *

I.

Dr. Stratienko's device is a modified catheter used for gaining medical access to blood vessels. Cordis explained the conventional medical practice associated with catheters in the following manner, which is consistent with the description of conventional practice in Dr. Stratienko's patent.

An interventional cardiology procedure generally begins by inserting a hollow needle into the femoral artery, which is located close to the surface of the skin in the groin area. A wire called a guidewire is then inserted through the needle into the artery, and the needle is withdrawn. Another device called a sheath is then inserted over the guidewire into the artery. A sheath is a 4–9 inch hollow tube with a valve at the end which remains outside the body ("proximal end"). The valve prevents excess blood loss. The sheath remains in place throughout the procedure.

Next, a 35–40 inch hollow tube called a guiding catheter is inserted through the sheath and into the artery. The guiding catheter has a soft, flexible tip at the end that is inserted into the patient ("distal end"). The distal end positions the catheter into a specific blood vessel within the heart ("coronary artery"). The guiding catheter also remains in place throughout the procedure. Other medical devices such as angioplasty balloons and stents can be inserted through the guiding catheter and into the patient's coronary artery to treat the blockage.

Dr. Stratienko submitted a patent application for a "sheath catheter." His design combines a sheath and a catheter with a preformed distal end. While the record is surprisingly unclear as to the benefits of the unified sheath-catheter, it appears that it allows a smaller puncture hole while providing necessary support during the invasive procedure. The preformed distal end is soft and flexible, which allows more precise engagement of targeted segments. His design also has holes at the end of the catheter, allowing direct delivery of x-ray contrast fluid to a segment of the targeted vessel; traditional delivery of contrast fluid must first displace blood to reach the intended segment.

On May 25, 1999, Dr. Stratienko, a Tennessee resident, sent a letter and Nondisclosure Agreement to Cordis Corporation. Cordis is a Florida corporation with its principal place of business in New Jersey, and is a subsidiary of Johnson & Johnson. In August 1999, Cordis' Associate Manager of Business Development William Scheessele proposed changes to the agreement and faxed them to Dr. Stratienko. Over a period of months, the parties negotiated the terms of the agreement. Cordis deleted portions regarding remedies for breach and regarding return of the materials. The agreement specifically provided that Dr. Stratienko's information was a trade secret. The parties executed the agreement in November 1999. On December 12, 1999, Dr. Stratienko submitted his patent application and a description of his "sheath catheter" to Scheessele.

Cordis' internal written policy states that "Reviews [of submitted proposals] will be conducted by members of New Business Development, New Product Strategy, Legal, and to a lesser degree, senior members of R & D. It is our goal to minimize exposing our innovative engineering talent pool to external ideas, to safeguard our interests to our own internal inventions." Scheessele provided Dr. Stratienko's submitted material to Cordis' in-house counsel Paul Coletti in mid-December 1999. Both Scheessele and Coletti declare that they discussed Dr. Stratienko's proposal, but they deny discussing the proposal with anyone else at Cordis or Johnson & Johnson. Scheessele declares that he kept the proposal in his locked file cabinet at all times, but Coletti cannot remember whether he placed the documents in a locked cabinet or safe. On January 17, 2000, Cordis advised Dr. Stratienko that Cordis was not interested in his proposal. Coletti returned the related documents, at the latest, by mid-February and kept no copies.

On April 7, 2000, Cordis submitted a combined sheath and guiding catheter, which it called the Vista Brite Tip Introducer Guiding Catheter, for FDA approval. The FDA approved it on April 28, 2000. Cordis sales documents establish that Cordis manufactured and shipped "seventy-eight Vista Brite Tip IG Catheters as of May 29, 2000."

* * *

Dr. Stratienko filed suit in Hamilton County Circuit Court on November 21, 2001, * * *. Dr. Stratienko alleged that Cordis had misappropriated, converted, and wrongfully benefitted from his ideas; breached the

Nondisclosure Agreement; and committed theft of a trade secret under Tennessee's Uniform Trade Secret Act * * *.

In March 2003, Cordis moved for summary judgment on all of Dr. Stratienko's claims. * * *

In October 2003, the district court granted Cordis' motion for summary judgment in full. The district court reasoned that, because this circuit requires direct evidence of use in trade-secret cases and because Dr. Stratienko offered only circumstantial evidence of use, Dr. Stratienko was unable to demonstrate that Cordis used his idea. Without evidence that Cordis used his secret, Dr. Stratienko was unable to rebut the evidence of Cordis' employees, who denied discussing his ideas with anyone else. Dr. Stratienko's claims for misappropriation, breach of contract, and wrongful benefit all failed, therefore, as a matter of law. * * *

III.

Cordis submitted declarations by Coletti and Scheessele, in which they deny sharing Dr. Stratienko's information with anyone else at Cordis. Although these declarations came from self-interested employees, Cordis can rely on those denials to demonstrate that no genuine issue of material fact exists because Dr. Stratienko has not impeached the declarants' credibility. * * *

Dr. Stratienko unsuccessfully contends that the following pieces of evidence so impeach or controvert the testimony of Scheessele and Coletti that their testimony is not sufficient for summary judgment: (1) Cordis did not follow its internal policy, (2) Coletti left his office unlocked, (3) Coletti retained Dr. Stratienko's information for weeks after he declined the proposal, (4) Cordis recommended changes to the Nondisclosure Agreement, and (5) Cordis provided several reasons for declining the proposal. Because none of these facts, however, impeach Scheessele and Coletti's testimony, the district court correctly relied upon Cordis' declarations.

Cordis followed its internal policy, and thus the internal policy has no bearing on the declarants' credibility. Dr. Stratienko argues that Cordis' policy, stating that reviews "will be conducted by members of New Business Development, New Product Strategy, Legal, and to a lesser degree, senior members of R & D [,]" impeaches the declarants' testimony that they were the only individuals to see his proposal. There is no inconsistency here. Cordis established the policy "to minimize exposing our innovative engineering talent pool to external ideas, to safeguard our interests to our own internal inventions." The policy does not mandate that other individuals read the proposal. Its purpose, as evidenced by "to a lesser degree," is to limit the individuals who have access to secrets. In this case, consistent with the policy, Scheessele, a member of New Business Development, and Coletti, a member of the legal department, examined the proposal. The fact that the policy may have permitted others to view the proposal does not create any evidence that they, in fact, viewed it.

Coletti's uncertainty as to whether he kept Dr. Stratienko's documents in a locked or unlocked office fails to impeach his testimony that he did not share Dr. Stratienko's information with others at Cordis. Dr. Stratienko contends that Coletti said that the documents were left in an unlocked office. But Coletti, instead, said that he was unsure whether the documents were locked away. The small possibility that the documents were stolen or viewed sub rosa by being in a potentially unlocked office does not impeach Coletti's testimony that he did not share Dr. Stratienko's information with anyone at Cordis.

Likewise, Coletti's retention of Dr. Stratienko's information for weeks after he declined the proposal does not contradict the declarations. Although Dr. Stratienko argues that Coletti's retention of the documents creates a genuine issue of material fact as to whether Cordis used the documents, the retention does not demonstrate in any way that Cordis used the information or that Coletti shared the information with anyone else. Any allowable inference that the retention of documents for a few weeks increases the probability that Cordis shared them with Research and Development is too tenuous to create a genuine issue of material fact as to use.

That Cordis had recommended changes to the Nondisclosure Agreement in no way impeaches the testimony of Scheessele and Coletti. Dr. Stratienko argues that, because Cordis' suggested changes affected the remedies and the return of documents, the declarants' credibility is impeached. Both Cordis and Dr. Stratienko negotiated the details of the agreement, and the agreement contains several provisions that protect Dr. Stratienko. Dr. Stratienko never explains how the revised terms, reached at arm's length, affect credibility or make it any more likely that Cordis used the proposal.

Dr. Stratienko's final argument-that Cordis' several reasons for declining the proposal impeach the declarants' testimony-also fails because the various reasons are not contradictory. According to Dr. Stratienko, Coletti gave only one reason: that the Hillstead patent disclosed the catheter-sheath combination. Scheessele gave three reasons: (1) that Cordis was not interested; (2) that the proposal did not meet Cordis' needs; and (3) that the proposal was not within Cordis' budget. Dr. Stratienko also alleges that Cordis later said that the Fernandez patent disclosed the catheter-sheath combination. None of these reasons is inconsistent with another. Cordis could have been uninterested because the proposal was not within its budget and did not meet its needs. Reliance on two other patents also raises no inconsistency because Cordis was not limited to only one patent from which to glean inspiration. Moreover, relying on two patents provides good reason why Cordis was uninterested. Even assuming that the recitation of several reasons creates credibility issues as to why Cordis declined the proposal, it does not make it any more likely that the proposal was given to others or used in any way. Dr. Stratienko's attempts to impeach the declarants' credibility thus are insufficient to require the conclusion that the district court could not consider the declarations submitted by Cordis in considering whether Cordis met its burden of demonstrating the absence of any genuine issue of material fact.

IV.

Because Cordis' declarations satisfied Cordis' burden, the burden of creating a genuine issue of material fact shifted to Dr. Stratienko, who failed to produce sufficient evidence of use to create a genuine issue of material fact as to whether Cordis used his secret. The district court held that Dr. Stratienko could not demonstrate that Cordis used his design through circumstantial evidence of (1) Cordis' access to Dr. Stratienko's secret and (2) the similarity between Dr. Stratienko's secret and Cordis' catheter. Even assuming that circumstantial evidence in the form of access and similarity may in some cases be sufficient evidence of use, such evidence is not sufficient here. Dr. Stratienko's evidence fails to identify which, if any, *innovative* features his and Cordis' designs share, and he is, therefore, unable to show sufficient relevant similarity to permit a circumstantial inference in this case. In light of the uncontested declarations of Cordis' employees and Dr. Stratienko's failure to produce sufficient evidence of shared innovative features, there is no genuine issue of material fact that Cordis used Dr. Stratienko's design.

The district court accurately described the four elements under Tennessee law for misappropriation of a trade secret: (1) the existence of a trade secret; (2) communication of the trade secret to the defendant while in a position of trust and confidence; (3) defendant's use of the communicated information; and (4) resulting detriment to the plaintiff. *See Hickory Specialties, Inc. v. B & L Labs., Inc.* (citing *Smith v. Dravo Corp.*). The issue in this case concerns the third element—whether Cordis used the confidential information that Dr. Stratienko communicated in his proposal. The parties have not referred to and we have not discovered any Tennessee cases considering whether parties may rely on circumstantial evidence to prove use of a trade secret. "Where the state supreme court has not spoken, our task is to discern, from all available sources, how that court would respond if confronted with the issue." * * *

Contrary to the district court's reasoning, a strong argument could be made that courts may properly consider circumstantial evidence concerning similarity of design plus access to the design to imply use by a defendant of a trade secret. Other circuit courts have permitted such an inference in trade-secret and nondisclosure cases. * * * Sufficient circumstantial evidence of use in trade-secret cases must demonstrate that (1) the misappropriating party had access to the secret and (2) the secret and the defendant's design share similar features. * * * These cases support the proposition that, once evidence of access and similarity is proffered, it is "entirely reasonable for [the jury] to infer that [defendant] used [plaintiff's] trade secret." * * *

Permitting an inference of use from evidence of access and similarity is sound because "[m]isappropriation and misuse can rarely be proved by convincing direct evidence." * * * Presented with "defendants' witnesses who directly deny everything," plaintiffs are often required to "construct a web of perhaps ambiguous circumstantial evidence from which the trier of fact may draw inferences which convince him that it is more probable than not that what the plaintiffs allege happened did in fact take place." * * * Thus, requiring direct evidence would foreclose most trade-secret claims from reaching the jury because corporations rarely keep direct evidence of their use ready for another party to discover. Caselaw from other circuits thus suggests that Tennessee law would most likely permit circumstantial evidence of use in trade-secret cases. * * *

In the case at bar, we assume that Dr. Stratienko produced sufficient evidence of access: Cordis' declarations demonstrate that Cordis, the entity that developed the Vista Brite IG Catheter, had access to the information. It would be very burdensome to require Dr. Stratienko to demonstrate that a particular inventor or designer had access. *See Sokol* (stating that any plaintiff "would be hard pressed to present direct proof of the flow of information inside the defendant's company").

Dr. Stratienko, however, has not presented sufficient circumstantial evidence of similarity to withstand summary judgment. His evidence does not reveal which novel features Cordis' device shares with Dr. Stratienko's device. His expert reports essentially state two facts: that (1) the Fernandez and Hillstead patents do not "teach" the features of Cordis' Vista Brite Tip IG Catheter and (2) the Stratienko device shares "all of the salient features found in the Cordis IG." Both of these conclusions are based on irrelevant comparisons. The experts' first conclusion that Cordis' catheter is dissimilar from the Fernandez and Hillstead catheters has no bearing on whether Cordis' and Stratienko's catheters are similar. The similarity inquiry is not a comparison of several products to determine which two products are the most similar. Dr. Stratienko must, instead, demonstrate similarity by comparing his secret with the features of Cordis' catheter, not the features of Cordis' catheter with the features of other catheters.

The experts' conclusions that the catheters share "all . . . salient features" except the holes at the distal end are also insufficient because their findings do not reveal which feature was the secret that Dr. Stratienko sought to protect. Misappropriation of a trade secret requires that an idea not be one that is already used by others. *See Hickory Specialties, Inc.* (stating that the device must give the creator "an opportunity to obtain an advantage over competitors who do not use it"). Dr. Stratienko must demonstrate similarity between his *secret idea* (not his product in general) and Cordis' device. * * * Instead, his experts state only that the Stratienko device has a catheter-sheath combination, a preformed tip, and holes at the distal end. At no point do his experts state which, if any, of these characteristics renders his idea innovative. It is entirely possible that the holes at the distal end, which the Cordis design lacked, distinguished Dr. Stratienko's device from prior art. We cannot find in the record that Dr. Stratienko has presented evidence of which features were novel to his design, and thus he has failed to show sufficient similarity between the innovative aspect of his idea and Cordis' device to provide enough of a circumstantial inference to create a genuine issue of material fact.

It is true that the parties have already conceded that Dr. Stratienko had a trade secret. But this does not mean that sufficient similarity has been shown to permit an inference of use. The parties' implicit concession that a trade secret exists does not identify the secret. Identifying the secret that provides Dr. Stratienko with an advantage in the market is necessary for determining whether the pertinent similarity implies that Cordis used his secret. The analysis of similarity evaluates only relevant, innovative features, not all possible congruence. Without evidence of the advantage of Dr. Stratienko's device over prior art, there is not a sufficient basis for a reasonable jury to make the circumstantial inference of use. Dr. Stratienko, therefore, has not presented sufficient evidence to establish that there is any genuine issue of material fact as to use, and summary judgment was proper as to Dr. Stratienko's claims for misappropriation, wrongful benefit, and breach of contract.

* * *

For the foregoing reasons, we AFFIRM the judgment of the district court.

> ### Reading Guidance
> *Can a co-owner of a trade secret be liable for misappropriating it?*

MORTON V. RANK AMERICA, INC.
United States District Court, C.D. of California, 1993.
812 F.Supp. 1062.

GADBOIS, DISTRICT JUDGE.

* * *

The Plaintiffs contend that the Defendants have utilized Hard Rock trade secrets to create the Planet Hollywood restaurants, and that these restaurants, which are allegedly knock-offs of the Hard Rock restaurants, constitute an infringement of the Plaintiffs' trade dress. The Plaintiffs further allege that the Defendants have stolen trade secrets and copied trade dress in an attempt to monopolize the market for entertainment/music themed restaurants in the United States. The Defendants have now moved to dismiss the entire complaint, pursuant to F.R.C.P. 12(b)(6). * * *

In Count 7 of the Complaint, the Plaintiffs allege that the Defendants have misappropriated Hard Rock trade secrets in connection with their development of the Planet Hollywood restaurant. * * *

The Defendants * * * maintain that, regardless of whether the information allegedly acquired by Defendant Earl constitutes "trade secrets," the Plaintiffs' claim still fails, because it does not allege "misappropriation." The Uniform Trade Secrets Act defines "misappropriation" as the "use of a trade secret of *another*."

The Defendants note that in paragraphs 38 and 39 of the Second Amended Complaint, the Plaintiffs allege that Plaintiff Morton (the owner of the rights to the Hard Rock mark in the Western half of the United States) and Rank (the corresponding owner in the Eastern half) jointly developed and own the alleged trade secrets. The Defendants then emphasize that Defendant Earl allegedly "learned" of the trade secrets while he was a director of the Hard Rock Licensing Corporation. Since the Complaint also alleges that Defendant Earl is the CEO of the Rank Hard Rock Cafes, the Defendants complete their logic by arguing that Defendant Earl could not have appropriated the trade secrets "of another" because he, as CEO of the Rank Hard Rock Cafes, is the joint owner of any alleged trade secrets.

The Plaintiffs refer the court to the Settlement Agreement that was executed between Morton and Tigrett (the original owners of the mark), and which allocated to Morton the rights to the mark in the Western half of the United States and to Tigrett the identical rights in the Eastern half. Section 2.8 of the Agreement provides that neither party may "engage in any use or exploitation of the HARD ROCK CAFE MARKS which would effectively preclude or limit [the other] . . . from engaging in the same or any other use or exploitation of the HARD ROCK CAFE MARKS in such other party's Domestic or Foreign Territories." The Plaintiffs contend that the "HARD ROCK CAFE MARKS" encompass the alleged trade secrets at issue here, and that the Defendants' alleged use of the trade secrets violates section 2.8 and constitutes a misappropriation under state law.

The Agreement between Morton and Tigrett specifically delineates the rights of each party in the Hard Rock Cafe Marks. Since these "Marks" likely encompass any trade secrets, it is reasonable to conclude that one party's use of the trade secrets that affects the other party's rights in the mark would constitute the misappropriation of the trade secrets "of another."

The Defendants have also failed to cite any authority indicating that the misappropriation of a trade secret by a joint owner of that trade secret does not constitute the misappropriation of the trade secret "of another." Indeed, a provision in the Civil Code cited by neither party appears to contemplate exactly this situation. Cal. Civ. Code § 3426.1(b) defines misappropriation as, *inter alia*, the

> . . . use of a trade secret of another without express or implied consent by a person who:
>
> (B) At the time of disclosure or use, knew or had reason to know that his or her knowledge of the trade secret was:
>
> * * *
>
> (ii) Acquired under circumstances giving rise to a duty to maintain its secrecy or limit its use. . . .

Given the circumstances of this case, it is possible that the Plaintiffs could prove a set of facts establishing that the Defendants misappropriated the Plaintiffs' trade secrets by using them when the Defendants knew or should have known that they were acquired under circumstances giving rise to a duty to maintain their secrecy or limit their use. Thus, the Defendants' arguments on this point are ineffectual and do not provide a basis upon which to dismiss this Count. * * *

IT IS SO ORDERED.

DID YOU GET IT?

1. What was the nature of the business relationship between the parties?

2. What is the misappropriation language from the California UTSA on which the plaintiff relies to make its claim?

3. Would these facts be appropriate for an "improper means" misappropriation analysis under the UTSA?

4. Does the court confuse the improper means analysis with the breach of confidentiality analysis, or do the two analyses overlap in some cases?

D. SPECIAL ISSUE: WHAT HAPPENS WHEN TRADE SECRETS ARE ACQUIRED BY A THIRD-PARTY?

As the foregoing cases make clear, when relying on the breach of a duty of confidentiality prong of trade secret misappropriation, it is not enough for the plaintiff to prove that the defendant possesses, used, or disclosed (or threatens to use or disclose) a trade secret. The plaintiff must also establish that the defendant owed a duty of confidentiality to the plaintiff and that he knew or should have known of the duty. This knowledge requirement poses problems when third-parties come to possess trade secrets that were earlier misappropriated by someone else (for example, when a former employee of a company transfers trade secret information to his new employer). The third-party usually has no direct relationship with the trade secret owner that gives rise to either an express or implied duty of confidentiality. Thus, unless there is another basis upon which to hold a third-party liable for trade secret misappropriation, the third-party is free to use information that they receive from another. Moreover, the "third-party doctrine" of trade secret law (similar to the third-party doctrine of Fourth Amendment jurisprudence) holds that information that is given to another without first imposing a duty of confidentiality loses any applicable trade secret status. *See Kewanee Oil Co. v. Bicron Corp.*, 416 U.S. 470, 475 (1974).

The court in *Metallurgical Industries, Inc. v. Fourtek, Inc.*, 790 F.2d 1195 (1986), explained the problem as follows:

> At this point we must devote separate attention to Smith, which stands in a different light from Bielefeldt. It had no significant dealings with Metallurgical and apparently was not heavily involved in the design of the furnace it purchased. The question therefore becomes whether Smith as purchaser, and thus a beneficiary of Bielefeldt's alleged misappropriation, can also be held liable for it.

Consistent with general tort theory, one way to impose liability on a third-party who comes to possess trade secrets is based upon a theory of direct liability whereby the third-party is shown to have engaged in a wrongful act that provides an independent basis for tort liability. *See* Sharon K. Sandeen, *The Third Party Problem: Assessing the Protection of Information through Tort Law*, in INTELLECTUAL PROPERTY PROTECTION OF FACT-BASED WORKS, COPYRIGHTS AND ITS ALTERNATIVES, pp. 278–304 (Robert Brauneis, ed. 2009). Another way is through some theory of indirect or secondary liability. For instance, under general agency principles an employer (the principal) may be held responsible for the wrongful acts of its employee (the agent). *See Restatement (Third) of Agency* § 7.03 (2016). However, as noted by Professor Robert Bone, unlike patent and copyright law, "there is no strong tradition of secondary liability in trade secret law." He explains:

> Although secondary liability doctrines of contributory infringement, vicarious liability, and active inducement play an important role in other areas of intellectual property law, especially copyright and patent, they do not play a significant role in trade secret law. The principal trade secret doctrine imposing liability on third parties is in fact based on a form of primary rather than secondary liability. This doctrine holds that a third

party is liable when the third party acquires a trade secret from another and then discloses or uses the secret under circumstances where he knows or should have known that the trade secret was wrongfully acquired. The third party is liable for his own use or disclosure, and the knowledge requirement assures some degree of individual culpability.

The one genuine example of secondary liability in trade secret law is the respondeat superior liability of employers for trade secret misappropriation by their employees. Yet even here the case law is quite thin and the opinions relatively recent. Notably, those judges who make an effort to analyze the issue struggle to square respondeat superior liability with traditional trade secret principles. These justificatory difficulties are instructive, for they suggest that there is no strong tradition of secondary liability in trade secret law. The question is why.

Robert G. Bone, *Secondary Liability for Trade Secret Misappropriation: A Comment*, 22 SANTA CLARA COMPUTER & HIGH TECH L. J. 529, 536–38 (2006).

Unlike patent, copyright, and trademark law, trade secret misappropriation is not in the nature of a strict liability tort where liability can be imposed on individuals and companies even if they do not know of the existence of the subject trade secrets or of the acts of misappropriation. At common law, a third-party could only be held liable for the misappropriation of trade secrets if it was shown that he used or disclosed the trade secrets with the requisite scienter. As set forth in the *Restatement (First) of Torts*, § 757:

> One who discloses or uses another's trade secret, without privilege to do so, is liable to the other if . . . (c) he learned the secret from a third person with notice of the facts that it was a secret and that the third person's disclosure of it was otherwise a breach of his duty to the other. . . .

The UTSA codified the knowledge requirement of the common law of trade secrets in Section 1(2) of the UTSA which sets forth five factual circumstances by which a third-party may be held liable for trade secret misappropriation (emphasis added):

1. Where the third-party *acquires* trade secrets of another with knowledge or reason to know that they were acquired [by another] by improper means. UTSA 1(2)(i);

2. Where the third-party *discloses or uses* trade secrets when he knows or has reason to know that they were derived from or through a person who used improper means to acquire them. UTSA 1(2)(ii)(B)(I);

3. Where the third-party *discloses or uses* trade secrets when he knows or has reason to know that they were acquired [by another] under circumstances giving rise to a duty to maintain or limit their use. UTSA 1(2)(ii)(B)(II);

4. Where the third-party *discloses or uses* trade secrets when he knows or has reason to know that they were derived from or through a person who owed a duty to maintain their secrecy or limit their use. UTSA 1(2)(ii)(B)(III)); and

5. Where the third-party, before a material change of his or her position, knows or has reason to know that the information disclosed to him is a trade secret and that knowledge of it was *acquired* by accident or mistake. UTSA 1(2)(ii)(C).

The key facts in each of the above-listed scenarios is that the third-party must actually know or have reason to know of the existence of "trade secrets of another" and that such trade secrets were misappropriated or, in the case of UTSA 1(2)(ii)(C), acquired by accident or mistake. *See also*, MILGRIM ON TRADE SECRETS, § 7.02 (2016) (summarizing the ways a "second user" may be liable for trade secret misappropriation).

As we have already seen, trade secret disclosures over the internet can raise very interesting third-party issues, especially in circumstances where an independent third-party, having no connection to or involvement with the original misappropriator who posted or disclosed the trade secret, discovers the trade secret and uses it. Professor Elizabeth Rowe has discussed the issue as follows:

> Having proved that the information [appearing on the Internet is its] trade secret, or likely to be a trade secret, the second hurdle to a trade secret owner whose proprietary information has been discovered on the Internet is proving misappropriation. This is difficult because, on the surface, the presence of the independent third party who has no duty to the trade secret owner to maintain his secret coupled with the public place discovery does not seem actionable. The view that any wrong to a trade secret owner occurs only at the time of the improper acquisition stems from the underlying construct of trade secret law that trade secrets are not property. Rather, the presence of a confidential relationship or good faith obligation is a necessary prerequisite, and it is that breach that triggers something akin to an enforceable property right in the trade secret. The key factors then appear to be whether the information was discovered by improper means and whether the third party should have known it was discovered by improper means.

> * * * This necessarily suggests a fact-intensive determination into the third party's state of mind, her level of knowledge that the

information was a trade secret, and whether it was acquired by improper means.

Elizabeth A. Rowe, *Saving Trade Secret Disclosures on the Internet Through Sequential Preservation*, 42 WAKE FOREST L. REV. 1, 21–22 (2007).

The California opinion in *DVD v. Bunner*, which follows, highlights some of the difficulties identified by Professor Rowe. Also, consider how third-parties may assert a defense based upon the First Amendment, as discussed in Chapter 9.

Food for Thought

How do you prove a third-party had knowledge (or a reason to know) that the information it received from another is the misappropriated trade secrets of someone else? If the trade secrets were misappropriated, isn't it likely the misappropriator will try to cover his tracks?

Reading Guidance

What knowledge must a third-party possess to be liable for trade secret misappropriation?

DVD COPY CONTROL ASSOCIATION INC. V. BUNNER

California Court of Appeals, Sixth District, 2004.
116 Cal.App.4th 241.

PREMO, ACTING P.J.

Plaintiff DVD Copy Control Association, Inc. (DVD CCA) sued defendant Andrew Bunner (Bunner) and others under California's Uniform Trade Secrets Act (UTSA) seeking an injunction to prevent defendants from using or publishing "DeCSS," a computer program allegedly containing DVD CCA's trade secrets.

The trial court granted DVD CCA's request for a preliminary injunction and entered an order prohibiting defendants from posting, disclosing, or distributing DeCSS or related proprietary material. Bunner appealed. * * *

The California Supreme Court granted review and held that the preliminary injunction did not violate the free speech clauses of the United States and California Constitutions "*assuming* the trial court properly issued the injunction under California's trade secret law." The Supreme Court remanded the matter to this court to determine whether the evidence in the record supports the factual findings necessary to establish that the preliminary injunction was warranted under the UTSA. We now conclude that it was not.

A. Introduction

Digital versatile disks (DVD's) are five-inch disks used to store large amounts of data in digital form. A single DVD may contain a full-length motion picture. Unlike motion pictures on videocassettes, motion pictures contained on DVD's may be copied without perceptible loss of video or audio quality. This aspect of the DVD format makes it particularly susceptible to piracy. For this reason, motion pictures stored on DVDs have been protected from unauthorized use by a content scrambling system referred to as CSS. Simply put, CSS scrambles the data on the disk and then unscrambles it when the disk is played on a compliant DVD player or computer. CSS does not allow the content on the DVD to be copied.

For obvious reasons, the motion picture industry desired to keep the CSS technology a secret. But to make DVD players and computer DVD drives that can unscramble and play a CSS-protected DVD, the manufacturers had to have the CSS "master keys" and an understanding of how the technology works. In an attempt to keep CSS from becoming generally known, the industries agreed upon a restrictive licensing scheme and formed DVD CCA to be the sole licensing entity for CSS. Under the CSS licensing scheme, each licensee receives a different master key to incorporate into its equipment and sufficient technical know how to permit the manufacture of a DVD-compliant device. All licensees must agree to maintain the confidentiality of CSS.

In spite of these efforts to maintain the secrecy of CSS, DeCSS appeared on the Internet sometime in October 1999 and rapidly spread to other Web sites, including those of the defendants. * * *

DVD CCA filed the instant complaint for injunctive relief on December 27, 1999, alleging that Bunner and the other defendants had misappropriated trade secrets by posting DeCSS or links to DeCSS on their Web sites, knowing that DeCSS had been created by improper means. The requested injunctive relief sought to prevent defendants from using DeCSS, from disclosing DeCSS or other proprietary CSS technology on their Web sites or elsewhere, and from linking their Web sites to other Web sites that disclosed DeCSS or other CSS technology. * * *

B. The Factual Record

The evidence before the trial court was submitted in the form of written declarations. John Hoy, president of DVD CCA explained that DeCSS first appeared on the Internet on October 6, 1999. That first posting was in machine-readable form referred to as object code. The DeCSS source code was posted about three weeks later, on or around October 25, 1999. Hoy declared that both postings contain CSS technology and the master key that had been assigned to DVD CCA's licensee, Xing Technology Corporation (Xing), a manufacturer of computer DVD drives. The intended inference is that DeCSS was created, at least in part, by reverse engineering the Xing software. Since Xing licensed its software pursuant to an agreement that prohibits reverse engineering, Hoy concludes that the CSS technology contained in DeCSS was "obtained in violation of the specific provision in the Xing end-user license 'click wrap' agreement which prohibits reverse engineering." Hoy stated on information and belief that Jon Johansen, a resident of Norway, was the author of the program.

Well before DeCSS was released on the Internet, a number of people had become interested in unraveling the CSS security system. Users of the Linux computer operating system had organized a forum dedicated to finding a way to override CSS. Apparently DVD CCA had not licensed CSS to anyone making DVD drives for the Linux system, so that computers using Linux were incapable of playing DVD's. CSS was widely analyzed and discussed in the academic cryptography community. Another exchange of information took place on www.slashdot.org (Slashdot), a news Web site popular with computer programmers. As early as July 1999 comments on Slashdot revealed a worldwide interest in cracking CSS. The gist of these communications is contained in the following excerpts of a discussion that took place on July 15, 1999:

> "Yes, it is true, we have now all needed parts for software decoding of DVDs, but any software doing so will be illegal and/or non-free. . . . The information about CSS was obtained by reverse engineering some DVD software decoder."

> "This code was released before anyone checked into the legal end of things. . . . Best idea now is to download the code. Get it spread around as widely as possible. It may not be able to be used legally when all is said and done, but at least it will be out there for others to work with."

> "Well, it might not be the most ethical thing on earth, but if the appropriate algorithms were to be found just lying on the web, once the coders have seen them, they don't have a 'forget' button for their brains. . . ."

Bunner first became aware of DeCSS on or about October 26, 1999 as a result of reading and participating in discussions on Slashdot. Bunner explained that he is a part-time user of Linux and supports its acceptance as a viable alternative to established computer operating systems such as Microsoft Windows. Bunner thought DeCSS would be useful to other Linux users. He claimed that at the time he posted the information on his Web site he had no information to suggest that the program contained any trade secrets or that it involved the misappropriation of trade secrets. There is no evidence as to the date Bunner first posted the program on his Web site.

Counsel representing the motion picture industry had become aware of the DeCSS posting on October 25, 1999. Beginning November 4, 1999, counsel sent letters to Web site operators and Internet service providers hosting

Web pages that contained DeCSS or links to DeCSS and demanded the information be taken down. Sixty-six such letters were sent between November 4 and November 23, 1999. None of the letters listed in counsel's declaration were addressed to Bunner or to his Web site address. About 25 of the 66 sites were taken down. DeCSS was also removed from Johansen's Web site on or around November 8, 1999, but a link to DeCSS reappeared on the same site on or around December 11, 1999. * * *

DVD CCA filed suit on December 27, 1999, naming as defendants the operators of every infringing Web site it could identify. A hearing for a temporary restraining order was to be held the following day. In support of that application, DVD CCA informed the court that since October 25, 1999, DeCSS had been displayed on or linked to at least 118 Web pages in 11 states and 11 countries throughout the world and that approximately 93 Web pages continued to publish infringing information.

The lawsuit outraged many people in the computer programming community. A campaign of civil disobedience arose by which its proponents tried to spread the DeCSS code as widely as possible before trial. Some of the defendants simply refused to take their postings down. Some people appeared at the courthouse on December 28, 1999 to pass out diskettes and written fliers that supposedly contained the DeCSS code. They made and distributed T-shirts with parts of the code printed on the back. There were even contests encouraging people to submit ideas about how to disseminate the information as widely as possible.

C.   The Trial Court's Findings

The trial court issued the preliminary injunction based upon the following findings: First, CSS is DVD CCA's trade secret and for nearly three years prior to the posting of DeCSS on defendants' Web sites, DVD CCA had exerted reasonable efforts to maintain the secrecy of CSS. The court stated that trade secret status should not be deemed destroyed merely because the information was posted on the Internet, because, "[t]o hold otherwise would do nothing less than encourage misappropriaters [sic] of trade secrets to post the fruits of their wrongdoing on the Internet as quickly as possible and as widely as possible thereby destroying a trade secret forever."

Second, the trial court found that the evidence was "fairly clear" that the trade secret had been obtained through a reverse engineering procedure that violated the terms of a license agreement and, based upon some defendants' boasting about their disrespect for the law, it could be inferred that all defendants knew that the trade secret had been obtained through improper means.

Third, the balancing of equities favored DVD CCA. The court determined that while the harm to defendants in being compelled to remove trade secret information from their Web sites was "truly minimal," the current and prospective harm to DVD CCA was irreparable in that DVD CCA would lose the right to protect CSS as a trade secret and to control unauthorized copying of DVD content. The court pointed out: "once this information gets into the hands of an innocent party, the Plaintiff loses their [sic] ability to enjoin the use of their [sic] trade secret. If the court does not immediately enjoin the posting of this proprietary information, the Plaintiff's right to protect this information as secret will surely be lost, given the current power of the Internet to disseminate information and the Defendants' stated determination to do so." The trial court did not expressly consider the harm to defendants' First Amendment rights.

DISCUSSION

* * *

The Existence of a Trade Secret.

In order to obtain an injunction prohibiting disclosure of an alleged trade secret, the plaintiff's first hurdle is to show that the information it seeks to protect is indeed a trade secret. * * *

In the instant matter, the secrecy element becomes important at two points. First, if the allegedly proprietary information contained in DeCSS was already public knowledge when Bunner posted the program to his Web site, Bunner could not be liable for misappropriation by republishing it because he would not have been disclosing a trade secret. Second, even if the information was not generally known when Bunner posted it, if it had become public knowledge by the time the trial court granted the preliminary injunction, the injunction (which only prohibits *disclosure*) would have been improper because DVD CCA could not have demonstrated interim harm.

1. The Likelihood of Prevailing on the Merits

The trial court did not make an express finding that the proprietary information contained in DeCSS was not generally known at the time Bunner posted it. Indeed, there is no evidence to support such a finding. Bunner first became aware of DeCSS on or around October 26, 1999. But there is no evidence as to when he actually posted it. Indeed, neither Bunner's name nor his Web site address appears among the 66 cease and desist letters counsel sent in November. We do know, however, that by the first week in November Internet news magazines were publicizing the creation of DeCSS and informing readers that the program was available to be downloaded for free on the Internet. As early as July 1999 people in the computer programming community were openly discussing the fact that the CSS code had been reverse engineered and were brainstorming ways to be able to use it legally. That means that when DeCSS appeared in October 1999 there was a worldwide audience ready and waiting to download and repost it.

DVD CCA urges us, in effect, to ignore the fact that the allegedly proprietary information may have been distributed to a worldwide audience of millions prior to Bunner's first posting. According to DVD CCA, so long as Bunner knew or should have known that the information he was republishing was obtained by improper means, he cannot rely upon the general availability of the information to the rest of the world to avoid application of the injunction to him. In support of this position, DVD CCA contends that the denial of an injunction would offend the public policies underlying trade secret law, which are to enforce a standard of commercial ethics, to encourage research and invention, and to protect the owner's moral entitlement to the fruits of his or her labors. DVD CCA points out that these policies are advanced by making sure that those who misappropriate trade secrets do not avoid "judicial sanction" by making the secret widely available.

The first problem with this argument is that by denying a preliminary injunction the court does not per se protect a wrongdoer from judicial sanction, which in most cases would come following trial on the merits.

Second, the evidence in this case is very sparse with respect to whether the offending program was actually created by improper means. Reverse engineering alone is not improper means. Here the creator is believed to be a Norwegian resident who probably had to breach a Xing license in order to access the information he needed. We have only very thin circumstantial evidence of when, where, or how this actually happened or whether an enforceable contract prohibiting reverse engineering was ever formed.

Finally, assuming the information was originally acquired by improper means, it does not necessarily follow that once the information became *publicly* available that everyone else would be liable under the trade secret laws for republishing it simply because they knew about its unethical origins. In a case that receives widespread publicity, just about anyone who becomes aware of the contested information would also know that it was allegedly created by improper means. Under DVD CCA's construction of the law, in such a case the general public could theoretically be liable for misappropriation simply by disclosing it to someone else. This is not what trade secret law is designed to do.

It is important to point out that we do not assume that the alleged trade secrets contained in DeCSS became part of the public domain simply by having been published on the Internet. Rather, the evidence demonstrates that in this case, the initial publication was quickly and widely republished to an eager audience so that DeCSS and the trade secrets it contained rapidly became available to anyone interested in obtaining them. Further, the record contains no evidence as to when in the course of the initial distribution of the offending program Bunner posted it. Thus, DVD CCA has not shown a likelihood that it will prevail on the merits of its claim of misappropriation against Bunner. * * *

DISPOSITION

The order granting a preliminary injunction is reversed. Defendant Andrew Bunner shall recover his appellate costs.

DID YOU GET IT?

1. What facts support the plaintiff's argument that Bunner knew or should have known that the information he was publishing was obtained by improper means?

2. What if Bunner and others knew about the "unethical origins" of how the information was obtained, and nonetheless disclosed it to others. Would they be liable for misappropriation as third parties under the UTSA?

3. Was the information a trade secret when Bunner posted it?

NOTES

1. **Third-party liability under the DTSA.** Because the DTSA adopts, verbatim, the definition of "misappropriation" that is specified in the UTSA, it appears to adopt its principles of third-party liability as well. The DTSA does not otherwise contain language imposing secondary liability.

2. **Third-party liability under the EU Trade Secret Directive.** Similar third-party liability language is included in the EU Trade Secret Directive, but without the same knowledge or reason to know language for all types of misappropriation and without mention of the acquisition by accident or mistake problem. (*See* Article 4, reprinted in Appendix B.) Like the DTSA, there are no separate provisions that set forth a basis for imposing secondary liability. The EU Trade Secret Directive does, however, define a new and additional wrong, heretofore unheard of under trade secret law.

Article 4(5) of the EU Trade Secret Directive states that the following behavior, in addition to the wrongful acquisition, disclosure, or use of trade secrets, is actionable:

> The production, offering or placing on the market infringing goods, or the importation, export or storage of infringing goods for those purposes, shall also be considered an unlawful use of a trade secret where the person carrying out such activities, knew, or ought, under the circumstance, to have known that the trade secret was unlawfully within the meaning of paragraph 3.

"Infringing goods" is defined broadly by the EU Trade Secret Directive to mean "goods, the design, characteristics, functioning, production process or marketing of which significantly benefits from trade secrets unlawfully acquired, used or disclosed." (Article 2(4)).

3. **Respondeat superior liability.** As noted above, respondeat superior is a theory of secondary liability that exists separate and apart from the above-cited provisions of trade secret law. Under this doctrine, an employer can be held liable for the wrongful acts of its employees that are committed within the course and scope of employment. *See* RESTATEMENT (THIRD) OF AGENCY § 7.07 (2016). At first glance, this would seem to apply to a situation where an employee breaches his duty to a former employer by disclosing trade secrets to his new employer or by using them in his new employment. However, imposing respondeat superior liability in such a situation seems at odds with the language and intent of the UTSA and the DTSA which clearly requires third-parties to have "knowledge or reason to know" of the initial misappropriation.

The court in *Infinity Products, Inc. v. Quandt*, 810 N.E.2d 1028, 1034 (2004), examined the apparent conflict between the knowledge requirement of trade secret law and the respondeat superior theory of liability and held that the former was precluded by Indiana's version of the UTSA. The court explained:

> As Infinity correctly points out, respondeat superior is a common law doctrine under which liability is imposed by law upon the master for acts done by the servant, regardless of the master's complicity in the acts. Indeed, it may impose liability even when the master directed the servant to the contrary. * * * Surely this doctrine must be thought as conflicting with the uniforms act's requirement that a claimant demonstrate that the defendant "knows or has reason to know" that the trade secret at issue was acquired by improper means. * * * It is thus displaced by the provisions of the uniform act.

Other courts have not followed the *Infinity* court's interpretation of the UTSA. *See, e.g., Newport News Indus. v. Dynamic Testing, Inc.,* 130 F.Supp.2d 745, 751 (E.D. Va. 2001).

4. **Idea submission policies and procedures vs. open innovation.** As the court hinted in *Burten,* it is important for companies to adopt idea submission policies and procedures that are designed to avoid the creation of an express, implied-in-fact, or implied-at-law duty of confidentiality. This is because creative and inventive people who come up with new ideas will always pitch their ideas and inventions to others, including large enterprises.

One way to avoid potential lawsuits from idea men and women is for companies to adopt an iron-clad policy that unsolicited ideas will not be accepted. However, as a practical matter, in order to implement such a policy a company would have to screen all incoming phone calls, e-mails, and other correspondence to be certain that no ideas are being received by employees, other than the limited few who are charged with screening the correspondence. It would also have to engage in an extensive campaign to educate its workforce in how to handle unsolicited ideas.

While some companies may choose an iron-clad policy, the reality is that many companies (particularly those that are engaged in research and development or the creative arts) want new ideas and are willing to pay a reasonable price for them. They just do not want to be surprised by a claim for compensation after the fact or be forced to pay someone for an idea that they, coincidentally, developed in-house. Thus, some companies are better served by "open innovation" policies and procedures. *See* Henry W. Chesbrough, *Why Companies Should Have Open Business Models*, 48 MIT SLOAN MGMT. REV. 22 (2007).

5. **Good faith or innocent acquirers.** The treatment of "good-faith (or innocent) acquirers" under the UTSA is at odds with the treatment that is accorded good-faith acquirers under the *Restatement (Third) of Unfair Competition*. Under the UTSA, a good-faith acquirer can avoid a finding of misappropriation by showing that he did not have the requisite knowledge before a material change in his position. Under the *Restatement (Third) of Unfair Competition*, the change in position goes to the issue of remedies and not to the issue of misappropriation. *See Restatement (Third) of Unfair Competition* § 45 cmt. e. As Richard Dole, the Reporter for the UTSA drafting project, has noted, UTSA § 1(2)(ii)(C) is derived from *Conmar Products Corporation v. Universal Slide Fastener Co.*, 172 F.2d 150 (1949). *See* Richard Dole, *The Uniform Trade Secrets Act—Trends and Prospects*, 33 Hamline L. Rev., 409, 428 (2010). In that case, Judge Learned Hand explained the underlying purposes of a limited third-party liability rule:

> We think, however, that the defendants had an excuse for exploiting that secret over that period, if they did so. As we have said, by November 16, 1940, they had invested $40,000 in the offending machine; that is, they had either paid or committed themselves to pay that much. The *Restatement of Torts* makes it an excuse for continued exploitation of a secret that at the time when one, who has theretofore been innocently exploiting it, first learns that he has induced the breach of an obligation, he has substantially changed his position. The opinions which support this are not very satisfactory; so far as we have found, in all but one or two it is doubtful whether what the judges say is more than dictum. However, they do all point the same way, for they assume that the situation is proper for the application of the doctrine that a bona fide purchaser takes free from a trust. *The act of inducing the breach is the wrong, and the inducer's ignorance is an excuse only because one is not ordinarily held liable for consequences which one could not have anticipated. Although it is proper to prevent any continued use of the secret after the inducer has learned of the breach, the remedies must not invade the inducer's immunity over the period while he was ignorant.*

See Conmar Products Corporation v. Universal Slide Fastener Co., 172 F.2d at 150 (emphasis added).

6.   **Bibliographic note:** In addition to the references noted above, for more information on the topics discussed in this chapter, *see* MILGRIM ON TRADE SECRETS §§ 3.03, 4.03, 7.01 (2016); Sharon K. Sandeen, *Lost in the Cloud: Information Flows and the Implications of Cloud Computing for Trade Secret Protection*, 19 VA. J. L. & TECH 1 (2014) (discussing the different meanings of "disclosure" under intellectual property laws); Jeff Paterson, *End User Liability for Software Developed with Trade Secrets*, 7 WASH. J. L. TECH & ARTS. 105 (2011); Mark Bartholomew, *Copyright, Trademark, and Secondary Liability After* Grokster, 32 COLUMBIA J. OF LAW & ARTS 445 (2009); Mark Bartholomew and John Tehranian, *The Secret Life of Legal Doctrine: The Divergent Evolution of Secondary Liability in Trademark and Copyright Law*, 21 BERKELEY TECH. L. J. 1363 (2006).

CHAPTER 8

PROTECTING TRADE SECRETS IN THE EMPLOYMENT CONTEXT

■ ■ ■

Anticipated Learning Outcomes

At the conclusion of this chapter, you will have a better understanding of some of the contractual provisions in employment agreements, such as non-disclosure agreements, non-competition agreements, and non-solicitation agreements, and how they implicate trade secret protection. This chapter also addresses the ownership of trade secrets created during an employment relationship and invention assignment agreements and policies.

A. INTRODUCTION

The employment relationship is a special relationship under the law with a number of statutory and implied obligations being imposed upon both the employer and the employee. *See, e.g.* Mark A. Rothstein, et al., EMPLOYMENT LAW 3 (5th ed. 2015). As was noted in Chapter 7, one implied obligation that is often imposed on employees is a duty of confidentiality with respect to employer-owned trade secrets. Employees are also usually subject to either an implied or statutory duty of loyalty. *See* Brian S. Malsberger, EMPLOYEE DUTY OF LOYALTY: A STATE-BY-STATE SURVEY (2015).

An issue that frequently arises with respect to both an employee's duty of confidentiality and duty of loyalty concerns the precise definition and scope of those duties. Understandably, employers assert that the duties of confidentiality and loyalty should be interpreted broadly to prohibit employees from disclosing and using a wide-variety of business information. Employers also argue that the duties of confidentiality and loyalty should be interpreted to limit the ability of employees to go to work for a competitor and solicit former clients. As we have seen elsewhere, however (for instance in the discussion of general skill and knowledge in Chapter 3), there are important public policy reasons why courts are reluctant to restrict the activities of employees too much. Generally, employee mobility is thought to benefit society.

In practice, how the duties of confidentiality and loyalty are defined in a given case will depend on the facts of the case and the applicable state law. Some states, most notably California, are much more solicitous of the rights of employees than others and, thus, are more apt to use public policy arguments to limit restrictions on employee mobility. Other states, while cognizant of the public policy issues, are more receptive to employer claims, particularly if the subject employee entered into a written confidentiality or non-compete agreement with his employer.

Employers who wish to strengthen their position with respect to current and former employees often attempt to do so contractually through the use of one or more agreements, including a confidentiality agreement (also known as a non-disclosure agreement of NDA), a non-solicitation agreement, or a non-compete agreement. However, because these agreements create a policy tension between the employer's freedom to contract and the employee's freedom to progress in their careers and seek new employment, courts will scrutinize the reasonableness of these agreements in deciding whether to enforce them. Rothstein, et al., EMPLOYMENT LAW, *supra,* Chapter 8 (discussing the enforceability of non-compete and similar agreements). Indeed, in some states, statutes have been adopted which dictate such scrutiny. *See e.g.,* Cal. Bus. & Prof. Code § 16600.

Whether or not a statute exists that limits the enforceability and scope of agreements with employees, the general rule is that confidentiality, non-solicitation, and non-compete agreements will not be enforced unless they are "reasonable." As with every other reasonableness standard under the law, what is reasonable ultimately depends upon the circumstances. In states that tend to favor employers, often such agreements are presumed to be reasonable unless shown to be unreasonable by the employee. In other states, such agreements are presumed to be unreasonable unless shown to be reasonable by the employer. When the agreements are designed to protect a legitimate interest of the employer, such as to protect trade secrets, they are more likely to be enforced. When they overreach and are seen as an effort to quell legitimate competition and employee mobility, they will not be enforced.

The first two cases of this chapter deal with the enforceability of non-compete agreements and show how courts of different states approach the same issue. The next two cases concern a related doctrine known as the "inevitable disclosure doctrine," and also present competing views on the topic.

The inevitable disclosure doctrine typically arises in cases where an employee of one company goes to work for a competitor and readily admits he is under an ongoing duty of confidentiality to his former employer. However, the former employer argues the circumstances of the employee's new employment make the disclosure of its trade secrets "inevitable." To prevent such disclosure, the employer typically is not satisfied with an injunction precluding the disclosure of its secrets. Instead, it wants an injunction to prevent its former employee from working for the competitor. In effect, an employer who asserts the inevitable disclosure doctrine is asking the court to imply a non-compete agreement. Thus, the inevitable disclosure doctrine raises the same policy issues as cases that consider the enforceability of non-compete agreements, but with the twist that the freedom to contract argument is missing.

The Special Issue of this chapter discusses the ownership of trade secrets. Typically, the trade secrets of a company will pre-exist the employment of an individual or be the work-product of management or other employees. In such cases, the employees to whom the information is disclosed have no claim of ownership in the information. In other cases, the trade secrets that are claimed by a company were actually created by the employee who is accused of misappropriation. Rules have developed to determine when these trade secrets are owned by the employee and when they are owned by the employer. However, the best practice is for employers to limit ownership disputes through the use of "reasonable" Invention Assignment Agreements. As is discussed below, in some states (and countries), including California, the allowable scope of these agreements are statutorily proscribed.

B. RESTRICTIVE COVENANTS

The common law of the United States and various statutes at both the state and federal level have long held that "unreasonable" restraints on trade (or "restrictive covenants") may violate antitrust laws or otherwise be unenforceable. However, restrictive covenants can come in many different forms and, depending on the needs and objectives of the contracting parties, are not always illegal. Generally, the key to the enforceability of restrictive covenants is the reasonableness of the restrictions (usually in terms of time and scope) and whether there is a "legitimate business purpose" for the restrictions, which in many states can include efforts to protect trade secrets and other confidential information.

In the employment context, the analysis of reasonableness often depends on the role of the employee within the organization; higher level employees may be subject to restrictive covenants because of their wider access to sensitive information than lower level employees. In general, restrictive covenants are a mechanism for employers to protect company assets and interests when an employee leaves. These interests must be balanced against the employee's freedom to earn a living and our societal interest in free competition. As summarized by a May 2016 White House Report titled, *Non-Compete Agreements: Analysis of Usage, Potential Issues, and State Responses*:

> In some cases, non-compete agreements can play an important role in protecting businesses and promoting innovation. They can also encourage employers to invest in training for their employees. However, as detailed in this report, non-competes can impose substantial costs on workers, consumers, and the economy more generally.

As also noted in the White House Report, not all states balance the interests of employers and employees in the same way.

Restrictive covenants can be provisions in employment agreements or they can be stand-alone agreements, including confidentiality agreements, non-competition agreements, invention assignment agreements, and non-solicitation agreements. Of these, the covenants that are most likely to be at issue in trade secret cases are confidentiality agreements and non-competition agreements. Confidentiality (or non-disclosure) agreements and non-compete agreements are discussed in the excerpt from an article by Professor Elizabeth Rowe (below) and in the cases that follow.

Non-solicitation agreements generally prevent former employees from "raiding" their former employers' clients or employees. These are usually upheld as long as they are reasonable and necessary to protect an employer's legitimate business interest. *See e.g., Lane Co. v. Taylor,* 330 S.E.2d 112, 117 (Ga. Ct. App. 1985*).* Because non-solicitation agreements usually do not affect the former employee's ability to earn a living, they tend to be less objectionable and raise fewer issues than non-competition agreements. However, the terms of non-solicitation agreements should clearly define the activities that are prohibited. Generally, courts draw a distinction between active solicitation of former clients (which can be the subject of reasonable restrictions) and merely announcing a change in employment or the opening of a new business (which is usually allowed in the interest of free competition and free speech). *See Kephart v. Hair Returns, Inc.,* 685 So.2d 959, 960 (Fla. Dist. Ct. App. 1996); *Rothstein, supra,* § 8.10, at 805–07.

WHEN TRADE SECRETS BECOME SHACKLES: FAIRNESS AND THE INEVITABLE DISCLOSURE DOCTRINE

Elizabeth A. Rowe.
7 Tul. J. Tech. & Intell. Prop. 167, 188–91 (2005).

Restrictive covenants enhance an employer's legitimate interests in its trade secrets and other assets, such as goodwill. Courts recognize the employer's need for such covenants to encourage investment, protect innovation, and promote free competition. Generally, carefully drafted post-employment covenants require that the employee maintain secrecy, refrain from soliciting customers or employees, and not engage in certain competitive activities. In addition, the agreements typically contain provisions recognizing that any breach of the employment agreement would cause irreparable harm for which the company would have no adequate remedy at law, and that in the event of any such breach the company would have the right to seek an injunction.

A.   Confidentiality/Nondisclosure Agreements

As a condition of employment, many employees, especially higher level employees, generally sign agreements acknowledging that the employment creates a relationship of confidence and trust with respect to confidential information. Confidential information may be broadly defined in these agreements to include trade secrets, processes, formulae, data and know-how, discoveries, developments, designs, improvements, inventions, techniques, marketing plans, strategies, forecasts, new products, software, software documentation, unpublished financial statements, budgets, projections, licenses, prices, costs, and customer and supplier lists. However, a confidentiality agreement cannot transform information that is generally known into a trade secret.

* * * A typical nondisclosure agreement may contain language similar to the following:

> All Confidential Information and rights relating to Confidential Information shall be the sole property of the company. I will not disclose to anyone outside the company or use for my own benefit or for the benefit of others any Confidential Information either during or after my employment without the company's prior written permission except as may be necessary in the ordinary course of performing my duties as an employee of the Company.

> Upon the termination of my employment with the Company for any reason, I will deliver to the Company all documents or other materials relating to my work with the Company and will not take with me any of the foregoing or any reproduction thereof or anything containing any, or relating to any, Confidential Information.

Confidentiality agreements express in writing the common law obligation of an employee to maintain the confidential nature of the employer-employee relationship. On a more practical level, confidentiality agreements are helpful for (1) delineating the confidentiality expectations between the employer and employee, (2) showing that the employer takes trade secret protection seriously, and (3) demonstrating the employer's reasonable efforts to maintain the secrecy of its confidential information. Employees typically do not need to provide additional consideration for nondisclosure agreements, and unlike noncompetition agreements, there is generally little or no hesitation to signing a nondisclosure agreement.

B.   Noncompetition Agreements

By entering into a noncompetition agreement, the employee usually agrees that for a specified period of time after the end of his employment not to work for any company that is a competitor of the employer. For instance, typical language may include the following:

> I agree that during the period of my employment by the Company I will not, without the Company's prior express written consent, engage in any employment, consulting or other business other than for the Company.

> I agree that during the period of my employment by the Company, and for a period of one year thereafter I will not, without the Company's prior express written consent, engage in, have an interest in, be employed by, or be in any way directly or indirectly connected with any business that is in competition with the Company.

However, such a covenant will generally be enforceable only if the employer can show that (1) it is necessary to protect a legitimate interest of the employer, (2) it is reasonably limited in duration, and (3) it is reasonably limited in geographic scope.

State law establishes the requirements for determining the validity of noncompetition agreements. Many states recognize and enforce noncompetition agreements as long as the restrictions are reasonable in view of the totality of the circumstances, including the scope of geographical, temporal, and competitive activity restrictions. Even in these jurisdictions courts also appear to take into consideration the financial hardship to the employee if the noncompetition agreement is enforced. Some states prohibit the use of noncompetition agreements entirely. Other states recognize these covenants under narrow and specified circumstances.

As with all contracts, a noncompetition agreement will not be enforced without valid consideration, and the employee must receive some benefit in exchange for the restriction. When an employee signs such a covenant upon being hired, the promise of at-will employment provides sufficient consideration. However, states are divided as to whether a covenant not to compete imposed after the commencement of at-will employment requires new and additional consideration.

> ### Reading Guidance
>
> *Does the former employer have a legitimate business interest to protect in this case?* [handwritten: Yes · Sensitive info re strategy, ads, finances, investments]

[handwritten: – Safely not added to reasonableness]

[handwritten: ***]

[handwritten: – preliminary injunction – ct. denied injunction]

CAMPBELL SOUP CO. V. DESATNICK

United States District Court, D. New Jersey, 1999.
58 F.Supp.2d 477.

[handwritten: – Stopping Campbell's from enjoining enforcing a non-compete against fmr. employee]

SIMANDLE, DISTRICT JUDGE.

This matter is before the court on the motion of Robert L. Desatnick ("Desatnick") for a preliminary injunction, pursuant to Federal Rule of Civil Procedure 65(a), enjoining Campbell Soup Company ("Campbell") from enforcing a 1997 non-competition agreement to prevent Desatnick from accepting an offer of employment from The Pillsbury Company ("Pillsbury"). Desatnick, who resigned from his position as Campbell's Vice President of Global Advertising and Promotion on April 8, 1999, argues that Campbell has no legitimate business interest in preventing him from joining Pillsbury as Chief Marketing Officer of Pillsbury North America because he does not possess any proprietary secrets or confidential information that require protection. * * *

FINDINGS OF FACT

From 1979 to 1994, Desatnick worked for an advertising agency, first as an account executive and then as a member of the agency's management team. For the last four years of his employment with this agency, Desatnick managed the Campbell account. [handwritten: ad agency]

In early 1994, Desatnick was offered a lucrative position by another advertising agency. In February 1994, when it learned that Desatnick was considering leaving his agency position as manager of the Campbell account for a position with another advertising agency, Campbell inquired whether Desatnick would be interested in joining Campbell in an in-house capacity. Thereafter, Desatnick and Gary Moss, then Campbell's Vice President of Global Advertising, engaged in a series of discussions about Campbell's ability to offer a compensation package that was competitive with the offer Desatnick had received from the advertising agency. [handwritten: in-house at Campbell's]

Desatnick Joins Campbell

Ultimately, Campbell extended Desatnick an offer of employment as Director—Advertising Services. The terms of Campbell's offer were set forth in a February 25, 1994 letter. The offer letter provided that Desatnick was to be paid a base salary of $140,000, a one-time signing bonus of $20,000, and standard medical and dental benefits. The offer letter further provided that Desatnick would be eligible to participate in a short-term management incentive program and a long-term executive stock option program. * * *

Desatnick signed Campbell's confidentiality agreement as he started employment in 1994, entitled the "Patent-Trade Secret Agreement," dated April 4, 1994, promising to keep confidential, both during and after his employment, such information as "confidential marketing plans or data" and "potential new product introductions." He testified that he refused to sign the "Employee Agreement Relating to Confidential and Proprietary Information" that contained a non-competition clause in 1994. * * *

[Desatnick signed another confidentiality agreement in 1995 and two non-competition agreements in 1996 and 1997. It is the 1997 agreement that is the focus of the court's attention.]

* * *

Campbell is * * * seeking to enforce * * * [the] "Nonqualified Stock Option and Non-Competition Agreement" that he signed without audible protest on July 25, 1997 ("the 1997 agreement"). The 1997 agreement provides that during Desatnick's employment with Campbell, and for 18 months after such employment (if he leaves voluntarily), he agrees not to become employed by any business that competes with the business of Campbell in any part of the world. A business "competes" if it "engages in, or plans to engage in, the production, marketing or selling of any product or service . . . which resembles or competes with a product or service of Campbell Companies . . . during [the employee's] employment [with Campbell]."

The 1997 agreement, quite significantly in this court's view, also provides a "safety net" in case Desatnick is unable to find employment with a non-competitor. Campbell agrees in this safety net to pay 100% of his base monthly salary (along with medical and dental benefits) beginning 90 days after his last employment at Campbell's and continuing for the 18-month duration of the non-competition provision or until he finds a suitable position, if sooner. The 1997 agreement also evidences Desatnick's acknowledgment that "the restrictions in this agreement are necessary to protect the legitimate interests of Campbell Companies, and impose no undue hardship on [him]." This "safety net" in the 1997 non-compete agreement provides a reasonable financial cushion to soften the financial impact of the executive employee's job search with a non-competitor for a reasonable period of time. The 18-month period is reasonably long in recognition that senior executive opportunities may not be easy to obtain overnight.

Meanwhile, Desatnick's base salary as a corporate Vice President continued to increase, reaching $185,000 as of January 1, 1999. Campbell granted Desatnick 4,488 stock options in June 1997, and 3,500 more stock options in 1998, which have not yet vested.

Desatnick's Exposure to Highly Sensitive Competitive Information

Throughout the hearing, Desatnick sought to minimize his duties in terms of exposure to strategic planning information, and he also sought to trivialize the competitive importance of the information that he received in the course of his duties. In fact, for the past two-plus years, Desatnick was a member of Campbell's Leadership Group, consisting of about 40 senior Campbell executives who meet on a monthly basis to discuss strategic planning, financial performance, financial forecasting, and resource allocations. Although Desatnick was not a member of the even more restrictive Senior Leadership Team consisting of a handful of the top executives, he was part of the important management team that planned and reviewed the company's performance.

[handwritten: Monthly mtgs]

Lisa Zakrajsek, Campbell Soup's Vice President of U.S. Soup, testified that the Leadership Team—of which she is a member—as consisting of very senior corporate officers who meet and communicate regularly with Campbell's CEO Dale Morrison to discuss how critical issues are being handled in the company. More detailed financial performance and projections are reviewed at the level of Campbell's various business components, in contrast to the generality of the corporate-level figures and documents that are released to financial analysts and shareholders. The monthly meeting topics are generally confidential including options under consideration by the Board or reasons for decisions made by the Board.
* * *

Mr. Desatnick asserts that the information he learned as Vice President is no longer confidential because Campbell executives disclose it to financial analysts, which in turn publish news of some upcoming developments and projections in newsletters to stock brokerage clients. Such analyst reports from brokers such as Salomon Smith Barney, Merrill Lynch, and others are in evidence. These financial analysts report their assessments of Campbell as an investment, based upon the data that can be gleaned through such information as is available, including in some instances meetings or interviews with CEO Dale Morrison and others. These brochures contain assessments and guesses and not the strategic planning that lies behind such developments. On various topics, Campbell refused to disclose further information to the analysts. The overall impression is that sketchy information has been made public regarding future plans and strategies, without disclosing the core confidentially planning and strategic information underlying it.

[handwritten: fmr. employee's argument for why info he knows is not confid.]

By focusing on these tidbits of information, Desatnick avoids the larger picture and the truly valid concerns of Campbell that his job at Pillsbury is exactly what is reasonably precluded by the non-competition agreement.
* * *

Competition Between Campbell and Pillsbury

Since Campbell seeks to invoke the 1997 agreement's non-compete clause, it is necessary to determine whether Pillsbury is a manufacturer and marketer of significantly competitive products. Desatnick points to some internal Campbell documents that do not list Pillsbury as a chief competitor against various lines, such as Campbell's Pepperidge Farm brands. It is clear, on balance, that Pillsbury is a significant competitor of Campbell in soups and Mexican salsa products, among others. Campbell considers Pillsbury's Progresso Soup brand as its principal domestic soup competitor. In fact, Pillsbury regards Campbell as its principal soup competitor, as Pillsbury recently launched a large advertising campaign expressly presenting its Progresso soup as a superior alternative to Campbell's. Desatnick in fact participated this year in formulating Campbell's plan to combat Progresso's advertising initiative, during the time when he was interviewing for the Pillsbury CMO position. Campbell's Chunky Soup is a direct competitor of Progresso Soup.

Campbell's Pace-brand Mexican salsa products compete directly with Pillsbury's Old El Paso products; Desatnick was not only ultimately responsible for Pace's creative advertising, he helped design the Pace initiatives for the coming year. These confidential initiatives include concepts being pursued and being dropped, and positioning recommendations being pursued at this time. * * *

It suffices to say that Pillsbury and Campbell are competitors in many product areas, and are direct and strenuous competitors in the huge markets for soups, salsas, and baked goods.

Desatnick's Proposed Duties at Pillsbury

Desatnick seeks to accept the offer of a "once-in-a-lifetime" opportunity with Pillsbury to become the Chief Marketing Officer. This position, reporting to the President of Pillsbury North America, includes responsibility for advertising and creating strategies for brand acceptance of Pillsbury's products, including those that compete with Campbell's brands in which Desatnick has sensitive competitive and trade secret information, such as Pillsbury's Progresso Soups and Old El Paso salsa products and Pillsbury refrigerated dough products. He points out that only two of the 44 food and beverage manufacturing companies listed in the Fortune 1000 have a Chief Marketing Officer. * * *

In November, 1998, Desatnick felt his duties at Campbell were being compressed and he sought new challenges elsewhere. He met with Pillsbury officials about this position in New York in December, 1998, and met with Pillsbury's Kathleen McArdle in Minneapolis to discuss the position in detail on February 19, 1999. (This latter trip happened while en route to Los Angeles on Campbell business involving Walt Disney company.)

Mr. Desatnick followed up on those interviews with letters to McArdle on February 25, 1999 and March 2, 1999. The latter helped Pillsbury to define the Chief Market Officer's roles and Desatnick's expectations, such as through achieving "new levels of excellence in the effectiveness and efficiency of the company's marketing activities," "creating broader experiential platforms that will let Pillsbury reach out to and surround the consumer in a seamlessly integrated fashion," and "leading the drive to create a world class marketing organization by enhancing Pillsbury's processes for recruiting, training, developing, evaluating, and promoting marketing personnel." He proposed to accomplish these aims through, among other things, "participating in decisions about brand positioning, strategy, execution and marketing staff," and he enclosed a summary of his ideas for how he would do this, including defining the "Key Roles & Initiatives" and the proposed revised organization structure for Pillsbury's advertising and business development functions.

On March 16, 1999, Pillsbury's President extended an offer to Desatnick to become the Vice President, Marketing, conditioned upon Desatnick's demonstration that the Campbell Non-Competition Agreement does not apply to his acceptance of this position, such as by a written waiver by Campbell. This offer was revised on March 26, 1999 to change the position title to Chief Marketing Officer, and it was again contingent upon the non-applicability of the Non-Competition Agreement. The offer would expire on May 15, 1999. Pillsbury apparently agreed to hold the offer open for a longer period to see whether the dispute regarding the non-compete agreement could be resolved in this litigation.

Desatnick accepted Pillsbury's offer even though he had not sought or obtained Campbell's waiver, and Pillsbury reiterated on April 14, 1999 that Desatnick's acceptance was not consistent with Pillsbury's conditional offer. Correspondence between the respective corporate counsel's offices of Campbell and Pillsbury confirmed that Desatnick had not disclosed to Campbell the conditional nature of Pillsbury's offer when he gave notice of his resignation from Campbell.

Desatnick has proposed that his new duties at Pillsbury could be temporarily scaled back and carved out to exclude responsibilities for marketing and advertising of Progresso and Old El Paso brands until Campbell's advertising campaigns are launched to the public. He points out that Progresso and Old El Paso comprise less than 6% of Pillsbury's sales overall, and that his new CMO duties could be temporarily restricted to the other dominant parts of Pillsbury's business. Under this temporary restructuring of the Pillsbury Chief Marketing Officer position, according to Desatnick, he would be unable to aid these competitive endeavors even if he possessed Campbell's secret information and plans for these products, which he denies.

There is no evidence that such a segmentation of duties would be acceptable to Pillsbury or that it would work in practice. First, when Pillsbury has expressed itself, it has repeatedly sought proof of Campbell's plenary waiver of the non-compete clause as it applies to the entire Chief Marketing Officer position, without reference to segmentation or balkanization of the duties of the CMO position. That is understandable, since the Pillsbury CMO position is expressly designed to integrate, across-the-board, the marketing strategy and its implementation through coordination of efforts in advertising, promotions, and packaging design across the entire brand portfolio for Pillsbury's North America's unit's $4.4 billion in sales.

Second, to insulate Desatnick at Pillsbury from duties dealing with Progresso, Old El Paso, and Pillsbury cookie and pastry products would require a great measure of trust that he could comport his conduct to the requirements of the non-compete clause. Campbell has demonstrated a sound basis for questioning whether such trust would be warranted. Although it is undisputed that he is bound by the 1995 "Employee Agreement" regarding trade secrets or other secret or confidential information, he disputes that even the precise items listed therein should be considered confidential, including "information concerning business plans, financial information, products, . . . strategic plans, advertising and marketing plans," choosing instead to regard this closely held information as disclosable and usable if in his view some parts of these plans, strategies, or brand positions have been disclosed; this narrow view of the confidentiality time line has been shown to be incorrect and his continued misinterpretation runs the serious risk of breaching confidentiality in his new position whether he intended to do so or not. He has shown the poor judgment of helping Pillsbury to restructure its responsibilities among its principal marketing officers, to the extent of providing detailed ideas for improving Pillsbury's competitiveness in March, 1999 while he was still employed by Campbell, to the possible competitive detriment of Campbell.
* * *

In short, the evidence of lack of candor further disinclines this court away from seeking to equitably cobble together some sort of duties that Mr. Desatnick might perform at Pillsbury while scrupulously adhering to his duties under the non-compete clause.

* * *

Analysis

Likelihood of Success on the Merits

Under New Jersey law, an agreement restricting an employee's ability to compete with his employer after the termination of his employment will generally be found to be reasonable and, therefore, enforceable " 'where it simply protects the legitimate interests of the employer, imposes no undue hardship on the employee, and is not injurious to the public.' " To minimize the hardship imposed on the employee, the geographic, temporal and subject-matter restrictions of an otherwise enforceable agreement not to compete will be enforced only to the extent reasonably necessary to protect the employer's legitimate business interests.

New Jersey courts "recognize as legitimate the employer's interest in protecting trade secrets, confidential information, and customer relations." * * * "Courts must evaluate the reasonableness of [a restrictive covenant] in light of the individual circumstances of the employer and employee" and "balance the employer's need for protection and the hardship on the employee that may result." Because "[t]he line between [protectable] information, trade secrets, and the general skills and knowledge of a highly sophisticated employee will be very difficult to draw," courts are expected to "narrowly" construe an employer's need for protection. "In cases where the employer's interests are strong, such as cases involving trade secrets or confidential information, a court will enforce a restrictive covenant." "Conversely, in cases where the employer's interests do not rise to the level of a proprietary interest deserving of judicial protection, a court will conclude that a restrictive agreement merely stifles competition and therefore is unenforceable."

This court finds that Campbell has proved that its corporate interests in enforcing the non-competition agreement as to Mr. Desatnick or any other senior executive in his position are deserving of judicial protection. The dominant purpose and effect of the restrictive covenant is to protect proprietary information and competitively sensitive plans and strategies and not to stifle competition. Campbell's interests are real and the enforcement of this contractual obligation is not unreasonable, nor does it result in undue hardship to the departing employee that is disproportional to the interests at stake. Further reasonableness is found in the "safety net" provision, which cushions the financial loss to the departing employee and which negates any intent to impose a punishment upon him.

In the present case, Desatnick argues that Campbell has no legitimate business interest in preventing him from joining Pillsbury because he does not possess any proprietary or confidential information that requires protection. As noted above, however, the record evidence in this matter reveals that during his tenure at Campbell Desatnick was exposed to a considerable amount of highly sensitive competitive information that is entitled to protection under New Jersey law.

According to his own resume, Desatnick was responsible for overseeing Campbell's $380 million global advertising, licensing and corporate promotion budget, and his functions included brand positioning, creative strategy, advertising and promotion campaigns, Campbell's Web site, corporate licensing, and media planning, buying and research. As a member of Campbell's Leadership Team, Desatnick was privy to high-level confidential discussions of such matters as Campbell's strategic planning, financial performance, financial forecasting, and resource allocation. Much of the information discussed at Leadership Team meetings is more detailed than that which is disclosed in publicly available sources or released to financial analysts and shareholders.

During the last six months of his employment with Campbell, Desatnick attended a number of meetings at which highly sensitive and confidential business information was discussed. For example, Desatnick attended meetings related to Campbell's soup strategies between November 1988 and January 1999, including sensitive strategy sessions with Campbell CEO Dale Morrison concerning a new direction Campbell's plans to take in its soup advertising. Desatnick contributed to these meetings by offering his analysis of the effectiveness of Campbell's current soup advertising. As a result of his participation in these meetings, Desatnick is generally aware of Campbell's plans for brand positioning and pricing in the marketplace, its plans for resource allocation among product lines within the company, and its perceptions of its brands' strengths and vulnerabilities. Desatnick attended a confidential meeting involving high-level Campbell executives and representatives of Campbell's advertising agencies in January 1999 during which aspects of Campbell's three-year strategic plan were discussed. In February, 1999, Desatnick participated in a highly confidential meeting with a consultant regarding the quality of Campbell's advertising. Desatnick also reviewed proposed "story boards" for eleven different commercials reflecting the brand positioning of various Pepperidge Farm products. These eleven commercials were eventually narrowed to three and will not be released until October 1999 through January 2000. * * *

* * * Accordingly, Desatnick has not met his burden of demonstrating that he is likely to succeed at trial on the merits of his claim that his non-competition agreement with Campbell is invalid and unenforceable. * * *

CONCLUSION

For these reasons, the court denies Desatnick's motion for a preliminary injunction enjoining Campbell from enforcing the non-competition agreement Desatnick executed in 1997 to prevent Desatnick from accepting an offer of employment from Pillsbury.

DID YOU GET IT?

1. What was Desatnick's main argument as to why his non-competition agreement with Campbell Soup was unenforceable?

2. On what facts did the court rely in support of its analysis on the question of whether Campbell Soup had a legitimate business interest to protect in preventing Desatnick from working for Pillsbury?

3. Why do you think Desatnick and not Campbell Soup was the plaintiff in this case?

Reading Guidance

How does this case express California's public policy on non-competition agreements?

EDWARDS V. ARTHUR ANDERSEN LLP

California Supreme Court, 2008.
44 Cal.4th 937.

CHIN, J.

We granted review to address the validity of noncompetition agreements in California. * * *

In January 1997, Raymond Edwards II (Edwards), a certified public accountant, was hired as a tax manager by the Los Angeles office of the accounting firm Arthur Andersen LLP (Andersen). Andersen's employment offer was made contingent upon Edwards's signing a noncompetition agreement, which prohibited him from working for or soliciting certain Andersen clients for limited periods following his termination. The agreement was required of all managers, and read in relevant part: "If you leave the Firm, for eighteen months after release or resignation, you agree not to perform professional services of the type you provided for any client on which you worked during the eighteen months prior to release or resignation. This does not prohibit you from accepting employment with a client. For twelve months after you leave the Firm, you agree not to solicit (to perform professional services of the type you provided) any client of the office(s) to which you were assigned during the eighteen months preceding release or resignation. You agree not to solicit away from the Firm any of its professional personnel for eighteen months after release or resignation." Edwards signed the agreement.

Between 1997 and 2002, Edwards continued to work for Andersen, moving into the firm's private client services practice group, where he handled income, gift, and estate tax planning for individuals and entities with large incomes and net worth. Over this period he was promoted to senior manager and was on track to become a partner. In March 2002, the United States government indicted Andersen in connection with the investigation into Enron Corporation, and in June 2002, Andersen announced that it would cease its accounting practices in the United States. In April 2002, Andersen began selling off its practice groups to various entities. In May 2002, Andersen internally announced that HSBC USA, Inc. (a New York-based banking corporation), through a new subsidiary, Wealth and Tax Advisory Services (WTAS), would purchase a portion of Andersen's tax practice, including Edwards's group.

In July 2002, HSBC offered Edwards employment. Before hiring any of Andersen's employees, HSBC required them to execute a "Termination of Non-compete Agreement" (TONC) in order to obtain employment with HSBC. Among other things, the TONC required employees to, inter alia, (1) voluntarily resign from Andersen; (2) release Andersen from "any and all" claims, including "claims that in any way arise from or out of, are based upon or relate to Employee's employment by, association with or compensation from" defendant; (3) continue indefinitely to preserve confidential information and trade secrets except as otherwise required by a court or governmental agency; (4) refrain from disparaging Andersen or its related entities or partners; and (5) cooperate with Andersen in connection with any investigation of, or litigation against, Andersen. In exchange, Andersen would agree to accept Edwards's resignation, agree to Edwards's employment by HSBC, and release Edwards from the 1997 noncompetition agreement.

* * *

Edwards signed the HSBC offer letter, but he did not sign the TONC. In response, Andersen terminated Edwards's employment and withheld severance benefits. HSBC withdrew its offer of employment to Edwards.

PROCEDURAL HISTORY

On April 30, 2003, Edwards filed a complaint against Andersen, HSBC and WTAS for intentional interference with prospective economic advantage and anticompetitive business practices under the Cartwright Act (Bus. & Prof. Code, § 16720 et seq.). Edwards alleged that the Andersen noncompetition agreement violated section 16600, which states "[e]xcept as provided in this chapter, every contract by which anyone is restrained from engaging in a lawful profession, trade, or business of any kind is to that extent void." * * *

Edwards settled with all parties except Andersen. * * *

The trial court heard argument from both parties, but took no evidence. The court determined all issues of law in favor of Andersen on the merits, and entered judgment in its favor. The court specifically decided that (1) the noncompetition agreement did not violate section 16600 because it was narrowly tailored and did not deprive Edwards of his right to pursue his profession * * *.

DISCUSSION

A.   Section 16600

Under the common law, as is still true in many states today, contractual restraints on the practice of a profession, business, or trade, were considered valid, as long as they were reasonably imposed. This was true even in California. * * * However, in 1872 California settled public policy in favor of open competition, and rejected the common law "rule of reasonableness," when the Legislature enacted the Civil Code. Today in California, covenants not to compete are void, subject to several exceptions discussed briefly below.

Section 16600 states: "Except as provided in this chapter, every contract by which anyone is restrained from engaging in a lawful profession, trade, or business of any kind is to that extent void." The chapter excepts noncompetition agreements in the sale or dissolution of corporations (§ 16601), partnerships (§ 16602), and limited liability corporations (§ 16602.5). In the years since its original enactment as Civil Code section 1673, our courts have consistently affirmed that section 16600 evinces a settled legislative policy in favor of open competition and employee mobility. * * *

* * *

Under the statute's plain meaning, therefore, an employer cannot by contract restrain a former employee from engaging in his or her profession, trade, or business unless the agreement falls within one of the exceptions to the rule. Andersen, however, asserts that we should interpret the term "restrain" under section 16600 to mean simply to "prohibit," so that only contracts that totally prohibit an employee from engaging in his or her profession, trade, or business are illegal. It would then follow that a mere limitation on an employee's ability to practice his or her vocation would be permissible under section 16600, as long as it is reasonably based.

Andersen contends that some California courts have held that section 16600 (and its predecessor statutes, * * * are the statutory embodiment of prior common law, and embrace the rule of reasonableness in evaluating competitive restraints. * * * Andersen claims that these cases show that section 16600 "prohibits only broad agreements that prevent a person from engaging entirely in his chosen business, trade or profession. Agreements that do not have this broad effect—but merely regulate some aspect of post-employment conduct, e.g., to prevent raiding [employer's personnel]—are not within the scope of [s]ection 16600."

As Edwards observes, however, the cases Andersen cites to support a relaxation of the statutory rule simply recognize that the statutory exceptions to section 16600 reflect the same exceptions to the rule against noncompetition agreements that were implied in the common law. * * *

* * * As the present Court of Appeal recognized, "Fairly read, the foregoing authorities suggest section 16600 embodies the original, strict common law antipathy toward restraints of trade, while the section 16601 and 16602 exceptions incorporated the later common law 'rule of reasonableness' in instances where those exceptions apply."

We conclude that Andersen's noncompetition agreement was invalid. As the Court of Appeal observed, "The first challenged clause prohibited Edwards, for an 18-month period, from performing professional services of the type he had provided while at Andersen, for any client on whose account he had worked during 18 months prior to his termination. The second challenged clause prohibited Edwards, for a year after termination, from 'soliciting,' defined by the agreement as providing professional services to any client of Andersen's Los Angeles office." The agreement restricted Edwards from performing work for Andersen's Los Angeles clients and therefore restricted his ability to practice his accounting profession. * * * The noncompetition agreement that Edwards was required to sign before commencing employment with Andersen was therefore invalid because it restrained his ability to practice his profession.

B.   Ninth Circuit's Narrow-restraint Exception

Andersen asks this court to adopt the limited or "narrow-restraint" exception to section 16600 that the Ninth Circuit discussed in *Campbell v. Trustees of Leland Stanford Jr. Univ.* and that the trial court relied on in this case in order to uphold the noncompetition agreement. In *Campbell*, the Ninth Circuit acknowledged that California has rejected the common law "rule of reasonableness" with respect to restraints upon the ability to pursue a profession, but concluded that section 16600 "only makes illegal those restraints which preclude one from engaging in a lawful profession, trade, or business." The court remanded the case to the district court in order to allow the employee to prove that the noncompetition agreement at issue completely restrained him from practicing his "profession, trade, or business within the meaning of section 16600."

The confusion over the Ninth Circuit's application of section 16600 arose in a paragraph in *Campbell*, in which the court noted that some California courts have excepted application of section 16600 " 'where one is barred from pursuing only a small or limited part of the business, trade or profession.' " The Ninth Circuit cited two California cases that it believed may have carved out such an exception to section 16600. (*See Boughton v. Socony Mobil Oil Co.* [interpreting deed restriction on land use] and *King v. Gerold* [rejecting manufacturer's argument that clause not to produce its product after license expiration was not an illegal restraint under section 16600].) Andersen relies on those cases, citing them as the underpinnings of the Ninth Circuit's exception to section 16600, and urges the court to adopt their reasoning here. * * *

* * * Section 16600 is unambiguous, and if the Legislature intended the statute to apply only to restraints that were unreasonable or overbroad, it could have included language to that effect. We reject Andersen's contention that we should adopt a narrow-restraint exception to section 16600 and leave it to the Legislature, if it chooses, either to relax the

statutory restrictions or adopt additional exceptions to the prohibition-against-restraint rule under section 16600. * * *

DISPOSITION

We hold that the noncompetition agreement here is invalid under section 16600, and we reject the narrow-restraint exception urged by Andersen. Noncompetition agreements are invalid under section 16600 in California even if narrowly drawn, unless they fall within the applicable statutory exceptions of sections 16601, 16602, or 16602.5. * * *

DID YOU GET IT?

1.   How does this case compare to *Campbell Soup*?

2.   Why did the California Supreme Court refuse to enforce the non-competition agreement that Edwards entered into freely?

3.   Earlier cases in California recognized that the interest of a company in trying to protect its trade secrets was a "legitimate business interest" that could justify a reasonable non-compete agreement. Is such a rule still viable in light of the California Supreme Court's decision in *Andersen?*

C. THE INEVITABLE DISCLOSURE DOCTRINE

The inevitable disclosure doctrine, where applied, allows a court to enjoin an employee from working for a company when that employment will result in the disclosure of a former employer's trade secret information. Thus, it provides a powerful weapon under trade secret law because it permits an employer to do that which it would not otherwise be entitled to do under the auspices of employment law: restrict an employee without an express non-competition agreement. Indeed, it appears to go against the employment at-will doctrine, an important tenet of employment law. The employment at-will doctrine generally provides that without an agreement to the contrary, an employee may leave his or her employer at any time and for any reason. Similarly, an employer may terminate an employee at any time, for any reason.

The precise history of the inevitable disclosure doctrine is not entirely clear. Some traces of the doctrine appear in the early 1900s. *See, e.g., Eastman Kodak Co. v. Powers Film Products, Inc.*, 179 N.Y.S. 325 (N.Y. App. Div. 1919). The doctrine's contemporary re-birth is attributed to the Seventh Circuit decision in *Pepsico v. Redmond,* below. While *Pepsico* applied the doctrine under the UTSA, the earliest inevitable disclosure cases pre-date the UTSA. This may explain why the doctrine, where accepted, has been used in both UTSA and *Restatement of Torts* jurisdictions.

While traces of the inevitable disclosure doctrine can be found in cases from the early 1900s, it remains controversial and the subject of much debate. Some people view it as an evidentiary tool for proving the threatened disclosure or use of trade secrets. Others, including an increasing number of courts, see the doctrine as allowing for an impermissible implied non-compete agreement and question the wisdom of such a doctrine when express non-compete agreements are so closely scrutinized.

Although the doctrine can be used in cases where a non-competition agreement was executed, its use in these cases is not as controversial as in cases where the employer did not obtain an explicit non-competition agreement from the employee. In those cases, the doctrine creates a policy tension between the employee's right to move freely and pursue his or her livelihood and the employer's right to protect its trade secrets. Indeed, the doctrine appears to "distort the terms of the employment relationship and upset the balance which courts have attempted to achieve in construing non-compete agreements." *EarthWeb, Inc. v. Schlack,* 71 F.Supp.2d 299, 310–311 (1999).

Because of the social importance of employee mobility, courts tend to approach inevitable disclosure cases with great care. For this reason, application of the doctrine, and its acceptance by states, is mired in variations and inconsistencies. Whether or not a particular court will accept the doctrine is often tied to the state's policies regarding non-competition agreements. Many states have adopted the doctrine, some have rejected it outright, and others recognize it in only very limited circumstances. You will see, for instance, California's view reflected in *Whyte v. Schlage Lock* which follows after *Pepsico v. Redmond.* Accordingly, it is very important to understand the view of each particular state before attempting to prove trade secret misappropriation using the inevitable disclosure doctrine. *Pepsico* and *Whyte* represent the two extremes.

Where does the DTSA stand on the inevitable disclosure doctrine? When the legislation that would lead to the enactment of the DTSA was first proposed in 2014, opposition was voiced to the fact that it might displace state laws and principles concerning employee mobility, including the strong public policy of California as expressed in both *Arthur Andersen* and *Whyte.* Responding to such concerns, California Senator Dianne Feinstein proposed an amendment to the legislation that restricts the scope of injunctive relief. The critical language in 18 USC § 1836(b)(3)(A)(i) provides that injunctive relief cannot be granted:

(I) [to] prevent a person from entering into an employment relationship, and that conditions placed on such employment shall be based on evidence of threatened misappropriation and not merely on the information the person knows; or

(II) otherwise conflict with an applicable State law prohibiting restraints on the practice of a lawful profession, trade, or business.

This language was probably intended to reject the inevitable disclosure doctrine, but it is arguably ambiguous. It states that an employee cannot be enjoined from "entering into an employment relationship" with another employer, but does not address whether the presence of a noncompetition agreement would affect such an outcome. With respect to the inevitable disclosure doctrine, if an employee cannot be enjoined this would suggest that the doctrine cannot be applied. Yet, the phrase "conditions placed on . . . employment shall be based on evidence of threatened misappropriation and not merely on the information the person knows" could be read to support application of the inevitable disclosure doctrine when there is evidence of threatened misappropriation (as is the view of some state courts). Going forward, these are all issues that will be subject to interpretation by the federal courts as the DTSA is applied.

Reading Guidance

What facts played an important role in the court's analysis of the inevitable disclosure doctrine in this case?

PEPSICO, INC. V. REDMOND

United States Court of Appeals, Seventh Circuit, 1995.
54 F.3d 1262.

affirmed
— Ct. grant of injunction

* * *

FLAUM, CIRCUIT JUDGE.

Plaintiff PepsiCo, Inc., sought a preliminary injunction against defendants William Redmond and the Quaker Oats Company to prevent Redmond, a former PepsiCo employee, from divulging PepsiCo trade secrets and confidential information in his new job with Quaker and from assuming any duties with Quaker relating to beverage pricing, marketing, and distribution. The district court agreed with PepsiCo and granted the injunction. We now affirm that decision.

I.

The facts of this case lay against a backdrop of fierce beverage-industry competition between Quaker and PepsiCo, especially in "sports drinks" and "new age drinks." Quaker's sports drink, "Gatorade," is the dominant brand in its market niche. PepsiCo introduced its Gatorade rival, "All Sport," in March and April of 1994, but sales of All Sport lag far behind those of Gatorade. Quaker also has the lead in the new-age-drink category. Although PepsiCo has entered the market through joint ventures with the Thomas J. Lipton Company and Ocean Spray Cranberries, Inc., Quaker purchased Snapple Beverage Corp., a large new-age-drink maker, in late 1994. PepsiCo's products have about half of Snapple's market share. Both companies see 1995 as an important year for their products: PepsiCo has developed extensive plans to increase its market presence, while Quaker is trying to solidify its lead by integrating Gatorade and Snapple distribution. Meanwhile, PepsiCo and Quaker each face strong competition from Coca Cola Co., which has its own sports drink, "PowerAde," and which introduced its own Snapple-rival, "Fruitopia," in 1994, as well as from independent beverage producers.

William Redmond, Jr., worked for PepsiCo in its Pepsi-Cola North America division ("PCNA") from 1984 to 1994. Redmond became the General Manager of the Northern California Business Unit in June, 1993, and was promoted one year later to General Manager of the business unit covering all of California, a unit having annual revenues of more than 500 million dollars and representing twenty percent of PCNA's profit for all of the United States.

Redmond's relatively high-level position at PCNA gave him access to inside information and trade secrets. Redmond, like other PepsiCo management employees, had signed a confidentiality agreement with PepsiCo. That agreement stated in relevant part that he w[ould] not disclose at any time, to anyone other than officers or employees of [PepsiCo], or make use of, confidential information relating to the business of [PepsiCo] . . . obtained while in the employ of [PepsiCo], which shall not be generally known or available to the public or recognized as standard practices.

Donald Uzzi, who had left PepsiCo in the beginning of 1994 to become the head of Quaker's Gatorade division, began courting Redmond for Quaker in May, 1994. Redmond met in Chicago with Quaker officers in August, 1994, and on October 20, 1994, Quaker, through Uzzi, offered Redmond the position of Vice President—On Premise Sales for Gatorade. Redmond did not then accept the offer but continued to negotiate for more money. Throughout this time, Redmond kept his dealings with Quaker secret from his employers at PCNA.

On November 8, 1994, Uzzi extended Redmond a written offer for the position of Vice President-Field Operations for Gatorade and Redmond accepted. Later that same day, Redmond called William Bensyl, the Senior Vice President of Human Resources for PCNA, and told him that he had an offer from Quaker to become the Chief Operating Officer of the combined Gatorade and Snapple company but had not yet accepted it. Redmond also asked whether he should, in light of the offer, carry out his plans to make calls upon certain PCNA customers. Bensyl told Redmond to make the visits.

Redmond also misstated his situation to a number of his PCNA colleagues, including Craig Weatherup, PCNA's President and Chief Executive Officer, and Brenda Barnes, PCNA's Chief Operating Officer and Redmond's immediate superior. As with Bensyl, Redmond told them that he had been offered the position of Chief Operating Officer at Gatorade and that he was leaning "60/40" in favor of accepting the new position.

On November 10, 1994, Redmond met with Barnes and told her that he had decided to accept the Quaker offer and was resigning from PCNA. Barnes immediately took Redmond to Bensyl, who told Redmond that PepsiCo was considering legal action against him.

True to its word, PepsiCo filed this diversity suit on November 16, 1994, seeking a temporary restraining order to enjoin Redmond from assuming his duties at Quaker and to prevent him from disclosing trade secrets or confidential information to his new employer. The district court granted PepsiCo's request that same day but dissolved the order *sua sponte* two days later, after determining that PepsiCo had failed to meet its burden of establishing that it would suffer irreparable harm. The court found that PepsiCo's fears about Redmond were based upon a mistaken understanding of his new position at Quaker and that the likelihood that Redmond would improperly reveal any confidential information did not "rise above mere speculation."

From November 23, 1994, to December 1, 1994, the district court conducted a preliminary injunction hearing on the same matter. At the hearing, PepsiCo offered evidence of a number of trade secrets and confidential information it desired protected and to which Redmond was privy. First, it identified PCNA's "Strategic Plan," an annually revised document that contains PCNA's plans to compete, its financial goals, and its strategies for manufacturing, production, marketing, packaging, and distribution for the coming three years. Strategic Plans are developed by Weatherup and his staff with input from PCNA's general managers, including Redmond, and are considered highly confidential. The Strategic Plan derives much of its value from the fact that it is secret and competitors cannot anticipate PCNA's next moves. PCNA managers received the most recent Strategic Plan at a meeting in July, 1994, a meeting Redmond attended. PCNA also presented information at the meeting regarding its plans for Lipton ready-to-drink teas and for All Sport for 1995 and beyond, including new flavors and package sizes.

Second, PepsiCo pointed to PCNA's Annual Operating Plan ("AOP") as a trade secret. The AOP is a national plan for a given year and guides PCNA's financial goals, marketing plans, promotional event calendars, growth expectations, and operational changes in that year. The AOP, which is implemented by PCNA unit General Managers, including Redmond, contains specific information regarding all PCNA initiatives for the forthcoming year. The AOP bears a label that reads "Private and

Confidential—Do Not Reproduce" and is considered highly confidential by PCNA managers.

In particular, the AOP contains important and sensitive information about "pricing architecture"—how PCNA prices its products in the marketplace. Pricing architecture covers both a national pricing approach and specific price points for given areas. Pricing architecture also encompasses PCNA's objectives for All Sport and its new age drinks with reference to trade channels, package sizes and other characteristics of both the products and the customers at which the products are aimed. Additionally, PCNA's pricing architecture outlines PCNA's customer development agreements. These agreements between PCNA and retailers provide for the retailer's participation in certain merchandising activities for PCNA products. As with other information contained in the AOP, pricing architecture is highly confidential and would be extremely valuable to a competitor. Knowing PCNA's pricing architecture would allow a competitor to anticipate PCNA's pricing moves and underbid PCNA strategically whenever and wherever the competitor so desired. PepsiCo introduced evidence that Redmond had detailed knowledge of PCNA's pricing architecture and that he was aware of and had been involved in preparing PCNA's customer development agreements with PCNA's California and California-based national customers. Indeed, PepsiCo showed that Redmond, as the General Manager for California, would have been responsible for implementing the pricing architecture guidelines for his business unit.

PepsiCo also showed that Redmond had intimate knowledge of PCNA "attack plans" for specific markets. Pursuant to these plans, PCNA dedicates extra funds to supporting its brands against other brands in selected markets. To use a hypothetical example, PCNA might budget an additional $500,000 to spend in Chicago at a particular time to help All Sport close its market gap with Gatorade. Testimony and documents demonstrated Redmond's awareness of these plans and his participation in drafting some of them.

Finally, PepsiCo offered evidence of PCNA trade secrets regarding innovations in its selling and delivery systems. Under this plan, PCNA is testing a new delivery system that could give PCNA an advantage over its competitors in negotiations with retailers over shelf space and merchandising. Redmond has knowledge of this secret because PCNA, which has invested over a million dollars in developing the system during the past two years, is testing the pilot program in California.

Having shown Redmond's intimate knowledge of PCNA's plans for 1995, PepsiCo argued that Redmond would inevitably disclose that information to Quaker in his new position, at which he would have substantial input as to Gatorade and Snapple pricing, costs, margins, distribution systems, products, packaging and marketing, and could give Quaker an unfair advantage in its upcoming skirmishes with PepsiCo. Redmond and Quaker countered that Redmond's primary initial duties at Quaker as Vice President—Field Operations would be to integrate Gatorade and Snapple distribution and then to manage that distribution as well as the promotion, marketing and sales of these products. Redmond asserted that the integration would be conducted according to a pre-existing plan and that his special knowledge of PCNA strategies would be irrelevant. This irrelevance would derive not only from the fact that Redmond would be implementing pre-existing plans but also from the fact that PCNA and Quaker distribute their products in entirely different ways: PCNA's distribution system is vertically integrated (i.e., PCNA owns the system) and delivers its product directly to retailers, while Quaker ships its product to wholesalers and customer warehouses and relies on independent distributors. The defendants also pointed out that Redmond had signed a confidentiality agreement with Quaker preventing him from disclosing "any confidential information belonging to others," as well as the Quaker Code of Ethics, which prohibits employees from engaging in "illegal or improper acts to acquire a competitor's trade secrets." Redmond additionally promised at the hearing that should he be faced with a situation at Quaker that might involve the use or disclosure of PCNA information, he would seek advice from Quaker's in-house counsel and would refrain from making the decision.

PepsiCo responded to the defendants' representations by pointing out that the evidence did not show that Redmond would simply be implementing a business plan already in place. On the contrary, as of November, 1994, the plan to integrate Gatorade and Snapple distribution consisted of a single distributorship agreement and a two-page "contract terms summary." Such a basic plan would not lend itself to widespread application among the over 300 independent Snapple distributors. Since the integration process would likely face resistance from Snapple distributors and Quaker had no scheme to deal with this probability, Redmond, as the person in charge of the integration, would likely have a great deal of influence on the process. PepsiCo further argued that Snapple's 1995 marketing and promotion plans had not necessarily been completed prior to Redmond's joining Quaker, that Uzzi disagreed with portions of the Snapple plans, and that the plans were open to re-evaluation. Uzzi testified that the plan for integrating Gatorade and Snapple distribution is something that would happen in the future. Redmond would therefore likely have input in remaking these plans, and if he did, he would inevitably be making decisions with PCNA's strategic plans and 1995 AOP in mind.

Moreover, PepsiCo continued, diverging testimony made it difficult to know exactly what Redmond would be doing at Quaker. Redmond described his job as "managing the entire sales effort of Gatorade at the field level, possibly including strategic planning," and at least at one point considered his job to be equivalent to that of a Chief Operating Officer. Uzzi, on the other hand, characterized Redmond's position as "primarily and initially to restructure and integrate our-the distribution systems for Snapple and for Gatorade, as per our distribution plan" and then to "execute marketing, promotion and sales plans in the marketplace." Uzzi also denied having given Redmond detailed information about any business plans, while Redmond described such a plan in depth in an affidavit and said that he received the information from Uzzi. Thus, PepsiCo asserted, Redmond would have a high position in the Gatorade hierarchy, and PCNA trade secrets and confidential information would necessarily influence his decisions. Even if Redmond could somehow refrain from relying on this information, as he promised he would, his actions in leaving PCNA, Uzzi's actions in hiring Redmond, and the varying testimony regarding Redmond's new responsibilities, made Redmond's assurances to PepsiCo less than comforting.

On December 15, 1994, the district court issued an order enjoining Redmond from assuming his position at Quaker through May, 1995, and permanently from using or disclosing any PCNA trade secrets or confidential information. * * * The court, which completely adopted PepsiCo's position, found that Redmond's new job posed a clear threat of misappropriation of trade secrets and confidential information that could be enjoined under Illinois statutory and common law. The court also emphasized Redmond's lack of forthrightness both in his activities before accepting his job with Quaker and in his testimony as factors leading the court to believe the threat of misappropriation was real. This appeal followed.

II.

Both parties agree that the primary issue on appeal is whether the district court correctly concluded that PepsiCo had a reasonable likelihood of success on its various claims for trade secret misappropriation and breach of a confidentiality agreement. We review the district court's legal conclusions in issuing a preliminary injunction *de novo* and its factual determinations and balancing of the equities for abuse of discretion.

The Illinois Trade Secrets Act ("ITSA"), which governs the trade secret issues in this case, provides that a court may enjoin the "actual or threatened misappropriation" of a trade secret. A party seeking an injunction must therefore prove both the existence of a trade secret and the misappropriation. The defendants' appeal focuses solely on misappropriation; although the defendants only reluctantly refer to PepsiCo's marketing and distribution plans as trade secrets, they do not seriously contest that this information falls under the ITSA.

The question of threatened or inevitable misappropriation in this case lies at the heart of a basic tension in trade secret law. Trade secret law serves to protect "standards of commercial morality" and "encourage [ ] invention and innovation" while maintaining "the public interest in having free and open competition in the manufacture and sale of unpatented goods." Yet that same law should not prevent workers from pursuing their livelihoods when they leave their current positions. It has been said that federal age discrimination law does not guarantee tenure for older employees. Similarly, trade secret law does not provide a reserve clause for solicitous employers.

This tension is particularly exacerbated when a plaintiff sues to prevent not the actual misappropriation of trade secrets but the mere threat that it will occur. While the ITSA plainly permits a court to enjoin the threat of misappropriation of trade secrets, there is little law in Illinois or in this circuit establishing what constitutes threatened or inevitable misappropriation. * * *

* * * [A] plaintiff may prove a claim of trade secret misappropriation by demonstrating that defendant's new employment will inevitably lead him to rely on the plaintiff's trade secrets. The defendants are incorrect that Illinois law does not allow a court to enjoin the "inevitable" disclosure of trade secrets. Questions remain, however, as to what constitutes inevitable misappropriation and whether PepsiCo's submissions rise above those of the *Teradyne* and *AMP* plaintiffs and meet that standard. We hold that they do.

PepsiCo presented substantial evidence at the preliminary injunction hearing that Redmond possessed extensive and intimate knowledge about PCNA's strategic goals for 1995 in sports drinks and new age drinks. The district court concluded on the basis of that presentation that unless Redmond possessed an uncanny ability to compartmentalize information, he would necessarily be making decisions about Gatorade and Snapple by relying on his knowledge of PCNA trade secrets. It is not the "general skills and knowledge acquired during his tenure with" PepsiCo that PepsiCo seeks to keep from falling into Quaker's hands, but rather "the particularized plans or processes developed by [PCNA] and disclosed to him while the employer-employee relationship existed, which are unknown to others in the industry and which give the employer an advantage over his competitors." * * *

Admittedly, PepsiCo has not brought a traditional trade secret case, in which a former employee has knowledge of a special manufacturing process or customer list and can give a competitor an unfair advantage by transferring the technology or customers to that competitor. PepsiCo has not contended that Quaker has stolen the All Sport formula or its list of distributors. Rather PepsiCo has asserted that Redmond cannot help but rely on PCNA trade secrets as he helps plot Gatorade and Snapple's new course, and that these secrets will enable Quaker to achieve a substantial advantage by knowing exactly how PCNA will price, distribute, and market its sports drinks and new age drinks and being able to respond strategically. This type of trade secret problem may arise less often, but it nevertheless falls within the realm of trade secret protection under the present circumstances.

Quaker and Redmond assert that they have not and do not intend to use whatever confidential information Redmond has by virtue of his former employment. They point out that Redmond has already signed an agreement with Quaker not to disclose any trade secrets or confidential information gleaned from his earlier employment. They also note with regard to distribution systems that even if Quaker wanted to steal information about PCNA's distribution plans, they would be completely useless in attempting to integrate the Gatorade and Snapple beverage lines.

The defendants' arguments fall somewhat short of the mark. Again, the danger of misappropriation in the present case is not that Quaker threatens to use PCNA's secrets to create distribution systems or co-opt PCNA's advertising and marketing ideas. Rather, PepsiCo believes that Quaker, unfairly armed with knowledge of PCNA's plans, will be able to anticipate its distribution, packaging, pricing, and marketing moves. Redmond and Quaker even concede that Redmond might be faced with a decision that could be influenced by certain confidential information that he obtained while at PepsiCo. In other words, PepsiCo finds itself in the position of a coach, one of whose players has left, playbook in hand, to join the opposing team before the big game. Quaker and Redmond's protestations that their distribution systems and plans are entirely different from PCNA's are thus not really responsive.

The district court also concluded from the evidence that Uzzi's actions in hiring Redmond and Redmond's actions in pursuing and accepting his new job demonstrated a lack of candor on their part and proof of their willingness to misuse PCNA trade secrets, findings Quaker and Redmond vigorously challenge. The court expressly found that:

> Redmond's lack of forthrightness on some occasions, and out and out lies on others, in the period between the time he accepted the position with defendant Quaker and when he informed plaintiff that he had accepted that position leads the court to conclude that defendant Redmond could not be trusted to act with the necessary sensitivity and good faith under the circumstances in which the only practical verification that he was not using plaintiff's secrets would be defendant Redmond's word to that effect.

The facts of the case do not ineluctably dictate the district court's conclusion. Redmond's ambiguous behavior toward his PepsiCo superiors might have been nothing more than an attempt to gain leverage in employment negotiations. The discrepancy between Redmond's and Uzzi's comprehension of what Redmond's job would entail may well have been a simple misunderstanding. The court also pointed out that Quaker, through Uzzi, seemed to express an unnatural interest in hiring PCNA employees: all three of the people interviewed for the position Redmond ultimately accepted worked at PCNA. Uzzi may well have focused on recruiting PCNA employees because he knew they were good and not because of their confidential knowledge. Nonetheless, the district court, after listening to the witnesses, determined otherwise. That conclusion was not an abuse of discretion. * * *

Thus, when we couple the demonstrated inevitability that Redmond would rely on PCNA trade secrets in his new job at Quaker with the district court's reluctance to believe that Redmond would refrain from disclosing these secrets in his new position (or that Quaker would ensure Redmond did not disclose them), we conclude that the district court correctly decided that PepsiCo demonstrated a likelihood of success on its statutory claim of trade secret misappropriation. * * *

For the same reasons we concluded that the district court did not abuse its discretion in granting the preliminary injunction on the issue of trade secret misappropriation, * * *.

* * *

III.

Finally, Redmond and Quaker have contended in the alternative that the injunction issued against them is overbroad. They disagree in particular with the injunction's prohibition against Redmond's participation in the integration of the Snapple and Gatorade distribution systems. The defendants claim that whatever trade secret and confidential information Redmond has, that information is completely irrelevant to Quaker's integration task. They further argue that, because Redmond would only be implementing a plan already in place, the injunction is especially inappropriate. A district court ordinarily has wide latitude in fashioning injunctive relief, and we will restrict the breadth of an injunction only where the district court has abused its discretion. Nonetheless, a court abuses its discretion where the scope of injunctive relief "exceed[s] the extent of the plaintiff's protectible rights."

While the defendants' arguments are not without some merit, the district court determined that the proposed integration would require Redmond to do more than execute a plan someone else had drafted. It also found that Redmond's knowledge of PCNA's trade secrets and confidential information would inevitably shape that integration and that Redmond could not be trusted to avoid that conflict of interest. If the injunction permanently enjoined Redmond from assuming these duties at Quaker, the defendants' argument would be stronger. However, the injunction against

Redmond's immediate employment at Quaker extends no further than necessary and was well within the district court's discretion.

For the foregoing reasons, we affirm the district court's order enjoining Redmond from assuming his responsibilities at Quaker through May, 1995, and preventing him forever from disclosing PCNA trade secrets and confidential information.

AFFIRMED.

DID YOU GET IT?

1. What facts were relevant to the district court's analysis of whether Redmond could be trusted?

2. According to the court, what facts made Redmond's disclosure of PepsiCo's trade secrets "inevitable"?

3. What role did the confidentiality agreement play in this case?

4. How much information do you think Pepsico and Quaker Oats learned about each other's business plans during the litigation process?

Reading Guidance

How does this court's view on inevitable disclosure differ from the PepsiCo court's view?

WHYTE V. SCHLAGE LOCK CO.

California Court of Appeal, Fourth District, 2002.
101 Cal.App.4th 1443.

FYBEL, J.

The doctrine of inevitable disclosure permits a trade secret owner to prevent a former employee from working for a competitor despite the owner's failure to prove the employee has taken or threatens to use trade secrets. Under that doctrine, the employee may be enjoined by demonstrating the employee's new job duties will inevitably cause the employee to rely upon knowledge of the former employer's trade secrets. No published California decision has accepted or rejected the inevitable disclosure doctrine.

In this opinion, we reject the inevitable disclosure doctrine. We hold this doctrine is contrary to California law and policy because it creates an after-the-fact covenant not to compete restricting employee mobility.

This holding leads us to affirm the trial court's order denying the application of Schlage Lock Company (Schlage) for a preliminary injunction and granting the motion of J. Douglas Whyte (Whyte) and Kwikset Corporation (Kwikset) to dissolve a temporary restraining order. We reach the issue of inevitable disclosure because we conclude certain information Schlage seeks to protect does constitute trade secret, but the evidence presented below, viewed (as it must be) through the lens of the applicable standard of review, fails to establish actual or threatened misappropriation.

Facts

Schlage is a subsidiary of defendant Ingersoll Rand Company (Ingersoll Rand). Kwikset and Schlage manufacture and sell locks and related products. They are fierce competitors and vie intensely for shelf space at The Home Depot, which is the major seller of locks and alone accounts for 38 percent of Schlage's sales.

Whyte worked as Schlage's vice-president of sales and was responsible for sales to The Home Depot and other "big box" retailers such as HomeBase, Lowe's, Menard's, and Sears. Whyte signed a confidentiality agreement to protect Schlage's proprietary information and agreed to abide by Schlage's code of ethics, which forbids disclosure of confidential information for personal or noncompany uses. Whyte did not sign a covenant not to compete.

The Home Depot periodically conducts a review of its suppliers' product lines, prices, pricing and marketing concessions, and ability to deliver product. The Home Depot uses this "line review" to determine which products it will sell and which products to remove from its shelves. As part of the line review, The Home Depot usually asks vendors, such as Kwikset and Schlage, to submit proposals for pricing and marketing concessions and for the amount of promotional discounts and advertising funds, and to present information about product changes and new products.

The Home Depot conducted a line review with Schlage in February 2000. The Home Depot followed Schlage's recommendation to remove Kwikset's Titan brand of locks and to expand Schlage's presence on its shelves. Whyte participated in the line review and in drafting the line review agreement confirming the business relationship between Schlage and The Home Depot.

Whyte's sales abilities impressed Kwikset's president, Christopher Metz. Metz realized Whyte "was killing my team," and asked him "what it would take to get him to leave Ingersoll Rand. . . ." Whyte apparently got what it took, for he accepted a position with Kwikset on June 3, 2000. He did not resign from Schlage, however, until June 14—after participating on behalf of Schlage in confidential meetings with The Home Depot on June 5.

Whyte departed Schlage on June 16, 2000. Schlage was not pleased with Whyte, and the parting was not amicable. Schlage contends Whyte left to revenge belittling comments made by Schlage's president, Robert Steinman, and contends Whyte disavowed a confidentiality agreement, stole trade secret information (including a copy on computer disk of the line review agreement with The Home Depot), and lied about returning company information. Whyte denies taking any trade secrets, claims he reaffirmed the confidentiality agreement, and contends that in the exit interview on June 16 Steinman vowed to destroy his career.

On June 25, 2000, Whyte became Kwikset's vice-president of sales for national accounts. His job duties at Kwikset are substantially similar to those at Schlage: handling the lock products account for The Home Depot and other "big box retailers."

Proceedings Below

* * *

On July 11, 2000, Schlage filed a cross-complaint for unfair competition, misappropriation of trade secrets, breach of contract, breach of fiduciary duty, intentional and negligent interference with economic relations, and conversion. The next day, Schlage brought an ex parte application to restrain Whyte temporarily from using or disclosing trade secrets, pending a hearing on an application for a preliminary injunction. The court granted the ex parte application on July 25 and issued a temporary restraining order enjoining Whyte from using or disclosing 20 categories of trade secret information and ordering Whyte to return any such information in his possession. In response, Whyte turned over a kitchen-sized garbage bag of shredded documents and a Ziploc bag containing seven destroyed "floppy" disks and nine destroyed "zip" disks.

The court permitted expedited discovery, and rapid-fire discovery ensued. The results of this discovery, as well as declarations, exhibits, and briefs were submitted in support of and in opposition to the application for preliminary injunction. At the first hearing on the application, the court rejected the inevitable disclosure doctrine, but took the matter under submission to consider issuing an injunction based upon actual or threatened misappropriation.

The parties submitted additional declarations, exhibits, requests for judicial notice, and briefs before the next hearing. Whyte filed a motion to dissolve the temporary restraining order, which Schlage opposed.

At a second hearing on October 24, 2000, the court stated it would deny the application for an injunction. In announcing the ruling, the court stated the information Schlage sought to protect was not trade secret: "I don't think these things rise I don't think these are trade secrets." The court reflected, "I think Mr. Whyte should be able to go about his business," but added, "[c]ertainly if it is proven somehow that he used specific information, well, there is money damages."

Later on October 24 the court entered a minute order denying the preliminary injunction and granting Whyte's motion to dissolve the temporary restraining order without stating its reasons. Schlage then filed (and withdrew) a lengthy motion for reconsideration.

* * *

Has Schlage Sufficiently Identified Information
Constituting Trade Secrets?

A "trade secret" is "information, including a formula, pattern, compilation, program, device, method, technique, or process that: (1) Derives independent economic value, actual or potential, from not being generally known to the public or to other persons who can obtain economic value from its disclosure or use; and (2) Is the subject of efforts that are reasonable under the circumstances to maintain its secrecy." (Civ. Code, § 3426.1, subd. (d).)

Schlage sought to enjoin use of a range of alleged trade secrets, identified in paragraph 1 of the temporary restraining order as: "a. Information about Schlage's new products; b. Pricing of Schlage's products sold to its customers; c. Profit margins on Schlage's products sold to its customers; d. Schlage's costs in producing the products it sells to its customers; e. The Home Depot Line Review Documents; f. Pricing concessions made by Schlage to its customers; g. Promotional discounts made by Schlage to its customers; h. Advertising allowances made by Schlage to its customers; i. Volume rebates made by Schlage on its products to its customers; j. Marketing concessions made by Schlage to its customers; k. Schlage's market research data; l. Advertising strategy plans for calendar year 2000; m. Trade Discounts made by Schlage to its customers; n. Payment terms offered by Schlage to its customers and offered by Schlage's vendors/suppliers to Schlage; o. Rebate Incentives made by Schlage to its customers; p. Schlage's advertising, sales and promotion budgets; q. Finishing processes for new and existing Schlage products; r. Composite material process technologies (i.e., the unique composite materials used by Schlage in its products and the processes applied to those composite materials); s. Schlage's 1, 3 and 5 year strategic plan documents; t. Schlage's personnel information. . . ."

Whyte contends these "broad" categories of business information are not described with sufficient particularity to deserve trade secret protection. He also contends, as the trial court stated orally, that none of these categories of information constitutes trade secrets. Schlage argues (1) it has described its trade secrets with the required specificity and (2) the information Schlage has identified is trade secret and Schlage made reasonable efforts to maintain the information's secrecy. We discuss these contentions in turn, and conclude, based upon the evidence submitted, that some of the information Schlage sought to protect was trade secret.

Our decision regarding trade secret status is based upon the appellate record and is not a final adjudication on the merits. The ultimate

determination of trade secret status is subject to proof presented at trial.
* * *

[The court's analysis of the trade secret status of the information identified by the plaintiff, *Schlage*, is deleted.]

Did Whyte Engage in Actual or Threatened Misappropriation?

We turn to the issue whether Whyte engaged in actual or threatened misappropriation. The court may enjoin "[a]ctual or threatened misappropriation" of a trade secret. Civ. Code, § 3426.2, subd. (a). "Misappropriation" is, generally speaking, improper acquisition of a trade secret or its nonconsensual use or disclosure. Civ. Code, § 3426.1.

Schlage contends direct and circumstantial evidence established Whyte engaged in actual or threatened misappropriation, including evidence that Whyte had access to its trade secrets, vowed to get even with Schlage's president, concealed his planned departure from Schlage to attend confidential meetings with The Home Depot, renounced his confidentiality agreement, lied about returning confidential information, lied about destroying Schlage confidential information, retained a copy of The Home Depot line review agreement downloaded onto disk, sent an e-mail attaching a confidential report to his personal e-mail address, and accepted a position with Kwikset with duties identical to those at Schlage in order to use Schlage's confidential information.

Whyte denies these charges. He argues nobody at Schlage testified to having personal knowledge that he misappropriated or threatened to misappropriate trade secrets. Whyte points to evidence showing that before he resigned from Schlage, he destroyed everything he had containing Schlage confidential information, and that he downloaded The Home Depot line review agreement at the request of Schlage's vice-president of marketing and left the disk on the vice-president's desk. In any event, Whyte disclaims any knowledge of Schlage's manufacturing technologies and processes. Whyte asserts that Kwikset instructed him not to disclose any Schlage trade secrets. Several Kwikset managers testified Whyte had disclosed no Schlage trade secrets.

The evidence is neatly divided. Both sides marshal declarations, exhibits, and deposition transcripts in support of their respective positions. But we need not, and cannot, resolve the conflicts in the evidence or reweigh it. The applicable standard of review dictates that we "interpret the facts in the light most favorable to the prevailing party and indulge in all reasonable inferences in support of the trial court's order," even though the evidence is presented by declaration. The trial court judges the credibility of the declarations. Accordingly, we must interpret the facts favorably to the order denying a preliminary injunction, and therefore conclude the evidence established Whyte did not threaten to or actually misappropriate Schlage's trade secrets.

We emphasize our decision is not a final adjudication of the issue of actual or threatened misappropriation and we have serious concerns over evidence in the record suggesting Whyte took Schlage's trade secrets or destroyed evidence. We are constrained, however, by the applicable standard of review and our limited role as a reviewing court to view the facts in favor of the trial court's order.

Is the Inevitable Disclosure Doctrine the Law of California?

As an alternative to proof of actual or threatened misappropriation, Schlage urges us to reverse and enjoin Whyte from working for the lock division of Kwikset under the doctrine of inevitable disclosure. Under the doctrine of inevitable disclosure, "a plaintiff may prove a claim of trade secret misappropriation by demonstrating that defendant's new employment will inevitably lead him to rely on the plaintiff's trade secrets." *PepsiCo, Inc. v. Redmond.* The inevitable disclosure doctrine results in an injunction prohibiting employment, not just use of trade secrets. The doctrine's justification is that unless the employee has "an uncanny ability to compartmentalize information" the employee will necessarily rely—consciously or subconsciously—upon knowledge of the former employer's trade secrets in performing his or her new job duties.

Courts applying the doctrine of inevitable disclosure have considered the degree of similarity between the employee's former and current positions, the degree of competition between the former and current employers, the current employer's efforts to safeguard the former employer's trade secrets, and the former employee's "lack of forthrightness both in his activities before accepting his job . . . and in his testimony."

PepsiCo is the leading case on inevitable disclosure. There, PepsiCo sought to enjoin its former employee, William Redmond, from working for a competitor, the Quaker Oats Company. PepsiCo and Quaker Oats were fierce competitors, particularly in "sports drinks" and "new age drinks." Redmond's high position at PepsiCo gave him access to its trade secrets regarding these products, including strategic plans, product innovations, "pricing architecture," selling and delivery innovations, and marketing " 'attack plans.' " To protect these trade secrets, PepsiCo had Redmond sign a confidentiality agreement. Quaker Oats courted Redmond, and he ultimately accepted a high-level position in that company. When Redmond resigned from PepsiCo, it immediately sought and obtained an injunction preventing him from assuming his duties at Quaker Oats.

PepsiCo did not contend Quaker Oats actually stole trade secrets, but asserted Redmond "cannot help but rely on [PepsiCo's] trade secrets as he helps plot [Quaker Oats'] new course." The Seventh Circuit agreed and applied the Illinois Trade Secrets Act to affirm an injunction preventing Redmond from working for Quaker Oats. The Seventh Circuit first concluded that Illinois law permits a court to enjoin employment based upon inevitable disclosure of trade secrets. The Seventh Circuit then agreed with the district court finding that "unless Redmond possessed an uncanny ability to compartmentalize information, he would necessarily be making decisions about [Quaker Oats' products] by relying on his knowledge of [PepsiCo's] trade secrets." Such inevitability of disclosure, coupled with Redmond's and Quaker Oats' "lack of candor on their part and proof of their willingness to misuse [PepsiCo's] trade secrets," led the Seventh Circuit to affirm the injunction barring Redmond from working for Quaker Oats.

Schlage asserts the facts here are "strikingly similar" to *PepsiCo*'s, and we are inclined to agree. Schlage and Kwikset are fierce competitors; Whyte's job duties at Kwikset are virtually identical to those he had at Schlage; Whyte knew of Schlage's trade secrets (in particular, those important to The Home Depot account); Whyte signed a confidentiality agreement; and, if we are to believe Schlage's evidence, Whyte was not "forthright" with Schlage. Whyte's evidence did show Kwikset made efforts to safeguard Schlage's trade secrets. Nonetheless, the similarity between this case and *PepsiCo* and other inevitable disclosure cases means we cannot distinguish those cases on the facts.

No published California decision has accepted or rejected the doctrine of inevitable disclosure. Two federal district courts in California recently concluded inevitable disclosure is not the law of this state. These federal decisions do not, of course, establish the law of the State of California or bind its courts. We are free to consider the inevitable disclosure doctrine, and we reject it.

* * *

The decisions rejecting the inevitable disclosure doctrine correctly balance competing public policies of employee mobility and protection of trade secrets. The inevitable disclosure doctrine permits an employer to enjoin the former employee without proof of the employee's actual or threatened use of trade secrets based upon an inference (based in turn upon circumstantial evidence) that the employee inevitably will use his or her knowledge of those trade secrets in the new employment. The result is not merely an injunction against the use of trade secrets, but an injunction restricting employment.

Business and Professions Code section 16600 generally prohibits covenants not to compete, and California public policy strongly favors employee mobility protects a person's right to "follow any of the common occupations of life" (*Continental Car-Na-Var Corp. v. Moseley*) and to pursue the " 'business or profession he may choose.' " We agree the doctrine of inevitable disclosure "creates a de facto covenant not to compete" and "runs[s] counter to the strong public policy in California favoring employee mobility." *Bayer Corp. v. Roche Molecular Systems, Inc.;* accord, *Globespan,*

Inc. v. O'Neill; PSC, Inc. v. Reiss [inevitable disclosure doctrine binds employee to implied-in-fact restrictive covenant that "runs counter to New York's strong public policy against such agreements"].

* * * The chief ill in the covenant not to compete imposed by the inevitable disclosure doctrine is its after-the-fact nature: The covenant is imposed *after* the employment contract is made and therefore alters the employment relationship without the employee's consent. When, as here, a confidentiality agreement is in place, the inevitable disclosure doctrine "in effect convert[s] the confidentiality agreement into such a covenant [not to compete]." *PSC, Inc. v. Reiss.* Or, as another federal court put it, "a court should not allow a plaintiff to use inevitable disclosure as an after-the-fact noncompete agreement to enjoin an employee from working for the employer of his or her choice."

The doctrine of inevitable disclosure thus rewrites the employment agreement and "such retroactive alterations distort the terms of the employment relationship and upset the balance which courts have attempted to achieve in construing non-compete agreements." *EarthWeb, Inc. v. Schlack.* The result, as the *EarthWeb* court explained, is "the imperceptible shift in bargaining power that necessarily occurs upon the commencement of an employment relationship marked by the execution of a confidentiality agreement. When that relationship eventually ends, the parties' confidentiality agreement may be wielded as a restrictive covenant, depending on how the employer views the new job its former employee has accepted. This can be a powerful weapon in the hands of an employer; the risk of litigation alone may have a chilling effect on the employee." *Id.* As a result of the inevitable disclosure doctrine, the employer obtains the benefit of a contractual provision it did not pay for, while the employee is bound by a court-imposed contract provision with no opportunity to negotiate terms or consideration.

Schlage and Whyte did not agree upon a covenant not to compete. We decline to impose one, however restricted in scope, by adopting the inevitable disclosure doctrine.

Lest there be any doubt about our holding, our rejection of the inevitable disclosure doctrine is complete. If a covenant not to compete (which would include, for example, a nonsolicitation clause), is part of the employment agreement, the inevitable disclosure doctrine cannot be invoked to supplement the covenant, alter its meaning, or make an otherwise unenforceable covenant enforceable. California law concerning enforcement of noncompetition agreements, not the inevitable disclosure doctrine, would measure the covenant's scope, meaning, and validity. Our opinion does not change that law. Under the circumstances presented in this case, an employer might prevent disclosure of trade secrets through, for example, an agreed-upon and reasonable nonsolicitation clause that is narrowly drafted for the purpose of protecting trade secrets. Thus, regardless whether a covenant not to compete is part of the employment agreement, the inevitable disclosure doctrine cannot be used as a substitute for proving actual or threatened misappropriation of trade secrets. * * *

Disposition

The order denying Schlage's application for a preliminary injunction and granting Whyte's motion to dissolve the temporary restraining order is affirmed. Whyte and Kwikset shall recover their costs on appeal.

DID YOU GET IT?

1. How does this court distinguish *PepsiCo v. Redmond*?

2. According to this court, is the rejection of the inevitable disclosure doctrine in California based solely on California's view on the enforcement of non-competition agreements?

3. If you were the plaintiff trade secret owner in a case with similar facts in California, how could you enhance your chances of success on a trade secret misappropriation claim?

Food for Thought

Now that you have read two cases concerning the inevitable disclosure doctrine (one which applied it and the other that rejected it), which approach do you think is correct? Why? Does your analysis differ depending upon whether you view trade secret misappropriation as a form of unfair competition or as a property tort?

D. SPECIAL ISSUE: WHO OWNS TRADE SECRETS CREATED BY AN EMPLOYEE?

When an individual goes to work for a company, he or she will often be provided with confidential information. As you have seen throughout this book, an employer's act of sharing trade secret information with an employee can create an implied duty of confidentiality, provided that the employee has notice of the employer's interest in confidentiality. At times, however, the information that a company claims as its trade secrets was not provided by the employer but, instead, was created by the employee. In these cases, a question arises about who owns the information that was created by the employee.

If you have taken a course on copyright law, you know that there are sections of the U.S. Copyright Act that specify the ownership of copyrights in works of authorship that are created by employees and independent contractors. Under U.S. copyright law, the creator of a work of authorship generally owns the copyrights therein. Exceptions to the general rule exist for works of joint authorship, works created by employees, and for certain specially commissioned works. *See* 15 U.S.C. § 201. There are no similar provisions in the UTSA or DTSA. Rather, the ownership of trade secrets (and other inventions) created by employees is governed either by state common law, state statutes, or by an enforceable agreement between the parties (typically labeled an "Invention Assignment Agreement").

Because "technical trade secrets" often take the form of inventions that may be patentable (as opposed to other types of trade secrets that are comprised of unpatentable ideas or information), many of the cases that have addressed the question of the ownership of trade secret information have arisen in patent cases. Unlike U.S. copyright law, U.S. patent law does not include provisions concerning the ownership of inventions. Rather, the question of patent ownership is governed largely by common law. As explained in the patent case of *Banks v. Unisys Corporation*:

> The general rule is that an individual owns the patent rights to the subject matter of which he is an inventor, even though he conceived it or reduced it to practice in the course of his employment. There are two exceptions to this rule: first, an employer owns an employee's invention if the employee is a party to an express contract to that effect; second, where an employee is hired to invent something or solve a particular problem, the property of the invention related to this effort may belong to the employer.

228 F.3d 1357, 1359 (2000).

While the particulars of each state's laws may vary, generally the key to determining whether an employer owns the ideas, inventions, and information that an employee creates concerns the nature of the employee's work. The *Restatement (Third) of Unfair Competition* sums up the rules governing the ownership of trade secrets as follows:

RESTATEMENT (THIRD) OF UNFAIR COMPETITION
Section 42, Comment e

e.   Allocation of ownership between employers and employees. The law of agency has established rules governing the ownership of valuable information created by employees during the course of an employment relationship. *See* Restatement, Second, Agency § 397. In the absence of a contrary agreement, the law ordinarily assigns ownership of an invention or idea to the person who conceives it. However, valuable information that is the product of an employee's assigned duties is owned by the employer, even when the information results from the application of the employee's personal knowledge or skill:

If, however, one is employed to do experimental work for inventive purposes, it is inferred ordinarily, although not so specifically agreed, that patentable ideas arrived at through the experimentation are to be owned by the employer. This is even more clear where one is employed to achieve a particular result which the invention accomplishes. On the other hand, if one is employed merely to do work in a particular line in which he is an expert, there is no inference that inventions which he makes while so working belong to the employer. Restatement, Second, Agency § 397, comment a.

An employee is ordinarily entitled to claim ownership of patents and trade secrets developed outside of the scope of the employee's assigned duties, even if the invention or idea relates to the employer's business and was developed using the employer's time, personnel, facilities, or equipment. In the latter circumstances, however, the employer is entitled to a "shop right"—an irrevocable, nonexclusive, royalty-free license to use the innovation. Similarly, employees retain ownership of information comprising their general skill, knowledge, training, and experience. *See* Comment d. The allocation of ownership between employers and employees is also subject to alteration by contract. *See* Comment g.

———

In the 1933 case of *U.S. v. Dubilier Condenser Corp.*, the United States Supreme Court explained the "hired to invent" principle and its limitations as follows:

One employed to make an invention, who succeeds, during his term of service, in accomplishing that task, is bound to assign to his employer any patent obtained. The reason is that he has only produced that which he was employed to invent. His invention is the precise subject of the contract of employment. A term of the agreement necessarily is that what he is paid to produce belongs to his paymaster. On the other hand, if the employment be general, albeit it covers a field of labor and effort in the performance of which the employee conceived the invention for which he obtained a patent, the contract is not so broadly construed as to require an assignment of the patent. * * *

The reluctance of courts to imply or infer an agreement by the employee to assign his patent is due to a recognition of the peculiar nature of the act of invention, which consists neither in finding out the laws of nature, nor in fruitful research as to the operation of natural laws, but in discovering how those laws may be utilized or applied for some beneficial purpose, by a process, a device, or a machine. It is the result of an inventive act, the birth of an idea and its reduction to practice; the product of original thought; a concept demonstrated to be true by practical application or embodiment in tangible form.

Though the mental concept is embodied or realized in a mechanism or a physical or chemical aggregate, the embodiment is not the invention and is not the subject of a patent. This distinction between the idea and its application in practice is the basis of the rule that employment merely to design or to construct or to devise methods of manufacture is not the same as employment to invent. Recognition of the nature of the act of invention also defines the limits of the so-called shop right, which, shortly stated, is that, where a servant, during his hours of employment, working with his master's materials and appliances, conceives and perfects an invention for which he obtains a patent, he must accord his master a nonexclusive right to practice the invention. This is an application of equitable principles. Since the servant uses his master's time, facilities, and materials to attain a concrete result, the latter is in equity entitled to use that which embodies his own property and to duplicate it as often as he may find occasion to employ similar appliances in his business. But the employer in such a case has no equity to demand a conveyance of the invention, which is the original conception of the employee alone, in which the employer had no part.

289 U.S. 178 (1933).

Food for Thought
Note how the foregoing quote refers to "technical trade secrets" and the value of an inventive mind. Do you think the same rules of ownership should apply to business information?

The first case that follows explores the ownership question; the second examines the reasonableness of an Invention Assignment Agreement.

Reading Guidance

Where an employee has not invented the trade secret but developed it in the context of the business, what rules apply?

NORTHERN ELECTRIC CO., INC. V. TORMA

Court of Appeals of Indiana, Fifth District, 2004.
819 N. E. 2d 417.

* * *

RILEY, JUDGE.

* * *

Northern Electric is a family-owned electric motor repair shop in South Bend, Indiana, employing approximately thirty employees. Northern Electric's president, Howard Dosmann (Dosmann), is also its sole shareholder. During the 1980s, Northern Electric began repairing servo motors for its customers. Unlike conventional motors, servo motors rely on a closed loop electrical system to achieve the precise velocities and positions required by manufacturing machinery used in robotic, computer numeric control, and other similarly sophisticated applications. Electrical signals travel between the servo motor, feedback devices, and a drive that instructs the motor to turn and stop in precise increments. While a malfunction in regular electric motors can often be diagnosed by visually inspecting the motor, repairing a computer malfunction in a servo motor requires between ten and fifteen bits of data that differ for each make and model.

Northern Electric continued to repair servo motors until the mid-1990s, when a customer's servo motor was not properly repaired. Torma, who had been an employee since 1990, approached Dosmann, seeking permission to continue the repair service for servo motors. Dosmann consented and placed Torma in charge of the servo motor department. While Torma supervised the department, the servo motor repair service grew, eventually accounting for approximately 33% of Northern Electric's business by the time Torma left the company.

As was his custom in previous positions, Torma assembled motor repair data in a spiral notebook. The compiled information included readings and settings that aid servo motor repair. He gathered the data from readings he took or discerned during the actual repair of the motor, and from data collected by other Northern Electric employees. Additionally, Torma also gained information from personal contacts with representatives of manufacturers and other servo motor shops, manuals, service bulletins maintained by Northern Electric, and various internet sites. As supervisor of the servo motor department, he directed the other technicians to similarly record and maintain data readings. This compilation of information proved helpful in repairing servo motors for Northern Electric's customers.

Although Torma initially maintained his data in a spiral notebook, after a while, he adopted a daily practice of assembling motor readings and other useful repair information on a photocopied job order, and entering the data into a word processing file, organized by manufacturer, stored on his home computer. He discarded the photocopied job order after he entered the data in his computer. He saved this compilation of data on his home computer and on a floppy disk (later on CD–ROM) which he used every day at work. His compilation is the result of seven years of data collection for more than 650 servo motors. He protected the data by locking it in his 500-pound toolbox, keeping it with him, or taking it home. Even though he allowed other Northern Electric employees to copy certain data, he never permitted another technician access to his entire compilation.

In June of 2002, Torma terminated his employment with Northern Electric after he was unable to reach an agreement with his employer on his compensation and duties. Prior to his resignation, Dosmann had unsuccessfully pursued a non-compete agreement with Torma. Upon leaving the company, Torma refused to return the data he had gathered during the course of his employment with Northern Electric. After his departure, Torma began working at Hy-Tech, a competing servo motor repair company he had founded before resigning his position at Northern Electric.

On July 15, 2002, Northern Electric filed a request for a temporary restraining order and temporary and permanent injunctions against Torma. During a hearing on the same day, the trial court ordered Torma to return all prototypes obtained by him while in Northern Electric's employment, to provide Northern Electric with a copy of all servo motor specifications developed while employed, and to keep complete records as to any use of these specifications by him and any economic advantage he derives from such use. From October 15 through October 17, 2003, a bench trial was held on Northern Electric's Complaint, alleging a violation of the Indiana Trade Secret Act, statutory conversion, and breach of fiduciary duty. On January 16, 2004, the trial court entered judgment in favor of Torma and Hy-Tech and issued Findings of Fact and Conclusions of Law.

Northern Electric now appeals. Additional facts will be provided as necessary.

DISCUSSION

Data Compilation

Northern Electric first contends several of the trial court's conclusions with regard to the data compilation [are in error]. Specifically, Northern Electric asserts that the trial court erred in concluding:

(1) that Torma is the owner of the data compilation stored on the computer discs;

(2) that the data compilation is not entitled to trade secret protection;

* * *

Ownership of the Compilation

Northern Electric first contends that the trial court clearly erred by concluding that it did not own the servo motor repair data collected by its agent, Torma. Specifically, Northern Electric asserts that, based on agency principles, the company owns the data compilation because Torma collected the data as part of his assigned duties as supervisor of the servo motor repair department. Conversely, Torma argues that unless an agreement to the contrary exists, the creator of the valuable information remains the owner of the information.

The question of whether an employee owns the compilation of data assembled in his own time but based upon raw data collected at his place of employment presents us with an issue of first impression in Indiana. In support of their respective arguments, both parties rely on the Restatements and out-of-state case law. In particular, the Restatement (Third) of Unfair Competition § 42 cmt. e., states with regard to allocation of ownership between employers and employees:

> [t]he law of agency has established rules governing the ownership of valuable information created by employees during the course of an employment relationship. In the absence of a contrary agreement, the law ordinarily assigns ownership of an invention or an idea to the person who conceives it. However, *valuable information that is the product of an employee's assigned duties is owned by the employer, even when the information results from the application of the employee's personal knowledge or skill:*
>
>> If however, one is employed to do experimental work for inventive purposes, it is inferred ordinarily, although not so specifically agreed, that patentable ideas arrived at through the experimentation are to be owned by the employer. This is even more clear where one is employed to achieve a particular result which the invention accomplishes. On the other hand, if one is employed merely to do work in a particular line in which he is an expert, there is no inference that inventions which he makes while so working belong to the employer.

Comment e further clarifies that "[a]lthough the rules governing ownership of valuable information created during an employment relationship are most frequently applied to inventions, the rules are also applicable to information such as customer lists, marketing ideas, and other valuable business information. *If an employee collects or develops such information as part of the assigned duties of the employment, the information is owned by the employer.*" (emphasis added). * * *

Clearly building upon the Restatements, the case law factually focuses on an employee's position and scope of assignment, including all reasonable inferences therefrom, to decide the issue of ownership of information. It is apparent that "assigned duties" is the decisive element, regardless of when the employee actually performs them.

In the instant case, our review of the trial court's conclusion, that Torma owns the data compilation, leaves us with a firm conviction that a mistake was made. Without citing any legal principle or authority for its conclusion, the trial court based its decision on the following findings: (1) Torma started and supervised Northern Electric's servo motor repair division; (2) during the repair of servo motors, Torma collected data from the servo motor that would aid him in diagnosing future malfunctions and formulating repair strategies; and (3) Torma and the other technicians made the data each collected and maintained individually available to one another for use in actual servo motor repair projects. Thus, by reaching its conclusion that Torma owned the data compilation, the trial court implicitly rejected the notion that data assembly is part and parcel of Torma's position.

Nonetheless, we are not persuaded. Overwhelming evidence presented at trial, including the trial court's own findings, establishes that data compilation falls squarely within the scope of a servo motor repair technician's assigned duties. Testimonial evidence by Torma indicates that virtually all information assembled in the data compilation was obtained during his working hours at Northern Electric. In particular, Torma testified that he gathered data from readings he took or discerned during the actual repair of the motors. He further stated that he would copy information out of manufacturers' manuals, received and maintained by Northern Electric, by using the company's copier. If the data was not readily available in the manual, Torma clarified that he would consult the manufacturers' internet site.

The evidence supports that initially Torma maintained this data collection in spiral notebooks; however, after a while he adopted a daily practice of assembling motor readings and other useful repair information on a photocopied job order. Torma testified that during his own time he entered all this assembled data into a word processing file, organized by manufacturer, and stored it on his home computer. He clarified that he would consult his compilation, which is the result of seven years of data collection for more than 650 servo motors, every day at work. During testimony, he not only admitted that ninety percent of his time dedicated to generating data was performed at work but also conceded that the data information compiled in the notebook belonged to Northern Electric.

Further review of the record shows that, as supervisor of the servo motor repair department, he directed the other employees to similarly collect, record, and maintain data readings. Employee Bill Alerding stated that Torma not only maintained his own data, but also requested a copy of the other employees' data when they worked on a servo motor unfamiliar to Torma. In sum, every trial witness, including Torma, testified to the importance of collecting servo motor data in the course of performing repairs. Everyone acknowledges that the quality of the maintained data resulted in more efficient and rapid repairs in the future. Moreover, Northern Electric's Vice President of Operations, Rick Meece, testified that during several conversations with Torma, they investigated the possibility of making the data collection readily accessible to all employees in the servo motor repair department by storing it on the company's server. The record reflects that Torma refused, pleading lack of time and computer illiteracy.

Nevertheless, Torma now contends that his data compilation should be characterized as an "invention" pursuant to § 397 cmt. a of the Restatement. Based on this section of the Restatement, Torma maintains that since he created the valuable compilation without being specifically assigned to do so by Northern Electric, he now owns the entire compilation. We find this argument to be without merit. The issue in the instant case does not revolve around the idea or invention of compiling the information according to the servo motor's manufacturer; instead, Northern Electric contests the ownership of the underlying raw data used in the compilation. From the evidence before us, it is apparent that this raw data resulted from readings of servo motors taken during repairs at Northern Electric and information collected from manuals and the internet. The record further reflects that collecting repair data is a standard practice in the industry, and compilations are even bought and sold. We find the fact that Torma might have organized the raw data more comprehensively does not amount to the sort of unanticipated invention or intellectual virtuosity that § 397 of the Restatement is intended to protect.

Therefore, mindful of the parties' respective arguments and the evidence presented at trial, we agree with Northern Electric that Torma's harvesting of raw data during work hours and the subsequent compilation of harvested data in his home computer during his own time does not make the data his. It is clear that but for Torma's employment at Northern Electric, he would not have had access to the wealth of servo motor repair data that he assembled in his compilation. Using his employer's facilities and opportunities, Torma not only supervised the motor servo repair department but was also instrumental in its success by directing all employees to collect and maintain data generated from the servo motors. This generated data resulted in more efficient diagnoses and formulation of repair strategies. Thus, given the facts before us, along with all reasonable inferences and applicable case law, we come to the opposite conclusion that Torma's compilation of Northern Electric's servo motor repair data clearly arose out of his assigned duties as supervisor of the department. Accordingly, we find that the trial court's conclusion is contrary to law and hold that Northern Electric is the owner of the data collected by Torma. * * *

Reversed.

DID YOU GET IT?

1. What was the defendant's argument as to why he owned the trade secrets in this case?

2. What facts were most persuasive to the court in ruling in favor of the employer, Northern Electric Co.?

3. What common law rules guided the court's reasoning in this case?

> ### Food for Thought
>
> *Do you think an employer should have trade secret rights in social media accounts, e.g. Twitter accounts, created and maintained by an employee for employment related purposes? If so, which aspects of such accounts do you think are best suited for trade secret protection?*

————

Because the various common law doctrines regarding ownership can be vague and nuanced and depend greatly upon the facts of each case, the simplest way to allocate ownership rights between an employer and its employees is by contract. Employers who are engaged in research and development efforts typically require employees to sign contracts by which the employees assign all inventions designed or conceived during the period of employment to the employer. However, for many of the same reasons that courts will closely scrutinize the reasonableness of Non-compete Agreements, courts will also scrutinize the reasonableness of Invention Assignment Agreements.

Questions concerning the reasonableness of Invention Assignment Agreements typically focus on the nature and the scope of the inventions that are covered by the agreement. Of particular concern to employees who are required to sign such agreements, and to the courts who are asked to enforce them, are provisions which require employees to assign inventions that do not relate to their scope of work or that are conceived of and developed after the subject employment terminates (sometimes referred to as "hold-over" or "claw-back" agreements).

Some states have statutes which place limits on the enforceability of such assignment contracts. *See* California Labor Code § 2870–72 (2015) and Minnesota Statutes § 181.78 (2015). California Labor Code § 2870 states the basic principle of California law as follows:

(a) Any provision in an employment agreement which provides that an employee shall assign, or offer to assign, any of his or her rights in an invention to his or her employer shall not apply to an invention that the employee developed entirely on his or her own time without using the employer's equipment, supplies, facilities, or trade secret information except for those inventions that either:

(1) Relate at the time of conception or reduction to practice of the invention to the employer's business, or actual or demonstrably anticipated research or development of the employer; or

(2) Result from any work performed by the employee for the employer.

(b) To the extent a provision in an employment agreement purports to require an employee to assign an invention otherwise excluded from being required to be assigned under subdivision (a), the provision is against the public policy of this state and is unenforceable.

As the next case demonstrates, in the absence of a statute like California's, courts must apply law and equitable principles to determine the reasonableness of Invention Assignment Agreements.

Reading Guidance

How should a court determine whether a former employee's Invention Assignment Agreement is enforceable?

INGERSOLL-RAND CO. V. CIAVATTA

Supreme Court of New Jersey, 1988.
110 N.J. 609.

* * *

GARIBALDI, JUDGE.

The issue in this appeal is the enforceability of an employee invention "holdover" agreement. Specifically, the issue presented is whether a "holdover" clause requiring an employee to assign a post-termination invention that does not involve an employer's trade secret or proprietary information is enforceable. The products relevant to this dispute are a new type of friction stabilizer, which defendant invented and patented, and a split-set friction stabilizer, manufactured and distributed by plaintiff. Both devices are used in the mining industry to prevent the fall of rock from the roof and walls of underground mines. * * *

The development of Ingersoll-Rand's roof stabilizer was well documented in the industry. Ingersoll-Rand, beginning in the mid-1970s, extensively marketed and promoted the product through advertisements, pamphlets, and technical articles. These publications thoroughly detailed the stabilizer's configuration, composition, method of operation, test results, performance capabilities, and sales information. The technology employed to manufacture the device is over fifty years old.

The split set stabilizer has been a very successful product for Ingersoll-Rand. It represented over half of all stabilizer units sold in the United States for metal and non-metal mines, with over one million units sold in 1984. Ingersoll-Rand controls over ninety percent of the sub-market for friction stabilizers. Ingersoll-Rand has never reduced the price of the split set below list in response to competition; and prior to 1983, when the defendant's company, Safeguard Energy Products, Inc., entered the market, only one other competitor was in the submarket: Atlas Copco Corporation. * * *

Defendant, Armand Ciavatta, is a 57-year-old engineer. He was graduated from the Rhode Island School of Design in 1953 with a Bachelor of Science degree in machine design. Subsequently, he took classes in mining, tunneling, and heavy construction engineering as well as graduate business classes. Since 1950, Ciavatta has held a number of technical engineering positions involving a variety of engineering principles, including: working for a division of General Signal Corporation on instrumentation used in weight and volume measurement; conducting quality control tests for instrumentation used in the first commercial nuclear reactor; as chief project engineer for the Revere Corporation of America where he worked with transducers and other force-measuring devices; and as Vice President of Engineering and Quality Control for Iona Corporation, where he was responsible for engineering development and testing of the company's line of kitchen and consumer appliances. * * *

Ciavatta joined the Millers Falls Division of Ingersoll-Rand as Director of Engineering and Quality Control in 1972. From 1972 to 1974, Ciavatta was responsible for quality control and materials management in the production of hand and electric tools. In the fall of 1974, the company terminated his employment in the Millers Falls Division, at which time he became Program Manager with Ingersoll-Rand Research, Inc. As a condition of his employment with Ingersoll-Rand Research, he executed an "Agreement Relating to Proprietary Matter" (Proprietary Agreement) in which he agreed, in pertinent part:

   1.   To assign and I hereby do assign, to the COMPANY, its successors and assigns, my entire right, title and interest in and to all inventions, copyrights and/or designs I have made

or may hereafter make, conceive, develop or perfect, either solely or jointly with others either

(a) during the period of such employment, if such inventions, copyrights and/or designs are related, directly or indirectly, to the business of, or to the research or development work of the COMPANY or its affiliates, or

(b) with the use of the time, materials or facilities of the COMPANY or any of its affiliates, or

(c) within one year after termination of such employment if conceived as a result of and is attributable to work done during such employment and relates to a method, substance, machine, article of manufacture or improvements therein within the scope of the business of the COMPANY or any of its affiliates.

Additionally, in Paragraph 4 of the Agreement, Ciavatta agreed:

4. Not to divulge, either during my employment or thereafter to any person, agency, firm or corporation, any secret, confidential or other proprietary information of the COMPANY or any of its affiliates which I may obtain through my employment without first obtaining written permission from the COMPANY.

* * *

While employed by Ingersoll-Rand Research as a Program Manager from October 1974 through March 1978, Ciavatta worked on a variety of development projects, other than those relevant to this litigation * * *. As a result of his participation in these development projects, Ciavatta became interested in underground mining and read extensively the industry literature on the subject. From 1974 to 1978, Ciavatta never was formally involved in or assigned to research or development relevant to the friction stabilizer. Nevertheless, Dr. McGahan, the Director of Research, encouraged the research staff to be creative, to discuss ideas for projects or potential projects beyond those to which they had been assigned. These ideas were to be submitted on disclosure forms. * * *

In March 1978, the company transferred Ciavatta to the Split Set Division of Ingersoll-Rand Equipment Corp. While there, he served as Manufacturing Manager and Quality Control Manager. * * *

During this period, the company did not employ Ciavatta to design, invent, or modify the basic configuration of its Split Set roof stabilizer, and in fact he did not do so. Ciavatta did, however, have access to Ingersoll-Rand's manufacturing drawings, materials, and specifications. Ingersoll-Rand considers all of that information confidential, although the information had been published in industry trade publications. * * *

In the spring of 1979, as a result of certain quality control problems, Ciavatta stopped certain shipments of the stabilizer and recommended that the vendors modify their production process. Ciavatta's superior countermanded this directive and directed the vendors to make their scheduled shipments. Subsequently, in June of that year, Ingersoll-Rand terminated Ciavatta's employment. * * *

After his termination, Ciavatta circulated more than one hundred resumes seeking employment with other engineering firms. From February to July 1980, he briefly obtained employment as general manager of a bankrupt company located in Michigan.

Ciavatta asserts, and the trial court found, that he first conceived of the invention in dispute in the summer of 1979 while unemployed and off the Ingersoll-Rand payroll. Apparently, he was installing a light fixture in his home when he first conceived of his invention, an elliptical metal tube designed to stabilize the roofs of mines. While searching for employment following his discharge from Ingersoll-Rand, Ciavatta intermittently worked on his design. He completed his first sketch of the stabilizing device on August 25, 1979, approximately two months after Ingersoll-Rand fired him. Ciavatta's stabilizer differs from Ingersoll-Rand's in two respects: its tubular portion is closed rather than split, and the tube is elliptical in shape.

* * *

After his brief employment with the bankrupt company in Michigan, Ciavatta returned to his work on the stabilizing device and began refining the system in a more systematic manner. Although still looking for employment, he "started to go through significantly more calculations," and obtained sample tubing to run experimental tests. In March 1980, nine months after his termination, Ciavatta filed for a United States patent on the device and was awarded U.S. Patent No. 4,316,677 in February 1982. Subsequently, in March 1982, Ciavatta received a second patent, U.S. Patent No. 4,322,183, which involved an improvement to the roof stabilizer protected by Ciavatta's first patent.

In July 1980, Ciavatta prepared a business plan and solicited venture capital from a number of firms, including Kerr McGee Co. and United Nuclear Corp. These financing efforts failed, however, and Ciavatta used his life savings and borrowed over $125,000 from his brother and a bank to take his invention to the marketplace. Ciavatta exhibited his now-patented invention at a trade show in October 1982, and sales of his product then began. He made his first sale in January 1983. Sales for 1983 totaled approximately $30,000. By the time that the trial of this case commenced in June 1985 his total sales approximated $270,000. * * *

In July 1982, Ciavatta received a letter from Ingersoll-Rand's patent counsel requesting that he assign his patent to the company. Ciavatta communicated to Ingersoll-Rand that his lawyer had advised him that he was not obligated to assign his patent to his former employer. * * *

In September 1983, after Ciavatta had sold his product to several Ingersoll-Rand customers, the company decided to lower the price of its split set stabilizer and to commence this lawsuit. Ingersoll-Rand initiated suit against Ciavatta on April 17, 1984, alleging that the defendant had violated the employment agreement by failing to assign the invention and related patents that he conceived after leaving Ingersoll-Rand. Specifically, Ingersoll-Rand sought assignment of the patent for Ciavatta's friction stabilizer and an accounting for profits. * * *

The trial court made detailed factual findings establishing that Ciavatta did not pirate any trade secrets or confidential information in conceiving his invention. Indeed, the trial court found that Ingersoll-Rand's split set technology "does not involve trade secrets or other confidential information since the specifications, methods of manufacture and operating principles relating to the device are available to the public or are easily discoverable." Ingersoll-Rand's "manufacturing process has been in existence for over 50 years. Anyone can buy plaintiff's product, observe it, measure it and analyze its steel content. In short, there does not appear to be anything secret about it or the principles it utilizes." Nevertheless, the trial court enforced the agreement[.] * * *

The Appellate Division * * * reversed the trial court's judgment and remanded the case to the Chancery Division for the dismissal of the company's complaint and for trial of the defendant's counterclaim. We granted Ingersoll-Rand's petition for certification.

Paragraph 1(c) of Ciavatta's Proprietary Agreement with Ingersoll-Rand comprises a one-year so-called "holdover" agreement under which the employee promises to assign his or her "entire right, title and interest" in any invention he or she creates during a one-year period following termination of employment if that invention is "conceived as a result of and is attributable to work done during such employment." The central question presented in this case is the enforceability of that covenant.

The common law regards an invention as the property of the inventor who conceived, developed, and perfected it. * * *

Thus, employment alone does not require an inventor to assign a patent to his employer. Absent a specific agreement, an employed inventor's rights and duties with respect to an invention or concept arise from the inventor's employment status when he actually designed the invention. Generally, where an employer hires an employee to design a specific invention or solve a specific problem, the employee has a duty to assign the resulting patent. Where the employee is not hired specifically to design or invent, but nevertheless conceives of a device during working hours with the use of the employer's materials and equipment, the employer is granted an irrevocable but non-exclusive right to use the invention under the "shop right rule." * * *

Since the common-law doctrines are vague and ambiguous in defining the rights of employers and employees in employees' inventions, most employers use written contracts to allocate invention rights. Such contracts requiring an employee to assign to the employer inventions designed or conceived during the period of employment are valid. * * *

Most large, technologically advanced companies today require their employees by contract to assign their patents to their employers. Courts, however, will not enforce invention assignment contracts that unreasonably obligate an employee in each and every instance to transfer the ownership of the employee's invention to the employer. Additionally, several states have recently adopted legislation that delimits employer-employee invention assignment agreements. Those statutes restrict the instances in which employers may compel the assignment of employee inventions. *See* Minn.Stat.Ann. § 181.78 (1980); N.C.Gen.Stat. § 66–57.1 to 57–2 (1981); Wash.Rev.Code Ann. § 49.44.140 (1987); Cal.Lab.Code § 2870 (West 1987). All of these statutes provide that any employee invention assignment agreement that purports to give employers greater rights than they have under the statute is against public policy and, consequently, unenforceable.

In the instant case, the contract involves the assignment of future or post-employment inventions. Contractual provisions requiring assignment of post-employment inventions are commonly referred to as "trailer" or "holdover" clauses. The public policy issues involved in the enforceability of these holdover clauses reflect the dichotomy of our views on the rights of an inventor and rights of an employer. Our society has long recognized the intensely personal nature of an invention and the importance of providing stimulation and encouragement to inventors. Some commentators believe that the existing patent system does not present sufficient motivation to an employee-inventor. These commentators allege that the United States is in danger of losing its position as technology leader of the world. They cite for support that America is experiencing a declining patent balance and is less patent-productive than many foreign countries. * * *

To encourage an inventor's creativity, courts have held that on terminating his employment, an inventor has the right to use the general skills and knowledge gained through the prior employment. Moreover, an employee may compete with his former employer on termination. Nonetheless, it is acknowledged that the inventive process is increasingly being supported and subsidized by corporations and governments. It is becoming a more collective research process, the collective product of corporate and government research laboratories instead of the identifiable work of one or two individuals. Employers, therefore, have the right to protect their trade secrets, confidential information, and customer relations. Thus, employees and employers both have significant interests warranting judicial attention.

In view of the competing interests involved in holdover agreements, courts have not held them void *per se.* Rather, the courts apply a test of reasonableness. Moreover, courts strictly construe contractual provisions that require assignment of post-employment inventions; they must be fair, reasonable, and just. Generally, a clause is unreasonable if it: (1) extends beyond any apparent protection that the employer reasonably requires; (2) prevents the inventor from seeking other employment; or (3) adversely impacts on the public. New Jersey courts previously have not specifically addressed the enforceability of a "holdover" clause. We have, however, addressed the enforceability of analogous employee noncompetition contracts. We find that our determination of the enforceability of those post-contracts is applicable to our determination in this case of the enforceability of "holdover" clauses. * * *

In *Solari* and *Whitmyer,* we articulated a three-part test to determine the validity of a noncompetition covenant in an employment contract. Under those cases, a court will find a noncompetition covenant reasonable if it "simply protects the legitimate interests of the employer, imposes no undue hardship on the employee and is not injurious to the public." *Solari* and *Whitmyer* both recognize as legitimate the employer's interest in protecting trade secrets, confidential information, and customer relations. * * *

Regardless of the results reached in the individual cases, all courts recognize the competing interests at stake. That is, the question of the enforceability of holdover covenants clearly presents the interest of the employee in enjoying the benefits of his or her own creation, on the one hand, and the interest of the employer in protecting confidential information, trade secrets, and, more generally, its time and expenditures in training and imparting skills and knowledge to its paid work force, on the other. Moreover, courts recognize that the public has an enormously strong interest in both fostering ingenuity and innovation of the inventor and maintaining adequate protection and incentives to corporations to undertake long-range and extremely costly research and development programs.

* * * Most courts have limited the legitimate protectible interests of an employer "to trade secrets and other proprietary information . . . and customer relations." The rationale offered for such a limitation is the broad definition of trade secret and other confidential information. There is no exact definition of a trade secret. Generally, cases rely on the broad

definition of trade secret found in the Restatement of Torts § 757 comment b (1939).

Ciavatta urges that holdover agreements also should be enforced only when the former employee has used the trade secrets or confidential information of the employer in developing his post-termination invention. Since it is undisputed that he did not do so in inventing his stabilizer, he argues, paragraph 1(c), the holdover clause, should not be enforced against him.

Ingersoll-Rand, however, argues that it is inequitable to limit an employer's "protectable interest" solely to trade secrets and other confidential information. Today, large corporations maintain at great expense modern research and development programs that involve synergistic processes. Such "think tanks" require the free and open exchange of new ideas among the members of a research staff using the employer's body of accumulated information and experiences. This creative process receives its impetus and inspiration from the assimilation of an employer's advanced knowledge and a spontaneous interaction among colleagues, co-employees, and superiors. Ingersoll-Rand argues that it maintains this creative atmosphere in its research and development effort at great expense and that it should be allowed to protect itself against a former employee who invents a unique, competing concept attributable to such brainstorming. Ingersoll-Rand contends that such creative brainstorming enriched Ciavatta and led to his invention and therefore that paragraph 1(c) of the proprietary agreement should be enforced.

We agree with Ingersoll-Rand that the protection afforded by holdover agreements such as the one executed by the parties in this lawsuit may under certain circumstances exceed the limitation of trade secrets and confidential information. We recognize that employers may have legitimate interests in protecting information that is not a trade secret or proprietary information, but highly specialized, current information not generally known in the industry, created and stimulated by the research environment furnished by the employer, to which the employee has been "exposed" and "enriched" solely due to his employment. We do not attempt to define the exact parameters of that protectable interest. We expect courts to construe narrowly this interest, which will be deemed part of the "reasonableness" equation. The line between such information, trade secrets, and the general skills and knowledge of a highly sophisticated employee will be very difficult to draw, and the employer will have the burden to do so.

Nevertheless, we do not hesitate to recognize what appears to us a business reality that modern day employers are in need of some protection against the use or disclosure of valuable information regarding the employer's business, which information is passed on to certain employees confidentially by virtue of the positions those employees hold in the employer's enterprise. Courts, however, must be aware that holdover agreements impose restrictions on employees. Such agreements clearly limit an employee's employment opportunities and in many instances probably interfere with an employee securing a position in which he could most effectively use his skills, at the same time depriving society of a more productive worker. How restrictive the clause is on a particular employee depends, of course, on the facts and circumstances of the case. Indeed, in many instances, the employee may have little choice but to sign a holdover agreement in order to secure employment. Conversely, some very talented or experienced individuals, pursued by several corporations, may bargain for highly lucrative positions in exchange for their promise to be bound by a holdover agreement. Accordingly, courts must evaluate the reasonableness of holdover agreements in light of the individual circumstances of the employer and employee. Courts must balance the employer's need for protection and the hardship on the employee that may result. * * *

We conclude that on the facts of this case, Ingersoll-Rand is not entitled to an assignment of the patent on Ciavatta's friction stabilizer. We find that Ingersoll-Rand has not substantiated that Ciavatta invented his friction stabilizer in violation of his contractual obligation under the holdover clause. Ingersoll-Rand has not established that Ciavatta "conceived" of his invention as a result of his employment at Ingersoll-Rand. The facts convince us that the holdover clause does not apply here however liberally we are willing to construe the protection afforded employers by such clauses. Furthermore, we also find that enforcement of the holdover agreement in this case would be unreasonable even if the contract by its terms applied to Ciavatta's invention.

The record shows that Armand Ciavatta was not hired to invent or to work on design improvements or other variations of the split set friction stabilizer. He was not directed by his employer into its research and development department, and even though Ciavatta himself submitted numerous product ideas to Ingersoll-Rand, the company never developed any of those ideas. Indeed, Ciavatta testified that as a result of plaintiffs' rejection of his submitted ideas, he was discouraged from creating or using his ingenuity to develop new ideas or suggest adaptations to existing Ingersoll-Rand products. Ingersoll-Rand did not assign Ciavatta to a "think tank" division in which he would likely have encountered on a daily basis the ideas of fellow Ingersoll-Rand personnel regarding how the split set stabilizer could be improved or how a more desirable alternative stabilizer might be designed.

More importantly, the information needed to invent the split set stabilizer is not that unique type of information that we would deem protectable even under our expanded definition of a protectable interest. All of the specifications and capabilities of the Ingersoll-Rand split set stabilizer were widely publicized throughout industry and trade publications. In fact, the general design of Atlas Copco's friction stabilizer, the leading competitor of the Ingersoll-Rand stabilizer, is identical to the general design of the Ingersoll-Rand product. Moreover, Ingersoll-Rand openly advertised the characteristics of its split set product. The uses of the product were well known throughout the mining industry as were the names of the particular users of the product. Production cost figures and pricing schedules were known in the industry as well. Furthermore, the technology behind the split set was no mystery; there was trial testimony that the technology behind the production of the split set was over fifty years old.

Thus, it is clear that Ingersoll-Rand has done little to guard the details of its friction stabilizer or maintain a secretive atmosphere surrounding corporate development and marketing of the product. Instead, the company deliberately created and perpetuated an open, public posture in the mining industry submarket in which it operated and in which it enjoyed a commanding market share. Matters of general knowledge throughout an industry cannot be claimed as secrets nor as "unique information" derived as a result of current, ongoing research of the employer. Ciavatta did not develop his stabilizer on the basis of valuable information about the Ingersoll-Rand product imparted to him because he held a special position with the company. His departure from Ingersoll-Rand and subsequent invention and development of his own competing product do not suggest that he purposefully left to develop a competing product on the basis of the knowledge he gained from his employment. We do not hold that the manner of an employee's departure is dispositive. It is a factor that the court should consider, however, and, in this case, that factor weighs heavily in defendant's favor.

Ciavatta was fired from Ingersoll-Rand and testified that he conceived of his invention while installing a light fixture at his home some months after he was terminated. Thereafter, he performed further, independent calculations to test and refine his concept. He worked intermittently on the product as he searched for employment. He developed the product based on his general skill, expertise, and knowledge. While Ciavatta employed certain skills and knowledge he undoubtedly gained during his employment by Ingersoll-Rand, his invention was not the result of any research currently being done by the company or any company research in which he personally was involved. Indeed, the technology Ciavatta employed was developed over fifty years ago and well known in the industry. Nor did he use any of Ingersoll-Rand's capital or materials in the development of his invention. When his attempts to lure capital failed, he borrowed and used his own savings to get the small business started.

These facts lead us to believe that the factors of the *Solari/Whitmyer* balancing test weigh heavily in favor of defendant, even assuming that paragraph 1(c) applies. Although we specifically hold today that reasonable holdover agreements may be enforceable, we decline to enforce the agreement between Ingersoll-Rand and Ciavatta because, as it relates to the patented invention in dispute, the restriction is unreasonable under *Solari/Whitmyer.* * * *

Accordingly, we affirm the judgment of the Appellate Division.

DID YOU GET IT?

1. On what basis would the plaintiff have a claim to ownership of the defendant's invention, which he created after leaving the plaintiff's employment?

2. What is the employer's policy rationale to justify a holdover agreement?

3. Should it matter whether the employee's post-employment invention was derived from the former employer's trade secrets or from his general skill and knowledge?

NOTES

1. **Employee mobility in the EU Trade Secret Directive.** The EU Trade Secret Directive is replete with language that is designed to preserve employee mobility and free competition, but there is no reference to the inevitable disclosure doctrine, which is principally a U.S. doctrine. The Directive also lacks details about how EU Member States should act to preserve employee mobility, meaning that each EU country (like each state in the U.S.) has the flexibility to determine what is best for itself.

2. **Inevitable confusion?** There is a wide variation among the states that have adopted or applied the inevitable disclosure doctrine. Putting aside the handful of states that have outright rejected the doctrine, the remainder fall along a broad continuum on how the doctrine should be applied. Some of the more prevalent issues separating the states' application of the doctrine include: (a) whether and how the doctrine relates to threatened misappropriation; (b) whether the doctrine is a substitute for proving actual misappropriation; (c) whether the doctrine should only be used to enforce non-competition agreements; (d) whether the doctrine should be used in the absence of a non-competition agreement; and (e) whether the doctrine should be used only when an employee had "intimate familiarity" with the former employer's trade secrets.

3. **Disloyalty and mobility in the workplace.** As you have learned in this chapter, employees, even without contractual restrictions, are subject to certain implied obligations to their employer, including a duty of loyalty. However, reality suggests that employees generally do not feel much loyalty to their employers, particularly with respect to changing norms in the workplace

and an economic climate that does not promote job security. Ultimately, this phenomenon is likely to have a negative effect on trade secret protection.

> [R]esearchers have, for a while, noted a general decline in loyalty in the workplace. This decline stems, in part, from the changing nature of expectations in the workplace, particularly the lack of job security. Indeed, as this Article goes to press the United States is in the midst of a recession. As a result, * * * [e]mployees are experiencing first-hand the effects of high unemployment rates and massive layoffs. The expectation of long-term employment until retirement with any company is a thing of the past. Most full time employees change jobs several times over the span of their careers. That mobility, in itself, creates more opportunities for employees to transfer trade secrets to new employers or to their own competing ventures.

Elizabeth A. Rowe, *A Sociological Approach to Misappropriation*, 58 U. KAN. L. REV. 1, 16 (2009).

4.   **Bibliographic note:** In addition to the references noted above, for more information on the topics discussed in this chapter, *see* MILGRIM ON TRADE SECRETS §§ 4.02, 5.02, 6.01 (2016); Robert W. Gomulkiewicz, *Leaky Covenants-Not-to-Compete as the Legal Infrastructure for Innovation*, 49 U.C. DAVIS L. REV. 251 (2015); Zoe Argento, *Whose Social Network Account: A Trade Secret Approach to Allocating Rights*, 19 MICH. TELECOMM. & TECH. L. REV. 201 (2013); Orly Lobel, TALENT WANTS TO BE FREE: WHY WE SHOULD LEARN TO LOVE LEAKS, RAIDS, AND FREE RIDING (2013); Jasmine McNealy, *Who Owns Your Friends:* Phonedog v. Kravitz *and Business Claims of Trade Secret in Social Media Information*, 39 RUTGERS COMPUTER & TECH. L. J. 30 (2013); Charles Tait Graves, *Analyzing The Non-Competition Covenant as a Category of Intellectual Property Regulation,* 3 HASTINGS SCI. & TECH. L.J. 69 (2011); Elizabeth A. Rowe, *When Trade Secrets Become Shackles: Fairness and the Inevitable Disclosure Doctrine*, 7 TULANE J. TECH. & INTELL. PROP. 167 (2005); Katherine V.W. Stone, *Knowledge at Work: Disputes over the Ownership of Human Capital in the Changing Workplace*, 34 CONN. L. REV. 721 (2002); Rachel S. Arnow-Richman, *Bargaining for Loyalty in the Information Age: A Reconsideration of the Role of Substantive Fairness in Enforcing Employee Noncompetes*, 80 OR. L. REV. 1163 (2001); Gillian Lester, *Restrictive Covenants, Employee Training, and the Limits of Transaction-Cost Analysis*, 76 IND. L.J. 49 (2001); Ronald J. Gilson, *The Legal Infrastructure of High Technology Industrial Districts: Silicon Valley, Route 128, and Covenants Not To Compete*, 74 N.Y.U. L. REV. 575 (1999).

CHAPTER 9

LITIGATION TACTICS AND DEFENSES

■ ■ ■

> ### Anticipated Learning Outcomes
>
> At the conclusion of this chapter, you will be able to articulate the primary defenses to a trade secret misappropriation claim and be able to differentiate between the following two defensive tactics: attacking plaintiff's *prima facie* case and pleading and proving affirmative defenses. You will also learn the importance of protecting trade secrets during and after trial and how a defendant might use the plaintiff's failure to identify trade secrets with specificity to its advantage.

A. INTRODUCTION

Up until now, the primary focus of this casebook has been on the essential elements of a claim for trade secret misappropriation. That is because to prevail in a trade secret misappropriation case the plaintiff bears the burden of pleading and proving all of the essential elements of a trade secret misappropriation claim, whereas the defendant need only disprove one element. By carefully examining the language of the UTSA and the DTSA and cases that have applied UTSA and *Restatement* principles, you should now be able to articulate the essential elements of a claim for trade secret misappropriation.

This chapter explores the principal substantive arguments and defensive tactics that a defendant in a trade secret misappropriation case might pursue to disprove such elements or otherwise avoid liability.

B. THE LIFE-CYCLE OF A TRADE SECRET CASE

In the United States, civil litigation typically begins with the filing and service of a complaint in which the plaintiff alleges the facts necessary to state one or more claims for relief. How detailed the recitation of facts must be depends upon the pleading rules of the court where the lawsuit is filed, but usually requires enough information to put the defendant on reasonable notice of the claims asserted. Federal Rule of Civil Procedure 8(a) has been interpreted to include a plausibility requirement that requires "a short and plain statement of the claim showing that the pleader is entitled to relief, in order to give the defendant fair notice of what the . . . claim is and the grounds upon which it rests." *Bell Atl. Corp. v.*

Twombly, 550 U.S. 544, 555 (2007); *see also, Ashcroft v. Iqbal,* 556 U.S. 662 (2009).

Until the recent adoption of the Defend Trade Secrets Act of 2016 (the DTSA), most trade secret cases were filed in state courts based upon state law, with federal court jurisdiction only being possible in diversity cases. Now it is possible for plaintiffs in most trade secret cases to file in either state or federal court because the DTSA specifies that federal courts have original (but not exclusive) jurisdiction of trade secret cases that meet the Commerce Clause requirement of the DTSA. Specifically, when filing a DTSA claim the plaintiff must allege that the subject trade secrets are "related to a good or service that is used in, or intended for use in, interstate or foreign commerce." *See* 18 U.S.C. § 1836(6)(1), reprinted in Appendix A.

Typically, in cases involving the alleged misappropriation of trade secrets, the principal cause of action will be a claim under the UTSA, the DTSA, or, in non-UTSA jurisdictions, a claim based upon common law. It is standard practice, however, for plaintiffs in trade secret cases to allege a variety of ancillary causes of action, such as: breach of contract; breach of fiduciary duty; unfair competition; conversion; violation of the Computer Fraud and Abuse Act; and interference with contract or prospective economic advantage. When responding to plaintiff's complaint, the defendant should address all of the causes of action alleged by the plaintiff.

The first two things that a defendant should do when it is served with a complaint are: (1) tender the claim to its insurance carrier to determine if insurance coverage is available and (2) hire an attorney. In trade secret misappropriation cases, this must be done quickly because the filing of the complaint is usually accompanied by a motion for temporary restraining order or a motion for preliminary injunction. Depending on the rules of court in which the case is filed, a hearing on the motion for a TRO may occur within days or hours of plaintiff filing its complaint with the court.

1.   SEEKING PRELIMINARY RELIEF

In cases where the alleged trade secret has not yet been publicly disclosed, and therefore lost, the plaintiff is likely to couple the filing of a complaint with the request for a temporary restraining order (TRO) or preliminary injunction (PI) in an effort to enjoin the threatened disclosure or use of the trade secret. The DTSA provides an additional form of preliminary relief in extraordinary situations (known as a Civil Seizure Order) whereby evidence of misappropriation and property associated with the threatened disclosure of trade secrets may be seized by federal law enforcement officers. 18 USC § 1836(b)(2). This new remedy can be sought "*ex parte,*" that is, without first giving notice to the defendant(s). (See more on the DTSA's Civil Order Seizure Order provision in Note 2 at the end of this chapter).

The focus of motions for a TRO and a PI is generally on the standards for granting preliminary relief, including the substantive merits of the plaintiff's claims. As discussed more fully in Chapter 10, most courts apply a four-part test for the grant of preliminary relief that requires the plaintiff to present sufficient evidence and argument to establish that: (1) plaintiff is likely to prevail on the merits; (2) plaintiff will be irreparably harmed if preliminary relief is not granted; (3) the balance of hardships tips in plaintiff's favor; and (4) the issuance of preliminary relief would not be inconsistent with the public interest. *See e.g., Williams-Sonoma Direct, Inc. v. Arhaus, LLC,* 109 F.Supp.3d 1009 (W.D. Tenn. 2015). Thus, the focus of a defendant's early efforts is often on garnering sufficient evidence to disprove the need for preliminary relief. Whereas the plaintiff will argue that trade secret misappropriation has occurred and there is an imminent threat of the disclosure or use of its trade secret, the defendant will argue that: there are no trade secrets; there was no misappropriation; and there is no immediate threat of the disclosure or use of trade secrets.

Unfortunately for many defendants in trade secret misappropriation cases, trade secret litigation is fraught with highly emotional claims about the importance and value of the plaintiff's information and the alleged wrongdoing of the defendant. It is not unusual for plaintiffs to claim that their business will be "ruined" unless the court acts quickly to enjoin the defendant. As an example, in the first case in this Chapter, the plaintiff (Boeing) referred to its trade secrets as the "life-blood" of its business. Thus, if there is evidence that the defendant engaged in activities that appear illegal or nefarious (such as copying documents late at night or going into restricted areas), preliminary relief may be granted first and questions about the trade secret status of information asked later.

When faced with seemingly bad facts, often the best a defendant can do at the preliminary relief stage is to argue that any injunctive relief should be limited in both time and scope. For reasons more fully explained below, the defendant will also want to argue that the plaintiff's trade secrets have not been identified with sufficient specificity. A defendant in a trade secret misappropriation case will not be able to argue anything before an *ex parte* Civil Seizure Order is granted because such orders can be sought, granted, and executed without notice to the defendant, However, the DTSA specifies that a fully-noticed hearing must be scheduled within seven days of the grant of a Civil Seizure Order, at which time the defendant's arguments against the Order will be heard and the Order may be rescinded.

A critical and intense part of the preliminary relief stage involves expedited discovery. As you will see in Chapter 10, the parties in a preliminary injunction case will generally agree to, or the judge will order, expedited discovery prior to a preliminary injunction hearing. This means that discovery will be conducted in a very compressed time frame. This is typically the defendant's first opportunity to request that the plaintiff produce evidence that the information which it claims is confidential is actually a trade secret. Depending on the nature of the claim and the aggressiveness of the parties, thousands of pages of documents could be exchanged, and several depositions conducted, within a very short time frame.

2.   THE INITIAL PLEADINGS

The preliminary relief stage of a trade secret case is followed by a continuation of the pleading stage. During this stage, the defendant has three courses of action. First, it can file a motion to dismiss (known as a demurrer in some jurisdictions) in which it argues that the plaintiff has not alleged sufficient facts to state one or more causes of action. For instance, in a case brought under the DTSA, it may be argued that sufficient facts have not been alleged to meet the Commerce Clause requirement. If successful, a motion to dismiss will result in either eliminating some of plaintiff's claims for relief or forcing the plaintiff to file an amended complaint in which it provides more details about the alleged wrongdoing. Second, the defendant can (and, unless the entire case is dismissed on a motion to dismiss, ultimately will have to) file an answer to the complaint. Third, in conjunction with filing an answer to the plaintiff's complaint, the defendant can allege one or more counter-claims.

There are two parts to any well-constructed answer. In the first part, the defendant admits or denies the facts alleged by the plaintiff. (In some courts this can be done through the use of what is known as a general denial. In other courts the defendant must specifically admit or deny each allegation.) *See* F.R.C.P. Rule 8(b). In the second part of an answer, the defendant asserts one or more affirmative defenses by alleging facts sufficient to give rise to those defenses. *See* F.R.C.P. Rule 8(c).

3.   FROM DISCOVERY TO TRIAL

After the pleading stage, civil litigation in the United States typically proceeds through a discovery phase, a pre-trial phase, the trial, and a post-trial phase. During the discovery phase, the focus of a defendant's efforts is on determining the nature and scope of the plaintiff's claims and gathering evidence sufficient to either: (1) disprove at least one of the essential elements of each of plaintiff's causes of action; or (2) prove at least one affirmative defense for each cause of action. In trade secret cases, a key defense strategy during or before the discovery phase is for defendants to force plaintiffs to identify their alleged trade secrets with particularity so that the existence or non-existence of trade secrets can be determined as soon as possible. Only by first identifying the specific information that the plaintiff claims as a trade secret can a defendant determine whether such information meets the requirements of trade secrecy.

The pre-trial phase of a trade secret misappropriation claim often includes a motion for summary judgment by either the plaintiff or the defendant. However, because a defendant need only disprove one essential element of each of the plaintiff's claims to prevail (for instance, that no trade secrets exist), it is usually easier for a defendant to prevail on a motion for summary judgment than it is for a plaintiff. If preliminary relief in the form of a PI or Civil Seizure Order is granted, the pre-trial phase may also include motions to dissolve or alter the preliminary injunction and Civil Seizure Order.

4. THE TRIAL

As should be clear from the numerous cases that you have already read, the trial of a trade secret misappropriation case begins with the plaintiff presenting evidence in an attempt to prove every element of at least one cause of action. During this part of the case, the defendant is allowed to cross-examine the plaintiff's witnesses in an effort to undermine the plaintiff's case, but cannot present its own evidence and witnesses. If at the conclusion of the plaintiff's case the defendant believes that the plaintiff has not presented sufficient evidence to meet the applicable burden of proof, the defendant should make a motion for non-suit. If the motion for non-suit is granted, judgment will be entered for the defendant and the defendant need not present its own witnesses and evidence.

If the defendant's motion for non-suit is denied, then it is up to the defendant to present its case by calling witnesses and introducing evidence to either: (1) disprove one or more of the essential elements of plaintiff's case; or (2) prove all of the essential elements of one or more of the defendant's affirmative defenses. The defendant also has the burden of proving all of the essential elements of any counterclaims or cross-claims.

At the conclusion of the defendant's case, the plaintiff is usually given the opportunity to present rebuttal evidence and testimony, after which the defendant (or the court *sua sponte*) may make a motion for a directed verdict (known as a motion for judgment as a matter of law in federal court). A directed verdict is a procedural device that essentially takes the decision out of the hands of the jury and puts it in the hands of the judge. It is similar to a motion for summary judgment in that the underlying basis for the motion is the insufficiency of plaintiff's evidence.

5. THE POST-TRIAL PHASE

When a defendant is successful in defending the case against it, judgment will be entered in its favor and any post-trial motions will focus on the possible award to defendant of attorney's fees and costs, as discussed in Chapter 10. If the plaintiff prevails, post-trial motions may concern all manner of remedies, including damages, injunctive relief, attorney's fees, and costs. Where injunctive relief is granted, later post-trial motions may be filed to hold individuals or companies in contempt for failing to abide by the terms of the injunction or to alter or dissolve the injunction. The post-trial phase may also include any appeals of orders and judgments that the parties choose to pursue.

C. ATTACKING PLAINTIFF'S *PRIMA FACIE* CASE

To determine what elements are part of plaintiff's *prima facie* case it is necessary to know what a given jurisdiction says about the essential elements of a trade secret misappropriation claim. While the adoption of the UTSA by most states has resulted in substantial uniformity concerning a trade secret claimant's burden of proof, some variations may exist, particularly in states that have not yet adopted the UTSA. Similarly, while the DTSA is modeled after the UTSA, it necessarily requires proof of additional facts, such as those that are required to establish federal court jurisdiction under the Commerce Clause.

Generally, in order to establish a claim for trade secret misappropriation under both the UTSA and the DTSA, a plaintiff has the burden of pleading and proving that: (1) it owns a trade secret; (2) that one or more of its trade secrets were misappropriated by the defendant; and (3) that it is entitled to a remedy. If the plaintiff seeks permanent injunctive relief, it will usually be required to prove irreparable harm, although some courts are willing to presume irreparable harm upon a showing of trade secret misappropriation. Where monetary relief is sought, the plaintiff must prove up the amount of damages and show that it was caused by the misappropriation.

Utilizing the UTSA's definitions of a trade secret and misappropriation to its advantage, a defendant in a trade secret case will argue that it is not liable for trade secret misappropriation because:

1. The information identified by the plaintiff as its putative trade secrets is either generally known or readily ascertainable. *See* Chapter 3;

2. The information does not have independent economic value. *See* Chapter 4;

3. The information was not subject to reasonable efforts to maintain its secrecy. *See* Chapter 5;

4. The information was not improperly acquired by the defendant (or, in the case of multiple-party claims, by anyone). *See* Chapter 6;

5. There was no duty of confidentiality between the plaintiff and defendant or, if there was, it was not breached. *See* Chapter 7; and

6. The defendant did not know or have reason to know that it had acquired trade secrets that had been misappropriated by someone else. *See* "Special Issue" in Chapter 7.

If a defendant succeeds in proving any one of the foregoing assertions, it should prevail on the trade secret claim because of the absence of a trade secret or an act of misappropriation. However, it will still have to separately address and disprove any ancillary claims for relief, such as breach of contract claims. Also, given the possibility that its assertions of fact are not accepted by the judge or jury, the defendant should also argue that the plaintiff is not entitled to any remedies. *See* Chapter 10 for a discussion of available remedies and possible defense arguments against the grant of such remedies.

D. ASSERTING AFFIRMATIVE DEFENSES

Although the essential elements of each cause of action are typically the focus of both the plaintiff's and defendant's efforts during civil litigation, all defendants should carefully consider whether affirmative defenses can be established. The principal difference between attacking plaintiff's *prima facie* case and asserting affirmative defenses is that a defendant who asserts an affirmative defense has the burden to plead and prove facts sufficient to support them. *See* Fed. R. Civ. P. 8(c).

In most courts, the failure to timely allege a cause of action or affirmative defense will preclude those issues from being raised at trial. Thus, in the same way that no plaintiff wants to fail to allege a cause of action that might apply to the relevant set of facts, no defendant wants to fail to allege an affirmative defense that might mean the difference between liability and non-liability.

When a defendant files an answer to a complaint it will typically include a series of possible defenses. Often, the affirmative defenses that are asserted include arguments that, technically, relate to the plaintiff's *prima facie* case and need not be alleged as affirmative defenses. For instance, the argument that the alleged trade secrets were acquired by reverse engineering technically relates to both the trade secret and misappropriation prongs of plaintiff's case and arguably need not be alleged as an affirmative defense. However, in an abundance of caution, most defendants will plead reverse engineering as an affirmative defense and some statutes might require such "special" pleading.

Despite the fact that any defense argument that relates to plaintiff's *prima facie* case need not be alleged as an affirmative defense, the principal defenses that are alleged in trade secret cases are:

(1) The non-existence or loss of trade secrecy;

(2) Proper acquisition of plaintiff's trade secrets, including through reverse engineering and independent development;

(3) Consent to acquire, disclose, or use plaintiff's trade secrets;

(4) Violation of the applicable statute of limitations;

(5) Section 7 preclusion of ancillary state claims; and

(6) Federal preemption of state claims.

In cases involving the actual or threatened disclosure of trade secrets and a request for injunctive relief, violation of the First Amendment rights to freedom of speech and the press may be alleged as an affirmative defense. Also, because trade secret cases typically seek equitable relief, a variety of equitable defenses, including unclean hands, laches, acquiescence, waiver, and estoppel, may be asserted. (*See* F.R.C.P. Rule 8(c) for a listing of other possible affirmative defenses.)

The first three of the above-listed "defenses" were examined in depth in Chapters 2 through 6 of this casebook when the elements of a claim for trade secret misappropriation were discussed. Also recall that the defense of federal preemption (which may arise when ancillary state claims or an overly broad interpretation of state trade secret rights are asserted) was discussed in Chapter 2. The remaining defenses are examined in the sub-sections that follow. But first, the *Boeing* case provides an overview of many of the arguments that a defendant will make in an effort to avoid liability for trade secret misappropriation.

Reading Guidance

Which of the defendant's arguments are attacking an element of plaintiff's prima facie case?

BOEING V. SIERRACIN CORP.

Washington Supreme Court, 1987.
108 Wash. 2d 38.

DORE, JUSTICE.

This appeal stems from a 2-month trial between the Boeing Company and Sierracin Corporation. Boeing alleged that Sierracin misappropriated its trade secrets concerning the design of airplane windows. Sierracin counterclaimed asserting that Boeing's actions to protect its designs violated Washington antitrust laws. A jury found for Boeing on its trade secrets claim and for Sierracin on its antitrust counterclaim. Both sides appeal. * * *

FACTS

This lawsuit concerns the manufacture and marketing of replacement cockpit windows for Boeing 707's, 727's and 737's, known as Triple Seven ("7/7/7") windows. Five of these windows lie on each side of the aircraft's nose, each performing multiple critical functions such as defogging, withstanding cabin pressurization, and providing a clear range of vision. Historically, only the appellant Boeing Company held the necessary Federal Aviation Administration Parts Manufacturer Authorization (hereinafter authorization), so only Boeing or its licensee could legally sell those windows.

Boeing's drawings for the 7/7/7 cockpit windows are unique, detailed blueprints containing approximately 500 critical tolerances, dimensions, specifications and material requirements. The basic design, which played an integral role in the production of the world's first commercial jet transport, has undergone minor changes since its inception in the 1950's, each requiring FAA reauthorization.

Because these drawings are the result of Boeing's original $16 million investment, and as they constitute Boeing's "lifeblood" in the commercial airplane business, Boeing always considered them proprietary trade secrets. For protection of its trade secrets Boeing requires in a standard contract provision that Boeing's outside suppliers, who receive these drawings, agree not to use them for any purpose other than exclusive Boeing manufacture.

Prior FAA authorization is needed for every spare part sold or installed on any commercial aircraft. Outside suppliers may manufacture and sell airplane parts by either: (1) selling to a manufacturer with prior FAA design authorization (like Boeing); or (2) selling directly to airlines after obtaining their own FAA authorization by (a) independent design and testing; (b) licensing from another authorized airplane manufacturer (like Boeing); or (c) showing that their own drawings and manufacturing processes are identical to those previously authorized (identicality). In granting an identicality, the FAA does not consider where the applicant obtained its drawings or derived its manufacturing process.

The three major suppliers of aircraft windows in the United States are PPG Industries, Inc.; Swedlow, Inc.; and Sierracin. Sierracin had supplied Boeing with other products for many years. In 1982, it began manufacturing Boeing's 7/7/7 windows after acquiring the business of Libbey-Owens-Ford Company, which had previously been a supplier of those windows. Boeing helped Sierracin enter the 7/7/7 window market by providing Sierracin with FAA authorized drawings, technical assistance and tooling, and by awarding it contracts for some of Boeing's 7/7/7 window needs in 1982 and 1983.

As a supplier, Sierracin received Boeing requests for quotations, which provided that all orders were subject to its confidential terms and conditions. Sierracin signed more than 270 Boeing contracts containing the same terms and conditions without objection, and signed and accepted Boeing purchase orders with a similar provision. Sierracin accepted Boeing's terms by letter, and after performance accepted payment under the purchase orders.

In 1984 after alleged breaches of contract because of late deliveries of windows, Boeing chose not to renew contracts with Sierracin, and instead signed a 5-year 100 percent requirements contract with PPG Industries, Inc. Sierracin decided, however, to continue manufacturing windows for sale on its own in the 7/7/7 "after market" (i.e., spare parts market). A Boeing official warned Sierracin against use of Boeing proprietary data for any purpose other than manufacturing parts for Boeing. Sierracin ignored the warning and used various Boeing engineering drawings and specifications to try to obtain its own authorization from the FAA. The FAA asked Boeing to make an identicality comparison between Boeing's 7/7/7 windows and those manufactured by Sierracin. Boeing refused and accused Sierracin of copying its drawings. Sierracin denied these accusations and Boeing filed this suit.

* * *

TRIAL AND APPEAL

Boeing's lawsuit against Sierracin alleged breach of contract, breach of confidential relationship, conversion and misappropriation of trade secrets in violation of the Uniform Trade Secrets Act, RCW 19.108. * * *

Sierracin asserted an antitrust affirmative defense and six counterclaims. Its counterclaim alleging "sham litigation" was dismissed by the trial court. The remaining counterclaims alleged that Boeing had violated the antitrust provisions of the Consumer Protection Act, RCW 19.86, by (1) engaging in an unlawful tying arrangement; (2) entering into a contract or combination which unreasonably restrains trade; (3) attempting to monopolize the relevant market; (4) monopolizing the relevant market; and (5) engaging in unfair trade practices or unfair methods of competition.

* * *

TRADE SECRETS

The Uniform Trade Secrets Act, RCW 19.108.030(1), provides that a plaintiff can receive actual damages for misappropriation of trade secrets. RCW 19.108.010(2)(a) defines "misappropriation" as "[a]cquisition of a trade secret of another by a person who knows or has reason to know that the trade secret was acquired by improper means . . ." Ample evidence was presented to the jury which indicated that Sierracin's actions in using the Boeing drawings to manufacture 7/7/7 windows for direct sales to other airlines, as well as to gain independent FAA authorization, violated this statute. Moreover, the jury also found that Sierracin breached its contract with Boeing and breached the confidential relationship between the two parties. As substantial evidence exists which supports all three of these claims, we affirm the jury verdicts. * * *

Sierracin signed over 270 contracts with Boeing, each containing the following proprietary language:

> CONFIDENTIAL DISCLOSURE. Seller shall keep confidential . . . all proprietary information including, but not limited to, designs, processes, drawings, specifications, reports, data, and other technical or business information and the features of all parts, equipment, tools, gauges, patterns, and other items furnished or disclosed to Seller by Buyer. . . . Seller shall use such information and items, and the features thereof, only in the performance of this Order; . . .

* * *

Despite this contractual language and warnings on the drawings indicating that this information was confidential, Sierracin asserts that the jury erred in finding for Boeing on its breach of contract, breach of confidential relationship, and misappropriation of trade secrets claims. Sierracin raises the following arguments in support of its assertion: (1) Boeing's claims should have been consolidated; (2) Boeing's trade secrets claim is preempted by federal law; (3) even if not preempted, Boeing had no "secrets" because the "secrets" were ascertainable from common tooling; and (4) if Boeing did have "secrets", they were lost into the public domain upon submission to the FAA at time of licensure, or were otherwise "published" through confidential disclosure of drawings to Libbey, and by use of exhibits at trial. All these arguments lack merit.

* * *

As its final attack on Boeing's jury verdict, Sierracin argues that its antitrust counterclaim constitutes an affirmative defense to Boeing's claims. We reject this argument, as we find no antitrust violation. * * *

DID YOU GET IT?

1. What arguments did defendant make to attack plaintiff's *prima facie* case?

2. What affirmative defenses did defendant assert?

3. What procedural arguments did the defendant make?

1. STATUTE OF LIMITATIONS

Section 6 of the UTSA sets forth the statute of limitations for trade secret misappropriation claims in UTSA jurisdictions. (The same three-year statute of limitations was adopted as part of the DTSA.) However, some states (obviously including non-UTSA states) have not adopted the UTSA's statute of limitations. In these states, the general statutes of limitations for the applicable state should be consulted and the applicable facts must be analyzed to determine when the statute of limitations begins to run.

[handwritten: – medical devices]

UNIFORM TRADE SECRETS ACT

Section 6

An action for misappropriation must be brought <u>within 3 years after the misappropriation</u> is discovered or by the exercise of reasonable diligence should have been discovered. For the purposes of this section, a continuing misappropriation constitutes a single claim.

> ### Reading Guidance
> *What triggers the running of the statute of limitations?* *[handwritten: Inquiry notice]*

[handwritten: – ct. affirmed stat. of lim. had run]
[handwritten: – started at 1999 letter P sent which showed inquiry notice]
[handwritten: – non-UTSA jx]

EPSTEIN V. C.R. BARD, INC.

United States Court of Appeals, First Circuit, 2006.
460 F.3d 183.

[Note: the following case is based on Massachusetts law. As of the publication of this casebook, Massachusetts was one of three states that has not enacted the UTSA. Thus, this case is an example of <u>how the statute of limitations defense is applied in non-UTSA jurisdictions.</u> The basis for the statute of limitations defense is not a special statute applicable only to trade secret cases, but a general statute of limitations that applies to a variety of claims.]

TORRUELLA, CIRCUIT JUDGE.

On October 15, 2003, plaintiff Scott M. Epstein ("Epstein") filed a ten-count complaint against Defendant C.R. Bard, Inc. ("Bard") in the Suffolk County Superior Court, requesting damages arising from Bard's alleged breach of contract and infringement of Epstein's intellectual property rights. * * *

I.

Epstein is a designer and manufacturer of medical devices and an officer and principal of SME Design Technology, Inc. ("SME"). At some point (the brief lacks dates), Epstein entered into a business relationship with Bard, a developer, manufacturer, and marketer of medical technology. According to the complaint, Epstein worked in cooperation with Bard Urological Division ("BUD") to develop improvements to certain medical devices, including catheters. Epstein agreed to provide a minimum of 50,000 of the improved catheters—marketed as the "Tigertail"—to BUD at a price of

$3.50 per catheter. Between December 23, 1994 and January 27, 1995, Epstein entered into a series of confidentiality agreements with Bard concerning the Tigertail technology.

At a later unspecified date, Epstein sought to sell or license his catheter technology to BUD. BUD declined and informed him that it was discontinuing the product line. But on October 10, 1999, Epstein wrote a letter ("the October 10, 1999 letter") to the president of BUD, noting that "it has been brought to my attention that Tigertail™ is still available through Bard Urology, which under the circumstances is confusing to me. We have not supplied BUD with product for about one year and therefore I have to wonder where additional inventory has come form [sic]. This letter is an attempt to ascertain this information because it has been established and is well defined that the BUD Tigertail™ technology and concept is the intellectual property of SME Design. Any second source manufacture utilizing SME Design technology which includes material and process information would have to be licensed form [sic] and approved by SME Design."

1999

On January 6, 2000, Epstein sent a follow-up letter ("the January 6, 2000 letter"), saying "I also want to voice my disappointment" regarding BUD's failure to "resolve this issue." Epstein observed that "I find myself dealing with people that I cannot trust. The issue is more and more complicated now that my Trade Secrets have been divulged and the Soft Tip product line is successful." Finally, Epstein warned that if there was no satisfactory response from BUD within 30 days, "we will end up in court."

Epstein did not commence litigation until October 15, 2003. The complaint alleged damages under the following legal theories, listed by count: 1) breach of contract; 2) tortious interference with contractual relations; 3) misappropriation of trade secrets; 4) conversion; 5) unjust enrichment; 6) misrepresentation; 7) negligent misrepresentation; 8) fraudulent concealment; 9) breach of the implied covenant of good faith and fair dealing; and 10) violation of Mass. Gen. Laws ch. 93A, §§ 2 and 11. * * *

II.

The district court dismissed Epstein's complaint under Rule 12(b)(6) of the Federal Rules of Civil Procedure. Under that rule, a complaint can properly be dismissed "for failure of the pleading to state a claim upon which relief can be granted." Fed.R.Civ.P. 12(b)(6). * * * We review a Rule 12(b)(6) dismissal *de novo,* considering all well-pleaded facts in the complaint to be true. * * *

A.   Statutes of Limitations

For statute of limitations purposes, the district court found that Epstein's cause of action accrued with the October 10, 1999 letter. Although Epstein claims that the district court's determination as to the accrual date was in error, we find no mistake.

The relevant statute of limitations periods are: three years for tort claims (Mass. Gen. Laws ch. 260, § 2A); four years for 93A violations (Mass. Gen. Laws ch. 260, § 5A); and four years for breach of contract claims governed by the Uniform Commercial Code (Mass. Gen. Laws ch. 106, § 2–725(1) and (2)). The limitations period begins to run "when a plaintiff discovers, or any earlier date when she should reasonably have discovered, that she has been harmed or may have been harmed by the defendant's conduct." * * * The so-called "discovery rule" provides that the limitations period is tolled until "events occur or facts surface which would cause a reasonably prudent person to become aware that she or he had been harmed." * * * A plaintiff is considered to be on "inquiry notice" when the first event occurs that would prompt a reasonable person to inquire into a possible injury at the hands of the defendant. * * *

The district court found that Epstein was on notice that BUD was improperly using his technology as of the October 10, 1999 letter. In the letter, Epstein stated in relevant part that "it has been brought to my attention that Tigertail™ is still available through Bard Urology" despite the fact that "[w]e have not supplied BUD with product for about one year." In the same letter Epstein wrote that the situation "is confusing to me" because "it is well defined that the BUD Tigertail technology and concept is the intellectual property of SME Design" and any use of that property "would have to be licensed form [sic] and approved by SME Design." From this language, the district court concluded that Epstein "was clearly on notice that BUD was improperly using his technology since he knew that BUD continued to sell the Tigertail™ and he, the sole supplier of the product, was not supplying it to BUD."

Epstein contends that the district court erred in its determination that the letter demonstrates that he was "clearly on notice" of a possible injury to his rights as of the October 10, 1999 letter because it was "merely an inquiry for more information." Epstein further maintains that the letter was a response to a "rumor" that might have been incorrect, and that he "neither knew, nor should have known that he had been harmed by Bard's conduct" as of October 10, 1999. He insists that "[o]nly after receiving a proper reply from Bard, or other reliable sources," could the statute of limitations begin to accrue. We find this argument to be wholly unpersuasive.

Epstein suggests that because he was uncertain as to the nature and extent of his injury when he wrote the October 10, 1999 letter, he could not have been on inquiry notice as of that date. This argument completely misunderstands the concept of inquiry notice. The discovery rule does not require that a plaintiff know the specific details pertaining to an alleged harm, but instead it imposes a "duty to investigate" on a plaintiff who has cause for concern. * * * Critically, knowledge of "every fact necessary to prevail on the claim" is not required to put the plaintiff on inquiry notice and trigger the accrual period. * * * In this case, we have no doubt that Epstein had cause for concern. The October 10, 1999 letter makes plain that Epstein had reason to believe that Bard was making unauthorized use of his intellectual property. In the letter, Epstein made clear his belief that SME owned the Tigertail, and that Bard was selling it despite the fact that SME was not providing it. In his own brief, Epstein admits that, by writing the letter, he "acted as a reasonably prudent person in his situation would, he inquired into the truth of the matter." We agree that a reasonable person would have inquired into the issue and therefore find that the district court properly deemed Epstein to have been on inquiry notice as of October 10, 1999.

* * *

B.   Tolling

Epstein next argues that even if his cause of action accrued on October 10, 1999, his claims are not time-barred because the doctrine of fraudulent concealment applied to toll the statutes of limitations. Fraudulent concealment is a tolling doctrine codified in Mass. Gen. Laws. ch. 260, § 12. Under that section, [i]f a person liable to a personal action fraudulently conceals the cause of such action from the knowledge of the person entitled to bring it, the period prior to the discovery of his cause of action by the person so entitled shall be excluded in determining the time limited for the commencement of the action. The Supreme Judicial Court of Massachusetts has held that, in the absence of a fiduciary relationship, the statute of limitations may be tolled under this doctrine "if the wrongdoer . . . concealed the existence of a cause of action through some affirmative act done with intent to deceive." * * * The district court found that the tolling doctrine did not apply because Epstein had not alleged that Bard acted affirmatively to deceive him. Epstein insists that determination was in error. In his complaint, Epstein claims that Bard acted to deceive him by 1) affirmatively concealing certain material facts about its use of his intellectual property; and 2) "making false promises" regarding its intention to undertake "further inquiry" into his concerns, inducing Epstein to delay taking legal action in reliance upon these promises.

In his complaint, Epstein alleged that Bard concealed and suppressed "material facts" as to 1) Bard's "notification to the Food and Drug Administration pertaining to the BUD Soft Tip Catheter"; 2) Bard's "filing a Master Design History for their internal records"; 3) Bard's "resubmitting the 510k to the FDA to substantiate additional claims like radiopacity and tip strength"; 4) Bard's "dissemination to third parties of Plaintiff's technology, intellectual property and trade secrets"; 5) Bard's "use of

Plaintiff's technology, intellectual property and trade secrets" without permission; and 6) Bard's "use of Plaintiff's technology, intellectual property, and trade secrets to apply for a Patent." There is no elaboration on any of these allegations.

Bard maintains that these allegations do not adequately support a claim for fraudulent concealment, and we agree. Under Rule 9(b) of the Federal Rules of Civil Procedure, it is incumbent upon the plaintiff "to plead with particularity the facts giving rise to the fraudulent concealment claim." * * * It is well-established that "[t]his rule entails specifying in the pleader's complaint the time, place, and content of the alleged false or fraudulent representations." * * * Epstein's complaint falls far short. He fails to explain the time, place, content or significance of the "facts" that Bard allegedly concealed and entirely fails to explain how Bard's actions constituted fraud as to him.

Epstein also contends that Bard affirmatively attempted to deceive him "by making false promises" regarding its intention to investigate the issues raised in Epstein's letters. It is Epstein's position that he acted in reliance upon "this delaying tactic" when he decided to postpone bringing suit. Specifically, Epstein explains that a letter from Bard's counsel dated November 10, 1999 indicated that "Bard seemed intent on initiating a dialogue," and although that letter stated that "Bard would come forward with affidavits to negate Mr. Epstein's assertions," ultimately "Bard entirely failed to forward any affidavits or answer any inquiries whatsoever." The district court did not find this argument persuasive, and neither do we. In Massachusetts, "[e]ven in cases of fraud . . . there is no concealment by mere failure to disclose if the aggrieved party has full means of detecting the fraud." * * *. Here, Epstein patently had the means to detect the alleged fraud. Regardless of what Bard might have suggested in its November 10, 1999 letter, Epstein should have detected at some point during the nearly four years before he finally filed suit that no affidavits were forthcoming. * * *

III.

For the foregoing reasons, we affirm the decision of the district court. Costs are awarded to the appellee.

Affirmed.

DID YOU GET IT?

1. According to the court, when did the statute of limitations begin to run? *1999 letter P sent*

2. On what basis did the plaintiff argue for a tolling of the statute of limitations? *— that D concealed their wrongdoing*

Reading Guidance
Is trade secret misappropriation a continuing tort?

[handwritten: use is only once; use the initial use]

CADENCE DESIGN SYSTEMS, INC. V. AVANT! CORP.

[handwritten: —software]

California Supreme Court, 2002.
29 Cal. 4th 215.

[handwritten: —fmr. employees → new co.]

MORENO, J.

We granted the request for certification of the United States Court of Appeals for the Ninth Circuit pursuant to California Rules of Court, rule 29.5, to address the following question:

> Under the California Uniform Trade Secrets Act (UTSA), Civil Code section 3426, when does a claim for trade secret infringement arise: only once, when the initial misappropriation occurs, or with each subsequent misuse of the trade secret? * * *

I.   Statement of Facts

The relevant facts, as stated in the Ninth Circuit's certification order to this court, are as follows:

Cadence Design Systems, Inc., and Avant! Corporation compete in the field of integrated circuit design automation. Both companies design "place and route" software, which enables computer chip designers to place and connect tiny components on a computer chip. Cadence formed in 1988 through the merger of several companies. Four senior employees left Cadence in 1991 to found Avant!, originally known as ArcSys.

In March 1994, Cadence vice-president Gerald Hsu resigned from Cadence to sign on with Avant!. Because Hsu possessed valuable business trade secrets and other confidential information, Cadence informed Hsu that it objected to his working at Avant!. Concerned that Hsu would reveal proprietary Cadence information when managing Avant!, Cadence sent Avant! a draft complaint naming Avant! and Hsu as defendants. Cadence alleged trade secret misappropriation and other causes of action. In negotiating a settlement of Cadence's claims, Cadence and Avant! apparently did not discuss Avant!'s alleged use of Cadence's Framework II (DFII) trade secret source code.

After extensive negotiations, in June 1994, the parties entered into a confidential settlement agreement (the Agreement or Release) that included a mutual general release, which provided in part:

> "Cadence, [Avant!] and Hsu . . . hereby forever release and discharge each other . . . of and from any and all manner of action, claim or cause of action, in law or in equity, suits, debts, liens, contracts, agreements, promises, liabilities, demands, losses, damages, costs or expenses, including without limitation court

costs and attorneys' fees, which they may have against each other at the time of the execution of this Agreement, known or unknown, including but not limited to any claims arising out of, or in connection with, or relating directly or indirectly to the following: Hsu's employment with Cadence, the cessation of Hsu's employment with Cadence, any wrongful termination of Hsu, any age or race discrimination by Cadence with respect to Hsu, any anticompetitive activity or unfair competition or trade secret misappropriation by Cadence, Hsu or [Avant!] with respect to Cadence, Hsu or [Avant!] with respect to Cadence, Hsu or [Avant!] . . . or any other actions taken by Cadence to with respect to Hsu or [Avant!] or by Hsu or [Avant!] with respect to Cadence."

* * *

[handwritten margin note: — Suing again — whether Release Agmt bars it.]

In the summer of 1995, a Cadence engineer discovered a "bug" (an error) in Avant!'s ArcCell software program that was similar to a bug he had inadvertently created several years earlier when writing source code for Cadence's DFII product. In December 1995, the Santa Clara County District Attorney executed a search of Avant!'s headquarters. Among the items seized was a log that showed line-by-line copying of Cadence source code in 1991 by a former Cadence employee and Avant! founder.

In December 1995, Cadence sued Avant! for theft of its copyrighted and trade secret source code and sought a preliminary order enjoining the sale of Avant!'s ArcCell and Aquarius products. In anticipation of trial, both sides filed cross-motions for partial summary judgment concerning the effect of the Release. Avant! argued that because Cadence had released all its claims existing at the time of the Release, any claims based on continuing or future misuse of trade secrets that were stolen prior to the date of the Release were now barred. Cadence maintained that the only claims it had released were those for misappropriation occurring before the effective date of the Release, and not claims to redress Avant!'s continuing or new misuses of its trade secrets after the date of the Release.

The federal district court ruled on these summary judgment motions on October 13, 1999. Reversing its initial order, the district court held that all of Cadence's trade secret claims for post-Release misuse of its DFII trade secrets taken before the Release were barred by the Release. Cadence now is appealing this decision to the Ninth Circuit. If the Release barred Cadence's claims existing at the time of the Agreement, but did not bar future claims, the question still remains: What claims existed at the time of the Agreement? Are all of Cadence's claims for Avant!'s trade secret misappropriation part of the same claim, or does each successive misuse of Cadence trade secret source code give rise to a separate claim?

II. Discussion

D's view

Avant! argues that a cause of action for misappropriation of a given trade secret by a particular plaintiff against a particular defendant arises only once, when the trade secret is initially misappropriated. In support of this position, it relies in large part on the rationale set forth in *Monolith Portland Midwest Co. v. Kaiser Aluminum & C. Corp.*, which applied the California common law of trade secrets. The *Monolith* court rejected the position exemplified by *Underwater Storage, Inc. v. United States Rubber Co.*, "that the wrong is the adverse use of the secret disclosed in confidence; each use is a new wrong, and a continuing use is a continuing wrong. Underlying this theory is the concept that a trade secret is in the nature of property, which is damaged or destroyed by the adverse use. . . . California does not treat trade secrets as if they were property. It is the *relationship* between the parties at the time the secret is disclosed that is protected. * * * The protected relationship, contractual or confidential, is one to which, as Mr. Justice Holmes observed, 'some rudimentary requirements of good faith' are attached. * * * (*E. I. Du Pont de Nemours Powder Co. v. Masland*) *The fabric of the relationship once rent is not torn anew with each added use or disclosure, although the damage suffered may thereby be aggravated. The cause of action arises but once. . . .*" (*Monolith*.)

P's view

On the other hand, Cadence asserts that the UTSA, which as discussed below was adopted by California in 1984, changed the common law view typified by *Monolith*, and now views trade secrets as property rather than simply as the protection of a confidential relationship. It further reasons that because trade secret misappropriation is the wrongful taking or use of protected property, *each* new use represents a new claim of misappropriation. As will be discussed, neither Cadence's nor Avant!'s position is entirely correct.

In order to answer the certified question, we must examine the pertinent language of the UTSA. * * *

The most critical section of UTSA for purposes of this case is section [6] which provides: "An action for misappropriation must be brought within three years after the misappropriation is discovered or by the exercise of reasonable diligence should have been discovered. *For the purposes of this section, a continuing misappropriation constitutes a single claim.*" (Italics added.)

As the Court of Appeal recognized in *Glue-Fold*, "[s]ection 3426.6 [of the California Civil Code] is derived almost verbatim from section 6 of the Uniform Act as originally drafted. It is therefore appropriate to accord substantial weight to the commissioners' comment on the construction of what is now section 3426.6. [Citations.] That comment is: 'There presently is a conflict of authority as to whether trade secret misappropriation is a continuing wrong. *Compare Monolith Portland Midwest Co. v. Kaiser*

Aluminum & Chemical Corp. (not a continuing wrong under California law-limitation period upon all recovery begins upon initial misappropriation) with *Underwater Storage, Inc. v. U.S. Rubber Co.,* (continuing wrong under general principles-limitation period with respect to a specific act of misappropriation begins at the time that the act of misappropriation occurs). This Act rejects a continuing wrong approach to the statute of limitations but delays the commencement of the limitation period until an aggrieved person discovers or reasonably should have discovered the existence of misappropriation. If objectively reasonable notice of misappropriation exists, three years is sufficient time to vindicate one's legal rights. (U. Trade Secrets Act, com. to § 6, p. 462.)"

The UTSA does not define the term "continuing misappropriation," but its meaning appears evident in light of the definition of "misappropriation." It is the continuing use or disclosure of a trade secret after that secret was acquired by improper means or as otherwise specified in section 3426.1, subdivision (b). Thus, for statute of limitations purposes, a continuing misappropriation is viewed as a single claim. The drafters of the UTSA explicitly affirmed *Monolith* and rejected the contrary view that misappropriation gives rise to multiple claims each time the trade secret is misused or improperly disclosed.

From our examination of the above statutes, a distinction between a "misappropriation" and a "claim" emerges. A *misappropriation* within the meaning of the UTSA occurs not only at the time of the initial acquisition of the trade secret by wrongful means, but also with each misuse or wrongful disclosure of the secret. But a *claim* for misappropriation of a trade secret arises for a given plaintiff against a given defendant only once, at the time of the initial misappropriation, subject to the discovery rule provided in section 3426.6. Each new misuse or wrongful disclosure is viewed as augmenting a single claim of continuing misappropriation rather than as giving rise to a separate claim.

Cadence makes much of the language in section 3426.6 that states, "[f]or *the purposes of this section*, a continuing misappropriation constitutes a single claim." (Italics added.) Based on that language, Cadence argues that a continuing misappropriation constitutes a single claim only for statute of limitations purposes. This argument cannot withstand scrutiny. The certified question asks when a *claim* for trade secret infringement arises. The term "claim" does not have some theoretical meaning apart from the context in which it is used. In the present case, the certified question is asked in the context of a release, which is intended to settle or prevent litigation. Therefore, "claim" must be defined in the context of litigation. If "continuing misappropriation" is viewed as a single claim for statute of limitations purposes (see *Glue-Fold*), then it is difficult to fathom how it could be treated as more than one claim for purposes of litigation generally. For example, a plaintiff could not legitimately plead separate claims of misappropriation for each misuse of a trade secret, for to do so would impermissibly evade the statute of limitations. Nor can it be asserted that separate "claims" accruing at different times can have the same limitations period, because that position is contrary to the rule that each civil action possesses its own statutorily prescribed limitations period. (*See* Code Civ. Proc., § 312.) The only other alternative is to hold that the term "claim" means one thing in the context of litigation and something else in the context of releases. There is no indication the Legislature intended this kind of inconsistency.

* * *

Another occasion in which an act of continuing misappropriation may be said to constitute more than one claim is when multiple defendants are involved. For example, in *PMC, Inc. v. Kadisha* officers, directors, and investors of a corporation were sued personally for a trade secret misappropriation initiated before their involvement in the corporation. They sought summary judgment in part on the grounds that they could not be held liable because the initial misappropriation had occurred before they assumed their positions. The Court of Appeal rejected that position, reasoning that the definition of misappropriation includes disclosure or use of a trade secret by persons who knew or had reason to know that the trade secret was acquired by improper means. (*Id.*) But Cadence's assertion that *Kadisha* advances its position is incorrect. That case holds only that there may be separate claims of continuing misappropriation among *different* defendants, with differing dates of accrual and types of tortious conduct—some defendants liable for initial misappropriation of the trade secret, others only for later continuing use. This holding does not conflict with our conclusion that there is only a single UTSA claim against a single defendant misappropriating a single plaintiff's trade secret.

* * *

Our answer to the certified question is narrow. As stated, we do not accept Avant!'s position, at least stated in its strongest form, that only the initial misappropriation of a trade secret via the breach of a confidential relationship constitutes misappropriation—the UTSA plainly states otherwise. The potential damages encompassed by a continuing misappropriation claim may expand with each illicit use or disclosure of the trade secret. Nor do we address how the parties intended to define the term "claim" in the present release. All we decide is that the UTSA views a continuing misappropriation of a trade secret of one party by another as a single claim.

III. Conclusion

We conclude that a plaintiff's claim for misappropriation of a trade secret against a defendant arises only once, when the trade secret is initially misappropriated, and each subsequent use or disclosure of the secret augments the initial claim rather than arises as a separate claim.

DID YOU GET IT?

1. Is trade secret misappropriation a continuing wrong? Why or why not?

2. What distinction does the court make between plaintiff's claims against Avant! and plaintiff's claims against others?

3. What is the statute of limitation for claims against third-parties who come to possess trade secrets months or years after the original misappropriation?

2. UTSA SECTION 7: PRECLUSION OF ANCILLARY STATE CLAIMS

The drafting history of the UTSA reveals that there was great concern about the possible over-assertion of trade secret rights (or more generally, information rights) not only because of fear that state trade secret law might be preempted by federal law if it was too broad (see discussion of the federal preemption doctrine in Chapter 2), but due to concerns that trade secret litigation might be used for anti-competitive purposes. *See* Sharon K. Sandeen, *The Evolution of Trade Secret Law and Why Courts Commit Error When They Do Not Follow the Uniform Trade Secrets Act,* 33 HAMLINE L. REV. 493 (2010).

While the drafters of the UTSA thought it was appropriate for state law to provide a remedy for the misappropriation of information that actually qualifies as a trade secret, they decided to preclude protection for lesser forms of business information. This was done in three ways. First, the UTSA carefully defines and limits the information that can qualify for trade secret protection by specifying three requirements for trade secrecy. Second, a provision similar to Section 759 of the *Restatement of Torts* (which provided protection for non-trade secret information when it is improperly acquired "for the purpose of advancing a rival business interest") was not included in the UTSA. Third, Section 7 of the UTSA was included to preclude the assertion of ancillary tort causes of action that provide remedies for the misappropriation of information. It reads:

UNIFORM TRADE SECRETS ACT

Section 7

(a) Except as provided in subsection (b), this Act displaces conflicting tort, restitutionary, and other law of this State providing civil remedies for misappropriation of a trade secret.

(b) This Act does not affect:

    (1) contractual remedies, whether or not based upon misappropriation of a trade secret;

    (2) other civil remedies that are not based upon misappropriation of a trade secret; or

    (3) criminal remedies, whether or not based upon misappropriation of a trade secret.

———

Although the authors of this casebook believe that the historical context and drafting history of the UTSA support the broad application of Section 7, not all courts agree. *See* John T. Cross, *UTSA Displacement of Other State Law Claims*, 33 HAMLINE L. REV. 445 (2010) (discussing the cases which have examined the purpose and meaning of Section 7). Also, not every state has adopted the identical language of Section 7 as set forth in the UTSA. For instance, in contrast to the foregoing language, California Civil Code § 3426.7 provides, in pertinent part:

    (a) Except as otherwise expressly provided, this title does not supersede any statute relating to misappropriation of a trade secret, or any statute otherwise regulating trade secrets.

    (b) This title does not affect (1) contractual remedies, whether or not based upon misappropriation of a trade secret, (2) other civil remedies that are not based upon misappropriation of a trade secret, or (3) criminal remedies, whether or not based upon misappropriation of a trade secret.

See also Ark. Code Ann. § 4–75–602 and Neb. Rev. St. § 87–507.

The following case presents the majority view concerning the meaning and application of Section 7 of the UTSA. For the minority view, see *Burbank Grease Services, LLC v. Sokolowski*, 294 Wis. 2d 274 (2006) and *Callaway Golf Co. v. Dunlop Slazenger Grp. Americas, Inc.*, 295 F.Supp.2d 430 (D. Del. 2003).

Reading Guidance

According to the court, why did the drafters of the UTSA include Section 7?

BLUEEARTH BIOFUELS, LLC V. HAWAIIAN ELEC. CO., INC.

Hawai'i Supreme Court, 2010.
123 Hawai'i 314.

Opinion of the Court by DUFFY, J.

The United States District Court for the District of Hawai'i (District Court) certified the following questions of law to the Hawai'i Supreme Court:

1. When are "tort, restitutionary, and other law[s] of this state" displaced because they "conflict" with [the Hawai'i Uniform Trade Secrets Act (HUTSA)], Hawaii Revised Statutes ("HRS") § 482B?

2. When a claim is found to "conflict" with HUTSA, what is the scope of the preemption, or displacement, of that claim under HRS § 482B–8?

3. May a claim that is found not to "conflict" with HUTSA still be preempted, or displaced, under HRS § 482B–8?

4. Does HUTSA also preempt, or displace, claims based upon the alleged misuse of "confidential information," which is determined, before or during trial, not to meet the definition of "trade secret" under HRS § 482B–2?

I.   BACKGROUND

A.   Factual Background

This case involves plans to create and construct a biodiesel production facility on Maui. Plaintiff-Appellee BlueEarth Biofuels, LLC (BlueEarth) specializes in the production of biodiesel production facilities. In or around March 2006, BlueEarth began talks with Hawaiian Electric Company, Inc. (HECO) and Maui Electric Company, Ltd. (MECO) to "jointly and exclusively develop a biodiesel production facility to be located on the Island of Maui [(the Project).]"

In furtherance of their discussions regarding the Project, BlueEarth executed a Mutual Non-Circumvention and Non-Disclosure Agreement (NDA) with both HECO and MECO. BlueEarth, HECO, and MECO also signed a confidential memorandum of understanding (Project Agreement), which set forth how the Project would be planned, developed, permitted, funded, constructed, maintained, and operated.

In 2007, BlueEarth, HECO, and MECO began discussions related to potential fuel subcontractors who would manage and run logistics for a fuel terminal, which would be used to store raw materials and fuel in connection with the Project. BlueEarth approached Aloha Petroleum, Ltd. (Aloha) as a potential subcontractor. In furtherance of their discussions, BlueEarth and Aloha executed a NDA on January 28, 2008. As with the HECO and MECO NDAs, the Aloha NDA contained a provision that information furnished by one of the parties would be kept confidential by the receiving party and its representatives. On July 14, 2008, BlueEarth and Aloha also executed a Mutual Confidentiality Agreement (Confidentiality Agreement), which provided that neither party shall use or disclose each other's confidential information to third parties or solicit business from each other's clients.

BlueEarth alleges that, contrary to the terms of the previously described Project Agreement, NDAs, and Confidentiality Agreement, HECO, MECO and Aloha engaged in undisclosed negotiations with each other concerning the development, investment, and ownership of the Project with the intent to cut BlueEarth out of the Project altogether. * * *

B. *Procedural Background*

* * * On May 29, 2009, BlueEarth filed its Second Amended Complaint (SAC), alleging the following causes of action: 1) breach of contract against HECO (HECO NDA); 2) breach of contract against MECO (MECO NDA); 3) breach of contract against HECO and MECO (Project Agreement); 4) quantum meruit/unjust enrichment against HECO and MECO; 5) breach of contract against Aloha (Aloha NDA and Confidentiality Agreement); 6) unfair competition against under Hawai'i Revised Statutes (HRS) § 480–2, *et seq.* against HECO, MECO, Stahlkopf, and Aloha; 7) tortious interference with existing contracts against HECO, MECO, Stahlkopf, and Aloha (all NDAs and the Confidentiality Agreement); 8) tortious interference with existing contract against Aloha (Project Agreement); 9) misappropriation of trade secrets against HECO, MECO, Stahlkopf, and Aloha; 10) conversion against HECO, MECO, Stahlkopf, and Aloha; and 11) breach of fiduciary duty against HECO and MECO.

On June 29, 2009, Aloha moved to dismiss the Sixth through Tenth causes of action. On the same day, HECO, MECO, and Stahlkopf (collectively the HECO defendants) moved to dismiss BlueEarth's SAC. * * *

II. *STANDARDS OF REVIEW*

* * *

B. *Statutory Construction*

It is a well-established rule of statutory construction that this court's foremost obligation is to ascertain and give effect to the intention of the legislature, which is to be obtained primarily from the language contained in the statute itself. And [this court] must read statutory language in the context of the entire statute and construe it in a manner consistent with its purpose. * * *.

III. *DISCUSSION*

In answering the Certified Questions, this court is required to determine the preemptive scope of the Hawai'i Uniform Trade Secrets Act (HUTSA) in HRS section 482B–1 *et seq.,* which is an issue of first impression in this jurisdiction. The HUTSA's preemption provision [HRS § 482B]. reads as follows:

> Effect on other law. (a) Except as provided in subsection (b) this chapter displaces conflicting tort, restitutionary, and other law of this State providing civil remedies for misappropriation of a trade secret.
>
> (b) This chapter does not affect:
>
>> (1) Contractual remedies, whether or not based upon misappropriation of a trade secret;
>>
>> (2) Other civil remedies that are not based upon misappropriation of a trade secret; or
>>
>> (3) Criminal remedies, whether or not based upon misappropriation of a trade secret.

. . . .

In order to answer the Certified Questions, it is necessary to first review the background of the Uniform Trade Secrets Act (UTSA) and HUTSA and analyze the decisions of other jurisdictions that have considered the scope of the UTSA's preemptive effect.

A. *Background of the UTSA and HUTSA*

The UTSA was drafted by the National Conference of Commissioners on Uniform State Laws (Commissioners) in 1979 and amended in 1985. The Commissioners gave the rationale behind drafting the UTSA as follows:

> Notwithstanding the commercial importance of state trade secret law to interstate business, this law has not developed satisfactorily. In the first place, its development is uneven . . . Secondly, even in states in which there has been significant litigation, there is undue uncertainty concerning the parameters of trade secret protection, and the appropriate remedies for misappropriation of a trade secret.

One commentator observed:

> "Under technological and economic pressures, industry continues to rely on trade secret protection despite the doubtful and

confused status of both common law and statutory remedies. Clear, uniform trade secret protection is urgently needed. . . ."

Comment, "Theft of Trade Secrets: The Need for a Statutory Solution."

To this end, the UTSA created a model statutory cause of action for misappropriation of trade secrets. * * * The Commissioners intended that the UTSA "be applied and construed to effectuate its general purpose to make uniform the law with respect to the subject of this Act among states enacting it."

* * * The HUTSA incorporates nearly verbatim the UTSA's definitions of "trade secret" and "misappropriation", as well as its remedies, statute of limitations and preemption provisions. * * * Though the HUTSA does not contain a uniformity provision of its own, HRS section 1–24 states that

> [a]ll provisions of uniform acts adopted by the State shall be so interpreted and construed as to effectuate their general purpose to make uniform the laws of the states and territories which enact them.

B. *The Scope of Preemption*

Courts that have considered the UTSA's preemption provision have "uniformly interpreted [it] to preempt previously existing misappropriation of trade secret actions, whether statutory or common law." * * * All the parties agree that HUTSA displaces Hawai'i's existing statutory and common law causes of action for misappropriation of a trade secret. Two questions regarding the scope of preemption remain: (1) whether the HUTSA displaces non-contract civil claims, where such claims are based on allegations of misappropriation of a trade secret; and (2) whether a non-contract civil claim is preempted when it is based on the misappropriation of confidential information that does not rise to the level of a statutorily-defined trade secret.

1. A non-contract civil claim conflicts with the HUTSA, and is therefore displaced, to the extent that it is based upon misappropriation of a trade secret.

* * *

The preemption provision of the HUTSA, like that of the UTSA, states that "[t]his chapter does not affect . . . [o]ther civil remedies that are not based upon the misappropriation of a trade secret[.]"HRS § 482B–8(b)(2). We agree with the *Hauck* court's analysis that the phrase "based upon" implies that "the UTSA's preemptive force reaches more than just claims *of* or *for* misappropriation of a trade secret." Otherwise, a plaintiff could state multiple different claims, all stemming from the same misappropriation of trade secret injury. This would undermine the purpose of the UTSA, which was to resolve the "uncertainty concerning the parameters of trade secret protection" and create a uniform law to remedy trade secret misappropriation. *See* 14 U.L.A. (prefatory note).

The "elements" test advocated by BlueEarth faces precisely the problem stated above. It would allow a party to raise multiple different claims based on the same trade secret misappropriation injury. Only a minority of courts apply the "elements" test to determine preemption. * * *

The majority of courts, however, have rejected the "elements" test and have instead examined the factual allegations underlying each claim to determine whether a claim, whatever its label, is based upon misappropriation of a trade secret.

BlueEarth's arguments to the contrary are not supported by the comment to the UTSA's preemption provision. BlueEarth contends that the comment's statement that "[t]his Act . . . is not a comprehensive statement of civil remedies [,]" means that "[b]eyond displacing previously existing common law actions for trade secret misappropriation . . . the Act does not displace other civil remedies." However, it appears that the comment is merely restating the substance of the preemption provision. The UTSA is not a comprehensive statement of civil remedies because "[i]t does not apply to a duty voluntarily assumed through an express or implied-in-fact contract." 14 U.L.A § 7 (comment). ("This Act does not affect . . . contractual remedies, whether or not based upon misappropriation of a trade secret[.]")

The comment further states that "[t]he Act also does not apply to a duty imposed by law that *is not dependent* upon the existence of competitively significant secret information, like an agent's duty of loyalty to his or her principal." * * * (emphasis added). BlueEarth argues that the comment's reference to "duties" implies a legal, rather than a factual, inquiry, and that the duty to refrain from misappropriating trade secrets is unrelated to and independent from, for example, the duty not to intentionally interfere with the contracts of others. Contrary to BlueEarth's argument, the language of the comment implies that the UTSA *does* apply to duties that *are* dependent upon the existence of competitively significant secret information, whatever their label. In analyzing whether a claim is preempted by the UTSA, "the court is to look beyond the label to the facts being asserted in support of the claims." *Weins* ("The majority of courts that have examined this issue have not relied upon the label attached to the claim, but have examined the facts underlying the claim to determine whether it is preempted by the UTSA.").

* * *

Though the majority of courts agree that an analysis of the plaintiff's allegations is necessary to determine whether a claim is based upon misappropriation of a trade secret, courts have differed on how the presence of facts relating to the improper acquisition, disclosure, or use of trade secrets within non-UTSA claims affects preemption. Some courts have imposed broad preemption, going so far as to wholly preempt claims that include trade secret misappropriation allegations. * * * Other courts suggest that the mere presence of facts in a claim that go beyond trade secret misappropriation prevents preemption. * * *

The UTSA's unitary definitions of "trade secret" and "misappropriation", its statutory remedies and statute of limitations for misappropriation of a trade secret, and its uniformity provision all evince the goal of eliminating uncertainty and creating a single action for misappropriation of a trade secret. * * *

The HUTSA was adopted by the Hawai'i State Legislature in furtherance of these goals, as evidenced by the fact that the language of the HUTSA is virtually identical to the UTSA. *See Kaho'ohanohano* (stating that "this court must read statutory language in the context of the entire statute and construe it in a manner consistent with its purpose" (brackets omitted)); * * * We find that the best approach to preemption, consistent with the goals of the UTSA and HUTSA, is the "same proof" standard articulated in *Hauck*. Under this standard, "if proof of a non-UTSA claim would also simultaneously establish a claim for misappropriation of trade secrets, it is preempted irrespective of whatever surplus elements of proof were necessary to establish it." *Hauck*. To the extent, however, that the claim is "based upon wrongful conduct[,] independent of the misappropriation of trade secrets[,]" it will not be preempted by the HUTSA. * * * In this way, the HUTSA will be the sole noncontractual civil remedy for misappropriation of a trade secret, while preserving "tort, restitutionary, and other law[s,]" HRS § 482B–8, that "seek[ ] to remedy an injury caused not by the misappropriation of proprietary information, but by separate conduct[.]" * * *

2. A non-contract civil claim that is based upon "confidential" information which does not rise to the level of a statutorily-defined trade secret is preempted.

* * *

Courts holding that non-UTSA, non-contract claims based upon "confidential" or "commercially valuable" information are not preempted have generally stated that their analysis is based on the "plain language" of the UTSA's preemption provision. * * *

In *Burbank Grease Services, LLC v. Sokolowski,* (hereinafter *Burbank Grease II*), for example, the Wisconsin Supreme Court noted at the outset that the allegedly misappropriated information underlying the plaintiff's claims did not qualify as a trade secret under the WUTSA's definition. * * * The Wisconsin Supreme Court held that the plain language of the WUTSA's preemption provision excepts from the class of unaffected remedies only those remedies based on the misappropriation of a statutorily-defined trade secret. It leaves available all other remaining civil remedies for the protection of confidential information. * * *

The purported "plain language" approach, exemplified in *Burbank Grease II,* has been criticized for disregarding the UTSA's uniformity directive. The dissent in *Burbank Grease II* described the majority's analysis as

> pay[ing] lip service to UTSA's uniformity goal and the corresponding legislative directive. It fails to engage in the necessary analysis to determine what is the uniform interpretation of the preemption provisions in UTSA or how cases decided by courts in other UTSA jurisdictions analyze the language in these provisions.

Burbank Grease II, (Bradley, J., dissenting); * * * The dissent found that, in contrast, the Wisconsin Court of Appeals analyzed the decisions of other jurisdictions to have considered the question and determined that "the prevailing rule in most UTSA jurisdictions is that UTSA is meant to replace tort claims for unauthorized use of confidential information with a single statutory cause of action." *Burbank Grease II,* (Bradley, J., dissenting).

* * *

The majority of the courts to have considered the issue have held that the UTSA's preemption provision abolish[es] all free-standing alternative causes of action for theft or misuse of confidential, proprietary, or otherwise secret information falling short of trade secret status (*e.g.* idea misappropriation, information piracy, theft of commercial information, etc.). * * *

The rationale for these decisions has been explained as follows:

> States adopting statutory provisions analogous to the UTSA's section 7 intend that at least some prior law relating to the protection of commercial information be displaced. Permitting litigants in UTSA states to assert common-law claims for the misappropriation or misuse of confidential data would reduce the UTSA to just another basis for recovery and leave prior law effectively untouched. Further, by expressly exempting "contractual remedies, whether or not based upon misappropriation of a trade secret" and "other civil remedies that are not based upon misappropriation of a trade secret" from its preemptive penumbra, the UTSA makes clear that only those claims addressing or arising out of wrongs distinct from pure information piracy survive passage of the trade secret statute. Indeed, contrary interpretations of the UTSA's "Effect on Other Law" provision ... effectively negate the UTSA's goal of promoting uniformity in "trade secrets" law. Additionally, these

contrary interpretations render the statutory preemption provision effectively meaningless.

* * *

Further, commentators have cautioned that information which is broader than the scope of information defined as a "trade secret" by the UTSA, and not the subject of reasonable efforts to maintain its secrecy does not deserve protection in the form of non-contract tort claims. * * *

* * * Similar to the court in *Burbank Grease II,* BlueEarth argues that

> the plain language of the preemption provision . . . refers only to "trade secrets" as defined by the Act . . . Since there is no statutory language regarding preemption of other confidential information not rising to the level of trade secrets, there is no reason to think such preemption was intended.

However, the HUTSA's preemption provision should not be considered "in a vacuum." *Burbank Grease II* (Bradley, J., dissenting). Rather, "this court must read statutory language in the context of the entire statute and construe it in a manner consistent with its purpose." *Kaho'ohanohano.* Here, the Hawai'i State Legislature has directed that "[a]ll provisions of uniform acts adopted by the State shall be so interpreted and construed as to effectuate their general purpose and to make uniform the laws of the states and territories which enact them." HRS § 1–24 (2009). As the foregoing analysis shows, courts in other jurisdictions have not been absolutely uniform in deciding whether non-contract claims based on information which does not rise to the level of a statutorily-defined trade secret are preempted under the UTSA. However, the conclusion that such claims are preempted, reached by the majority of courts to have considered the issue, comports with the HUTSA's goal of uniformity in the area of trade secret misappropriation.

* * *

The court in *Mortgage Specialists* noted that, along with the contribution of unitary definitions of "trade secret" and "misappropriation" [t]he UTSA "also arose to create a uniform business environment that created more certain standards for protection of commercially valuable information." [*Auto Channel*.] "[T]he purpose of the preemption provision is to preserve a single tort action under state law for misappropriation of a trade secret as defined in the statute and thus to eliminate other tort causes of action founded on allegations of misappropriation of information that may not meet the statutory standard for a trade secret." [*Burbank I.*] * * *

The *Mortgage Specialists* court's analysis is persuasive and consistent with the Hawai'i State Legislature's goals in adopting the HUTSA. *See* HRS § 1–24 (2009) Accordingly, we hold that the HUTSA preempts non-contract, civil claims based on the improper acquisition, disclosure or use of confidential and/or commercially valuable information that does not rise to the level of a statutorily-defined trade secret.

* * *

DID YOU GET IT?

1. What information did the court rely upon in interpreting the Hawaii statute that the Wisconsin court in *Burbank Grease* did not?

2. Why did the court find that Section 7 precluded other civil claims for the misappropriation of information not meeting the definition of a trade secret?

3. Does Section 7 preclude all other civil causes of action that a trade secret owner might bring? If not, how must those causes of action differ from the causes of action that are precluded?

> ### *Food for Thought*
> *Which affirmative defense is likely to be at issue in Wisconsin because of the* Burbank Grease *court's narrow interpretation of Section 7 of the UTSA?*

---

3. VIOLATION OF THE FIRST AMENDMENT

The First Amendment to the U.S. Constitution states, in part, that "Congress shall adopt no laws which . . . abridge freedom of the press or freedom of speech." Although not all trade secret cases will implicate the First Amendment, when the defendant's alleged wrongdoing involves the actual or threatened disclosure (as opposed to the actual or threatened acquisition or use) of trade secrets, a First Amendment issue may arise because the disclosure is a form of speech. For instance, defendants who did not engage in the initial wrongful acquisition or disclosure of the alleged trade secrets but merely found the information on the internet often assert a First Amendment defense. When weighing First Amendment rights against the commercial interests in protecting trade secrets, courts are usually reluctant to enjoin the use of trade secrets. This is especially so where the trade secrets have already been publicly disclosed and, therefore, no longer qualify for trade secret protection.

As you will read in *Ford Motor Co. v. Lane*, in the absence of proof that the defendant owed a fiduciary duty to keep the information secret, or entered into a confidentiality agreement not to publish trade secret information, a court could rule that the First Amendment prevails and treat an injunction to prevent the defendant from publishing trade secrets as an impermissible prior restraint. However, if the First Amendment always trumps an owner's right to protect against disclosure, then trade secret law would be powerless to enforce non-disclosure agreements or otherwise prevent disclosure of secret information. Accordingly, in one case, *DVD v. Bunner* (which you read in Chapter 7), the California Supreme Court ruled that an injunction against disclosure of information that qualifies as a trade secret does not always violate the First Amendment.

As you read the case that follows, consider when it is appropriate under the First Amendment to enjoin speech that takes the form of a disclosure of trade secrets and when it is not.

Reading Guidance

What factual scenario gives rise to a First Amendment argument in a trade secret case?

FORD MOTOR COMPANY V. LANE

United States District Court, E.D. Michigan, 1999.
67 F.Supp.2d 745.

EDMUNDS, DISTRICT JUDGE.

Thirty years ago, on September 2, 1969, computer scientists at UCLA introduced a system which allowed one computer to speak to another. The birth of the Internet, inauspicious at the time, presaged a revolution in worldwide communications. In the realm of law, we are only beginning to grapple with the impact of the communications revolution, and this case represents just one part of one skirmish-a clash between our commitment to the freedom of speech and the press, and our dedication to the protection of commercial innovation and intellectual property. In this case, the battle is won by the First Amendment.

This matter is before the Court on Plaintiff's Motion for a Preliminary Injunction. Although Defendant has stipulated to certain provisions of the injunction, including a prohibition on the infringing publication of copyrighted materials, Defendant challenges the provision which would enjoin him from using, copying, or disclosing any internal document of Ford Motor Company (including information contained therein). * * *

I.   Facts

Plaintiff, Ford Motor Company, is an internationally-known automobile manufacturer. Ford closely guards its strategic, marketing, and product development plans. These plans are "trade secrets," which include program structures and vehicle cycle plans, engineering data, profitability and pricing data, and blueprints for manufacturing vehicles and their parts. * * *

Defendant, Robert Lane, is a student. Doing business as Warner Publications, he publishes a website with the domain name "*blueovalnews.com*," formerly "*fordworldnews.com*." The website publishes information about Ford and its products on the Internet, and has featured the Ford blue oval mark. Some time prior to the events at issue in this case,

Lane applied for and received authorization to access Ford's press release website.

In the fall of 1998, Ford became aware of Lane's website, which then operated under the domain name *fordworldnews.com*. Ford objected to Lane's use of the name "Ford" as part of the domain name and blocked Lane's access to Ford's press release website. In response, Lane wrote Ford a letter, dated October 30, 1998, in which Lane advised Ford that he possessed several "sensitive" photographs, including one of the upcoming Ford Thunderbird, which purportedly were provided to Lane by one of Ford's employees. The photos allegedly showed pictures of Ford products that were confidential and had not been released to the public. In a letter dated November 3, 1998, Lane threatened to publish materials on his website that Ford would find "disturbing." In both letters, Lane threatened to encourage Ford employees to disclose confidential information. Ford met with Lane and requested that Lane obtain Ford's approval prior to posting any Ford documents on the Internet. Lane agreed to do so.

Lane later changed his mind. On July 13, 1999, Lane posted an article on his website discussing and quoting from confidential documents that Lane received from an anonymous source relating to quality issues concerning the Ford Mustang Cobra engine. On July 27, 1999, Lane published information from another document that Lane received from an anonymous source, a document entitled "Powertrain Council Strategy & Focus." This was an internal Ford memo containing Ford's strategies relating to fuel economy, vehicle emissions through the year 2010, and powertrain technology advances. Lane also published a Ford engineering blueprint on his site, and stated that he planned to offer other blueprints for sale. In addition, Lane stated that he possessed other confidential Ford documents. When Ford advised Lane that the Company intended to file a lawsuit and to seek an injunction against him, Lane responded by posting approximately forty Ford documents online, including materials with high competitive sensitivity.

Lane testified that he did not know the identity of anyone who provided him with the confidential Ford information that he wrote about and posted verbatim on his website. These anonymous sources, likely former and current Ford employees, gave Ford documents to Lane by delivering them to his house or to his truck or by using the U.S. mail. Lane was aware of the confidential nature of the Ford documents that he published. Ford representatives informed Lane that Ford employees are bound by a confidentiality agreement. Lane testified that, with respect to some of the documents, he knew that the Ford employees who gave them to him were breaching their duty to Ford. Further, many of the documents were marked "confidential," "property of Ford," "proprietary," or "copyright protected." In addition, Lane acknowledged the confidential nature of the Ford documents when he wrote on his website, "Ford must take steps to make sure that from the design state until the time of market—their products undergo the utmost of secrecy. The whole reason behind all of this secrecy? To maintain a competitive advantage."

Because of Lane's publishing activities, on August 25, 1999, Ford Motor Company filed a Complaint and a Motion for a Temporary Restraining Order against him. The Complaint alleges copyright infringement, statutory conversion, intentional interference with contractual relations, misappropriation of trade secrets, misappropriation, trademark infringement, and unfair competition. * * * Ford also alleges that Lane solicited and received trade secrets that were misappropriated; that is, Ford employees gave the trade secrets to Lane in breach of their confidentiality agreements with Ford.

On August 25, 1999, the Court issued a Temporary Restraining Order, which provides as follows:

> Robert Lane . . . [is] enjoined and ordered as follows:
>
> A. Defendant is restrained from destroying, despoiling or electronically deleting or erasing documents in his possession originated by or for Ford Motor Company.
>
> B. Defendant is ordered to file with the Court, and serve upon Ford Motor Company, within ten (10) days, a sworn statement (1) identifying with particularity all documents within his possession, custody or control which were originated by or for Ford Motor Company, (2) the source (by name or description) of each document, and (3) provide details as to how defendant Robert Lane acquired each document.
>
> C. *Defendant is restrained from (1) using, copying or disclosing any internal document of Ford Motor Company (including the information contained therein),* (2) committing any acts of infringement of Ford Motor Company's copyrights, including unpublished works known by defendant Robert Lane to have been prepared by a Ford Motor Company employee within the scope of his or her employment, or specially ordered or commissioned by Ford Motor Company, if not an employee, (3) interfering with Ford's contractual relationship with its employees by soliciting Ford employees to provide Ford trade secrets or other confidential information.

(Emphasis added). * * * The Court also ordered the Defendant to show cause why the Temporary Restraining Order should not be entered as a preliminary injunction. Ford subsequently filed a motion seeking such relief.

Lane filed a response to the order to show cause and to Ford's motion for preliminary injunction. In the response, Lane agreed to the entry of the preliminary injunction in the same form as the temporary restraining order, except with respect to section C1, highlighted above.

II.   Standard for Preliminary Injunction

The availability of injunctive relief is a procedural question that is governed by federal law. * * * The Sixth Circuit has held that a court generally must consider four factors in deciding whether to issue a TRO or preliminary injunction:

(1)   whether the movant has shown a strong or substantial likelihood of success on the merits;

(2)   whether the movant has demonstrated irreparable injury;

(3)   whether the issuance of a preliminary injunction would cause substantial harm to others; and

(4)   whether the public interest is served by the issuance of an injunction.

* * * In cases involving prior restraint of pure speech, however, the Court is directed to consider whether publication "threaten[s] an interest more fundamental than the First Amendment itself" and to forego the prerequisites from the realm of "everyday resolution of civil disputes governed by the Federal Rules." * * * Only if a plaintiff can meet this substantially higher standard can a court issue an injunction prohibiting publication of pure speech. * * *

III.   Analysis

A.   Misappropriation of Trade Secrets and the Prior Restraint Doctrine

* * *

Count IV of Ford's Complaint alleges that Lane violated the Michigan Uniform Trade Secrets Act, Mich. Comp. Laws Ann. § 445.1901–1910 (the "Act"). The Act provides that actual or threatened misappropriation of trade secrets may be enjoined. * * * Section 445.1902(b) of the Act defines "misappropriation" as:

(i)   Acquisition of a trade secret of another by a person who knows or has reason to know that the trade secret was acquired by improper means, or

(ii)   Disclosure or use of a trade secret of another without express or implied consent by a person who did 1 or more of the following:

(A)   *Used improper means to acquire knowledge of the trade secret.*

> (B) *At the time of disclosure or use, knew or had reason to know that his or her knowledge of the trade secret was derived from or through a person who had utilized improper means to acquire it, acquired under circumstances giving rise to a duty to maintain its secrecy or limit its use, or derived from or through a person who owed a duty to the person to maintain its secrecy or limit its use.*
>
> (C) Before a material change of his or her position, knew or had reason to know that it was a trade secret and that knowledge of it had been acquired by accident or mistake.

(Emphasis added). Ford alleges that Lane violated section 1902(b)(ii)(A) & (B) because at the time Lane published Ford's trade secrets he used improper means to acquire knowledge of the trade secret, or he knew or had reason to know that his knowledge of the trade secret was derived from or through a person who had utilized improper means to acquire it, acquired it under circumstances giving rise to a duty to maintain its secrecy or limit its use, or it derived from or through a person who owed a duty to the person to maintain its secrecy or limit its use. * * *

Although Ford has presented evidence to establish that Lane is likely to have violated the Michigan Uniform Trade Secrets Act, the Act's authorization of an injunction violates the prior restraint doctrine and the First Amendment as applied under these circumstances.[6]

The First Amendment protects freedom of speech and freedom of the press by providing, "Congress shall make no law . . . abridging the freedom of speech, or of the press. . . ." The First Amendment applies to speech on the Internet. *Reno v. American Civil Liberties Union.* The primary purpose of the guarantee of freedom of the press is to prevent prior restraints on publication. * * * Even a temporary restraint on pure speech is improper absent the "most compelling circumstances." * * *

In the seminal case on prior restraints, *Near v. Minnesota,* the defendant was the publisher of "The Saturday Press," a newspaper containing anti-semitic articles which were critical of local officials. Applying a state statute which authorized an injunction of "malicious, scandalous, and defamatory" publications, the district court issued a permanent injunction against the defendant. The state supreme court affirmed the injunction, and the publisher appealed to the U.S. Supreme Court. The Court reversed, finding that the state statute violated freedom of the press because it was

---

[6] The Michigan Uniform Trade Secrets Act is not unconstitutional on its face, as an injunction may issue against one who plans to reveal a trade secret in violation of an employment contract or in breach of a fiduciary duty. Use of trade secrets in violation of a confidentiality agreement or in breach of a fiduciary duty is not protected by the First Amendment. * * * Note also that the Act permits monetary recovery. * * *

the "essence of censorship." * * * The *Near* Court explained that prior restraints may be issued only in rare and extraordinary circumstances, such as when necessary to prevent the publication of troop movements during time of war, to prevent the publication of obscene material, and to prevent the overthrow of the government. * * *

> Although the prohibition against prior restraints is by no means absolute, the gagging of publication has been considered acceptable only in "exceptional cases." Even where questions of allegedly urgent national security, or competing constitutional interests, are concerned, we have imposed this "most extraordinary remedy" only where the evil that would result from the reportage is both great and certain and cannot be militated by less intrusive measures. *CBS v. Davis.*

The broad parameters of the prior restraint doctrine were further explained in the Pentagon Papers case, *New York Times Co. v. United States.* There, the federal government sought to enjoin The New York Times and The Washington Post from publishing a classified study on U.S. policy-making in Vietnam. The Vietnam conflict was ongoing, and the government argued that the publication of the classified information might damage the national interest. The Court observed that, because any prior restraint on speech is presumptively invalid under the First Amendment, the government bore a heavy burden of showing a justification for the restraint. Finding that the government had not met its burden, the Court denied the injunction. * * * The government failed to demonstrate that the injury to the national interest was both great and certain to occur. * * *

The Sixth Circuit has recently applied the prior restraint doctrine to overturn an injunction against the publication of trade secrets and other confidential material in *Procter & Gamble Co. v. Bankers Trust Co.* Procter & Gamble and Bankers Trust were parties to civil litigation and had stipulated to the entry of a protective order, which prohibited disclosure of trade secrets and other confidential documents obtained during the discovery process. A journalist from Business Week magazine obtained some of those documents. Procter & Gamble and Bankers Trust sought an injunction prohibiting Business Week from publishing or disclosing any information contained in the documents. The district court held an evidentiary hearing and found that Business Week had knowingly violated the protective order by obtaining the documents. The district court therefore enjoined Business Week from using the confidential materials it had obtained unlawfully.

Business Week appealed. In reversing the district court, the Sixth Circuit held that Business Week's planned publication of the documents did not constitute a grave threat to a critical government interest or to a constitutional right sufficient to justify a prior restraint. To justify a prior restraint on pure speech, "publication must threaten an interest more fundamental than the First Amendment itself." * * * The court found that Procter & Gamble and Bankers Trusts' commercial interest in the confidential documents was insufficient to justify an injunction. "The private litigants' interest in protecting their vanity or their commercial self-interest simply does not qualify as grounds for imposing a prior restraint." * * * Further, the court held that Business Week's allegedly improper conduct in obtaining the documents did not justify imposing a prior restraint, and that the district court was misguided when it inquired into the issue, stating, "[T]he [district] court inquired painstakingly into how Business Week obtained the documents and whether or not its personnel had been aware that they were sealed. While these might be appropriate lines of inquiry for a contempt proceeding or a criminal prosecution, they are not appropriate bases for issuing a prior restraint." * * *

Although there are distinctions one can draw between the case brought by Ford and the existing precedent on prior restraint, those distinctions are defeated by the strength of the First Amendment. While it may be true that Ford's trade secrets here are more competitive in nature and more carefully protected than those at issue in *Procter & Gamble,* they are certainly not more volatile than those at issue in the Pentagon Papers case. While it may be true that publication on the Internet is subject to fewer editorial restraints than The New York Times, Business Week, or The Washington Post, the material here is not more inflammatory than the anti-semitic tabloid at issue in *Near.* And while the reach and power of the Internet raises serious legal implications, nothing in our jurisprudence suggests that the First Amendment is circumscribed by the size of the publisher or his audience.

The more troubling aspect of this case is whether Lane utilized the power of the Internet to extort concessions or privileges from Ford, by threatening to sell blueprints or other confidential documents. It is apparent from Lane's October 30, 1998 letter that he threatened Ford with the release of sensitive photographs when Ford first blocked his access to Ford's press release website, and that Lane raised the stakes and published more highly confidential documents in response to Ford's announcement of legal action. He also threatened in the October 30 letter to solicit trade secret material from Ford employees, although no evidence was submitted to establish that he actually did so, and Lane has since testified that he does not know the identity of anyone who provided him with documents. Finally, although the documents he published in July, having to do with problems in Mustang engines and with Ford's approach to emission standards, do address issues of public concern, the documents published more recently appear to be design and product information more useful to Ford's competitors-published for the purpose of flexing First Amendment muscle. Although the Sixth Circuit in *Procter & Gamble* has held that a defendant's improper conduct in obtaining confidential information does not justify a prior restraint, the legal system may yet provide redress through criminal prosecution, if such is found to be warranted by the underlying facts.

With respect to this proceeding, however, this Court is bound by existing precedent, and, under the broad holdings of the Pentagon Papers case and *Procter & Gamble,* may not enjoin Lane's publication of Ford's trade secrets and other internal documents. In the absence of a confidentiality agreement or fiduciary duty between the parties, Ford's commercial interest in its trade secrets and Lane's alleged improper conduct in obtaining the trade secrets are not grounds for issuing a prior restraint. Accordingly, Ford's request for preliminary injunction of Lane's using, copying, or disclosing Ford's internal documents must be DENIED.

* * *

IV. Conclusion

The last century has seen substantial advances in communications, of which the Internet is only the most recent development. Each new medium, as it was introduced, changed the balance of power in the constitutional equation involving the First Amendment. Every advance in mass communication has enhanced the immediate and widespread dissemination of information, often resulting in great potential for immediate and irreparable harm. With the Internet, significant leverage is gained by the gadfly, who has no editor looking over his shoulder and no professional ethics to constrain him. Technology blurs the traditional identities of David and Goliath. Notwithstanding such technological changes, however, the Courts have steadfastly held that the First Amendment does not permit the prior restraint of speech by way of injunction, even in circumstances where the disclosure threatens vital economic interests.

Being fully advised in the premises, having read the pleadings, taken testimony and heard the arguments of counsel, and for the reasons set forth above, the Court hereby orders as follows:

The August 25, 1999 Temporary Restraining Order is DISSOLVED.

Ford's motion for preliminary injunction is GRANTED IN PART AND DENIED IN PART.

> 1) Ford's request for preliminary injunction of Lane's using, copying, or disclosing Ford's internal documents is DENIED * * *.
>
> 2) The other aspects of Ford's request for a preliminary injunction are GRANTED since Lane stipulated to the entry of a preliminary injunction * * *.

DID YOU GET IT?

1. Did Lane engage in trade secret misappropriation?

2. What was the speech?

3. Why did the court refuse to enjoin the speech?

4. According to the court, are there cases where an injunction to prevent the disclosure of trade secrets would not be considered a prior restraint? If so, why?

4. WHISTLEBLOWER DEFENSE

The DTSA recognizes a new defense for trade secret misappropriation which is applicable in both civil and criminal trade secret cases whether brought in state or federal court. Known as the "whistleblower defense" or the "whistleblower immunity," this defense is based upon the public's interest in learning about illegal behavior. It applies when trade secrets are disclosed "in confidence" to Federal, State or local government officials or to attorneys for specified purposes. It does not immunize disclosure of trade secrets to the media.

The relevant provision of the DTSA, which amended 18 U.S.C. § 1833, has three principal parts. The first part details the immunity that individuals enjoy under the statute, as follows:

(b) IMMUNITY FROM LIABILITY FOR CONFIDENTIAL DISCLOSURE OF A TRADE SECRET TO THE GOVERNMENT OR IN A COURT FILING.—

    (1) IMMUNITY.—An individual shall not be held criminally or civilly liable under any Federal or State trade secret law for the disclosure of a trade secret that—

        (A) is made—

            (i) in confidence to a Federal, State, or local government official, either directly or indirectly, or to an attorney; and

            (ii) solely for the purpose of reporting or investigating a suspected violation of law; or

        (B) is made in a complaint or other document filed in a lawsuit or other proceeding, if such filing is made under seal.

The second part of the whistleblower defense concerns disclosures within the context of retaliation lawsuits. It provides:

    (2) USE OF TRADE SECRET INFORMATION IN ANTI-RETALIATION LAWSUIT.—An individual who files a

lawsuit for retaliation by an employer for reporting a suspected violation of law may disclose the trade secret to the attorney of the individual and use the trade secret information in the court proceeding, if the individual—

(A) files any document containing the trade secret under seal; and

(B) does not disclose the trade secret, except pursuant to court order.

The third part of the whistleblower defense is of particular import to employers because it requires that employees be given notice of the whistleblower immunity. Failure to provide such notice as required will adversely affect the availability of remedies in trade secret actions against employees. It provides:

(3) NOTICE.—

(A) IN GENERAL.—An employer shall provide notice of the immunity set forth in this subsection in any contract or agreement with an employee that governs the use of a trade secret or other confidential information.

(B) POLICY DOCUMENT.—An employer shall be considered to be in compliance with the notice requirement in subparagraph (A) if the employer provides a cross-reference to a policy document provided to the employee that sets forth the employer's reporting policy for a suspected violation of law.

(C) NON-COMPLIANCE.—If an employer does not comply with the notice requirement in subparagraph (A), the employer may not be awarded exemplary damages or attorney fees under subparagraph (C) or (D) of section 1836(b)(3) in an action against an employee to whom notice was not provided.

(D) APPLICABILITY.—This paragraph shall apply to contracts and agreements that are entered into or updated after the date of enactment of this subsection.

For purpose of the foregoing, an employee is defined broadly to include "any individual performing work as a contractor or consultant for an employer." 18 U.S.C. § 1833(b)(4). The statute further provides that: "Except as expressly provided for under this subsection, nothing in this subsection shall be construed to authorize, or limit liability for, an act that is otherwise prohibited by law, such as the unlawful access of material by unauthorized means." 18 U.S.C. § 1833(b)(5). This is potentially a huge exception given that employers might contractually prevent employees from having "authorized access" to certain information.

Food for Thought

What potential abuses or ambiguities do you think might arise under this new whistleblower provision?

E. PROTECTING TRADE SECRETS BEFORE, DURING, AND AFTER TRIAL

As a practical matter, when presenting its case at trial (either to a judge or jury) the plaintiff will have to explain what its trade secrets are as part of its *prima facie case*. However, the specification of trade secrets only at trial would make it difficult for the defendant to fashion a defense. For this reason, defendants in trade secret cases are typically allowed (usually subject to a protective order) to learn the details of plaintiff's trade secrets during the discovery phase of a case, if not earlier.

Because of the right of defendants in trade secret cases to learn the identification and details of the plaintiff's putative trade secrets, there is an obvious risk that whatever trade secrets exist will be revealed during the course of the litigation. This explains why many plaintiffs are reluctant to identify their trade secrets with particularity and why they will often fight hard to delay the disclosure of any information concerning their alleged secrets (although it may also be the case that they cannot identify their trade secrets because none exist). To facilitate the discovery process, most courts will issue protective orders that are designed to protect plaintiff's information during the pendency of litigation. Indeed, both the UTSA and the DTSA require courts to do so.

UNIFORM TRADE SECRETS ACT
Section 5

In an action under this [Act], a court shall preserve the secrecy of an alleged trade secret by reasonable means, which may include granting protective orders in connection with discovery proceedings, holding in-camera hearings, sealing the records of the action, and ordering any person involved in the litigation not to disclose an alleged trade secret without prior court approval.

Despite the ability of courts to enter protective orders to facilitate the discovery process, the early stages of trade secret litigation can be consumed by costly and time-consuming disagreements regarding the appropriate language of protective orders and the appropriate scope of discovery. A typical topic of dispute is how and to whom the information will be revealed. The plaintiff will usually argue for a very restrictive protective order (such as an "attorney's eyes only" order) that precludes any individual defendant or the employees of a corporate defendant from seeing the alleged trade secret information. The plaintiff may even insist that the disclosure of its secrets only occur at a secure facility, such as plaintiff's offices, and that otherwise the information be kept under lock and key. The defendant will argue that it needs to be able to show the information to potential witnesses, including expert witnesses, and that it can and will hold the information in confidence.

The challenge for courts is to figure out how to accommodate the demands of due process (i.e., that defendants should know the details of the claims being made against them) while protecting plaintiff's putative trade secrets. Sometimes, plaintiffs will request that defendants or their representatives be excluded from hearings and other proceedings in order to protect the trade secrets at issue. The fear is that a defendant's agent who learns the plaintiff's trade secrets from testimony might use it for competitive advantage. In such cases, defendants often assert their due process rights to be present and hear the evidence. However, such a right is not absolute, and the court must hear the arguments on both sides and decide when it is appropriate to exclude defendants or impose other limitations to protect the plaintiff's trade secrets. *See, e.g., In re M–I L.L.C.*, 2016 WL 2981342 (Texas Sup. Ct. 2016) (concluding that trial court had discretion to exclude defendant's representative from portions of temporary injunction hearing involving trade secret information).

The process of drafting protective orders is further complicated by the fact that the act of defining the information that is subject to a protective order does not, and should not, constitute a finding that trade secrets actually exist. That fact remains to be determined based upon the evidence that the plaintiff is required to present to prove the existence of trade secrets. Thus, defendants should make sure that the protective order is not perceived as an admission of the existence of trade secrets. Nonetheless, a protective order will typically cover both information that the plaintiff *claims* to be its trade secrets and other confidential business information and is often a reciprocal agreement between the parties.

Protecting trade secrets during and after trial may be more difficult due to the simple fact that public court proceedings are supposed to be open to public viewing. Thus, while a court is likely to impose confidentiality obligations on the parties to litigation and their attorneys and agents (including expert witnesses) during the pre-trial and discovery phases of litigation, they are less likely to impose such obligations at trial. The decision that follows provides some of the reasoning why. Consider how this reasoning would apply in criminal cases involving alleged trade secret misappropriation, discussed in Chapter 12.

Reading Guidance

Why is the court reluctant to allow documents to be filed with the court under seal?

CITIZENS FIRST NAT. BANK OF PRINCETON v. CINCINNATI INS. CO.

United States Court of Appeals, Seventh Circuit, 1999.
178 F.3d 943.

* * *

POSNER, CHIEF JUDGE.

In the course of the litigation from which these appeals arise, the district judge, in accordance with a stipulation by the parties, issued an order authorizing either party to designate as confidential, and thus keep out of the public record of the litigation, any document "believed to contain trade secrets or other confidential or governmental information, including information held in a fiduciary capacity." One of the parties has now asked us to permit it to file an appendix under seal. In support of this motion it submits the protective order just described that the district judge issued. That order was issued in March of 1997, however, two years ago, and we do not know enough about the case to be able to assess the order's current validity without the advice of the district judge, to whom, therefore, we remand the case for the limited purpose of enabling him to advise us whether in his view good cause exists for our allowing the appendix to be filed under seal. *Caterpillar, Inc. v. NLRB*, and cases cited there. * * *

There is a deeper issue of confidentiality in this case than the currency of the protective order, and we must address it in order to make clear the judge's duty on remand. That issue is the judge's failure to make a determination, as the law requires * * * of good cause to seal any part of the record of a case. Instead of doing that he granted a virtual carte blanche to either party to seal whatever portions of the record the party wanted to seal. This delegation was improper. The parties to a lawsuit are not the only people who have a legitimate interest in the record compiled in a legal proceeding.

It is true that pretrial discovery, unlike the trial itself, is usually conducted in private. * * * But in the first place the protective order that was entered in this case is not limited to the pretrial stage of the litigation, and in the second place the public at large pays for the courts and therefore has an interest in what goes on at all stages of a judicial proceeding. * * * That interest does not always trump the property and privacy interests of the litigants, but it can be overridden only if the latter interests predominate in the particular case, that is, only if there is good cause for sealing a part or the whole of the record in that case. * * * The determination of good cause cannot be elided by allowing the parties to seal whatever they want, for then the interest in publicity will go unprotected unless the media are interested in the case and move to unseal. The judge is the primary representative of the public interest in the judicial process and is duty-bound therefore to review any request to seal the record (or part of it). *See* Arthur R. Miller, "Confidentiality, Protective Orders, and Public Access to the Courts." He may not rubber stamp a stipulation to seal the record. * * *

The order that the district judge issued in this case is not quite so broad as "seal whatever you want," but it is far too broad to demarcate a set of documents clearly entitled without further inquiry to confidential status. The order is not limited to trade secrets, or even to documents "believed to contain trade secrets," which anyway is too broad both because "believed" is a fudge and because a document that contains trade secrets may also contain material that is not a trade secret, in which case all that would be required to protect a party's interest in trade secrecy would be redaction of portions of the document. Also much too broad is "other confidential . . . information," not further specified, and all "governmental information," a category absurdly overbroad. The order is so loose that it amounts, as we suggested at the outset, to giving each party carte blanche to decide what portions of the record shall be kept secret. Such an order is invalid. * * * The order in this case is invalid for the additional reason that it is not limited to pretrial discovery; it seals the documents covered by it even after they are introduced at trial. * * *

We are mindful of the school of thought that blanket protective orders ("umbrella orders"), entered by stipulation of the parties without judicial review and allowing each litigant to seal *all* documents that it produces in pretrial discovery, are unproblematic aids to the expeditious processing of complex commercial litigation because there is no tradition of public access to discovery materials. * * * The weight of authority, however, is to the contrary. Most cases endorse a presumption of public access to discovery materials, * * *, and therefore require the district court to make a determination of good cause before he may enter the order. * * * Rule 26(c) would appear to require no less. And we note that both the First and Third Circuits, which used to endorse broad umbrella orders * * * have moved away from that position * * *.

We do not suggest that all determinations of good cause must be made on a document-by-document basis. In a case with thousands of documents, such a requirement might impose an excessive burden on the district judge or magistrate judge. There is no objection to an order that allows the parties to keep their trade secrets (or some other properly demarcated category of legitimately confidential information) out of the public record, provided the judge (1) satisfies himself that the parties know what a trade secret is and are acting in good faith in deciding which parts of the record are trade secrets and (2) makes explicit that either party and any interested member of the public can challenge the secreting of particular documents. Such an order would be a far cry from the standardless, stipulated, permanent, frozen, overbroad blanket order that we have here.

Thus it will not be enough for the district judge on remand to point to the protective order as authority for allowing a portion of the appellate record to be filed under seal in this court. He must determine what parts of the appendix contain material that ought, upon a neutral balancing of the relevant interests, be kept out of the public record.

DID YOU GET IT?

1. What distinctions does the court make between the types of materials that can and cannot be sealed?

2. Is the sealing of documents allowed during the discovery process?

3. Whose interest is advanced by the presumption that court records should not be sealed?

———

Based upon the foregoing case and others like it (*see e.g.*, *Hammock v. Hoffman-LaRoche, Inc.*, 142 N.J. 356, 662 A.2d 546 (1995) (discussing the policies concerning the sealing of court records under state law and detailing recent efforts by state legislature to curb such practices)), the risk that the initiation of trade secret litigation will result in the disclosure of plaintiff's trade secrets cannot be ignored. Thus, trade secret owners need to think carefully before bringing such claims. As a practical matter, the risk of disclosure during trial should be an added incentive for the plaintiff to settle the case before it gets to trial.

F. SPECIAL ISSUE: WHAT CAN A DEFENDANT DO IF THE PLAINTIFF FAILS TO IDENTIFY ITS TRADE SECRETS WITH SPECIFICITY?

Due to the unique nature of trade secret litigation (namely, that a plaintiff cannot disclose the details of its trade secrets in its complaint for fear of losing them), there is a post-pleading procedural tactic that a defendant may use to prevail. If the plaintiff fails to timely identify its trade secrets with sufficient particularity, the defendant can file a motion either before or during trial and assert that such failure is fatal to plaintiff's claim. The plaintiff cannot complain that the identification of its trade secrets will destroy their secrecy because it is common practice in trade secret litigation for courts to enter protective orders that are designed to ensure the continued confidentiality of plaintiff's trade secrets.

> ### *Food for Thought*
> *What are the policy concerns that underlie the requirement that trade secrets be identified with specificity or reasonable particularity?*

> ### *Reading Guidance*
> *Why is plaintiff's disclosure of its trade secrets deficient?*

NILSSEN V. MOTOROLA, INC.
United States District Court, N.D. Illinois, 1997.
963 F.Supp. 664.

* * *

SHADUR, SENIOR DISTRICT JUDGE.

Ole Nilssen ("Nilssen") has brought suit against Motorola, Inc. and its subsidiary Motorola Lighting, Inc. ("Lighting") (collectively "Motorola" * * *) in connection with Motorola's alleged theft of Nilssen's trade secrets before Motorola's 1989 entry into the electronic ballast industry. Nilssen asserts claims for (1) breach of confidential relationship, (2) theft of trade secrets under the Illinois Trade Secrets Act ("Act" or "Illinois Act," 765 ILCS 1065/1 to /9) and (3) quantum meruit/implied contract/unjust enrichment.

Both sides have now filed summary judgment motions under Rule 56, with Nilssen seeking partial summary judgment only as to liability (and not as to damages) and with Motorola asking for a total victory as a matter of law. * * *

Summary Judgment Standards

Familiar Rule 56 principles impose on a party seeking summary judgment the burden of establishing the lack of a genuine issue of material fact * * *. For that purpose this Court is "not required to draw every conceivable inference from the record—only those that are reasonable"—in the light most favorable to the non-moving party * * *. Whereas here cross-motions are involved, it is necessary to adopt a dual perspective—one that this Court has often described as Janus-like—that sometimes involves the denial of both motions. And as the discussion in the body of this opinion will show, that is unfortunately true here in spades. * * *

What follows in the *Background* section is limited to an undisputed version of events. Other facts that fit better into the substantive legal discussion will be included later in this opinion.

Background

[The court's detailed recitation of the undisputed facts is deleted. In summary, it tells the story of plaintiff's repeated attempts to get Motorola interested in the electronic ballast technology that he developed. The first such effort began in July of 1982. Every time that Motorola informed plaintiff that it was not interested, plaintiff persisted in presenting his ideas further. A second pitch was made to Motorola in February of 1986, and a third in mid-1987. As a result of the third-pitch, Motorola conducted what appears to have been an extensive investigation of the electronic ballast industry generally and Nilssen's technology in particular, including the review of numerous documents that plaintiff marked "confidential" and provided pursuant to a written non-disclosure agreement between the parties. In May of 1988, after Motorola again decided not to proceed, Nilssen made another pitch and further discussions and disclosures ensued. However, due in part to the inability of Nilssen and Motorola to reach an agreement on how Nilssen would be compensated for the use of his technology, discussions ended and Motorola decided to pursue other opportunities. Ultimately, in February 1989 Motorola entered the electronic ballast industry using technology that it asserts was not acquired from Nilssen.]

Nilssen's Illinois Act Claim

Nilssen's Illinois Act claim against Motorola for theft of trade secrets requires that he demonstrate (1) the existence of a protectable "trade secret" (as defined in Act § 2(d)) and (2) Motorola's "misappropriation" (as defined in Act § 2(b)) of that trade secret * * *. Nilssen suggests that he has proved each of those elements as a matter of law, while Motorola correspondingly argues that Nilssen's claim fails as a matter of law with respect to each element. * * *

As a preliminary matter, Motorola suggests that Nilssen's failure to identify a *particular* trade secret is fatal to his claim. As *Composite Marine Propellers. Inc. v. Van Der Woude* (per curiam) has warned.

> It is not enough to point to broad areas of technology and assert
> that something there must have been secret and misappropriated.
> The plaintiff must show concrete secrets.

Hence Nilssen cannot state a claim for trade secret protection under the Act by simply "producing long lists of general areas of information which contain unidentified trade secrets" (*AMP Inc. v. Fleischhacker*). Instead he must articulate protectable trade secrets with specificity or suffer dismissal of his claim (see *Lear Siegler, Inc. v. Glass Plastics Corp.*).

Motorola's attack on that basis stems from interrogatory answers that Nilssen provided when asked to specify the precise scope of his alleged trade secrets. N. Interrog. Ans. 18 "contends that the information he provided Motorola in the 1987 and 1988 time period, and prior thereto, constituted a package of trade secret and confidential information." On that score this Court has spoken plainly of the legal insufficiency under

AMP of such a "blunderbuss statement that 'Everything you got from us was a trade secret.' " * * *

And Nilssen's other interrogatory responses similarly fail the specificity requirement. N. Interrog. Ans. 24 says:

> More particularly, Nilssen's trade secrets consisted of an extensive interwoven combination of a large number of individual elements of information relevant to the technology and business of electronic ballasts as well as to how these elements of information fitted together and how they pertained to Motorola and its prospective participation in the electronic ballast business. These individual elements of information related to and/or included a wide variety of pertinent facts, data, test results, evaluations, graphs, analyses, specifications, drawings, product samples, product requirements, product prototypes, product improvement potentials, circuit diagrams, graphs, types and identities of prospective customers, types and identities of product users, types and identities of key sources, industry standards, industry issues, industry expectations, competitors, revenue potentials, profit projections, social issues and values, patent positions and prospects, etc.; all of which were aimed such as to make Motorola sufficiently understand the significant advantages and appropriateness for it to enter the electronic ballast business.

N. Interrog. Ans. 24 goes on to identify "some" of the confidential information to which that description refers—a 35-element list (including Nilssen's supplemental response) that occupies some five pages.

But other Nilssen submissions to Motorola and to this Court have more specifically identified his claimed trade secrets. N. Mem. 11–20 details a substantial amount of both technical and nontechnical information that Nilssen assertedly divulged—and that he argues was necessary for Motorola's timely entry into the electronic ballast industry. In terms of technical information relating to the design of electronic ballasts, Nilssen suggests that he disclosed four key circuit elements to Motorola in confidence:

* A series resonant inverter driven by a half-bridge,

* Ballast output capable of driving more than two lamps in a series,

* Means for reducing the cathode heating voltage after lamp ignition and

* A slow-down capacitor used across the inverter output.

And N. Mem. 12–15 and 17–20 substantially narrow Nilssen's identification of nontechnical trade secret information from the 35-element list of N. Interrog. Ans. 24 to a more articulable set. Relying primarily on the expert report of Horace DePodwin ("DePodwin"), Nilssen identified these items of nontechnical information that he claims were—along with Nilssen's technical knowledge of electronic ballast circuits—the "very basis for Motorola's decision to enter the business and its entry strategy" (N. Mem.12, 17–20):

* Information concerning the reliability, cost of manufacture and efficiency of Nilssen's ballast design, often in comparison to existing commercial electronic ballasts,

* Detailed information and analyses of the comparative performance of competitors' ballasts, based on tests Nilssen had conducted,

* Detailed information and analyses of competitive ballasts, including their relative economic advantages and disadvantages,

* Detailed analyses of potential channels for distributing electronic ballasts,

* Information concerning the size and structure of the electronic ballast market, including the prevailing methods of distribution and generally accepted product specifications,

* Estimates of electrical efficiencies that Motorola could expect to achieve with electronic ballast technology in the future, and

* Research and analysis concerning expected profitability following entry into the electronic ballast market and related markets.

This Court finds that level of specificity suffices to withstand Motorola's attack, though not nearly to the extent that Nilssen would have it. Decisions such as *Roton Barrier, Inc. v. Stanley Works* (applying the Illinois Act) provide generally that a "trade secret" under that statute may include a compilation of confidential business and financial information. And Nilssen has documented each of those nontechnical items, at least to some extent, by referring to appropriate papers from the voluminous record in this case. Similarly, Nilssen's identification of his claimed technical trade secrets—the four key circuit elements of his electronic ballast—is quite specific. In sum, Nilssen's trade secrets as presently articulated are not so lacking in specificity as to require dismissal of his Illinois Act claim.

That being said, Motorola correctly urges that Nilssen's Illinois Act claim is also *limited* to trade secrets that are supported by the particular documents that he has specified in his memoranda on the current motions. As already said, Nilssen's claimed "definition" of his trade secret package was truly amorphous throughout the discovery process. It was not until Mem. 11–20 that Nilssen even attempted to "discuss in detail" the precise scope of his trade secret claim (see also his R. Mem. 14–15). Motorola properly relied on that first-time-specified particularity when fashioning its own submissions on the current motions, just as this Court has properly relied on Nilssen's statements when deciding these motions.

In that respect *AMP* has spoken in terms of requiring an identified list of trade secrets "[p]rior to trial," and such cases as *Publishers Resource, Inc. v. Walker-Davis Publications. Inc.*, citing and quoting from this Court's opinion in *Keene Corp. v. International Fidelity Ins. Co.*, clearly teach that a motion for summary judgment is the "functional equivalent" of a trial in which it is asserted that material facts are not in dispute. In responding to Motorola's motion for summary judgment on Nilssen's Illinois Act claim, a motion that rested in critical part on Motorola's contention that the claim should be rejected because of Nilssen's lack of specificity in identifying his purported trade secrets, Nilssen stood in no position to "hold back" on any of the things that he contended met the legal requirement of such specificity. Thus Nilssen's package of alleged trade secrets will be limited at trial to the four circuit elements of his technical claim and to those documents that are expressly identified at his Mem. 11–20 as constituting the basis of his nontechnical claims.

[The court's detailed examination of each of plaintiff's claims with respect to the alleged trade secrets that were identified by plaintiff is deleted. The court reached the following conclusion:]

* * *

Conclusion

As to Nilssen's Illinois Act claim, genuine issues of material fact exist as to (1) whether or not Nilssen's alleged trade secrets were sufficiently secret to be of value, (2) whether or not Motorola owed a duty to Nilssen to maintain the confidentiality of various of his disclosures and (3) whether or not Motorola misappropriated any of Nilssen's alleged trade secrets. Both Rule 56 motions are denied as to Nilssen's Illinois Act claim.

Nilssen's other claims at common law—for breach of confidential relationship and on theories of quantum meruit/implied contract/unjust enrichment—are preempted by the Illinois Act. Motorola is therefore entitled to a judgment as a matter of law as to those claims, which are accordingly dismissed. Nilssen's motion for summary judgment as to those claims is of course denied.

* * *

DID YOU GET IT?

1. Why did the court limit the plaintiff in the identification of trade secrets that it could assert on Motion for Summary Judgment and at trial?

2. What should the plaintiff have done to prevent its case from being limited in the manner ordered by the court?

3. When, according to the court, was the plaintiff required to disclose its trade secrets with specificity?

NOTES

1. **Defenses to DTSA claims.** All of the defenses that are asserted in state trade secret cases can also be asserted in cases brought under the DTSA, particularly those that are based upon provisions of the DTSA itself, such as a statute of limitations defense. As noted previously, however, the DTSA added an important defense that applies to all manner of trade secret claims (state, federal, civil, and criminal) known as the Whistleblower immunity.

2. **The DTSA's civil seizure order requirements.** Section 2(b)(2) of the DTSA (18 USC § 1836(b)(2)) provides for the granting of *ex parte* civil seizure orders in extraordinary circumstances based on the filing of an affidavit or verified complaint. The objective is to prevent the dissemination of the trade secrets at issue in the litigation, and permits seizure of "property necessary to prevent the propagation" of such trade secrets.

In attempting to limit the circumstances under which these seizure orders may be granted, the DTSA requires a showing that other forms of equitable relief (such as a TRO or preliminary injunction) would be inadequate to prevent dissemination of the trade secret because the defendant would evade or fail to comply. It further requires a showing, similar to that under Rule 65, of immediate and irreparable injury, harm to the applicant that would outweigh harm to the defendant if the seizure order is denied, and likelihood of success on the merits. The applicant must also: (1) establish that the defendant has "actual possession" of the trade secret and any related property to be seized; (2) describe with reasonable particularity what is to be seized; and (3) identify the location of the property to be seized.

Importantly, the applicant cannot publicize the fact that it applied for or received a seizure order, it must post a bond sufficient to cover damages for wrongful seizure, and neither the applicant nor its agent may participate in the seizure with law enforcement officials. Any materials seized shall remain in the custody of the court.

3. **The debate concerning the applicability of the First Amendment defense.** Cases like *Ford* have prompted a debate among legal scholars about when and whether the First Amendment defense should be used in trade secret cases. As detailed by Professor Pamela Samuelson, at one end of the spectrum are those who argue that trade secrets and the injunctions that

are issued to protect them should be "categorically immune (or nearly so) from First Amendment scrutiny." Pamela Samuelson, *Principles for Resolving Conflicts Between Trade Secrets and the First Amendment*, 58 HASTINGS L.J. 777 (2007), *citing*, Andrew Beckerman-Rodau, *Prior Restraints and the First Amendment: The Clash Between Intellectual Property and the First Amendment from an Economic Perspective*, 12 FORDHAM INTELL. PROP., MEDIA & ENT.L.J. (2001), among others. On the other end of the spectrum are those who believe that it is appropriate to consider the applicability of the First Amendment in some trade secret cases. Professor Samuelson summarizes the cases where she believes First Amendment scrutiny is appropriate:

> When defendants are under a contractual or other obligations not to disclose secrets to others, holding them to their promises is generally consistent with the First Amendment. When defendants have misappropriated information, preventing disclosure of wrongfully acquired information is also generally consistent with the First Amendment. * * * First Amendment defenses to trade secret claims are most likely to succeed as to those who did not participate in misappropriating the information, who acquired the information lawfully, and who seek to make public disclosures as to matters of public concern.

Samuelson, *Principles for Resolving Conflicts Between Trade Secrets and the First Amendment*, 58 HASTINGS L. J. 777, at 846 (2006).

Although the First Amendment defense may not work in all cases, it should always be considered as a potential defense in cases where the defendant has or wishes to "speak" about the plaintiff's trade secrets by disclosing them to the public.

4. **Identifying trade secrets before discovery.** Although it is recognized under the law of most states that a plaintiff need not identify its trade secrets with specificity in its complaint and such specification ordinarily occurs during the discovery phase of a case, California has enacted a statute that requires the alleged trade secrets be disclosed before discovery can commence. California Code of Civil Procedure, § 2019.210 reads:

> In any action alleging the misappropriation of a trade secret under the Uniform Trade Secrets Act, before commencing discovery relating to the trade secret, the party alleging the misappropriation shall identify the trade secret with reasonable particularity subject to any orders that may be appropriate under [Section 5 of the UTSA].

An issue that arises both in California (before discovery) and other states (during or after discovery) is whether the plaintiff's disclosure has been adequate. *See e.g.*, *Perlan Therapeutics v. Superior Court of San Diego County*, 178 Cal.App.4th 1333 (2009).

Since the DTSA is a new federal law, it remains to be seen when specificity regarding the alleged trade secrets will be required, but in keeping with federal court practice, this issue should be addressed in the required Scheduling Order. *See* F.R.C.P., Rule 16(b).

5.   **Bad faith claims.** When a plaintiff files an action knowing, for instance, that it does not have a protectable trade secret, it can be subject to liability on a bad faith claim by the defendant or sanctioned under F.R.C.P., Rule 11. These findings are generally made when plaintiffs have failed to produce sufficient evidence of the existence of a trade secret and it was apparent that plaintiff had this knowledge prior to initiating the lawsuit. The *Gemini Aluminum* case in Chapter 10 discusses the defendant's entitlement to attorney's fees when a trade secret misappropriation claim is brought in bad faith.

6.   **Costs of trade secret litigation.** Trade secret cases can have high tangible and intangible costs. Due to the fact-intensive nature of trade secret litigation, the actual dollar cost of filing and maintaining a trade secret misappropriation action can be very high, over $2 million in larger stakes cases. *See*, AIPLA, REPORT OF THE ECONOMIC SURVEY 2015 (reporting survey results showing trade secret litigation costs ranging from $500,000 to $2.6 million depending upon the amount at risk). Moreover, because of the costs associated with the injunction process, a trade secret misappropriation plaintiff will be required to spend more money earlier in the litigation process. Ultimately, both parties must bear the costs associated with temporary restraining order hearings and briefs, expedited discovery, and preliminary injunction hearings and briefs.

There are also a variety of indirect costs associated with trade secret litigation. Key employees with relevant knowledge and information will likely need to devote a substantial amount of time to the investigation and discovery process as the litigation continues. Other employees may also be distracted by the litigation, which can negatively affect employee morale and productivity. Similarly, an even greater concern for plaintiffs may be jeopardizing their relationships with third parties who are important to their business. Customers, vendors, or even investors may need to become involved in the litigation as reluctant witnesses, and the mere mention of the trade secret misappropriation may cause the company to suffer a loss in stock value and may trigger SEC reporting requirements. Also, there is always a risk that the trade secrets will be disclosed during the litigation process. Accordingly, the decision to proceed with a trade secret misappropriation case is not one to be made lightly, especially if the nature and value of the information does not warrant it.

7.   **Bibliographic note:** For more information on the topics discussed in this chapter, see Peter S. Menell, *Tailoring a Public Policy Exception to Trade Secret Protection*, 105 CAL. L. REV. (forthcoming); MILGRIM ON TRADE SECRETS CHAPTERS 15 AND 16 (2016); Kyle J. Mendenhall, *Can You Keep a Secret—The Court's Role in Protecting Trade Secrets and Other Confidential Business Information from Disclosure in Litigation*, 62 DRAKE L. REV. 885 (2014); Randall E. Kahnke and Kerry L. Bundy, THE SECRETS TO WINNING

TRADE SECRET CASES (2013); Charles Tait Graves, *Trade Secrets and the Problem of Common Law Confidentiality, in* THE LAW AND THEORY OF TRADE SECRECY: A HANDBOOK OF CONTEMPORARY RESEARCH, (Rochelle C. Dreyfuss & Katherine J. Strandburg, eds. 2011); Elizabeth A. Rowe, *Trade Secret Litigation and Free Speech: Is It Time to Restrain the Plaintiffs?*, 50 BOSTON COLLEGE L. REV. 1425 (2009); Mark Lemley and Eugene Volokh, *Freedom of Speech and Injunction in Intellectual Property Cases*, 48 DUKE L. J. 147 (1998); Lloyd Doggett & Michael J. Mucchetti, *Public Access to Public Courts: Discouraging Secrecy in the Public Interest*, 69 TEX. L. REV. 643 (1991); Arthur M. Miller, *Confidentiality, Protective Orders, and Public Access to the Courts*, 105 HARV. L. REV. 427 (1991); Thomas M. Morgan & Ruth C. Schoenbeck, *Trade Secret Preliminary Hearings: Does the Press Have a Right to Know*, 3 SANTA CLARA COMPUTER & HIGH TECH. L.J. 329 (1987).

CHAPTER 10

REMEDIES FOR TRADE SECRET MISAPPROPRIATION

■ ■ ■

Anticipated Learning Outcomes

At the conclusion of this chapter, you will be able to identify the remedies that are available for trade secret misappropriation and will understand the basics of what a plaintiff in a trade secret misappropriation case must prove to be awarded such remedies. You will also understand what a plaintiff must prove to obtain preliminary injunctive relief, the standards for determining the appropriate length of injunctive relief, and what a defendant must prove to be awarded attorney's fees.

A. INTRODUCTION

To appreciate the scope of remedies that are available for trade secret misappropriation under the UTSA, it is important to first consider the scope of remedies that are generally available for civil wrongs (torts and breach of contract claims) under common law. Usually, even if a plaintiff in a civil case proves that the defendant engaged in a wrongful act, the case will be dismissed and judgment entered for the defendant unless the plaintiff also proves that he has been harmed in some compensable way. Traditional courts of equity had wider latitude to grant relief that was designed to "do justice," including enjoining various activities either by prohibiting the defendant from engaging in an activity (known as a prohibitory injunction) or requiring the defendant to do something (known as a mandatory injunction).

Today it is generally understood that equitable relief, if granted at all, is more appropriate in tort cases than in contract cases. In both types of cases, however, the focus of the remedies analysis is on determining whether, and to what extent, the plaintiff suffered actual harm caused by the alleged wrongdoing. A central question is how such harm is to be shown and measured and whether the plaintiff can prove both the existence of actual harm and the amount of harm suffered.

In the case of contract disputes, the principal remedy is an award of damages that is designed to put the plaintiff in the same position (and no better) than he would have been in if the breach of contract had not occurred. According to the *Restatement (Second) of Contracts*, Section 347,

447

these "expectation damages" are measured by: (a) the loss in value to the plaintiff of the defendant's performance caused by its failure or deficiency, plus (b) any other loss, including incidental or consequential loss, caused by the breach, less (c) any cost or other loss that he has avoided by not having to perform. Injunctive relief is generally not available to enjoin the threatened or actual breach of contract, but in the rare case where a damage award is not adequate to protect the expectations of the plaintiff, specific performance of a contract may be ordered in a court's discretion.

Under tort law, the available remedies depend upon the type of tort alleged but generally include compensatory damages measured by the actual harm suffered by the plaintiff, including out-of-pocket expenses such as property damage, medical expenses and lost wages or (in the case of business torts) lost profits. Depending upon the tort that was alleged and the evidence that was presented, the plaintiff may also be entitled to an award of damages for such things as pain and suffering, emotional distress, and loss of consortium. Preliminary or permanent injunctive relief is available, but only upon a showing that court intervention is needed to prevent irreparable harm.

The general rule under both tort and contract law (known as "the American Rule") is that attorney's fees are not awarded to the prevailing party, but two exceptions are recognized: (1) in contract cases where the subject contract includes an attorney's fees provision; or (2) where a statute allows for the award of attorney's fees for specified claims. Similarly, punitive damages (also known as exemplary damages) are not available for a breach of contract but are generally available in tort cases upon a showing of willful and malicious behavior.

B. REMEDIES UNDER THE UTSA AND THE DTSA

In many respects, the remedies that are available for trade secret misappropriation under both the UTSA and the DTSA (which adopted the UTSA's remedies) mirror the remedies that are available under common law tort principles, as described above. But there are some important differences. Most importantly, although the plaintiff in a trade secret case can seek an award of damages, he does not have to prove actual harm to prevail in a trade secret misappropriation case. The threatened use or disclosure of a trade secret can provide the grounds for preliminary and permanent injunctive relief even if the proven acts of trade secret misappropriation did not cause the trade secret owner to suffer actual harm. For this reason, the focus of many trade secret cases is on injunctive relief and attorney's fees rather than compensatory and punitive damages.

The basic principles of injunctive relief that were developed at common law and in courts of equity pre-date both the *Restatement of Torts* and the UTSA and continue to be applied in both UTSA and non-UTSA jurisdictions and are likely to be applied under the DTSA. Generally, before a preliminary injunction will be granted, the plaintiff must establish: (1) a likelihood of success on the merits; (2) a substantial threat that the plaintiff will suffer irreparable injury if the injunction is denied; (3) that the balance of hardships favors the plaintiff; and (4) that the injunction will not disserve the public interest. Also, in the case of preliminary injunctive relief, the plaintiff is usually required to post a bond (also known as "security" or "an undertaking") that will compensate the defendant in the event that preliminary relief was improvidently granted. *See* F.R.C.P. § 65(c). Special and more detailed requirements apply to any request for an *ex parte* Civil Seizure Order under the DTSA. *See* 18 U.S.C. § 1836(b)(2), reprinted in Appendix A.

Although a request for injunctive relief is central to most trade secret cases, plaintiffs who successfully prove that their trade secrets have been wrongly used or disclosed (as opposed to merely acquired) can also seek an award of monetary relief. Because actual harm can be difficult to prove in trade secret cases, both the UTSA and the DTSA give the plaintiff flexibility in how to prove such harm, including: (1) the traditional measure of lost profits; (2) defendant's unjust enrichment; and (3) a reasonable royalty measure of damages for the disclosure or use of the trade secret.

What constitutes "actual harm" in trade secret cases logically refers to the wrongful disclosure or use of the trade secrets, not its mere acquisition, but plaintiffs in trade secret cases have been known to seek an award of monetary damages even in cases where trade secrets remain secret and are not used. Two questions are raised by such an approach: (1) whether trade secret misappropriation is a trespassary tort like trespass to real property; and, if so, (2) how such damages are to be measured. Without actual and measurable harm to the trade secrets, usually the remedy for mere wrongful acquisition is an injunction and possible criminal responsibility.

Under both the UTSA and the DTSA, exemplary damages can be awarded in the case of "willful and malicious misappropriation," but not to exceed 2 times the award of damages. Finally, the UTSA and DTSA create an exception to "the American Rule" by providing for the award of attorney's fees to the prevailing party in certain cases of bad faith or willful and malicious misappropriation.

Food for Thought

Consider why the drafters of the UTSA felt it was important to broaden the measure of damages and to modify the rule that an award of attorney's fees is not generally available to the prevailing party. What societal goals are achieved by a broader and more flexible concept of damages and the possible award of attorney's fees?

THE UNIFORM TRADE SECRETS ACT

Section 2
Injunctive Relief

(a) Actual or threatened misappropriation may be enjoined. Upon application to the court, an injunction shall be terminated when the trade secret has ceased to exist, but the injunction may be continued for an additional reasonable period of time in order to eliminate commercial advantage that otherwise would be derived from the misappropriation.

(b) In exceptional circumstances, an injunction may condition future use upon payment of a reasonable royalty for no longer than the period of time for which use could have been prohibited. Exceptional circumstances include, but are not limited to, a material and prejudicial change of position prior to acquiring knowledge or reason to know of misappropriation that renders a prohibitive injunction inequitable.

(c) In appropriate circumstances, affirmative acts to protect a trade secret may be compelled by court order.

Section 3
Damages

(a) Except to the extent that a material and prejudicial change of position prior to acquiring knowledge or reason to know of misappropriation renders a monetary recovery inequitable, a complainant is entitled to recover damages for misappropriation. Damages can include both the actual loss caused by misappropriation and the unjust enrichment caused by misappropriation that is not taken into account in computing actual loss. In lieu of damages measured by any other methods, the damages caused by misappropriation may be measured by imposition of liability for a reasonable royalty for a misappropriator's unauthorized disclosure or use of a trade secret.

(b) If willful and malicious misappropriation exists, the court may award exemplary damages in an amount not exceeding twice an award made under subsection (a).

Section 4
Attorney's Fees

If (i) a claim of misappropriation is made in bad faith, (ii) a motion to terminate an injunction is made or resisted in bad faith, or (iii) willful and malicious misappropriation exists, the court may award reasonable attorney's fees to the prevailing party.

The cases that follow provide some examples of the factual and legal issues that courts face when trying to fashion remedies for trade secret misappropriation. What remedies are granted ultimately depends upon what the plaintiff (or the defendant in the case of attorney's fees) requests and can prove.

1.   PRELIMINARY INJUNCTIVE RELIEF

Generally, and pursuant to the rules of court of both state and federal courts, there are two forms of preliminary injunctive relief: a temporary restraining order and a preliminary injunction. *See e.g.,* F.R.C.P. Rule 65. The DTSA introduces a new type of preliminary relief known as an *ex parte* Civil Seizure Order which, if granted, requires the U.S. Marshal's Service to seize the property specified in the Order, which may include not only the alleged trade secrets, but property that might be used to disseminate such trade secrets. (Discussed below.) As discussed in Chapter 8, the DTSA also limits the scope and nature of available injunctive relief in employment related cases.

Typically, temporary restraining orders (TROs) are sought in emergency situations when quick relief is needed to prevent imminent harm (as some judges have opined, TROs will only be issued in life and death situations). In trade secret cases, a motion for a TRO is usually made when a plaintiff fears the public disclosure (and death) of its trade secrets. Sometimes, depending upon the applicable rules of court, motions for a TRO are brought on an "*ex parte*" basis without notice to the defendant. If issued, TROs last for only a short period of time, usually no more than a week or two or until such time as a hearing on a Motion for Preliminary Injunction can be held, and are usually made subject to the posting of adequate security.

Preliminary injunction motions, like TROs, are usually filed at the same time as the plaintiff's complaint and seek the same type of relief. They differ from TROs in the length of time that the defendant is given to respond to the motion. If issued, preliminary injunctions typically last until a decision on the merits, although such injunctions may be dissolved earlier if the subject trade secrets cease to exist.

Reading Guidance

In addition to having to establish a prima facie case for trade secret misappropriation, what does a plaintiff have to prove to obtain a preliminary injunction?

SI HANDLING SYSTEMS, INC. V. HEISLEY

Court of Appeals, Third Circuit, 1985.
753 F.2d 1244.

INTRODUCTION

This is an appeal pursuant to 28 U.S.C. § 1292(a)(1) (1982) from an interlocutory order of the district court preliminarily enjoining the use and disclosure of certain trade secrets. * * *

I.

BACKGROUND

* * *

A.   *SI Handling and CARTRAC*

Appellee SI Handling Systems, Inc. ("SI"), founded in 1958 by its current Chairman and Chief Executive Officer L. Jack Bradt, is a Pennsylvania corporation with headquarters and principal manufacturing facilities located in Easton, Pennsylvania. * * * SI is in the business of designing, manufacturing, and installing "materials handling systems." "Materials handling" is a generic term describing the transportation of materials, by any mechanized means, between locations in a factory or warehouse. * * * This litigation involves only one of SI's product lines, known by the trade name "CARTRAC".

* * *

B.   *The Appellants and ROBOTRAC*

Appellant Michael E. Heisley was an officer of SI from 1973 to mid-1978, serving as president for nearly all of that period. In that capacity he was involved in early discussions concerning SI's entry into the automotive manufacturing market. * * * After leaving SI in 1978 Heisley formed appellant Heico, Inc. ("Heico"), an Illinois corporation.

Appellant Philip L. Bitely, then SI's vice-president for finance, left the company and joined Heico shortly thereafter. Bitely had been with SI since 1971, and had also been involved in the early development of automotive CARTRAC.

Appellant Thomas H. Hughes joined SI in 1976 as manager of field sales. In March 1977 he was promoted to vice-president of marketing, and in January of 1979 he became vice-president in charge of the computer controls division. It appears that in the latter two positions he had significant responsibility for the development of automotive CARTRAC. In July of 1981 Hughes left SI, with a number of other controls division employees, to form appellant Sy-Con Technology, Inc. ("Sy-Con"), a subsidiary of Heico. * * *

The watershed event leading to this litigation took place on April 17, 1982. On that date chief executive officer Bradt fired SI's vice-president of operations, appellant Richard O. Dentner. Dentner, it is fair to say, was the "father" of SI's automotive CARTRAC, with responsibility for coordinating both the engineering and marketing of this product. According to Bradt, he fired Dentner reluctantly, only after efforts to resolve tensions between Dentner and other SI officers had failed.

Dentner remained as vice-president of operations until May 9, 1982, and continued to receive severance pay until September 30, 1982. During that period he also did some consulting for SI on a per diem basis. Despite this continuing relationship with SI, Dentner was already making plans, in association with Heico, to market a competing spinning tube car-on-track system, ROBOTRAC.

* * *

C. *Proceedings in the District Court*

On March 21, 1983 SI filed a complaint against the aforementioned corporate and individual appellants, alleging violations of the Sherman Act and the Racketeering Influenced and Corrupt Organizations Act, and stating a variety of common law claims sounding in contract and tort, including misappropriation of trade secrets. SI moved for a preliminary injunction against use and disclosure of its trade secrets on October 20, 1983, and a hearing on this motion commenced November 7. * * *

In an opinion handed down on March 1, 1984, the district court found that SI had made the requisite showings for preliminary injunctive relief, and in particular had demonstrated a reasonable probability of success on the merits of its trade secrets claim.

The district court's order enjoining appellants from use and disclosure of SI's trade secrets reads, in pertinent part:

1.   all defendants are enjoined from the use and disclosure of any mechanisms developed by them or any of them to design around the Jacoby patent;

2.   all defendants are enjoined from the use and disclosure of any detailed drawings of car-on-track materials handling products not revealed by the CARTRAC hardware;

3. the defendants Dentner, Bitely and Possinger are enjoined from engaging in any costing/pricing of a car-on-track materials handling system;

4. the defendants Scheel, Gutekunst and Ziegenfus are enjoined from concepting, designing, manufacturing, marketing or installing of any car-on-track materials handling system except as may be necessary to complete the General Motors Livonia Plant installation;

5. this injunction being preliminary in nature is limited in time until final hearing and the issuance thereafter of an order pertaining to plaintiff's application for a final and permanent injunction; subject, however, to earlier termination, upon appropriate application, if the confidential information in question comes into the possession of defendant by legitimate means.

This appeal followed.

II.

DISCUSSION

In considering a motion for preliminary injunctive relief, a court must carefully weigh four factors: (1) whether the movant has shown a reasonable probability of success on the merits; (2) whether the movant will be irreparably injured by denial of such relief; (3) whether granting preliminary relief will result in even greater harm to the nonmoving party; and (4) whether granting preliminary relief will be in the public interest. * * *

A. *Probability of Success On The Merits*

[First, the court found that some of the information claimed to be trade secret information qualified for trade secret protection, while other information did not. With respect to the trade secrets, it ruled that the plaintiff (SI) had shown a reasonable probability of success on the merits.]

B. *Equitable Considerations*

In exercising its discretion in the issuance of a preliminary injunction, a district court must weigh, in addition to the movant's probability of success on the merits: (1) the threat of irreparable harm to the movant if relief is denied; (2) the balance of harms; and (3) the public interest. * * * Appellants contend that the district court abused its equitable discretion because none of these factors militate in favor of a preliminary injunction here. We disagree. * * *

Appellants contend that there has been no showing that SI will suffer irreparable harm in the absence of a preliminary injunction. They rely on the fact that SI did not move for a preliminary injunction until seven months after filing their complaint. (SI attributes this delay to appellants' failure to comply with discovery.) We do not understand appellants to be asserting the defense of laches, but rather to be suggesting an estoppel-*i.e.,* SI's conduct is inconsistent with a claim of immediate and irreparable harm. We do not, however, think it is important whether the movant considered a preliminary injunction necessary at the time of filing the complaint. The relevant inquiry is whether the movant is in danger of suffering irreparable harm at the time the preliminary injunction is to be issued. Here SI made an ample showing that appellants intended to use its trade secrets, and did not intend to take reasonable measures to preserve their secret status. * * *

Appellants further contend that had the district court properly balanced the harm they would suffer if an injunction was granted against the harm to SI if an injunction was denied, it could not have issued a preliminary injunction. They claim that the harm appellants suffer is "catastrophic" and that for Scheel, Gutekunst and Ziegenfus it is "the equivalent of economic capital punishment". We do not find any evidence in the record that would support these claims. Heico, the parent of Sy-Con and Eagle, appears to be a corporation of roughly equal size to SI, with the advantage of greater diversity. Though it is clear that individual appellants Scheel, Gutekunst and Ziegenfus are prevented by the injunction from exploiting valuable expertise, we cannot find by judicial notice that they have been subjected to economic capital punishment. It appears that they continue to be employed by Heico, and we surmise that their considerable talents have found a productive outlet.

Finally, appellants ask us to hold that the district court failed to properly weigh the public interest when it stated that "the preservation of commercial morality far outweighs any negative impact on free competition which might result from any order emanating from this litigation." Appellants point to the numerous statutes and cases embodying the strong public policies favoring competition and economic mobility, apparently implying that these are overriding interests. Appellants do not, however, explain why this case is different from numerous other trade secret cases, all implicating similar "commercial morality" issues and thus these same public policy concerns, where injunctions have issued. * * * Appellants here are not concerned about raising the morality of capitalism; rather their sole concern is raising the profitability of their ventures predicated on utilizing a competitor's trade secrets.

A classic statement of the competing policies appears in *Wexler v. Greenberg* where the court found that trade secrets cases bring to the fore a problem of accommodating competing policies in our law: the right of a businessman to be protected against unfair competition stemming from the usurpation of his trade secrets and the right of an individual to the unhampered pursuit of the occupations and livelihoods for which he is best suited. There are cogent socio-economic arguments in favor of either position. Society as a whole greatly benefits from technological improvements. Without some means of post-employment protection to assure that valuable developments or improvements are exclusively those of the employer, the businessman could not afford to subsidize research or improve current methods. In addition, it must be recognized that modern economic growth and development has pushed the business venture beyond the size of the one-man firm, forcing the businessman to a much greater degree to entrust confidential business information relating to technological development to appropriate employees. While recognizing the utility in the dispersion of responsibilities in larger firms, the optimum amount of "entrusting" will not occur unless the risk of loss to the businessman through a breach of trust can be held to a minimum.

On the other hand, any form of post-employment restraint reduces the economic mobility of employees and limits their personal freedom to pursue a preferred course of livelihood. The employee's bargaining position is weakened because he is potentially shackled by the acquisition of alleged trade secrets; and thus, paradoxically, he is restrained, because of his increased expertise, from advancing further in the industry in which he is most productive. Moreover, as previously mentioned, society suffers because competition is diminished by slackening the dissemination of ideas, processes and methods. *See also Kewanee Oil Co. v. Bicron Corp.* It was not necessary for the district court to engage in extended analysis of the public interest-extensive precedent supports an injunctive remedy where the elements of a trade secret claim are established. * * *

C. *The Scope of the Injunction*

The district court found:

> It will be virtually impossible for the various individual defendants not to use their CARTRAC systems engineering knowledge if they continue to work in car-on-track materials handling systems. Further, continued use of it by them would inevitably result in disclosure to fellow employees and potential customers. For these reasons a limited injunction against disclosure and use of the information is not sufficient.

It is clear that under Pennsylvania law a court of equity may fashion a trade secret injunction that is broad enough to ensure that the information is protected. * * * Because we have rejected several of the district court's most significant trade secret findings, it is necessary that this preliminary injunction be vacated. * * * In view of our holding, it will be necessary for the district court to reconsider its conclusion that it will be "virtually impossible" for appellants to work on car-on-track systems without compromising SI's proprietary information. In particular, the district court should consider whether, with regard to the eighth trade secret findings that we have affirmed, *all* appellants are equally situated, or that work by appellants on *any* car-on-track system—as opposed to merely *spinning tube* car-on-track systems—is threatening to SI's proprietary interests. * * *

For the guidance of the district court on remand, we set out here two additional concerns relating to the breadth and specificity of the original order.

Paragraph four of the preliminary injunction enjoins appellants Scheel, Gutekunst, and Ziegenfus from, among other things, "concepting" any car-on-track materials handling system. The term "concepting", though it was used by a number of witnesses and appears to be part of the jargon of the trade, is probably one that ought to be eschewed in judicial orders. Our concern is in part linguistic. * * * [W]e doubt, whatever exactly is meant by "concepting", that it is something that can be enjoined by judicial fiat. A court of equity should not issue an order that it cannot enforce.

The fifth paragraph of the preliminary injunction provides that it will terminate upon disposition of the application for a final injunction, "subject, however to earlier termination, upon appropriate application, if the confidential information in question comes into the possession of defendant by legitimate means." To the extent this means that, should SI's trade secrets be publicly disclosed, the injunction would terminate, we think this is a salutary and necessary provision. *Cf. Kewanee Oil Co. v. Bicron Corp.* To the extent it means, as SI suggests, that appellants should have to retrace every step SI has taken in developing CARTRAC before they can market a similar product, we believe it would be a wasteful and unduly punitive requirement. A court of equity should not require one who knows that Los Angeles is west of Chicago to look at a map before going to Los Angeles. We endorse the current trend toward so-called "lead time" injunctions, whereby the trade secret injunction lasts only so long as is necessary to negate the advantage the misappropriator would otherwise obtain by foregoing independent development. * * *

CONCLUSION

For the reasons set forth above, the order of the district court will be vacated and the case remanded for proceedings consistent with this opinion.

DID YOU GET IT?

1. What are the claimed trade secrets and who owns them?

2. Did the court consider the public interest or dismiss it?

3. Why did the court vacate the order of the trial court and remand the matter to the trial court for further consideration? What was wrong with the trial court's order?

Reading Guidance

Why do the rules of various courts require that the plaintiff post a bond [or undertaking] before a preliminary injunction goes into effect?

ABBA RUBBER CO. v. SEAQUIST

California Court of Appeal, Fourth District, 1991.
235 Cal. App. 3d 1.

MCKINSTER, J.

In an action concerning the alleged misappropriation of trade secrets, the trial court issued a preliminary injunction, restraining the defendants from soliciting any former customers of the plaintiff. The defendants challenge the plaintiff's entitlement to injunctive relief, the form and scope of the injunction, and the adequacy of the amount of the undertaking specified by the trial court. * * *

Factual Background

Roy J. Seaquist began manufacturing rubber rollers under the name of ABBA Rubber Company in 1959. He sold the business in 1980. The plaintiff bought the business in 1982.

J.T. "Jose" Uribe began working at ABBA in 1973. He remained there through the various changes of ownership, rising to vice-president and general manager in 1987. His brother, J.A. "Tony" Uribe began working for the company in 1985, and later was promoted to sales manager. In these capacities, both Uribes became very familiar with the identities of ABBA's customers.

Meanwhile, Mr. Seaquist had started a metal fabrication business known as Seaquist Company (Seaquist). In 1985, following the expiration of the noncompetition clause in the agreement by which he had sold ABBA, Seaquist also began manufacturing rubber roller products. However, it had no sales force, and did not significantly expand.

On September 11, 1989, Jose Uribe either quit or was fired from ABBA. The same day, he was hired by Seaquist, which simultaneously leased a new building from which to operate an expanded rubber roller business. Several weeks later, Seaquist hired Tony Uribe as a salesman. He had been fired by the plaintiff in early 1989, and since then had been working for yet another manufacturer of rubber rollers.

While the Uribes deny taking any records from ABBA, they admit to soliciting business from some ABBA customers. They did this in part by means of a letter which announced Jose Uribe's relocation from ABBA to Seaquist, and which invited the recipient to contact him regarding Seaquist's "ability to provide . . . an advantage in price, quality and service."

Procedural Background

The plaintiff filed a complaint on June 13, 1990, which alleged misappropriation of trade secrets, unfair competition, intentional inference with business relations, breach of contract, and other theories. It named as defendants Mr. Seaquist, Jose Uribe, and Tony Uribe, and prayed for preliminary and permanent injunctive relief and damages.

Six days later, the plaintiff made an ex parte application for a temporary restraining order (TRO) and for an order to the defendants to show cause why a preliminary injunction should not issue. Ultimately, the trial court denied the application for the TRO, but granted the application for the preliminary injunction.

The preliminary injunction was signed on August 20, 1990, and issued on August 24, 1990, when the plaintiff filed the requisite $1,000 undertaking.

* * *

Contentions

The defendants contend that the trial court abused its discretion in issuing the injunction, because the identity of the plaintiff's customers was not a trade secret. They also attack the form of the injunction, on the grounds that it does not allow them to determine, in advance and with certainty, what conduct is permissible and what conduct is prohibited. Similarly, they contend that the injunction is impermissibly overbroad, because it proscribes the solicitation of businesses which are not customers of the plaintiff or the identities of which are otherwise not secret. Finally, they assert that the amount of the undertaking specified in the injunction is inadequate.

We conclude that the undertaking is insufficient, and therefore reverse the trial court's order granting the preliminary injunction. For the guidance of the trial court and the parties in the event that any further injunctions, either preliminary or permanent, are issued in this matter, we also address the defendants' contentions concerning the merits, form, and scope of the injunction.

Discussion

A.   Is the Undertaking Too Low?

* * *

While no hearing was held concerning the form of the order, the defendants submitted to the judge written objections to the form proposed by the plaintiff. Those objections raised the lack of any provision for an undertaking, and proposed the sum of $315,000, based upon the evidence which the plaintiff had previously submitted concerning Seaquist's income from former customers of the plaintiff. The plaintiff responded that the defendants had waived their right to "request" an undertaking, and that in any event an undertaking was not required. As an aside, it noted that an undertaking of only $1,000 had been specified in the exemplar which it had provided to the court. The trial court amended the form of order proposed by the plaintiff by adding the requirement of a $1,000 undertaking, and signed the injunction.

On appeal, the defendants renew their objection to the lack of a sufficient bond.

1. *Did the Defendants Waive Their Objection?*

As its initial response to the defendants' attack on the amount of the undertaking, the plaintiff again contends that the objection has been waived. Specifically, the plaintiff argues, without authority, that they waived their right to make such a challenge because they failed to raise the issue prior to the issuance of the trial court's ruling on the application for the preliminary injunction. Although not specifically raised by the plaintiff, we also consider whether a waiver resulted from the defendants' failure to contest the adequacy of the undertaking by a noticed motion.

a. *No Waiver by Failing to Request Undertaking in Advance.*

The conditioning of the issuance of a preliminary injunction upon the posting of an undertaking is statutorily required: "On granting an injunction, the court or judge *must* require an undertaking on the part of the applicant. . . ." (Code Civ. Proc., § 529, subd. (a), italics added.) That duty is mandatory, not discretionary. * * * Nothing in the statute conditions the trial court's obligation to require such an undertaking upon a request from the parties. To the contrary, an injunction does not become effective until an undertaking is required and furnished * * * and must be dissolved if an undertaking is not filed within the time allowed by statute (§ 529, subd. (a)). * * *

Under these facts, we find that the defendants' ex parte objection substantially complied with the statutory procedure for contesting the sufficiency of the bond. Since neither the trial court nor the plaintiff insisted upon strict compliance with section 995.930, that substantial compliance is sufficient to prevent the waiver provided by subdivision (c) of that section. Therefore, the defendants did not waive their right to have this court review the adequacy of the amount of that bond on appeal.

2. *Is the Undertaking Insufficient?*

Section 529, subdivision (a), requires that the amount of the undertaking be sufficient to "pay to the party enjoined such damages . . . as the party may sustain by reason of the injunction, if the court finally decides that the applicant was not entitled to the injunction." Thus, the trial court's function is to estimate the harmful effect which the injunction is likely to have on the restrained party, and to set the undertaking at that sum. * * * That estimation is an exercise of the trial court's sound discretion, and will not be disturbed on appeal unless it clearly appears that the trial court abused its discretion by arriving at an estimate that is arbitrary or capricious, or is beyond the bounds of reason.

In reviewing the trial court's estimation, the first step is to identify the types of damages which the law allows a restrained party to recover in the event that the issuance of the injunction is determined to have been unjustified. The sole limit imposed by the statute is that the harm must have been proximately caused by the wrongfully issued injunction. * * * Case law adds only the limitation that the damages be reasonably foreseeable.

When an injunction restrains the operation of a business, foreseeable damages include "the profits which [the operator] would have made had he not been prevented by the injunction from carrying on his business." * * * Thus, the defendants correctly sought to have the undertaking include the losses which they will incur by reason of the prohibition against their continued solicitation of business from former customers of the plaintiff. In their objection, the defendants argued that, by the plaintiff's own analysis of the evidence, those customers accounted for 87.7 percent of Seaquist's invoices, representing $26,000 in sales per month, or $315,000 per year. The plaintiff did not dispute their interpretation of the evidence, either below or on appeal. Therefore, while those lost sales will undoubtedly be offset to some degree by savings resulting from reduced sales expenses or costs of goods sold, it is undisputed that the injunction will cause the defendants to incur very substantial lost profits.

At the final hearing on the application for the injunction, the trial court appeared to believe that it would be a simple matter for the defendants to locate new customers for their products, and that the proposed injunction, restraining them from soliciting further orders from the plaintiff's customers, would be only a "minor inconvenience. . . ." This may have been the trial court's rationale for setting the undertaking at the nominal sum of $1,000. Certainly, it is the ground upon which the plaintiff seeks to justify that action.

That reasoning, however, ignores the fact that section 529 requires that the potential damages be estimated on the assumption that the preliminary injunction was wrongfully issued, i.e., that the plaintiff did not have the right to keep the defendants from soliciting its customers. Under that hypothetical circumstance, the defendants would be entitled to solicit business from both the plaintiff's former customers and entirely new customers, and thus would be entitled to retain all profits from sales to both subsets of potential buyers. Therefore, the losses which they are likely to suffer from being precluded from soliciting business from their existing customer base cannot be offset by any profits they may make from sales to new customers. A nominal undertaking cannot be justified on the ground that the defendants' profitability could remain constant, when their sales and profitability might have risen in the absence of the injunction.

Furthermore, the plaintiff's analysis ignores another type of damage which the undertaking must take into account: attorney's fees. "It is now well settled that reasonable counsel fees and expenses incurred in successfully procuring a final decision dissolving the injunction are recoverable as 'damages' within the meaning of the language of the undertaking, to the extent that those fees are for services that relate to such dissolution [citations]." * * * Thus, "a successful appeal from an order granting an injunction, after notice and hearing, gives rise to liability on the bond for damages" in the amount of the attorney's fees incurred in prosecuting that appeal. * * * If the preliminary injunction is valid and regular on its face, requiring the defendant to defend against the main action in order to demonstrate that the injunction was wrongfully issued, the prevailing defendant may recover that portion of his attorney's fees attributable to defending against those causes of action on which the issuance of the preliminary injunction had been based.

Thus, in calculating the amount of the undertaking to be required in this case, the trial court should have considered at least (1) the profits to be lost by the defendants from the elimination of the vast majority of their existing customers, and (2) the attorney's fees and expenses to be incurred in either prosecuting an appeal of the preliminary injunction, or defending at trial against those causes of action upon which the preliminary injunctive relief had been granted. * * * By setting that undertaking at $1,000, the trial court impliedly estimated that those two classes of damages would total no more than that sum.

That estimation is not within the bounds of reason. Even ignoring the lost profits, there is no reasonable possibility that the attorney's fees and expenses necessary to dissolve the injunction, either through appeal or trial, would not exceed $1,000. It is well known that litigation is extraordinarily expensive. That is especially true in commercial litigation such as this, in which two businesses are fighting over the right to sell to a particular customer base amid allegations of misappropriation of trade secrets and unfair competition. Such a battle is likely to be vigorously fought, as shown by the number and length of the submissions by both sides concerning the application for preliminary injunction below. Expenses alone would be likely to substantially exhaust the liability limit created by the trial court. Indeed, in the current appeal, filing fees and the costs of the preparation of the clerk's and reporters' transcripts have certainly consumed over half of that sum. When attorney's fees and lost profits are added into the equation, the utter inadequacy of the undertaking is clear.

* * *

Disposition

An injunction cannot remain in effect without an adequate undertaking. Therefore, the preliminary injunction is reversed. No further preliminary injunction shall be issued unless its issuance is conditioned upon the furnishing of an adequate undertaking. * * *

Any preliminary or permanent injunction issued in this case in the future shall both clearly and narrowly define the scope of the proscribed activities, in accordance with the views expressed in this opinion.

Appellants shall recover their costs on appeal.

DID YOU GET IT?

1. Why did the court reverse the grant of preliminary injunction? Was it on procedural or substantive grounds?

2. Who has the burden of proof on the issue of the amount of a proper undertaking [or bond]?

3. How can a defendant in a trade secret misappropriation case use the bond requirement to its advantage? What evidence should the defendant produce to bolster its arguments?

2. EX PARTE CIVIL SEIZURE ORDER UNDER THE DTSA

As first discussed in Chapter 9, the Defend Trade Secrets Act of 2016 (DTSA), which was effective as of May 11, 2016, adds another potential remedy for trade secret misappropriation to the arsenal of remedies already available under the UTSA. Known as a "Civil Seizure Order," this remedy allows trade secret owners to seek an order that the U.S. Marshal's Service (or specified other law enforcement personnel) seize property related to the alleged trade secret misappropriation. Although such a remedy can (and has been successfully sought) under F.R.C.P., Rule 65, this new remedy is significant because it is specific to trade secret misappropriation claims and can be sought and granted without notice to the target of the Order, provided that the stringent requirements of the remedy are met. *See* 18 U.S.C. § 1836 (b)(2), reprinted in Appendix A.

Food for Thought

When you read the ex parte Civil Seizure Order provision of the DTSA, consider these questions:

a. What does a plaintiff in a trade secret misappropriation case have to prove for a court to grant a Civil Seizure Order?

b. What property can be the subject of a Civil Seizure Order?

c. Is the potential target of a Civil Seizure Order limited to the alleged misappropriator?

d. What remedies does the target of a Civil Seizure Order have if an Order is improvidently granted?

e. Can a Civil Seizure Order be granted by a state court?

---

3. "PERMANENT" INJUNCTIVE RELIEF

For reasons that are explained in the Special Issue section of this chapter, injunctive relief that is granted in trade secret misappropriation cases after a decision on the merits (a trial or a hearing on plaintiff's motion for summary judgment) is not actually "permanent." An order that grants injunctive relief in a trade secret misappropriation case (and indeed in any case) can be dissolved after it is issued. In practice, the "permanent" label simply refers to injunctions that are issued after a decision on the merits of a case, whereas injunctive relief issued before a final decision on the merits is referred to as "preliminary relief" or a "preliminary injunction."

The following case sets forth some of the issues that courts consider when deciding whether to grant a permanent injunction.

Reading Guidance

Do the standards for a permanent injunction differ from the standards for preliminary relief?

GENERAL ELECTRIC CO. v. SUNG
United States District Court, D. Mass, 1994.
843 F.Supp. 776.

GORTON, DISTRICT JUDGE.

Pending before this Court is the motion of plaintiff, General Electric Company ("GE"), filed on August 18, 1993, for injunctive relief against Iljin Corporation, Iljin Diamond Manufacturing Company and Chin-Kyu Huh (collectively, "Iljin"). * * *

I.   Background

Chien-Min Sung ("Sung"), a geochemistry Ph.D., ended a seven-year employment relationship with GE Superabrasives in March 1984. When he left GE, Sung took with him an abundance of documents, including drawings and process instructions relating to the production of industrial synthetic diamond. In 1988, Sung and Iljin entered into several agreements under which Sung agreed to transfer to Iljin technology related to the production of industrial diamond.

GE filed an action against Iljin in 1989, alleging, *inter alia,* that they misappropriated GE trade secrets relating to the technology for manufacturing saw grade industrial diamond. After protracted discovery and pre-trial motions, the case was tried to a jury in July, 1993. * * * On July 30, 1993, the jury returned a verdict in favor of GE and against Iljin for misappropriation of GE trade secrets.

GE waived its legal remedy with respect to its alleged lost profits and Iljin's alleged unjust enrichment when it chose not to offer evidence of such monetary damages at trial. On November 15, 1993, this Court denied GE's Motion for Reconsideration of its Request for an Equitable Accounting.

II.   Discussion

It is well settled that equity will protect against the unwarranted use of a trade secret. * * * The purpose of an injunction in a trade secret case is to protect the secrecy of the misappropriated information, eliminate the unfair advantage obtained by the wrongdoer and reinforce the public policy of commercial morality. *Kewanee Oil Co. v. Bicron Corp.* An injunction to protect against the use of a trade secret is the appropriate remedy in a trade secret case if, absent such relief, plaintiff will suffer irreparable injury. * * *

The jury found that Iljin misappropriated GE trade secrets and the evidence at trial clearly indicated that Iljin's use of those trade secrets enabled them to produce saw grade diamond for commercial sale and thereby to compete with GE in the industrial diamond industry before it would have been otherwise possible. This Court concludes that GE will suffer irreparable injury if Iljin is allowed to continue to use the technology it wrongfully acquired from GE, and an injunction is therefore the appropriate remedy in this case. The only remaining issues to be decided by this Court relate to the scope, nature and duration of that injunction.

A.   *Scope of Injunction*

The jury found that Iljin misappropriated 487 pages of documents that were GE trade secrets. Trade secret protection, however, extends not only to the misappropriated trade secret itself but also to materials "substantially derived" from that trade secret. * * * This Court must, therefore, determine whether an injunction in this case should be limited to the documents contained in trial Exhibit A or extend to cover Iljin's IJ–77 process.

The IJ–77 process is a 5,000-ton apparatus and specifications for its operation. It is designed and used to produce saw grade diamond on a commercial scale. The evidence at trial indicates that it took GE more than twenty years to develop its comparable, 5,000-ton "GE V" design for commercial production of saw grade diamond. Taek-Jung Shin ("Shin"), the Engineering Manager of Iljin Diamond, admitted at trial that 1) the IJ–77 design was developed by Iljin engineers with explicit reference to the GE trade secrets and 2) in creating the IJ–77, Iljin engineers modified the GE V design to make it "less aggressive". Shin himself was intimately familiar with the GE trade secret technology and supervised the development of the IJ–77 design. Under Massachusetts trade secret law, these facts give rise to a compelling inference that the IJ–77 was substantially derived from GE trade secrets.

* * *

The physical evidence sustains the inference. The evidence adduced from pretrial depositions, expert trial testimony and post-trial affidavits indicates that the dimensions and material specifications of the IJ–77 are substantially similar, and in some respects identical, to GE's L–5000 and M–3000 designs in Exhibit A. * * * Moreover, specific expert testimony indicated that 25% of the dimensions of the IJ–77 die and anvil are identical to the GE V dimensions.

* * *

This Court concludes that the IJ–77 was substantially derived from the 487 pages of documents determined by the jury to be GE trade secrets. Any injunction to preclude Iljin from exploiting their wrongfully obtained competitive advantage must therefore enjoin Iljin from, among other things, using the IJ–77.

B.   *Nature of Injunction*

There are two kinds of trade secret injunctions potentially applicable in this case. The Court could permanently enjoin Iljin from using the misappropriated information, i.e., impose a "use injunction". Because the Court has determined that the IJ–77 was substantially derived from the GE trade secrets in Exhibit A, any use injunction would necessarily enjoin Iljin from using the IJ–77. Alternatively, the Court could enjoin Iljin from manufacturing saw grade diamond for a certain amount of time, i.e., impose a "production injunction". For the reasons stated below, the Court concludes that a production injunction is the most effective and appropriate way to remedy the misappropriation of trade secrets in this case.

Courts have imposed production injunctions in circumstances where a use injunction would be ineffective in eliminating the competitive advantage gained by the misappropriator. *See, e.g., Viscofan, S.A. v. U.S. Int'l Trade Comm'n* (prohibition on sale of sausage casings); *Aerosonic Corp. v. Trodyne Corp.* (injunction against making or selling pressure sensing devices); *Head Ski Co. v. Kam Ski Co.* (prohibition on manufacturing adhesively bonded metal skis); *Eastern Marble Products Corp. v. Roman Marble, Inc.* (injunction against manufacturing two-tone, one-piece marble sinks). The common rationale for imposing a production injunction is that, where the misappropriated trade secrets are "inextricably connected" to the defendant's manufacture of the product, a use injunction is ineffective because the misappropriator cannot be relied upon to "unlearn" or abandon the misappropriated technology. * * *

An "inextricable connection" is found where the trade secrets form such an integral and substantial part of a comprehensive manufacturing process or technology that, absent the misappropriated trade secrets, the defendant would not be able independently to manufacture or design a comparable product. * * * In that respect, it is pertinent whether the defendant had a significant and comparable, pre-existing design of its own prior to the misappropriation of the trade secrets. * * *

Shin admitted at trial that, at the time they acquired GE's trade secrets from Sung in 1988, Iljin had neither manufactured nor developed a commercial process for producing saw grade diamond. The evidence at trial indicates that without the GE trade secrets stolen by Sung, Iljin would not have been able to manufacture *any* saw grade diamond, let alone commercially salable saw grade diamond. By use of the stolen GE trade secrets, Iljin was able to produce in two years what it had taken GE and its few legitimate competitors twenty years to produce.

This Court concludes that Iljin's production of saw grade diamond was inextricably connected to the technology found by the jury to be GE trade secrets and that Iljin's saw grade diamond process was entirely dependent upon that misappropriated technology. Under these circumstances, a production injunction is warranted. * * *

C.   *Duration of Injunction*

The appropriate measure for determining the duration of the production injunction in this case is the amount of time it would have taken Iljin independently to develop or reverse engineer a technology for commercial production of high-grade saw diamond. * * * Because it is both logical and within the discretion of the Court that a production injunction run from the date of the Court's Order rather than from the date of misappropriation, it shall be so imposed in this case. * * *

GE argues that it would have taken Iljin a minimum of ten years to produce independently a commercially viable, high-grade saw diamond technology. Iljin, on the other hand, contends that they could have independently produced such a technology in three years. Based upon the evidence presented at trial, and affidavits submitted since the trial, this Court concludes that it would have taken Iljin a minimum of seven years to develop independently a commercially viable, high-grade saw diamond technology.

* * *

In determining that a seven-year production injunction is appropriate, the Court has taken into account the technological advances that have occurred and come into the public domain during the interceding decades since GE and its competitors began developing the technology. In the Court's view, those advances indicate that GE's proposed ten-year ban is too long. At the same time, this Court is mindful of the fact that Iljin was a willful, rather than innocent, wrongdoer. Iljin made a calculated decision to circumvent the expensive and difficult process of developing their own saw grade diamond technology by purchasing stolen GE trade secrets. * * *

By enjoining Iljin from the manufacture of saw grade diamond for seven years, this Court intends to promote the policies underlying trade secret protection by 1) reversing the headstart that Iljin achieved at GE's expense, 2) depriving Iljin of the advantages of their wrongdoing and 3) placing GE in the same position it would have occupied had Iljin not misappropriated its trade secrets. The injunction also should encourage commercial morality by its deterrent effect.

For the duration of the injunction, Iljin is free to conduct research on any diamond technology and to manufacture and sell diamond products other than saw grade diamond. Iljin may, however, with leave of Court and under appropriate conditions, license from another manufacturer technology or equipment to produce and sell saw grade diamond.

III. Conclusion

For the foregoing reasons, plaintiff's motion for injunctive relief is hereby ALLOWED, in part. A production injunction for seven years, as more fully described in the Order entered herewith, will become effective upon the entry of that Order.

* * *

DID YOU GET IT?

1. What was the irreparable harm that GE suffered? Would an award of actual damages measured by GE's lost profits suffice to compensate GE for the defendant's wrongdoing?

2. Is irreparable harm presumed from the wrongdoing itself, or were there other facts that established irreparable harm?

3. Is irreparable harm presumed when, after trial or the plaintiff's motion for summary judgment, there is a finding of trade secret misappropriation?

4. MONETARY RELIEF: DAMAGES, EXEMPLARY RELIEF AND ATTORNEY'S FEES

When a trade secret misappropriation case is brought and tried before the plaintiff's trade secrets become generally known or readily ascertainable, it is understandable that the focus of the plaintiff's request for remedies will be on injunctive relief. In such cases, the plaintiff wants to do everything it can to limit the disclosure or use of its trade secrets and preliminary and permanent injunctive relief are the best ways to accomplish that goal. However, the plaintiff may also be entitled to monetary relief caused by the misappropriation, for instance, if it can show that the defendant used or profited from its trade secrets during the period of time which generally runs from date of the misappropriation to the date that the injunction is issued.

In some trade secret misappropriation cases, the plaintiff's trade secrets cease to qualify for trade secret protection either before the case is filed or during the time it takes for the case to reach a conclusion. When this happens, injunctive relief is no longer needed to prevent the loss of trade secrecy and the focus of the plaintiff's remedies request is likely to be on monetary relief in the form of damages, exemplary relief (also known as punitive damages), and attorney's fees. As discussed in the Special Issue section of this chapter, the plaintiff may also request a limited permanent injunction that is designed to prevent the defendant from enjoying any "lead-time advantage."

The *Roton Barrier* case that follows provides an overview of the types of monetary relief that are available to a prevailing plaintiff in a trade secret misappropriation case. It is also an example of a case where both permanent injunctive relief and monetary damages were awarded. The *Gemini* case shows how a prevailing defendant in a trade secret misappropriation case can use the remedies provisions of the UTSA to be awarded attorney's fees. In recent years, several trade secret owners have been awarded monetary awards in excess of $500 million. A substantial monetary award is more likely in cases where the misappropriated trade secrets are used in competing products or, in the case of trade secrets that are disclosed, where a pre-disclosure value can be set.

Reading Guidance

How were plaintiff's damages measured?

ROTON BARRIER, INC. V. STANLEY WORKS

U.S. Court of Appeals, Federal Circuit, 1996.
79 F.3d 1112.

RICH, CIRCUIT JUDGE.

The Stanley Works (Stanley) appeals from the judgment of the United States District Court for the Eastern District of Missouri finding trade secret misappropriation under the law of Illinois and awarding actual and exemplary damages therefor, * * * awarding prejudgment interest and attorney fees, and enjoining Stanley from disclosing any of Roton's trade secret information and from participating or otherwise engaging in the continuous pinless hinge business for four years from the date of the judgment.

* * *

I.   BACKGROUND

A.   The Technology

In 1963, Austin R. Baer (Baer), the owner of Roton Corporation, a predecessor in interest to appellee Roton Barrier, Inc. (Roton), obtained U.S. Patent No. 3,092,870 directed to a hinge comprising two intermeshed geared hinge members, a so-called continuous pinless hinge. In 1968, Baer obtained another patent, U.S. Patent No. 3,402,422, directed to an improvement in pinless hinges in which thrust bearings are placed in recesses along the length of the hinge leaves. In 1990, Baer secured yet another patent, the '008 patent in suit, which discloses adding bearing inserts above and below each thrust bearing "for enhancing hinge performance by reducing frictional sliding contact between the hinge members" and each thrust bearing. Through the course of the years, Baer developed and refined his process for manufacturing Roton hinges and Roton became the market leader in continuous pinless hinges.

B.   Contact Between Stanley and Roton

As early as 1976, Stanley was interested in manufacturing Roton-type hinges. Stanley concluded, however, that "[a]s a product, the Roton hinge does not lend itself to Stanley manufacturing capabilities" and "is limited to an extruded process requiring extremely close tolerances." In 1988, Stanley was again interested in "adding a commercial continuous hinge as a product line." At that time, Stanley estimated that "95% of all commercial continuous hinge applications are Roton" hinges.

In 1989, Stanley considered acquiring Roton. Stanley's Vice President of Marketing (Bannell) first contacted Baer and in April 1989, Roton and

— one yr of negotiations

Stanley entered into a Confidentiality Agreement which barred the disclosure or use by Stanley of any of the "Evaluation Material" provided to it by Roton except for purposes of Stanley's evaluation of Roton for acquisition. In June of that year, Stanley's Vice President of Manufacturing (Martino), Comptroller (Gallagher), and President (Martin) inspected the Roton facility. Gallagher and Martin also reviewed Roton's financial statements and discussed the information with Roton's accountant. Various conferences took place between Stanley and Roton and there was what can be characterized as a free flow of information from Roton to Stanley seemingly concerning every aspect of Roton's business.

In July 1989, Stanley made an offer to purchase Roton, which Roton rejected. On August 1, Roton terminated negotiations with Stanley and requested the return or destruction of all confidential materials. Later that month, Stanley corresponded with Roton about a possible distributorship arrangement. During these negotiations Stanley sought to amend the Confidentiality Agreement to provide:

— Δ offered to buy π

> Notwithstanding anything to the contrary contained in this Agreement or the April 10, 1989 [Confidentiality Agreement], Stanley specifically represents to Roton that Stanley currently possesses the capability of manufacturing and selling continuous hinges for use on architectural/commercial grade exterior and interior doors. This capability was developed independently by Stanley without use of any Evaluation Material.

Baer found this proposed amendment inconsistent with his understanding of Stanley's capabilities prior to its evaluation of Roton and for this reason broke off all discussions with Stanley.

In January 1990, Roton was acquired by C. Hager & Sons Hinge Manufacturing Co. (Hager), a chief competitor of Stanley, and became Roton Barrier. When Stanley learned of Hager's acquisition of Roton, it embarked on a self-styled "aggressive project plan" in which it sought to "develop [its] own product line of continuous extruded hinges." In response to perceived "weaknesses in the life cycle of the Roton product," Stanley intended to "focus on an improved weight bearing system." As a result, Stanley introduced into the market its own continuous pinless hinge, the LS500.

— Δ's competitor bought π

C.   District Court Proceedings

Roton sued Stanley for patent infringement, misappropriation of trade secrets, and breach of contract. Stanley counterclaimed seeking a declaratory judgment of patent invalidity, and unenforceability and noninfringement. The suit was tried in the district court without a jury. The court found misappropriation of trade secrets and awarded $2,791,677 in actual damages and the same amount in exemplary damages. * * * Attorney fees were also awarded as was prejudgment interest on the actual damages portion of the award from June 1, 1991. Additionally, Stanley was barred from participating in the continuous pinless hinge business for four years from the date of the judgment and was also permanently enjoined from using, disclosing, or otherwise disseminating any of Roton's trade secrets.

II.   *TRADE SECRET MISAPPROPRIATION*

[After reviewing the applicable law (the UTSA as enacted in Illinois, referred to by the court as ITSA) and the findings of fact, the court affirmed the district court's finding of trade secret misappropriation and turned its attention to the appropriateness of the remedies that were awarded.]

E.   *Actual Damages for Trade Secret Misappropriation*

* * *

"A trial judge's assessment of damages 'will not be set aside unless it is manifestly erroneous.'" * * * "[A] party seeking damages must supply a reasonable basis for the computation of those damages." * * * The trial court found that the "actual damages plaintiffs have sustained include both lost sales and price erosion." The price erosion damages included historical price erosion and future price erosion.

Stanley contends that the trial court failed to "separate the damages that resulted from the lawful entry of a powerful competitor . . . from damages that resulted from particular forms of misconduct." We find this not to be the case; in fact it is unclear that Stanley would have entered the market at all absent Roton's trade secret information. Indeed Stanley had considered such entry before, but had rejected it. Here it appears that though Stanley was motivated by competition with Hager, it was armed with Roton's proprietary information when it embarked on its aggressive project plan.

From our review of the record, we conclude that the trial court's assessment of damages was not manifestly erroneous. The record amply supports the award of lost profits owing to Roton's loss of market share attributable to Stanley's entry in the market.

The record also supports the award of historical price erosion damages. Roton reduced its prices in response to Stanley's entry in the market. Though there were others in the market, Zero and Pemko, with lower prices, Roton perceived their products to be inferior and saw no need to lower its prices in response to their entry.

Finally, respecting the award of future price erosion damages, Baer testified that a substantial period of time will be required for Roton to reestablish its prices and margins. No evidence requires rejection of this testimony. We affirm the trial court's award of actual damages for trade secret misappropriation.

F. *Exemplary Damages*

Section 4(b) of ITSA provides that "[i]f willful and malicious misappropriation exists, the court may award exemplary damages in an amount not exceeding twice any award made under subsection (a).

"Whether to award punitive damages is an issue for the sound discretion of the trial court, and its decision will not be set aside absent an abuse of discretion." * * * However, "punitive damages are not favored in the law, and the courts must take caution to see that punitive damages are not improperly or unwisely awarded." * * * Additionally, punitive damages are penal in nature and their "purpose is to deter the defendant and others from committing the same offense in the future." Such damages should be "allowed with caution and confined within narrow limits." * * *

Under ITSA, in order for there to be misappropriation, there must be knowing disclosure of a trade secret. By its very terms, therefore, trade secret misappropriation under ITSA requires a "bad act": the disclosure of someone else's trade secret. For an award of exemplary damages, that misappropriation must in addition be willful *and* malicious. In this regard, the trial court stated only that "Stanley's misappropriation was willful and malicious." From our review of the record, such a finding is not legally supportable.

— CA held it was not willful + malicious

Illinois courts have distinguished between motivation by malice and motivation by competition and have awarded punitive damages in the former situation, but not in the latter. * * * In this case, it is clear that Stanley was motivated by competition when it embarked on its aggressive project plan to enter the continuous pinless hinge market. One of its biggest rivals, Hager, had just acquired Roton, and Stanley sought to compete. Other courts have recognized that competition by its very nature "is ruthless, unprincipled, uncharitable, unforgiving—and a boon to society." * * *

— policy of whether competition is "malicious"

Because Stanley was motivated by competition with its biggest rival, rather than by any malice against either Hager or Roton, we conclude that the trial court's award of exemplary damages was an abuse of discretion. By our decision we certainly do not condone the actions of Stanley in its dealings with Roton. Indeed, Stanley is guilty of misappropriation; the record simply does not support a finding that the misappropriation was willful and malicious.

G. *Attorney Fees*

Section 5 of ITSA provides that "[i]f . . . willful and malicious misappropriation exists, the court may award reasonable attorney's fees to the prevailing party." Inasmuch as we have reversed the trial court's finding of willful and malicious misappropriation, we necessarily vacate the award of attorney fees predicated on such a finding.

* * *

J. *Conclusion as to Trade Secret Misappropriation*

We affirm the trial court's holding of trade secret misappropriation and the award of actual damages. However, because the trial court erred in finding willful and malicious misappropriation, we vacate the awards of exemplary damages and attorney fees. Additionally, we remand on the issue of injunctive relief for the trial court to tailor such relief to the specific facts of this case. Finally, we do not disturb the trial court's exclusion of Stanley's "trade secret" witnesses.

DID YOU GET IT?

[handwritten: – Lost profits sales etc. Avg. price erosion]

1. How was the award of monetary relief measured? *[handwritten: Actual, exemplary, att'y's fees, injunction.]*

2. What did the plaintiff fail to prove in order to be entitled to exemplary relief and attorney's fees? *[handwritten: "Willful + Malicious" misappropriation]*

3. What constitutes willful and malicious misappropriation of trade secrets? *[handwritten: Malicious as opposed to being Motivated by market competition.]*

[handwritten left margin: Motivation]

> ### Reading Guidance
> What does a party have to prove to be entitled to an award of attorney's fees in a trade secret misappropriation case? *[handwritten: Motivation]*

GEMINI ALUMINUM CORP. V. CALIFORNIA CUSTOM SHAPES, INC.

California Court of Appeal, Fourth District, 2002.
95 Cal. App. 4th 1249.

MCCONNELL, J.

Plaintiff Gemini Aluminum Corporation (Gemini) appeals a judgment in favor of defendant California Custom Shapes, Inc. (CCS), entered after a jury rejected Gemini's claim that CCS intentionally interfered with its prospective economic advantage. * * *

Gemini also appeals a postjudgment order awarding CCS $160,200 in attorney fees under Civil Code section 3426.4 for the "bad faith" prosecution of a claim for misappropriation of trade secrets. * * *

Factual and Procedural Background

Ray Williams, who was a principal of Taskmaster Industries Corporation (Taskmaster), invented the "Taskmaster workbench." In the spring of 1995 Taskmaster and Makita entered into a contract under which Taskmaster would manufacture the workbenches under the Makita name and Makita would market them to the public. * * *

Gemini and CCS are both extruders and finishers of aluminum parts. Taskmaster hired Gemini to extrude and paint, or "powder coat," aluminum parts for the workbenches. Gemini subcontracted with CCS to perform the powder coating.

Gemini began shipping aluminum parts to Taskmaster in June 1995. In July or August 1995, CCS discovered defects in parts it had powder coated for Gemini. CCS and Gemini blamed the problem on each other's workmanship. The parties were unable to resolve the dispute, and by September 21, 1995, CCS ceased coating the Taskmaster parts, put Gemini on a credit hold and demanded a COD payment for parts it had finished but not delivered to Gemini. However, in response to Gemini's threatened lawsuit, CCS delivered the materials to Gemini on a credit basis.

Taskmaster experienced financial problems, and by mid-September 1995 was $326,219.21 in arrears to Gemini. Gemini had stopped shipping materials to Taskmaster the previous month. Unaware of these facts, on September 27, 1995, CCS's principal, Richard Price, instructed one of his salespersons, Larry Jackson, to "go get the [Taskmaster] business." Price believed that in addition to powder coating, CCS was capable of extruding the aluminum parts for the Taskmaster workbench. On the same date, Jackson sent Taskmaster a letter soliciting its account.

In late September 1995 CCS filed a small claims action against Gemini, seeking $4,600.28 for unpaid invoices. On November 9, 1995, four days before the scheduled trial date, Gemini sued CCS in municipal court for breach of contract and related counts. CCS cross-complained against Gemini for breach of contract and related counts. On November 30, 1995, CCS filed another small claims action against Gemini, seeking an additional $930.30 in damages.

In mid-November 1995 Gemini sued Taskmaster for $326,219.21 in unpaid invoices.

In January 1996 Taskmaster first ordered aluminum parts for the workbench from CCS. Between then and early June 1996 CCS billed Taskmaster $25,053.29 for materials it ordered. Taskmaster paid only $6,156.53 of that amount, and, by June 1996 CCS refused to perform additional work for it.

In September 1996 Taskmaster filed for bankruptcy protection under Chapter 7, and its $324,219.21 debt to Gemini was presumably discharged. In any event, Taskmaster never paid Gemini the arrearages.

In December 1996 Gemini sued CCS in superior court for misappropriation of trade secrets, unfair competition and conversion. Gemini alleged that CCS used the die drawings Gemini provided it, which drawings identify Taskmaster as its customer and are used to fabricate the aluminum parts for the workbench, to solicit Taskmaster's business. The parties stipulated to consolidate the various actions in superior court. In June 1998 Gemini filed a first amended complaint, adding a cause of action for interference with prospective economic advantage. In its answer, CCS raised the privilege of competition as an affirmative defense.

A jury trial began in August 1999. At the outset, Gemini decided to pursue only its causes of action for conversion and interference with prospective economic advantage. However, it stated that its misappropriation of trade secrets claim "would be encompassed within the interference claim."

At the close of Gemini's case-in-chief, CCS moved for nonsuit. The court granted the motion as to the conversion cause of action, but denied it as to the interference cause of action.

After several days of testimony, the jury deliberated less than one hour before unanimously finding that CCS did not intentionally interfere with Gemini's prospective economic relationship with Taskmaster. As an advisory matter, the jury also determined Gemini acted in bad faith in pursuing its claim for misappropriation of trade secrets. The jury awarded CCS $4,600 on its cross-complaint. Judgment was entered for CCS on the complaint and cross-complaint on September 17, 1999. Gemini unsuccessfully moved for a new trial.

CCS then moved for attorney fees under section 3426.4, arguing Gemini pursued its claim for misappropriation of trade secrets in bad faith. The court granted the motion based on the "history of this lawsuit," stating "the claim for misappropriation was a not uncommon kind of knee-jerk response" to CCS's small claims collection action, and finding a lack of evidence to support the claim. The court awarded CCS $160,200 after determining that a minimum of 90 percent of its attorney fees was related to the misappropriation claim.

Discussion

* * *

II.   Attorney Fees Under Section 3426.4

A

Gemini challenges the propriety of the attorney fees award to CCS. The court relied on section 3426.4, a provision of the Uniform Trade Secrets Act (UTSA) (§ 3426 et seq.), which provides: "If a claim of misappropriation is made in bad faith, a motion to terminate an injunction is made or resisted in bad faith, or willful and malicious misappropriation exists, the court may award reasonable attorney's fees to the prevailing party."

The UTSA does not define "bad faith" as used in section 3426.4, and apparently there is no reported California case interpreting the term. In *Stilwell Development, Inc. v. Chen* * * * (*Stilwell*), a federal court noted the legislative history of section 3426.4 shows it is intended to " 'allow[ ] a court to award reasonable attorney fees to a prevailing party in specified circumstances as a *deterrent* to *specious* claims of misappropriation. . . .' "

* * * The court concluded that "[a]s to deterrence, . . . it requires conduct more culpable than mere negligence. To be deterrable, conduct must be at least reckless or grossly negligent, if not intentional and willful. Webster's defines specious as, among other things, 'apparently right or proper: superficially fair, just, or correct but not so in reality. . . .' Thus, the claim must have been without substance in reality, if not frivolous." * * *

The *Stilwell* court interpreted "bad faith" under section 3426.4 to require objective speciousness of the plaintiff's claim and its subjective misconduct in bringing or maintaining a claim for misappropriation of trade secrets. * * * The court awarded attorney fees in *Stilwell*, finding that as to the objective component, the plaintiffs produced no evidence of confidentiality of the information or misappropriation. As to the subjective component, the court inferred from the complete failure of proof that the plaintiffs must have knowingly and intentionally prosecuted a specious claim. * * *

Gemini contends that in interpreting section 3426.4, we should apply the standard of Code of Civil Procedure section 128.5, subdivision (a), which provides: "Every trial court may order a party, the party's attorney or both to pay any reasonable expenses, including attorney's fees, incurred by another party as a result of bad-faith actions or tactics that are frivolous or solely intended to cause unnecessary delay." Whether an action is "frivolous" under Code of Civil Procedure section 128.5 "is governed by an objective standard: Any reasonable attorney would agree it is totally and completely without merit. But there must also be a showing of an improper purpose, i.e., *subjective* bad faith on the part of the attorney or party to be sanctioned." * * *

Unlike Code of Civil Procedure section 128.5, subdivision (a), however, section 3426.4 does not contain the word "frivolous." Moreover, in enacting section 3426.4 the Legislature was concerned with curbing "specious" actions for misappropriation of trade secrets, and such actions may superficially appear to have merit. We find *Stilwell* persuasive and conclude that "bad faith" for purposes of section 3426.4 requires objective speciousness of the plaintiff's claim, as opposed to frivolousness, and its subjective bad faith in bringing or maintaining the claim.

An award of attorney fees for bad faith constitutes a sanction * * * and the trial court has broad discretion in ruling on sanctions motions. * * * "Assuming some evidence exists in support of the factual findings, the trial court's exercise of discretion will not be disturbed unless it exceeds the bounds of reason. * * * In reviewing the facts which led the trial court to impose sanctions, we must accept the version thereof which supports the trial court's determination, and must indulge in the inferences which favor its findings." * * *

We cannot say the court abused its discretion. The UTSA defines a trade secret as information that "(1) *Derives independent economic value, actual or potential*, from not being generally known to the public or to other persons who can obtain economic value from its disclosure or use; and [¶] (2) Is the subject of efforts that are reasonable under the circumstances to maintain its secrecy." (§ 3426.1, subd. (d), italics added.) When information has no independent economic value, a claim for misappropriation lacks merit.

Gemini alleged that CCS misappropriated the identity of Taskmaster and die drawings needed for the extrusion of aluminum parts for the workbench. Customer lists and related information may constitute protectable trade secrets. * * * However, Gemini filed its complaint for misappropriation and related counts in December 1996, long after the identity of Taskmaster and die drawings for the workbench parts arguably held any economic value, actual or potential, to Gemini, CCS or any other competitor. By September 1995 Taskmaster was $326,219.21 in arrears to Gemini, and by the summer of 1996 it was $18,896.76 in arrears to CCS. Further, in September 1996 Taskmaster filed a bankruptcy proceeding. Gemini's case was objectively specious, if not frivolous, from its inception.

The timing of Gemini's action also raises an inference of subjective bad faith. "*Good faith*, or its absence, involves a factual inquiry into the plaintiff's subjective state of mind: Did he or she believe the action was valid? What was his or her intent or purpose in pursuing it? A subjective state of mind will rarely be susceptible of direct proof; usually the trial court will be required to infer it from circumstantial evidence." * * * " '[B]ad faith' means simply that the action or tactic is being pursued for an improper motive. Thus, if the court determines that a party had acted with the intention of causing unnecessary delay, or for the sole purpose of harassing the opposing side, the improper motive has been found, and the court's inquiry need go no further." * * *

The legal requirement of economic value in a misappropriation case is well established and straightforward, and, by December 1996, Gemini could not have reasonably believed that Taskmaster's identity and die drawings retained any economic value. Moreover, before trial CCS brought the infirmities in Gemini's misappropriation claim to its attention, but its counsel "stat[ed] curtly that he did not want to reveal his theories of liability or the evidence supporting those theories," and "CCS [did not] have a clue about this case and [he had] no desire to educate [it]." "Bad faith may be inferred where the specific shortcomings of the case are identified by opposing counsel, and the decision is made to go forward despite the inability to respond to the arguments raised." * * *

Despite the lack of any proof of economic value, Gemini persisted with its misappropriation claim through trial, in conjunction with its cause of action for intentional interference with prospective economic advantage. Gemini, in fact, requested a jury instruction that the interference may consist of misappropriation. Yet, at the hearing on the motion for attorney fees, Gemini's counsel argued "[w]e did not attempt to prove that it was a trade secret," presumably conceding the lack of merit. Further, during his testimony Hardy revealed his hostility toward CCS and its principal, Price. Hardy referred to CCS as "snaky"; to Price twice as a "snake"; to Price and Williams, Taskmaster's principal, as "two snakes in a paper sack"; and to Williams as having "had a snake [Price] hid[den]." Under all the circumstances, we cannot fault the court for finding both objective speciousness and subjective bad faith and awarding CCS attorney fees under section 3426.4.

B

CCS seeks attorney fees on appeal. " '[I]t is established that fees, if recoverable at all—pursuant either to statute or [the] parties' agreement— are available for services at trial *and on appeal.*'" * * * CCS is the prevailing party on appeal, and thus it is entitled to fees under section 3426.4. "Although this court has the power to fix attorney fees on appeal, the better practice is to have the trial court determine such fees." * * *

Disposition

The judgment and order are affirmed. The matter is remanded to the trial court for its determination of an award to CCS for attorney fees on appeal. CCS is also awarded costs on appeal.

DID YOU GET IT?

1. What does a defendant have to prove to be entitled to an award of attorney's fees under the UTSA? How does that differ from what a plaintiff must prove?

2. What evidence did the court rely on to meet the objective and subjective standards it articulates?

Food for Thought

How does the "bad faith" standard of UTSA, sections 4(i) and 4(ii), differ from the "willful and malicious" standard of section 4(iii)?

---

5. AWARD OF REASONABLE ROYALTIES

There are two places in the UTSA and the DTSA where courts can grant reasonable royalties in lieu of other relief. However, because the factual circumstances that give rise to such remedies and the standards for granting such relief are different, they should not be confused with one another.

The first reference to a reasonable royalty in the UTSA is in Section 2(b) which states, in part, that: "[i]n exceptional circumstances, an injunction may condition future use upon payment of a reasonable royalty."

See also, the DTSA, 18 U.S.C. § 1836 (b)(3)(A)(iii), reprinted in Appendix A. The official comments to the UTSA explain the purpose of this provision as follows:

> Section 2(b) deals with the special situation in which a future use by a misappropriator will damage a trade secret owner but an injunction against future use nevertheless is inappropriate due to exceptional circumstances. Exceptional circumstances include the existence of an overriding public interest which requires the denial of a prohibitory injunction against future damaging use and a person's reasonable reliance upon acquisition of a misappropriated trade secret in good faith and without reason to know of its prior misappropriation that would be prejudiced by a prohibitory injunction against future damaging use. * * * The [second] justification for withholding prohibitory injunctive relief can arise upon a trade secret owner's notification to a good faith third party that the third party has knowledge of a trade secret as a result of misappropriation by another. This notice suffices to make the third party a misappropriator thereafter under Section 1(2)(ii)(B)(I).

As noted by Professor Richard Dole, the Reporter on the UTSA drafting project, members of the Patent, Trademark, and Copyright Committee of the ABA (now known as the IPL Section) advocated for the "exceptional circumstances" language in Section 2 "in order to preclude routine judicial licensing of misappropriated trade secrets." *See* Richard F. Dole, Jr., *The Uniform Trade Secrets Act—Trends and Prospects*, 33 HAMLINE L. REV. 409, 437 (2010). Thus, the provision did not create a new remedy that was not recognized at common law, but rather, limited the circumstances under which reasonable royalties could be granted in lieu of an injunction.

The second place where the UTSA allows the grant of a reasonable royalty is set forth at the end of Section 3, the damages provision. It provides, in pertinent part, that: "[i]n lieu of damages measured by any other methods, the damages caused by misappropriation may be measured by imposition of liability for a reasonable royalty." *See also*, the DTSA, 18 U.S.C. § 1836(b)(3)(B)(ii). The case that follows, although based upon the common law of New York rather than the UTSA, provides an example of the award of damages as measured by a reasonable royalty.

> ### Reading Guidance
> *What prompted the award of a reasonable royalty in this case?*

- reasonable royalty when lost profits + unjust enrichment are not accurate measures of damages.

LINKCO, INC. V. FUJITSU LTD.

U. S. District Court, S.D. New York, 2002.
232 F.Supp.2d 182.

- fmr. employee goes to new co.

SCHEINDLIN, DISTRICT JUDGE.

I.   INTRODUCTION

LinkCo, Inc. ("LinkCo") was formed in 1995 as an Internet content company with a mission to become the preeminent world-wide provider of comprehensive information about Japan's public companies delivered in an electronic format. The company was created in response to the Japanese Ministry of Finance's announcement that the government was adopting an electronic corporate disclosure reporting system. * * * Although LinkCo designed various computer systems for two years, it never commercialized a product.

After LinkCo ceased operations in December 1997, one of its former directors, Kyoto Kanda, began working for Fujitsu Ltd. ("Fujitsu"), a large Japanese company that in addition to its many other products, became interested in developing programs related to corporate disclosure. On March 31, 1999, Fujitsu publicly announced the development of DisclosureVision—a software package that performs some of the same functions as the computer system designed by LinkCo. As a result, on September 25, 2000, LinkCo sued Fujitsu on the ground "that certain elements of DisclosureVision are copies of its technology, 'virtually identical in design and substance.'" Indeed, LinkCo claimed that "'virtually every significant element of Fujitsu's DisclosureVision was stolen from LinkCo's technology.'" LinkCo brought this action, alleging that Fujitsu engaged in misappropriation of trade secrets, unfair competition, and tortious interference with contract.

Both parties proposed competing jury instructions concerning the appropriate measure of damages for each claim. During the trial, I made an oral ruling as to the appropriate measure of damages in a trade secret case. I write now to fully set forth the reasoning supporting that decision.

The parties differ as to whether damages for the alleged misappropriation of a trade secret should be measured by (1) LinkCo's losses, (2) Fujitsu's unjust enrichment, or (3) a reasonable royalty. For the reasons below, I conclude [applying New York law] that a reasonable royalty is the proper measure of damages. * * *

II.   APPROPRIATE MEASURE OF DAMAGES

A.   Plaintiff's Losses, Defendant's Unjust Enrichment, or a Reasonable Royalty

Once it is established that a trade secret has been misappropriated, there are two obvious ways to calculate plaintiff's damages. * * * *First,* damages may be measured according to any losses plaintiff suffered from the alleged misappropriation. Plaintiff's losses may include the cost of developing the trade secret and the revenue plaintiff would have made but for the defendant's wrongful conduct. *Second,* damages may be measured by the defendant's unjust enrichment as a result of the misappropriation. Unjust enrichment is measured by the profits the defendant obtained from using the trade secret. * * *

In certain circumstances, these damage calculations provide inadequate compensation to the plaintiff. Courts have therefore developed a third measure of damages: a reasonable royalty. "A reasonable royalty award attempts to measure a hypothetically agreed value of what the defendant wrongfully obtained from the plaintiff." * * * To measure this value, "the Court calculates what the parties would have agreed to as a fair licensing price at the time that the misappropriation occurred." * * * Because the plaintiff's loss or the defendant's gain may be very difficult to calculate in intellectual property cases, a reasonable royalty is "a common form of award in both trade secret and patent cases." * * * Moreover, a reasonable royalty is ideal when the commercial context in which the misappropriation occurred requires consideration of multiple factors in order to compensate the plaintiff adequately. * * *

B.   Reasonable Royalty Applies to this Case

Neither LinkCo's losses nor Fujitsu's unjust enrichment can serve as an adequate method of calculating damages. *First,* LinkCo's losses are an inadequate measure of damages because the company ceased operations very close to the time of the alleged misappropriation, making losses difficult to establish. Measuring LinkCo's damages after it was already out of business would require a fact-finder to speculate as to the revenue LinkCo may have made if it had remained in business. In addition, losses measured solely by LinkCo's development costs would not adequately compensate the company for its loss of the potentially valuable trade secret. *Second,* Fujitsu's unjust enrichment is impossible to measure because the company did not make any profits from DisclosureVision. Nevertheless, "the lack of actual profits does not insulate the defendants from being obliged to pay for what they have wrongfully obtained." * * * Under these circumstances, a reasonable royalty avoids the danger of an inadequate measure of damages by enabling the jury to consider various relevant factors to reach the most practical and sensible award. Therefore, a reasonable royalty is the best measure of damages in a case where the alleged thief made no profits.

C.   Form of Royalty

A reasonable royalty may be computed in various ways, including a lump-sum royalty based on expected sales or a running royalty based on a percentage of actual sales. The choice of the proper form of the royalty is dependent upon what would have been the most likely agreement during the hypothetical negotiation. A jury may award damages based on a lump-sum if there is sufficient evidence that lump-sum license structures are common in the industry. * * * Although Fujitsu and LinkCo disagree on the prevalence of lump-sum licence fees in the industry, the jury should decide whether there is sufficient evidence to warrant the award of a lump-sum or running royalty.

III. ADMISSIBLE EVIDENCE

* * *

A.   Evidence Relevant to a Reasonable Royalty Award

1.   Sales Projections

An infringer's projected sales are often used as a basis for a reasonable royalty when the projections would have been available at the time of the hypothetical negotiation. * * * Although these projections are not an exact measurement of a trade secret's value, these estimates are relevant to the parties' perceived value of the trade secret at the time of misappropriation. For example, in *Interactive Pictures,* the infringer's sales projections were created two months before the infringement began. As a result, the court held that a reasonable royalty could be based on these projections because "those projections would have been available to [defendant] at the time of the hypothetical negotiation" and were not outdated.

In contrast, post-negotiation sales projections are an after-the-fact assessment that the negotiating parties could not have considered. These estimates do not reflect the parties perceived value of the trade secret during the negotiation. Therefore, sales projections are only relevant in a reasonable royalty calculation when they are available before the time of the misappropriation and would have been considered by the parties.

2.   Actual Sales

While an infringer's actual sales are often used to determine damages, there are advantages and disadvantages to allowing this proof to be presented to a jury. On the one hand, when an infringer has not done well on the product developed through use of the trade secret, it argues that the only way to calculate the damages is to apply a reasonable royalty to the actual sales. * * * On the other hand, when an infringer has done very well on its sales, it argues that proof of the actual sales is prejudicial because the amount of actual sales could not have been anticipated at the time of the hypothetical negotiations. * * *

The victims, or plaintiffs, are equally mercurial. When the infringer's product has not done well in the market, the victims argue that the sales should not be presented to the jury because they occurred after the date of the hypothetical meeting and therefore do not reflect the value the infringer placed on the product at the time of the meeting. * * * The victims also argue that the actual sales are highly prejudicial because the infringer may have done a poor job of marketing the product. * * * When the product does well on the market, however, the victims argue that actual sales represent the best measure of damages. * * *

Each of these arguments has some merit and the case law on this issue reflects a high level of confusion and inconsistency. Occasionally, courts allow proof of actual sales and in other instances they do not. Apparently, no governing principle informs the court's decision. The key, of course, is what the parties would have believed to be the reasonable value of the alleged trade secret at the time it was stolen.

* * *

3.   Lack of Profits

A reasonable royalty may also be based on the infringer's profits. *See Trans-World* ("Evidence of the infringer's profits generally is admissible as probative of his anticipated profits."). It is not surprising that when the infringer has profited from its wrongful use of a competitor's intellectual property, and sometimes quite handsomely, the injured party urges that those profits reflect the damages it has suffered. Many cases recognize this self-evident proposition.

The situation is entirely different when the infringer has not profited from its wrongful conduct. The absence of profits does not preclude the victim from obtaining damages based on the loss of its intellectual property. * * * Indeed, that is the genesis of the damage calculation based on the hypothetical negotiation at the time of misappropriation. * * * These cases demonstrate that when there are no profits, an event that the parties could not have anticipated at the time of the hypothetical negotiations, admission of this evidence would be highly prejudicial to the victim of the alleged infringement. The intellectual property had a theoretical value at the time it was stolen. There are many reasons why the infringer may not have profited once it commercialized the idea and sold the product. These intangible factors, such as the infringer's efficiency in bringing the product to market, the quality of its product and its marketing efforts, all contribute to the conclusion that proof of no profits by the infringer is unreliable, highly prejudicial, and inadmissible.

* * *

V. CONCLUSION

For the reasons discussed above, the appropriate measure of damages for plaintiff's misappropriation of trade secrets claim, where defendant did not profit from the alleged infringement, is a reasonable royalty. Depending on the evidence presented at trial, the royalty may result in a lump-sum payment based on a reasonable royalty as applied to expected sales or a running royalty based on actual sales. If damages are awarded, pre-judgment interest is mandatory under New York law because a claim for damages is legal in nature.

SO ORDERED

DID YOU GET IT?

1. Why was a reasonable royalty measure of damages used? *measure here.*

   B/c lost profits + unjust enrich. inaccurate measure here.

2. What evidence supported entitlement to a reasonable royalty? *near time of*

   Alleged infringer made no profits + Company stopped operating near time of misapp.

3. What evidence was there that the trade secret misappropriation "caused" harm?

4. How did the court calculate the reasonable royalty? *infringer+ pockets*

   — Sales projections, actual sales, lack of infringer pockets

5. For what period of time should the reasonable royalty apply? *When negotiations would have taken place. At time TS was stolen. Directly prior to misapp.*

Food for Thought

What if the only evidence of misappropriation of a trade secret is the improper acquisition or threatened use or disclosure of the trade secret; should the plaintiff in such a case be entitled to an award of damages measured by reasonable royalties if the trade secret was never used or disclosed?

C. SPECIAL ISSUE: HOW LONG SHOULD AN INJUNCTION LAST?

Assuming a plaintiff in a trade secret case succeeds in proving it is entitled to injunctive relief, the court (as it did in *Sung, supra*) must consider the proper scope and length of the injunction. Typically, the plaintiff (as the prevailing party) will draft a proposed injunction order which sets forth the preferred restrictions (including the persons and entities that will be subject to the injunction) and the court will either approve the proposed injunction as drafted by the plaintiff or modify it as it deems necessary.

There are three different factual scenarios that give rise to issues concerning the length of an injunction. The first concerns the proper length of an injunction in cases where plaintiff's trade secrets continue to exist at the time the injunction order is granted. In such cases, a "permanent" injunction with no specified time limit makes sense because there is no telling how long the trade secrets will last. *See*, Richard F. Dole, *Permanent*

*Injunctive Relief for Trade Secret Misappropriation without an Express Limit upon its Duration: The Uniform Trade Secrets Act Reconsid*ered, 17 B.U. J. SCI. & TECH. L. 173 (2011).

The second scenario involves the post-injunction loss of trade secrecy. In such cases, trade secret principles and applicable procedural rules allow parties who are subject to an injunction to make a motion to dissolve the injunction on the grounds that the underlying trade secrets no longer exist. The *Carus* case, *infra,* is an example of this scenario.

In the final factual scenario, the plaintiff's trade secrets cease to exist either before or during the pendency of the trade secret misappropriation case. The loss of trade secrecy may occur due to the wrongful actions of the defendant (in which case the plaintiff would be entitled to an award of damages as a remedy for the loss of its trade secrets) or because the plaintiff voluntarily disclosed its trade secrets to the public. Plaintiff's trade secrets may also cease to exist because of the independent development and reverse engineering activities of another, followed by the disclosure of the results of such activities. Under this scenario, the question is whether injunctive relief is needed at all.

Before the adoption of the UTSA, some courts viewed injunctive relief in trade secret cases both as a penalty for defendant's wrongdoing and as a means to protect plaintiff's trade secrets in the future. Thus, there are cases in which the court granted or continued injunctive relief even after the plaintiff's trade secrets ceased to exist. The *Shellmar* case in Chapter 1 is an example. Although the information that the plaintiff had disclosed to the defendant was a trade secret at the time of the initial disclosure to defendant, it was subsequently disclosed to the world. In granting the requested injunctive relief anyway, the court reasoned:

> The jurisdiction of equity to protect such trade secrets is founded upon trust or confidence. The court "fastens the obligation upon the conscience of the party, and enforces it against him in the same manner as it enforces against a party to whom a benefit is given, the obligations of performing a promise on the faith of which the benefit has been conferred." * * * Whether the subject-matter is patentable or not, if the designer discovers and keeps secret a process of manufacture, though he will not have an exclusive right to it as against the public, after he shall have published it, or against those who in good faith acquire knowledge of it, yet he has a property right, which a court of chancery will protect against one who in bad faith and breach of confidence undertakes to apply it to his own use.

Allen-Qualley v. Shellmar Products Co., 31 F.2d 293, 296 (N.D. Ill. 1929).

Roughly four years after the grant of an injunction against it, Shellmar Products Co. initiated further proceedings asking the District Court to dissolve the injunction because the plaintiff (Allen-Qualley) had disclosed its secrets in a published patent. *See Shellmar Products Co. v. Allen-Qualley Co.,* 87 F.2d 104 (7th Cir. 1937). The request was denied by the court which originally granted the injunction and, on appeal, by the Seventh Circuit Court of Appeals. Explaining the significance of plaintiff's patent, the Circuit court stated:

> [The patent], however, did not add to the inviolability of the confidential communication as between [Shellmar] and Allen-Qualley, nor did it detract from it. It merely gave to Allen-Qualley a monopoly against the world. . . . In that event, anyone, except appellant, could have infringed it if he desired to do so and thereby hazard an action for infringement at the hands of Allen-Qualley. But not so the appellant, for the consensus of authority is that by its inequitable conduct appellant has precluded itself from enjoying the patent disclosure. . . .

One of the purposes of the UTSA was to clarify the law concerning the proper length of injunctions in trade secret cases and, in so doing, reject the reasoning and result of "the *Shellmar* line of cases" in favor of what had become known as "the *Conmar* line of cases" *See Conmar Prods. Corp. v. Universal Slide Fastener Co.,* 172 F.2d 150 (2nd Cir. 1949); *see also* Comment, *Trade Secrets after Patent Publication: A Punitive Injunction,* 32 Fordham L. Rev. 313 (1963). The comment to section 2 of the UTSA reads:

> Injunctions restraining future use and disclosure of misappropriated trade secrets frequently are sought. Although punitive perpetual injunctions have been granted, * * * , Section 2(a) of this Act adopts the position of the trend of authority limiting the duration of injunctive relief to the extent of the temporal advantage over good faith competitors gained by a misappropriator. *See e.g., K–2 Ski Co. v. Head Ski Co., Inc.,* 506 F.2d 471 (CA9, 1974) (maximum appropriate duration of both temporary and permanent injunctive relief is period of time it would have taken defendant to discover trade secrets lawfully through either independent development or reverse engineering of plaintiff's products.)
>
> The general principle of Section 2(a) and (b) is that an injunction should last for as long as is necessary, but no longer than is necessary, to eliminate the commercial advantage or "lead time" with respect to good faith competitors that a person has obtained through misappropriation. Subject to any additional period of restraint necessary to negate lead time, an injunction accordingly should terminate when a former trade secret becomes either generally known to good faith competitors or generally knowable

to them because of the lawful availability of products that can be reversed engineered to reveal a trade secret.

* * *

If a misappropriator either has not taken advantage of the lead time or good faith competitors already have caught up with a misappropriator at the time a case is decided, future disclosure and use of a former trade secret by a misappropriator will not damage a trade secret owner and no injunctive restraint of future disclosure and use is appropriate. * * *

The cases that follow provide examples of how courts apply the foregoing principles.

Food for Thought

What is the purpose of injunctive relief in civil cases? Should it be designed to punish the defendant? Is punishment typically a goal of tort law? If not, what are the goals of tort law?

Reading Guidance

Why did the trade secrets cease to exist?

CARUS CHEMICAL CO. V. CALCIQUEST, INC.

Appellate Court of Illinois, Third District, 2003.
341 Ill.App.3d 897.

JUSTICE LYTTON delivered the opinion of the court:

Plaintiff, Carus Chemical Company, sued defendants, John Charlton and Calciquest, Inc., for breach of contract and violation of the Illinois Trade Secret Act. Carus obtained a preliminary injunction prohibiting defendants from comparing the products manufactured by Carus and Calciquest. After discovering that Carus itself had published a comparison between the products in a bid proposal, defendants petitioned the court to dissolve the preliminary injunction and to sanction Carus. The trial court denied the motions and defendants filed this interlocutory appeal. We reverse the trial court's decision on the motion to dissolve and affirm its refusal to order sanctions.

John Charlton testified that he held a number of technical and marketing positions with Carus that gave him unique access to certain trade secrets and confidential information. Charlton signed a confidentiality agreement as a condition of his employment with Carus, in which he agreed not to use or disclose (directly or indirectly) any confidential information after his employment ended. The agreement defined "confidential information" as all processes, techniques, compositions, etc., which "are in the possession of Carus and which have not been published or disclosed to the general public."

Charlton ended his employment with Carus and went to work for Calciquest. Carus and Calciquest manufacture similar chemical products used in community water supplies to control corrosion. Charlton was in the process of selling Calciquest's product to a customer when he sent a letter which included the following language:

> Please find enclosed a product data sheet for CalciQuest Liquid, our primary liquid phosphate blend for corrosion control and sequestering. It is, essentially, identical to Aqua Mag [Carus' product], both in specifications and in chemical composition. Chromatographic analysis shows the two compounds to be virtually identical. The thermal process used to make these liquid blends is also identical. As a chemist, I have no doubt that the two compounds are interchangeable.

Carus filed a motion for a temporary restraining order alleging that defendants used and revealed confidential and trade secret information by divulging Carus' proprietary thermal process. Carus claimed that disclosure of the information could result in enormous economic losses, and that by disclosing the thermal process, Charlton breached his confidentiality agreement. In support of its motion, Carus vice-president Len Kubera testified that: "[a]sserting that the thermal process used to make the two competing products is identical, necessarily demonstrates that Mr. Charlton has used and disclosed Carus' trade secret information for the benefit of Calciquest and to Carus Chemical's detriment."

The court entered a temporary restraining order and on July 16, 2002, granted a preliminary injunction prohibiting "defendants from making comparisons to the Aqua Mag thermal process and/or production process."

Meanwhile, Carus had attached a copy of the Charlton letter to a bid proposal Carus submitted to Miami-Dade County on June 19, 2002. In that proposal, Kubera wrote that "[i]t should be noted that our products continue to be used as a 'bench mark' by our competitor, your current supplier, who has issued written statements that their product is 'identical' to the Carus Chemical Company product." Kubera referenced the letter as support for that claim.

When defendants became aware that Carus had used Charlton's letter in its Miami-Dade negotiations, they filed a motion to dissolve the injunction and to impose sanctions on Carus * * *. During the hearing on the motion to dissolve, Carus admitted that no confidential information or trade secrets were disclosed in Charlton's letter. The trial court denied the motion to dissolve and the motion for sanctions.

I.

The defendants argue that the trial court abused its discretion when it denied defendants' motion to dissolve the preliminary injunction. * * *

In order to obtain a preliminary injunction, a party must establish four factors: (1) a clearly ascertainable right in need of protection, (2) the risk of irreparable harm if the injunction is not granted, (3) the lack of any adequate legal remedy, and (4) the likelihood of success on the merits. * * * The failure to establish any of the four factors will preclude the court from issuing the injunction.

We believe that Carus' disclosure of Charlton's letter vitiated the need for a preliminary injunction. When Carus sent the letter to Miami-Dade county, the information was no longer confidential. In effect, Carus had republished the letter, putting it into the public domain. Since the information became public by Carus' own hand, defendants' further use of it cannot be said to cause Carus irreparable harm. * * *

In *Campbell Soup Co. v. ConAgra, Inc.*, the plaintiff obtained an injunction prohibiting defendant from using or exploiting the plaintiff's product preparation process. The defendant became familiar with the process while employed by plaintiff. The plaintiff obtained a patent for the process before suit was filed; in the patent application, the details of the process were disclosed. The appellate court found that further disclosure of facts already revealed could not constitute irreparable harm and reversed the award for injunctive relief. * * *

Our supreme court decided a similar issue in *ILG Industries, Inc. v. Scott*, where the plaintiff obtained an injunction preventing former employees from using its trade secrets. The court, in determining whether the documents used by defendants were indeed trade secrets, made the following observation: "[t]hat which is of general knowledge within an industry cannot be a trade secret; something which is fully and completely disclosed by a business through its catalogs or literature disseminated throughout an industry cannot be a trade secret." * * * Although we are not determining the existence of a trade secret in this case, the principle remains the same. Charlton's letter comparing the two formulas ceased to be proprietary or protectable when Carus republished it.

Furthermore, under the terms of the preliminary injunction, Carus is free to compare the thermal processes of the two companies, but defendants are not. The threat of irreparable harm is belied by Carus' ability to use the letter as a sword in its competition with defendants while relying on the preliminary injunction as a shield against them. Thus, while the preliminary injunction improperly protects Carus, it also acts as an unreasonable restraint on competition. * * *

Since the information is not confidential, no threat of irreparable harm exists, and Carus is not entitled to injunctive relief. The preliminary injunction must be dissolved. * * *

We make no comment on other issues pending in the trial court.

* * *

Reversed in part and affirmed in part.

DID YOU GET IT?

1. What are the claimed trade secrets and who owns them?

2. Why did the trade secrets cease to exist?

3. Why didn't the court continue the injunction for at least a brief period of time?

Reading Guidance

Did plaintiff's trade secrets continue to exist at the time the injunction order was issued?

MICROSTRATEGY INC. v. BUSINESS OBJECTS, S.A.

United States District Court, E.D. Virginia, 2005.
369 F.Supp.2d 725.

* * *

FRIEDMAN, DISTRICT JUDGE.

Pending before the court is the motion of the defendants, Business Objects, S.A. and Business Objects Americas, Inc., (collectively "Business Objects"), to dissolve the injunction entered by the court on August 6, 2004 that presently enjoins Business Objects from using, disclosing or possessing certain trade secrets of the plaintiff, MicroStrategy, Inc. ("MicroStrategy"). * * *

I.   Background and Procedural History

The history of the underlying litigation between the two parties is lengthy and has been fully detailed by the court in prior orders. * * * An extensive review of this history is not necessary for the purposes of addressing the instant motion. In brief encapsulation, among the numerous claims alleged by MicroStrategy against Business Objects at the onset of this litigation was that the latter had misappropriated the trade secrets of the former, in violation of the Virginia Uniform Trade Secrets Act. *See* Va.Code. Ann. 59.1–336 et seq.

* * * The court determined that Business Objects had misappropriated two of the many documents claimed by MicroStrategy to constitute trade secrets, specifically, the documents referred to as the "Business Objects Competitive Recipe" and the "Volume Discount Schedule." * * * As a

remedy, the court granted MicroStrategy's request for an injunction, narrowly tailored to prohibiting Business Objects from possessing, disclosing, or using either of the two documents.

In discussing the necessary scope of injunctive relief, the court recognized in the August 6, 2004 order that the two documents in question might no longer constitute trade secrets due to their age. * * * Beyond making this observation, however, the court expressed no affirmative opinion as to whether the two documents currently constituted trade secrets. Rather, the court noted that the Virginia Uniform Trade Secrets Act permits a defendant to petition the court to dissolve the injunction when the information has lost trade secret status. * * * Indeed, the VUTSA specifies that an injunction shall terminate when the trade secret ceases to exist. As the court also recognized in the August 6, 2004 order, however, section 59.1–337 also permits the court to extend the injunction for a reasonable period of time in order to eliminate any commercial advantage derived from the misappropriation. * * * Consequently, in the August 6, 2004 order, the court issued a permanent injunction but advised Business Objects that it could, at the end of a six-month period, petition the court to dissolve the injunction on the basis that the documents in question no longer constitute trade secrets.

* * *

II.   Discussion

Business Objects contends that the injunctive relief provided by the August 6, 2004 order should be terminated because the Business Objects Competitive Recipe and the Volume Discount Schedule can no longer be viewed trade secrets. Business Objects claims that the information in both of these documents is now stale, such that neither document has any economic value. Furthermore, Business Objects argues that to the extent the information in such documents may have passed into the public domain, Business Objects should not be subject to contempt if it should come into possession of this information. Business Objects also claims that it would be unfairly penalized if it was prohibited from obtaining what would amount to legitimate business intelligence to which the public now has access.

* * *

C.   Motion to Dissolve the Injunction

Federal Rule of 60(b)(5), upon which Business Objects relies in support of the instant motion, provides "[o]n motion and upon such terms as are just, the court may relieve a party or a party's legal representative from a final judgment, order, or proceeding for the following reasons: . . . (5) the judgment has been satisfied, released, or discharged . . . or it is no longer equitable that the judgment should have prospective application."

Fed.R.Civ.P. 60(b)(5). In order to grant a Rule 60(b)(5) motion to modify a prior order, the court must find "a significant change either in factual conditions or in law." * * *

The court ordered the injunction in reliance on Virginia law. * * * "Where federal courts are called upon to adjudicate a claim predicated on state law . . . the ultimate issue of whether injunctive relief may issue must be decided under applicable state law." * * *

* * * Although the decision to grant the injunction was rooted in state law, the court is free to follow the procedures stemming from the federal rules in determining this motion to dissolve, even though a similar method of analysis for dealing with motions to dissolve is not readily apparent under the state scheme. * * *

The parties agree that the governing federal standard in reviewing a motion to dissolve focuses on six factors:

   (1)   the circumstances leading to entry of the injunction and the nature of the conduct sought to be prevented;

   (2)   the length of time since entry of the injunction;

   (3)   whether the party subject to its terms has complied or attempted to comply in good faith with the injunction;

   (4)   the likelihood that the conduct or conditions sought to be prevented will recur absent the injunction;

   (5)   whether the moving party can demonstrate a significant, unforeseen change in the facts or law and whether such changed circumstances have made compliance substantially more onerous or have made the decree unworkable; and

   (6)   whether the objective of the decree has been achieved and whether continued enforcement would be detrimental to the public interest.

* * * In applying this framework, which is linked to Federal Rule of Civil Procedure 60(b), the court also considers the substantive state law that authorized this injunction-specifically, Virginia Code section 59.1–337. This statute provides that an injunction shall terminate, upon application to the court, when the trade secret has ceased to exist. * * * Even if the trade secret has ceased to exist, however, the court may continue the injunction for an additional reasonable period of time in order to eliminate the commercial advantage that otherwise would be derived from the misappropriation. * * *

From the above standards of review * * * two factors stand out. One, in both state and federal schemes it is clear that it is the defendant's burden to show changed circumstances, which in this case requires a showing that the documents are no longer trade secrets. Second, the court can continue the injunction on one of two findings: (1) that the documents still constitute trade secrets; and (2) even if the documents are not trade secrets, if the court finds that a reasonable period of time is needed to eliminate commercial advantage that has accrued to the defendant as a result of its possession of such documents. * * *

Although the court did recognize in its August 6, 2004 order that the Business Objects Competitive Recipe and Volume Discount Schedule might no longer constitute trade secrets, it determined that injunctive relief was appropriate without definitively deciding whether trade secret status still existed. The reason for this was that Virginia Code section 59.1–337, which authorizes injunctive relief, also provides that even when trade secret status ceases, such that the injunction shall terminate, an injunction may be continued for "an additional reasonable period of time in order to eliminate commercial advantage." * * * Thus, injunctive relief was permitted under section 59.1–337 regardless of whether the documents still constituted trade secrets at the time of the August 6, 2004 order.

The court, however, also followed the provision of section 59.1–337 that provides that the party enjoined should make application to the court for a dissolution of the injunction based on the loss of trade secret status. In keeping with this provision, the court, in its August 6, 2004 order, placed the burden on Business Objects to show that the documents at issue no longer constitute trade secrets. Accordingly, in the posture of the instant motion to dissolve the injunction and considering the aforementioned standards of review, the court must assume that the documents at issue continue to be trade secrets and that it is Business Objects' burden to prove otherwise. This inquiry into whether Business Objects has established changed circumstances is, of course, different than the court's initial inquiry as to whether the Business Objects Competitive Recipe and the Volume Discount Schedule constituted trade secrets at the time of misappropriation.

* * *

1.   Virginia Code Section 59.1–337

In establishing that the documents no longer constitute trade secrets, Business Objects must put forward an evidentiary basis sufficient for the court to find that the documents (1) no longer have economic value; and (2) are no longer the subject of efforts that are reasonable under the circumstances to maintain their secrecy. * * *

The court finds that Business Objects has failed to make such a showing. There is no evidence, beyond argument based on the age of the documents, that these documents have lost economic value. Although Business Objects argues that the Business Objects Competitive Recipe is tied to outdated products, there is no showing the analysis and information that went into developing the Business Objects Competitive Recipe was or is exclusively tied to the products available at the time that document was authored. Furthermore, Business Objects has not shown that MicroStrategy no longer relies on either document in either competing against Business Objects or in offering discounts to customers.

* * *

Moreover, Business Objects has not shown that either document is no longer the subject of efforts by MicroStrategy to retain its confidential status. The Virginia Supreme Court has recognized that "[t]he characteristic of a trade secret is secrecy rather than novelty." * * * There has been no showing that MicroStrategy has allowed these documents to become public or failed to take other steps to secure them. Accordingly, Business Objects has not established that the injunction should cease to exist based on a loss of trade secret status.

2.   Rule 60(b)(5)

Application of the general framework that governs a Rule 60(b)(5) motion to dissolve an injunction also support the denial of the instant motion. "When confronted with any motion invoking [Rule 60(b)(5)], a district court's task is to determine whether it remains equitable for the judgment at issue to apply prospectively and, if not, to relieve the parties of some or all of the burdens of that judgment on such terms as are just." * * *

a.   Circumstances of Injunction and Nature of Conduct

The circumstances leading to the entry of the injunction and the nature of the conduct sought to be prevented are set forth in the August 6, 2004 order and need not be repeated. The harm the court sought to prevent in its prior order was the improper advantage Business Objects gained and would continue to gain commercially through its improper possession and use of MicroStrategy's confidential trade secrets. Business Objects possessed these documents for nearly three years prior to the imposition of the injunction.

b.   Length of Time Since Entry of the Injunction

Business Objects claims that, considering the outdated nature of the documents, a significant period of time has passed since the entry of the injunction. The mere passage of time, however, is not a sufficient reason to terminate an injunction. * * * The Supreme Court of Virginia has indicated that "[t]he crucial characteristic of a trade secret is secrecy rather than novelty." * * * Thus, Business Objects must not only show that the documents are old, but that they are no longer kept secret. The relatively brief duration of the injunction does not allow for such a finding and, thus, does not warrant dissolution at this time. * * * Given the nearly three years that Business Objects was in possession of the documents, the court does not find that the nine months that have passed since the entry of the injunction supports a showing of dramatic change in the circumstances underlying its issuance. * * *

This is not to suggest that the age of the documents is not relevant to the question of changed circumstances. In view, however, of the fact that Business Objects has not established that the documents no longer constitute trade secrets, the court does not believe that nine months is a sufficient amount of time to undercut any commercial advantage that Business Objects may have gained through their three year possession and use of the documents. * * *

c.   Business Objects' Compliance with the Injunction

Business Objects also claims that it has fully complied with the terms of the injunction. In the court's view, this merits little consideration as compliance is what the law expects. * * * Furthermore, the time of compliance is too brief to warrant dissolution when balanced against the time that Business Objects possessed the documents.

d.   Likelihood of Repeat of Conduct that Prompted Injunction

Although there is no indication that the misappropriation will reoccur absent the injunction, or that Business Objects will somehow again obtain the documents at issue, the court is not convinced that a sufficient period of time has passed in order to eliminate any commercial advantage Business Objects might have obtained through its possession or use of the documents. * * *

e.   Significant Change in Facts or Law That Have Made Compliance Difficult

As has been discussed, Business Objects has not demonstrated that any significant, unforseen change of fact or law has occurred that would make compliance with the injunction more difficult. * * * There has been no showing, other than reliance on the passage of time and certain nonspecific MicroStrategy releases, that the documents have lost significant economic value or have entered into the public domain in the past nine months since the court issued the injunction. Nor has Business Objects demonstrated that it is any more difficult for it to comply with the injunction. In fact, Business Objects admits in its memoranda, and also did so at the hearing, that it is not interested in reacquiring the documents at issue.

* * *

f.   Objectives of the Injunction and the Public Interest

Business Objects argues that the injunction has served its purpose and that it is no longer in the public interest to prevent Business Objects from obtaining what might be legitimate competitive intelligence. This latter argument, that Business Objects should not be deprived from using intelligence that is available to any other competitor, is at odds with

Business Objects' repeated contention that the documents at issue are stale and without value.

The purposes of the injunction were twofold: (1) to prevent Business Objects from possessing, using and disclosing the described misappropriated trade secrets, and (2) to eliminate any commercial advantage Business Objects may have obtained through its possession and use of the documents. Based on the foregoing discussion, the court cannot find that the injunction has run its course because Business Objects has failed to demonstrate that the Business Objects Competitive Recipe and the Volume Discount Schedule are no longer trade secrets. Even were the court to rely on the largely speculative assertions made by Business Objects in support of its motion to dissolve and find that the trade secrets have ceased to exist, the court is not convinced that enough time has passed to completely eliminate the commercial advantage Business Objects obtained by having these documents. * * *

The court finds that there is certainly a significant public interest in maintaining the confidentiality of trade secrets and preventing their misappropriation. Business Objects argues, however, that competition in the software industry thrives on the free flow of information and is stymied when outdated documents are given trade secret protection. Once again, this argument is in tension with Business Objects' claims that the documents are too stale to constitute trade secrets.

Moreover, in the course of the hearing, it became apparent that Business Objects' motivation to dissolve the injunction stems, at least in part, from its concern over a negative market perception that this injunction has created. Business Objects claims that MicroStrategy, in its advertising, has taken advantage of the fact that its competitor is subject to an injunction. As a result, Business Objects contends that it operates under a cloud of impropriety that is no longer justifiable. While such considerations certainly have their place in the commercial market in which both Business Objects and MicroStrategy operate, they relate more to Business Objects' own interests than to those of the public. As such, the court cannot find that continued enforcement would be in any way detrimental to the public interest. * * *

II. Conclusion

The court does not anticipate that this injunction will exist permanently into perpetuity. A reading of section 59.1–337 makes clear that the objectives of an injunction covering trade secrets will be met when both the trade secrets cease to exist and any residual commercial advantage is eliminated. * * * As the court suggested in the August 6, 2004 order, at some point the documents at issue cease to be economically valuable or become publicly available and, thus, cease to be trade secrets. * * * Both section 59.1–337 and the caselaw interpreting the reach of Rule 60(b)(5) indicate that it is Business Objects' burden to make these showings.

The court concludes that Business Objects has failed to do so. * * *

* * *

Accordingly, the defendant's motion to dissolve the injunction is DENIED. * * * As set forth and in the manner described in the August 6, 2004 order, the defendant remains enjoined from possessing, disclosing or using the Business Objects Competitive Recipe and the Volume Discount Schedule.

* * *

It is so ORDERED.

DID YOU GET IT?

1.   What are the claimed trade secrets?

2.   Did the plaintiff's trade secrets cease to exist before the court issued its injunction order?

3.   On a motion to dissolve an injunction, who has the burden of proof to prove the non-existence of trade secrets?

4.   Is the lapse of time, alone, sufficient grounds for dissolving an injunction in a trade secret case?

NOTES

1.   **Remedies under the DTSA.** As noted previously, the remedies provisions of the DTSA substantially mirror the UTSA, but with the addition of the Civil Seizure Order provision and the limitations that the DTSA imposes on the scope and nature of allowable injunctive relief. *See* the DTSA, 18 U.S.C. § 1836(b)(2) and (b)(3)(A)((i)(I) and (II), reprinted in Appendix A.

2.   **Remedies under the EU Trade Secret Directive.** One of the principal reasons for the EU Trade Secret Directive was the stated need for better and more consistent remedies for trade secret misappropriation throughout the EU. In large part, the remedies specified in the EU Trade Secret Directive are identical to the remedies that are specified in the UTSA and DTSA, but there are some notable differences. First, the EU Trade Secret Directive includes explicit provisions that are apparently designed to address the problem of misappropriated trade secrets being used to produce goods by allowing courts to order the destruction of such goods. Significantly, the focus is not solely on the trade secrets themselves, but on any "infringing goods" that may be tainted by such trade secrets. Another difference is that the EU Trade Secret Directive does not include an ex parte Civil Seizure Order provision, although such remedy may be available under the preexisting laws and procedural rules of EU Member States.

3.   **Can irreparable harm be presumed for purposes of a permanent injunction?** Prior to the U.S. Supreme Court's decision in *Ebay,*

Inc. v. MercExchange, LLC, 547 U.S. 388 (2006), it was assumed by many attorneys and courts that a permanent injunction would issue upon a finding of patent infringement, at least in cases where the patent remained valid and there was an ongoing threat of infringement. In *Ebay*, however, the Supreme Court used the explicit language of the injunction provision of U.S. patent law to hold that injunctive relief can only be granted in patent cases "in accordance with principles of equity." In *Automated Merchandising Systems v. Crane Co.*, 357 Fed. Appx. 297 (Fed. Cir. 2009), the Federal Circuit Court of Appeals went one step further and, applying the reasoning of *Ebay,* held that there is no presumption of irreparable harm based "just on proof of infringement."

The question of whether irreparable harm can be presumed from a finding of trade secret misappropriation has also arisen in trade secret cases. Many courts (particularly before *Ebay*) applied a presumption of irreparable harm once there was a finding of trade secret misappropriation. For instance, in *Boeing v. Sierracin Corp.* (reprinted, in part, in Chapter 9), the court rejected the defendant's argument that a permanent injunction should not have been granted without a showing of irreparable harm. The court explained:

> Sierracin argues that a finding of irreparable harm must be entered in order to support the trial court's injunction. We disagree. Neither the Uniform Trade Secrets Act nor the civil rules about injunctions require such a finding. RCW 19.108.020(1); CR 65(d). To allow Sierracin in this case to continue to manufacture cockpit windows after deciding that it had misappropriated the information from Boeing would permit Sierracin to profit from its own wrongful conduct. The trial judge found that an injunction would not be unreasonable (finding of fact 10), and we agree. No finding of irreparable harm need be found to support this decision.

In light of *Ebay*, whether the *Sierracin* approach will continue to be applied in trade secret cases remains to be seen. *See* MILGRIM ON TRADE SECRETS, § 15.02[1][a], n. 2 (2016).

In *Faiveley Transport Malmo AB v. Wabtec Corp.*, 559 F.3d 110 (2d Cir. 2009) (reprinted, in part, in Chapter 6), the court considered whether a finding of irreparable harm could be presumed at the preliminary injunction stage following a finding that the plaintiff was likely to succeed on the merits of its claim. In refusing to apply a presumption of irreparable harm for purposes of a preliminary injunction, the court explained:

> We have previously observed that "the loss of trade secrets cannot be measured in money damages" where that secret, once lost, is "lost forever." *FMC Corp. v. Taiwan Tainan Giant Indus. Co.*, 730 F.2d 61, 63 (2d Cir. 1984) (per curiam). Some courts in this Circuit have read this passing observation to mean that a presumption of irreparable harm automatically arises upon the determination that a trade secret has been misappropriated. * * * That reading is not correct. A rebuttable presumption of irreparable harm might be warranted in cases where there is a danger that, unless enjoined, a

misappropriator of trade secrets will disseminate those secrets to a wider audience or otherwise irreparably impair the value of those secrets. Where a misappropriator seeks only to use those secrets—without further dissemination or irreparable impairment of value—in pursuit of profit, no such presumption is warranted because an award of damages will often provide a complete remedy for such an injury.

Indeed, once a trade secret is misappropriated, the misappropriator will often have the same incentive as the originator to maintain the confidentiality of the secret in order to profit from the proprietary knowledge. As Judge Conner has observed, where there is no danger that a misappropriator will disseminate proprietary information, "the only possible injury that [the] plaintiff may suffer is loss of sales to a competing product . . . [which] should be fully compensable by money damages."

Significantly, however, the *Faiveley* case is based upon New York law which follows the *Restatement of Torts* rather than the UTSA. Whether its reasoning would be applied under the UTSA and the DTSA, and with respect to permanent injunctions, is an open question.

Unlike the facts in *Ebay*, there is no language in either the UTSA or DTSA which directly and explicitly invokes principles of equity. In jurisdictions that have not adopted the UTSA (or otherwise enacted a statute to allow injunctive relief for trade secret misappropriation), common law principles of equity clearly apply. But do they apply to the injunction provisions of the UTSA and DTSA? Given the common law origins of trade secret law and the stated intent of the UTSA to codify the pre-existing common law, it may be argued that the equitable principles applicable to the grant of an injunction at common law also apply to the UTSA and the DTSA.

Food for Thought

If you were the plaintiff's attorney in a trade secret misappropriation case, what arguments would you make to support your client's claim for injunctive relief? Should irreparable harm be presumed from the finding of trade secret misappropriation? Should the balance of harms and the public interest be considered?

---

4. **Bibliographic note:** In addition to the references noted above, for more information on the topics discussed in this chapter, see MILGRIM ON TRADE SECRETS § 14.01, 15.02 (2016); Richard F. Dole, *Statutory Royalty Damages Under the Uniform Trade Secrets Act and the Federal Patent Code*, 16 VAND. J. ENT. & TECH L. 223 (2014); David S. Almeling, *Seven Reasons Why Trade Secrets Are Increasingly Important*, 27 BERKELEY TECH. L.J. 1091 (2012); David W. Quinto and Stuart H. Singer, TRADE SECRETS, § 2.11 (2014); Comment, *Trade Secrets: How Long Should an Injunction Last?*, 26 UCLA L. REV. 203 (1978).

CHAPTER 11

MANAGEMENT OF TRADE SECRETS

■ ■ ■

Anticipated Learning Outcomes

At the conclusion of this chapter, you will better understand some of the specific steps that companies can utilize to manage and protect their trade secrets, including a review of what constitutes "reasonable efforts" to maintain secrecy. You will also be introduced to some of the special considerations related to companies providing trade secret information to the government and how companies should approach the protection of trade secrets in countries other than the United States.

A. INTRODUCTION

We learned in Chapter 5 that a company's reasonable efforts to protect trade secrets are critical. But no company wants to be in the position of having to prove that it engaged in reasonable efforts because it would mean that the company is in litigation and that its trade secrets may already have been misappropriated. Thus, in addition to employing enough reasonable efforts to establish the existence of trade secrets, trade secret owners should try to prevent trade secret misappropriation in the first instance.

The safest and most conservative approach for any company that owns trade secrets is to be prepared for the day when it may have to prove its efforts to a court. This means that trade secret protection should not be an afterthought. Instead, the protection of trade secrets requires a conscious risk assessment approach that is part of a broader information governance strategy. This strategy should anticipate, and ultimately stem, the inappropriate dissemination or disclosure of trade secrets and other business information, including the personally identifiable information of customers. As a practical matter, companies must weigh the costs of available protection measures with the risks of loss and determine how much they are willing to pay for security.

The widespread availability and use of computers together with an apparent decline in employee loyalty provides fertile ground for the improper dissemination of trade secrets and other business information. Losses due to theft of proprietary information can potentially cost companies millions of dollars annually, but the non-financial costs are often more significant and harder to quantify. The misappropriation of a trade secret is particularly devastating when it results in public disclosure because a trade secret, once lost, is lost forever.

The lesson for trade secret owners is that they must be vigilant and proactive in maintaining and protecting their trade secrets both internally and externally. Not only should companies be mindful of protecting trade secrets against internal and external threats, but they should also be cautious about circumstances when they share their trade secrets with outside parties. This is especially the case when dealing with governmental entities and foreign enterprises.

This chapter is organized to progress from a micro to a macro presentation of trade secret management. It will first discuss the management of trade secrets at the company level with respect to both internal and external threats. It then follows with a section on company trade secrets and the government. Finally, the Special Issue section addresses the protection of trade secrets in other countries.

B. MANAGING THREATS FROM EMPLOYEES

The biggest threat to a company's trade secrets is from its own employees. Many employees have legitimate access to trade secret information by virtue of their employment status and can take advantage of that access to misappropriate trade secrets. The motivation to do so need not be a desire to go into a competitive business, but can be the act of a disgruntled current or former employee who wants a measure of revenge against his employer. Thus, a corporate security program cannot overlook the threat posed by employees. Granted, it is often a delicate balance to view employees both as valued members of the corporate family and as threats to the company's trade secrets. However, in addition to the high risks associated with blind trust, arguably the employer would not be taking "reasonable steps" to protect its trade secrets if the employee threat is ignored or not effectively addressed.

Vigilance is an ongoing process that requires comprehensive security measures. Employers should consider establishing and implementing trade secret protection programs tailored to their specific needs. The first part of any such program is to identify the specific information that the business wishes to protect, including information that may qualify for trade secret protection. The second step is to determine an appropriate information governance strategy for each type of information. It is important that companies do not take the position that every bit of information they utilize in their business is a trade secret because such a claim is untrue and, more importantly, it fails to put employees on notice of the actual information that qualifies for trade secret protection. Moreover, for the public policy reasons discussed throughout this casebook, courts are reluctant to sanction the overbroad assertion of trade secret rights when to do so would limit the mobility of employees.

For information that is identified for trade secret protection, the next step in the information governance process requires the implementation of "reasonable efforts" that are designed to secure the secrecy of such information. It is with regard to this component of the test of trade secrecy that the threats posed by employees should be understood and addressed.

As the cases you have read throughout this casebook reveal, there are a variety of efforts that can be utilized in the management of trade secrets that are shared with employees. However, which efforts are used necessarily depends on the organization and the nature and form of its trade secrets. For instance, the tactics that are used to maintain the secrecy of a recipe that only needs to be known by a few people will be different from the tactics that should be used to protect computer code that is embedded in mass-distributed software. It is generally recommended, however, that a policy of "need to know," rather than "nice to know," be implemented with respect to most business information, meaning that only employees that need to know certain information are given access to it.

Computer monitoring of employees is one option available to employers who wish to keep a close eye on their trade secrets. Generally, employers may engage in various levels of employee computer monitoring that range from tracking key strokes and data outflows, to monitoring e-mails, as long as they provide notice to employees that they are subject to such monitoring. The decision to monitor must be balanced against the need to maintain a workplace where employees feel comfortable and are thus able to be productive. It is also important to establish clear policies regarding personal use of computers for e-mail and other internet activities, such as web browsing and the downloading of videos. Employers should also be mindful of their policies governing telecommuting employees and should restrict others whose work outside of the office permits access to trade secrets.

But simply establishing policies is usually not enough. Employees also have to be educated about the scope and nature of their duties of confidentiality and sensitized about potential external threats. Fraudulent e-mail communications addressed to employees (often referred to as phishing scams) should be of particular concern, since outsiders have gained company information from employees who thought they were communicating with a superior. Also, in their zeal to tout the benefits of a company, employees (particularly those in the marketing department) have been known to disclose information that was intended to be kept secret. The point of both of these examples is that the loss of trade secrets can occur without any intent on the part of an employee to do the wrong thing.

The following excerpt from an article by Victoria Cundiff details strategies that companies may use to protect their trade secrets from misappropriation by departing employees.

MAXIMUM SECURITY: HOW TO PREVENT DEPARTING EMPLOYEES FROM PUTTING YOUR TRADE SECRETS TO WORK FOR YOUR COMPETITOR

Victoria A. Cundiff.
8 Santa Clara Computer & High Tech. L. J. 301, 303–323 (1992).

A company intent on protecting its trade secrets must first identify those secrets. It must then take steps to place its employees on reasonable notice that such information is to be kept confidential, both during employment and afterwards. Otherwise, employees cannot be expected to maintain the information in confidence. The company must establish appropriate procedures to limit access to confidential information to the minimum number of employees or consultants reasonably consistent with the business needs of the company. Finally, when the employee or consultant departs, the company must get continuing agreement that the information will remain confidential.

Particular circumstances may dictate more rigorous protective measures. State law permitting, restrictive covenants may be appropriate to prevent certain employees from working in competitive positions for a reasonable period of time. Upon learning of new employment that threatens to place the first employer's trade secrets at risk, it may be necessary to commence detailed negotiations with the new employer to ensure that the employee will not be assigned to areas that inevitably put the company's secrets at risk. If these strategies fail, it may be necessary to commence litigation seeking an injunction against activities likely to lead to use or disclosure of trade secrets.

While different secrets may dictate somewhat different strategies, the company's overriding concern—before hiring the new employee or consultant, during employment, and upon departure—must always be to determine the most reasonable and effective way of protecting its confidential information. * * *

Take Inventory

It is difficult for a company to protect trade secrets it does not formally recognize. Perhaps the best way to identify the company's trade secrets is to periodically ask managers, scientists, technical gurus and the sales force a series of questions. What does the company know that gives it an advantage over its competitors? Is there reason to believe that others do not know this information? Is the information something competitors would be likely to want to know? Was the information difficult or expensive or time-consuming to gain? Would the company suffer significant damage if competitors obtained the information? Where is that information resident (by department, or by job description)? The answers to these questions will likely point the way to the company's current secrets. Remember that most companies regularly add to their store of trade secrets. Running this inquiry periodically to determine both whether new information qualifies for protection and whether old information no longer qualifies is a solid practice.

Install Appropriate Protections

    1.   Restrict Access to Confidential Information

The best way to protect confidential information is to make sure that as few people within the company learn the details of the information as possible. What an employee—past or current—does not know, he cannot disclose to others.

Restricting access to confidential information does not mean that a company must keep its employees in the dark about its essential plans. It does mean, however, that while many employees may need to know that the company's major product push for the next year will be to design a faster computer that will achieve specified results more efficiently than competitive products currently on the market, not as many need to know precisely how work is progressing and the details of such varied aspects of the product development as sources of supply, costs of components, prospective upgrades, protocols and interfaces, coding sequences, projected market dates, pricing strategy, planned distribution network, and so forth. Advise the company to make sure that each employee knows what he needs to be a contributing member of the team, but consider whether every employee truly needs to know every detail of what every team is working on. The watchword is "think." Do not allow trade secrets to be disclosed to anyone without determining whether disclosure is necessary.

    2.   Tell Employees and Consultants What Information is Confidential

If employees are given access to confidential information, make sure they know it. Departing or current employees cannot be expected to protect trade secrets if they have not been made aware that certain information is restricted. Courts are apt to deny employers injunctive relief against use or disclosure of information if the employees were not made aware that the information was confidential.

It is obvious that, without clear guidance, employees may have a very different view from their employers of what information is confidential—or may say they do upon leaving the company. Therefore, in anticipation of such likely-to-occur differences, employers should be advised to find opportunities to inform and remind employees about the kinds of information the employer regards as confidential. Give concrete examples.

When particularly sensitive information is given to employees, employers should underscore the importance of maintaining it in confidence. Finally, where practicable, employers should document these advices as discussed below. Being able to offer documentary proof that the company clearly identified confidential information to the former employee will make subsequent negotiation or litigation much more likely to succeed.

3. Use Confidentiality Agreements

Most states imply a duty to keep an employer's confidential information secret whether or not the employee has signed a confidentiality agreement. Requiring employees to enter into a written confidentiality agreement, however, serves a number of valuable purposes. First, it is an explicit reminder that the company has developed its own information that is not to be freely disclosed to others. The contract may therefore help guide the employee's future actions. Second, the agreement has later evidentiary value. It is difficult for an employee who leaves a company after signing such an agreement to contend that he was never told not to disclose the company's valuable secrets. Conversely, the absence of a confidentiality agreement can be an indication that particular matter is not a trade secret. Third, an employee who participates in identifying secrets to be subject to the protections of such an agreement may later be estopped to deny that such information is protectible under trade secret law.

Advise employers that if they use confidentiality agreements, they should insist that every employee who is given access to confidential information actually signs the confidentiality agreement. A trade secret protection program that is implemented only sporadically may be found to be no protection at all.

Keep in mind that a confidentiality agreement cannot transform information that is generally known into a trade secret, or, in most instances, extend the obligation to maintain confidentiality beyond the time that a trade secret becomes generally known. Nor can a confidentiality agreement substitute for identifying trade secrets and taking necessary steps to protect them. Finally, be sure not to draft a confidentiality agreement so narrowly that it protects only a small portion of the company's confidential information. While trade secrets are protectible even in the absence of an agreement, a too narrowly drafted agreement may foreclose broad relief.

4. Use Confidentiality Legends and Document Controls

Applying a confidentiality legend to confidential documents not only serves as a warning that particular information is confidential, but also reinforces the company's overriding concern for protecting its confidential information. The legend may be as simple as the word "CONFIDENTIAL."

Instruct your clients to avoid over-legending. Routinely marking documents or other things (e.g., computer tapes) confidential that clearly are not may be seen as giving the employee no guidance at all as to what documents are in fact confidential. Conversely, employers should isolate and legend all critical information. While, if necessary, an employer may well be able to offer extrinsic evidence that an employee knew or should have known particular information was confidential, legending some but not all matters may give trade secret defendants grounds for argument, thereby driving up costs and slowing resolution of the matter. Advise your client to consider adding a feature to the company's word processing system inquiring each time a document is created whether the legend should be applied. This step will require thought about confidentiality before the document is even printed.

Suggest that your client consider numbering critical documents as well as legending them, maintaining a log showing where each copy is at a given time. Recommend that computer records be established showing who has accessed password protected documents and for how long. This information should be maintained as important company records. Particularly sensitive documents can be printed on distinctive paper to make it easier to detect unauthorized use.

Maintaining such safeguards for confidential documents can prove extremely useful if an employee does leave. First, the confidentiality legending should give the employee certainty that the information in those documents is not to be used or disclosed outside the company. It will be difficult for a former employee to contend that he did not know information was confidential and should not be shown to his new employer if the information is clearly marked "CONFIDENTIAL" (assuming, of course, that the employer has not "cried wolf" by careless or indiscriminate legending). Second, a log can give the company guidance as to what sensitive documents the employee may have in his possession that should be returned upon departure. Finally, the use of legending and document control procedures can often make it easier to resolve any disputes once an employee leaves. A court or a competitive employer faced with proof that a company has taken extensive precautions to protect particular information from dissemination will be more likely to agree that the first employer's information is entitled to protection.

Consider Using Restrictive Covenants

Confidentiality agreements are an important tool for almost any company having significant confidential information. Restrictive covenants, which attempt to protect trade secrets by restricting a former employee from engaging in competitive activity for a specified period of time, present more difficult philosophical and legal issues. However, there is no doubt that a valid restrictive covenant is among the most effective ways of protecting confidential information. If a former employee cannot work for competitors for a period of time, competitors will not be in as good a position to receive the benefits of the former employer's trade secrets. Even if the former employee eventually works for a competitor when the restrictive covenant has expired, time spent away from activities in which he would be most likely to use the first employer's trade secrets lessens the risk that when he eventually can work for a competitor, he will use or disclose the secrets.

Despite the advantages of restrictive covenants, some companies nonetheless decide not to use them because of independent concerns, such as a potential change in the corporate atmosphere. Some employers fear that current or potential employees will feel "trapped" if asked to sign a restrictive covenant. They also worry about the impact on recruiting efforts. While these concerns can usually be addressed and solved by sensitive presentation of the rationale for restrictive covenants, restrictive covenants may not be appropriate for your client's needs. Be sure, however, to give the matter careful thought. * * *

The Exit Interview

How a company responds to an employee's (or, in some situations, even a consultant's) resignation is of critical importance in determining whether trade secrets will be put at risk and whether resulting negotiations or litigation will be successful.

1. Staffing

Upon being informed of impending resignation, a company should promptly arrange to conduct an exit interview. If the departing employee knows important company secrets, this exit interview should be conducted by the employee's supervisor together with a member of the legal staff or outside counsel. The supervisor will be able to provide details about the proprietary information the employee knows. Further, his presence should lessen the risk that the lawyer will be disqualified from serving as litigation counsel if the matter should later go to trial.

2. Preparing for the Exit Interview

Be prepared for the exit interview. It will go more smoothly if, during the course of the employee's work, a file has been assembled containing all confidentiality agreements and restrictive covenants the employee has signed; the employee's initial application and resumé, which can be an indication of what constitutes the employee's general skills, knowledge and experience, as opposed to the trade secrets learned from your company; and detailed job descriptions and evaluations. With this background, the exit interviewers will be prepared to determine what competitive activities are of particular concern to the company as well as what documents the departing employee is likely to have in his possession.

3. Purposes of the Exit Interview

The exit interview is not a trial. Maintaining an even tone is very important. Until his resignation, the individual was presumably viewed as a valued employee. Resignation does not turn him into a corporate traitor. It does, however, raise concerns—which may be heightened depending on what is known about the prospective employment—that must be jointly addressed to protect the company's valuable information.

The exit interview should serve three major purposes. First, it should remind the departing employee of his confidentiality obligations and obtain a continued agreement to honor them. Identify for the departing employee examples of confidential information. If practicable, furnish a moderately detailed list of specific categories of information which the departing employee has seen, so there will be no lingering doubt as to whether the company views that particular information as confidential. Many companies formalize this portion of the exit interview by asking the employee to sign a written statement acknowledging that confidential information of the company may not be used or disclosed outside the company, unless it has become generally known. This document is useful even if the employee has already signed a confidentiality agreement, because it underscores that earlier agreement's importance.

Second, the exit interview should be the occasion for obtaining from the employee all confidential documents in his possession. If some of these documents are of the premises, the employee should itemize those documents and agree in writing to return them, together with all copies, by a specified date. Explain that it is in the employee's interest, as well as the company's, for all confidential documents to be returned so there will be no possibility for confusion or misunderstanding later on.

The third purpose of the exit interview is to give the company sufficient information to determine whether the new employment is likely to put the company's trade secrets at risk. Determine the name and address of the new employer. Ask the employee what he expects to be doing in the new position. While many employees may be reluctant to give a comprehensive description of their new duties, perhaps in part out of concern that so doing may improperly expose their new employer's trade secrets, the departing employee should at a minimum be asked to provide a functional listing of his proposed activities.

Food for Thought

The foregoing article by Victoria Cundiff was written in 1992, before the commercial use of the internet began in 1995. Consider what additional strategies are needed to protect information that is stored and maintained on computer systems and transmitted over the internet.

C. EXTERNAL THREATS: TECHNOLOGY AND PEOPLE

While most trade secret misappropriation cases involve current or former employees, the possibility of external threats cannot be ignored. This is particularly true with respect to the growing threat of cyber-hacking, cyber-espionage, and a variety of internet and email based scams. In the ongoing struggle to protect trade secrets, the use of technological tools will be an important component of any security plan. *See* Elizabeth A. Rowe, *RATs, TRAPs, and Trade Secrets*, 57 B.C. L. REV. 381, 412–17 (2016). However, such tools alone, divorced from consideration of human behavior, are not sufficient. "[H]uman error accounts for 35%–53.5% of cyber breaches caused by preventable employee error or sabotage from within a company." Devin C. Streeter, *The Effect of Human Error on Modern Security Breaches*, STRATEGIC INFORMER: STUDENT PUBL'N OF THE STRATEGIC INTELLIGENCE SOC'Y, 2013, at 5, 6. Thus, the primary line of defense in protecting trade secrets must account for human tendencies.

While the use of firewalls, passwords, and encryption are widely used to protect data that is stored on computers, reliance on these tools alone is not optimal. Among other reasons, technological tools tend to be reactive and are not capable of the intelligence and risk assessments that could avoid inappropriate access to trade secret information in the first instance. The question is not simply whether a company has used technology to secure its information, it is whether a company has used tools (both technological and non-technological) that address the actual risks that are posed to its trade secrets.

Beyond careless or accidental disclosures, companies need to protect against those who maliciously or intentionally set out to acquire trade secrets and other business information. These threats include, but are not limited to, phishers and hackers who often outsmart the technological barriers because their motivation is strong or because they enjoy a challenge. Information technology departments usually rely on security technology like firewalls to regulate what information is allowed on a corporate network and to detect suspicious behavior. However, because these systems work in predictable ways, they are vulnerable to attack. Using such sophisticated hacking tools as "crackers," "Trojans," and "worms," those wanting to do so can take over another's computer. Hackers are also skilled at covering their tracks by, for example, making it look like they're someone they're not, and by leaving "backdoors" in a system that will allow them to access it again later.

Defensive measures related to computer security include firewalls, encryption, automated detection of intrusions, and education of employees and users of computer systems. In the parlance of cybersecurity, these are considered passive measures. Somewhere between these passive measures and more active defense measures are approaches that, for instance, use decoy sites to attract hackers. On the other end of the spectrum from passive defense mechanisms are active defenses. More active and offensive measures are beginning to emerge as companies become more proactive against hacking. An active defense allows a company to detect an intrusion, trace it, and actively respond to the threat. This could include interrupting an attack in progress in order to lessen the damage that it may cause, all the way to counter-striking the attacker (aka "hacking back"). However, the pursuit of active defense is currently very controversial and raises many complicated and unresolved issues, including its legality.

Companies must be mindful of the interaction and influence of human behavior in a comprehensive information governance scheme. They should identify sensitive data, monitor where it goes, audit who has access to it, and restrict access in order to better assess risks. They should also be mindful of what information they choose to collect and store because, for instance, the handling of the trade secrets of another may expose them to liability for trade secret misappropriation. Additionally, some information may simply be too valuable to store in a computer.

Since many companies already conduct risk assessments of their security strategies, augmenting technological approaches with strategies to address human behavior can go a long way toward planning for trade secret security in a proactive rather than a reactive framework. The trade secret owner needs an infrastructure in place to protect its secrets, one that includes specific processes and technological measures. Conducting a risk analysis of potential threats to the company's trade secrets should be comprehensive, paying attention to people, processes, and technology.

Food for Thought

Do you think companies should receive immunity for hacking back or counterstrikes against hackers? Is striking against an attack analogous to self-defense?

D. DEALING WITH THE GOVERNMENT

Federal and state governments collect and store a large amount of information from companies they regulate and also in relation to their business relationships with companies that serve as vendors or contractors to the government. Thus, companies that conduct business with the government must be clear about whether they can protect confidential and trade secret information that they disclose to government agencies and, if so, how such protection can be secured. As with the sharing of trade secret information generally, if information is submitted to a governmental entity without first asserting trade secret rights or the need for confidentiality, the default assumption under both state and federal freedom of information laws is that the information is not protected as a trade secret, is publicly available, and can be publicly disclosed.

Before submitting information to an entity of government, it should first be determined if the applicable laws, regulations, or rules of that governmental entity allow businesses to designate their trade secret (or other proprietary information) for special, confidential handling by government officials. If so, such materials must usually be labeled and designated to indicate that they are not for public distribution or viewing. When submitting information to government agencies or courts, attorneys should consult the applicable laws, rules and regulations to determine how to submit confidential information, including the precise language of required confidentiality legends. Usually, it will be necessary to make a motion to "seal" information before it is a lodged with a court, including if one wants to take advantage of the "whistleblower immunity" that is discussed in Chapter 9.

Each of the federal agencies has enacted regulations that describe how they will treat confidential information submitted to them by companies. However, the procedures are different for each agency and not all information that is submitted to a federal agency is protected for all purposes or for all time. Moreover, even with government processes in place to protect trade secret information, inadvertent disclosures can and do occur. Accordingly, there is always a risk when submitting trade secret information to the government that the trade secret status of the information will be lost due to an inadvertent disclosure by a governmental official.

The excerpt below briefly summarizes the Freedom of Information Act (FOIA), which is the main mechanism by which one can request business information, including trade secret information, which is in the hands of the federal government. In addition, it also discusses the uncertainty of a trade secret owner's recourse against the government in the event of the inappropriate use or disclosure of trade secret information. The cases that follow, including *Ruckleshaus v. Monsanto*, illustrate the potential consequences of the government's disclosure of trade secrets.

STRIKING A BALANCE: WHEN SHOULD TRADE-SECRET LAW SHIELD DISCLOSURES TO THE GOVERNMENT?

Elizabeth A. Rowe.
96 Iowa L. Rev. 791, 800–07 (2011).

[The Freedom of Information Act—FOIA]

Under FOIA, anyone may request copies of documents that form the records of agencies of the Executive Branch. One does not need to show standing, legitimate interest, or any other threshold requirement to be entitled to the information. Most FOIA requests come from businesses seeking information on their competitors. If trade secret information is disclosed through a FOIA request, it could become the kind of private use of information that constitutes a taking under the Fifth Amendment Takings Clause. FOIA therefore presents a considerable risk of loss to trade-secret holders.

FOIA contains exemptions against disclosure of trade secrets. However, it is significant to note that the Supreme Court has found these exemptions to be permissive, not mandatory. Thus, while FOIA permits the agencies to withhold company records containing trade secrets, it does not require them to do so. Most relevant to this discussion, subsection 3 of 5 U.S.C. § 552(b) ("Exemption 3"), exempts information that is "specifically exempted from disclosure by statute," and subsection 4 ("Exemption 4") exempts "trade secrets and commercial or financial information obtained from a person and privileged or confidential." Note that Exemption 4 applies to a wider category of information beyond trade secrets, i.e., "commercial or financial information." This would presumably be information that is confidential and proprietary to the company, but not necessarily a trade secret. Exemption 4 is the category most applicable and most often used in FOIA litigation to protect trade secrets and confidential information. None of the exemptions, however, apply to Congress. There is thus the risk that Congress could request information from an agency, increasing the chances that the information could be leaked or that a member of Congress could * * * discuss the information openly on the congressional floor and thereby destroy its trade secret status.

According to the Director of the Office of Public Information and Library Services, it is only through FOIA that the general public would be able to access a copy of an agency record. When a request is received, the Office of Public Information and Library Services will assign the request to the agencies with jurisdiction over the record(s) at issue. There are trained staff within each of these component offices who are responsible for searching for the requested records, reviewing these records to determine whether they should be released, and redacting nonreleasable information (subject to both FOIA and the agency's implementing regulations). In making a disclosure decision, the FOI officer of the particular agency would consider the records in light of the FOIA statute and the agency's implementing regulations.

When a submitter of trade secrets to an agency seeks to prevent the agency from disclosing the trade secrets to a third-party FOIA requester, the mechanism for doing so within the courts is known as a reverse-FOIA action. The process of a reverse-FOIA action occurs in two major sequential stages. In the first stage the submitter objects to the prospective disclosure directly to the agency, and in the second stage the submitter can appeal an unfavorable determination by the agency in federal court. * * *

[The Cost of Disclosure by the Government]

If a company submitted trade-secret information to the government and that information was disclosed by the government to the public, it is the trade-secret owner who would ultimately bear the cost of the government's misguided action. This is in part because when a trade secret is revealed, it loses all of its value, the loss is irreparable, and the company may not be made whole by monetary damages. An aggrieved trade-secret owner may have a trade-secret-misappropriation claim or constitutional-takings claim against the government. There may also be a possible criminal action under the Trade Secrets Act against an individual government employee who discloses a trade secret. However, none of these options may provide a satisfactory remedy, and legal recourse against the government may also be tenuous.

The Trade Secrets Act does not provide a private right of action. Moreover, a claim under the Act could only be against an individual, and any fine may not exceed $1000. It therefore provides practically no compensation to a company that may have suffered a multimillion dollar loss as a result of an inappropriate disclosure of its trade secret. Accordingly, the more feasible option with a better chance for damages may be a takings claim.

Reading Guidance

Why did the court find a taking of property under one version of FIFRA but not the other?

RUCKELSHAUS V. MONSANTO CO.

United States Supreme Court, 1984.
467 U.S. 986.

JUSTICE BLACKMUN delivered the opinion of the Court.

In this case, we are asked to review a United States District Court's determination that several provisions of the Federal Insecticide, Fungicide, and Rodenticide Act (FIFRA), 61 Stat. 163, as amended, 7 U.S.C. § 136 et seq., are unconstitutional. The provisions at issue authorize the Environmental Protection Agency (EPA) to use data submitted by an applicant for registration of a pesticide in evaluating the application of a subsequent applicant, and to disclose publicly some of the submitted data.

I

* * *

Because of mounting public concern about the safety of pesticides and their effect on the environment and because of a growing perception that the existing legislation was not equal to the task of safeguarding the public interest, Congress undertook a comprehensive revision of FIFRA through the adoption of the Federal Environmental Pesticide Control Act of 1972,

86 Stat. 973. The amendments transformed FIFRA from a labeling law into a comprehensive regulatory statute. * * *

For purposes of this litigation, the most significant of the 1972 amendments pertained to the pesticide-registration procedure and the public disclosure of information learned through that procedure. Congress added to FIFRA a new section governing public disclosure of data submitted in support of an application for registration. Under that section, the submitter of data could designate any portions of the submitted material it believed to be "trade secrets or commercial or financial information." Another section prohibited EPA from publicly disclosing information which, in its judgment, contained or related to "trade secrets or commercial or financial information." * * *

The 1972 amendments also included a provision that allowed EPA to consider data submitted by one applicant for registration in support of another application pertaining to a similar chemical, provided the subsequent applicant offered to compensate the applicant who originally submitted the data. In effect, the provision instituted a mandatory data-licensing scheme. The amount of compensation was to be negotiated by the parties, or, in the event negotiations failed, was to be determined by EPA, subject to judicial review upon the instigation of the original data submitter. The scope of the 1972 data-consideration provision, however, was limited, for any data designated as "trade secrets or commercial or financial information" exempt from disclosure under § 10 [of FIFRA] could not be considered at all by EPA to support another registration application unless the original submitter consented.

* * *

Under FIFRA, as amended in 1978, applicants are granted a 10-year period of exclusive use for data on new active ingredients contained in pesticides registered after September 30, 1978. All other data submitted after December 31, 1969, may be cited and considered in support of another application for 15 years after the original submission if the applicant offers to compensate the original submitter. * * * Data that do not qualify for either the 10-year period of exclusive use or the 15-year period of compensation may be considered by EPA without limitation.

Also in 1978, Congress added a new subsection [to FIFRA] that provides for disclosure of all health, safety, and environmental data to qualified requesters, notwithstanding the prohibition against disclosure of trade secrets * * *. The provision, however, does not authorize disclosure of information that would reveal "manufacturing or quality control processes" or certain details about deliberately added inert ingredients unless "the Administrator has first determined that the disclosure is necessary to protect against an unreasonable risk of injury to health or the environment." * * *

II

Appellee Monsanto Company (Monsanto) is an inventor, developer, and producer of various kinds of chemical products, including pesticides. Monsanto, headquartered in St. Louis County, Mo., sells in both domestic and foreign markets. It is one of a relatively small group of companies that invent and develop new active ingredients for pesticides and conduct most of the research and testing with respect to those ingredients.

* * *

Monsanto, like any other applicant for registration of a pesticide, must present research and test data supporting its application. The District Court found that Monsanto had incurred costs in excess of $23.6 million in developing the health, safety, and environmental data submitted by it under FIFRA. The information submitted with an application usually has value to Monsanto beyond its instrumentality in gaining that particular application. Monsanto uses this information to develop additional end-use products and to expand the uses of its registered products. The information would also be valuable to Monsanto's competitors. For that reason, Monsanto has instituted stringent security measures to ensure the secrecy of the data.

It is this health, safety, and environmental data that Monsanto sought to protect by bringing this suit. The District Court found that much of these data "contai[n] or relate to trade secrets as defined by the Restatement of Torts and Confidential, commercial information."

Monsanto brought suit in District Court, seeking injunctive and declaratory relief from the operation of the data-consideration provisions of FIFRA's § 3(c)(1)(D), and the data-disclosure provisions of FIFRA's § 10 and the related § 3(c)(2)(A). Monsanto alleged that all of the challenged provisions effected a "taking" of property without just compensation, in violation of the Fifth Amendment. * * *

III

* * *

This Court never has squarely addressed the applicability of the protections of the Taking Clause of the Fifth Amendment to commercial data of the kind involved in this case. In answering the question now, we are mindful of the basic axiom that " '[p]roperty interests . . . are not created by the Constitution. Rather, they are created and their dimensions are defined by existing rules or understandings that stem from an independent source such as state law.' " *Webb's Fabulous Pharmacies, Inc. v. Beckwith,* quoting *Board of Regents v. Roth.* Monsanto asserts that the health, safety, and environmental data it has submitted to EPA are property under Missouri law, which recognizes trade secrets, as defined in § 757, Comment b, of the Restatement of Torts, as property. * * *

[This portion of the court's decision is reprinted in part in Chapter 1 of this casebook. Based upon the court's reasoning, it held: "to the extent that Monsanto has an interest in its health, safety, and environmental data cognizable as a trade-secret property right under Missouri law, that property right is protected by the Taking Clause of the Fifth Amendment."]

IV

Having determined that Monsanto has a property interest in the data it has submitted to EPA, we confront the difficult question whether a "taking" will occur when EPA discloses those data or considers the data in evaluating another application for registration. * * *

As has been admitted on numerous occasions, "this Court has generally 'been unable to develop any "set formula" for determining when "justice and fairness" require that economic injuries caused by public action' " must be deemed a compensable taking. The inquiry into whether a taking has occurred is essentially an "ad hoc, factual" inquiry. The Court, however, has identified several factors that should be taken into account when determining whether a governmental action has gone beyond "regulation" and effects a "taking." Among those factors are: "the character of the governmental action, its economic impact, and its interference with reasonable investment-backed expectations." It is to the last of these three factors that we now direct our attention, for we find that the force of this factor is so overwhelming, at least with respect to certain of the data submitted by Monsanto to EPA, that it disposes of the taking question regarding those data.

A

A "reasonable investment-backed expectation" must be more than a "unilateral expectation or an abstract need." We find that with respect to any health, safety, and environmental data that Monsanto submitted to EPA after the effective date of the 1978 FIFRA amendments—that is, on or after October 1, 1978—Monsanto could not have had a reasonable, investment-backed expectation that EPA would keep the data confidential beyond the limits prescribed in the amended statute itself. Monsanto was on notice of the manner in which EPA was authorized to use and disclose any data turned over to it by an applicant for registration.

Thus, with respect to any data submitted to EPA on or after October 1, 1978, Monsanto knew that, for a period of 10 years from the date of submission, EPA would not consider those data in evaluating the application of another without Monsanto's permission. It was also aware, however, that once the 10-year period had expired, EPA could use the data without Monsanto's permission. Monsanto was further aware that it was entitled to an offer of compensation from the subsequent applicant only until the end of the 15th year from the date of submission. In addition, Monsanto was aware that information relating to formulae of products could be revealed by EPA to "any Federal agency consulted and [could] be revealed at a public hearing or in findings of fact" issued by EPA "when necessary to carry out" EPA's duties under FIFRA. The statute also gave Monsanto notice that much of the health, safety, and efficacy data provided by it could be disclosed to the general public at any time. If, despite the data-consideration and data-disclosure provisions in the statute, Monsanto chose to submit the requisite data in order to receive a registration, it can hardly argue that its reasonable investment-backed expectations are disturbed when EPA acts to use or disclose the data in a manner that was authorized by law at the time of the submission.

* * *

Thus, as long as Monsanto is aware of the conditions under which the data are submitted, and the conditions are rationally related to a legitimate Government interest, a voluntary submission of data by an applicant in exchange for the economic advantages of a registration can hardly be called a taking. * * *

C

The situation may be different, however, with respect to data submitted by Monsanto to EPA during the period from October 22, 1972, through September 30, 1978. Under the statutory scheme then in effect, a submitter was given an opportunity to protect its trade secrets from disclosure by designating them as trade secrets at the time of submission. When Monsanto provided data to EPA during this period, it was with the understanding, embodied in FIFRA, that EPA was free to use any of the submitted data that were not trade secrets in considering the application of another, provided that EPA required the subsequent applicant to pay "reasonable compensation" to the original submitter. But the statute also gave Monsanto explicit assurance that EPA was prohibited from disclosing publicly, or considering in connection with the application of another, any data submitted by an applicant if both the applicant and EPA determined the data to constitute trade secrets. Thus, with respect to trade secrets submitted under the statutory regime in force between the time of the adoption of the 1972 amendments and the adoption of the 1978 amendments, the Federal Government had explicitly guaranteed to Monsanto and other registration applicants an extensive measure of confidentiality and exclusive use. This explicit governmental guarantee formed the basis of a reasonable investment-backed expectation. If EPA, consistent with the authority granted it by the 1978 FIFRA amendments, were now to disclose trade-secret data or consider those data in evaluating the application of a subsequent applicant in a manner not authorized by the version of FIFRA in effect between 1972 and 1978, EPA's actions would frustrate Monsanto's reasonable investment-backed expectation with respect to its control over the use and dissemination of the data it had submitted.

* * *

In summary, we hold that EPA's consideration or disclosure of data submitted by Monsanto to the agency prior to October 22, 1972, or after September 30, 1978, does not effect a taking. We further hold that EPA consideration or disclosure of health, safety, and environmental data will constitute a taking if Monsanto submitted the data to EPA between October 22, 1972, and September 30, 1978; the data constituted trade secrets under Missouri law; Monsanto had designated the data as trade secrets at the time of its submission; the use or disclosure conflicts with the explicit assurance of confidentiality or exclusive use contained in the statute during that period; and the operation of the arbitration provision does not adequately compensate for the loss in market value of the data that Monsanto suffers because of EPA's use or disclosure of the trade secrets.

* * *

DID YOU GET IT?

1. How did the court treat Monsanto data submitted to EPA before October 1972 or after September 1978? Why?

2. How did the court treat Monsanto data submitted to EPA between October 1972 and September 1978? Why?

3. What role did Monsanto's "reasonable investment-based expectations" play in the court's reasoning?

Food for Thought

What steps should a company take if a government agency accidentally discloses its trade secret?

Reading Guidance

Can a state pass legislation requiring a company to disclose its trade secrets?

PHILIP MORRIS V. REILLY

United States Court of Appeals, First Circuit, 2002.
312 F.3d 24.

EN BANC OPINION

TORRUELLA, CIRCUIT JUDGE.

Unquestionably, tobacco is subject to heavy regulation by federal and state governments. This case concerns one attempt, by Massachusetts, to further regulate tobacco products by requiring tobacco companies to submit to Massachusetts the ingredient lists for all cigarettes, snuffs, and chewing tobaccos sold in the state. For each brand, the manufacturer must list, by relative amount, all ingredients besides tobacco, water, or reconstituted tobacco sheet. Mass. Gen. Laws ch. 94, § 307B (2002). Currently, the appellees, a group of tobacco companies, treat these ingredient lists as trade secrets and either do not disclose brand-specific information at all or do not disclose it without some guarantee of confidentiality.

The tobacco companies brought suit claiming that the Massachusetts statute, which allows the public disclosure of these ingredient lists whenever such disclosure "could reduce risks to public health," creates an unconstitutional taking. * * * The district court concurred and granted summary judgment in favor of the tobacco companies. A divided panel of this Court rejected appellees' arguments and reversed the district court's judgment. After en banc review, however, Judge Selya and I agree with the district court and, therefore, affirm its grant of summary judgment and award of injunctive and declaratory relief in favor of plaintiffs-appellees.

Factual Background

Appellees are various manufacturers of cigarettes and smokeless tobacco products. They all currently sell their products in Massachusetts and are potentially subject to the requirements of Mass. Gen. Laws ch. 94, § 307B ("Disclosure Act"). * * * Defendants-appellants are the Attorney General of Massachusetts and the Massachusetts Commissioner of Public Health.

The Ingredient Lists

All of the tobacco products manufactured by appellees include a variety of additives (in addition to tobacco, water, and reconstituted tobacco sheet). For example, common ingredients include sugars, glycerin, propylene glycol, cocoa, and licorice. These various additives are used as solvents, processing aids, pH modifiers, formulation aids for reconstituted tobacco, preservatives, humectants, tobacco protection aids, "plasticizing" agents, and, perhaps most importantly, flavorings. It is undisputed that appellees have spent millions of dollars developing formulas for their different brands, and when successful, those brands are worth billions of dollars. A major factor of each brand's success is its distinctive flavor, taste, and aroma.

While appellants argue that the added ingredients are neither pre-approved by regulators nor tested for safety, it is undisputed that most of the added ingredients are approved for consumption in food or "Generally Recognized As Safe" by the Food and Drug Administration. The one additive not found on either list is denatured alcohol, and this has been approved by the Bureau of Alcohol, Tobacco, and Firearms for use in the manufacture of tobacco products.

Each of the appellees closely guards its valuable ingredient lists. For example, within each company, only a few individuals are privy to the entire formula for any one brand. Suppliers are subject to confidentiality agreements and ship their products in packages which disguise their contents.

It is true that some ingredients of particular brands are known, and all ingredients used in any tobacco product are publicly available. However, this does not mean that complete brand-specific ingredient information can be obtained. In fact, various appellees have tried to "reverse engineer" the formulas of their competitors, but these attempts have been unsuccessful. Apparently, they have been able to determine the chemical composition of the various brands, but this information does not translate into a formula to recreate the product. Appellees assert, however, that if they were able to combine the chemical composition derived from this "reverse engineering" with a list of specific ingredients, arranged by relative amount, it would be much easier to discover a competitor's formula. Therefore, the tobacco companies argue that publication of their ingredient lists, organized by relative amount, on a brand-by-brand basis would likely destroy the secrecy of their formulas. This contention is not disputed by appellants.

Current Federal and State Disclosure Requirements

Tobacco companies currently have to disclose their ingredient lists to both the federal government and at least two state governments.

The federal government requires only that an aggregate list of all ingredients used in cigarettes and smokeless tobacco products be provided to the Department of Health and Human Services. 15 U.S.C. § 1335a(a). These lists, each of which contains hundreds of ingredients, neither identify the ingredients in any particular brand nor reveal which ingredients are used by which manufacturer. The Department of Health and Human Services can study and report to Congress on the health effects of tobacco additives, including information on specific ingredients which may pose a health risk to consumers. However, without further legislation and disclosure, the federal government has no ability to warn consumers of the use of harmful additives in specific brands.

The Disclosure Act

In 1996, Massachusetts enacted the Disclosure Act, ostensibly to promote public health. Citing the fact that various tobacco product additives may have adverse health effects when burned, either alone or in combination with other additives, Massachusetts expressed an interest in being able to study more accurately the health effects of tobacco products on consumers. Massachusetts was also concerned that certain additives may increase nicotine delivery and that those additives might be used in cigarettes advertised as having a lower nicotine content.

In Massachusetts' view, previous disclosure requirements did not allow it to investigate adequately these public health concerns. * * * Therefore, Massachusetts could not study the interaction of additives and know whether those additives are actually combined. Nor could Massachusetts study the additives used in more popular brands and those brands targeted to younger consumers. No one disputes that these suggested studies are laudable and within the health and safety realm of the state's traditional police powers.

Massachusetts, however, has an additional goal to be realized through the Disclosure Act: it hopes to publicize the ingredient lists of various brands. This information, Massachusetts believes, will help consumers make more informed choices about the tobacco products they choose to consume. The envisioned effect is greater public awareness about the potential health effects of tobacco additives. With these considerations in mind, Massachusetts enacted the Disclosure Act, which reads, in relevant part:

> For the purpose of protecting the public health, any manufacturer of cigarettes, snuff or chewing tobacco sold in the commonwealth shall provide the department of public health with an annual report, in a form and at a time specified by that department, which lists for each brand of such product sold the following information:
>
> > (a) The identity of any added constituent other than tobacco, water or reconstituted tobacco sheet made wholly from tobacco, to be listed in descending order according to weight, measure, or numerical count; and
>
> . . . [Any] information in the annual reports with respect to which the department determines that there is a reasonable scientific basis for concluding that the availability of such information *could* reduce risks to public health, *shall* be public records; provided, however, that before any public disclosure of such information the department shall request the advice of the attorney general whether such disclosure would constitute an unconstitutional taking of property, and shall not disclose such information unless and until the attorney general advises that such disclosure would not constitute an unconstitutional taking.

Therefore, the Disclosure Act establishes two threshold requirements before an ingredient list "shall" be made public: (1) there must be a finding that publication "could reduce risks to public health;" and (2) the Massachusetts Attorney General must find that disclosure would not be an unconstitutional taking. * * *

Takings Analysis

The tobacco companies allege, and the district court found, that the Disclosure Act unconstitutionally takes the tobacco companies' property when it requires the tobacco companies to disclose their ingredient lists to Massachusetts, which may, in turn, publish those lists. To support this claim, the tobacco companies first argue that their ingredient lists are trade secrets and, as such, are property protected by the Takings Clause. Second, they argue that the public disclosure of these trade secrets destroys their value, thereby effecting a taking. Appellants counter with two separate arguments. First, they claim that the tobacco companies' interest in keeping their ingredient lists secret does not defeat the state's ability to require public disclosure where, as here, the requirement is "rationally related to a legitimate governmental interest." *Ruckelshaus v. Monsanto Co.*. The asserted legitimate governmental interest is the health and safety of its citizens. Second, appellants dispute that Massachusetts law creates a property interest in trade secrets that are required by law to be disclosed to public agencies. I begin with analysis of the question of whether Massachusetts law protects the tobacco companies' ingredient lists as trade secrets.

Trade Secret Protection in Massachusetts

In most states, trade secrets are property protected by the Takings Clause, *see Monsanto* (holding that Missouri law, which follows the Restatement of Torts, creates cognizable property right in trade secrets), and neither side disputes that Massachusetts has long recognized and protected trade secrets. Also, neither side suggests that Massachusetts treats trade secrets differently from other states or argues that the district court's application of the Restatement (First) of Torts was incorrect. Finally, appellants do not contest that the tobacco companies' ingredient lists are trade secrets.

Rather, appellants make a more subtle, but nonetheless ultimately ineffective, argument. Despite recognizing that Massachusetts' laws provide a remedy for misappropriation of trade secrets by private actors, appellants argue that Massachusetts has long established that it can require public disclosure of trade secrets to advance public health and safety.

In support of this argument, appellants first point to the Restatement (First) of Torts which says that the law may require the disclosure of a trade secret to "promote some public interest." § 757, cmt. d (1939). Certainly, courts have long recognized that trade secrets generally can be subject to disclosure under certain limited circumstances. However, the fact that the public interest can sometimes override private property interests does not establish that the tobacco companies have *no* cognizable property interest when a state decides that publication of their trade secrets will further public health. In fact, Massachusetts continues to protect the integrity of many trade secrets despite the potentially valuable impact on the public interest if those trade secrets were to be placed in the public sphere. *See, e.g., Gen. Chem. Corp. v. Dep't of Env't Quality Eng'g,* (discussing Massachusetts statute which specifically guarantees confidentiality of trade secrets belonging to hazardous waste industries and submitted pursuant to regulations). Instead, the potential for mandated disclosure in the public interest forms part of the inquiry as to whether a particular disclosure requirement is constitutional. Finally, the Supreme Court specifically found that jurisdictions which follow the Restatement create a cognizable property interest in trade secrets. *Monsanto.*

Second, appellants argue that *General Chemical Corp.* establishes that the state may generally seize trade secrets in the public interest. That case established no such proposition. Rather, the court only assumed, *arguendo,* that the state legislature could deprive hazardous waste industries of certain trade secrets in the context of regulating those industries. Therefore, the case provides no notice that trade secrets are subject to disclosure.

Third, appellants point to the Massachusetts public records law which establishes that when a law requires trade secret information to be filed with a state agency, nothing requires those trade secrets to be treated as confidential. In fact, the public records law makes such information publicly available. Therefore, appellants argue that the tobacco companies have no property interest in their ingredient lists once a law requires them to submit that information to the state. Whether Massachusetts guarantees the confidentiality of trade secrets once they have been submitted to a state agency has no bearing on whether Massachusetts creates a property interest in trade secrets that is protected by the Takings Clause. Holders of trade secrets can always voluntarily submit their information to a state, consequently losing their property right. *See, e.g., Monsanto* (noting that Monsanto had voluntarily submitted its trade secrets information, knowing it was subject to public disclosure, as part of a regulatory scheme). The question is not whether trade secrets can be lost but whether trade secrets are a protected property interest in Massachusetts.

And the answer to that question is clear. Massachusetts protects trade secrets, and appellants fail to identify any background principles of state law that successfully obviate appellees' property interest in their trade secrets. The fact that trade secrets are potentially subject to disclosure does not destroy the tobacco companies' interest because trade secrets still enjoy general protection. Specific laws simply cannot destroy property interests. In fact, this is precisely what the Takings Clause is designed to prevent: "a State, by *ipse dixit,* may not transform private property into public property without compensation. This is the very kind of thing that the Taking Clause of the Fifth Amendment was meant to prevent. That clause stands as a shield against the arbitrary use of governmental power." Massachusetts cannot provide trade secret protection to some parties and then refuse others the same protections. Therefore, it is clear that the tobacco companies have a property interest in their trade secrets that is implicated by the Disclosure Act. In light of this, I turn to the question of whether the Disclosure Act violates the Takings Clause.

The Takings Clause

The Supreme Court has distinguished between two branches of Takings Clause cases: physical takings and regulatory takings. * * * A regulatory taking transpires when some significant restriction is placed upon an owner's use of his property for which "justice and fairness" require that compensation be given. For the most part, courts apply a three-part "ad hoc, factual inquiry" to evaluate whether a regulatory taking has occurred: (1) what is the economic impact of the regulation; (2) whether the government action interferes with reasonable investment-backed expectations; and (3) what is the character of the government action. *Penn Central*. However, the Supreme Court has developed at least one per se rule in the regulatory takings sphere. When a regulation denies all economically beneficial or productive uses of land, it is a taking.

Here, there is an alleged taking of intellectual property-trade secrets. The Supreme Court has addressed an alleged taking of trade secrets only once, in *Monsanto*. There, the Court simply applied the multi-factored regulatory takings analysis enunciated in Penn Central.[5] * * *

Reasonable Investment-Backed Expectations

* * * Monsanto complained about current and future disclosures of *already submitted* data. *Monsanto* ("Having determined that Monsanto has a property interest in the data it *has submitted* to EPA, we confront the difficult question whether a 'taking' will occur when EPA discloses those data. . . ." (emphasis added)). In answering that challenge, the Court measured Monsanto's reasonable investment-backed expectations at the time it submitted the data. Because there was no promise by the government under these two schemes to keep the data confidential, Monsanto had no basis on which to expect that its data would remain secret. In essence, Monsanto had "constructive notice" that its trade secrets might later be made public. Here, the tobacco companies challenge the ability of Massachusetts to compel future submissions of data which would be subject to disclosure. The tobacco companies have not voluntarily

---

[5]   * * * The tobacco companies are challenging the Disclosure Act before complying with its provisions. They point to general laws protecting trade secrets as evidence of a reasonable investment-backed expectation that those trade secrets will remain protected property. The concurrence * * * wants to take that reasonable investment-backed expectation and say that Massachusetts can never override the tobacco companies' property interest without violating the Takings Clause:

> [A]ctions speak louder than words. Once the *Monsanto* Court found that the trade secret holder possessed a reasonable investment-backed expectation in its trade secrets, the Court determined that such a taking, if not justly compensated, would be unconstitutional. *Monsanto*. * * *

provided their ingredient lists. Therefore, their situation is fundamentally different from two of the scenarios that confronted Monsanto.

The second scheme addressed by the *Monsanto* Court does shed some light on the current case, but it is not entirely dispositive. There, FIFRA provided Monsanto with an explicit guarantee of confidentiality. This guarantee established a reasonable investment-backed expectation that Monsanto's trade secrets would remain protected. When the Court decided that the government could not disclose submitted data which had been guaranteed confidentiality, the Court simply enforced the terms of the statute. Here, Massachusetts only generally protects trade secrets, establishing a right to recovery when a third party discloses or uses a trade secret without permission, and the Disclosure Act only provides for publication of submitted data. It explicitly disclaims any long-term confidentiality. This distinction is important because a trade secret is lost if its holder gives the trade secret to another without extracting a guarantee of confidentiality. Monsanto preserved its trade secrets because there was a promise of confidentiality.[11] The tobacco companies will lose their trade secrets because there is no similar promise here. Therefore, a slightly different question is posed by the current case. In *Monsanto,* the question was whether the government could disclose trade secrets it had previously agreed to keep secret. Here, the question is whether Massachusetts can force the tobacco companies to cede their trade secrets.

To answer that question I must look at the tobacco companies' reasonable investment-backed expectations that they can maintain the integrity of their trade secrets. The fact that the Disclosure Act has been enacted is not dispositive because, as discussed above, Massachusetts cannot simply redefine property rights without regard to previously existing protections. I must examine the tobacco companies' reasonable investment-backed expectations "in light of the whole of our legal tradition," * * * not just in light of the provisions of the Disclosure Act.

* * *

More recent regulation, of both tobacco and other products, supports the idea that "fair information" is not always a complete ingredient list. While the federal government and other states worry about the health effects of tobacco additives, none of their regimes requires the publication of brand-specific ingredient lists. They either do not require brand-specific disclosures, or they grant the tobacco companies protections against public disclosure of ingredient lists submitted to the states. Furthermore,

---

[11] * * * Furthermore, as this opinion addresses later, the tobacco companies are currently placed in the untenable position of having to choose between relinquishing their valuable trade secrets or pulling their products out of Massachusetts. This is an unconstitutional condition. However, the fact that Massachusetts is creating an unconstitutional condition has little, if anything, to do with whether the tobacco companies have a reasonable investment-backed expectation that their trade secrets will remain protected.

regulations governing other products recognize the difference between requiring accurate labeling and protecting secret formulas. For example, the Food, Drug, and Cosmetic Act allows additives to be grouped as "spices, flavoring, and coloring" without specifically identifying the individual ingredients. 21 U.S.C. § 343(i)(2). This allows many manufacturers to maintain their secret formulas.

Given this complex background and the fact that Massachusetts has long protected trade secrets, I cannot hold that the tobacco companies have no reasonable investment-backed expectation that their ingredient lists will remain secret. * * *

Economic Impact

In contrast to reasonable investment-backed expectations, the law regarding economic impact is fairly straightforward. The inquiry is whether the regulation "impair[s] the value or use of [the] property" according to the owners' general use of their property. Not only is the use to which the property owner puts her property important, but the economic impact needs to be considered in the context of other laws and regulatory schemes.

The evidence presented here is similarly straightforward. The appellees' have spent millions of dollars developing the formulas for different brands. The evidence shows that public disclosure of the appellees' ingredient lists, even in part, will make it much easier to reverse engineer those formulas. If competitors can obtain these formulas, they can replicate appellees' products, undermining the value of appellees' brands. Some of those brands, such as Marlboro, are worth billions of dollars. While it is impossible to predict the exact economic impact that the Disclosure Act will have, it is potentially tremendous.

Character of the Government Action

In this last section, I delve into how the Disclosure Act regulates and what that regulation does to the tobacco companies' trade secrets. As mentioned above, the tobacco companies believe that the Disclosure Act regulations are so egregious that they rise to the level of a per se taking. They ground this claim on the fact that the Disclosure Act gives Massachusetts the right to publish the ingredient lists. The Act, in essence, prevents the tobacco companies from excluding others from their trade secrets, destroying their essential attribute. It also, allegedly, destroys the entire value of the trade secrets. I now address those arguments in full. However, I will also balance the effects of the Disclosure Act against Massachusetts' interests. Here, the asserted state interest is the promotion of public health.

I begin with the tobacco companies' argument that they will lose the right to exclude others from their trade secrets and, consequently, their trade secrets will lose all value. It appears paradigmatic that these assertions are true. In *Monsanto,* the Supreme Court recognized that, "[i]f an individual discloses his trade secret to others who are under no obligation to protect the confidentiality of the information, or otherwise publicly discloses the secret, his property right is extinguished." That is exactly what happens here. The Disclosure Act requires the tobacco companies to share their trade secrets with Massachusetts, which is under no obligation to keep the information secret. In fact, the Disclosure Act spells out the terms under which Massachusetts will publish those trade secrets. It, thus, provides specific notice to the tobacco companies that Massachusetts need not respect their property rights. Therefore, if the tobacco companies comply with the requirements of the Disclosure Act, their property right will be extinguished. In the future, should a competitor use published data, the tobacco companies will have no ability to enforce their rights. Similarly, the value of the trade secrets will be lost because their value lies in the ability of the tobacco companies to exclude others. *See Monsanto.* The Disclosure Act essentially destroys the tobacco companies' trade secrets.

* * *

Appellants urge us, however, to consider the asserted state interest, promoting public health, as a counterbalance. I recognize that appellants have asserted a significant, perhaps compelling, state interest: a right for Massachusetts to protect and promote the health of its citizens. If I was convinced that this regulation was tailored to promote health and was the best strategy to do so, I might reconsider our analysis. Numerous cases show that a crucial part of the regulatory takings equation is the government interest. However, the cases also show that the means should bear some reasonable relationship to the ends.

I simply am not convinced that the Disclosure Act, particularly the provisions about which the tobacco companies complain, really helps to promote public health. The Disclosure Act allows for full disclosure of the ingredient lists when doing so "could" further public health. This places an extremely low burden on Massachusetts. Frankly, for a state to be able to completely destroy valuable trade secrets, it should be required to show more than a *possible* beneficial effect. The tremendous individual loss is simply not justified by such a speculative public gain. Furthermore, it is not at all clear that protecting the overall integrity of the tobacco companies' ingredient lists will interfere with Massachusetts' goal of promoting public health. * * *

Conclusion

For the reasons discussed above, I find that the Disclosure Act violates the Takings Clause. Therefore, I affirm the district court's judgment. * * *

DID YOU GET IT?

1. What was the Commonwealth's argument as to why it could require the cigarette companies to disclose their trade secrets?

2. What was the court's response to the Commonwealth's argument?

3. What is an unconstitutional condition?

Food for Thought

How should we balance the public's right to access information submitted to a government agency, like the FDA, versus a company's right to protect its trade secrets? How heavily should we weigh the public's interest in knowing all of the ingredients contained in the food and drugs they consume?

SECRECY AND UNACCOUNTABILITY: TRADE SECRETS IN OUR PUBLIC INFRASTRUCTURE

David S. Levine.
59 Florida L. Rev. 135, 136–40 (2007).

There has always been tension between the interests of the public and commerce. * * * The public and private sector do not operate without regard for the operations or interests of the other; rather, they increasingly can and do regard the other as a direct partner in achieving their vastly different goals. * * *

Fixed at the intersection of these increasingly intertwined worlds is trade secret law. Private businesses are increasingly displacing the government in providing and operating public infrastructure, but these private businesses are utilizing commercial law standards and norms, including the key tool of trade secrecy, to do so. Countless examples of modern infrastructure, from telecommunications in the form of the Internet, to traditional government operations in the form of voting machines, are now being provided by the private sector. Because of this shift to private provision of public infrastructure, the trade secrecy doctrine has intruded into activities that traditionally have been conducted in the relatively open realm of public institutions like government. I argue in this Article that public access to information should prevail over trade secrecy protection in this sphere.

Secrecy, and its attendant goals of pecuniary gain and commercial competition, conflict with the methods and purpose of transparent and accountable democratic governance. This conflict is crystallized in the private distribution of voting machines. Voting machines are perhaps the signature example of a device designed to advance governmental and democratic interests. Diebold Election Systems, Inc. (Diebold), by its own estimation, is currently providing over 130,000 voting machines to states.

These machines, replacing older (but not necessarily less reliable) pull-lever and punch-card systems, are the public infrastructure through which elections are conducted, votes are counted, and the results are verified. They form the backbone upon which one can exercise the right to vote; they instill confidence that one's vote will not be disregarded, lost, or erroneously tabulated.

* * * [H]owever, public access to the internal workings of these machines is difficult, or in some cases impossible, to obtain. North Carolina's experience with Diebold illustrates this problem. The North Carolina State Board of Elections, charged by statute to procure voting machines for use in its elections, is legally required to have access to the inner workings of potential vendors' machines. This requirement exists to guarantee that the Board meets its responsibilities to conduct error-free and fraud-free elections, and that the vendors supply the information. The disclosure of this information helps to provide legitimacy to, and trustworthiness in, the very system of conducting elections—a bedrock requirement of a transparent democratic society.

But in late 2005, potential vendor Diebold, when faced with this law's requirements, responded differently and focused instead on its commercial property rights. Rather than comply with the law, it brought a declaratory judgment action against the state, arguing that it could not supply the required information. Diebold explained that some of the inner workings of its voting machines were a third party's intellectual property, likely trade secrets, to which it did not have access. Therefore, Diebold claimed the information could not be shared with the state or the public without violating intellectual property rights or intellectual property licensing agreements with third parties, even if it had access to this information.

Was this a legitimate objection based upon Diebold's trade secret rights? From a business perspective, it would appear so; but exercising those rights frustrated the goals of public transparency and accountability. Rather than comply with the law, Diebold chose to keep its secrets and withdraw from competition for the state's contract. The Diebold story is one of many. Today, more and more public infrastructure is provided by the private sector while the use of trade secrecy by the business world is expanding. * * *

Should we want or expect private companies like Diebold to adhere to public values like transparency and accountability in the provision of public infrastructure, and, if so, can this goal be achieved under the current trade secrecy framework? I argue here that we can and should expect such public disclosure when companies step out of the purely private commercial world and seek to reap the financial benefits of providing essential public infrastructure, and that trade secret law stands in the way of this goal.

The people and the government, in these contexts, are not simply buying a product or service where the product legitimately incorporates trade secrets. Rather, the products or services being procured—and their attendant trade secrets—are themselves the public infrastructure that people have traditionally turned to a publicly accountable government to provide, like the ability to vote, communicate, and access governmental services. If we do nothing, it will be the infrastructure itself—owned and operated by private interests with commercial values like business advantage and secrecy of corporate information—that will direct the law involving public activity, rather than the law creating the conditions under which public infrastructure operates.

Trade secrecy law and practices serve many useful and important purposes in private industry, but, as I argue here, their use in the public infrastructure context is inappropriate, unexpectedly powerful, and doctrinally unsound. When private firms provide public infrastructure, commercial trade secrecy should be discarded (at least in its pure form) and give way to more transparency and accountability. Industry's broad definition of "trade secrets," derived from trade secrecy theory, caselaw, and statutes, is inapplicable to a transparent democratic society. * * *

Food for Thought

If governmental entities want to enhance transparency and accountability, how must they draft their laws and regulations to ensure that government contractors will not assert trade secret rights and make a takings claim? What are the potential consequences to the government of not protecting the trade secrets of companies with whom it does business?

E. SPECIAL ISSUE: HOW ARE TRADE SECRETS PROTECTED IN OTHER COUNTRIES?

By now it should be obvious that the easiest and best way to protect a trade secret is not to share it with anyone. For a small enterprise this strategy may be possible, but for larger enterprises trade secrets usually have to be shared with others to have any value. This is why the "relative secrecy doctrine" exists in the U.S. so that trade secrets can be shared in the context of a confidential relationship.

While businesses that possess trade secrets are well-advised to limit the disclosure of trade secrets within the confines of their facilities, this is not always possible. Often, trade secret owners must disclose their trade secrets to individuals and companies that are located off-site. If a trade secret owner elects to "outsource" any part of its operations to foreign countries, it is the substantive laws and procedural rules of the other countries, rather than the laws and procedures of the United States that are likely to define whether the information is protected.

1. THE TRIPS AGREEMENT

During the negotiations that led to the World Trade Organization (WTO) Agreement on Trade-related Aspects of Intellectual Property Law (known as the TRIPS Agreement), the delegation from the United States fought hard to include trade secrets among the mix of intellectual property rights (referred to in international circles as "IPR") that would be covered. Initially, a number of developing countries argued that trade secrets were not a form of intellectual property and, therefore, should not be included in the TRIPS Agreement. Ultimately, as explained in the following excerpt of a work by Professor Sharon Sandeen, the position of the United States won out and, for the first time, trade secrets were included in a major and widespread international treaty.

THE LIMITS OF TRADE SECRET LAW: ARTICLE 39 OF THE TRIPS AGREEMENT AND THE UNIFORM TRADE SECRETS ACT ON WHICH IT IS BASED

Sharon K. Sandeen.
Chapter 20, The Law and Theory of Trade Secrecy.
Edward Elgar, 2011.

* * * The effort to add trade secrets to the mix of IPRs that would be a part of the Uruguay Round negotiations, and ultimately the TRIPS Agreement, began well before the first meeting of the TRIPS Negotiating Group (NG11). As detailed in several accounts, it was a group of U.S. industry leaders who conceived of the idea of tying IPRs to international trade and who advocated for an international system for the protection of IPRs that was based upon the laws of the United States. This advocacy led to efforts by the United States to ensure that the Punte del Este Declaration included the protection of IPRs within its scope.

When NG11 met for the first time in March 1987, the United States quickly staked out its position, calling for a comprehensive, enforceable agreement for the protection of IPRs "including patents, trademarks, trade dress, copyrights, mask works and trade secrets." In a submission later that year, the Office of the United States Trade Representative detailed its proposed negotiating objectives with respect to trade secrets:

> Trade secrets should be broadly defined to include undisclosed valuable business, commercial, technical or other proprietary data as well as technical information. Misappropriation, including the unauthorized acquisition, use or disclosure of a trade secret, must be prevented.

> Trade secrets submitted to governments as a requirement to do business shall not be disclosed except in extreme circumstances involving national emergencies or, in the case of public health and safety, provided that such disclosure does not impair actual or potential markets of the submitter or the value of the submitted trade secrets.

From late 1987 until late 1989, most conversations concerning the TRIPS Agreement revolved around the proper scope of NG11's work. The United States argued that strong and enforceable protection of IPRs was essential to free trade and economic development and, therefore, it was appropriate for the TRIPS Agreement to contain standards for the protection of IPRs. Other countries, principally India and Brazil, argued that the focus of the TRIPS Agreement should be on how IPRs impact free trade and that it should not be used as a means to establish or strengthen IP standards. In their view, it was up to the World Intellectual Property Organization (WIPO) to establish substantive IP standards.

As a consequence of the debate concerning the scope of NG11's work, substantive discussions regarding standards for the protection of IPRs were delayed for more than eighteen months. Once they occurred, they were dominated by developed countries and most of the attention was focused on issues of counterfeiting, enforcement, and IPRs other than trade secrets, leaving little time for the parties to gain a complete understanding of the purpose, scope, and limitations of trade secret protection. * * *

———

As ultimately adopted, the TRIPS Agreement includes a provision that requires all WTO member countries to provide protection for "undisclosed information." Article 39(1) begins with a statement of the pre-existing obligation under Article 6*bis* in the Paris Convention (1967) that requires "effective protection against unfair competition." Using language that is modeled after the UTSA, Article 39(2) then defines a specific instance of unfair competition. Article 39.3 does not concern trade secrets, but a lesser form of protection known as "data exclusivity."

THE TRIPS AGREEMENT

Article 39.1

In the course of ensuring effective protection against unfair competition as provided in Article 10*bis* of the Paris Convention (1967), Members shall protect undisclosed information in accordance with paragraph 2 and data submitted to governments or governmental agencies in accordance with paragraph 3.

Article 39.2

Natural and legal persons shall have the possibility of preventing information lawfully within their control from being disclosed to, acquired by, or used by others without their consent in a manner contrary to honest business practices[10] so long as such information:

(a) is secret in the sense that it is not, as a body or in the precise configuration and assembly of its components, generally known among or readily accessible to persons within the circles that normally deal with the kind of information in question;

(b) has commercial value because of its secret; and

(c) has been subject to reasonable steps under the circumstances, by the person lawfully in control of the information, to keep it secret.

Article 39.3

Members, when requiring, as a condition of approving the marketing of pharmaceutical or of agricultural chemical products which utilize new chemical entities, the submission of undisclosed test or other data, the origination of which involves a considerable effort, shall protect such data against unfair commercial use. In addition, Members shall protect such data against disclosure, except where necessary to protect the public, or unless steps are taken to ensure that the data are protected against unfair commercial use.

––––––

While the existence of Article 39.2 may give U.S. trade secret owners hope that they can protect their trade secrets abroad, there are a number of reasons why they should not assume that such is the case. First and foremost, although the TRIPS Agreement was designed, in part, to increase the harmonization of intellectual property protection throughout the world, some differences in intellectual property laws are still allowed. Thus, to truly understand how trade secrets are protected in other WTO member countries, the laws of those countries must be consulted. *See, e.g.,* Elizabeth A. Rowe & Sharon K. Sandeen, TRADE SECRECY AND INTERNATIONAL TRANSACTIONS (2015). Second, where trade secrets laws exist in a given

---

[10] For purposes of this provision, "a manner contrary to honest business practices" shall mean at least practices such as breach of contract, breach of confidence and inducement to breach, and includes the acquisition of undisclosed information by third parties who knew, or were grossly negligent in failing to know, that such practices were involved in the acquisition.

country, there is always the question of whether and to what extent such laws have extraterritorial effect.

2. EXTRATERRITORIAL APPLICATION OF U.S. LAW

There is no established framework for addressing extraterritoriality in trade secret law. Accordingly, courts have struggled to find consistency, which, in turn, has left trade secret owners unsure of the extent of their enforceable rights. *See* Elizabeth A. Rowe and Daniel M. Mahfood, *Trade Secrets, Trade, and Extraterritoriality*, 66 ALABAMA L.REV. 63, 69–73 (2014). In addition to the uncertainty already attendant to trade secret enforcement, trade secret owners must address unpredictable procedural hurdles (like personal jurisdiction and choice of law) wholly independent from substantive trade secret law.

The enactment of the DTSA provides a stronger basis for applying a federal statute (rather than the previous state trade secret laws) extraterritorially, but certain challenges, both practical and legal, are likely to remain. (*See* Note 1 at the end of this chapter). The first case below, *BP Chemicals Ltd. v. Formosa*, illustrates these procedural hurdles. The case that follows, *TianRui Group Co. v. International Trade Commission*, presents the alternative of seeking redress for foreign misappropriation of trade secrets before a quasi-judicial federal agency known as the United States International Trade Commission (ITC), when the allegedly infringing goods are imported into the United States.

Reading Guidance
What country's law applies to the relationship between the parties?

BP CHEMICALS LTD. V. FORMOSA CHEMICAL & FIBRE CORPORATION

U.S. Court of Appeals, Third Circuit, 2000.
229 F.3d 254.

STAPLETON, CIRCUIT JUDGE.

This is a trade secret case filed in the United States District Court for the District of New Jersey by BP Chemicals Ltd. (BP), a British corporation, against Formosa Chemical & Fibre Corporation (FCFC), a Taiwanese corporation, and Joseph Oat Corporation (JOC), a Pennsylvania corporation with its principal place of business in New Jersey. * * *

The undisputed facts are as follows. FCFC is a publicly-traded Taiwanese corporation with its principal place of business in Taipei, Taiwan. FCFC is a subsidiary of a Taiwanese conglomerate known as the Formosa Plastics Group (FPG), which is owned by Y.C. Wang. In 1996, FPG's U.S. operations produced revenue of $2.58 billion. FCFC has a 3.51% stock interest in

Formosa Plastics Corporations (FPC), a Delaware corporation with headquarters in New Jersey. * * *

FCFC has a contract with JOC under which JOC will fabricate vessels in New Jersey for delivery to FCFC in Taiwan. It is performance of this contract that the instant action seeks to enjoin. * * *

FCFC has contracts for the purchase of equipment for its acetic acid plant with at least eight U.S. vendors in addition to JOC. These vendors received "bid packages" containing specifications that allegedly incorporate misappropriated trade secrets. The process for soliciting bids was that FCFC's engineering team would prepare a bid package and send it to a purchasing group. BP asserts, and FCFC does not dispute, that the purchasing group was actually the purchasing group of FPG, not FCFC. The purchasing group would then send the bid packages to the Taiwanese agents of U.S. vendors, who would in turn send them to their U.S. clients. All meetings between FCFC representatives and representatives of equipment vendors and their agents took place in Taiwan. No FCFC personnel visited the United States for any purpose in connection with the design or construction of the acetic acid plant. There is no evidence that any U.S. vendor received bid packages directly from FCFC, or even from FPG's purchasing group, rather than through Taiwanese agents of the U.S. vendors.

* * *

FCFC argues on appeal that the District Court did not have personal jurisdiction over it. Both FCFC and JOC further argue that the District Court erred in issuing the preliminary injunction by (1) determining the likelihood of success on the merits under the law of New Jersey rather than Taiwan, and (2) finding that the injunction was necessary to prevent imminent, irreparable harm. BP cross-appeals, asserting that the District Court erred in limiting the duration of the injunction to thirty months.

* * *

II.

"In order to obtain a preliminary injunction, the moving party must show (1) irreparable injury, (2) a reasonable probability of success on the merits, (3) the harm to it outweighs the possible harm to other interested parties, and (4) harm to the public." * * * A District Court then balances these four factors to determine if an injunction should issue. * * * JOC asserts that the District Court erred in finding that BP had demonstrated both imminent and irreparable injury and a likelihood of success on the merits.

A.

We find that the record supports the District Court's conclusion that an injunction was necessary to prevent imminent and irreparable harm. * * *

B.

In determining whether BP had shown a likelihood of success, however, the District Court concluded that New Jersey had the most significant relationship with the case and applied New Jersey law in analyzing each issue. We conclude that it erred in doing so.

* * * [W]hile it appears to be undisputed that New Jersey law governs the issues of JOC's knowledge and conduct, this does not necessarily signify that New Jersey law—as opposed to Taiwanese law—applies to the two additional issues necessary to BP's case against JOC.

JOC has tendered affidavits tending to show that Taiwanese law governing the protectability of commercially valuable information and what constitutes a tortious conversion of such a protectable interest is different from, and more difficult for BP than, the New Jersey law governing those issues. As to the issue of protectability, the affidavits indicate, for example, that "[a] single unprotected disclosure [by either BP, Monsanto, CPDC or other Monsanto licensees] of the secret terminates its trade secret status immediately (like a needle hits a balloon)," * * *, and that "BP is required to show that CPDC actually took steps to safeguard the information," * * *. As to the issue of whether FCFC tortiously acquired the information from Tu, the affidavits indicate that:

> BP is required to show that CPDC actually entered into a confidentiality agreement with Mr. Tu. There must be evidence that Mr. Tu was put on notice or instructed as to what materials he should consider confidential. Under Taiwanese law, corporate obligations do not attach to a corporation's employee. The employee has to be subject to [sic] specific agreement or clear instructions as to exactly what he was required to keep confidential.

We recognize that BP has tendered conflicting affidavits tending to show that JOC's affidavits do not accurately characterize Taiwanese law and that Taiwanese and New Jersey law are the same as to these issues. It is enough for present purposes, however, to find that there is record evidence that, if believed, would support a finding that there are relevant differences in the laws of the two sovereigns that the parties claim to be governing. This requires us to determine whether Taiwan or New Jersey has the more substantial interest in determining:

(1) whether proprietary information licensed by its purported owner for use in Taiwan was protectable and whether at the time of its alleged conversion in Taiwan it had been returned to the public domain; and

(2) whether FCFC's acquisition of the alleged trade secret in Taiwan was wrongful.

In both instances, we conclude based on the current record that Taiwan had the more substantial interest in having its law applied and that a New Jersey court would apply that law in a case like this.

We believe Taiwan has the greater interest in setting the standards regarding whether information that has been licensed by a British company to a Taiwanese company has been sufficiently safeguarded to warrant legal protection or whether it has entered the Taiwanese public domain. This issue implicates policy judgments regarding the appropriate balance between protecting trade secrets, thereby encouraging both the development of new technology and the willingness of foreign companies to share their technology with Taiwanese businesses, and free interchange and access to information, which also has profound implications for the health of the Taiwanese economy. New Jersey's interest, on the other hand, would appear to be virtually nil.

As we have previously pointed out, BP, the purported owner of the trade secret, is not a resident of New Jersey and, while it may suffer some marginal injury there, New Jersey is assuredly not the principal situs of either the direct or the indirect injury inflicted. Moreover, we are doubtful that a New Jersey court would apply New Jersey law even if BP were a New Jersey corporation. A state's interest in protecting its citizens from injury by protecting intellectual property which they choose to license to foreign companies cannot outweigh the interests of the foreign sovereign in setting the standards for the protection of intellectual property within its own borders. * * *

The New Jersey Superior Court's decision in *O'Connor* is instructive. There, a New Jersey resident was injured in Virginia. The injuries were allegedly caused by both the New Jersey plaintiff's and the Virginia defendant's negligence. The issue was whether the court should apply Virginia's strict rule of common-law contributory negligence or New Jersey's comparative negligence rule, which afforded more protection to the injured plaintiff. The court held that:

> New Jersey's concern for its injured citizens is also legitimate, but it cannot exempt them from other states' law setting standards for local conditions and conduct. If New Jersey's comparative negligence doctrine followed [the plaintiff] [i]nto . . . Virginia, it would follow her into every other state as well, and would supplant local liability rules wherever she went. That would be an impermissible intrusion into the affairs of other states.

* * * Similarly, in this case, neither New Jersey nor Great Britain's concern for their injured citizens can outweigh Taiwan's interest in setting standards for the protection of intellectual property in Taiwan.

Similarly, Taiwan has the greater interest in having its law applied to determine whether FCFC, a Taiwanese company, acted tortiously in acquiring information in Taiwan from CPDC, another Taiwanese company, and, in particular, as to the circumstances under which a Taiwanese company's actions have created a duty of confidentiality in its employees. Again the law in this area reflects a delicate balance of competing interests that has the capacity to profoundly affect the Taiwanese economy, and any interest that New Jersey would have in protecting trade secret holders who export their intellectual property to Taiwan is greatly outweighed by Taiwan's interest in setting the standards that govern the conduct of its own citizens regarding intellectual property that is present within its borders.

* * *

The vast majority of the conduct that is relevant to these two issues occurred in Taiwan. BP licensed the trade secrets to CPDC in Taiwan. To the extent that BP and CPDC took measures to safeguard those secrets in CPDC's hands, those measures were taken in Taiwan. FCFC acquired whatever information it acquired in Taiwan, designed its plant in Taiwan, prepared the bid packages with the specifications for the equipment in Taiwan, and delivered those packages to Taiwanese agents of U.S. companies in Taiwan.

Moreover, while neither BP nor JOC is Taiwanese, which by itself weighs against the application of Taiwanese law, both have established significant relationships with Taiwan, BP by licensing its technology to a Taiwanese company and JOC by maintaining agents in Taiwan for the purpose of soliciting Taiwanese business. These relationships are centered in Taiwan, and these relationships gave rise to the events that are at issue here.

We hold that Taiwan has the greater interest in having its law govern the issues of whether BP had a protectable interest in the information licensed to CPDC and whether FCFC acted unlawfully in acquiring it. Therefore, to the extent that there is a conflict of law on these issues, Taiwanese law should govern.

As we have previously noted, there is evidence in the current record that, if believed, would support a conclusion that Taiwanese and New Jersey law do not differ in any respect material here. The District Court had no occasion to resolve the conflict presented in the affidavits before it because it erroneously concluded that New Jersey law governed all issues. While we conclude that we are authorized to resolve that conflict, * * *, we believe the District Court is in the best position to determine what at this point is essentially a credibility issue—i.e., which expert to believe. The District Court will thus be required to determine hereafter whether Taiwanese law differs from that of New Jersey. It may address this issue in the context of a renewed application for a preliminary injunction and/or in the context of a merits determination. In either context, it will have discretion to supplement the existing record with testimony or otherwise and/or to conduct its own independent investigation regarding Taiwanese law. * * *

III.

We will reverse the District Court's order of May 14, 1999, and direct that it: (a) dismiss FCFC for want of personal jurisdiction, and (b) conduct further proceedings with respect to BP's claim against JOC in a manner consistent with this opinion.

DID YOU GET IT?

1. Which country's law did the court hold applicable to the relationship between plaintiff and defendant JOC? Why?

2. Is the trade secret law of Taiwan the same as the trade secret law of New Jersey?

3. Given the parties' attenuated relationship with New Jersey, why do you think the lawsuit was filed in New Jersey? Why wasn't it filed in Great Britain or Taiwan?

———

The next case illustrates how the United States International Trade Commission (ITC) can be used to enforce trade secret rights in some situations.

Reading Guidance

Can an importation statute apply American trade secret law to conduct that occurs in a foreign country?

TIANRUI GROUP CO. LTD. v. INTERNATIONAL TRADE COMMISSION

U.S. Court of Appeals, Federal Circuit, 2011.
661 F.3d 1322.

BRYSON, CIRCUIT JUDGE.

This appeal arises from a determination by the International Trade Commission that the importation of certain cast steel railway wheels violated section 337 of the Tariff Act of 1930, 19 U.S.C. § 1337. The Commission found that the wheels were manufactured using a process that was developed in the United States, protected under domestic trade secret law, and misappropriated abroad. We are asked to decide whether the Commission's statutory authority over "[u]nfair methods of competition and unfair acts in the importation of articles . . . into the United States," as provided by section 337(a)(1)(A), allows the Commission to look to conduct occurring in China in the course of a trade secret misappropriation investigation. We conclude that the Commission has authority to investigate and grant relief based in part on extraterritorial conduct insofar as it is necessary to protect domestic industries from injuries arising out of unfair competition in the domestic marketplace.

We are also asked to decide whether the Commission erred by finding that the imported wheels would injure a domestic industry when no domestic manufacturer is currently practicing the protected process. In light of the evidence before the Commission regarding the marketplace for cast steel railway wheels, we affirm the Commission's determination that the wheel imports threaten to destroy or substantially injure an industry in the United States, in violation of section 337.

I

A

Amsted Industries Inc. is a domestic manufacturer of cast steel railway wheels. It owns two secret processes for manufacturing such wheels, the "ABC process" and the "Griffin process." Amsted previously practiced the ABC process at its foundry in Calera, Alabama, but it no longer uses that process in the United States. Instead, Amsted uses the Griffin process at three of its domestic foundries. Amsted has licensed the ABC process to several firms with foundries in China.

TianRui Group Company Limited and TianRui Group Foundry Company Limited (collectively, "TianRui") manufacture cast steel railway wheels in China. In 2005, TianRui sought to license Amsted's wheel manufacturing technology, but the parties could not agree on the terms of a license. After the failed negotiations, TianRui hired nine employees away from one of Amsted's Chinese licensees, Datong ABC Castings Company Limited. Some of those employees had been trained in the ABC process at the Calera plant in Alabama, and others had received training in that process at the Datong foundry in China.

Datong had previously notified those employees through a written employee code of conduct that information pertaining to the ABC process was proprietary and confidential. Each employee had been advised that he had a duty not to disclose confidential information. Eight of the nine employees had also signed confidentiality agreements before leaving Datong to begin working for TianRui. In the proceedings brought by Amsted before the International Trade Commission, Amsted alleged that the former Datong employees disclosed information and documents to TianRui that revealed the details of the ABC process and thereby misappropriated Amsted's trade secrets.

TianRui partnered with Standard Car Truck Company, Inc., ("SCT") to form the joint venture Barber TianRui Railway Supply, LLC. SCT and Barber have marketed TianRui wheels to United States customers and have imported TianRui wheels into the United States. Other than Amsted,

SCT and Barber are the only companies selling or attempting to sell cast steel railway wheels in the United States.

B

Amsted filed a complaint with the Commission alleging a violation of section 337 based on TianRui's misappropriation of trade secrets. Section 337(a)(1)(A) prohibits "[u]nfair methods of competition and unfair acts in the importation of articles . . . into the United States, . . . the threat or effect of which is . . . to destroy or substantially injure an industry in the United States."

TianRui moved to terminate the proceedings on the ground that the alleged misappropriation occurred in China and that Congress did not intend for section 337 to be applied extraterritorially. An administrative law judge at the Commission denied that motion based on his view that section 337 focuses not on where the misappropriation occurs but rather on the nexus between the imported articles and the unfair methods of competition. The administrative law judge also rejected TianRui's argument that Chinese courts would provide a better forum for Amsted's complaint.

At the merits stage, the administrative law judge analyzed the alleged misappropriation under Illinois trade secret law. * * * He applied Illinois law because Amsted, SCT, and Barber all have their principal place of business in Illinois. He noted, however, that "the Illinois law relating to trade secrets does not differ substantially from the law applied in previous Commission trade secret investigations," and he then applied general principles of trade secret law, including the six factors defining a trade secret set forth in the comments to section 757 of the Restatement (First) of Torts.

Following a 10-day evidentiary hearing, the administrative law judge found that TianRui had misappropriated 128 trade secrets relating to the ABC process from Datong. That conclusion was based on evidence that included an admission by TianRui's expert that TianRui's foundry used the asserted trade secrets; his only contention was that the trade secrets were not actually secret. In addition, the administrative law judge compared TianRui's manufacturing specifications with secret Datong documents outlining the ABC process and found them essentially identical. In fact, some of the TianRui specifications contained the same typographical errors that were found in the Datong documents. The administrative law judge also relied on similarities in foundry layout between the Datong and TianRui plants. The administrative law judge summarized the evidence as to the appropriation of the trade secrets by saying that "there is overwhelming direct and circumstantial evidence that TianRui obtained its manufacturing process for cast steel railway wheel[s] through the misappropriation of [Amsted's] ABC Trade Secrets."

Besides contesting the Commission's authority to apply section 337 extraterritorially, TianRui contended that Amsted did not satisfy the domestic industry requirement of section 337 based on the fact that Amsted no longer practiced the ABC process in the United States. Because none of Amsted's domestic operations used the ABC process, TianRui argued that there was no "domestic industry" that could be injured by the misappropriation of trade secrets relating to that process.

The administrative law judge rejected that argument, holding that it was not essential that the domestic industry use the proprietary process, as long as the misappropriation of that process caused injury to the complainant's domestic industry. Applying that standard, the administrative law judge concluded that Amsted's domestic industry would be substantially injured by the importation of TianRui wheels.

The Commission decided not to review the administrative law judge's initial determination and issued a limited exclusion order. TianRui then appealed to this court.

II

The main issue in this case is whether section 337 authorizes the Commission to apply domestic trade secret law to conduct that occurs in part in a foreign country.

Section 337 authorizes the Commission to exclude articles from entry into the United States when it has found "[u]nfair methods of competition [or] unfair acts in the importation of [those] articles." 19 U.S.C. § 1337(a)(1)(A). The Commission has long interpreted section 337 to apply to trade secret misappropriation. TianRui does not challenge that interpretation. Nor does it dispute the Commission's factual finding that proprietary information belonging to Amsted was disclosed to TianRui in breach of obligations of confidentiality imposed on the former Datong employees or the finding that the information was used in manufacturing the imported railway wheels. Instead, TianRui focuses on the fact that the disclosure of the trade secret information occurred in China. According to TianRui, section 337 cannot apply to extraterritorial conduct and therefore does not reach trade secret misappropriation that occurs outside the United States.

Amsted argues that the Commission did not apply section 337 extraterritorially, because trade secrets were misappropriated in the United States as a legal matter when railway wheels made by exploiting those trade secrets were imported into the United States and sold to customers or disclosed to the Association of American Railroads for certification purposes. Amsted argues that Illinois law defines trade secret misappropriation very broadly and that under Illinois law any unauthorized "use" of an article embodying a trade secret constitutes misappropriation. That definition of misappropriation, according to Amsted, is broad enough to encompass any use of articles produced by the misappropriated process, not simply the acts that constitute a direct breach of the duty of confidentiality. Amsted concludes that the administrative law judge therefore had sufficient evidence to find trade secret misappropriation based on TianRui's importation of the wheels and its disclosure of those wheels for certification purposes.

Like Amsted, the Commission argues that it applied section 337 based on TianRui's conduct in the United States and did not apply the statute extraterritorially to conduct occurring in China. In the alternative, the Commission contends that section 337 applies to imported articles produced with misappropriated trade secrets, even if the disclosure of the proprietary information occurred outside the United States.

A

At the outset, we reject Amsted's argument that Illinois trade secret law governs the section 337 inquiry in this case. The question of what law applies in a section 337 proceeding involving trade secrets is a matter of first impression for this court. We hold that a single federal standard, rather than the law of a particular state, should determine what constitutes a misappropriation of trade secrets sufficient to establish an "unfair method of competition" under section 337.

The administrative law judge acknowledged that in previous section 337 proceedings involving trade secret misappropriation, the Commission has applied general principles of trade secret law, not the law of any particular state. The administrative judge, however, felt bound to apply state law because of a statement by this court that issues of trade secret misappropriation are ordinarily matters of state law. That statement is, of course, true as a general matter * * * , [b]ut where the question is whether particular conduct constitutes "unfair methods of competition" and "unfair acts" in importation, in violation of section 337, the issue is one of federal law and should be decided under a uniform federal standard, rather than by reference to a particular state's tort law.

* * *

Fortunately, trade secret law varies little from state to state and is generally governed by widely recognized authorities such as the Restatement of Unfair Competition and the Uniform Trade Secrets Act. Moreover, the federal criminal statute governing theft of trade secrets bases its definition of trade secrets on the Uniform Trade Secrets Act, so there is no indication of congressional intent to depart from the general law in that regard. In any event, there is no dispute in this case pertaining to the substantive law of trade secrets. The administrative law judge's findings establish that TianRui obtained access to Amsted's confidential information through former Datong employees, who were subject to duties of confidentiality imposed by the Datong code of employee conduct, and that TianRui exploited that information in producing the subject goods.

TianRui does not take issue with those findings, which are sufficient to establish the elements of trade secret misappropriation under either Illinois law or the generally understood law of trade secrets, as reflected in the Restatement, the Uniform Trade Secrets Act, and previous Commission decisions under section 337. Therefore, the choice of law issue, although it could be important in other cases, does not affect the outcome of this case.

In this case, TianRui argues that section 337 is inapplicable because Amsted's confidential information was disclosed in China. The legal issue for us to decide is thus whether section 337 applies to imported goods produced through the exploitation of trade secrets in which the act of misappropriation occurs abroad. To answer that question, we must review the principles that apply to federal statutes that create causes of action based in part on conduct that occurs overseas.

B

* * *

The presumption against extraterritoriality does not govern this case, for three reasons. First, section 337 is expressly directed at unfair methods of competition and unfair acts "in the importation of articles" into the United States. As such, "this is surely not a statute in which Congress had only 'domestic concerns in mind.' " *Pasquantino v. United States.* The focus of section 337 is on an inherently international transaction—importation. In that respect, section 337 is analogous to immigration statutes that bar the admission of an alien who has engaged in particular conduct or who makes false statements in connection with his entry into this country. In such cases, the focus is not on punishing the conduct or the false statements, but on preventing the admission of the alien, so it is reasonable to assume that Congress was aware, and intended, that the statute would apply to conduct (or statements) that may have occurred abroad. * * *

Second, in this case the Commission has not applied section 337 to sanction purely extraterritorial conduct; the foreign "unfair" activity at issue in this case is relevant only to the extent that it results in the importation of goods into this country causing domestic injury. In light of the statute's focus on the act of importation and the resulting domestic injury, the Commission's order does not purport to regulate purely foreign conduct. Because foreign conduct is used only to establish an element of a claim alleging a domestic injury and seeking a wholly domestic remedy, the presumption against extraterritorial application does not apply.

The dissent disregards the domestic elements of the cause of action under section 337 and characterizes this case as involving "conduct which entirely occurs in a foreign country." That characterization accurately describes most of the events constituting the misappropriation, but the determination of misappropriation was merely a predicate to the charge that TianRui committed unfair acts in importing its wheels into the United

States. In other words, the Commission's interpretation of section 337 does not, as the dissent contends, give it the authority to "police Chinese business practices." It only sets the conditions under which products may be imported into the United States.

Under the dissent's construction of section 337, the importation of goods produced as a result of trade secret misappropriation would be immune from scrutiny if the act of misappropriation occurred overseas. That is, as long as the misappropriating party was careful to ensure that the actual act of conveying the trade secret occurred outside the United States, the Commission would be powerless to provide a remedy even if the trade secret were used to produce products that were subsequently imported into the United States to the detriment of the trade secret owner. We think it highly unlikely that Congress, which clearly intended to create a remedy for the importation of goods resulting from unfair methods of competition, would have intended to create such a conspicuous loophole for misappropriators.

* * *

C

TianRui argues that the Commission should not be allowed to apply domestic trade secret law to conduct occurring in China because doing so would cause improper interference with Chinese law. We disagree. In the first place, as we have noted, the Commission's exercise of authority is limited to goods imported into this country, and thus the Commission has no authority to regulate conduct that is purely extraterritorial. The Commission does not purport to enforce principles of trade secret law in other countries generally, but only as that conduct affects the U.S. market. That is, the Commission's investigations, findings, and remedies affect foreign conduct only insofar as that conduct relates to the importation of articles into the United States. The Commission's activities have not hindered TianRui's ability to sell its wheels in China or any other country.

Second, TianRui has failed to identify a conflict between the principles of misappropriation that the Commission applied and Chinese trade secret law. * * * We cannot discern any relevant difference between the misappropriation requirements of TRIPS article 39 and the principles of trade secret law applied by the administrative law judge in this case. We therefore detect no conflict between the Commission's actions and Chinese law that would counsel denying relief based on extraterritorial acts of trade secret misappropriation relating to the importation of goods affecting a domestic industry.

Finally, even apart from the acts of importation, the conduct at issue in this case is not the result of the imposition of legal duties created by American law on persons for whom there was no basis to impose such duties. The former Datong employees had a duty not to disclose Amsted's trade secrets arising from express provisions in the Datong employee code and, in the case of most of the employees, from confidentiality agreements that they signed during their employment with Datong. Thus, the question in this case is whether the disclosure of protected information in breach of that duty is beyond the reach of section 337 simply because the breach itself took place outside the United States. To answer that question in the affirmative would invite evasion of section 337 and significantly undermine the effectiveness of the congressionally designed remedy.

* * *

AFFIRMED.

MOORE, CIRCUIT JUDGE, dissenting.

The majority in this case expands the reach of both 19 U.S.C. § 1337 (§ 337) and trade secret law to punish TianRui Group Company Limited (TianRui) for its completely extraterritorial activities. As a court, however, we must act within the confines set out by the text of the law. Here, there is no basis for the extraterritorial application of our laws to punish TianRui's bad acts in China. As a result, I respectfully dissent.

The majority in this case holds that 19 U.S.C. § 1337(a)(1)(A), which applies to "unfair acts in the importation of articles . . . into the United States," allows the International Trade Commission (Commission) to bar imports because of acts of unfair competition occurring entirely in *China*. The majority states the issue: "The main issue in this case is whether § 337 authorizes the Commission to apply domestic trade secret law to conduct that occurs in part in a foreign country." With all due respect, that is not the issue. The issue is whether § 337 authorizes the Commission to apply domestic trade secret laws to conduct which *entirely* occurs in a foreign country.

The facts of this case are not disputed. A Chinese company, Datong, had a license from a United States company, Amsted, to use in China a process which Amsted kept secret. TianRui, the Chinese company accused of violating § 337 in this case, hired several employees from its Chinese competitor, Datong. These employees disclosed the trade secrets to TianRui in *China* who used them *in China* to make railway wheels *in China*. The acts which arguably constitute misappropriation (theft of a trade secret) all occurred in China.

To be clear, I agree that trade secret misappropriation falls squarely within the terms of § 337: if TianRui carried out its acts of misappropriation in the United States—namely if TianRui came to the United States and stole Amsted's trade secrets here—then § 337 could be used to bar import of any goods made with the stolen technology. But, as the majority concedes, these are not the facts of this case, and to the extent there was a misappropriation of any Amsted trade secret that misappropriation occurred abroad. In this case, *none* of the acts which constitute misappropriation occurred in the United States. While TianRui is certainly not a sympathetic litigant—it poached employees to obtain confidential information—none of the unfair acts occurred in the United States and, as such, there is no violation of United States law which amounts to an unfair trade practice under the statute.

DID YOU GET IT?

1. What is TianRui's argument as to why section 337 should not be applied in this case?

2. Why does the majority find that in this case the International Trade Commission could consider trade secret misappropriation that occurred in China?

3. Why is the dissent not persuaded by the majority's reasoning on the extraterritorial application of trade secret law in this case?

3. THE EU TRADE SECRET DIRECTIVE

On July 5, 2016, the *Directive (EU) 2016/943 of the European Parliament and of the Council of 8 June 2016 on the protection of undisclosed know-how and business information (trade secrets) against their unlawful acquisition, use and disclosure* (the EU Trade Secret Directive) entered into force, requiring all EU Member States to conform their laws to the Directive by June 9, 2018. (*See* Appendix B of this book). This Directive will lead to more uniformity in trade secret principles throughout Europe. Thus, whereas Article 39 of the TRIPS Agreement provides a helpful baseline for understanding the trade secret laws of countries that are members of the WTO, the EU Trade Secret Directive provides a more detailed explanation of the trade secret principles that are to be applied throughout the EU.

For the most part, the EU Trade Secret Directive tracks the UTSA and the DTSA, but there are some significant differences with respect to the limitations that are placed upon the scope of trade secret rights and the list of potential wrongdoing. *See* Sharon K. Sandeen, *Trade Secret Harmonization and the Search for Balance*, in the INTERNET AND THE EMERGING IMPORTANCE OF NEW FORMS OF INTELLECTUAL PROPERTY (2016). How the EU Trade Secret Directive is implemented in each EU Member State remains to be seen. Thus, as with all EU Directives, the individual laws of each EU Member State should be consulted to determine how the Directive is being implemented.

4. THE ENFORCEMENT OF TRADE SECRET RIGHTS

Knowing which country's laws apply to a particular business dispute and what those laws say about the protection of undisclosed information is only part of the process of determining if trade secret protection will be accorded in another country. Consideration must also be given to how those laws are applied and enforced.

As we have seen within the United States with respect to trade secret law as enforced under state law, even if the laws of two states are word-for-word identical, the actual implementation of the laws within a particular state may differ due to a number of factors. The same is true with respect to foreign countries, even if they are members of the WTO or the EU. For instance, there may be differences in how each country defines protectable information. Also, the nature of relationships that give rise to a duty of confidentiality may differ. Courts in some countries, like courts in some of the United States, may be more solicitous toward employees and be unwilling to grant broad injunctive relief that limits employee mobility. Procedural rules, including the scope of discovery, may limit the evidence that is available to prove misappropriation. Additionally, the judicial systems of some countries may not have the financial and court resources to consider a trade secret misappropriation claim in what the trade secret owner would consider to be timely manner. For a comparative review of the trade secret laws of Brazil, Canada, China, India, Japan, Mexico, and the United Kingdom, *see* Elizabeth A. Rowe & Sharon K. Sandeen, TRADE SECRECY AND INTERNATIONAL TRANSACTIONS (2015).

Given the uncertainties of protecting trade secrets outside of the United States, trade secret owners should think carefully about where their trade secrets are used and disclosed. As with disclosures that are made within the United States, the best practice is to obtain a written agreement of confidentiality before any disclosures are made. However, as a general matter, the fewer instances of disclosure, the better.

NOTES

1.   **The DTSA and extraterritoriality.** In *Tianrui*, an issue was raised concerning the law that should be applied, with the Administrative Law Judge feeling bound to follow Illinois law and the ITC ruling that it could apply a "single federal standard" to determine what constitutes an "unfair method of competition." This was a significant ruling given the fact that, at the time, there was no federal civil cause of action for trade secret misappropriation and, therefore, no federal jurisprudence on the issue of trade secrecy. With the enactment of the Defend Trade Secrets Act of 2016 (DTSA), the federal judiciary will now begin to develop a body of federal trade secret jurisprudence which may or may not conform to existing principles of state law.

One issue concerning the DTSA that the federal courts will be called upon to determine is the reach of the extraterritorial provision of the Economic Espionage Act of 1996 (EEA), which now applies to both federal criminal and civil claims for trade secret misappropriation. Title 18 of the United States Code, Section 1837 reads:

This chapter also applies to conduct occurring outside the United States if—

(1) the offender is a natural person who is a citizen or permanent resident alien of the United States, or an organization organized under the laws of the United States or a State or political subdivision thereof; or

(2) an act in furtherance of the offense was committed in the United States.

This provision has not proven sufficiently useful to be widely utilized by prosecutors under the EEA. Part of the reason is because prosecutors do not have the appropriate enforcement and service mechanisms to use against individuals who are outside of the United States. In other words, even if a lawsuit can be brought in the U.S. against an individual or company located outside of the U.S., how will any judgment in that case be enforced in the foreign country?

2. **Trade secrets in franchises.** Similar to the typical employer-employee relationship, the franchisor-franchisee relationship also involves the sharing of trade secrets. Franchisors, in allowing independent businesses to serve as franchisees, necessarily rely on a model wherein the franchisor must share details about its business operations in order for it to be replicated by the franchisee. Much of this information could be trade secret information about formulas, recipes, suppliers, etc. Accordingly, franchise agreements will often contain provisions regarding the use or disclosure of such confidential information. *See generally* Mark S. VanderBroek and Christian B. Turner, *Protecting and Enforcing Franchise Trade Secrets*, 25 FRANCHISE LAW JOURNAL 191 (2006).

3. **Reverse FOIA actions.** If a government agency receives a FOIA request for production of documents that the owner believes is a trade secret, and the agency intends to produce the document, the owner of the trade secret is entitled to file a "reverse FOIA action" against the agency in federal court to block the release of the information. In reviewing the agency's action, the court will examine the record developed by the agency to determine whether the agency's actions in determining whether the information was exempt from disclosure was arbitrary and capricious. The focus in reverse FOIA cases tends to be on the government agency's actions and on whether the agency created the appropriate record rather than on a trade-secret analysis. The substantive analysis is driven by whether the information was required or submitted voluntarily to the government. Accordingly, the trade-secret status of the information carries almost no relevance. *See* Elizabeth A. Rowe, *Striking a Balance: When Should Trade Secret Law Shield Disclosures to the Government?*, 96 IOWA L. REV. 791, 823–25 (2011).

4. **Data exclusivity and Article 39.3 of the TRIPS Agreement.** The federal law involved in *Ruckleshaus v. Monsanto Co.* is an example of a data exclusivity law whereby the government agrees to keep confidential for a

period of time information or data that is submitted to it as part of a regulatory process. The information is not necessarily trade secret information but is nonetheless protected by the government so that competitors of the submitter will not be able to use the same information to support their applications for regulatory approval. In this way, the companies that originate the information enjoy a statutory lead-time advantage of a fixed number of months or years. For instance, pursuant to the Federal Food, Drug, and Cosmetic Act, sections 505(c)(3)(E) and 505(j)(5)(F), data that is submitted to the Food and Drug Administration in relation to an application for a new pharmaceutical may be entitled to a period of exclusivity from 3 to 5 years.

In the negotiations that led to the TRIPS Agreement, the pharmaceutical and agro-chemical industries pushed for a provision which would require WTO-member countries to provide data exclusivity for information submitted to the government. *See* Aaron Xavier Fellmeth, *Secrecy, Monopoly, and Access to Pharmaceuticals in International Trade Law: Protection of Marketing Approval Data Under the TRIPS Agreement*, 45 HARV. INT'L L.J. 443 (2004). The end result of these efforts is a limited data exclusivity requirement as set forth in Article 39.3 of the TRIPS Agreement (set forth above). Greater data exclusivity rights are specified in subsequent Free Trade Agreements entered into by the United States.

Food for Thought

How does the information that is required to be protected under Article 39.3 of the TRIPS Agreement differ from the information that is required to be protected under Article 39.2? Is the scope of protected information under Article 39.3 greater or lesser than that which is protected under Article 39.2?

---

5. **Lessons from employee theft research.** In addition to the legal and technical considerations discussed in this chapter and in Chapter 8, the effective management and protection of trade secrets in the workplace could benefit from a holistic approach, incorporating lessons from the social sciences to better guide employer's protection strategies. Professor Elizabeth Rowe has studied how sociological theories about employee theft can offer useful insights into trade secret misappropriation and assist trade secret owners in devising strategies for trade secret protection.

> Employee theft theories have provided guidance to researchers in suggesting various prevention measures against theft. * * * A corporate culture that includes a focus on honesty and the benefits of and respect for intellectual property, including trade secrets, could reinforce to all workers, both management and non-management personnel, the importance of intellectual property protection and the consequences for misappropriation. Research has demonstrated that when the work environment is egotistic or based on self-interest, employees are more likely to engage in unethical behavior. Thus, * * * [employers should] promot[e] values that focus less on self-interest

and competitive goals, and more on the consequences of misappropriation. * * *

Punishment has a deterrent effect on other employees who might want to steal from an employer. Moreover, when punishment is inconsistent or unseen, it might have the opposite effect and encourage theft. Punishment for trade secret misappropriation generally involves two steps: first, termination from employment (frequently, however, the misappropriation is not discovered until the employee has left the company), and second, litigation against the employee, and possibly the new employer, for trade secret misappropriation. Taking such steps is consistent with * * * theories about punishment, and helps to send a message to remaining employees and to the new employer that such conduct will not be tolerated. It is also a highly visible way to raise awareness among employees about the risks of trade secret misappropriation, and to emphasize that the company takes protection of its secrets seriously.

The screening out of potential hires that might be most likely to steal trade secrets is intriguing. Indeed, there is a new measurement tool called an integrity test that purports to identify individuals' attitudes towards a variety of unacceptable behaviors, including stealing. Some researchers believe that integrity tests are a reliable and valid tool to determine who is likely to steal or display hostile tendencies. Others, however, question the validity of the tests.

Whether integrity tests will be a good predictor for trade secret theft is left to be seen. However, this kind of test, in combination with appropriate information gathering about prospective employees— such as the reason for leaving their previous employment or even their offering to use their previous employer's trade secrets in their new position—could be a useful predictive tool. It is worth a note of caution, however, that screening out broad classes of people is not advisable * * * [and] could * * * subject an employer to liability.

Elizabeth A. Rowe, *A Sociological Approach to Misappropriation*, 58 U. KAN. L. REV. 1, 28–30 (2009).

6.   **Bibliographic note:** For more information on the topics discussed in this chapter, see Elizabeth A. Rowe, *RATs, TRAPs, and Trade Secrets*, 57 B.C. L. REV. 381 (2016); Elizabeth A. Rowe and Sharon K. Sandeen, TRADE SECRECY AND INTERNATIONAL TRANSACTIONS (2015); John Craven, *Note: Fracking Secrets: The Limitations of Trade Secret Protection in Hydraulic Fracturing*, 16 VAND. J. ENT. & TECH. L. 395 (2014); Robert J. Rohrberger, *Trade Secret Issues in the Era of LinkedIn, Facebook and Blogs*, 2014 N.J. LAW. 42 (2014); Elizabeth A. Rowe and Daniel M. Mahfood, *Trade Secrets, Trade, and Extraterritoriality*, 66 ALABAMA L. REV. 63 (2014); Carlos M. Correa, *Test Data Protection: Rights Conferred Under the TRIPS Agreement and Some Effects of TRIPS-Plus Standards*, *in* Dreyfuss, R.C. & Strandburg, K.J., THE LAW AND THEORY OF TRADE SECRECY: A HANDBOOK OF CONTEMPORARY

RESEARCH, (Rochelle C. Dreyfuss & Katherine J. Strandburg, eds. 2011); Rebecca S. Einsenberg, *Data Secrecy in the Age of Regulatory Exclusivity*, *in* THE LAW AND THEORY OF TRADE SECRECY: A HANDBOOK OF CONTEMPORARY RESEARCH; David S. Levine, *The Impact of Trade Secrecy on Public Transparency*, THE LAW AND THEORY OF TRADE SECRECY: A HANDBOOK OF CONTEMPORARY RESEARCH; Christopher G. Blood, *Holding Foreign Nations Civilly Accountable for Their Economic Espionage Practices*, 42 IDEA 227 (2002); Carlos Correa, *Unfair Competition Under the Trips Agreement: Protection of Data Submitted for the Registration of Pharmaceuticals*, 3 CHI. J. INT'L L. 69 (2002).

CHAPTER 12

CRIMINAL CONSEQUENCES FOR TRADE SECRET MISAPPROPRIATION

■ ■ ■

Anticipated Learning Outcomes

At the conclusion of this chapter, you will understand the principal differences between a civil trade secret misappropriation case and a criminal trade secret misappropriation action. The bulk of the chapter focuses on the federal criminal statute governing trade secret theft, the Economic Espionage Act (EEA). The level of intent necessary for a conviction under the EEA, in addition to the various definitions utilized in the statute, will serve as useful contrasts to civil trade secret claims.

A. INTRODUCTION TO CRIMINAL TRADE SECRET ACTIONS UNDER STATE LAW

In addition to each state recognizing a claim for civil trade secret misappropriation under either the UTSA or common law, half of the states have enacted criminal laws that are specifically directed at trade secret theft. In these jurisdictions, it is therefore possible for a defendant in a civil trade secret misappropriation case to also face state criminal charges for the same alleged misappropriation. In states which do not have specific criminal trade secret statutes, statutes which prohibit larceny, property theft, or the receipt of stolen property may cover trade secret-claims, particularly if the alleged trade secrets are embodied in a tangible form. The difficulty in such cases often relates to the question of whether trade secrets can be considered property for the purpose of such crimes.

While an individual who misappropriates trade secrets may be subject to criminal prosecution, state criminal actions for trade secret theft are not very common. Among other reasons, state prosecutors are unlikely to use their limited resources to prosecute an economic crime where the victim-company has a readily available, and perhaps better suited, civil cause of action and remedy. When criminal actions are brought by state and federal prosecutors, they tend to involve egregious (or apparently egregious) instances of corporate or foreign espionage and cyber-hacking.

When a criminal trade secret action is filed, the prosecutors must prove that the information in question is a trade secret in much the same way as would be required in a civil action (unless the language of the statute suggests otherwise). Accordingly, the same kinds of evidence, such as efforts to preserve secrecy, are required. However, one important requirement under the criminal statutes is the *mens rea* (or "guilty mind") requirement. Generally, the defendant must have "knowingly" or "intentionally" misappropriated the trade secret which is considered to be a higher standard than the civil requirement that the defendant "know or have reason to know" that the trade secrets were misappropriated.

There may also be significant definitional differences between the civil trade secret statute and the criminal trade secret statute in the same state. For example, in a *Restatement of Torts* jurisdiction, the civil definition of a trade secret or of misappropriation may differ from that state's criminal statute (especially, if the state's criminal statute is modeled after the federal Economic Espionage Act or the UTSA). Sometimes in a civil UTSA jurisdiction, the criminal statute may define a trade secret to include only scientific or technical information, thus narrowing the scope of subject matter that can be prosecuted under the criminal statute. This appears to be the case, for instance, in Arkansas, New Hampshire, and Utah.

Notice in *Schalk v. State,* which follows, that the criminal definition of a trade secret in Texas does not appear to contain the "use" requirement of the *Restatement of Torts* definition. (This issue is not addressed in the opinion.) In *Clark v. State* you can also compare Texas' approach to Florida's, where the state criminal statute adopts a UTSA-like definition of a trade secret. Following these two cases, the remainder of the chapter addresses the federal Economic Espionage Act of 1996 (as amended by the Defend Trade Secrets Act of 2016 (the DTSA)) and a few of the cases in which courts have interpreted various provisions of that statute. The Special Issue section discusses whether a defendant in a trade secret case can refuse to answer questions or produce information based on the Fifth Amendment privilege against self-incrimination.

> ### Reading Guidance
> *How does the analysis in this case compare to that in a typical civil misappropriation case?*

SCHALK V. STATE OF TEXAS

Court of Appeals of Texas, Dallas, 1988.
767 S.W. 2d 441.

MCCLUNG, JUSTICE.

This is an appeal from a jury trial for the theft of trade secrets. Appellant was found guilty and assessed punishment at two years confinement and a fine of $5,000, probated for two years. Specifically, appellant was indicted under Texas Penal Code section 31.05 for knowingly making a copy of five separately identified computer programs that were the trade secrets of his employer.

Appellant contends that: 1) the evidence is insufficient to establish that the five computer programs listed in the indictment were, in fact, trade secrets; [and] 2) the evidence is insufficient to prove that appellant knowingly committed the offense charged. * * *

FACTS

The complainant, appellant's former employer, is a major corporation with world-wide facilities and engaged primarily in the electronics industry in various capacities. This case involves a computer programming area sometimes referred to as speech synthesis, or voice recognition. It can be described in an oversimplified manner as a computer software program that causes a device to respond in a specified manner to commands issued orally or by voice. The complainant is generally understood to be a pioneer in this field and an industry leader in the research and development of this type of programming for various applications.

The complainant kept and maintained a facility on their premises in Dallas designated as the "speech research laboratory" where this type of programming, research and development was conducted. Appellant had been employed by the complainant for approximately twelve years as an engineer in the speech laboratory. The laboratory was kept physically separated from other facilities within the confines of the overall premises. Access to the laboratory was limited to only certain authorized personnel, estimated to be something less than one hundred out of the several thousand that were admitted daily through the gates of the fences around the perimeter. The exterior gates were monitored by security guards around the clock. Speech laboratory employees were required to wear a certain type identity badge to gain access to the laboratory. Appellant, as an employee in this speech laboratory, was provided with the appropriate identity badge and was one of the limited group of employees granted access to the laboratory. * * *

As was customary with all laboratory employees, appellant had a "directory" designated as his and identified as such. Appellant's work product was saved or stored under this directory in the memory bank of the computer in the speech laboratory. Appellant also could, and did, store other data, programs and information in this same directory, some of which was personal to him. The speech laboratory computer equipment had the capability of receiving from, sending to, or copying to another medium, such as magnetic tape, any information stored in the memory when the appropriate instructions or commands were entered. Whenever a computer memory was accessed, the date, time, and identification of the user and the terminal was automatically logged into the memory. Appellant was experienced and very sophisticated in the use of this equipment and was a top level employee in the laboratory, working at a computer terminal regularly on a full time basis.

Appellant resigned his position with the complainant company to take a position as a vice-president with another company that also engaged in voice recognition and speech synthesis research and development. Although this new company was much smaller in overall size and scope and said to be utilizing a different method or system, the new employer was in fact a direct competitor of the complainant in the area of voice control technology. Appellant's background, knowledge, and experience in this field was a major factor in making the new job available to him.

Over a period of a few years, several other speech laboratory personnel had left the complainant's employment to take positions with this same new employer, primarily because their specialized knowledge in this field gave them unique qualifications that competitive companies would seek out. One such employee had occasion to see some information stored in the memory of the computer he was using on his new job that he believed he recognized and he thought belonged to his former employer, the complainant. Feeling something was amiss, this employee contacted complainant's company security to report what he had seen. (This informant acknowledged that he felt that he had been wrongfully terminated previously by the complainant and that he hoped that bringing this information to the complainant's attention would help get his old job back.) A series of meetings between security personnel and the informant took place and during these meetings, additional information was delivered. The informant was also recruited to act as a "mole" to search his employer's premises and equipment for further information or like material. The mole took several photos of various offices and their contents and made copies of some documents he thought belonged to the complainant and contained sensitive material. One of the photographs taken in appellant's office revealed a shelf containing one or more magnetic tapes of the type used to store computer data. Although the contents of the tapes were unknown at that time, at least one of them bore a label with the names of certain programs which the mole recognized from his former employment and job assignments with the complainant.

The information from the informant was passed along through the complainant's corporate structure, and an internal investigation within the speech laboratory took place. From the automatic entries made when the computer memory was accessed, the complainant determined that only a few hours before appellant left complainant's employ, a copy of the entire directory assigned to appellant was made onto a magnetic tape by someone using the personal access code assigned to the appellant. Imbedded within that directory and the information copied onto that tape from that directory were programs identified by the complainant to be trade secrets. Among these were the five programs that were ultimately made the subject of this indictment.

Armed with this information, complainant contacted the District Attorney. A search warrant for the premises of appellant's employer was obtained and executed shortly thereafter. During this search, the tape in question was among the items seized from appellant's office. Examination of the data recorded on the tape using compatible equipment revealed that it did, in fact, contain the five programs listed on the indictment. Appellant was arrested at the time the search warrant was executed at his place of employment.

Appellant does not dispute the fact that he did copy the directory that had a plethora of data recorded on it, or that the programs on the indictment were included, or that he took the tape with him when he left complainant's employ.

TRADE SECRET

Section 31.05(b)(2) of the Texas Penal Code, entitled "Theft of Trade Secrets," provides:

> A person commits an offense if, without the owner's effective consent, he knowingly makes a copy of an article representing a trade secret.

Section 31.05 defines a trade secret in subsection (a):

> "Trade secret" means the whole or any part of any scientific or technical information, design, process, procedure, formula or improvement that has value and that the owner has taken measures to prevent from becoming available to persons other than those selected by the owner to have access for limited purposes.

To be a "trade secret" within the clear meaning of this section, the information, design, process, procedure, formula or improvement must not only be a secret, but must also be generally unavailable to the public and it must give one who uses it an advantage over competitors that do not know of or use the trade secret. A fair reading of this section suggests that to qualify as a "trade secret," the article in question must meet a three prong test:

1) Be all or part of scientific or technical information,

2) Be of value to the owner,

3) Be protected by measures taken by the owner from access, except; those selected by the owner for limited purposes.

Appellant does not contest the first two prongs of the test, that is, the fact that the programs are a "part of any scientific or technical information . . .

that has value. . . ." Rather, he asserts in his first point of error that the evidence is insufficient to support the third prong: He contends that the complainant failed to designate the computer programs as trade secrets or prevent access to the computer where this information was stored; therefore, the complainant did not take measures to prevent access to them. Appellant argues that the programs in question were not trade secrets at the time he made the copy, or, if they had been, they had lost their status as trade secrets because the complainant had not protected them. Clearly, if an article that is a trade secret becomes known to the community, it loses its status as a trade secret. However, a limited disclosure to others pledged to secrecy will not destroy the trade secret's status as such. There is no question but that appellant was one of the limited persons that had been granted limited access to this information since his job function required him to work with this data on a regular basis. We must determine, therefore, if the data was ever a trade secret and, if so, whether it had lost its status as such for some reason at the time it was copied by appellant.

Appellant points out that several persons had been granted guest/user codes, including a summer intern who was allowed to utilize the laboratory equipment to write his college thesis. That intern testified, however, that he felt the information and codes entrusted to him were a secret and were not to be disclosed. Appellant argues that access could be gained through use of a telephone modem, but recognizes that it took the right kind of computer and user password to do so. Appellant claims that his superior, the Chief Speech Scientist and Branch Manager of the Speech Research Laboratory, had made a ten minute presentation at a seminar where he discussed the "concepts" involved concerning the series of programs listed on the indictment. Although concepts were briefly discussed, the algorithms used in the creations of the programs were not mentioned or disclosed. Appellant further maintains that certain data base programs were released to the National Bureau of Standards to aid them in establishing an industry standard. These programs were unrelated to those in the indictment. Appellant further argues that data was released to a university engaged in similar research. This release was only under a nondisclosure agreement. Appellant insists that the internal procedures manual provided to all employees set out the manner that trade secrets were to be identified and handled and these programs were not so identified. Significantly, the basic programs from which the items in question were derived were, in fact, listed in the Trade Secret Register kept by the complainant. While appellant points out certain areas that he feels show complainant's weaknesses in the security of the information, he presents no evidence to suggest that any of the series of programs in the indictment had ever been released to anyone outside the speech laboratory. The complainant vigorously and steadfastly denied that any of these programs and the algorithms had ever been published or given out to anyone and that none of complainant's speech recognition, speech synthesis, speaker verification, or voice verification software had ever been released nor had anyone ever been authorized to do so. Finally, appellant admitted that he had personally told fellow employees that such programs had not been given out. * * *

Turning to the statute, the pertinent portion reads *"that the owner has taken measures to prevent from becoming available to persons other than those selected by the owner. . . ."* This statute does not deal with the degree or extent to which an owner must go to protect a secret but simply specifies that for it to be an offense to copy information without the owners' permission, the owner must have taken some measures to protect the information from unauthorized disclosure. Although appellant's attack is directed more toward the type, degree, or extent of the measures taken to protect the data than it is toward the question of whether the ". . . owner has taken measures . . . " we, nevertheless, will treat this point as one of factual insufficiency and address the record under that standard.

The relevant question is whether, after viewing the evidence in the light most favorable to the prosecution, a rational trier of fact could find the essential elements of the offense beyond a reasonable doubt. * * *

This voluminous record is replete with evidence detailing the strict security measures taken by the complainant to prevent any and all information emanating from the speech laboratory from falling into the hands of unauthorized persons. All employees, including appellant, signed nondisclosure agreements when hired. This was a necessary condition of the employment of the appellant. Various applications of identification badges were provided to all employees and these badges had to be displayed at all times and places while on or about the premises. Different levels of security were applied to different areas and the badges carried features to delineate whether a particular employee was cleared to enter a particular area. The full time security guards, regular employees, receptionist, and so forth, were required to remain alert for anyone they might observe without a proper identification badge for a particular section or area. Visitors were subjected to sign-in procedures and were provided escorts and special identification badges. The entry gates were manned by security guards. Security guards were stationed in selected locations, and closed circuit television monitors were used throughout the building. Entry to the speech laboratory was limited to only a very small segment of the total employee population, and was contained in a separate wing or building and isolated with security doors from other areas. Within this area, all print-outs or hard copies of any data were kept put away. Night time security checks were made for data left out on desks. In the event any documents were seen by security personnel during routine off-hour inspections, they were put away and the incident made the subject of a report.

Appellant was assigned a password or access code which allowed limited access to some information stored in the computer memory but other data stored in restricted directories was not available. Any access at all required certain code clearance or password information to be given before the computer would respond. A highly confidential Trade Secret Register was kept and maintained as a permanent record in the legal department which contained reference to the "speech processing" programs being utilized in the laboratory. Employees in the laboratory were given an admonition that they were to protect any software programs being used, developed, or being researched by the laboratory. In addition, an "exit" interview was conducted with any employee whose job involved sensitive proprietary and confidential information by a member of the Legal Department staff for the specific purpose of re-emphasizing their non-disclosure responsibility upon termination.

We conclude that these facts are sufficient for this jury, as a rational trier of fact, to find beyond a reasonable doubt that these elaborate security precautions were taken by the owner/complainant to protect its information, that such information was secret and intended by the owner to remain so. Having determined that the evidence is sufficient to meet the test of "measures taken by the owner to protect," we hold the programs listed in the indictment were trade secrets as defined in Texas Penal Code section 31.05(a). Appellant's point of error number one is overruled.

KNOWLEDGE

In his second point of error, appellant maintains that the evidence is insufficient to prove that he "knowingly" made copies of trade secrets. Appellant having admitted that he made the copy, and our having previously held the items to be trade secrets, we then come to the question of whether appellant "knew" the items were trade secrets when he made the copy, thus that he acted knowingly as set out in Texas Penal Code section 31.05(b)(2). The necessary culpable mental state is described in Texas Penal Code section 6.03(b) thusly:

> A person acts knowingly, or with knowledge, with respect to the nature of his conduct or to circumstances surrounding his conduct when he is aware of the nature of his conduct or that the circumstances exist. A person acts knowingly, or with knowledge, with respect to a result of his conduct when he is aware that his conduct is reasonably certain to cause the result.

* * *

Because appellant had been a full time, high level employee in the speech laboratory for twelve years, he had been subjected to the elaborate security precautions implemented by his employer every day. The controlled physical access to the plant through the use of guards, employee identification badges, visitor escorts and special sign-in procedures, confidential materials kept locked up or destroyed when no longer needed, closed circuit television monitoring, and the necessity of the regular use of secret identity codes on the computer all served as a constant reminder of the restricted environment in which appellant worked. Appellant signed a nondisclosure agreement when he was hired. He discussed the need for secrecy and the nature of the confidential aspects of their work with his immediate superior and fellow employees on a regular basis during his employment. Periodic staff meetings were held where the nature and progress of their work was discussed and the subject of much of the discussions was the secret and confidential aspects of work appellant and his fellow employees were doing. The value of work and how it did or would affect the complainant's competitive position in the general market place was a significant factor discussed in the regular staff meetings.

Appellant, during his testimony at trial, stated that it would have taken hours to have gone through the numerous programs and data in his directory to selectively pick out items for copying, so in the interest of time, he intentionally entered the commands that would copy all files in the directory, knowing that all files would be copied. He further stated that he had worked on the files that were in his directory and was familiar with them and what they were, but that he did not consider them to be trade secrets; that they were not so marked or designated in the computer and that they were readily accessible to him.

Significantly, appellant not only copied his own entire directory, but also copied one other directory called the "speech utility" directory. He did so very close to his last day on the job, and used his secret identity code to gain access to all of this data for copying. In his exit interview, which took place as one of the last official events on the job, he signed a document titled Trade Secret Listing for Termination of Employment where he acknowledged that his nondisclosure responsibility and the confidentiality of his work was discussed. Appellant testified he felt he had a right to copy and take anything he was interested in because he never had any intention of using this information. The issue of whether the data and information in question was wrongfully used is not before us. There was also testimony that during the time appellant was in the employ of the new company, he was heard to make reference to items belonging to the complainant as the "stolen data base" and the "stolen files," on a periodic basis.

We hold this evidence is sufficient to support the finding by the jury that appellant knowingly made copies of protected programs that were of value to his employer. Appellant's second point of error is overruled.

* * *

DID YOU GET IT?

1. What is the appellant's argument as to the trade secret status of the information at issue in this case?

2.   What facts supported the courts finding on the appellant's level of intent in this case?

3.   In what way is the definition of trade secret under this statute more limited than under the UTSA?

Food for Thought

Why is the intent requirement for a crime typically greater than it is for a related civil action? What other features of criminal law make it more difficult to obtain a criminal conviction than a civil judgment?

Reading Guidance

How does the Florida criminal statute in this case compare to the Texas statute in Schalk?

CLARK V. STATE

District Court of Appeal, 2nd District Florida, 1996.
670 So.2d 1056.

PATTERSON, ACTING CHIEF JUDGE.

Noel Clark appeals from his conviction for theft of trade secrets in violation of section 812.081, Florida Statutes (1993). We reverse Clark's conviction because the materials at issue are not "trade secrets."

Norman Frick owned and operated "Resale Specialists," a company engaged in the sale of mobile homes on leased lots. In December 1993, Frick hired Clark to manage his rental division. Soon after, upon Clark's request, Frick also allowed him to make sales. Clark was a licensed real estate salesperson, and he obtained authorization to sell mobile homes on leased lots.

Frick's business operated much like a standard real estate sales office based on exclusive listings, or right of sale agreements. From these listing agreements were compiled information sheets for the use of Frick's employees, and others, as an aid in the sale of mobile homes. The information sheets contained the name and address of the owner and general information on the property such as the number and size of rooms and amenities. Copies of the information sheets were compiled in several books kept in the office. Frick gave one of these books to Clark at the time of his employment.

Clark proved to be an effective salesperson and obtained contracts for sale on several units within a number of weeks. Prior to the closings, Clark alleges that he obtained information from the State of Florida that Frick's license to sell mobile homes, issued by the Department of Motor Vehicles, had not been timely renewed. Clark asserts that he confronted Frick with the information and questioned the legal right to close the transactions and receive commissions. No immediate resolution was reached.

On January 15, 1994, Clark went to the business office, collected certain of his personal property, and waited for Frick to arrive. A confrontation resulted wherein Clark told Frick he was retaining the information sheets "as evidence" which Frick could obtain through "court proceedings." He then demanded that Frick close the pending sales through a licensed dealer and deposit the commission proceeds in the court registry. Frick refused and Clark left.

Frick contacted the Lee County Sheriff's Department and reported that Clark had burglarized the office and stolen various items of property, including the information sheets. Clark was interviewed, waived his constitutional right to remain silent, and basically recounted the above facts. Clark and Frick then filed civil lawsuits against one another.

For reasons not apparent to this court, this civil dispute of modest proportions escalated into a criminal prosecution wherein Clark was charged with theft of trade secrets (a third-degree felony), petit theft (a misdemeanor), and burglary of a structure (a third-degree felony). A jury trial resulted in his conviction for theft of trade secrets and his acquittal on the remaining two offenses.

Clark has raised numerous issues on appeal. The only issue we need to address to reverse Clark's conviction is whether the "information sheets" are protected materials under section 812.081, Florida Statutes (1993), which provides in pertinent part:

> 812.081 Trade secrets; theft, embezzlement; unlawful copying; definitions; penalty.—
>
> . . . .
>
> (c) "Trade secret" means the whole or any portion or phase of any formula, pattern, device, combination of devices, or compilation of information which is for use, or is used, in the operation of a business and which provides the business an advantage, or an opportunity to obtain an advantage, over those who do not know or use it.

Confining our determination to the facts of this case, the "information sheets" neither provide Frick's business an advantage or an opportunity to obtain an advantage over competitors. They are of little or no significance because the underlying exclusive sales agreement is the document from which Frick derives his advantage. In fact, these "information sheets," much like the same written materials in the real estate trade, derive their value from their use in effecting sales to which Frick is the benefactor. The sheets were available for inspection and use by outside salespersons showing the homes. One such person testified that she would hold "open houses" of the listed properties and pass out copies of the sheets to prospective buyers. Clearly, these materials were not secret or confidential and do not constitute "trade secrets." We, therefore, reverse Clark's conviction for theft of trade secrets and direct that he be discharged.

Reversed.

* * *

ALTENBERND, JUDGE, concurring specially.

I agree the state failed to prove that these specific information sheets were "trade secrets" taken with the "intent to deprive" as required in section 812.081(2), Florida Statutes (1993). I write only to emphasize that similar documents could be in the nature of a "list of customers," as discussed in section 812.081(1)(c), and could contain information providing a business advantage. An entire book of such information sheets might be a trade secret, even though individual sheets were shared with potential buyers. Thus, I do not regard this case as holding, as a matter of law, that a realtor's book of information sheets is never a trade secret.

DID YOU GET IT?

1. What are the main differences in the definition of a trade secret between this Florida statute and the Texas statute in *Schalk*?

2. Why was the defendant's conviction overturned in this case?

3. Would the definition of a trade secret in this statute be consistent with one that was adopted in large part from a civil UTSA jurisdiction?

B. BACKGROUND OF THE ECONOMIC ESPIONAGE ACT

In addition to available criminal sanctions under state law, there are a number of federal statutes that aim to punish behavior associated with trade secret misappropriation. The most directly applicable federal statute is the Economic Espionage Act of 1996 (EEA), as amended, which makes trade secret misappropriation a federal crime under specified situations. Criminal defendants who wrongfully access computer databases may also be charged with a violation of the federal Computer Fraud and Abuse Act (18 U.S.C. § 1030) or the federal wire and mail fraud statutes (18 U.S.C. §§ 1341 and 1443). Also, based upon changes made to the EEA by the DTSA, criminal trade secret misappropriation is now a predicate act under the Racketeer Influenced and Corrupt Organization Act (18 U.S.C. §§ 1961–1968). Finally, as with state law, a variety of other federal criminal statutes might apply related to possession of stolen property and the movement of such property over state lines.

Unlike state civil trade secret schemes, like the UTSA, the EEA is a relative newcomer to the scene. It was signed by President Bill Clinton on

October 11, 1996 and was subsequently amended twice, most recently by the DTSA.

Prior to the enactment of the EEA, federal prosecutors wanting to charge a defendant with theft of trade secrets had to utilize other federal criminal statutes such as those prohibiting mail fraud and wire fraud. However, one limitation of the mail and wire fraud statutes was that the alleged trade secret theft had to utilize mail or wire services. The stated intent of the EEA was to protect "trade secrets of all businesses operating in the United States, foreign and domestic alike, from economic espionage and trade secret theft." Economic Espionage Act of 1996, Pub. L. No. 104–294, 110 Stat.3488 (Statement by President William Clinton upon signing.)

The legislative history of the EEA suggests that it was motivated by three concerns. First, trade secrets were of growing importance to the United States' economy and this economic strength had national security implications. Second, reported incidents of trade secret theft, especially by foreign companies and foreign governments, were increasing. Finally, the existing federal criminal statutes were not suitable for addressing trade secret theft, especially in light of the rise of new digital technologies. The political climate was also supportive. The end of the Cold War brought fears that foreign governments would use their military spying capabilities to steal trade secrets from United States companies.

Ultimately, the enactment of the EEA signified a recognition that the protection of trade secrets is in the national interest of the United States. *See* Chris Carr *et al., The Economic Espionage Act: Bear Trap or Mouse Trap?*, 8 Tex. Intell. Prop. L. J. 159, 161 (2000). Trade secret theft, both foreign and domestic, whether conducted by individuals or corporations (corporate espionage), has wide reaching implications. It can affect national security, the economic stability of businesses, and threaten research and development efforts. The following excerpt by Professor Elizabeth Rowe discusses how the internet and technology have heightened the problem of cyber espionage, especially as it pertains to foreign actors.

RATs, TRAPs, and Trade Secrets
Elizabeth A. Rowe.
57 Boston College L. Rev. 381, 394–400 (2016).

Because it is easier to access intangible information from anywhere in the world, and to do so in a manner that is unlikely to be detected, the Internet has vastly expanded the potential threat of actors successfully reaching and accessing American trade secrets. Even when foreign offenders are identified and espionage charges may be filed under the EEA, prosecution in the United States can be severely hindered. Complicating prosecution is the fact that offenders who live outside the United States would need to be extradited back to the United States, and not all countries permit extradition for these types of offenses. Although the EEA includes a provision for extraterritorial jurisdiction for acts of trade secret misappropriation even if outside the United States, in practice it is not a meaningful remedy. Prosecutors do not have the appropriate enforcement and service mechanisms with which to serve individuals and entities that are not located in the United States. In reality, violators cannot fully be charged and indicted under a system unless and until they are within its borders. * * *

Threats from cyber espionage have been framed as threats to our national security. According to President Obama, it is "one of the most serious economic and national security challenges," and a "rapidly growing threat." Heads of the FBI and national intelligence agencies have identified the cyber threat as the top global threat facing America, rivaling and even surpassing that of terrorism. * * *

Foreign governments have used strategic cyberattacks in growing numbers, and some view these as geopolitical assaults on the United States. * * * Many countries, including Russia, France, Israel, India, Japan, Taiwan, and China, allegedly engage in cyber espionage against U.S. companies. In our rhetoric of war, however, one public enemy emerges in the narrative, and that appears to be China. According to one public official, "[The Chinese] are stealing everything that isn't bolted down, and it's getting exponentially worse." One report accuses the Chinese of being "the world's most active and persistent perpetrators of economic espionage." The close relationship between the Chinese military and its state-owned companies might also contribute to its position as chief culprit. The U.S. government believes that up to fifty percent of the Chinese economy is controlled by the state, and that industrial espionage is an articulated mission of its intelligence services. Both the government and private companies have also implicated China in alleged thefts of proprietary and trade secret information.

China has denied the allegations and has stated its official position against hacking. Chinese Premier Li Keqiang also seeks an end to the "groundless accusations," and Chinese diplomats have denounced reports of Chinese espionage as "baseless, unwarranted and irresponsible." Moreover, because hackers can disguise the source of their attacks by spoofing an Internet Provider address ("IP address"), it is possible that attacks that appear to be coming from China might actually have originated elsewhere, including within the United States. Whether the enemy is a Chinese attacker, a Russian crime group, or an angry former employee, a focus on protecting and defending one's own proprietary information, rather than relying on the government to fight an enemy or battle, is ultimately the most productive and effective way to stem the loss of company trade secrets.

C. OVERVIEW OF THE ECONOMIC ESPIONAGE ACT OF 1996

The first two sections of the EEA, 18 U.S.C. §§ 1831 and 1832, establish two different types of offenses under the Act. Section 1831 is the provision on foreign economic espionage. It prohibits targeting or acquiring trade secrets to benefit a foreign government or agent. It reads as follows:

§ 1831. Economic espionage

(a) In general. Whoever, intending or knowing that the offense will benefit any foreign government, foreign instrumentality, or foreign agent, knowingly—

  (1) steals, or without authorization appropriates, takes, carries away, or conceals, or by fraud, artifice, or deception obtains a trade secret;

  (2) without authorization copies, duplicates, sketches, draws, photographs, downloads, uploads, alters, destroys, photocopies, replicates, transmits, delivers, sends, mails, communicates, or conveys a trade secret;

  (3) receives, buys, or possesses a trade secret, knowing the same to have been stolen or appropriated, obtained, or converted without authorization;

  (4) attempts to commit any offense described in any of paragraphs (1) through (3); or

  (5) conspires with one or more other persons to commit any offense described in any of paragraphs (1) through (3), and one or more of such persons do any act to effect the object of the conspiracy,

  shall, except as provided in subsection (b), be fined not more than $5,000,000 or imprisoned not more than 15 years, or both.

(b) Organizations. Any organization that commits any offense described in subsection (a) shall be fined not more than $10,000,000 or 3 times the value of the stolen trade secret to the organization, including expenses for research and design and other costs of reproducing the trade secret that the organization has thereby avoided.

Section 1832 of the EEA (as amended by the DTSA) prohibits the same type of conduct as in section 1831, except that it does not require a benefit to a foreign government, instrumentality, or agent. Accordingly, this is the section that is used in most prosecutions. It reads:

§ 1832. Theft of trade secrets

(a) Whoever, with intent to convert a trade secret, that is related to or included in a product that is produced for or placed in interstate or foreign commerce, to the economic benefit of anyone other than the owner thereof, and intending or knowing that the offense will, injure any owner of that trade secret, knowingly—

    (1) steals, or without authorization appropriates, takes, carries away, or conceals, or by fraud, artifice, or deception obtains such information;

    (2) without authorization copies, duplicates, sketches, draws, photographs, downloads, uploads, alters, destroys, photocopies, replicates, transmits, delivers, sends, mails, communicates, or conveys such information;

    (3) receives, buys, or possesses such information, knowing the same to have been stolen or appropriated, obtained, or converted without authorization;

    (4) attempts to commit any offense described in paragraphs (1) through (3); or

    (5) conspires with one or more other persons to commit any offense described in paragraphs (1) through (3), and one or more of such persons do any act to effect the object of the conspiracy, shall, except as provided in subsection (b), be fined under this title or imprisoned not more than 10 years, or both.

(b) Any organization that commits any offense described in subsection (a) shall be fined not more than the greater of $5,000,000 or 3 times the value of the stolen trade secret to the organization, including expenses for research and design and other costs of reproducing the trade secret that the organization has thereby avoided.

In recent years, changes have been made to enhance the penalty provisions under the EEA. The Foreign and Economic Espionage Penalty Enhancement Act of 2013 provides that if convicted of a violation of section 1831 of the EEA, an individual is subject to a sentence of 15 years in prison and a fine of $5,000,000 (formerly $500,000), while a corporation can be fined not more than the greater of $10 million or 3 times the value of the stolen trade secret to the organization (formerly $10 million). The DTSA increased the financial penalties under section 1832. The penalty under section 1832 specifies: 10 years in prison for an individual, or a fine of up to the greater of $5 million for a corporation or 3 times the value of the stolen trade secret to the organization. Unlike in section 1831, the maximum fine for an individual is not specified. Having not provided a specified fine, the maximum fine of $250,000 set in 18 U.S.C. § 3571(b)(3) for felony offenses is likely to serve as the ceiling.

The EEA also contains a forfeiture provision, section 1834, which provides that, in addition to any sentence imposed, the court shall order that the defendant forfeit any property constituting the alleged trade secret, derived from it, or used to commit the violation.

Food for Thought

Note the mens rea required under both sections 1831 and 1832. Does it differ from the type of intent or knowledge required under the UTSA and the DTSA? If so, how?

The intent requirement of the EEA can be difficult to meet. However, because both sections 1831 and 1832 make it a crime to attempt or conspire to commit any of the offenses delineated in those sections, in practice, prosecutors often charge trade secret offenses as attempts or conspiracies. *See e.g., U.S. v. Hsu,* 40 F.Supp.2d 623 (E.D. Pa. 1999). A question that prosecutions under the EEA raise is whether the defendants who must have intended to misappropriate information that constitutes trade secrets or whether it need only be shown that the defendants thought that the targeted information constituted trade secrets. *Compare U.S. v. Chung,* 633 F.Supp.2d 1134 (C.D. Cal 2009) with *U.S. v. Hanjuan Jin,* 833 F.Supp.2d 977 (N. D. Ill 2012) (holding that the defendant need only know that the information is "proprietary.")

In keeping with the due process requirement that criminal statutes not be vague, the EEA has its own definition of a trade secret which, while modeled after the UTSA's definition, is slightly different. Section 1839 of the EEA, as amended by the DTSA, states:

§ 1839. Definitions

As used in this chapter [18 USCS §§ 1831 et seq.]

* * *

(3)   the term "trade secret" means all forms and types of financial, business, scientific, technical, economic, or engineering information, including patterns, plans, compilations, program devices, formulas, designs, prototypes, methods, techniques, processes, procedures, programs, or codes, whether tangible or intangible, and whether or how stored, compiled, or memorialized physically, electronically, graphically, photographically, or in writing if—

(A)   the owner thereof has taken reasonable measures to keep such information secret; and

(B) the information derives independent economic value, actual or potential, from not being generally known to, and not being readily ascertainable through proper means by, another person who can obtain economic value from the disclosure or use of the information;

(4) the term "owner," with respect to a trade secret, means the person or entity in whom or in which rightful legal or equitable title to, or license in, the trade secret is reposed:

* * *

Food for Thought

Identify the ways that the EEA's (and therefore the DTSA's) definition of a trade secret differs from the UTSA's definition of a trade secret. Why do you think the EEA definition is more detailed than the UTSA's definition?

Finally, the EEA has an extraterritoriality provision, allowing it to reach conduct occurring outside the United States in specified situations. Section 1837 reads:

§ 1837. Applicability to conduct outside the United States

This chapter also applies to conduct occurring outside the United States if

(1) the offender is a natural person who is a citizen or permanent resident alien of the United States, or an organization organized under the laws of the United States or a State or political subdivision thereof; or

(2) an act in furtherance of the offense was committed in the United States.

While the EEA always empowered courts to enter protective orders to protect the confidentiality of the trade secrets (18 U.S.C. § 1835), companies were often reluctant to report incidents of trade secret theft to the government for fear that their trade secrets would not be protected during the government's prosecution of the case, thus leading to a potential loss of trade secrets. To address this concern, the DTSA added a new subsection to section 1835 which reads:

(b) RIGHTS OF TRADE SECRET OWNERS.—The court may not authorize or direct the disclosure of any information the owner asserts to be a trade secret unless the court allows the owner the opportunity to file a submission under seal that describes the interest of the owner in keeping the information confidential. No submission under seal made under this subsection may be used in a prosecution under this chapter for any purpose other than those set forth in this section, or otherwise required by law. The provision of information relating to a trade secret to the United States or the court in connection with a prosecution under this chapter shall not constitute a waiver of trade secret protection, and the disclosure of information relating to a trade secret in connection with a prosecution under this chapter shall not constitute a waiver of trade secret protection unless the trade secret owner expressly consents to such waiver.

> ### Food for Thought
> *Read section 1835(b) in the context of the entire section. Are the rights of trade secret owners that it describes limited to criminal prosecutions or might they also apply in civil cases?*

As with any statute, the provisions of the EEA contain some ambiguity and the constitutionality of the Act has been challenged. As you will see from the cases that follow, the courts have had to wrestle with some of the same trade secrecy requirements that arise in civil cases. The first case to be tried under the EEA was *United States v. Hsu*.

> ### Reading Guidance
> *On what basis do these defendants challenge the Economic Espionage Act?* vagueness

UNITED STATES V. HSU

United States District Court, E.D. Pennsylvania, 1999.
40 F.Supp.2d 623.

– Ct. denies motion to dismiss
– held the terms were not uncon. vague
– facts – Hsu's behavior showed he knew it was not "generally known" "readily ascer."

[Note that the jurisdictional clause at issue in *Hsu* was subsequently amended by Congress pursuant to the Theft of Trade Secret Clarification Act of 2012 which went into effect on December 28, 2012. The new language is reflected in Appendix A of this book.]

* * *

DALZELL, DISTRICT JUDGE.

Defendant Kai-Lo Hsu argues that the recently-enacted Economic Espionage Act, 18 U.S.C. § 1831 *et seq.* ("EEA"), is unconstitutionally vague. Hsu's motion to dismiss the EEA charges in Counts Ten and Eleven of the Indictment raises serious concerns about the scope and clarity of the EEA that we at some length address here.

Defendant's Vagueness Argument

Hsu is charged in the Indictment with, *inter alia,* conspiracy to steal trade secrets in violation of 18 U.S.C. § 1832(a)(5) (Count Ten), and attempted theft of trade secrets in violation of 18 U.S.C. § 1832(a)(4) (Count Eleven).

[margin note: — D's arguments for vagueness]

In his motion to dismiss Counts Ten and Eleven of the Indictment, Hsu argues that the EEA is unconstitutionally vague in two respects. First, he contends that the statute is unlawfully vague in that it fails to define the term "related to or included in" a product that is produced for or placed in interstate or foreign commerce. Second, Hsu argues that the definition of "trade secret" in 18 U.S.C. § 1839(3) offends due process with its vagueness because it does not define either "reasonable measures" to keep the information secret, or what is meant by information not being "generally known" or "readily ascertainable" to the public.

The Legal Landscape

It is well-recognized that due process requires a penal statute to "define [a] criminal offense with sufficient definiteness that ordinary people can understand what conduct is prohibited and in a manner that does not encourage arbitrary and discriminatory enforcement." The void for vagueness doctrine, however, does not mean that a statute is unconstitutionally vague where "Congress might, without difficulty, have chosen 'clearer and more precise language' equally capable of achieving the end which it sought."

It has also been the experience, as Professor Anthony Amsterdam observed almost forty years ago, that "legislation creating 'new' crimes (which does not generically tend to be unclear, but is likely to represent affirmative legislative intrusion into realms previously left to individual freedom) is particularly vulnerable to vagueness attack." The EEA certainly constitutes such legislation, criminalizing, as it does, conduct that heretofore was thought best left to the civil law of unfair competition and cognate jurisprudence.

The developed case law recognizes that when, as here, the First Amendment is not implicated, a void for vagueness challenge must be unconstitutional as applied to the defendant and "must be examined in light of the facts of the case at hand."

Analysis

* * *

"Related to or included in"

[margin note: — Ct. rejects D's argument]

We reject Hsu's argument that the term "related to or included in a product that is produced for or placed in interstate or foreign commerce" is unacceptably vague. The cases he cites in support of his argument are all First Amendment decisions in which the only connection to what is at stake here is the fact that the cases involve the use of the term *related.* We believe the term "related to or included in" is readily understandable to one of ordinary intelligence, particularly here where the defendant appears to be well versed as to the relationship (and technological differences) between "first generation" and "second generation" taxol technology [the technology that defendant Hsu is accused of attempting and conspiring to steal].

"Reasonable Measures"

Similarly, we also find that the EEA's definition of "trade secret"—requiring, in part, that the owner take "reasonable measures" to keep such information secret—is also not for use of that locution void for vagueness. First, a statute is not void for vagueness merely because it uses the word "reasonable" or "unreasonable". In sustaining the antitrust "rule of reason" as sufficiently definite even in a criminal prosecution, Justice Holmes observed, with his customary sensitivity to human frailty, that "the law is full of instances where a man's fate depends on his estimating rightly, that is, as the jury subsequently estimates it, some matter of degree. If his judgment is wrong, not only may he incur a fine or a short imprisonment . . . ; he may incur the penalty of death."

The Government has here pointed out that the definition of "trade secret" is taken, "with only minor modifications," from the definition used in the Uniform Trade Secret Act (UTSA), which has apparently been adopted in forty states and the District of Columbia, and the language has withstood at least one vagueness attack.

Finally, as applied here, it is clear that Hsu and his alleged co-conspirator, Jessica Chou, were told on several occasions (in e-mails, telephone conversations, and in-person meetings) that the taxol technology in question was proprietary to BMS and Phyton, could not be acquired via a license or joint venture (as the cost would be too high), and that they would have to "get [it] another way," namely, through an allegedly corrupt BMS employee. Hsu thus knew that BMS had taken many steps to keep its technology to itself, and therefore he will not be heard to quibble with the ductility of "reasonable measures" as applied to him in this case.

how D knew it wasn't generally known to public / read ascert.

"Generally known to" and "not being readily ascertainable" through proper means by the public

At the outset, the issue of whether "second generation" taxol technology is "generally known to" and not "readily ascertainable" to the public is a question that we (and the parties) have struggled with since the inception of this case. After the June 14, 1997 sting operation at the Four Seasons Hotel, in August, 1997 two BMS scientists, Dr. Nikhil Mehta and Dr. Norman Lacroix, were enlisted by BMS and the Government to review the documents shown to the defendant at the Four Seasons Hotel ("the June 14th documents") and to redact all "confidential" information contained therein. As our February 16, 1999 Memorandum illustrates, even Dr. Mehta and Dr. Lacroix could not agree about what information in the June 14th documents was "confidential" and what information was public.

After an interlocutory appeal in which the Government soothingly assured the Court of Appeals panel that the redactions to the June 14th documents "consist of technical information that constitutes trade secrets under any definition," BMS enlisted Dr. Pallaiah Thammana, the Associate Director of Biotechnical Development at BMS, to undertake a complete reevaluation of the redactions to the June 14th documents. After Dr. Thammana's reevaluation of the June 14th documents, over *one hundred* pages that had previously been redacted by Dr. Mehta and Dr. Lacroix were then unredacted as public information.

Finally, at the urging of our Court of Appeals, we undertook an *in camera* review of the redactions made to the June 14th documents. While we (perhaps immodestly) consider ourselves of "ordinary" intelligence, after an *in camera* review of the June 14th documents, in both their newly-redacted and unredacted forms, it became clear to us that "the issue of whether the June 14th documents had been properly redacted to exclude only trade secret information required technical expertise far beyond our capabilities." Accordingly, with the consent of the parties, we enlisted the assistance of Dr. Kenneth Snader from the National Cancer Institute as our technical advisor to review the June 14th documents in both their redacted and unredacted forms. After his exhaustive analysis, Dr. Snader suggested that we unredact yet another ten pages in the June 14th documents because they are truly public information.

At oral argument on the current motion, we asked counsel for the Government to explain how the terms "generally known" and not "readily ascertainable" by the public could be anything but vague in relation to taxol technology, particularly given the ever-shrinking redactions to the June 14th documents against the very same "trade secret" definition. In response, counsel for the Government argued that while it was a difficult undertaking to determine whether the June 14th documents actually contained trade secret information within the meaning of the EEA, ultimately the trade secret status of the June 14th documents did not matter to the outcome of this case because Hsu is charged only with the inchoate offenses of attempt and conspiracy. At oral argument, the Government pointed to our Court of Appeals' August, 1998 decision in which the panel made it clear that the Government need not prove at trial that an actual trade secret was used during the investigation, because the defendant's culpability for a charge of attempt depends only on the circumstances as the defendant *believes* them to be and not as they really are.

While the Government's position is legally accurate, it is quite troubling in the context of this particular statute. Unlike statutes that prohibit, for example, murder (or attempted murder), bribery (or attempted bribery), or distribution of cocaine (or conspiracy to distribute cocaine), where there is a clearly defined end (*e.g.*, the definitions of murder, bribery, and cocaine are fixed), here, where a "trade secret" is based on intangible and evolving concepts and ideas, and where the definition of a "trade secret" is based, in part, on what is "generally known" or "readily ascertainable" to the public, the analysis is considerably more problematic.

A hypothetical illustrates the difficulty of the Government's argument. Assume Congress passed a statute making it a crime to be "bad" or to "attempt to be bad" and the definition of "bad" was "what people generally know as really bad or evil." On its face, such a statute is palpably and unlawfully vague. Yet as applied to Dr. Hannibal "the cannibal" Lecter (in *The Silence of the Lambs*), such a statute would not be unconstitutionally vague, as all but the criminally insane would agree that Dr. Lecter is "bad."[6] As applied to Little Mary Sunshine, however, such a statute would be unconstitutionally vague because no reasonable person would call her morally "bad."[7]

Turning specifically to the EEA, it is in many ways more problematic than our badness statute because, unlike our imagined law, what is "generally known" and "reasonably ascertainable" about ideas, concepts, and technology is constantly evolving in the modern age. With the proliferation of the media of communication on technological subjects, and (still) in so many languages, what is "generally known" or "reasonably ascertainable" to the public at any given time is necessarily never sure.

Furthermore, when the EEA states that the information must be generally known and not readily ascertainable "by the public," to whom does it refer? The "general" public? The "scientific" public? The "commercial" public? The "judicial" public? Prior to this case we had not heard of the cancer drug Taxol (and had never heard of the plant cell culture process to produce it)- does that ignorance in and of itself make taxol technology not "generally known"? If a large quantity of information about taxol technology is available on the Internet and in published journals (which it is), or if those subjects were discussed at scientific conferences abroad (they were), do those realities make it "readily ascertainable"?

While we are thus much troubled by the EEA's vaporous terms, as applied to the facts of *this* case and *this* defendant we nevertheless find that the term "generally known to, and not being readily ascertainable through

---

[6]   Theoretically, Dr. Lecter's conviction for the completed offense of badness would be based, in part, on a battle of expert witnesses over what the public "knows" and whether the general public would regard Dr. Lecter as really bad or evil.

[7]   We hasten to add that we make no judgment as to her taste, however. We do note that if Little Mary Sunshine decided that she wanted to be in her heart bad, and really *believed* that she was then being bad, she could be prosecuted under our hypothetical statute for attempted badness. At oral argument we posed a similar question to the Assistant United States Attorney (albeit in a hypothetical involving the recipe for an angel food cake), to which he answered that the U.S. Attorney's office would use its discretion and not prosecute such cases. It is precisely this type of prosecutorial discretion, however, that is so unsettling. We are indeed aware of no instance in which a vague statute has been deemed constitutionally safe because we can all rest easy trusting the goodness and wisdom of our prosecutors.

proper means by, the public," 18 U.S.C. § 1839(3), is not unconstitutionally vague. Based upon a careful review of the evidence that the Government will offer at trial, including e-mails, telephone conversations, and tape recordings of in-person meetings, it appears that Hsu knew (or at a minimum believed) that the "second generation" taxol information he was seeking to acquire was not "generally known to" or "readily ascertainable through proper means by, the public." The e-mails, telephone calls, and conversations show a pattern whereby Hsu, along with his indicted co-conspirator, Jessica Chou, realized that they could not license or acquire the "second generation" taxol technology through legal or public means, and that they would have to acquire it from an allegedly corrupt BMS employee. In several of the conversations Hsu and Chou are unambiguously told that this undertaking is illegal. Yet, despite these warnings, Hsu and his co-conspirator continued with their pursuit of taxol technology and, on April 22, 1997, Jessica Chou offered undercover FBI Agent John Hartmann (posing as "John Mano") "US $400,000 which is a combination of cash payment, stock shares and royalties" for the taxol technology.

Therefore, as applied to the conduct of this particular defendant and given the fact that he is charged *only* with the inchoate offenses of attempt and conspiracy (rather than completed offenses), we put aside our considerable disquiet about the EEA's language and deny defendant's motion to dismiss Counts Ten and Eleven of the Indictment.[8]

DID YOU GET IT?

1. What statutory terms did the defendants challenge as part of the vagueness argument?

2. How do the challenged definitions under the EEA compare to the UTSA?

3. The court notes its "considerable disquiet" with the language of the EEA. Based on what you have learned about civil trade secret misappropriation, are any parts of the EEA/DTSA troubling to you?

---

[8] We take some solace from our recognition of an aspect of the EEA that the Government did not mention in its papers or in oral argument. To be convicted under the EEA, a defendant must "knowingly" set out to violate the statute. Therefore, a person who takes a "trade secret" because of ignorance, mistake, or accident should not be successfully prosecuted.

Reading Guidance

How did the defendant in this case "conspire" under the EEA to steal trade secrets?

UNITED STATES V. MARTIN

United States Court of Appeals, First Circuit, 2000.
228 F.3d 1.

BACKGROUND

TORRUELLA, CHIEF JUDGE.

* * *

This case arises out of an electronic mail "pen-pal" relationship between a dissatisfied Maine chemist, Caryn Camp, and a California scientist, Dr. Stephen Martin. * * *

Camp's Employment at IDEXX

Camp first began work at IDEXX, Inc. ("IDEXX"), a manufacturer of veterinary products headquartered in Portland, Maine, in May of 1995. Camp's responsibilities as an IDEXX chemist included mixing chemicals for diagnostic test kits for both pets and livestock. At the time of her employment, she signed non-disclosure and non-competition agreements, promising in part not to "disclose to others, or use for [her] own benefit or the benefit of others, any of the Developments or any confidential, proprietary or secret information owned, possessed or used by [IDEXX] or its customers or contractors." The proprietary information included, but was not limited to, "trade secrets, processes, data, know-how, marketing plans, forecasts, unpublished financial statements, budgets, licenses, prices, costs, and employee, customer and supplier lists." Camp also signed the IDEXX policy on ethics and business conduct, which prohibited employees from revealing "proprietary knowledge or data" without prior authorization.

Martin's Communication with IDEXX

In May 1997, Martin, as CEO of Wyoming DNA Vaccine ("WDV"), contacted IDEXX with a proposal involving research into human immunodeficiency virus (HIV) and feline immunodeficiency virus (FIV). Although IDEXX ultimately rejected Martin's proposal, he signed a confidentiality agreement during his conversations with IDEXX.

Camp's Initial Contact with Martin

By early 1998, Camp was dissatisfied and bored with her job. In January 1998, she began researching other potential job opportunities. She found the Internet web site for WDV and sent an electronic mail message with an attached resumé. Martin responded immediately via electronic mail, praising Camp's credentials and touting the beauty of Cody, Wyoming (the future site of WDV). Martin also noted the existence of the WDV–IDEXX confidentiality agreement and the fact that WDV had chosen to "develop [its] own program ... with respect to veterinary diagnostics." After receiving Martin's response, Camp sent Martin a letter providing more detail about her qualifications.

Between January and March of 1998, Martin and Camp continued their correspondence. Based partly on Martin's encouragement and partly on her own interests, Camp contacted the Director of Regulatory Affairs at IDEXX and obtained permission to "volunteer [her] free time" to learn that end of the business. Martin indicated that despite Camp's preference for laboratory work, she would be more useful to WDV for her regulatory experience and knowledge. Martin briefed Camp on his own work at WDV, while Camp continued to update Martin on her professional success, in particular her promotion to a technical position in IDEXX's Livestock/Poultry unit.

Camp and Martin's early correspondence established several themes that would permeate their e-mails: contained within the small talk was on-going discussion of Camp's future employment with Martin's company, as well as a willingness by Camp to relay IDEXX information and gossip to Martin. Camp described her promotion as preparation "for making a strong contribution to the success of WDV" within four to six months. Her February 27 letter contained information regarding a manual that "IDEXX ... [is] not exactly supposed to have." And throughout this period, Camp's correspondence included light-hearted remarks about the weather, life in Maine, and a potential future in Wyoming.

Camp and Martin's correspondence became more and more frequent during March and April of 1998. Camp continued to apprise Martin of her problems with IDEXX management, the changes associated with her new position in technical support, and her interest in new employment, both at WDV and elsewhere. At times she included information about IDEXX's internal strategic weaknesses and customer complaints. Camp noted in an April 12 e-mail that the information she had transmitted was to some extent confidential. Martin reciprocated the information exchange: he told Camp about conflicts within WDV that ultimately resulted in his formation of a separate company called "Maverck"; he also relayed "confidential" WDV information. Martin continued to discuss Camp's future, noting that she could "have a job with either [WDV or Maverck]," that he thought she "belong[ed] in Tahoe/Reno," and that she might "become CEO [her]self one day."

As the two corresponded more frequently, their communications became more personal. Camp began to refer to Martin as "Steve." They discussed their families and social lives, and even shared the messages with family members. As their relationship grew more personal, both Camp and Martin, but particularly Martin, spoke jokingly of the "spy" aspect of the correspondence. For example, Martin referred to Camp's gossip as "IDEXX Files" and described the events at WDV as a "palace coup." Martin also continued to praise Camp's "aggressiveness" and exhorted her to work only in her own interest and to continue to accumulate relevant knowledge.

On April 14, Martin indicated that he "had much to tell" Camp, but that he wanted her to sign a confidentiality agreement first. Camp considered signing the agreement immediately, but ultimately postponed signing because of potential ethical concerns, including potential competition between WDV and IDEXX.[1]

On April 22, Camp sent Martin an e-mail discussing the poultry and livestock industries, noting problems IDEXX customers had been having with particular diagnostic kits, and mentioning that customers "loved" the IDEXX free software program "x-Chek." Camp continued to discuss IDEXX's poor customer service approach in her May 1 "travelogue," written during a business trip to the Midwest. Throughout her "travelogue," Camp repeatedly expressed her happiness in being away from IDEXX and her willingness to move on to new employment. * * *

On May 4, Camp wrote concerning IDEXX's legal problems. She also included "lots & lots of goodies for your next rainy day," including internal memoranda. Camp noted that the internal memoranda may have been confidential. "I feel like a spy," she commented. In a letter the next day, Camp regretted her actions, promising to "be good . . . and send no more dirty secrets from IDEXX. . . ." Martin responded, claiming that he did "not want to know anything confidential about IDEXX," and asking only for "public information."

Despite Camp's repentance and Martin's denial of any desire for confidential or proprietary information, Camp continued to assemble and pass on information, an activity which she apparently viewed as ethically suspect.[2] * * *

On July 12, Camp sent Martin a large package of information via Priority Mail, including various devices, product inserts, USDA course materials,

---

[1]   In an April 19 e-mail message, Camp wrote: "I'm not certain of how comfortable I am with signing the agreement as long as I am working for another company-particularly a company which is or could be a potential competitor, nor I am I[sic] comfortable with you sharing with me anything which you feel needs to be covered by this agreement."

[2]   Camp's May 7 e-mail noted that "the fun part of my week has been putting together packages of information for you . . . " and celebrated "the intrigue of being Agent Ace." On June 22, she "couldn't resist playing Ace-the-Spy today . . . and so I am dropping a few more things in the mail." But her fun did not come without guilt: "I know I should be shot. But I just can't resist sending you this chain of internal IDEXX e-mails regarding concern of a certain competitor;" "I am probably crossing the line with this [but] I've crossed lines worse than this one." However, Camp re-assured herself that she was doing nothing wrong, that she was forwarding "nothing proprietary" but simply the "dirty secrets of an IDEXX Livestock and Poultry weekly meeting."

information on her own projects, miscellaneous IDEXX product information, and "Examples of My Work," labeled "Confidential." Camp also promised to send an actual test kit, if Martin wished. The mailing and receipt of this package formed the basis of a mail fraud charge, of which Martin was ultimately convicted. After receiving the package, Martin once more praised Camp's aggressiveness, encouraged her to "keep on charging," to "keep on thinking about the competition, and how we can beat them," and promised that "lips are sealed." * * *

In several e-mails between July 19 and July 21, Camp outlined a proposal for customer-friendly additions and modifications to current IDEXX technology. Martin explained how such a test might be constructed, telling Camp that if it could be marketed successfully, she would receive "enough bonus money to buy [a] house for cash." Camp clearly understood that the proposal was for technology competitive with that of IDEXX, as she suggested the possibility that "[she and Martin would] own the whole market."

Camp's proposal also prompted Martin to ask about the relevance and applicability of x-Chek or similar software. Camp offered to send Martin a copy of the software IDEXX had developed for poultry and livestock testing. Martin responded the same day, writing that "he would like to play with the software you mentioned." Camp immediately replied, promising "lots of cool goodies," including the x-Chek disks. Camp also indicated that she was on the verge of "cleaning out her office" and leaving IDEXX; however, she noted that she was speaking to headhunters in addition to Martin.

Martin's response to this last message re-affirmed his intention to compete with IDEXX. Moreover, Martin acknowledged Camp's potentially illicit activity, and exhorted her to continue in her final few days at work. "Before you bag IDEXX (I am embarrassed to ask this), absorb as much information, physically and intellectually, as you can. I never had a spy before." Camp's answer bemoaned the constraints on her information gathering (because co-workers knew she was preparing to leave), detailed her continued efforts to take home both information and property, and admitted the illegality (or at least inappropriateness) of her actions.[5] However, Camp noted that she had as of yet been unwilling to copy "confidential" documents, although she admitted that she had copied "semi-confidential" internal e-mail. The next day, Camp promised to send Martin additional kits as her last "secret agent" act.

In Camp's last several days at IDEXX, she continued to collect products and information, which she forwarded to Martin on July 24. The package

---

[5]   "I have been filling my briefcase every day with all the stuff that I want to keep. . . . Aren't I awful? I'm liking this spy business way too much. . . . The problem [with hiring other IDEXX employees] is they'll see what a thief I am. . . . My biggest 'inheritance' from IDEXX is a multi-channel pipettor. . . . I am still feeling guilty about [taking the pipets]. I don't know where all this lawlessness in me is coming from."

included operating manuals, IDEXX marketing materials, research and development data, a sales binder prepared by an independent contractor, as well as a binder labeled "Competition."

Unfortunately for Camp and Martin, Camp inadvertently sent her July 25 e-mail (acknowledging that July 24 was her last day and detailing the contents of her second package) to John Lawrence, the global marketing manager for Poultry/Livestock at IDEXX. Camp informed Martin of what she had done, and continued on her vacation. According to Camp, Martin later recommended that she lie to IDEXX, i.e., that she tell them that he was interested only in limited information unrelated to IDEXX core businesses. Upon her return to Maine, Camp was intercepted and interviewed by an FBI agent at the Portland airport. An August 9, 1998 search of Martin's home found the contents of Camp's second package, including the x-Chek software.

DISCUSSION

* * *

Conspiracy to Steal Trade Secrets

The jury found Martin guilty of count 13, which charged him with conspiracy to steal trade secrets in violation of the Economic Espionage Act of 1996, specifically 18 U.S.C. § 1832(a)(5). In order to find a defendant guilty of conspiracy, the prosecution must prove (1) that an agreement existed, (2) that it had an unlawful purpose, and (3) that the defendant was a voluntary participant. The government must prove that the defendant possessed both the "intent to agree and [the] intent to commit the substantive offense." In addition, the government must prove that at least one conspirator committed an "overt act," that is, took an affirmative step toward achieving the conspiracy's purpose.

The agreement need not be express, however, as long as its existence may be inferred from the "defendants' words and actions and the interdependence of activities and persons involved." A so-called "tacit" agreement will suffice. Moreover, the conspirators need not succeed in completing the underlying act, nor need that underlying act even be factually possible. * * *

Martin contends that the evidence is factually insufficient to establish a "meeting of the minds" or agreement to violate § 1832(a), because (1) insufficient evidence exists to establish an agreement between Martin and Camp; (2) insufficient evidence exists to prove that Martin had the necessary intent to commit an act prohibited by § 1832(a), i.e., injure the owner of the trade secret (IDEXX); and (3) the information provided by Camp to Martin did not meet the statutory definition of a trade secret under § 1839(3). As we explain below, none of these arguments are persuasive.

First, the evidence is sufficient for a reasonable jury to conclude that Martin and Camp formed an agreement regarding the theft of trade secrets. Martin's argument against the existence of an agreement relies on the facts that (a) his early e-mails specifically requested that Camp *not* send him confidential information, and (b) Camp did not seem to know the distinction between confidential information, proprietary information, and office gossip. However, while Martin's disclaimer and Camp's confusion indicate the lack of an explicit agreement *at that time,* they do not necessarily negate the existence of *an* agreement. A rational jury could have plausibly concluded on the basis of the evidence presented at trial that an agreement existed. By July 21, Martin had received extensive correspondence from Camp that she had either marked "confidential" or "proprietary," or had expressed some hesitation in forwarding. Despite his previous protestations that he wanted nothing to do with IDEXX or its confidential information, Martin asked Camp on July 21 to "absorb as much information, physically and intellectually, as you can," and included a set of questions to direct Camp's research. Throughout June and July, Martin referred to Camp as "Agent Ace," or as his "spy." Given the type of information that Martin had already received, a reasonable jury could have concluded that, whatever Martin's original intentions, as of July 21, Camp and Martin had reached a tacit agreement by which she would send him items and information that potentially fell under the trade secret definition of 18 U.S.C. § 1839(3). In other words, sufficient evidence exists to show an agreement between Camp and Martin to violate § 1832(a).

Second, the evidence is sufficient to show that Martin intended to injure IDEXX by obtaining IDEXX trade secrets and competing against IDEXX. Although Martin consistently claimed that he had no interest in developing products that competed with IDEXX, and hence had no intention of injuring IDEXX economically, his correspondence with Camp detailed a plan of competition. Martin had, among other things, considered the possibility of starting a competing veterinary lab and had asked Camp to think, in particular, about ways to compete with tests that IDEXX manufactured. A reasonable jury could have found that Martin intended to use the information gained from Camp, particularly information on IDEXX's costs and customer dissatisfaction with IDEXX, to create a more successful competitor with greater capability to injure IDEXX.

Third, Martin's final argument-that he actually received no trade secrets-even if true, is irrelevant. Martin has only been found guilty of a conspiracy to steal trade secrets, rather than the underlying offense. The relevant question to determine whether a conspiracy existed was whether Martin *intended* to violate the statute. The key question is whether Martin intended to steal trade secrets. A rational jury, considering the information Camp had already sent Martin, could have concluded that his further queries indicated such an intention.

A reasonable jury could therefore have concluded that Martin and Camp formed an agreement by which Camp conveyed information and property to Martin that potentially fell under the definition of a trade secret in 18 U.S.C. § 1839. As a result, sufficient evidence existed to convict Martin of conspiracy to steal trade secrets. * * *

DID YOU GET IT?

1. What evidence supports Martin's intent to injure IDEXX in this case?

2. How does the court resolve Martin's argument that he did not actually receive any "trade secrets"?

Reading Guidance
How is section 1831 of the EEA applied in this case?

UNITED STATES V. CHUNG

United States District Court, C.D. California, 2009.
633 F.Supp.2d 1134.

CORMAC J. CARNEY, DISTRICT JUDGE.

* * *

FACTUAL BACKGROUND

Mr. Chung, a naturalized United States citizen, worked as an engineer for his entire adult life. At the beginning of his career, Boeing hired him as a stress analyst on the airframe and rotor hub for the CH–47 helicopter. In 1969, Mr. Chung moved to another company, McDonnell Douglas, where he worked as a strength engineer on the wing structure of the DC–10 airliner and on the wing and armament support for the F–15 fighter. In 1972 and part of 1973, Mr. Chung returned to Boeing and worked at its facility in Wichita, Kansas on the B–52 Life Extension Program. In the fall of 1973, Mr. Chung moved to Rockwell International ("Rockwell") in Downey, California and worked there for the next twenty-six years. Boeing acquired Rockwell's space division in 1996. In 1999, Mr. Chung moved to Boeing's plant in Huntington Beach. For most of his career at Rockwell and Boeing, Mr. Chung worked as a stress analyst on the forward fuselage section of the Space Shuttle. Mr. Chung held a secret clearance from 1973 until 2002.

In 2002, Boeing moved parts of its Space Shuttle program to Houston, Texas. Mr. Chung declined to move, and Boeing laid him off in September 2002. After the crash of the Columbia orbiter in February 2003, however, Mr. Chung came back to Boeing as a contractor to assist in the evaluation of the crash. He remained at Boeing until September 11, 2006.

Federal agents first suspected that Mr. Chung was spying for the PRC [the People's Republic of China] during its 2005 investigation of another engineer named Chi Mak, who worked for a naval defense contractor. Mr. Chung had significant contact with Chi Mak over the years, and the federal agents were concerned that their relationship was more than purely social. Federal agents knew that Chi Mak was using his position and security clearance to pass sensitive naval technology to the PRC. In 2007, a jury convicted Chi Mak of conspiring to export defense articles, attempting to export defense articles, acting as an unregistered agent of a foreign government, and making a false statement. This Court sentenced Chi Mak to approximately twenty-four years in prison for his crimes.

During a search of Chi Mak's home in October 2005, federal agents found address books containing contact information for Mr. Chung. As part of the investigation in the Chi Mak case, Mr. Chung was interviewed on April 24, 2006. Mr. Chung told federal agents he first met Chi Mak in 1992 through a mutual friend "Mr. Gu" (later identified as Gu Weihao of the Chinese Ministry of Aviation), whom he described as an exchange scholar from China. In June 2006, during a second search of Chi Mak's home, federal agents discovered letters to Mr. Chung from Gu Weihao. In one letter, dated May 2, 1987, Gu Weihao asked Mr. Chung to provide information on airplanes and the Space Shuttle and referred to information that Mr. Chung had previously provided to the PRC.

Following the discovery of the letter to Mr. Chung from Gu Weihao, federal agents conducted surveillance and trash searches at Mr. Chung's home. In August and September 2006, federal agents discovered that Mr. Chung had disposed of technical documents taken from work by secreting them within the pages of newspapers. The documents included design drawings and diagrams, structural and material specifications, project management data, and engineering modification reports for the Space Shuttle and the International Space Station.

Based on the information found in Mr. Chung's trash, federal agents believed that it was necessary to take a closer look at him and his activities. On September 11, 2006, federal agents interviewed Mr. Chung and searched his home. Federal agents were astonished at what they found. Mr. Chung had over 300,000 pages of sensitive and proprietary documents belonging to Boeing. More specifically, federal agents found a veritable treasure trove of Boeing's documents relating to the Space Shuttle, Delta IV Rocket, F–15 fighter, B–52 bomber, CH–46/47 Chinook helicopter, and other proprietary aerospace and military technologies. Federal agents also found numerous letters, tasking lists, and journals detailing Mr. Chung's communications with officials in the PRC. As federal agents sifted through the hundreds of thousands of pages of documents in Mr. Chung's home, the story of Mr. Chung's secret life became clear. He was a spy for the PRC.

* * *

Economic Espionage Act Counts

Mr. Chung is charged with six counts of possessing a trade secret with the intent to benefit the PRC under the EEA. The EEA provides, in pertinent part:

> (a) In general.—Whoever, intending or knowing that the offense will benefit any foreign government, foreign instrumentality, or foreign agent, knowingly—
>
> > (3) receives, buys, or possesses a trade secret, knowing the same to have been stolen or appropriated, obtained, or converted without authorization . . .
>
> shall . . . be fined not more than $500,000 or imprisoned not more than 15 years, or both.

18 U.S.C. § 1831.

* * * It is not explicitly clear from the language of section 1831(a)(3) whether the word "knowingly" modifies the "trade secret" element of the offense. The Government argues that it does not, and therefore it does not have to prove that Mr. Chung knew the information that he possessed was a trade secret. Mr. Chung contends that the Government must prove that he had such knowledge. The Court agrees with Mr. Chung.

* * *

Contrary to the Government's assertion, requiring it to prove that Mr. Chung knew the information he possessed was a trade secret does not impose an insurmountable or even difficult burden of proof. The Government must prove that Mr. Chung knew that the information he possessed was a trade secret, but not that he knew his behavior was illegal. The statutory definition of a trade secret is not overly technical and requires no specialized knowledge or expertise to understand. Proving that a defendant knows that the owner of a trade secret takes reasonable measures to protect it and that the information has economic value is not exceedingly difficult. A defendant charged with economic espionage will necessarily have some understanding of the measures that have been taken to protect the information he possesses. He will know whether the facility he acquired the information from was gated. He will know if the information in his possession has proprietary, trade secret, or classified markings. If he is an employee, he will know his company's policy about whether documents can be taken home. The Government need not prove that a defendant knew all of the security measures taken to protect the information. Likewise, proving that a defendant charged with economic espionage knows that the information he possesses has economic value is not exceedingly difficult. A spy does not deal in worthless or readily ascertainable information. He collects information without authorization precisely because it has independent economic value. He passes this information to a foreign government that cannot obtain the information lawfully.

Accordingly, under Section 1831(a)(3), the Government must prove five elements: (1) Mr. Chung intended to benefit a foreign government; (2) Mr. Chung knowingly possessed trade secret information; (3) Mr. Chung knew that the information was obtained without authorization; (4) the information Mr. Chung possessed was, in fact, a trade secret; and (5) Mr. Chung knew the information was a trade secret. * * * The Government proved each of these elements beyond a reasonable doubt with respect to all six documents charged in the indictment.

* * *

All six of the documents charged in the indictment contain trade secret information. Boeing took more than reasonable measures to protect the documents. Armed guards secured the Boeing facility, and employees had to show their identification to enter the building. Boeing reserved the right to search its employees' belongings and their cars for violations of its security policies. Access to the documents was restricted to those engineers who needed access and had approval from their managers. Rockwell and Boeing disseminated written guidelines and conducted trainings in which the companies made clear the importance of not sharing the documents with outside parties. Boeing took even further precautions with respect to the TSM documents. Hard copies of the TSM documents had to be locked up at night and could not be removed from the facility.

The information contained in the six documents charged in the indictment also has independent economic value. None of the information in the six documents is available in the public domain. The TSM documents found in Mr. Chung's library constitute a "do-it-yourself kit" that would allow another engineer to build the system. The TSM assembly took a large team of engineers five years to develop, and its development cost Boeing close to $50 million. The TSM system is currently in use, and Boeing hopes to place the system at Vandenberg Air Force Base. If Boeing's competitors were to acquire a "do-it-yourself" kit to recreate this technology, Boeing would be at a serious competitive disadvantage. Similarly, the four Phased Array Antenna documents reveal information that would allow a competitor to determine the number of elements needed and Boeing's cost to produce the Phased Array Antenna. Based on this information, a competitor would be able to undermine Boeing's ability to win competitive contracts. Although the first two Phased Array Antenna documents are not marked proprietary, they are never published or distributed by the company. This information has both actual and potential economic value to Boeing. Rockwell spent considerable time and well over a million dollars developing this technology. Although the Phased Array Antenna is not currently used on the Space Shuttle, the work done by Rockwell was successful and the technology is currently in use in a number of "black programs" at Boeing. Additionally, the Phased Array Antenna may be viable technology for the Space Shuttle in the future.

The Court also has no doubt that Mr. Chung knew that he possessed trade secret information. Mr. Chung, a long-time employee of Boeing and Rockwell, was well aware of the numerous security measures in place to protect all of Boeing's information. Mr. Chung had to show his identification each day to enter the building. Most of the documents Mr. Chung possessed were stamped proprietary. Mr. Chung signed agreements confirming his understanding that he could not disclose any of the information developed by Boeing. Mr. Chung also did not request his supervisor's permission to take any of the documents home. Had Mr. Chung requested permission to bring home the TSM and Phased Array Antenna documents, his supervisor would have denied Mr. Chung's request because Boeing simply did not allow engineers to keep any of its proprietary documents at home-much less its highly valuable trade secret ones.

Mr. Chung also knew that the information derived value from being not readily available to the public. If the information were worthless or readily available in the public domain, Mr. Chung surely would not have gathered it for the PRC in violation of well-established Boeing policies and subjected himself to immediate termination by the company. Mr. Chung knew that the PRC could not obtain the information and that it desperately wanted to get its hands on it. Tragically, Mr. Chung was willing to betray the trust Boeing placed in him to safeguard the information in the documents. The reason for that betrayal is obvious to the Court. Mr. Chung was a devoted spy for the PRC.

Accordingly, the Court finds Mr. Chung guilty beyond a reasonable doubt on all six counts of economic espionage. Mr. Chung possessed six trade secret documents for the benefit of the PRC. Boeing took more than reasonable measures to protect the information in the documents, and the information in the documents derived substantial value because it was not known to Boeing's competitors. And finally, Mr. Chung knew the information in the documents was trade secret information.

* * *

For the foregoing reasons, the Court finds Mr. Chung guilty on all counts * * *.

DID YOU GET IT?

1. Why do you think this case was charged under section 1831 instead of section 1832?

2. According to this court, what knowledge must the government prove under the statute?

3.   What evidence supports the finding on the knowledge requirement in this case?

Reading Guidance

What effect did the section 1831 charge (economic espionage) have on the defendant's sentence?

UNITED STATES V. HANJUAN JIN

United States District Court, Seventh Circuit, 2013.
733 F.3d 718.

POSNER, CIRCUIT JUDGE.

The defendant was charged with theft of trade secrets and economic espionage, both being offenses under the Economic Espionage Act. *See* 18 U.S.C. §§ 1831, 1832. A bench trial resulted in her conviction of theft of trade secrets but acquittal of economic espionage. The judge imposed a 48-month prison sentence. Her appeal challenges both her conviction and her sentence.

The defendant, a naturalized American citizen of Chinese origin who has a bachelor's degree in physics from a Chinese university and master's degrees in both physics and computer science from American universities, was employed by Motorola as a software engineer from 1998 to 2007 at the company's global headquarters in a Chicago suburb. Her duties primarily involved a cellular telecommunications system manufactured and sold by Motorola called iDEN, an acronym for Integrated Digital Enhanced Network.

She spent a protracted period in China in 2006 and 2007 while on a year-long medical leave from Motorola, and while there sought a job with a Chinese company called Sun Kaisens, which develops telecommunications technology for the Chinese armed forces. Shortly after returning to the United States in February 2007 she bought a one-way ticket to China on a plane scheduled to leave Chicago a few days later. In the interval before her scheduled departure she downloaded thousands of internal Motorola documents, all stamped proprietary, disclosing details of the iDEN technology. The government based its prosecution on three of these documents.

As her purchase of a one-way ticket to China indicated, along with the large amount of currency ($31,000) that she was carrying when stopped by Customs agents at the airport, she intended to live in China and work there for Sun Kaisens. Asked by Customs and later the FBI what she was doing with thousands of Motorola documents relating to the iDEN system, she said she needed them in order to refresh her knowledge of it.

* * *

iDEN is a mobile telecommunications system developed by Motorola in the early 1990s. It is on its way out, supplanted by more advanced systems. But in 2007, when the theft occurred, Motorola still had many customers for iDEN—indeed about 20 million, spread over 22 countries including China.

iDEN's most notable feature is "push to talk," which allows handsets to operate as walkie-talkies but provides conventional cellular phone capabilities as well, such as texting and Internet access. Push-to-talk made iDEN systems attractive to law enforcement, emergency responders, taxicab dispatchers, and the like; the Israeli and South Korean armed forces were among iDEN's customers. Other manufacturers besides Motorola offered push-to-talk capability, but iDEN was a complete end-to-end system that one witness testified had the fastest push-to-talk capability. Because the technology was treated by Motorola as a trade secret, iDEN could be bought from and serviced only by Motorola or its licensees.

The defendant argues that because iDEN was rapidly losing its commercial cachet, the theft could not have harmed Motorola; no one would have tried to sell copies of iDEN, as keeping the iDEN technology secret conferred no economic benefit on Motorola. But as an engineer intimately familiar with iDEN, the defendant had to know that had she been able to fly to China with the iDEN documents in her luggage, Motorola, as soon as it discovered the theft, would have had to warn its customers of the risk that privacy of communications over the iDEN network had been or would be compromised. And it would have had to take counter-measures at some expense to itself. Moreover, once it learned that the defendant was going to work for a company that provides telecommunications services to the Chinese armed forces, it would have had to assume that there was a good chance that the defendant would show the stolen documents to the company, which in turn might use them to help the Chinese government hack into iDEN networks. The danger might be illusory, but Motorola could not assume that.

The defendant must also have known that Sun Kaisens or some other Chinese company would discover in those thousands of documents that she had stolen information that would make it easier to duplicate the iDEN system and thus create new iDEN networks, to compete with Motorola's network. Competitors could peel off some of those 20 million Motorola customers by offering a usable substitute at a lower price, being able to offer a lower price, yet still make a profit, by virtue of not having incurred costs of research and development.

Motorola had taken elaborate precautions, albeit skillfully circumvented by the defendant, to keep the iDEN technology secret. It wouldn't have incurred the cost of those precautions had it not feared adverse consequences if the technology became public. The secrecy of the technology gave Motorola a monopoly. Maybe not a terribly valuable monopoly, in view of technological advances that would soon make iDEN obsolete, but a temporary monopoly generating supracompetitive profits that competition, enabled by the loss of secrecy, would erode.

* * *

The government doesn't have to prove that the owner of the secret actually lost money as a result of the theft. For remember that the "independent economic value" attributable to the information's remaining secret need only be "potential," as distinct from "actual." 18 U.S.C. § 1839(3)(B). * * *

Coming closer to home, suppose a company in New Orleans had stolen the iDEN technology and was about to sell its first subscription to its brand-new iDEN network when Hurricane Katrina destroyed the company. Would that mean that the company had stolen something that had no economic value? No; for what it stole had economic value though for extraneous reasons the value couldn't be monetized. The theft in the present case, as in our hypothetical case, might have injured Motorola by revealing that it couldn't keep secrets or prevent rivals from stealing its technology.

So there was adequate evidence of the defendant's guilt, and we turn to her challenge to the sentence.

The district judge acquitted her of the other crime that she was charged with—economic espionage, which required the government to prove that she had stolen the trade secrets intending to, or knowing that the theft would, benefit a foreign government, instrumentality, or agent. 18 U.S.C. § 1831(a). He thought her guilty of the offense, but not that it had been proved beyond a reasonable doubt. Nevertheless at sentencing he added two levels to her base offense level, pursuant to section 2B1.1(b)(5) of the sentencing guidelines, which requires such an increase "if the offense involved misappropriation of a trade secret and the defendant knew or intended that the offense would benefit a foreign government, foreign instrumentality, or foreign agent." A judge need determine guilt of an offense only by a preponderance of the evidence in order to be allowed to factor that determination into his decision regarding the appropriate sentence for the offense of which the defendant has been convicted.

The addition of the two levels brought the defendant's total offense level to 28, making her guidelines sentencing range 78 to 97 months. The sentence the judge gave her—48 months—was much lower. Given her egregious conduct, which included repeatedly lying to federal agents (for which she could have been prosecuted but was not), she was fortunate to be the recipient of discretionary sentencing lenity based on her ill health and inability to join her family, now in China. The judge gave her a further, surprising break by reducing her offense level (by two levels) for acceptance of responsibility, U.S.S.G. § 3E1.1(a), despite her having pleaded not guilty and gone to trial.

AFFIRMED.

DID YOU GET IT?

1. Was the defendant convicted on the section 1831 charge?

2. How did the section 1831 charge affect the defendant's sentence?

3. Why does the appellate court affirm the finding below on guilt and sentencing?

D. SPECIAL ISSUE: CAN A DEFENDANT IN A TRADE SECRET CASE (CRIMINAL OR CIVIL) "PLEAD THE FIFTH"?

The Fifth Amendment to the U.S. Constitution states that: "No person . . . shall be compelled in any criminal case to be a witness against himself." Known as the privilege against self-incrimination, this Constitutional right has been held to apply any time "a witness can show any possibility of prosecution which is more than fanciful." *See Warford v. Medeiros,* 160 Cal.App.3d 1035, 1043–44 (1984). As the U.S. Supreme Court explained in *Hoffman v. United States*:

> The Fifth Amendment declares in part that "[n]o person . . . shall be compelled in any Criminal Case to be a witness against himself." This guarantee against testimonial compulsion, like other provisions of the Bill of Rights, "was added to the original Constitution in the conviction that too high a price might be paid even for the unhampered enforcement of the criminal law and that, in its attainment, other social objects of a free society should not be sacrificed." This provision of the Amendment must be accorded liberal construction in favor of the right it was intended to secure.

> The privilege afforded not only extends to answers that would in themselves support a conviction under a federal criminal statute, but likewise embraces those which would furnish a link in the chain of evidence needed to prosecute the claimant for a federal crime. But this protection must be confined to instances where the witness has reasonable cause to apprehend danger from a direct answer. The witness is not exonerated from answering merely because he declares that in so doing he would incriminate himself-his say-so does not of itself establish the hazard of incrimination. It is for the court to say whether his silence is justified, and to require him to answer if "it clearly appears to the court that he is mistaken." However, if the witness, upon interposing his claim,

were required to prove the hazard in the sense in which the claim is usually required to be established in court, he would be compelled to surrender the very protection which the privilege is designed to guarantee. *To sustain the privilege, it need only be evident from the implications of the question, in the setting in which it is asked, that a responsive answer to the question or an explanation of why it cannot be answered might be dangerous because injurious disclosure could result.*

341 U.S. 479, 486–87 (1951) (emphasis added).

The Fifth Amendment privilege against self-incrimination was held applicable to the states in *Malloy v. Hogan,* 378 U.S. 1 (1964). The following case provides an example of compelled testimony in a criminal action for trade secret misappropriation under state law.

Reading Guidance

What is the procedural device that makes Heddon's testimony "compelled"?

HEDDON V. STATE OF FLORIDA

District Court of Appeal of Florida, Second District, 2001.
786 So. 2d 1262.

NORTHCUTT, JUDGE.

David Heddon's petition for a writ of certiorari challenges the circuit court's refusal to quash a subpoena which requires Heddon's attorney to produce a document to the State. We conclude that the order denying Heddon's motion to quash departed from the essential requirements of law, and we grant the writ.

After Heddon left his job at West World Telecommunications Systems, Inc., a principal of West World complained to the state attorney that Heddon was misappropriating the company's trade secrets. The State began investigating Heddon for a violation of section 812.081, Florida Statutes (1999). In conjunction with its investigation, the State subpoenaed numerous records from Heddon's corporation, which he provided. The State then served an investigative subpoena on Stephen Artman, Heddon's former lawyer, requiring Artman to "provide all documents including vendor/customer list(s) of West World . . . in your possession that were obtained from David Heddon." Artman acknowledged that Heddon consulted him for legal advice and that he possessed a file concerning this previous representation, but he asserted the attorney-client privilege as to the file's contents. Nevertheless, the circuit court denied the attorney's motion to quash the subpoena.

Heddon argues that if he were in possession of any such list he could not be compelled to furnish it in violation of his Fifth Amendment privilege against self-incrimination. Further, he maintains, the attorney-client privilege protects any such documents he may have given to his attorney. In *Fisher v. United States*, the Court held that if a document in the hands of the client is unobtainable by subpoena, and the client transfers the document to his attorney for the purpose of obtaining legal advice, the document can not be obtained by subpoena from the attorney by reason of the attorney-client privilege. As in this case, the clients in *Fisher* contended that the Fifth Amendment barred enforcement of a subpoena for the documents in their hands.

The *Fisher* Court noted that the Fifth Amendment does not shield every kind of incriminating evidence; rather, it only precludes forcing an accused to produce incriminating testimonial communications. * * * The Court further observed that the very act of producing a subpoenaed document can have a testimonial aspect apart from the content of the document itself. Compliance with the subpoena concedes the existence of the document and the fact that the accused possesses or controls it. * * * *See also United States v. Doe* (approving Fifth Amendment privilege against compelled production of documents when the act of producing the documents involved testimonial self-incrimination).

We applied these principles in *Briggs v. Salcines*, in which we issued a writ of certiorari commanding the circuit court to quash a subpoena requiring production of testimonial evidence. In that case, the state attorney was investigating whether certain audio tapes were recorded in violation of Florida law. Mr. Joseph, who supposedly made the tapes, had given them to his attorney in the course of receiving legal advice. The State issued a subpoena requiring the attorney to produce the tapes. We determined that if the tapes were in Joseph's hands, forced production of them would amount to a compelled incriminating testimonial communication because his possession of the tapes would implicate him in their making, a potential violation of the law. Relying on both *Fisher* and section 90.502, Florida Statutes, we held that because the tapes were entitled to Fifth Amendment protection in the hands of the client, the attorney-client privilege also protected them in the hands of the attorney.

Such is the case here. The state attorney is investigating Heddon for a violation of Florida's Trade Secrets Act. A trade secret includes a list of customers. * * * The statute further provides:

> Any person who, with intent to deprive or withhold from the owner thereof the control of a trade secret, or with an intent to appropriate a trade secret to his or her own use or to the use of another, steals or embezzles an article representing a trade secret or without authority makes or causes to be made a copy of an

article representing a trade secret is guilty of a felony of the third degree. . . .

§ 812.081(2). Thus, Heddon's possession of an original customer list of West World, or a copy of such a list, would tend to incriminate him. Further, production of such a document would be testimonial, in that it would concede the existence of the list and Heddon's possession of it. Accordingly, the Fifth Amendment would prohibit forcing Heddon to produce any such document, and the attorney-client privilege shields any such document Heddon gave his attorney in the course of seeking legal advice.

We issue a writ of certiorari and direct the circuit court to quash the State's subpoena.

DID YOU GET IT?

1. What was Heddon being compelled to do?

2. How was Heddon being compelled to testify against himself?

3. How might the documents be incriminating?

———

Although the Fifth Amendment privilege against self-incrimination specifically refers to criminal cases, in *Kastigar v. United States*, the U.S. Supreme Court held that the privilege against self-incrimination "can be asserted in any proceeding, civil or criminal, administrative or judicial, investigatory or ajudicatory." 406 U.S. 441, 444 (1972). Thus, the factual circumstance which triggers the possible application of the privilege is not the nature of the legal proceeding, but whether: (1) the person who might invoke the privilege is being compelled to testify against himself; and (2) there is the possibility of criminal prosecution. For instance, in *Arminius Schleifmittel GMBH v. Design Industrial, Inc.*, 2008 WL 819032 (M.D.N.C. 2008), an individual defendant in a civil trade secret misappropriation case was allowed to invoke the privilege against self-incrimination in his answer to plaintiff's complaint rather than having to specifically admit or deny plaintiff's allegations.

Based upon the foregoing, a very real consequence of making trade secret misappropriation a crime is that individual defendants will invoke the privilege against self-incrimination in civil trade secret cases. *See* Sharon K. Sandeen, *Conflicting Rights: Intellectual Property Litigation and the Privilege Against Self Incrimination*, 3 PROPRIETARY RTS. J. 9 (Dec. 1991). In fact, if employed correctly, the invocation of the privilege against self-incrimination in a civil trade secret misappropriation case can bring the case to a screeching halt. This is particularly true where there is an ongoing criminal investigation by state or federal authorities. In such cases, the companion civil case may be stayed until the criminal investigation is concluded. *See Afro-Lecon, Inc. v. United States*, 820 F.2d

1198 (Fed. Cir. 1987). However, the privilege only applies to individuals. Pursuant to the collective entity doctrine, it does not apply to corporate entities (no matter the size) or to other forms of business entities. *See Bellis v. United States,* 417 U.S. 85 (1974).

If an individual is subpoenaed to be a witness at a deposition or at trial or to answer written interrogatories, it is easy to see how he might be compelled to be a witness against himself. The questions he is asked may require him to admit criminal wrongdoing of some sort or, at least, one or more of the elements of a crime. In trade secret cases, for instance, if an individual is asked whether he is in possession of certain documents, an affirmative answer would effectively admit that he possessed the documents and may be used as a piece of evidence that he also misappropriated them. However, as the *Heddon* case reveals, direct questioning in a legal proceeding is not the only form of compelled testimony. A subpoena that requires the production of documents may also elicit compelled testimony where the production itself "has communicative aspects of its own, wholly apart from the contents of the papers produced." 786 So. 2d 1262, quoting *Fisher v. United States*, 425 U.S. 391, 410 (1976). For instance, if a defendant in a civil trade secret case is asked to produce all of the documents that he took with him when he left his prior employment, his production of any documents in response to the discovery request would admit that he took documents with him when he left his former employer. As the Court in *Fisher* explained:

> The act of producing evidence in response to a subpoena nevertheless has communicative aspects of its own, wholly aside from the contents of the papers produced. Compliance with the subpoena tacitly concedes the existence of the papers demanded and their possession or control by the [defendant]. It would also indicate the [defendant's] belief that the papers are those described in the subpoena.

In a different case, Judge Kennedy (now Justice Kennedy) explained:

> It is important to state that a subpoena to produce documents may elicit testimonial assertions that pertain to matters quite aside from authentication. By complying with the subpoena, a witness may be forced to communicate his state of mind, his memory, his perception, or his cognition; and such evidence may relate either to documents to be produced or to entirely different matters. Articulation of this evidence may arise either by the act of delivering the requested materials or by responding to inquiries necessary to insure that there has been full compliance with the subpoena.

In the Matter of the Grand Jury Subpoena of Fred Witte Center Glass No. 3, 544 F.2d 1026 (9th Cir. 1976).

There are a number of ways that the production of documents may be compelled in the course of a civil action for trade secret misappropriation. They may be requested from a party to the litigation pursuant to a discovery request, they may be subpoenaed during the discovery phase from a third party, or they may be subpoenaed for production at trial. They may also be the subject of a temporary restraining order, a preliminary injunction order, or a permanent injunction order, for instance, if the judge mandates the return of certain documents. In the case of discovery requests and subpoenas, the individual who is requested to produce the documents can simply invoke the privilege against self-incrimination as a response to the production request. It would then be up to the requesting party to move to compel production based upon a showing that the invocation of the Fifth Amendment was not proper.

Invocation of the privilege against self-incrimination in response to a court order is a bit trickier because it requires the person who was enjoined to refuse to abide by the order on the grounds that compliance with the injunction may incriminate him. Such a refusal may lead to contempt proceedings being brought by the party who successfully obtained the injunction or by the judge who issued the order, but based upon Fifth Amendment jurisprudence, the court should respect the invocation of the privilege against self-incrimination if compliance with the injunction is testimonial and there is a possibility of criminal prosecution. In *Maness v. Meyers*, the U.S. Supreme Court held that an attorney may not be held in contempt for advising his client to refuse to comply with a court order when the lawyer believes in good faith that such compliance may tend to incriminate his client. 419 U.S. 449 (1975).

There is an important and significant difference between the invocation of the Fifth Amendment in a civil case versus a criminal case. In a criminal case, the invocation of the privilege cannot be referred to or used by prosecutors to infer guilt. *See* Wayne R. LaFave *et al.*, CRIMINAL PROCEDURE § 24.5(b), at 1163–65 (5th ed. 2009). This is not true with respect to civil cases. The invocation of the Fifth Amendment in a civil case can be used to infer liability. The United States Supreme Court in *Baxter v. Palmigiano* explained:

> Our conclusion is consistent with the prevailing rule that the Fifth Amendment does not forbid adverse inferences against parties to civil actions when they refuse to testify in response to probative evidence offered against them: the Amendment "does not preclude the inference where the privilege is claimed by a party to a Civil cause." 8 J. Wigmore, Evidence 439. In criminal cases, where the stakes are higher and the State's sole interest is to convict, *Griffin* prohibits the judge and prosecutor from suggesting to the jury that it may treat the defendant's silence as substantive evidence of guilt. 425 U.S. 308, 318–19 (1976) .

Thus, individual defendants in civil trade secret cases should not invoke the privilege against self-incrimination without carefully considering the potential consequences. However, whether or not to assert Constitutional rights is a personal choice and not one that should be made by an individual defendant's employer or attorney.

Food for Thought

If you are hired to represent a corporation and its new employee against trade secret misappropriation claims and the issue of the Fifth Amendment privilege against self-incrimination comes up, what should you do? What can a plaintiff's attorney do to reduce the number of Fifth Amendment issues that may arise in a civil trade secret misappropriation case?

NOTES

1. **Criminal law and the DTSA.** The DTSA amended the pre-existing criminal provisions of the EEA in at least 4 ways, as reflected in Appendix A of this book. First, the penalties for a violation of Section 1832 were increased Second, the whistleblower immunity was added (18 U.S.C. § 1833(b)), providing a defense to both civil and criminal trade secret misappropriation claims. Third, a "Rights of Trade Secrets Owners" provision (18 U.S.C. § 1835(b)) was added that allows trade secret owners to intervene in criminal prosecutions in order to protect their trade secrets. Lastly, the last provision of the DTSA makes trade secret misappropriation a predicate act under RICO, 18 U.S.C. § 1961(1).

2. **A note on the CFAA.** Another criminal cause of action that may be available when a computer has been used inappropriately to transmit or intercept information is the Computer Fraud and Abuse Act ("CFAA"). 18 U.S.C. § 1030. The Act prohibits accessing a computer without authorization to obtain information. The phrase "without authorization" is not defined in the Act and it is questionable whether it would cover an employee who at the time of accessing the information was permitted to access the computers, even if the later use of the information were unauthorized. *See Diamond Power Int'l, Inc. v. Davidson,* 540 F.Supp.2d 1322, 1341–44 (N.D. Ga. 2007) (recognizing a split among the courts on the interpretation of "without authorization," but holding that "a violation does not depend upon the defendant's unauthorized use of information, but rather upon the defendant's unauthorized use of access"). It may therefore be applicable where employees use the employer's computer to send "unauthorized" e-mail with confidential information to others, including prospective new employers. *See* Graham M. Liccardi, *The CFAA: A Vehicle for Litigating Trade Secrets in Federal Court,* 8 J. MARSHALL REV. INTELL. PROP. L. 155 (2008). In *United States v. Nosal (Nosal II),* 2016 WL 3608752 (9th Cir. July 5, 2016), the Ninth Circuit Court of Appeals even held that it can be a violation of the CFAA to use another person's password in violation of a company policy.

The CFAA provides both criminal and civil remedies, including a private right of action against a person who intentionally causes damage to a protected computer. A "protected computer" is a computer "which is used in or affecting interstate or foreign commerce or communication, including a computer located outside the United States that is used in a manner that affects interstate or foreign commerce or communication of the United States." 18 U.S.C. § 1030(e)(2)(B).

3. **The Taborsky story.** As you have seen throughout the cases in this book, trade secret law intersects with many other areas of law such as property law, criminal law, tort law, and contract law. The facts of *Taborsky v. State of Florida*, 659 So.2d 1112 (1995), present a criminal trade secret case involving employment law and patent law at an academic institution. As reported in the case:

> The essential facts are that in August 1987, USF [the University of South Florida] contracted with Progress Technologies Corporation (PTC) to provide research in the area of municipal wastewater management and treatment. The research project focused, in part, on improving the use of clinoptilolite (clino) in the wastewater treatment process. PTC and USF executed an agreement requiring that the research remain proprietary and confidential. Progress Water Technologies Corporation (PWT), an affiliate of PTC, subsequently contracted with USF to continue and expand the clino research. That agreement also required the research to remain proprietary and confidential.

> Taborsky, an undergraduate research assistant, worked on this research project * * *. He entered into a confidentiality agreement with PWT, which the parties intended would apply to all research relating to the project. * * * Following a Christmas vacation break, Taborsky left USF and never returned as a student. He took with him laboratory notebooks containing proprietary and confidential research. Taborsky refused to respond to repeated requests for return of the notebooks and other information and, in July 1989, was charged with violating section 812.014(2)(b), Florida Statutes (1987), in one count of second degree grand theft and with violating section 812.081(2), Florida Statutes (1987), in one count of theft of trade secrets. In January 1990, a jury convicted Taborsky of the second degree grand theft charge of violating section 812.014(2)(b), and a lesser included count of theft of trade secrets. Taborsky was sentenced to one year of house arrest, fifteen years' probation and 500 hours of community service. As a condition of Taborsky's probation, the judge expressly prohibited him from using the stolen research for any purpose. * * *

> In violation of the circuit court's sentencing order, Taborsky obtained a patent that included or was related to the research he stole from USF. In response, the state attorney's office moved to revoke his

probation. The criminal court ruled that Taborsky willfully and intentionally violated his probation and, accordingly, revoked his probation and sentenced him to three-and-one-half years of incarceration, suspended, and placed him on fifteen years' probation. The criminal court further directed Taborsky to assign his patent to USF as restitution.

Taborsky refused to assign his patents to the university. As a result, his probation was revoked and he was sent to prison for three and one-half years. He refused to accept a pardon from the governor of Florida. What lessons do you think can be learned from this story?

4. **The Aleynikov story.** Sergey Aleynikov was a Vice President in Goldman Sach's Equities Division. He was responsible for developing some of the source code for Goldman's high frequency trading platform. A startup, Teza Technologies, offered him a $1.2 million position as Executive Vice President, so that he could develop a high frequency trading business for Teza. In June 2009, on his way out of Goldman, Aleynikov copied more than 500,000 lines of source code for Goldman's high frequency trading platform and uploaded them to a server in Germany. He then copied the code to his home computers and a flash drive. He brought the code with him to Chicago for meetings with Teza. On his way back from Chicago the FBI arrested him at the Newark Airport.

Aleynikov was indicted for violating the EEA and the National Stolen Property Act (NSPA). After a two-week trial, the jury convicted him on all counts in December 2010. His bail was revoked and he was held in jail until his sentencing in March 2011. He was sentenced to eight years and one month in prison, and fined $12,500. About a year into his prison term, the Second Circuit Court of Appeals overturned his conviction, finding that neither the EEA or the NSPA applied in his case. *See United States v. Aleynikov,* 737 F.Supp.2d 173 (S.D.N.Y. 2010); *United States v. Aleynikov,* 676 F.3d 71 (2d. Cir. 2012).

At the time of his conviction, section 1832 of the EEA made it a crime to convert a trade secret "that is related to or included in a product that is produced for or placed in interstate or foreign commerce." The appeals court held that since Goldman's code was kept secret, it was not "produced for" or "placed in" interstate or foreign commerce. In addition, because this trade secret was not tangible property it could not be "stolen property" under the NSPA. Congress responded swiftly to Aleynikov's acquittal by amending the language of the EEA. The Trade Secret Clarification Act of 2012 made the EEA applicable to a trade secret "that is related to a *product or service used in or intended for use in* interstate or foreign commerce." This is the same language which now serves as the Commerce Clause hook for an action under the DTSA.

Unfortunately for Aleynikov, he was not home free. State prosecutors in Manhattan (after receiving evidence from the federal prosecutors) charged him with violating two New York Statutes: Unlawful Use of Secret Scientific Material and Unlawful Duplication of Computer Material. A trial was held in April 2015 and the jury found him guilty on one count of the Unlawful Use of

Scientific Material charge. However, the trial court granted Aleynikov's motion to dismiss the count on which he was convicted. In short, the court reasoned that Aleynikov's making a copy of computer code did not violate the language of the NY statutes. Prosecutors have appealed the decision. Aleynikov's defense costs for his over five-year battle in federal and state court was estimated to exceed $7 million. *See People v. Aleynikov*, No. 04447/12, slip. op. 1 (N.Y. Sup.Ct. July 6, 2015).

5.   **Trade secrets and racial profiling.** Many of the prosecutions that have been brought under the EEA involved individuals who were either immigrants to the United States or who are of Asian descent. This is due in part to provable facts, but also reflects fears about China acquiring trade secrets from U.S. companies. As a result, questions have been raised about whether such prosecutions involve aspects of racial profiling. The recent dismissal of a case against a professor at Temple University provides a case in point and spurred the National Asian Pacific American Bar Association to express its concerns. *See 70+ Asian Pacific American, Civil Rights, and Civil Liberties Organizations Urge U.S. Attorney General to Investigate Possible Profiling of Asian American Scientists*, available at: http://www.napaba.org/ news/news.asp?id=260541&hhSearchTerms=%22trade+and+secrets%22.

6.   **Bibliographic note:** In addition to the references noted above, for more information on the topics discussed in this chapter, *see* MILGRIM ON TRADE SECRETS, § 12.06 (2016); Melanie Reid, *A Comparative Approach to Economic Espionage: Is Any Nation Effectively Dealing with this Global Threat?*, 70 U. MIAMI L.REV. 757 (2016); Elizabeth A. Rowe and Sharon K. Sandeen, TRADE SECRECY AND INTERNATIONAL TRANSACTIONS (2015); Elizabeth A. Rowe and Daniel M. Mahfood, *Trade Secrets, Trade, and Extraterritoriality*, 66 ALABAMA L.REV. 63 (2014); Adam Cohen, *Securing Trade Secrets in the Information Age: Upgrading the Economic Espionage Act After* United States v. Aleynikov, 30 YALE J. ON REG. 189 (2013); R. Mark Halligan, *Protection of U.S. Trade Secret Assets: Critical Amendments to the Economic Espionage Act of 1996*, 7 J. MARSHALL REV. INTELL. PROP. L. 656 (2008); James H.A. Pooley et al., *Understanding the Economic Espionage Act of 1996*, 5 TEX. INTELL. PROP. L.J. 177 (1997); Robert Heidt, *The Conjurer's Circle—The Fifth Amendment Privilege in Civil Cases*, 91 YALE L. J. 1062 (1982); Robert Heidt, *The Fifth Amendment Privilege and Documents—Cutting Fischer's Tangled Line*, 49 MISSOURI L. REV. 440 (1984).

APPENDIX A

THE "NEW" ECONOMIC ESPIONAGE ACT, AS AMENDED BY THE DEFEND TRADE SECRETS ACT OF 2016

■ ■ ■

[The Defend Trade Secrets Act of 2016 is "An Act to Amend chapter 90 of title 18, United States Code, to provide Federal jurisdiction for the theft of trade secrets, and for other purposes" that was signed by President Obama and effective on May 11, 2016. *See* Pub. L. 114–529. The following shows the amendments as made to the pre-existing Economic Espionage Act of 1996, as earlier amended in 2012. The "New" sections are numbered as they are in the DTSA.]

18 U.S.C. § 1831. Economic espionage

(a) **IN GENERAL.**—Whoever, intending or knowing that the offense will benefit any foreign government, foreign instrumentality, or foreign agent, knowingly—

    (1) steals, or without authorization appropriates, takes, carries away, or conceals, or by fraud, artifice, or deception obtains a trade secret;

    (2) without authorization copies, duplicates, sketches, draws, photographs, downloads, uploads, alters, destroys, photocopies, replicates, transmits, delivers, sends, mails, communicates, or conveys a trade secret;

    (3) receives, buys, or possesses a trade secret, knowing the same to have been stolen or appropriated, obtained, or converted without authorization;

    (4) attempts to commit any offense described in any of paragraphs (1) through (3); or

    (5) conspires with one or more other persons to commit any offense described in any of paragraphs (1) through (3), and one or more of such persons do any act to effect the object of the conspiracy, shall, except as provided in subsection (b), be fined not more than $5,000,000 or imprisoned not more than 15 years, or both.

(b) **ORGANIZATIONS.**—Any organization that commits any offense described in subsection (a) shall be fined not more than the greater of $10,000,000 or 3 times the value of the stolen trade secret to the organization, including expenses for research and design and other costs of reproducing the trade secret that the organization has thereby avoided.

(Added Pub. L. 104–294, title I, § 101(a), Oct. 11, 1996, 110 Stat. 3488; amended Pub. L. 112–269, § 2, Jan. 14, 2013,126 Stat. 2442.)

18 U.S.C. § 1832. Theft of trade secrets

(a) Whoever, with intent to convert a trade secret, that is related to a product or service used in or intended for use in interstate or foreign commerce, to the economic benefit of anyone other than the owner thereof, and intending or knowing that the offense will, injure any owner of that trade secret, knowingly—

   (1) steals, or without authorization appropriates, takes, carries away, or conceals, or by fraud, artifice, or deception obtains such information;

   (2) without authorization copies, duplicates, sketches, draws, photographs, downloads, uploads, alters, destroys, photocopies, replicates, transmits, delivers, sends, mails, communicates, or conveys such information;

   (3) receives, buys, or possesses such information, knowing the same to have been stolen or appropriated, obtained, or converted without authorization;

   (4) attempts to commit any offense described in paragraphs (1) through (3); or

   (5) conspires with one or more other persons to commit any offense described in paragraphs (1) through (3), and one or more of such persons do any act to effect the object of the conspiracy, shall, except as provided in subsection (b), be fined under this title or imprisoned not more than 10 years, or both.

(b) Any organization that commits any offense described in subsection (a) shall be fined not more than $~~5,000,000~~ the greater of $5,000,000 or 3 times the value of the stolen trade secret to the organization, including expenses for research and design and other costs of reproducing the trade secret that the organization has thereby avoided.

(Added Pub. L. 104–294, title I, § 101(a), Oct. 11, 1996, 110 Stat. 3489; amended Pub. L. 112–236, § 2, Dec. 28, 2012,126 Stat. 1627; [Also amended by the Defend Trade Secrets Act of 2016].)

18 U.S.C. § 1833. Exceptions to prohibitions

~~This chapter~~(a)   IN GENERAL.—This chapter does not prohibit or create a private action for—

immunity to disclosure of TS to a lawyer or govt agency

(1)   any otherwise lawful activity conducted by a governmental entity of the United States, a State, or a political subdivision of a State; or

(2)   ~~the reporting of a suspected violation of law to any governmental entity of the United States, a State, or a political subdivision of a State, if such entity has lawful authority with respect to that violation.~~ the disclosure of a trade secret in accordance with subsection (b).

(b)   IMMUNITY FROM LIABILITY FOR CONFIDENTIAL DISCLOSURE OF A TRADE SECRET TO THE GOVERNMENT OR IN A COURT FILING.—

(lawyer)

(1)   IMMUNITY.—An individual shall not be held criminally or civilly liable under any Federal or State trade secret law for the disclosure of a trade secret that—

(A) is made—

(i)   in confidence to a Federal, State, or local government official, either directly or indirectly, or to an attorney; and

(ii) solely for the purpose of reporting or investigating a suspected violation of law; or

(B) is made in a complaint or other document filed in a lawsuit or other proceeding, if such filing is made under seal.

(2)   USE OF TRADE SECRET INFORMATION IN ANTI-RETALIATION LAWSUIT.—An individual who files a lawsuit for retaliation by an employer for reporting a suspected violation of law may disclose the trade secret to the attorney of the individual and use the trade secret information in the court proceeding, if the individual—

(A) files any document containing the trade secret under seal; and

(B) does not disclose the trade secret, except pursuant to court order.

(3)   NOTICE.—

(A) IN GENERAL.—An employer shall provide notice of the immunity set forth in this subsection in any contract or

-if employer has you sign NDA, they must give you notice of this immunity

agreement with an employee that governs the use of a trade secret or other confidential information.

(B) POLICY DOCUMENT.—An employer shall be considered to be in compliance with the notice requirement in subparagraph (A) if the employer provides a cross-reference to a policy document provided to the employee that sets forth the employer's reporting policy for a suspected violation of law.

(C) NON-COMPLIANCE.—If an employer does not comply with the notice requirement in subparagraph (A), the employer may not be awarded exemplary damages or attorney fees under subparagraph (C) or (D) of section 1836(b)(3) in an action against an employee to whom notice was not provided.

(D) APPLICABILITY.—This paragraph shall apply to contracts and agreements that are entered into or updated after the date of enactment of this subsection.

(4) EMPLOYEE DEFINED.—For purposes of this subsection, the term 'employee' includes any individual performing work as a contractor or consultant for an employer.

(5) RULE OF CONSTRUCTION.—Except as expressly provided for under this subsection, nothing in this subsection shall be construed to authorize, or limit liability for, an act that is otherwise prohibited by law, such as the unlawful access of material by unauthorized means.

(Added Pub. L. 104–294, title I, § 101(a), Oct. 11, 1996, 110 Stat. 3489; [Also amended by the Defend Trade Secrets Act of 2016].)

18 U.S.C. § 1834. Criminal forfeiture

Forfeiture, destruction, and restitution relating to this chapter shall be subject to section 2323, to the extent provided in that section, in addition to any other similar remedies provided by law.

(Added Pub. L. 104–294, title I, § 101(a), Oct. 11, 1996, 110 Stat. 3489; amended Pub. L. 110–403, title II, § 207, Oct. 13, 2008, 122 Stat. 4263.)

18 U.S.C. § 1835. Orders to preserve confidentiality

~~In any prosecution~~ (a) IN GENERAL.—In any prosecution or other proceeding under this chapter, the court shall enter such orders and take such other action as may be necessary and appropriate to preserve the confidentiality of trade secrets, consistent with the requirements of the Federal Rules of Criminal and Civil Procedure, the Federal Rules of Evidence, and all other applicable laws. An interlocutory appeal by the United States shall lie from a decision or order of a district court authorizing or directing the disclosure of any trade secret.

(b) RIGHTS OF TRADE SECRET OWNERS.—The court may not authorize or direct the disclosure of any information the owner asserts to be a trade secret unless the court allows the owner the opportunity to file a submission under seal that describes the interest of the owner in keeping the information confidential. No submission under seal made under this subsection may be used in a prosecution under this chapter for any purpose other than those set forth in this section, or otherwise required by law. The provision of information relating to a trade secret to the United States or the court in connection with a prosecution under this chapter shall not constitute a waiver of trade secret protection, and the disclosure of information relating to a trade secret in connection with a prosecution under this chapter shall not constitute a waiver of trade secret protection unless the trade secret owner expressly consents to such waiver.

(Added Pub. L. 104–294, title I, § 101(a), Oct. 11, 1996, 110 Stat. 3490; [Also amended by the Defend Trade Secrets Act of 2016].)

18 U.S.C. § 1836. Civil proceedings ~~to enjoin violations~~

(a) The Attorney General may, in a civil action, obtain appropriate injunctive relief against any violation of this chapter.

(b) ~~The district courts of the United States shall have exclusive original jurisdiction of civil actions under this section.~~

(b) PRIVATE CIVIL ACTIONS.—

(1) IN GENERAL.—An owner of a trade secret that is misappropriated may bring a civil action under this subsection if the trade secret is related to a product or service used in, or intended for use in, interstate or foreign commerce.

(2) CIVIL SEIZURE.—

(A) IN GENERAL.—

(i) APPLICATION.—Based on an affidavit or verified complaint satisfying the requirements of this paragraph, the court may, upon ex parte application but only in extraordinary circumstances, issue an order providing for the seizure of property necessary to prevent the propagation or dissemination of the trade secret that is the subject of the action.

(ii) REQUIREMENTS FOR ISSUING ORDER.—The court may not grant an application under clause (i) unless the court finds that it clearly appears from specific facts that—

(I) an order issued pursuant to Rule 65 of the Federal Rules of Civil Procedure or another form of equitable relief would be inadequate to achieve the purpose of this paragraph because the party to which the order would be issued would evade, avoid, or otherwise not comply with such an order;

(II) an immediate and irreparable injury will occur if such seizure is not ordered;

(III) the harm to the applicant of denying the application outweighs the harm to the legitimate interests of the person against whom seizure would be ordered of granting the application and substantially outweighs the harm to any third parties who may be harmed by such seizure;

(IV) the applicant is likely to succeed in showing that—

(aa) the information is a trade secret; and

(bb) the person against whom seizure would be ordered—

(AA) misappropriated the trade secret of the applicant by improper means; or

(BB) conspired to use improper means to misappropriate the trade secret of the applicant;

(V) the person against whom seizure would be ordered has actual possession of—

(aa) the trade secret; and

(bb) any property to be seized;

(VI) the application describes with reasonable particularity the matter to be seized and, to the extent reasonable under the circumstances, identifies the location where the matter is to be seized;

(VII) the person against whom seizure would be ordered, or persons acting in concert with such person, would destroy, move, hide, or otherwise make such matter inaccessible to the court, if the applicant were to proceed on notice to such person; and

(VIII) the applicant has not publicized the requested seizure.

(B) ELEMENTS OF ORDER.—If an order is issued under subparagraph (A), it shall—

(i)   set forth findings of fact and conclusions of law required for the order;

(ii) provide for the narrowest seizure of property necessary to achieve the purpose of this paragraph and direct that the seizure be conducted in a manner that minimizes any interruption of the business operations of third parties and, to the extent possible, does not interrupt the legitimate business operations of the person accused of misappropriating the trade secret;

(iii) (I) be accompanied by an order protecting the seized property from disclosure by prohibiting access by the applicant or the person against whom the order is directed, and prohibiting any copies, in whole or in part, of the seized property, to prevent undue damage to the party against whom the order has issued or others, until such parties have an opportunity to be heard in court; and

(II) provide that if access is granted by the court to the applicant or the person against whom the order is directed, the access shall be consistent with subparagraph (D);

(iv) provide guidance to the law enforcement officials executing the seizure that clearly delineates the scope of the authority of the officials, including—

(I) the hours during which the seizure may be executed; and

(II) whether force may be used to access locked areas;

(v) set a date for a hearing described in subparagraph (F) at the earliest possible time, and not later than 7 days after the order has issued, unless the party against whom the order is directed and others harmed by the order consent to another date for the hearing, except that a party against whom the order has issued or any person harmed by the order may move the court at any time to dissolve or modify the order after giving notice to the applicant who obtained the order; and

(vi) require the person obtaining the order to provide the security determined adequate by the court for the payment of the damages that any person may be entitled to recover as a result of a wrongful or excessive seizure or wrongful or excessive attempted seizure under this paragraph.

(C) PROTECTION FROM PUBLICITY.—The court shall take appropriate action to protect the person against whom an order under this paragraph is directed from publicity, by or at the behest of the person obtaining the order, about such order and any seizure under such order.

(D) MATERIALS IN CUSTODY OF COURT.—

(i) IN GENERAL.—Any materials seized under this paragraph shall be taken into the custody of the court. The court shall secure the seized material from physical and electronic access during the seizure and while in the custody of the court.

(ii) STORAGE MEDIUM.—If the seized material includes a storage medium, or if the seized material is stored on a storage medium, the court shall prohibit the medium from being connected to a network or the Internet without the consent of both parties, until the hearing required under subparagraph (B)(v) and described in subparagraph (F).

(iii) PROTECTION OF CONFIDENTIALITY.—The court shall take appropriate measures to protect the confidentiality of seized materials that are unrelated to the trade secret information ordered seized pursuant to this paragraph unless the person against whom the order is entered consents to disclosure of the material.

(iv) APPOINTMENT OF SPECIAL MASTER.—The court may appoint a special master to locate and isolate all misappropriated trade secret information and to facilitate the return of unrelated property and data to the person from whom the property was seized. The special master appointed by the court shall agree to be bound by a non-disclosure agreement approved by the court.

(E) SERVICE OF ORDER.—The court shall order that service of a copy of the order under this paragraph, and the submissions of the applicant to obtain the order, shall be made by a Federal law enforcement officer who, upon making service, shall carry out the seizure under the order. The court may allow State or local law enforcement officials to participate, but may not permit the applicant or any agent of the applicant to participate in the seizure. At the request of law enforcement officials, the court may allow a technical expert who is unaffiliated with the applicant and who is bound by a court-approved non-disclosure agreement to participate in the seizure if the court determines that the participation of the expert will aid the efficient execution of and minimize the burden of the seizure.

(F) SEIZURE HEARING.—

(i) DATE.—A court that issues a seizure order shall hold a hearing on the date set by the court under subparagraph (B)(v).

(ii) BURDEN OF PROOF.—At a hearing held under this subparagraph, the party who obtained the order under subparagraph (A) shall have the burden to prove the facts supporting the findings of fact and conclusions of law necessary to support the order. If the party fails to meet that burden, the seizure order shall be dissolved or modified appropriately.

(iii) DISSOLUTION OR MODIFICATION OF ORDER.—A party against whom the order has been issued or any person harmed by the order may move the court at any time to dissolve or modify the order after giving notice to the party who obtained the order.

(iv) DISCOVERY TIME LIMITS.—The court may make such orders modifying the time limits for discovery under the Federal Rules of Civil Procedure as may be necessary to prevent the frustration of the purposes of a hearing under this subparagraph.

(G) ACTION FOR DAMAGE CAUSED BY WRONGFUL SEIZURE.—A person who suffers damage by reason of a wrongful or excessive seizure under this paragraph has a cause of action against the applicant for the order under which such seizure was made, and shall be entitled to the same relief as is provided under section 34(d)(11) of the Trademark Act of 1946 (15 U.S.C. 1116(d)(11)). The security posted with the court under subparagraph (B)(vi) shall not limit the recovery of third parties for damages.

(H) MOTION FOR ENCRYPTION.—A party or a person who claims to have an interest in the subject matter seized may make a motion at any time, which may be heard ex parte, to encrypt any material seized or to be seized under this paragraph that is stored on a storage medium. The motion shall include, when possible, the desired encryption method.

(3) REMEDIES.—In a civil action brought under this subsection with respect to the misappropriation of a trade secret, a court may—

(A) grant an injunction—

(i) to prevent any actual or threatened misappropriation described in paragraph (1) on such terms as the court deems reasonable, provided the order does not—

(I) prevent a person from entering into an employment relationship, and that conditions placed on such employment shall be based on evidence of threatened misappropriation and not merely on the information the person knows; or

(II) otherwise conflict with an applicable State law prohibiting restraints on the practice of a lawful profession, trade, or business;

(ii) if determined appropriate by the court, requiring affirmative actions to be taken to protect the trade secret; and

(iii) in exceptional circumstances that render an injunction inequitable, that conditions future use of the trade secret upon payment of a reasonable royalty for no longer than the period of time for which such use could have been prohibited;

(B) award—

    (i) (I) damages for actual loss caused by the misappropriation of the trade secret; and

        (II) damages for any unjust enrichment caused by the misappropriation of the trade secret that is not addressed in computing damages for actual loss; or

    (ii) in lieu of damages measured by any other methods, the damages caused by the misappropriation measured by imposition of liability for a reasonable royalty for the misappropriator's unauthorized disclosure or use of the trade secret;

(C) if the trade secret is willfully and maliciously misappropriated, award exemplary damages in an amount not more than 2 times the amount of the damages awarded under subparagraph (B); and

(D) if a claim of the misappropriation is made in bad faith, which may be established by circumstantial evidence, a motion to terminate an injunction is made or opposed in bad faith, or the trade secret was willfully and maliciously misappropriated, award reasonable attorney's fees to the prevailing party.

(c) JURISDICTION.—The district courts of the United States shall have original jurisdiction of civil actions brought under this section.

(d) PERIOD OF LIMITATIONS.—A civil action under subsection (b) may not be commenced later than 3 years after the date on which the misappropriation with respect to which the action would relate is discovered or by the exercise of reasonable diligence should have been discovered. For purposes of this subsection, a continuing misappropriation constitutes a single claim of misappropriation.

(e) EFFECTIVE DATE.—The amendments made by this section shall apply with respect to any misappropriation of a trade secret (as defined in section 1839 of title 18, United States Code, as amended by this section) for which any act occurs on or after the date of the enactment of this Act.

(f) RULE OF CONSTRUCTION.—Nothing in the amendments made by this section shall be construed to modify the rule of construction under section 1838 of title 18, United States Code, or to preempt any other provision of law.

(g) APPLICABILITY TO OTHER LAWS.—This section and the amendments made by this section shall not be construed to be a law pertaining to intellectual property for purposes of any other Act of Congress.

(Added Pub. L. 104–294, title I, § 101(a), Oct. 11, 1996, 110 Stat. 3490; amended Pub. L. 107–273, div. B, title IV, § 4002(e)(9), Nov. 2, 2002, 116 Stat. 1810; [also amended by the Defend Trade Secrets Act of 2016] .)

18 U.S.C. § 1837. Applicability to conduct outside of the United States

This chapter also applies to conduct occurring outside the United States if—

(1) the offender is a natural person who is a citizen or permanent resident alien of the United States, or an organization organized under the laws of the United States or a State or political subdivision thereof; or

(2) an act in furtherance of the offense was committed in the United States.

(Added Pub. L. 104–294, title I, § 101(a), Oct. 11, 1996, 110 Stat. 3490.)

18 U.S.C. § 1838. Constructions with other laws

~~This chapter~~ Except as provided in section 1833(b), this chapter shall not be construed to preempt or displace any other remedies, whether civil or criminal, provided by United States Federal, State, commonwealth, possession, or territory law for the misappropriation of a trade secret, or to affect the otherwise lawful disclosure of information by any Government employee under section 552 of title 5 (commonly known as the Freedom of Information Act).

(Added Pub. L. 104–294, title I, § 101(a), Oct. 11, 1996, 110 Stat. 3490; [Also amended by the Defend Trade Secrets Act of 2016].)

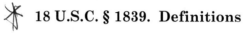 18 U.S.C. § 1839. Definitions

As used in this chapter—

(1) the term "foreign instrumentality" means any agency, bureau, ministry, component, institution, association, or any legal, commercial, or business organization, corporation, firm, or entity that is substantially owned, controlled, sponsored, commanded, managed, or dominated by a foreign government;

(2) the term "foreign agent" means any officer, employee, proxy, servant, delegate, or representative of a foreign government;

(3) the term "trade secret" means all forms and types of financial, business, scientific, technical, economic, or engineering information, including patterns, plans, compilations, program devices, formulas, designs, prototypes, methods, techniques, processes, procedures, programs, or codes, whether tangible or intangible, and whether or how stored, compiled, or memorialized physically, electronically, graphically, photographically, or in writing if—

   (A) the owner thereof has taken reasonable measures to keep such information secret; and

   (B) the information derives independent economic value, actual or potential, from not being generally known to, and not being readily ascertainable through proper means by, the public another person who can obtain economic value from the disclosure or use of the information; and

(4) the term "owner", with respect to a trade secret, means the person or entity in whom or in which rightful legal or equitable title to, or license in, the trade secret is reposed;.

(5) the term 'misappropriation' means—

   (A) acquisition of a trade secret of another by a person who knows or has reason to know that the trade secret was acquired by improper means; or

   (B) disclosure or use of a trade secret of another without express or implied consent by a person who—

      (i) used improper means to acquire knowledge of the trade secret;

      (ii) at the time of disclosure or use, knew or had reason to know that the knowledge of the trade secret was—

         (I) derived from or through a person who had used improper means to acquire the trade secret;

         (II) acquired under circumstances giving rise to a duty to maintain the secrecy of the trade secret or limit the use of the trade secret; or

         (III) derived from or through a person who owed a duty to the person seeking relief to maintain the secrecy of the trade secret or limit the use of the trade secret; or

(iii) before a material change of the position of the person, knew or had reason to know that—

(I)   the trade secret was a trade secret; and

(II)   knowledge of the trade secret had been acquired by accident or mistake;

(6)   the term 'improper means'—

(A)   includes theft, bribery, misrepresentation, breach or inducement of a breach of a duty to maintain secrecy, or espionage through electronic or other means; and

(B)   does not include reverse engineering, independent derivation, or any other lawful means of acquisition; and

(7)   the term 'Trademark Act of 1946' means the Act entitled 'An Act to provide for the registration and protection of trademarks used in commerce, to carry out the provisions of certain international conventions, and for other purposes, approved July 5, 1946 (15 U.S.C. 1051 et seq.) (commonly referred to as the 'Trademark Act of 1946' or the 'Lanham Act')'.

(Added Pub. L. 104–294, title I, § 101(a), Oct. 11, 1996, 110 Stat. 3490; [Also amended by the Defend Trade Secrets Act of 2016].)

[New] Sec. 4. Report on Theft of Trade Secrets Occurring Abroad

(a)   DEFINITIONS.—In this section:

(1)   DIRECTOR.—The term "Director" means the Under Secretary of Commerce for Intellectual Property and Director of the United States Patent and Trademark Office.

(2)   FOREIGN INSTRUMENTALITY, ETC.—The terms "foreign instrumentality", "foreign agent", and "trade secret" have the meanings given those terms in section 1839 of title 18, United States Code.

(3)   STATE.—The term "State" includes the District of Columbia and any commonwealth, territory, or possession of the United States.

(4)   UNITED STATES COMPANY.—The term "United States company" means an organization organized under the laws of the United States or a State or political subdivision thereof.

(b)   REPORTS.—Not later than 1 year after the date of enactment of this Act, and biannually thereafter, the Attorney General, in consultation with the Intellectual Property Enforcement Coordinator, the Director, and the heads of other appropriate agencies, shall submit to the Committees on the Judiciary of the House of Representatives and the Senate, and make publicly available on the Web site of the Department of Justice and disseminate to the public through such other means as the Attorney General may identify, a report on the following:

(1) The scope and breadth of the theft of the trade secrets of United States companies occurring outside of the United States.

(2) The extent to which theft of trade secrets occurring outside of the United States is sponsored by foreign governments, foreign instrumentalities, or foreign agents.

(3) The threat posed by theft of trade secrets occurring outside of the United States.

(4) The ability and limitations of trade secret owners to prevent the misappropriation of trade secrets outside of the United States, to enforce any judgment against foreign entities for theft of trade secrets, and to prevent imports based on theft of trade secrets overseas.

(5) A breakdown of the trade secret protections afforded United States companies by each country that is a trading partner of the United States and enforcement efforts available and undertaken in each such country, including a list identifying specific countries where trade secret theft, laws, or enforcement is a significant problem for United States companies.

(6) Instances of the Federal Government working with foreign countries to investigate, arrest, and prosecute entities and individuals involved in the theft of trade secrets outside of the United States.

(7) Specific progress made under trade agreements and treaties, including any new remedies enacted by foreign countries, to protect against theft of trade secrets of United States companies outside of the United States.

(8) Recommendations of legislative and executive branch actions that may be undertaken to—

(A) reduce the threat of and economic impact caused by the theft of the trade secrets of United States companies occurring outside of the United States;

(B) educate United States companies regarding the threats to their trade secrets when taken outside of the United States;

(C) provide assistance to United States companies to reduce the risk of loss of their trade secrets when taken outside of the United States; and

(D) provide a mechanism for United States companies to confidentially or anonymously report the theft of trade secrets occurring outside of the United States.

[New] Sec. 5. Sense of Congress

It is the sense of Congress that—

(1) trade secret theft occurs in the United States and around the world;

(2) trade secret theft, wherever it occurs, harms the companies that own the trade secrets and the employees of the companies;

(3) chapter 90 of title 18, United States Code (commonly known as the "Economic Espionage Act of 1996"), applies broadly to protect trade secrets from theft; and

(4) it is important when seizing information to balance the need to prevent or remedy misappropriation with the need to avoid interrupting the—

(A) business of third parties; and

(B) legitimate interests of the party accused of wrongdoing.

[New] Sec. 6. Best Practices

(a) IN GENERAL.—Not later than 2 years after the date of enactment of this Act, the Federal Judicial Center, using existing resources, shall develop recommended best practices for—

(1) the seizure of information and media storing the information; and

(2) the securing of the information and media once seized.

(b) UPDATES.—The Federal Judicial Center shall update the recommended best practices developed under subsection (a) from time to time.

(c) CONGRESSIONAL SUBMISSIONS.—The Federal Judicial Center shall provide a copy of the recommendations developed under subsection (a), and any updates made under subsection (b), to the—

(1) Committee on the Judiciary of the Senate; and

(2) Committee on the Judiciary of the House of Representatives.

Amendments to Provisions of the Law Other than the EEA

(b) RICO PREDICATE OFFENSES.—Section 1961(1) of title 18, United States Code, is amended by inserting "sections 1831 and 1832 (relating to economic espionage and theft of trade secrets)," before "section 1951".

APPENDIX B

DIRECTIVE (EU) 2016/943 OF THE EUROPEAN PARLIAMENT AND OF THE COUNCIL

of 8 June 2016

on the protection of undisclosed know-how and business information (trade secrets) against their unlawful acquisition, use and disclosure

(Text with EEA relevance)

■ ■ ■

THE EUROPEAN PARLIAMENT AND THE COUNCIL OF THE EUROPEAN UNION,

Having regard to the Treaty on the Functioning of the European Union, and in particular Article 114 thereof,

Having regard to the proposal from the European Commission,

After transmission of the draft legislative act to the national parliaments,

Having regard to the opinion of the European Economic and Social Committee[1],

Acting in accordance with the ordinary legislative procedure[2],

Whereas:

(1) Businesses and non-commercial research institutions invest in acquiring, developing and applying know-how and information which is the currency of the knowledge economy and provides a competitive advantage. This investment in generating and applying intellectual capital is a determining factor as regards their competitiveness and innovation-related performance in the market and therefore their returns on investment, which is the underlying motivation for business research and development. Businesses have recourse to different means to appropriate the results of their innovation-related activities when openness does not allow for the full exploitation of their investment in research

---

[1]   OJ C 226, 16.7.2014, p. 48.

[2]   Position of the European Parliament of 14 April 2016 (not yet published in the Official Journal) and decision of the Council of 27 May 2016.

and innovation. Use of intellectual property rights, such as patents, design rights or copyright, is one such means. Another means of appropriating the results of innovation is to protect access to, and exploit, knowledge that is valuable to the entity and not widely known. Such valuable know-how and business information, that is undisclosed and intended to remain confidential, is referred to as a trade secret.

(2) Businesses, irrespective of their size, value trade secrets as much as patents and other forms of intellectual property right. They use confidentiality as a business competitiveness and research innovation management tool, and in relation to a diverse range of information that extends beyond technological knowledge to commercial data such as information on customers and suppliers, business plans, and market research and strategies. Small and medium-sized enterprises (SMEs) value and rely on trade secrets even more. By protecting such a wide range of know-how and business information, whether as a complement or as an alternative to intellectual property rights, trade secrets allow creators and innovators to derive profit from their creation or innovation and, therefore, are particularly important for business competitiveness as well as for research and development, and innovation-related performance.

(3) Open innovation is a catalyst for new ideas which meet the needs of consumers and tackle societal challenges, and allows those ideas to find their way to the market. Such innovation is an important lever for the creation of new knowledge, and underpins the emergence of new and innovative business models based on the use of co-created knowledge. Collaborative research, including cross-border cooperation, is particularly important in increasing the levels of business research and development within the internal market. The dissemination of knowledge and information should be considered as being essential for the purpose of ensuring dynamic, positive and equal business development opportunities, in particular for SMEs. In an internal market in which barriers to cross-border collaboration are minimised and cooperation is not distorted, intellectual creation and innovation should encourage investment in innovative processes, services and products. Such an environment conducive to intellectual creation and innovation, and in which employment mobility is not hindered, is also important for employment growth and for improving the competitiveness of the Union economy. Trade secrets have an important role in protecting the exchange of knowledge between businesses, including in particular SMEs, and research institutions both within and across the borders of the internal

market, in the context of research and development, and innovation. Trade secrets are one of the most commonly used forms of protection of intellectual creation and innovative know-how by businesses, yet at the same time they are the least protected by the existing Union legal framework against their unlawful acquisition, use or disclosure by other parties.

(4) Innovative businesses are increasingly exposed to dishonest practices aimed at misappropriating trade secrets, such as theft, unauthorised copying, economic espionage or the breach of confidentiality requirements, whether from within or from outside of the Union. Recent developments, such as globalisation, increased outsourcing, longer supply chains, and the increased use of information and communication technology contribute to increasing the risk of those practices. The unlawful acquisition, use or disclosure of a trade secret compromises legitimate trade secret holders' ability to obtain first-mover returns from their innovation-related efforts. Without effective and comparable legal means for protecting trade secrets across the Union, incentives to engage in innovation-related cross-border activity within the internal market are undermined, and trade secrets are unable to fulfil their potential as drivers of economic growth and jobs. Thus, innovation and creativity are discouraged and investment diminishes, thereby affecting the smooth functioning of the internal market and undermining its growth-enhancing potential.

(5) International efforts made in the framework of the World Trade Organisation to address this problem led to the conclusion of the Agreement on Trade-related Aspects of Intellectual Property Rights (the TRIPS Agreement). The TRIPS Agreement contains, inter alia, provisions on the protection of trade secrets against their unlawful acquisition, use or disclosure by third parties, which are common international standards. All Member States, as well as the Union itself, are bound by this Agreement which was approved by Council Decision 94/800/EC[3].

(6) Notwithstanding the TRIPS Agreement, there are important differences in the Member States' legislation as regards the protection of trade secrets against their unlawful acquisition, use or disclosure by other persons. For example, not all Member States have adopted national definitions of a trade secret or the unlawful acquisition, use or disclosure of a trade secret, therefore knowledge on the scope of protection is not readily accessible and that scope differs across the Member States. Furthermore, there

---

[3]   Council Decision 94/800/EC of 22 December 1994 concerning the conclusion on behalf of the European Community, as regards matters within its competence, of the agreements reached in the Uruguay Round multilateral negotiations (1986–1994) (OJ L 336, 23.12.1994, p. 1).

is no consistency as regards the civil law remedies available in the event of unlawful acquisition, use or disclosure of trade secrets, as cease and desist orders are not always available in all Member States against third parties who are not competitors of the legitimate trade secret holder. Divergences also exist across the Member States with respect to the treatment of a third party who has acquired the trade secret in good faith but subsequently learns, at the time of use, that the acquisition derived from a previous unlawful acquisition by another party.

(7) National rules also differ as to whether legitimate trade secret holders are allowed to seek the destruction of goods produced by third parties who use trade secrets unlawfully, or the return or destruction of any documents, files or materials containing or embodying the unlawfully acquired or used trade secret. Furthermore, applicable national rules on the calculation of damages do not always take account of the intangible nature of trade secrets, which makes it difficult to demonstrate the actual profits lost or the unjust enrichment of the infringer where no market value can be established for the information in question. Only a few Member States allow for the application of abstract rules on the calculation of damages based on the reasonable royalty or fee which could have been due had a licence for the use of the trade secret existed. Additionally, many national rules do not provide for appropriate protection of the confidentiality of a trade secret where the trade secret holder introduces a claim for alleged unlawful acquisition, use or disclosure of the trade secret by a third party, thereby reducing the attractiveness of the existing measures and remedies and weakening the protection offered.

(8) The differences in the legal protection of trade secrets provided for by the Member States imply that trade secrets do not enjoy an equivalent level of protection throughout the Union, thus leading to fragmentation of the internal market in this area and a weakening of the overall deterrent effect of the relevant rules. The internal market is affected in so far as such differences lower the incentives for businesses to undertake innovation-related cross-border economic activity, including research cooperation or production cooperation with partners, outsourcing or investment in other Member States, which depends on the use of information that enjoys protection as trade secrets. Cross-border network research and development, as well as innovation-related activities, including related production and subsequent cross-border trade, are rendered less attractive and more difficult

within the Union, thus also resulting in Union-wide innovation-related inefficiencies.

(9) In addition, there is a higher risk for businesses in Member States with comparatively lower levels of protection, due to the fact that trade secrets may be stolen or otherwise unlawfully acquired more easily. This leads to inefficient allocation of capital to growth-enhancing innovation within the internal market because of the higher expenditure on protective measures to compensate for the insufficient legal protection in some Member States. It also favours the activity of unfair competitors who, subsequent to the unlawful acquisition of trade secrets, could spread goods resulting from such acquisition across the internal market. Differences in legislative regimes also facilitate the importation of goods from third countries into the Union through entry points with weaker protection, when the design, production or marketing of those goods rely on stolen or otherwise unlawfully acquired trade secrets. On the whole, such differences hinder the proper functioning of the internal market.

(10) It is appropriate to provide for rules at Union level to approximate the laws of the Member States so as to ensure that there is a sufficient and consistent level of civil redress in the internal market in the event of unlawful acquisition, use or disclosure of a trade secret. Those rules should be without prejudice to the possibility for Member States of providing for more far-reaching protection against the unlawful acquisition, use or disclosure of trade secrets, as long as the safeguards explicitly provided for in this Directive for protecting the interests of other parties are respected.

(11) This Directive should not affect the application of Union or national rules that require the disclosure of information, including trade secrets, to the public or to public authorities. Nor should it affect the application of rules that allow public authorities to collect information for the performance of their duties, or rules that allow or require any subsequent disclosure by those public authorities of relevant information to the public. Such rules include, in particular, rules on the disclosure by the Union's institutions and bodies or national public authorities of business-related information they hold pursuant to Regulation (EC) No 1049/2001 of the European Parliament and of the Council[4], Regulation (EC) No 1367/2006 of the European Parliament and of

---

[4] Regulation (EC) No 1049/2001 of the European Parliament and of the Council of 30 May 2001 regarding public access to European Parliament, Council and Commission documents (OJ L 145, 31.5.2001, p. 43).

the Council[5] and Directive 2003/4/EC of the European Parliament and of the Council[6], or pursuant to other rules on public access to documents or on the transparency obligations of national public authorities.

(12) This Directive should not affect the right of social partners to enter into collective agreements, where provided for under labour law, as regards any obligation not to disclose a trade secret or to limit its use, and the consequences of a breach of such an obligation by the party subject to it. This should be on the condition that any such collective agreement does not restrict the exceptions laid down in this Directive when an application for measures, procedures or remedies provided for in this Directive for alleged acquisition, use or disclosure of a trade secret is to be dismissed.

(13) This Directive should not be understood as restricting the freedom of establishment, the free movement of workers or the mobility of workers as provided for in Union law. Nor is it intended to affect the possibility of concluding non-competition agreements between employers and employees, in accordance with applicable law.

(14) It is important to establish a homogenous definition of a trade secret without restricting the subject matter to be protected against misappropriation. Such definition should therefore be constructed so as to cover know-how, business information and technological information where there is both a legitimate interest in keeping them confidential and a legitimate expectation that such confidentiality will be preserved. Furthermore, such know-how or information should have a commercial value, whether actual or potential. Such know-how or information should be considered to have a commercial value, for example, where its unlawful acquisition, use or disclosure is likely to harm the interests of the person lawfully controlling it, in that it undermines that person's scientific and technical potential, business or financial interests, strategic positions or ability to compete. The definition of trade secret excludes trivial information and the experience and skills gained by employees in the normal course of their employment, and also excludes information which is generally known among, or is readily

---

[5]   Regulation (EC) No 1367/2006 of the European Parliament and of the Council of 6 September 2006 on the application of the provisions of the Aarhus Convention on Access to Information, Public Participation in Decision-making and Access to Justice in Environmental Matters to Community institutions and bodies (OJ L 264, 25.9.2006, p. 13).

[6]   Directive 2003/4/EC of the European Parliament and of the Council of 28 January 2003 on public access to environmental information and repealing Council Directive 90/313/EEC (OJ L 41, 14.2.2003, p. 26).

accessible to, persons within the circles that normally deal with the kind of information in question.

(15) It is also important to identify the circumstances in which legal protection of trade secrets is justified. For this reason, it is necessary to establish the conduct and practices which are to be regarded as unlawful acquisition, use or disclosure of a trade secret.

(16) In the interest of innovation and to foster competition, the provisions of this Directive should not create any exclusive right to know-how or information protected as trade secrets. Thus, the independent discovery of the same know-how or information should remain possible. Reverse engineering of a lawfully acquired product should be considered as a lawful means of acquiring information, except when otherwise contractually agreed. The freedom to enter into such contractual arrangements can, however, be limited by law.

(17) In some industry sectors, where creators and innovators cannot benefit from exclusive rights and where innovation has traditionally relied upon trade secrets, products can nowadays be easily reverse-engineered once in the market. In such cases, those creators and innovators can be victims of practices such as parasitic copying or slavish imitations that free-ride on their reputation and innovation efforts. Some national laws dealing with unfair competition address those practices. While this Directive does not aim to reform or harmonise the law on unfair competition in general, it would be appropriate that the Commission carefully examine the need for Union action in that area.

(18) Furthermore, the acquisition, use or disclosure of trade secrets, whenever imposed or permitted by law, should be treated as lawful for the purposes of this Directive. This concerns, in particular, the acquisition and disclosure of trade secrets in the context of the exercise of the rights of workers' representatives to information, consultation and participation in accordance with Union law and national laws and practices, and the collective defence of the interests of workers and employers, including co-determination, as well as the acquisition or disclosure of a trade secret in the context of statutory audits performed in accordance with Union or national law. However, such treatment of the acquisition of a trade secret as lawful should be without prejudice to any obligation of confidentiality as regards the trade secret or any limitation as to its use that Union or national law imposes on the recipient or acquirer of the information. In particular, this

Directive should not release public authorities from the confidentiality obligations to which they are subject in respect of information passed on by trade secret holders, irrespective of whether those obligations are laid down in Union or national law. Such confidentiality obligations include, inter alia, the obligations in respect of information forwarded to contracting authorities in the context of procurement procedures, as laid down, for example, in Directive 2014/23/EU of the European Parliament and of the Council[7], Directive 2014/24/EU of the European Parliament and of the Council[8] and Directive 2014/25/EU of the European Parliament and of the Council[9].

(19) While this Directive provides for measures and remedies which can consist of preventing the disclosure of information in order to protect the confidentiality of trade secrets, it is essential that the exercise of the right to freedom of expression and information which encompasses media freedom and pluralism, as reflected in Article 11 of the Charter of Fundamental Rights of the European Union ('the Charter'), not be restricted, in particular with regard to investigative journalism and the protection of journalistic sources.

(20) The measures, procedures and remedies provided for in this Directive should not restrict whistleblowing activity. Therefore, the protection of trade secrets should not extend to cases in which disclosure of a trade secret serves the public interest, insofar as directly relevant misconduct, wrongdoing or illegal activity is revealed. This should not be seen as preventing the competent judicial authorities from allowing an exception to the application of measures, procedures and remedies in a case where the respondent had every reason to believe in good faith that his or her conduct satisfied the appropriate criteria set out in this Directive.

(21) In line with the principle of proportionality, measures, procedures and remedies intended to protect trade secrets should be tailored to meet the objective of a smooth-functioning internal market for research and innovation, in particular by deterring the unlawful acquisition, use and disclosure of a trade secret. Such tailoring of measures, procedures and remedies should not jeopardise or undermine fundamental rights and freedoms or the public

---

[7]　Directive 2014/23/EU of the European Parliament and of the Council of 26 February 2014 on the award of concession contracts (OJ L 94, 28.3.2014, p. 1).

[8]　Directive 2014/24/EU of the European Parliament and of the Council of 26 February 2014 on public procurement and repealing Directive 2004/18/EC (OJ L 94, 28.3.2014, p. 65).

[9]　Directive 2014/25/EU of the European Parliament and of the Council of 26 February 2014 on procurement by entities operating in the water, energy, transport and postal services sectors and repealing Directive 2004/17/EC (OJ L 94, 28.3.2014, p. 243).

interest, such as public safety, consumer protection, public health and environmental protection, and should be without prejudice to the mobility of workers. In this respect, the measures, procedures and remedies provided for in this Directive are aimed at ensuring that competent judicial authorities take into account factors such as the value of a trade secret, the seriousness of the conduct resulting in the unlawful acquisition, use or disclosure of the trade secret and the impact of such conduct. It should also be ensured that the competent judicial authorities have the discretion to weigh up the interests of the parties to the legal proceedings, as well as the interests of third parties including, where appropriate, consumers.

(22) The smooth-functioning of the internal market would be undermined if the measures, procedures and remedies provided for were used to pursue illegitimate intents incompatible with the objectives of this Directive. Therefore, it is important to empower judicial authorities to adopt appropriate measures with regard to applicants who act abusively or in bad faith and submit manifestly unfounded applications with, for example, the aim of unfairly delaying or restricting the respondent's access to the market or otherwise intimidating or harassing the respondent.

(23) In the interest of legal certainty, and considering that legitimate trade secret holders are expected to exercise a duty of care as regards the preservation of the confidentiality of their valuable trade secrets and the monitoring of their use, it is appropriate to restrict substantive claims or the possibility of initiating actions for the protection of trade secrets to a limited period. National law should also specify, in a clear and unambiguous manner, from when that period is to begin to run and under what circumstances that period is to be interrupted or suspended.

(24) The prospect of losing the confidentiality of a trade secret in the course of legal proceedings often deters legitimate trade secret holders from instituting legal proceedings to defend their trade secrets, thus jeopardising the effectiveness of the measures, procedures and remedies provided for. For this reason, it is necessary to establish, subject to appropriate safeguards ensuring the right to an effective remedy and to a fair trial, specific requirements aimed at protecting the confidentiality of the litigated trade secret in the course of legal proceedings instituted for its defence. Such protection should remain in force after the legal proceedings have ended and for as long as the information constituting the trade secret is not in the public domain.

(25) Such requirements should include, as a minimum, the possibility of restricting the circle of persons entitled to have access to evidence or hearings, bearing in mind that all such persons should be subject to the confidentiality requirements set out in this Directive, and of publishing only the non-confidential elements of judicial decisions. In this context, considering that assessing the nature of the information which is the subject of a dispute is one of the main purposes of legal proceedings, it is particularly important to ensure both the effective protection of the confidentiality of trade secrets and respect for the right of the parties to those proceedings to an effective remedy and to a fair trial. The restricted circle of persons should therefore consist of at least one natural person from each of the parties as well as the respective lawyers of the parties and, where applicable, other representatives appropriately qualified in accordance with national law in order to defend, represent or serve the interests of a party in legal proceedings covered by this Directive, who should all have full access to such evidence or hearings. In the event that one of the parties is a legal person, that party should be able to propose a natural person or natural persons who ought to form part of that circle of persons so as to ensure proper representation of that legal person, subject to appropriate judicial control to prevent the objective of the restriction of access to evidence and hearings from being undermined. Such safeguards should not be understood as requiring the parties to be represented by a lawyer or another representative in the course of legal proceedings where such representation is not required by national law. Nor should they be understood as restricting the competence of the courts to decide, in conformity with the applicable rules and practices of the Member State concerned, whether and to what extent relevant court officials should also have full access to evidence and hearings for the exercise of their duties.

(26) The unlawful acquisition, use or disclosure of a trade secret by a third party could have devastating effects on the legitimate trade secret holder, as once publicly disclosed, it would be impossible for that holder to revert to the situation prior to the loss of the trade secret. As a result, it is essential to provide for fast, effective and accessible provisional measures for the immediate termination of the unlawful acquisition, use or disclosure of a trade secret, including where it is used for the provision of services. It is essential that such relief be available without having to await a decision on the merits of the case, while having due respect for the right of defence and the principle of proportionality, and having regard to the characteristics of the case. In certain instances, it should be possible to permit the alleged infringer, subject to the

lodging of one or more guarantees, to continue to use the trade secret, in particular where there is little risk that it will enter the public domain. It should also be possible to require guarantees of a level sufficient to cover the costs and the injury caused to the respondent by an unjustified application, particularly where any delay would cause irreparable harm to the legitimate trade secret holder.

(27) For the same reasons, it is also important to provide for definitive measures to prevent unlawful use or disclosure of a trade secret, including where it is used for the provision of services. For such measures to be effective and proportionate, their duration, when circumstances require a limitation in time, should be sufficient to eliminate any commercial advantage which the third party could have derived from the unlawful acquisition, use or disclosure of the trade secret. In any event, no measure of this type should be enforceable if the information originally covered by the trade secret is in the public domain for reasons that cannot be attributed to the respondent.

(28) It is possible that a trade secret could be used unlawfully to design, produce or market goods, or components thereof, which could be spread across the internal market, thus affecting the commercial interests of the trade secret holder and the functioning of the internal market. In such cases, and when the trade secret in question has a significant impact on the quality, value or price of the goods resulting from that unlawful use or on reducing the cost of, facilitating or speeding up their production or marketing processes, it is important to empower judicial authorities to order effective and appropriate measures with a view to ensuring that those goods are not put on the market or are withdrawn from it. Considering the global nature of trade, it is also necessary that such measures include the prohibition of the importation of those goods into the Union or their storage for the purposes of offering or placing them on the market. Having regard to the principle of proportionality, corrective measures should not necessarily entail the destruction of the goods if other viable options are present, such as depriving the good of its infringing quality or the disposal of the goods outside the market, for example, by means of donations to charitable organisations.

(29) A person could have originally acquired a trade secret in good faith, but only become aware at a later stage, including upon notice served by the original trade secret holder, that that person's knowledge of the trade secret in question derived from sources using or disclosing the relevant trade secret in an unlawful manner. In order to avoid, under those circumstances, the

corrective measures or injunctions provided for causing disproportionate harm to that person, Member States should provide for the possibility, in appropriate cases, of pecuniary compensation being awarded to the injured party as an alternative measure. Such compensation should not, however, exceed the amount of royalties or fees which would have been due had that person obtained authorisation to use the trade secret in question, for the period of time for which use of the trade secret could have been prevented by the original trade secret holder. Nevertheless, where the unlawful use of the trade secret would constitute an infringement of law other than that provided for in this Directive or would be likely to harm consumers, such unlawful use should not be allowed.

(30) In order to avoid a person who knowingly, or with reasonable grounds for knowing, unlawfully acquires, uses or discloses a trade secret being able to benefit from such conduct, and to ensure that the injured trade secret holder, to the extent possible, is placed in the position in which he, she or it would have been had that conduct not taken place, it is necessary to provide for adequate compensation for the prejudice suffered as a result of that unlawful conduct. The amount of damages awarded to the injured trade secret holder should take account of all appropriate factors, such as loss of earnings incurred by the trade secret holder or unfair profits made by the infringer and, where appropriate, any moral prejudice caused to the trade secret holder. As an alternative, for example where, considering the intangible nature of trade secrets, it would be difficult to determine the amount of the actual prejudice suffered, the amount of the damages might be derived from elements such as the royalties or fees which would have been due had the infringer requested authorisation to use the trade secret in question. The aim of that alternative method is not to introduce an obligation to provide for punitive damages, but to ensure compensation based on an objective criterion while taking account of the expenses incurred by the trade secret holder, such as the costs of identification and research. This Directive should not prevent Member States from providing in their national law that the liability for damages of employees is restricted in cases where they have acted without intent.

(31) As a supplementary deterrent to future infringers and to contribute to the awareness of the public at large, it is useful to publicise decisions, including, where appropriate, through prominent advertising, in cases concerning the unlawful acquisition, use or disclosure of trade secrets, on the condition that such publication does not result in the disclosure of the trade

secret or disproportionally affect the privacy and reputation of a natural person.

(32) The effectiveness of the measures, procedures and remedies available to trade secret holders could be undermined in the event of non-compliance with the relevant decisions adopted by the competent judicial authorities. For this reason, it is necessary to ensure that those authorities enjoy the appropriate powers of sanction.

(33) In order to facilitate the uniform application of the measures, procedures and remedies provided for in this Directive, it is appropriate to provide for systems of cooperation and the exchange of information as between Member States on the one hand, and between the Member States and the Commission on the other, in particular by creating a network of correspondents designated by Member States. In addition, in order to review whether those measures fulfil their intended objective, the Commission, assisted, as appropriate, by the European Union Intellectual Property Office, should examine the application of this Directive and the effectiveness of the national measures taken.

(34) This Directive respects the fundamental rights and observes the principles recognised in particular by the Charter, notably the right to respect for private and family life, the right to protection of personal data, the freedom of expression and information, the freedom to choose an occupation and right to engage in work, the freedom to conduct a business, the right to property, the right to good administration, and in particular the access to files, while respecting business secrecy, the right to an effective remedy and to a fair trial and the right of defence.

(35) It is important that the rights to respect for private and family life and to protection of personal data of any person whose personal data may be processed by the trade secret holder when taking steps to protect a trade secret, or of any person involved in legal proceedings concerning the unlawful acquisition, use or disclosure of trade secrets under this Directive, and whose personal data are processed, be respected. Directive 95/46/EC of the European Parliament and of the Council[10] governs the processing of personal data carried out in the Member States in the context of this Directive and under the supervision of the Member States' competent authorities, in particular the public independent

---

[10] Directive 95/46/EC of the European Parliament and of the Council of 24 October 1995 on the protection of individuals with regard to the processing of personal data and on the free movement of such data (OJ L 281, 23.11.1995, p. 31).

authorities designated by the Member States. Thus, this Directive should not affect the rights and obligations laid down in Directive 95/46/EC, in particular the rights of the data subject to access his or her personal data being processed and to obtain the rectification, erasure or blocking of the data where it is incomplete or inaccurate and, where appropriate, the obligation to process sensitive data in accordance with Article 8(5) of Directive 95/46/EC.

(36) Since the objective of this Directive, namely to achieve a smooth-functioning internal market by means of the establishment of a sufficient and comparable level of redress across the internal market in the event of the unlawful acquisition, use or disclosure of a trade secret, cannot be sufficiently achieved by Member States but can rather, by reason of its scale and effects, be better achieved at Union level, the Union may adopt measures in accordance with the principle of subsidiarity as set out in Article 5 of the Treaty on European Union. In accordance with the principle of proportionality, as set out in that Article, this Directive does not go beyond what is necessary in order to achieve that objective.

(37) This Directive does not aim to establish harmonised rules for judicial cooperation, jurisdiction, the recognition and enforcement of judgments in civil and commercial matters, or deal with applicable law. Other Union instruments which govern such matters in general terms should, in principle, remain equally applicable to the field covered by this Directive.

(38) This Directive should not affect the application of competition law rules, in particular Articles 101 and 102 of the Treaty on the Functioning of the European Union ('TFEU'). The measures, procedures and remedies provided for in this Directive should not be used to restrict unduly competition in a manner contrary to the TFEU.

(39) This Directive should not affect the application of any other relevant law in other areas, including intellectual property rights and the law of contract. However, where the scope of application of Directive 2004/48/EC of the European Parliament and of the Council[11] and the scope of this Directive overlap, this Directive takes precedence as *lex specialis*.

(40) The European Data Protection Supervisor was consulted in accordance with Article 28(2) of Regulation (EC) No 45/2001 of the

---

[11] Directive 2004/48/EC of the European Parliament and of the Council of 29 April 2004 on the enforcement of intellectual property rights (OJ L 157, 30.4.2004, p. 45).

European Parliament and of the Council[12] and delivered an opinion on 12 March 2014,

HAVE ADOPTED THIS DIRECTIVE:

CHAPTER I

Subject matter and scope

Article 1

Subject matter and scope

1.   This Directive lays down rules on the protection against the unlawful acquisition, use and disclosure of trade secrets.

Member States may, in compliance with the provisions of the TFEU, provide for more far-reaching protection against the unlawful acquisition, use or disclosure of trade secrets than that required by this Directive, provided that compliance with Articles 3, 5, 6, Article 7(1), Article 8, the second subparagraph of Article 9(1), Article 9(3) and (4), Article 10(2), Articles 11, 13 and Article 15(3) is ensured.

2.   This Directive shall not affect:

(a)   the exercise of the right to freedom of expression and information as set out in the Charter, including respect for the freedom and pluralism of the media;

(b)   the application of Union or national rules requiring trade secret holders to disclose, for reasons of public interest, information, including trade secrets, to the public or to administrative or judicial authorities for the performance of the duties of those authorities;

(c)   the application of Union or national rules requiring or allowing Union institutions and bodies or national public authorities to disclose information submitted by businesses which those institutions, bodies or authorities hold pursuant to, and in compliance with, the obligations and prerogatives set out in Union or national law;

(d)   the autonomy of social partners and their right to enter into collective agreements, in accordance with Union law and national laws and practices.

---

[12]   Regulation (EC) No 45/2001 of the European Parliament and of the Council of 18 December 2000 on the protection of individuals with regard to the processing of personal data by the Community institutions and bodies and on the free movement of such data (OJ L 8, 12.1.2001, p. 1).

3.   Nothing in this Directive shall be understood to offer any ground for restricting the mobility of employees. In particular, in relation to the exercise of such mobility, this Directive shall not offer any ground for:

    (a)   limiting employees' use of information that does not constitute a trade secret as defined in point (1) of Article 2;

    (b)   limiting employees' use of experience and skills honestly acquired in the normal course of their employment;

    (c)   imposing any additional restrictions on employees in their employment contracts other than restrictions imposed in accordance with Union or national law.

Article 2

Definitions

For the purposes of this Directive, the following definitions apply:

(1)   'trade secret' means information which meets all of the following requirements:

    (a)   it is secret in the sense that it is not, as a body or in the precise configuration and assembly of its components, generally known among or readily accessible to persons within the circles that normally deal with the kind of information in question;

    (b)   it has commercial value because it is secret;

    (c)   it has been subject to reasonable steps under the circumstances, by the person lawfully in control of the information, to keep it secret;

(2)   'trade secret holder' means any natural or legal person lawfully controlling a trade secret;

(3)   'infringer' means any natural or legal person who has unlawfully acquired, used or disclosed a trade secret;

(4)   'infringing goods' means goods, the design, characteristics, functioning, production process or marketing of which significantly benefits from trade secrets unlawfully acquired, used or disclosed.

CHAPTER II

Acquisition, use and disclosure of trade secrets

Article 3

Lawful acquisition, use and disclosure of trade secrets

1.   The acquisition of a trade secret shall be considered lawful when the trade secret is obtained by any of the following means:

(a) independent discovery or creation;

(b) observation, study, disassembly or testing of a product or object that has been made available to the public or that is lawfully in the possession of the acquirer of the information who is free from any legally valid duty to limit the acquisition of the trade secret;

(c) exercise of the right of workers or workers' representatives to information and consultation in accordance with Union law and national laws and practices;

(d) any other practice which, under the circumstances, is in conformity with honest commercial practices.

2. The acquisition, use or disclosure of a trade secret shall be considered lawful to the extent that such acquisition, use or disclosure is required or allowed by Union or national law.

Article 4

Unlawful acquisition, use and disclosure of trade secrets

1. Member States shall ensure that trade secret holders are entitled to apply for the measures, procedures and remedies provided for in this Directive in order to prevent, or obtain redress for, the unlawful acquisition, use or disclosure of their trade secret.

2. The acquisition of a trade secret without the consent of the trade secret holder shall be considered unlawful, whenever carried out by:

(a) unauthorised access to, appropriation of, or copying of any documents, objects, materials, substances or electronic files, lawfully under the control of the trade secret holder, containing the trade secret or from which the trade secret can be deduced;

(b) any other conduct which, under the circumstances, is considered contrary to honest commercial practices.

3. The use or disclosure of a trade secret shall be considered unlawful whenever carried out, without the consent of the trade secret holder, by a person who is found to meet any of the following conditions:

(a) having acquired the trade secret unlawfully;

(b) being in breach of a confidentiality agreement or any other duty not to disclose the trade secret;

(c) being in breach of a contractual or any other duty to limit the use of the trade secret.

4. The acquisition, use or disclosure of a trade secret shall also be considered unlawful whenever a person, at the time of the acquisition, use

or disclosure, knew or ought, under the circumstances, to have known that the trade secret had been obtained directly or indirectly from another person who was using or disclosing the trade secret unlawfully within the meaning of paragraph 3.

5.   The production, offering or placing on the market of infringing goods, or the importation, export or storage of infringing goods for those purposes, shall also be considered an unlawful use of a trade secret where the person carrying out such activities knew, or ought, under the circumstances, to have known that the trade secret was used unlawfully within the meaning of paragraph 3.

Article 5

Exceptions

Member States shall ensure that an application for the measures, procedures and remedies provided for in this Directive is dismissed where the alleged acquisition, use or disclosure of the trade secret was carried out in any of the following cases:

(a)   for exercising the right to freedom of expression and information as set out in the Charter, including respect for the freedom and pluralism of the media;

(b)   for revealing misconduct, wrongdoing or illegal activity, provided that the respondent acted for the purpose of protecting the general public interest;

(c)   disclosure by workers to their representatives as part of the legitimate exercise by those representatives of their functions in accordance with Union or national law, provided that such disclosure was necessary for that exercise;

(d)   for the purpose of protecting a legitimate interest recognised by Union or national law.

CHAPTER III

Measures, procedures and remedies

Section 1

General provisions

Article 6

General obligation

1.   Member States shall provide for the measures, procedures and remedies necessary to ensure the availability of civil redress against the unlawful acquisition, use and disclosure of trade secrets.

2.   The measures, procedures and remedies referred to in paragraph 1 shall:

(a) be fair and equitable;

(b) not be unnecessarily complicated or costly, or entail unreasonable time-limits or unwarranted delays; and

(c) be effective and dissuasive.

Article 7

Proportionality and abuse of process

1.   The measures, procedures and remedies provided for in this Directive shall be applied in a manner that:

(a) is proportionate;

(b) avoids the creation of barriers to legitimate trade in the internal market; and

(c) provides for safeguards against their abuse.

2.   Member States shall ensure that competent judicial authorities may, upon the request of the respondent, apply appropriate measures as provided for in national law, where an application concerning the unlawful acquisition, use or disclosure of a trade secret is manifestly unfounded and the applicant is found to have initiated the legal proceedings abusively or in bad faith. Such measures may, as appropriate, include awarding damages to the respondent, imposing sanctions on the applicant or ordering the dissemination of information concerning a decision as referred to in Article 15.

Member States may provide that measures as referred to in the first subparagraph are dealt with in separate legal proceedings.

Article 8

Limitation period

1.   Member States shall, in accordance with this Article, lay down rules on the limitation periods applicable to substantive claims and actions for the application of the measures, procedures and remedies provided for in this Directive.

The rules referred to in the first subparagraph shall determine when the limitation period begins to run, the duration of the limitation period and the circumstances under which the limitation period is interrupted or suspended.

2.   The duration of the limitation period shall not exceed 6 years.

Article 9

Preservation of confidentiality of trade secrets in the course of legal proceedings

1.   Member States shall ensure that the parties, their lawyers or other representatives, court officials, witnesses, experts and any other person participating in legal proceedings relating to the unlawful acquisition, use or disclosure of a trade secret, or who has access to documents which form part of those legal proceedings, are not permitted to use or disclose any trade secret or alleged trade secret which the competent judicial authorities have, in response to a duly reasoned application by an interested party, identified as confidential and of which they have become aware as a result of such participation or access. In that regard, Member States may also allow competent judicial authorities to act on their own initiative.

The obligation referred to in the first subparagraph shall remain in force after the legal proceedings have ended. However, such obligation shall cease to exist in any of the following circumstances:

(a) where the alleged trade secret is found, by a final decision, not to meet the requirements set out in point (1) of Article 2; or

(b) where over time, the information in question becomes generally known among or readily accessible to persons within the circles that normally deal with that kind of information.

2.   Member States shall also ensure that the competent judicial authorities may, on a duly reasoned application by a party, take specific measures necessary to preserve the confidentiality of any trade secret or alleged trade secret used or referred to in the course of legal proceedings relating to the unlawful acquisition, use or disclosure of a trade secret. Member States may also allow competent judicial authorities to take such measures on their own initiative.

The measures referred to in the first subparagraph shall at least include the possibility:

(a) of restricting access to any document containing trade secrets or alleged trade secrets submitted by the parties or third parties, in whole or in part, to a limited number of persons;

(b) of restricting access to hearings, when trade secrets or alleged trade secrets may be disclosed, and the corresponding record or transcript of those hearings to a limited number of persons;

(c) of making available to any person other than those comprised in the limited number of persons referred to in points (a) and

(b) a non-confidential version of any judicial decision, in which the passages containing trade secrets have been removed or redacted.

The number of persons referred to in points (a) and (b) of the second subparagraph shall be no greater than necessary in order to ensure compliance with the right of the parties to the legal proceedings to an effective remedy and to a fair trial, and shall include, at least, one natural person from each party and the respective lawyers or other representatives of those parties to the legal proceedings.

3.   When deciding on the measures referred to in paragraph 2 and assessing their proportionality, the competent judicial authorities shall take into account the need to ensure the right to an effective remedy and to a fair trial, the legitimate interests of the parties and, where appropriate, of third parties, and any potential harm for either of the parties, and, where appropriate, for third parties, resulting from the granting or rejection of such measures.

4.   Any processing of personal data pursuant to paragraphs 1, 2 or 3 shall be carried out in accordance with Directive 95/46/EC.

Section 2

Provisional and precautionary measures

Article 10

Provisional and precautionary measures

1.   Member States shall ensure that the competent judicial authorities may, at the request of the trade secret holder, order any of the following provisional and precautionary measures against the alleged infringer:

    (a)   the cessation of or, as the case may be, the prohibition of the use or disclosure of the trade secret on a provisional basis;

    (b)   the prohibition of the production, offering, placing on the market or use of infringing goods, or the importation, export or storage of infringing goods for those purposes;

    (c)   the seizure or delivery up of the suspected infringing goods, including imported goods, so as to prevent their entry into, or circulation on, the market.

2.   Member States shall ensure that the judicial authorities may, as an alternative to the measures referred to in paragraph 1, make the continuation of the alleged unlawful use of a trade secret subject to the lodging of guarantees intended to ensure the compensation of the trade secret holder. Disclosure of a trade secret in return for the lodging of guarantees shall not be allowed.

Article 11

Conditions of application and safeguards

1.   Member States shall ensure that the competent judicial authorities have, in respect of the measures referred to in Article 10, the authority to require the applicant to provide evidence that may reasonably be considered available in order to satisfy themselves with a sufficient degree of certainty that:

(a)   a trade secret exists;

(b)   the applicant is the trade secret holder; and

(c)   the trade secret has been acquired unlawfully, is being unlawfully used or disclosed, or unlawful acquisition, use or disclosure of the trade secret is imminent.

2.   Member States shall ensure that in deciding on the granting or rejection of the application and assessing its proportionality, the competent judicial authorities shall be required to take into account the specific circumstances of the case, including, where appropriate:

(a)   the value and other specific features of the trade secret;

(b)   the measures taken to protect the trade secret;

(c)   the conduct of the respondent in acquiring, using or disclosing the trade secret;

(d)   the impact of the unlawful use or disclosure of the trade secret;

(e)   the legitimate interests of the parties and the impact which the granting or rejection of the measures could have on the parties;

(f)   the legitimate interests of third parties;

(g)   the public interest; and

(h)   the safeguard of fundamental rights.

3.   Member States shall ensure that the measures referred to in Article 10 are revoked or otherwise cease to have effect, upon the request of the respondent, if:

(a)   the applicant does not institute legal proceedings leading to a decision on the merits of the case before the competent judicial authority, within a reasonable period determined by the judicial authority ordering the measures where the law of a Member State so permits or, in the absence of such determination, within a period not exceeding 20 working days or 31 calendar days, whichever is the longer; or

    (b)   the information in question no longer meets the requirements of point (1) of Article 2, for reasons that cannot be attributed to the respondent.

4.   Member States shall ensure that the competent judicial authorities may make the measures referred to in Article 10 subject to the lodging by the applicant of adequate security or an equivalent assurance intended to ensure compensation for any prejudice suffered by the respondent and, where appropriate, by any other person affected by the measures.

5.   Where the measures referred to in Article 10 are revoked on the basis of point (a) of paragraph 3 of this Article, where they lapse due to any act or omission by the applicant, or where it is subsequently found that there has been no unlawful acquisition, use or disclosure of the trade secret or threat of such conduct, the competent judicial authorities shall have the authority to order the applicant, upon the request of the respondent or of an injured third party, to provide the respondent, or the injured third party, appropriate compensation for any injury caused by those measures.

Member States may provide that the request for compensation referred to in the first subparagraph is dealt with in separate legal proceedings.

Section 3

Measures resulting from a decision on the merits of the case

Article 12

Injunctions and corrective measures

1.   Member States shall ensure that, where a judicial decision taken on the merits of the case finds that there has been unlawful acquisition, use or disclosure of a trade secret, the competent judicial authorities may, at the request of the applicant, order one or more of the following measures against the infringer:

    (a)   the cessation of or, as the case may be, the prohibition of the use or disclosure of the trade secret;

    (b)   the prohibition of the production, offering, placing on the market or use of infringing goods, or the importation, export or storage of infringing goods for those purposes;

    (c)   the adoption of the appropriate corrective measures with regard to the infringing goods;

    (d)   the destruction of all or part of any document, object, material, substance or electronic file containing or embodying the trade secret or, where appropriate, the delivery up to the applicant of all or part of those documents, objects, materials, substances or electronic files.

2.   The corrective measures referred to in point (c) of paragraph 1 shall include:

     (a)   recall of the infringing goods from the market;

     (b)   depriving the infringing goods of their infringing quality;

     (c)   destruction of the infringing goods or, where appropriate, their withdrawal from the market, provided that the withdrawal does not undermine the protection of the trade secret in question.

3.   Member States may provide that, when ordering the withdrawal of the infringing goods from the market, their competent judicial authorities may order, at the request of the trade secret holder, that the goods be delivered up to the holder or to charitable organisations.

4.   The competent judicial authorities shall order that the measures referred to in points (c) and (d) of paragraph 1 be carried out at the expense of the infringer, unless there are particular reasons for not doing so. Those measures shall be without prejudice to any damages that may be due to the trade secret holder by reason of the unlawful acquisition, use or disclosure of the trade secret.

Article 13

Conditions of application, safeguards and alternative measures

1.   Member States shall ensure that, in considering an application for the adoption of the injunctions and corrective measures provided for in Article 12 and assessing their proportionality, the competent judicial authorities shall be required to take into account the specific circumstances of the case, including, where appropriate:

     (a)   the value or other specific features of the trade secret;

     (b)   the measures taken to protect the trade secret;

     (c)   the conduct of the infringer in acquiring, using or disclosing the trade secret;

     (d)   the impact of the unlawful use or disclosure of the trade secret;

     (e)   the legitimate interests of the parties and the impact which the granting or rejection of the measures could have on the parties;

     (f)   the legitimate interests of third parties;

     (g)   the public interest; and

(h) the safeguard of fundamental rights.

Where the competent judicial authorities limit the duration of the measures referred to in points (a) and (b) of Article 12(1), such duration shall be sufficient to eliminate any commercial or economic advantage that the infringer could have derived from the unlawful acquisition, use or disclosure of the trade secret.

2.   Member States shall ensure that the measures referred to in points (a) and (b) of Article 12(1) are revoked or otherwise cease to have effect, upon the request of the respondent, if the information in question no longer meets the requirements of point (1) of Article 2 for reasons that cannot be attributed directly or indirectly to the respondent.

3.   Member States shall provide that, at the request of the person liable to be subject to the measures provided for in Article 12, the competent judicial authority may order pecuniary compensation to be paid to the injured party instead of applying those measures if all the following conditions are met:

(a) the person concerned at the time of use or disclosure neither knew nor ought, under the circumstances, to have known that the trade secret was obtained from another person who was using or disclosing the trade secret unlawfully;

(b) execution of the measures in question would cause that person disproportionate harm; and

(c) pecuniary compensation to the injured party appears reasonably satisfactory.

Where pecuniary compensation is ordered instead of the measures referred to in points (a) and (b) of Article 12(1), it shall not exceed the amount of royalties or fees which would have been due, had that person requested authorisation to use the trade secret in question, for the period of time for which use of the trade secret could have been prohibited.

Article 14

Damages

1.   Member States shall ensure that the competent judicial authorities, upon the request of the injured party, order an infringer who knew or ought to have known that he, she or it was engaging in unlawful acquisition, use or disclosure of a trade secret, to pay the trade secret holder damages appropriate to the actual prejudice suffered as a result of the unlawful acquisition, use or disclosure of the trade secret.

Member States may limit the liability for damages of employees towards their employers for the unlawful acquisition, use or disclosure of a trade secret of the employer where they act without intent.

2.   When setting the damages referred to in paragraph 1, the competent judicial authorities shall take into account all appropriate factors, such as the negative economic consequences, including lost profits, which the injured party has suffered, any unfair profits made by the infringer and, in appropriate cases, elements other than economic factors, such as the moral prejudice caused to the trade secret holder by the unlawful acquisition, use or disclosure of the trade secret.

Alternatively, the competent judicial authorities may, in appropriate cases, set the damages as a lump sum on the basis of elements such as, at a minimum, the amount of royalties or fees which would have been due had the infringer requested authorisation to use the trade secret in question.

Article 15

Publication of judicial decisions

1.   Member States shall ensure that, in legal proceedings instituted for the unlawful acquisition, use or disclosure of a trade secret, the competent judicial authorities may order, at the request of the applicant and at the expense of the infringer, appropriate measures for the dissemination of the information concerning the decision, including publishing it in full or in part.

2.   Any measure referred to in paragraph 1 of this Article shall preserve the confidentiality of trade secrets as provided for in Article 9.

3.   In deciding whether to order a measure referred to in paragraph 1 and when assessing its proportionality, the competent judicial authorities shall take into account, where appropriate, the value of the trade secret, the conduct of the infringer in acquiring, using or disclosing the trade secret, the impact of the unlawful use or disclosure of the trade secret, and the likelihood of further unlawful use or disclosure of the trade secret by the infringer.

The competent judicial authorities shall also take into account whether the information on the infringer would be such as to allow a natural person to be identified and, if so, whether publication of that information would be justified, in particular in the light of the possible harm that such measure may cause to the privacy and reputation of the infringer.

CHAPTER IV

Sanctions, reporting and final provisions

Article 16

Sanctions for non-compliance with this Directive

Member States shall ensure that the competent judicial authorities may impose sanctions on any person who fails or refuses to comply with any measure adopted pursuant to Articles 9, 10 and 12.

The sanctions provided for shall include the possibility of imposing recurring penalty payments in the event of non-compliance with a measure adopted pursuant to Articles 10 and 12.

The sanctions provided for shall be effective, proportionate and dissuasive.

Article 17

Exchange of information and correspondents

For the purpose of promoting cooperation, including the exchange of information, among Member States and between Member States and the Commission, each Member State shall designate one or more national correspondents for any question relating to the implementation of the measures provided for by this Directive. It shall communicate the details of the national correspondent or correspondents to the other Member States and the Commission.

Article 18

Reports

1. By 9 June 2021, the European Union Intellectual Property Office, in the context of the activities of the European Observatory on Infringements of Intellectual Property Rights, shall prepare an initial report on the litigation trends regarding the unlawful acquisition, use or disclosure of trade secrets pursuant to the application of this Directive.

2. By 9 June 2022, the Commission shall draw up an intermediate report on the application of this Directive, and shall submit it to the European Parliament and to the Council. That report shall take due account of the report referred to in paragraph 1.

The intermediate report shall examine, in particular, the possible effects of the application of this Directive on research and innovation, the mobility of employees and on the exercise of the right to freedom of expression and information.

3. By 9 June 2026, the Commission shall carry out an evaluation of the impact of this Directive and submit a report to the European Parliament and to the Council.

Article 19

Transposition

1.   Member States shall bring into force the laws, regulations and administrative provisions necessary to comply with this Directive by 9 June 2018. They shall immediately communicate the text of those measures to the Commission.

When Member States adopt those measures, they shall contain a reference to this Directive or be accompanied by such a reference on the occasion of their official publication. Member States shall determine how such reference is to be made.

2.   Member States shall communicate to the Commission the text of the main provisions of national law which they adopt in the field covered by this Directive.

Article 20

Entry into force

This Directive shall enter into force on the twentieth day following that of its publication in the *Official Journal of the European Union*.

Article 21

Addressees

This Directive is addressed to the Member States.

Done at Strasbourg, 8 June 2016.

For the European Parliament

The President

M. SCHULZ

For the Council

The President

A.G. KOENDERS